HANDBOOK OF
SEX THERAPY

PERSPECTIVES IN SEXUALITY
Behavior, Research, and Therapy

Series Editor: RICHARD GREEN
State University of New York at Stony Brook

NEW DIRECTIONS IN SEX RESEARCH
Edited by Eli A. Rubinstein, Richard Green, and Edward Brecher

PROGRESS IN SEXOLOGY
Edited by Robert Gemme and Connie Christine Wheeler

HANDBOOK OF SEX THERAPY
Edited by Joseph LoPiccolo and Leslie LoPiccolo

THE PREVENTION OF SEXUAL DISORDERS: Issues and Approaches
Edited by C. Brandon Qualls, John P. Wincze, and David H. Barlow

A Continuation Order Plan is available for this series. A continuation order will bring delivery of each new volume immediately upon publication. Volumes are billed only upon actual shipment. For further information please contact the publisher.

HANDBOOK OF SEX THERAPY

Edited by

Joseph LoPiccolo
and Leslie LoPiccolo
State University of New York at Stony Brook

PLENUM PRESS · NEW YORK AND LONDON

Library of Congress Cataloging in Publication Data

Main entry under title:

Handbook of sex therapy.

    (Perspectives in sexuality)
    Includes bibliographies and index.
    1. Sex therapy—Addresses, essays, lectures. I. LoPiccolo, Joseph. II.
LoPiccolo, Leslie.
RC555.H36   616.6'06   77-18818
ISBN 0-306-31074-0

© 1978 Plenum Press, New York
A Division of Plenum Publishing Corporation
227 West 17th Street, New York, N.Y. 10011

Printed in the United States of America

ACKNOWLEDGMENTS

The editors and publisher would like to thank the following copyright holders for permission to reprint previously published articles in this volume.

The American Academy of Psychosomatic Medicine
Treatments of male potency disorders: The present status, by Alan J. Cooper [pp. 323-336], originally published in *Psychosomatics*, 1971, *12*, 235-244.

American Psychological Association
Orgasm during intercourse: A treatment strategy for women, by Antonette M. Zeiss, Gerald M. Rosen, and Robert A. Zeiss [pp. 219-225], originally published in *Journal of Consulting and Clinical Psychology*, 1977, *45*(5), 891-895.

Annals of Internal Medicine
Impotence in diabetes: The neurologic factor, by Max Ellenberg [pp. 421-432], originally published in *Annals of Internal Medicine*, 1971, *75*, 213-219.

Archives of Sexual Behavior
The sexual interaction inventory: A new instrument for assessment of sexual dysfunction, by Joseph LoPiccolo and Jeffrey C. Steger [pp. 113-122], originally published in 1974, *3*(6), 585-595.

The role of masturbation in the treatment of orgasmic dysfunction, by Joseph LoPiccolo and W. Charles Lobitz [pp. 187-194], originally published in 1972, *2*(2), 163-17.

Secondary orgasmic dysfunction. I. Analysis and strategies for treatment, by Kevin B. McGovern, Rita Stewart McMullen, and Joseph LoPiccolo [pp. 209-218], originally published in 1975, *4*(3), 265-275.

Group treatment of premature ejaculation, by Helen S. Kaplan, Richard N. Kohl, Wardell B. Pomeroy, Avodah K. Offit, and Barbara Hogan [pp. 277-285], originally published in 1974, *3*(5), 443-452.

Systematic desensitization of erectile impotence: A controlled study, by G. Kockott, F. Dittmar, and L. Nusselt [pp. 337-343], originally published in 1975, *4*(5), 493-500.

Group therapy for nonorgasmic women: Two age levels, by Barbara Schneidman and Linda McGuire [pp. 467-475], originally published in 1976, *5*(3), 239-247.

Vivian Cadden
The psychiatrists versus Masters and Johnson, by Vivian Cadden [pp. 485-490], originally published in J. and J. Robbins (Eds.), *An Analysis of Human Sexual Inadequacy*. New York: Signet, 1970, pp. 299-307.

Division 17, the Division of Counseling Psychology of the American Psychological Association
Desensitization procedures in dealing with female sexual dysfunction, by June R. Husted [pp. 195-208], originally published in *The Counseling Psychologist*, 1975, *5*(1), 30-37.

Helping elderly couples become sexually liberated: Psychosocial issues, by Mary Ann P. Sviland [pp. 351-360], originally published in *The Counseling Psychologist*, 1975, *5*(1), 67-72.

A program for enhancing the sexual relationship of normal couples, by Joseph LoPiccolo and Vinnie H. Miller [pp. 451-458], originally published in *The Counseling Psychologist*, 1975, *5*(12), 41-45.

The Division of Psychotherapy, American Psychological Association
Issues in the treatment of sexually dysfunctioning couples of Afro-American descent, by Gail E. Wyatt, Richard G. Strayer, and W. Charles Lobitz [441-450], originally published in *Psychotherapy: Theory, Research and Practice*, 1976, *13*(1), 44-50 (revised for this volume).

Elsevier/North-Holland Biomedical Press
Direct treatment of sexual dysfunction, by Joseph LoPiccolo [pp. 1-17], originally published in J. Money and H. Musaph (Eds.), *Handbook of Sexology*. Amsterdam: ASP Biological & Medical Press B. V., 1977. Pp. 1227-1244.

Insight Publishing Company, Inc.
Training dual sex teams for rapid treatment of sexual dysfunction: A pilot program by Raymond W. Waggoner, Emily H. Mudd, and Marshall L. Shearer [pp. 499-509], originally published in *Psychiatric Annals*, 1973, *3*(5), 61-76.

Journal of Marriage and Family Counseling
A behavioral group treatment program for sexually dysfunctional couples, *by* Kevin B. McGovern, Carole C. Kirkpatrick, and Joseph LoPiccolo [pp. 459–466], originally published in *Journal of Marriage and Family Counseling*, 1976, *2*(4), 397–404.

McGraw-Hill Book Company
Overcoming sexual inadequacy, *by* Arnold A. Lazarus [pp. 19–34], originally published in Arnold A. Lazarus, *Behavior Therapy and Beyond*. New York: McGraw-Hill, 1971. Pp. 141–162.

The New England Journal of Medicine
Sexual behavior in pregnancy, *by* Don A. Solberg, Julius Butler, and Nathaniel N. Wagner [pp. 361–371], originally published in *New England Journal of Medicine*, 1973, *288*, 1098–1103.

W. W. Norton & Company, Inc.
Types of female orgasm, *by* Josephine Singer and Irving Singer [pp. 175–186], originally published in Irving Singer, *The Goals of Human Sexuality*. New York: Norton, 1973. Pp. 66–82. Paperback edition published by Shocken Books, New York. An earlier version of the article appeared in *The Journal of Sex Research*, 1972, *8*(4), 255–267.

NYM Corp.
The question of surrogates in sex therapy, *by* Linda Wolfe [pp. 491–497], originally published in *New York Magazine*, December 3, 1973, pp. 120–127.

Pergamon Press Ltd.
Ejaculatory incompetence treated by deconditioning anxiety, *by* Javad Razani [pp. 287–290], originally published in *Journal of Behavior Therapy and Experimental Psychiatry*, 1972, *3*, 65–67.

A case of ejaculatory incompetence treated with a mechanical aid, *by* Adrian G. Newell [pp. 291–293], originally published in *Journal of Behavior Therapy and Experimental Psychiatry*, 1976, *7*, 193–194.

Treatment of erectile failure and ejaculatory incompetence of homosexual etiology, *by* Joseph LoPiccolo, Rita Stewart McMullen, and Bruce Watkins [pp. 345–350], originally published in *Journal of Behavior Therapy and Experimental Psychiatry*, 1972, *3*, 233–236.

Physicians Postgraduate Press
Impotence in diabetics, *by* Domeena C. Renshaw [pp. 433–440], originally published in *Diseases of the Nervous System*, 1975, *36*(7), 369–371 (additional new material added for this volume).

Psychological Reports
Use of written material in learning self-control of premature ejaculation, *by* John C. Lowe and William L. Mikulas [pp. 271–275], originally published in *Psychological Reports*, 1975, *37*, 295–298.

Society
The professionalization of sex therapy: Issues and problems, *by* Joseph LoPiccolo [pp. 511–526], originally published in *Society*, 1977, *14*(5), 60–68. © 1977 by Transaction, Inc.

The Society for Clinical and Experimental Hypnosis
Hypnodesensitization therapy of vaginismus: Part I. In vitro method. Part II. In vivo method, *by* K. Fuchs, Z. Hoch, E. Paldi, H. Abramovici, J. M. Brandes, I. Timor-Tritsch, and M. Kleinhaus [pp. 261–270], originally published in *International Journal of Clinical and Experimental Hypnosis*, 1973, *21*(3), 144–156.

Society for the Psychological Study of Social Issues
Factors in marital orgasm *by* Paul H. Gebhard [pp. 167–174], originally published in *Journal of Social Issues*, 1966, *22*(2), 88–95.

Weekly Psychiatry Update Division, Biomedia, Inc.
Advances in the psychophysiological evaluation of male erectile impotence, *by* Ismet Karacan [pp. 137–145], originally published in *Weekly Psychiatry Update Series*, 1977, *1*, 43.

The Williams & Wilkins Company
Sexual functioning in patients with chronic renal failure, *by* Harry S. Abram, L. R. Hester, W. F. Sheridan, and G. M. Epstein [pp. 411–419], originally published in *Journal of Nervous and Mental Disease*, 1975, *160*(3), 220–226.

Year Book Medical Publishers, Inc.
Impotence as a practical problem, *by* John Reckless and Nancy Geiger [pp. 295–321], originally published in Harry F. Dowling (Ed.), *Disease-a-Month*, Chicago: Year Book Medical Publishers, May, 1975. Pp. 1–40.

Foreword

When is it timely to publish a synthesis of previously published and original materials from a specific discipline? I believe it to be timely when one has a sufficient amount of high-quality material covering the critical areas of that topic, when the previously published material is scattered over a wide range of journals and books, and when there is no single book that synthesizes the discipline.

The treatment of sexual dysfunction emerged to the front lines of health delivery only during the past decade with the pioneering work of William Masters and Virginia Johnson. In spite of the rash of sex clinics and sex therapists that followed, preciously little solid research has been conducted on the various strategies of therapy, the means of assessing complex interpersonal sexual relationships, and the manner by which clinical change is objectively assessed.

No one reader can keep pace with the multitude of journals that publish key material by sophisticated investigators. And no one investigator can cover these salient areas alone with his or her original work in a single volume.

The critical papers have now been written. Ten were written specifically for this volume and thirty-three have previously appeared. This volume laces them together into a coherent pattern.

Thus, the time for a synthesis in sexual dysfunction.

Richard Green

Preface

Sex therapy, or the rapid treatment of sexual dysfunction, entered into the mainstream of the professional world and gained widespread public attention in 1970, with the landmark publication of William Masters and Virginia Johnson's *Human Sexual Inadequacy*. In the years since 1970, sex therapy has become a major specialty within the fields of psychology, psychiatry, and medicine, and is beginning to assume, for better or worse, some aspects of an independent profession. With this expansion of interest, there has come an explosion of professional literature. There are now at least two professional journals focusing on sex therapy, three other journals that are devoted exclusively to sexuality, and relevant articles appearing in dozens of other professional journals. This information explosion makes it difficult, if not impossible, for anyone to stay abreast of what has become a rapidly developing field, especially given that sex therapists and sex researchers represent several different professions.

The aim of this volume is to pull together the most definitive information available on sexual dysfunction. Ten of the articles in this volume were written at the editors' invitation, to cover especially important issues in sex therapy. These articles include surveys of particular areas in sex therapy and reports of the latest developments in these areas.

The other thirty-three articles are taken from a wide variety of sources—four different books, nineteen different journals, and one convention presentation. Each article represents, in the editors' judgment, the best available material on a particular topic. If the quality of these papers varies, this variation is to be expected in an emergent field where much more research is needed on many issues.

This volume is designed to be a comprehensive text for students and practicing clinicians who are interested in the field of sex therapy. While we feel that this book is broad in scope, it does not, and was not meant to, stand alone. Anyone beginning work in the area of sexual dysfunction should certainly read the Masters and Johnson volumes—*Human Sexual Response*, *Human Sexual Inadequacy*, and *The Pleasure Bond*. These monumental works, together with the more recent material included in this volume, will acquaint the reader with the best information available on the etiology and treatment of sexual dysfunction.

Joseph LoPiccolo
Leslie LoPiccolo

Stony Brook

Contributors

A. R. Abarbanel, M.D., Medical Director, Fertility Institute, and Independent Practice, Obstetrics and Gynecology, Los Angeles, California

Harry S. Abram, M.D., Deceased, Department of Psychiatry, Vanderbilt University Medical Center, Nashville, Tennessee

H. Abramovici, M.D., Rambam University Hospital, Aba Khoushy School of Medicine, Haifa, Israel; and Assaf Harofeh Hospital, Tel-Aviv University Medical School, Tel-Aviv, Israel

Jack S. Annon, Ph.D., Department of Psychology, University of Hawaii, Honolulu, Hawaii

J. M. Brandes, M.D., Rambam University Hospital, Aba Khoushy School of Medicine, Haifa, Israel; and Assaf Harofeh Hospital, Tel-Aviv University Medical School, Tel-Aviv, Israel

Julius Butler, M.D., Department of Obstetrics and Gynecology, University of Washington, School of Medicine, Seattle, Washington

Vivian Cadden, *McCall's* Magazine, New York, New York

Alan J. Cooper, M.D., M.R.C. Psych., D.P.M., Department of Psychiatry, St. Mary's Hospital Medical School, University of London, London, England

F. Dittmar, M.D., Max Planck Institut für Psychiatrie, München, West Germany

Max Ellenberg, M.D., Department of Medicine, Mount Sinai Hospital, New York, New York

Gerald M. Epstein, B.A., Department of Psychology, George Peabody College for Teachers, Nashville, Tennessee

Jerry M. Friedman, M.S., Department of Psychology and Department of Psychiatry and Behavioral Science, State University of New York, Stony Brook, New York

K. Fuchs, M.D., Rambam University Hospital, Aba Khoushy School of Medicine, Haifa, Israel; and Assaf Harofeh Hospital, Tel-Aviv University Medical School, Tel-Aviv, Israel

Paul H. Gebhard, Ph.D., Institute for Sex Research, Indiana University, Bloomington, Indiana

Nancy Geiger, B.S.N., Trouro Infirmary, New Orleans, Louisiana

Benjamin Graber, M.D., Department of Psychiatry, University of Wisconsin Medical School, Madison, Wisconsin

Julia R. Heiman, Ph.D., Long Island Research Institute, and Department of Psychiatry and Behavioral Science, School of Medicine, State University of New York, Stony Brook, New York

Larry R. Hester, D. Min., Department of Psychiatry, Vanderbilt University Medical Center, Nashville, Tennessee

Glenn E. Higgins, Jr., M.S., Department of Psychology, State University of New York, Stony Brook, New York

Z. Hoch, M.D., Rambam University Hospital, Aba Khoushy School of Medicine, Haifa, Israel; and Assaf Harofeh Hospital, Tel-Aviv University Medical School, Tel-Aviv, Israel

Barbara Hogan, M.D., Department of Psychiatry, Cornell University Medical College, and Payne Whitney Psychiatric Clinic, New York Hospital Medical Center, New York, New York

Douglas R. Hogan, B.A., Department of Psychology, Sexual Dysfunction Clinic, and Department of Psychiatry and Behavioral Science, State University of New York, Stony Brook, New York.

June R. Husted, Ph.D., Veterans Administration Hospital, Long Beach, California

Helen S. Kaplan, M.D., Department of Psychiatry, Cornell University Medical College; and Payne Whitney Psychiatric Clinic, New York Hospital Medical Center, New York, New York

Ismet Karacan, M.D., (Med.) D.Sc., Professor of Psychiatry, Director of Sleep Disorders Center, Baylor College of Medicine, Houston, Texas

Carole C. Kirkpatrick, Ph.D., Independent Practice, Psychology, Eugene, Oregon

M. Kleinhaus, M.D., Rambam University Hospital, Aba Khoushy School of Medicine, Haifa, Israel; and Assaf Harofeh Hospital, Tel-Aviv University Medical School, Tel-Aviv, Israel

Georgia Kline-Graber, R.N., B.A., Nurse Specialist, Department of Psychiatry, University of Wisconsin Medical School, Madison, Wisconsin

G. Kockott, M.D., Max Planck Institut für Psychiatrie, München, West Germany

Richard N. Kohl, M.D., Department of Psychiatry, Cornell University Medical College, and Payne Whitney Psychiatric Clinic, New York Hospital Medical Center, New York, New York

Arnold A. Lazarus, Ph.D., Graduate School of Applied and Professional Psychology, Rutgers University, New Brunswick, New Jersey

Gretchen K. Lobitz, Ph.D., Department of Psychology, University of Denver, Denver, Colorado

W. Charles Lobitz, Ph.D., Division of Clinical Psychology, Department of Psychiatry, University of Colorado School of Medicine, Denver, Colorado

Joseph LoPiccolo, Ph.D., Department of Psychiatry and Behavioral Science, School of Medicine, State University of New York, Stony Brook, New York

Leslie LoPiccolo, M.S., Department of Psychiatry and Behavioral Science, School of Medicine, State University of New York, Stony Brook, New York

John C. Lowe, M.A., Department of Psychology, University of West Florida, Pensacola, Florida

Kevin B. McGovern, Ph.D., Columbia Psychiatric Clinic, Portland, Oregon

Linda McGuire, Ph.D., Department of Obstetrics and Gynecology and Department of Psychiatry, School of Medicine, University of Washington, Seattle, Washington

Rita Stewart McMullen, Ph.D., Desert Counseling Clinic, Inc., Ridgecrest, California

William L. Mikulas, Ph.D., Department of Psychology, University of West Florida, Pensacola, Florida

Vinnie H. Miller, Ph.D., Counseling Center, University of Oregon, Eugene, Oregon

Patricia Morokoff, M.S., Department of Psychology, State University of New York, Stony Brook, New York

Emily H. Mudd, M.S.W., Ph.D., Department of Psychiatry, University of Pennsylvania, School of Medicine, Philadelphia, Pennsylvania

Adrian G. Newell, Ph.D., Department of Clinical Psychology, St. James's Hospital, Leeds, England

L. Nusselt, M.D., Max Planck Institut für Psychiatrie, München, West Germany

Avodah K. Offit, M.D., Payne Whitney Psychiatric Clinic, New York Hospital Medical Center, New York, New York

E. Paldi, M.D., Rambam University Hospital, Aba Khoushy School of Medicine, Haifa, Israel; and Assaf Harofeh Hospital, Tel-Aviv University Medical School, Tel-Aviv, Israel

Wardell B. Pomeroy, Ph.D., Independent Practice, Psychology, San Francisco, California

Javad Razani, M.D., Department of Psychiatry, University of Southern California, School of Medicine, Los Angeles, California

John Reckless, M.D., John Reckless Clinic, P.A., and Lecturer, School of Nursing, Duke University Medical Center, Durham, North Carolina

Domeena C. Renshaw, M.D., Professor of Psychiatry, Loyola University, Stritch School of Medicine, Maywood, Illinois

Craig H. Robinson, Ph.D., Department of Psychology, University of Hawaii, Honolulu, Hawaii

Gerald M. Rosen, Ph.D., Providence Family Medical Center, Seattle, Washington

Barbara Schneidman, M.D., M.P.H., Department of Obstetrics and Gynecology, United States Public Health Service Hospital, Seattle, Washington

Marshall L. Shearer, M.D., Department of Psychiatry, University of Michigan Medical School, Ann Arbor, Michigan

William F. Sheridan, M.D., Department of Psychiatry, Vanderbilt University Medical Center, Nashville, Tennessee

Irving Singer, Ph.D., Department of Linguistics and Philosophy, Massachusetts Institute of Technology, Cambridge, Massachusetts

Josephine Singer, Boston, Massachusetts

Don A. Solberg, B.A., Department of Psychology, University of Washington, Seattle, Washington

Jeffrey C. Steger, Ph.D., Department of Rehabilitation Medicine, University of Washington, Seattle, Washington

Richard G. Strayer, Ph.D., The Wheeler Clinic, Plainville, Connecticut

Mary Ann P. Sviland, Ph.D., Clinical Psychologist, Private Practice, Canoga Park, California, and Lecturer, California State University, Northridge, California

I. Timor-Tritsch, M.D., Rambam University Hospital, Aba Khoushy School of Medicine, Haifa, Israel; and Assaf Harofeh Hospital, Tel-Aviv University Medical School, Tel-Aviv, Israel

Raymond W. Waggoner, M.D., D.Sc., Department of Psychiatry, University of Michigan Medical School, Ann Arbor, Michigan

Nathaniel N. Wagner, Ph.D., Department of Psychology, University of Washington, Seattle, Washington

Bruce Watkins, Ph.D., Department of Psychology, University of Oregon, Eugene, Oregon

Martin H. Williams, Ph.D., Berkeley Sex Therapy Group, Berkeley, California

Linda Wolfe, New York Magazine, New York, New York

Gail E. Wyatt, Ph.D., Neuropsychiatric Institute, University of California at Los Angeles, School of Medicine, Los Angeles, California

Antonette M. Zeiss, Ph.D., Department of Psychology, Arizona State University, Tempe, Arizona

Robert A. Zeiss, Ph.D., Valle del Sol, Phoenix, Arizona, and Department of Psychology, Arizona State University, Tempe, Arizona

Contents

Part III—Female Orgasmic Dysfunction
A—Determinants of Female Orgasm

B—Treatment of Female Orgasmic Dysfunction

Part IV—Dyspareunia and Vaginismus

Part V—Male Orgasmic Dysfunction

Part VI—Male Erectile Dysfunction

Part VII—Sexual Dysfunction in Special Populations

Part X—Professional Issues

The field of sex therapy is one in which practical applications have been much more emphasized than basic research. Paradoxically, sex therapy consists of a variety of procedures that are demonstrably effective, but the reasons for this effectiveness are not known. Thus, different therapists use very different theoretical viewpoints to "explain" why their sex therapy procedures work. In this chapter, an attempt is made to find the common elements in different sex therapy programs, and so arrive at a set of common basic principles of sex therapy. In addition, this chapter provides a brief overview and summary of the etiology and treatment of the common sexual dysfunctions that are more thoroughly discussed in other chapters of this volume.

1

Direct Treatment of Sexual Dysfunction

Joseph LoPiccolo

The prevailing view of the best therapeutic approach to sexual dysfunction has undergone a remarkable revolution over the past ten years. Until recently, sexual dysfunctions were widely accepted as symptoms of a deep-seated personality conflict, reflecting the influence of instinctual drives, maturational changes in focus of sexual responsiveness from the oral to the anal to the genital zone, and crucial early childhood experiences (Freud, 1905/1962; Fenichel, 1945). Within this view, sexual dysfunctions could be treated only through individual, insight-oriented psychotherapy requiring "an appointment several times a week for a minimum of eight months" (Bergler, 1947). This requirement, of course, is not a realistic possibility for a large segment of the population. Given this viewpoint, it logically followed that most people suffering from sexual dysfunction could not be helped, or as it has been phrased, "as a mass problem, the question of frigidity is unfortunately not to be solved" (Bergler, 1951).

The general public first became aware of the effectiveness of an alternative approach to treatment of sexual dysfunction with the landmark publication of

Preparation of this chapter was supported in part by a grant from the National Institute of Mental Health, U.S. Public Health Service.

Joseph LoPiccolo • Department of Psychiatry and Behavioral Science, School of Medicine, State University of New York, Stony Brook, New York

1

Masters and Johnson's *Human Sexual Inadequacy* (1970). This approach involves brief, time-limited directive counseling of the couple aimed at symptom removal rather than attainment of insight, uncovering of repressions, or resolution of unconscious conflict. While the direct, symptomatic treatment of sexual dysfunction has received tremendous publicity in the last five years, the roots of this "new" therapy actually go back over two hundred years. Writing in the mid-eighteenth century, a British physician, Sir John Hunter (cited in Comfort, 1965), described a treatment approach for erectile failure (impotence) that is virtually identical with that described by Masters and Johnson (1970). More recently, effective direct approaches to sexual dysfunction were described by Semans (1956), Hastings (1963), Brown (1966), and a number of behavior therapists (Wolpe, 1958; Lazarus, 1963; Brady, 1966; Kraft and Al-Issa, 1968). It was, however, the publication of Masters and Johnson's (1970) unquestionable data on the effectiveness of the direct approach that led to its general acceptance.

This chapter will describe the basic principles of direct treatment of sexual dysfunction in the couple and review recent work on each of the major types of sexual dysfunctions.

Researchers writing on the treatment of sexual dysfunction tend to use different theoretical labels for rather similar therapy procedures. The virtually standarized treatment procedures now used for erectile failure may alternatively be described as a means of reducing performance demands and the spectator role (Masters and Johnson, 1970), as in vivo systematic desensitization of anxiety through reciprocal inhibition by sexual arousal (Wolpe, 1958), as a way of stopping the couple's attempt to voluntarily control an involuntary behavior (erection) through the use of quasi-hypnotic specific instructions (Haley, 1973), as a way of disrupting a self-maintaining "vicious cycle" of fear of erectile failure *producing* erectile failure by preventing sexual arousal (LoPiccolo and Lobitz, 1973), or as anxiety reduction through specific suggestions based on paradoxical intention or successive approximation (Annon, 1974). Rather than attempt to resolve such differences, it seems more reasonable to conceive of direct therapy procedures as complex and multifaceted packages of many different components. Lacking factorial research testing the relative effectiveness of these different components, it is premature to begin theoretical discussion of the underlying mechanisms that account for the effectiveness of the total package (Lobitz and LoPiccolo, 1972). At this point, the "active ingredients" and "inert fillers" in the direct therapy package cannot be distinguished, and the explanations offered for the effectiveness of the approach are simply speculations rather than data-based interpretations. With this in mind, it is possible to describe the common elements in various sex therapy programs, avoiding theoretical interpretation and simply focusing on the actual procedures used.

Basic Principles of Direct Treatment of Sexual Dysfunction

In varying degrees, the following principles are used by most clinicians who follow the direct treatment approach. Relative emphasis placed on each procedure depends partly on the clinician's theoretical viewpoint and partly on the needs, history, and specific dysfunction of the particular patient couple.

Mutual Responsibility. It must be stressed that all sexual dysfunctions are *shared disorders;* that is, the husband of an inorgasmic woman is partially responsible for creating or maintaining her dysfunction, and he is also a patient in need of help. Regardless of the cause of the dysfunction, both partners are responsible for future change and the solution of their problems. Some patients will resist the notion of mutual responsibility quite vigorously, in a defensive attempt to protect their self-image as sexually adept, or to maintain a position of power and control in their marital relationship. Reassurance, distinction of "responsibility" from "blame," and prognosis of successful outcome will usually deal with the self-image issue. Use of sexual dysfunction in a power struggle may be an indication for more general marital therapy instead of sex therapy. If reassurance does not eliminate resistence, *raising* the defensive spouse's anxiety about his sexual ability may motivate him to enter therapy on an equal basis with his spouse. Therapeutic anxiety can be engendered by such statements as "I agree that your spouse has severe and long-standing sexual problems, but I know from clinical experience that had you responded differently, she could have overcome these difficulties, and sex therapy would never have been needed." Further details of this procedure can be found in Lobitz, LoPiccolo, Lobitz, and Brockway (1974). Involving both spouses is also made easier by the use of a male–female, cotherapy team, which gives each patient someone to identify with. Such cotherapy is common in most sex therapy programs but does not seem to be essential (Kaplan, 1974).

Information and Education. Most patients suffering from sexual dysfunction are woefully ignorant of both basic biology and effective sexual techniques. Sometimes this ignorance can directly lead to the development of anxiety, which in turn produces sexual dysfunction. For example, a recent patient dated the onset of her aversion to sex as beginning when she first noted that her clitoris "disappeared" during manipulation. She interpreted this normal retraction of the clitoral shaft during the plateau phase of arousal (Masters and Johnson, 1966) as a pathological sign that she was *not* becoming aroused. This anxiety led to a complete loss of her arousal and enjoyment of sexuality. Similarly, many cases of vaginismus seem to begin as a result of the husband's forceful attempts to accomplish intromission in spite of his uncertainty about the exact location of the vagina. The wife's anticipation of painful battering about her vaginal introitus directly leads to the involuntary spastic contraction of the vaginal musculature called vaginismus. In direct therapy, therefore, the therapist ensures that the patients have accurate knowledge of the sexual response cycle through verbal discussion, providing the patient with appropriate reading materials, and the use of educational films. In addition, specific information is provided (again, by lecture, books, and films) on the general principles of effective sexual techniques of kissing, manual and oral foreplay, positions of intercourse, and so forth. While this specific information alone is probably not *sufficient* to produce symptom remission, it appears to be *necessary* for treatment to succeed, and its absence may be partially responsible for the generally low success rate of nondirective or dynamic treatment approaches (Lorand, 1934; Moore, 1961).

Attitude Change. Negative societal and parental attitudes toward sexual expression, past traumatic experiences, and the current acute distress combine to make the dysfunctional patients approach each sexual encounter with anxiety or, in extreme cases, with revulsion and disgust. Because of the double-standard type of morality Western nations adhere to (Christensen and Gregg, 1970), these negative attitudes seem to be considerably more common in women than in men. It may be that such negative attitudes toward sex are not really more common but are only more visible in women than in men. Discussions with the urologists and gynecologists who refer patients to the author's clinical treatment program indicate that males are much more reluctant to accept a referral for sex therapy than are females. Sex therapy may be more threatening to a male's self-image than to a female's, or women may put less pressure on their dysfunctional spouses to enter therapy than do men. The women's liberation movement has rejected *Kinder, Küche, Kirche* (children, kitchen, church) as the role model for the ideal woman, and now stresses that a "decent" woman can also be sexually interested, aroused, assertive, and orgasmic (Lydon, 1971; Bardwick, 1971). This revolution, however, has occurred too recently and has been accepted by too small a minority of urban, liberal, and educated women to have much impact on the overall incidence of negative attitudes toward female sexuality. Thus, the therapist must directly induce attitude change in such patients. Procedures used may involve having the patient read positive material on sexuality, arranging consultations with sympathetic clergy in the case of religiously based negative attitudes, instructing the husband to make it clear to his wife that he will value and respect her *more*, not less, if she becomes more sexual (which usually involves resolving the husband's lingering ambivalence about female sexuality and his fears about her becoming unfaithful or too demanding sexually), having the patients attend lectures or workshops on sexuality and sexual values which may be offered by local colleges, churches, or social-interest groups, and use of the therapeutic relationship itself. The psychotherapist in our culture is a respected authority figure. It is also to be hoped that the patients will personally like and respect their therapists. The therapists can use this role and relationship to produce attitude change in the patients through self-disclosure (Jourard, 1964) about their own enjoyment of sexuality (Lobitz and LoPiccolo, 1972). Given that the patient has a negative attitude toward sex and a positive attitude toward the therapist, the self-disclosure that the therapist enjoys sex creates cognitive dissonance (Festinger, 1957) for the patient: "Someone that I like and respect enjoys something I think is reprehensible, immoral, and disgusting." The resolution of this dissonance can lead to acceptance of sex as decent, moral, and enjoyable. Alternatively, if such self-disclosure is too extreme or used too early in therapy, the patients may resolve the dissonance by losing respect for the therapist or by deciding that the therapist is simply a different type of person. For this reason, self-disclosure probably produces the most attitude change when used by the female cotherapist with the female patient, and by the male cotherapist with the male patient.

Eliminating Performance Anxiety. In the culture of the 1970s, with its heavy emphasis on youth, beauty, and sexual attractiveness, demands for sexual competence and expertise seem to be assuming a larger role in the development of sexual dysfunction. Accordingly, for therapy to succeed, the dysfunctional patients must be freed from anxiety about their sexual performance. Patients, regardless of presenting complaint, are told to stop "keeping score," to stop being so *goal-centered* on erection, orgasm, or ejaculation, and instead to focus on enjoying the *process* rather than trying for a particular end result. For example, the therapeutic procedure of forbidding intercourse in the treatment of erectile failure makes it possible for the patients to enjoy mutual kissing, hugging, body massage, and manual or oral stimulation of the genitals without anxiety about whether erection sufficient for intercourse will occur. Other techniques include reassuring a woman that she need not feel that she must reach orgasm in order to enjoy intercourse or to confirm her husband's belief that he is a good lover for her, and instructing patients that they can each provide sexual satisfaction for each other through manual and oral stimulation, even when they are not capable or desirous of having intercourse. Giving one partner "permission" to masturbate as a legitimate route to sexual satisfaction will also reduce demands for performance in some cases.

Increasing Communication and Effectiveness of Sexual Technique. Dysfunctional couples tend to be unable to clearly communicate their sexual likes and dislikes to each other, due to inhibitions about discussing sex openly, excessive sensitivity to what is perceived as hostile criticism by the spouse, inhibitions about trying new sexual techniques, and the incorrect assumption that a person's sexual responsiveness is unchanging, i.e., that an activity that is pleasurable on one occasion will always be pleasurable. Accordingly, direct therapy encourages sexual experimentation and open, effective communication about technique and response. Procedures that are used include having the patient couple share their sexual fantasies with each other, read explicit erotic literature, and see explicit sexual movies that model new techniques, and training the couple to communicate during their sexual interaction. Patients are advised to train each other to be effective sexual partners through demonstrating their own effective masturbation techniques to each other (LoPiccolo and Lobitz, 1972), by guiding their partner's hands during genital caressing (Masters and Johnson, 1970), and by giving each other effective feedback during sex. Patients are taught the difference between ineffective, threatening communication (e.g., "Stop, I don't like that") and effective information-rich feedback (e.g., "It feels better if you rub a little more lightly and over here instead of there"). It is stressed that patients are to simply ask and tell each other what they would like to do during each particular sexual encounter.

Changing Destructive Life-Styles and Sex Roles. Direct therapy for sexual dysfunction often involves the therapist's stepping outside the usual therapeutic posture of *responding* to the patient, and instead taking an active, directive, and initiating role with the patient in regard to general life-style and sex-role issues. For example, many dysfunctional patients make sex the lowest priority item in their life. Sex occurs only when all career, housework, child-rearing, home management, friendship, and family responsibilities have been met. This usually ensures that sex occurs infrequently, hurriedly, late at night, and when both partners are physically and mentally fatigued. In such a case, patients may be instructed to make "dates" with each other for relaxing days or evenings (Annon, 1974). These dates may involve dinner and the theater, a day in the sun at a park or a beach, or simply sending the children to the baby-sitter and staying home with the telephone disconnected and a "Do Not Disturb" sign on the door. This simple change in itself tends to make sex a more positive experience. Similarly, patients may be advised to disengage from parents or others who are a destructive influence on their sexuality (Snyder, LoPiccolo, and LoPiccolo, 1975), to enter bankruptcy to solve hopeless financial troubles that consume all their emotional energy, or, as in a recent case, to quit a job that requires the husband to commute four hours daily to and from work.

Rigid and unsatisfying sex-role separation is also a major negative influence on many couples' sexual relationship. If a husband and wife spend virtually no time together and have no mutual, shared responsibility for the tasks of day-to-day living, it is unlikely that they will find sex to be a rewarding, close, sharing experience. The most common problem of this type involves the "housewife's lament" syndrome. In this syndrome, an educated, intelligent woman has given up her career or education to become a homemaker, maid, cook, and mother. When her husband comes home from work, he is tired and overstimulated. He wants peace, quiet, the newspaper, and a chance to do nothing. In a sense, his day is over. The woman, on the other hand, is also tired from a long day of household and child-rearing responsibilities but still has dinner to prepare, the dishes to do, the children to bathe and put to bed, etc. At the same time, she would like conversation and interaction from her husband after a day of children and housework. If he is unwilling to help reduce her evening work load and increase her life satisfaction, a poor, unrewarding sex life is perhaps the *best* he can hope for in the continuing progress of their relationship. While many men would usually resist taking on more household responsibilities, in the context of sex therapy a change can be produced *if the therapists take a strong, directive position on this issue.* An effective therapist statement to open discussion is, "You say your wife never wants sex anymore and doesn't enjoy it. It's clear to us that her work load in the evening *prevents* her getting in touch with her sex drive and her sexual responsiveness. Are you willing to make some changes that will lead to a good sex life for both of you, but will require some effort on your part?"

Prescribing Changes in Behavior. If there is any one procedure that is the hallmark of direct treatment of sexual dysfunction, it is the prescription by the therapist of a series of gradual steps of specific sexual behaviors to be performed by the patients in their own home. These behaviors are often described as "sensate focus" or "pleasuring" exercises. Typically, intercourse and, indeed, breast and genital touching are initially prohibited, and the patients only examine, discuss, and sensually massage each other's bodies. Forbidding more intense sexual expression allows the patients to enjoy kissing, hugging, body massage, and other sensual pleasures without the disruption that would occur if the patient anticipated these activities would be followed by intercourse or other sexual behaviors that have not been pleasurable in the past. The couple's sexual relationship is then rebuilt in a graduated series of successive approximations to full sexual intercourse. At each step, anxiety reduction, skill training, elimination of performance demands, and the other components described above are used to keep the couple's interactions pleasurable and therapeutic experiences. Exactly what specific behaviors are prescribed and how the other six components discussed above are integrated into these prescriptions will be described in the following section on specific types of sexual dysfunction.

Obviously, in prescribing some activities for the patients to perform and forbidding others, the question arises of how the therapist ensures patient compliance with these prescriptions and prohibitions. While some clinicians videotape or actually observe their patients' sexual behavior (Hartman and Fithian, 1972), this approach seems unlikely to be acceptable to the majority of sexually inhibited couples. Alternatively, patients may be required to keep separate written records of their "homework" activities and to pay the therapists a deposit in advance of treatment. This deposit is refunded in full if the patients comply with mutually agreed-upon therapeutic instructions. However, they forfeit (to charity, not to the therapist) increasingly larger portions of this deposit for each successive violation of therapeutic prescriptions. This "penalty deposit" system seems to work well in maintaining patient compliance with therapist instructions (Lobitz and LoPiccolo, 1972).

Types of Sexual Dysfunction

Premature Ejaculation

There are no objective criteria for what constitutes premature ejaculation. The problem of an objective definition is complicated by the fact that 27.5% of women will experience orgasm on 90% to 100% of coital opportunities even when the duration of coitus is less than one minute. At the other extreme, 10.2% of women will never or rarely experience coital orgasm even with coitus lasting longer than sixteen minutes (Gebhard, 1966). However, data do indicate that increasing ejaculatory latency beyond seven minutes is not strongly associated with increased incidence of coital orgasm for women, and that the median duration of intercourse for men is somewhere between four and seven minutes (Gebhard, 1966). Thus, one might suggest that a latency to ejaculation of less than four minutes may be a tentative indicator for treatment. Such a definition must be tempered by several other factors: How much manual and oral foreplay stimulation of his genitals can the male tolerate without ejaculation; whether the male is unrestrained in intercourse or can only delay ejaculation by slowing thrusting, thinking unpleasant, antierotic thoughts, biting his tongue, or wearing a condom; frequency of intercourse; age of the patient; and use of alcohol, drugs, and even topical anesthetic creams to dull sexual responsivity and delay ejaculation. It is therefore easier to describe what is *not* premature ejaculation: Both husband and wife agree that the quality of their sexual encounters is not influenced by efforts to delay ejaculation.

Since ejaculation is a response that is innervated by the sympathetic nervous system (Kaplan, 1974), one approach to premature ejaculation involves systematic desensitization (Wolpe, 1958). In systematic desensitization, muscle relaxation is used to elicit parasympathetic arousal, which then reduces sympathetic arousal through reciprocal inhibition. Procedurally, the patient practices deep muscle relaxation while visualizing items from a hierarchy of sexually arousing situations. This procedure is moderately successful in treating premature ejaculation (Cooper, 1968; Kraft and Al-Issa, 1968).

Far more effective is the procedure originally developed by James Semans (1956). Basically, the problem in premature ejaculation is the male's low threshold for amount of stimulation required to elicit the ejaculation response. In the Semans procedure, the penis is stimulated until ejaculation is imminent. At this point, stimulation is stopped. The male pauses until the sensation of high arousal subsides, then begins stimulation of the penis again. This procedure is repeated over and over again, until the male has experienced a massive amount of stimulation, *but without the occurrence of ejaculation.* The number of pauses required to sustain stimulation and delay ejaculation rapidly decreases over successive occasions with this procedure, and the male soon gains the capacity for penile stimulation of great duration without any pauses at all. The underlying mechanism in the Semans procedure may be Guthrie's "crowding the threshold" process for extinguishing stimulus–response connections—in this case, the connection between minimal stimulation and ejaculation. According to Guthrie, such extinction is produced by gradually exposing the subject to progressively more intense and more prolonged stimulation, but always keeping the intensity and duration of the stimulus just below the threshold for elicitation of the response (Guthrie, 1952).

Masters and Johnson (1970) have modified this procedure by having the wife stimulate the husband's penis and squeeze firmly on the frenulum when a pause in stimulation is needed. This "squeeze technique" is said to immediately eliminate the urge to ejaculate, and it may also cause the male to lose 10% to 30% of his erection. While there has not been a controlled experimental study of the relative effectiveness of the pause procedure versus the squeeze procedure, at a clinical level, both procedures seem to be quite effective. If the squeeze procedure is used, the patient should be cautioned to release the squeeze immediately if he ejaculates as a result of not stopping stimulation early enough. Ejaculation while physically holding the urethra closed can, in rare instances, produce retrograde ejaculation with concomitant risk of physiological problems in the bladder, prostate, or seminal vesicles.

There is one additional procedure that may enhance the effectiveness of the pause procedure. Contraction of the scrotum and elevation of the testicles occurs during high arousal and orgasm (Masters and Johnson, 1966). Indeed, for some men, cupping the scrotum and pressing it against the perineum will trigger orgasm during high arousal. Conversely, pulling down on the scrotum and testes seems to work like the squeeze procedure to reduce arousal and the urge to ejaculate in many men.

In prescribing homework assignments for the premature ejaculation patient, the first step involves masturbation with the pause procedure, to learn when to pause and to identify the signals of approaching ejaculation. The advantages of beginning with masturbation are threefold: (1) The male gains confidence and reduces his anxiety by learning some ejaculatory control before resuming sexual activity with his wife; (2) the male can focus exclusively on learning when and how to pause or squeeze, free of any pressure to also communicate this information to his wife; and (3) the spouse's eagerness to learn and cooperate is enhanced by the husband's report of the success of the procedure. Contrary to what has been reported elsewhere (Masters and Johnson, 1970, p. 113), data from patients treated in the author's clinical research program indicate good transfer of increased latency from masturbation to manipulation by the wife.

Next, the patient may be instructed to try the squeeze procedure, to see if this is more or less effective for him than the simple pause. In the next sessions, the male patient will teach this procedure to his wife. When good tolerance for manual and oral stimulation by the wife is achieved, the couple uses the pause (or squeeze) procedure during stationary vaginal containment of the penis, during slow pelvic thrusting, and finally during, full, unrestrained intercourse.

If the patient couple progresses through this procedure on a daily basis, the need to use the pause or squeeze will quickly diminish. Part of this gain is artifactual, however, as latency to ejaculation is greatly increased by frequent ejaculation. Such patients need to be placed on a "maintenance program," which includes occasional training sessions with the pause–squeeze procedures, to ensure that relapse does not occur following the intensive therapy period (Lobitz et al., 1974).

Erectile Failure

If the definition of premature ejaculation is complex, the definition of erectile failure is simple: inability of the male to attain or maintain an erection sufficient for intercourse.

The treatment program for erectile failure consists of two basic components: (1) ensuring that the patient is receiving a high level of physical and psychological sexual stimulation from his wife and (2) eliminating anxiety and performance demands that interfere with erection despite such adequate stimulation. Illustrating the mutual responsibility of both spouses for a sexual dysfunction, some cases of erectile failure are at least partially the result of the wife's poor sexual technique and her placing strong demands on the male to have erections. For example, in one recent case (Lobitz et al., 1974), the patients were a couple in their fifties, both married for the second time. The wife's first husband had always had an erection *before* beginning lovemaking, and did not want her to touch his genitals at all. The male patient had been previously married to a woman who manually and orally stimulated his genitals a great deal before intercourse. When the patient couple began their sexual relationship, their very different expectations about the role of foreplay in producing an erection led to conflict. Because of communication difficulties, these conflicts were never resolved. Instead, the wife became quite bitter, frustrated, and hostile about "his" sexual dysfunction.

In such cases of insufficient stimulation and excessive demands for performance by either the wife's or the husband's own expectations, a number of therapeutic tactics are indicated. The therapist should instruct the couple that erection is not subject to voluntary control and is neither spontaneous nor instantaneous (especially in older males) but will automatically occur given sufficient stimulation in an anxiety-free setting. Performance demands on the husband and the wife's frustration can be reduced through instructing the couple to assure orgasm for the female by means of manual, oral, or electric vibrator stimulation of her genitals, none of which requires the male to have an erect penis. Explicit films and books can be used to train the wife in effective stimulation techniques. If the wife makes demanding or derogatory statements about her husband's sexual abilities, the therapist should emphasize that such demands or criticism are counterproductive and increase the anxiety that causes the male's erectile failure. In extreme cases, when all else has failed to change the wife's attitude, an effective statement is, "Most men would find it very difficult to have erections in a sexual relationship with you at this time. We know you can change and learn to be a more skilled lover and less demanding. Are you willing to accept responsibility and make these changes, with our help?"

An equally powerful source of anxiety, independent of the spouse's reaction, stems from the male's own attitude toward sex, once erectile failure has begun to occur. That is, a male with erectile failure tends to enter his sexual encounters as an anxious observer rather than as an aroused participant. That is, he watches closely for signs of erection, is upset by any lag in gaining erection or any signs of partial loss of erection. Since this anxiety about erection obviously prevents erection from occurring, one therapeutic approach is to use systematic desensitization to eliminate anxiety (Cooper, 1963; Friedman, 1968; Kushner, 1965; Lazarus, 1965). Since erection is mediated by the parasympathetic nervous system, the state of sympathetic arousal associated with anxiety interferes with erection, and the parasympathetic arousal produced by muscle relaxation in systematic desensitization presumably facilitates erection.

Alternatively, anxiety reduction can be accomplished by prescribing a course of homework activities for the couple which preclude performance anxiety and ensure adequate stimulation for the male. Paradoxical instructions (Annon, 1974) can be utilized in prescribing these activities to further eliminate anxiety. For example, the first set of activities might require the couple only to examine and massage each other's nude bodies, not including any stimulation of the male's genitals. The male is paradoxically instructed that "the purpose of this exercise is for you to learn to enjoy *sensual* pleasures, without focusing on *sexual* goals. Therefore, you should try to *not* get an erection. Erection would mean you are being sexual rather than sensual." Obviously, a nude massage is a sexually stimulating experience. The paradoxical demand *not* to get an erection in this setting effectively frees the man from anxiety about getting an erection.

Over successive occasions, the couple's repertoire of sexual activities can now be rebuilt. The next assignment might be for the wife to manually or orally stimulate the male's penis but to stop such stimulation immediately should an erection occur. Only when the penis is flaccid should stimulation be resumed. This procedure, which has been called the "teasing technique" (Masters and Johnson, 1970), convinces the couple that if erection is lost, it can be regained. Next, penile insertion into the vagina is allowed, but only with the female physically pushing the male's flaccid penis into her vagina while she sits astride his supine body. Again, the couple is told, "This procedure works best with a flaccid penis. If you can't avoid an erection, it's all right, although not as good, to go ahead and insert anyway. But please try *not* to have an erection." Once the male has been unable to avoid an erection during vaginal containment, slow pelvic thrusting by each partner, mutual slow thrusting, vigorous intercourse, and finally coital ejaculation can be prescribed. The timing of these activities is such that they are only prescribed after the patients have seen that they naturally and automatically occur if the male is stimulated and not anxious. For example, ejaculation is "allowed" only after the male has been unable to restrain himself from ejaculating intravaginally (LoPiccolo and Lobitz, 1973).

While this procedure works well with most cases, it has not been found successful in cases where the male has a homosexual orientation (Masters and Johnson, 1970, p. 273). In such cases, lack of psychological stimulation (rather than the male's anxiety and the wife's poor technique) may be a factor. That is, if a male is more aroused by men than by women, removing his performance anxiety may still leave him unaroused in response to his wife's lovemaking, regardless of how nondemanding and skilled she may be. For such cases, addition of a classical conditioning procedure to increase heterosexual arousal seems to increase effectiveness of the basic treatment strategy (LoPiccolo, Stewart, and Watkins, 1972). In this procedure, the male masturbates with his currently arousing homosexual fantasies and explicit stimuli, such as pictures of nude males. Just prior to orgasm, the male is instructed to switch his focus to fantasies of heterosexual activities with his spouse, and to look at erotic photographs of her. Such photos can be discreetly obtained by supplying the couple with a Polaroid self-developing camera. This procedure ensures that the pleasure of orgasm occurs in a heterosexual context. On subsequent occasions, this switch can be made earlier in masturbation until fantasies and photos of the wife become effective sexual stimuli in their own right. This stimulus-switching procedure can also be used by the couple in their series of prescribed sexual activities.

While all patients seeking sex therapy should receive a complete physical examination before entering treatment, such an examination is especially important in erectile failure cases. Unlike premature ejaculation and female orgasmic dysfunction, there are many organic causes (such as diabetes and vascular disease) for erectile failure (Belt, 1973; Dengrove, 1971).

Ejaculatory Incompetence

Ejaculatory incompetence involves the inability of the male to reach orgasm through stimulation by his wife. While failure to reach orgasm is common in women, it is quite rare in men. For example, while Kinsey, Pomeroy, Martin, and Gebhard (1953) found that up to 15% of women remain inorgasmic even after many years of marriage, the incidence of orgasmic failure in males is too low to permit statistical study. There may be an evolutionary basis for this difference, in that there is selective pressure on males but not on females to have orgasm. That is, for a male's genes to continue in the gene pool, he must ejaculate (have orgasm) while mating. On the other hand, ovulation and fertilization of the ovum are not related to occurrence of female orgasm.

Treatment of the ejaculatory incompetent couple follows a paradigm that combines elements from the premature ejaculation and the erectile failure programs. As in cases of premature ejaculation, the couple is instructed in the technique of providing massive amounts of stimulation of the male's penis, but without use of the pause or squeeze procedures. Similar to treatment of erectile failure, the wife is trained to be an effective sexual partner for her husband, and, perhaps most importantly, all performance demands upon him for ejaculation are eliminated through the same procedures used to reduce performance anxiety in erectile failure. To increase stimulation, an electric vibrator may be used by the wife or her husband. The previously discussed procedure of cupping the testicles to elicit orgasm may be used, as well as the body posture and muscular procedures used to trigger female orgasm, as described in the following section.

In treating ejaculatory incompetence, it should be ascertained that the patient is not receiving any tranquilizing drugs, especially phenothiazines. Ejaculation is a sympathetic response, and ejaculatory incompetence can be a side effect of these sympathetic blocking agents.

Orgasmic Dysfunction

There are several types of orgasmic dysfunction in women. *Primary* orgasmic dysfunction applies to the woman who has never experienced an orgasm through any means of sexual stimulation. *Secondary* orgasmic dysfunction applies to a woman who usually cannot experience orgasm during coitus but who is able to have orgasm through masturbation or through her husband's manual or oral stimulation of her genitals. In discussing a lack of coital orgasm, it must be emphasized that "coital" orgasm is not synonomous with "vaginal" orgasm. Psychoanalytic theory makes a specious and now discredited distinction between "clitoral" and "vaginal" orgasm (Kinsey et al., 1953; Lydon, 1970; Weisstein, 1971; Sherfey, 1966). In this view, a woman who achieves orgasm through her husband's manipulation of her genitals is considered neurotic, immature, and "frigid" (Fenichel, 1945). Research has now made it clear that *all* orgasms are physiologically identical and derive from clitoral stimulation (Masters and Johnson, 1966). If a woman has orgasm during coitus, this orgasm is produced in large part by indirect stimulation of the clitoris from the husband's pubis, and by penile thrusting causing the labia to pull on the clitoral hood. Obviously, such stimulation can also be directly produced if the husband (or the woman herself) manually manipulates the clitoris during intercourse. To argue that orgasm produced by direct clitoral stimulation during coitus is somehow more immature and less phychologically healthy than orgasm produced by indirect clitoral stimulation is to draw almost mystical distinctions between the male pubis and the male hand. It should be stressed, therefore, that a woman who can have coital orgasm if she receives concurrent manual stimulation of her clitoris *does not* have secondary orgasmic dysfunction; she is normal. Similarly, a woman who regularly has orgasm during manual or oral stimulation by her husband, and who enjoys intercourse even though orgasm does not occur during coitus, is a candidate for reassurance about her normality rather than for sex therapy. The therapist must take care, however, that reassurance does not have the effect of making a patient couple feel that they cannot or should not want to change sexual patterns that are unsatisfying to them.

In addition to the primary–secondary distinction, a distinction can be drawn between those inorgasmic women who are *inhibited* and those who suffer from performance anxiety. The inhibited woman approaches the stereotype of the "frigid" woman. Such a woman has a history of negative parental or religious

indoctrination about sex, finds sex repulsive, does not become aroused, and enters therapy reluctantly, perhaps primarily to keep her husband from leaving her. These women need heavy exposure to the *information and education* and *attitude change* procedures previously described. The woman with *performance anxiety*, on the other hand, often has an unremarkable parental and religious history, enjoys sex, becomes aroused, and enters therapy eager for the experience of orgasm for her own gratification. These cases have often been exposed to mass media demands to be multiorgasmic and supersexual if they are "real" women. Alternatively, the husbands of such women often have profound doubts about their own masculinity and abilities as lovers, and put their wives under extreme pressure to have orgasms to reassure themselves on this issue. Such cases need more emphasis on the principles of *eliminating performance anxiety* and *increasing communication and effectiveness of sexual techniques* described above.

The role of the husband as an effective and nondemanding sexual partner for his wife is obviously crucial in orgasmic dysfunction, especially secondary orgasmic dysfunction. In one sense, it can be argued that if a woman can produce orgasm for herself through masturbation but cannot have orgasm with her husband, he is the dysfunctional one. This relates to the old maxim that "there are no frigid women, only clumsy men." In many cases, this is true: The woman's sexual responsiveness is entirely normal, but her husband is quite inept as a lover. The principle of mutual responsibility, however, points out that such a woman has failed to *train* her husband to be an effective lover *for her*. This suggests a revision of the old maxim: "There are both frigid women and clumsy men, and they are usually married to each other."

The treatment program for orgasmic dysfunction involves four different components. First, for the woman who has never experienced an orgasm, a program of directed masturbation is indicated (LoPiccolo and Lobitz, 1972). The rationale for the use of masturbation includes the fact that it is the sexual technique most likely to produce an orgasm. According to Kinsey et al. (1953), for the average woman the probabilities of orgasm are .95 for masturbation and .74 for coitus. In prescribing masturbation, LoPiccolo and Lobitz (1972) describe a nine-step program. In step one, the woman visually examines her genitals with the aid of a hand mirror and diagrams. At this time, she is also placed on a program of Kegel's (1952) exercises to enhance her orgasmic potential through increasing strength and vascularity of the pelvic musculature. In steps two and three, the woman tactually explores her genitals to locate pleasure-sensitive areas. In steps four and five, the woman learns to intensely stimulate these areas while using erotic fantasies or explicit literature and photos to enhance arousal. She is also taught to label her physiologic responses to such intense stimulation as sexual arousal and pleasure, rather than, as often occurs, other states such as anxiety, discomfort, or tension. If orgasm has not yet occurred, in step six the woman masturbates using the electric vibrator.

Steps seven through nine of this program involve the second major component of treatment for orgasmic dysfunction—skill training for the husband. In step seven, he observes his wife's masturbation to learn what is effective for her. In step eight, he learns to manipulate her to orgasm, and in step nine this manipulation is paired with coitus. While this program has produced good results, it should be

emphasized that it is not used in isolation. Typically, the male is also placed on the same masturbation program to ensure his cooperation and support of the female. Also throughout this program the couple has a series of prescribed *mutual* activities to engage in, starting with simple nondemanding body massage and progressing through kissing and hugging, breast stimulation, genital stimulation, penile insertion, and slow thrusting, and ending in full intercourse.

A third major component of treatment or orgasmic dysfunction involves disinhibition of arousal. Many inorgasmic women are inhibited from reaching orgasm by fear of loss of control or embarrassment about displaying intense sexual arousal and pleasure in front of their husbands. Such a woman may be able to reach high levels of arousal (but not orgasm) in masturbation, or to masturbate to orgasm when alone but not in the presence of her husband. In such cases, the patient is instructed to repeatedly role-play a grossly exaggerated orgasm with violent convulsions, screaming, and other extreme behavior. Knowing that she is merely acting, the couple can engage in this activity quite readily. With repeated role play of exaggerated orgasm during the couple's prescribed homework activities, the initial fear and embarrassment turns into amusement and eventually boredom (Lobitz and LoPiccolo, 1972).

Obviously, all procedures for disinhibiting a woman about displaying her sexuality depend ultimately upon the husband's ability to respond in an unambivalent, positive manner to his wife's increased sexual responsiveness. Many male patients, however, in a seeming paradox, become unenthusiastic, derogatory, negativistic, or even hostile as their previously unresponsive wives show treatment gains. Inquiry typically reveals that these men fear that their wives will become too sexually demanding or promiscuous. Therapist reassurance that these fears are normal, common at this point in therapy, and unfounded will usually allay the husband's anxieties. Failure to deal with these issues will often lead to the husband negating the treatment effects.

The fourth component of therapy for orgasmic dysfunction involves teaching the woman certain behaviors that, if performed during high sexual arousal, will often trigger the orgasm response. These behaviors tend to occur spontaneously or involuntarily during intense orgasm (Singer and Singer, 1972) and, when performed voluntarily, may initiate orgasm. These "orgasm triggers" include pelvic thrusting, pointing the toes, tensing the thigh muscles, holding the breath, pushing down with the diaphragm, contracting the vaginal musculature, and throwing the head back to displace the glottis.

All four of the components described above seem to be most effective in cases of primary orgasmic dysfunction. It has been suggested that secondary orgasmic dysfunction is associated with a distressed marital relationship, and that it may be a symptom and result of this distress rather than a sexual problem in its own right (McGovern, Stewart, and LoPiccolo, 1975). Such cases may respond better to a combination of sex therapy and marital counseling than to pure sex therapy (Snyder et al., 1975).

Vaginismus

Vaginismus refers to involuntary spastic contraction of the vaginal musculature such that intromission cannot be accomplished or can only take place with

great difficulty and pain. If physical examination reveals no organic basis, vaginismus is usually an anxiety response. The woman may fear penetration because of prior painful attempts at coitus due to lack of lubrication, rape, extreme fear or guilt during the first attempt at coitus, or in rare instances, an extremely naïve couple who mistake the anus or the urethral opening for the vagina. In treating vaginismus, one addition is made to the usual program for orgasmic dysfunction. A graduated series of dilators is used to enable the woman to learn to tolerate vaginal intromission. This dilation program may be carried out by the gynecologist in the office or by the woman or her husband at home. Such dilation can also be accomplished with the woman's (or her husband's) fingers (Haslam, 1965; Wolpe, 1969; Masters and Johnson, 1970; Fuchs, Hoch, Paldi, Abramouici, Brandes, Timor-Tritsch, and Kleinhaus, 1973). In addition, the Kegel (1952) exercises may be utilized not to strengthen the vaginal musculature but as a means of enabling the woman to attain voluntary control of these muscles.

The Future: Current Trends in Direct Therapy for Sexual Dysfunction

While the recent rapid acceptance of direct action modes of therapy for sexual dysfunction has brought effective treatment to many distressed couples, the results of this rapid growth are not unmixed. If the publicity sex therapy has received in recent years has made many couples aware that there is hope for them, it has also attracted many unqualified people into the field and led to outrageous fees being charged for sex therapy. While years of study and strict legal and professional requirements must be met to legally represent oneself as a psychiatrist or clinical psychologist, virtually anyone can legally enter practice as a "sex therapist." It must be realized that direct therapy is still a form of psychotherapy, and that psychotherapy training is needed to help the acutely distressed couples who seek sex therapy. Unfortunately, sex educators, counselors, sociologists, clergy, and other people with little or no formal psychotherapy training are now springing up as sex therapists. Often these people have an impressive (to the unsuspecting patient) diploma, complete with gold seal and blue ribbon certifying their status as sex therapists. Such diplomas can be obtained by anyone willing to pay a fee and attend a brief workshop. It is also remarkable to consider that in the United States, fifteen hours of psychotherapy cost between $450 and $600. The same fifteen hours of therapy from one of the myriad "sex therapy centers" cost $2,500 to $3,000.

On the positive side, a number of investigators are now working on group therapy, instructional books and films, and self-help programs for dysfunctional couples. These procedures should provide wider availability of effective help for many couples who cannot afford the current fees. Similarly, there is a small but growing trend for medical schools and graduate programs in clinical psychology to include sexual therapy in their curricula, which should lead to an increase in the number of qualified therapists and a decrease in the fees currently charged.

It is to be hoped that the need for sex therapy will eventually disappear entirely. Perhaps in the future our society will come to value sexuality as an expression of one of the least destructive and most loving components of the human personality, and will communicate this clearly to our children. Children raised in such a culture would presumably find the idea of "sexual dysfunction" to be emotionally incomprehensible. It is the responsibility of the current generation of researchers and clinicians who work in the area of human sexuality to foster this change in our society.

References

Annon, J. S. *The behavioral treatment of sexual problems.* Honolulu: Kapiolani Health Services, 1974.

Bardwick, J. *Psychology of women.* New York: Harper & Row, 1971.

Belt, B. G. Some organic causes of impotence. *Medical Aspects of Human Sexuality*, 1973, *7*, 152–161.

Bergler, E. Frigidity in the female: Misconceptions and facts. *Marriage Hygiene*, 1947, *1*, 16–21.

Bergler, E. *Neurotic counterfeit-sex.* New York: Grune and Stratton, 1951.

Brady, J. P. Brevital relaxation treatment of frigidity. *Behaviour Research and Therapy*, 1966, *4*, 71–77.

Brown, D. G. Female orgasm and sexual inadequacy. In R. and E. Brecher (Eds.), *An analysis of human sexual response.* New York: New American Library, 1966.

Christensen, H. T., and Gregg, C. F. Changing sex norms in America and Scandinavia. *Journal of Marriage and the Family*, 1970, *32*, 616–627.

Comfort, A. *The anxiety makers.* Camden, New Jersey: T. Nelson & Sons, 1965.

Cooper, A. J. A case of fetishism and impotence treated by behavior therapy. *British Journal of Psychiatry*, 1963, *109*, 649–652.

Cooper, A. J. A factual study of male potency disorders. *British Journal of Psychiatry*, 1968, *114*, 719–731.

Dengrove, E. The urologic aspects of impotence. *Journal of Sex Research*, 1971, *7*, 163–168.

Fenichel, O. *The psychoanalytic theory of neurosis.* New York: Norton, 1945.

Festinger, L. *A theory of cognitive dissonance.* Stanford: Stanford University Press, 1957.

Freud, S. *Three essays on the theory of sexuality.* Standard Ed., Vol. 7. London: Hogarth, 1962. (Originally published 1905.) P. 125.

Friedman, D. The treatment of impotence by Brevital relaxation therapy. *Behavior Research and Therapy*, 1968, *6*, 257–261.

Fuchs, K., Hoch, E., Paldi, H., Abramouici, H., Brandes, J., Timor-Tritsch, I., and Kleinhaus, M. Hypno-desensitization of vaginismus. *International Journal of Clinical and Experimental Hypnosis*, 1973, *21* (3), 144–156.

Gebhard, P. Factors in marital orgasm. *Journal of Social Issues*, 1966, *22* (2), 88–96.

Guthrie, E. R. *The psychology of learning.* New York: Harper, 1952.

Haley, J. *Uncommon therapy.* New York: Ballantine Books, 1973.

Hartman, W. E., and Fithian, M. A. *Treatment of sexual dysfunction.* Long Beach: California Center for Marital and Sexual Studies, 1972.

Haslam, M. T. The treatment of psychogenic dyspareunia by reciprocal inhibition. *British Journal of Psychiatry*, 1965, *111*, 280–282.

Hastings, D. W. *Impotence and frigidity.* Boston: Little, Brown, 1963.

Jourard, S. M. *The transparent self.* Princeton: D. Van Nostrand, 1964.

Kaplan, H. S. *The new sex therapy.* New York: Brunner/Mazel, 1974.

Kegel, A. H. Sexual functions of the pubococcygeus muscle. *Western Journal of Obstetrics and Gynecology*, 1952, *60*, 521.

Kinsey, A. C., Pomeroy, W. B., and Martin, C. E. *Sexual behavior in the human male.* Philadelphia: W. B. Saunders, 1948.

Kinsey, A. C., Pomeroy, W. B., Martin, C. E., and Gebhard, P. H. *Sexual behavior in the human female.* Philadelphia: W. B. Saunders, 1953.

Kraft, T., and Al-Issa, I. Behavior therapy and the treatment of frigidity. *American Journal of Psychotherapy*, 1967, *21*, 116–120.

Kraft, T., and Al-Issa, I. The use of methahexitone sodium in the systematic desensitization of premature ejaculation. *British Journal of Psychiatry*, 1968, *114*, 351–352.

Kushner, M. The reduction of long standing fetish by means of aversive conditioning. In L. P. Ullmann and L. Krasner (Eds.), *Case studies in behavior modification*. New York: Holt, Rinehart & Winston, 1965. Pp. 239–242.

Lazarus, A. A. The treatment of chronic frigidity by systematic desensitization. *Journal of Nervous and Mental Disease*, 1963, *136*, 272–278.

Lazarus, A. A. The treatment of a sexually inadequate man. In L. P. Ullmann and L. Krasner (Eds.), *Case studies in behavior modification*. New York: Holt, Rinehart & Winston, 1965. Pp. 243–245.

Lobitz, W. C., and LoPiccolo, J. New methods in the behavioral treatment of sexual dysfunction. *Journal of Behavior Therapy and Experimental Psychiatry*, 1972, *3* (4), 265–271.

Lobitz, W. C., LoPiccolo, J., Lobitz, G., and Brockway, J. A closer look at "simplistic" behavior therapy for sexual dysfunction: Two case studies. In H. J. Eysenck (Ed.), *Case studies in behavior therapy*. London: Routledge & Kegan Paul, 1974.

LoPiccolo, J., and Lobitz, W. C. The role of masturbation in the treatment of orgasmic dysfunction. *Archives of Sexual Behavior*, 1972, *2*, 153–164.

LoPiccolo, J., and Lobitz, W. C. Behavior therapy of sexual dysfunction. In L. A. Hammerlynck, L. C. Handy and E. J. Mash (Eds.), *Behavior change: Methodology, concepts, and practice*. Champaign, Illinois: Research Press, 1973. Chapter 13.

LoPiccolo, J., Stewart, R., and Watkins, B. Case study: Treatment of erectile failure and ejaculatory incompetence in a case with homosexual etiology. *Journal of Behavior Therapy and Experimental Psychiatry*, 1972, *3*, 233–236.

Lorand, S. Contribution to the problem of vaginal orgasm. *International Journal of Psychoanalysis*, 1934, *20*, 432–438.

Lydon, S. The politics of orgasm. In N. Garskof (Ed.), *Roles women play*. Monterey, California: Brooks/Cole, 1971.

Masters, W. H., and Johnson, V. E. *Human sexual response*. Boston: Little, Brown, 1966.

Masters, W. H., and Johnson, V. E. *Human sexual inadequacy*. Boston: Little, Brown, 1970.

McGovern, L., Stewart, R., and LoPiccolo, J. Secondary orgasmic dysfunction I: Analysis and strategies for treatment. *Archives of Sexual Behavior*, 1975, *4* (3), 265–275.

Moore, Burness E. Frigidity in women. *Journal of the American Psychoanalytic Association*, 1961, *9*, 571–584.

Semans, J. H. Premature ejaculation: A new approach. *Southern Medical Journal*, 1956, *49*, 353–357.

Sherfey, J. J. The evolution and nature of female sexuality in relation to psychoanalytic theory. *Journal of the American Psychoanalytic Association*, 1966, *14*, 28–128.

Singer, I., and Singer, J. Types of female orgasm. *Journal of Sex Research*, 1972, *8*, 255–267.

Snyder, A., LoPiccolo, L., and LoPiccolo, J. Secondary orgasmic dysfunction II: Case study. *Archives of Sexual Behavior*, 1975, *4* (3), 277–283.

Weisstein, N. Psychology constructs the female, or the fantasy life of the male psychologist. In N. Garskof (Ed.), *Roles women play*. Monterey, California: Brooks/Cole, 1971.

Wolpe, J. *Psychotherapy by reciprocal inhibition*. Stanford University Press, 1958. Pp. 130–135.

Wolpe, J. *The practice of behavior therapy*. New York: Pergamon Press, 1969.

Sex therapy is often described as nothing more than a set of behavioral procedures and techniques. Lazarus points out in this article that just the use of such procedures alone is often not enough to produce change. The need for assertion training and behavioral rehearsal as well as deconditioning of anxiety responses in men with erectile failure is an example of the need for a broad-spectrum approach to the treatment of sexual problems.

In this article Lazarus also stresses the importance of attitudinal and prior learning factors in therapy, in terms of both the cause of sexual dysfunction and the influence of these factors on the success or failure of treatment procedures. A common criticism of behavioral procedures is that they are based on an oversimplified and mechanistic view of personality. This article addresses these concerns and offers an example of an eclectic, broad-spectrum approach to sexual problems.

2

Overcoming Sexual Inadequacy

Arnold A. Lazarus

Effective psychotherapy frequently necessitates an appreciation of the subtle interplay between biological, psychological, and sociological factors. Nowhere is this more fundamental than in the treatment of sexual problems. To consider sexual intercourse merely the expression of a "drive" or "need" is to ignore the network of social values, cultural taboos, and personal attitudes that permeate every aspect of this frenetic embrace. Very few sexual problems stem entirely from structural, hormonal, or neuronic deficiencies. The overwhelming majority of sexual problems stem from psychological (attitudinal) determinants.

Sexual information, despite the efforts of many enlightened educators, remains confusingly fragmentary and contradictory. Many forces favoring sexual obscurantism still retain an unhealthy measure of support in our society. Puritanism, although waning, is still responsible for disseminating sexual myths and superstitions. It is hardly necessary to labor the point that many people are uninformed and uncertain about sexual matters. But as Fromme (1966, p. 7) points out, the situation is not easily remedied. "Although sex is here to stay there are

When this chapter was originally published, Arnold A. Lazarus was visiting professor and director of clinical training in the Department of Psychology, Yale University, New Haven, Connecticut.

Arnold A. Lazarus • Graduate School of Applied and Professional Psychology, Rutgers University, New Brunswick, New Jersey

many people and many forces attempting to drive it underground. In addition to legal censorship, we have religious bans and, probably most pervasive of all, just plain common prudishness."

The strongly inhibitory sex training that predominates in North American society is described by Bandura and Walters (1963, p. 149) as being "accomplished mainly by the transmission to children of parental anxiety reactions to the exploratory, manipulative and curiosity behavior that inevitably occur during childhood." Consequently, it is not surprising that even in this supposedly enlightened era, clinicians' caseloads are replete with sexually disturbed individuals. In this chapter we are concerned with the understanding and correction of sexual insufficiency or inadequacy (commonly referred to as "frigidity" in the case of females and "impotence" and "premature ejaculation" in the case of males).

Forms of Sexual Inadequacy

In general, the terms *frigidity* and *impotence* refer to the inability to initiate, enjoy, or complete sexual intercourse. Successful coitus presupposes that this most intimate act be taken to the point of mutual fulfillment. Obviously, there are degrees of impotence and frigidity. Some men display almost complete absence of sexual arousal. Others, although easily aroused, nevertheless lose their erections before reaching orgasm. Similarly, sexual problems in women range from those who find coitus completely revolting to those who experience difficulty in reaching a climax.

While the term *impotence* usually implies various degrees of difficulty in obtaining and/or maintaining erections, it also refers to those males who are capable of prolonged coitus but who have difficulty in achieving orgasm or ejaculation (known as retarded ejaculation or ejaculatory impotence). The term also describes those men who report minimal or limited pleasure in sex, especially ejaculation without sensation. Some authorities view premature ejaculation as a form of impotence, whereas others regard it as a separate condition. Kinsey, Pomeroy, Martin, and Gebhard (1948, p. 580) consider rapid ejaculation a superior biological trait! But the man who ejaculates too soon is obviously unable to maintain an erection to the satisfaction of the female and is certainly considered "impotent" in her eyes.

It is uncommon to find women who find all sexual contacts anathema. Most "frigid" women occasionally experience mild but essentially fleeting pleasure during sex. Frigidity parallels the features of impotence in several respects. Some women fail to become sexually aroused; others tend to lose their response before reaching orgasm (corresponding to loss of erection in the male); and some, although adequately aroused, experience great difficulty in achieving orgasm. However, whereas "orgasmic impotence" is common in women, it is rare in men, and whereas premature orgasms are common in men, this condition is probably nonexistent in women. Absence of pleasure in sex is the most common feature of frigidity. Some writers (e.g., Kant, 1969) define frigidity as the absence of orgasmic response. But surely, those women who enjoy coitus by obtaining sensual pleasure, emotional closeness, and physical excitement, and who feel satisfied despite the lack of a true orgasm, should not be called "frigid." Unfortunately the term *frigid* is often used in a pejorative manner.

In broad outline, impotent men usually desire or even crave sexual intercourse but are unable to perform the act; frigid women usually have no desire for sex and derive little or no pleasure from the act, but are generally able to go through with it. A condition known as vaginismus (conditioned involuntary spasm of the perivaginal and circumvaginal muscles) makes intercourse painful or impossible for certain frigid women. But whereas the impotent male is usually traumatized by his condition, the frigid female may sometimes be proud of herself.

Causal Factors in Impotence and Frigidity

The causes of sexual inadequacy are varied. Numerous drugs, chemicals, or toxins may impair sexual functioning. Most physical illnesses that produce general malaise tend to decrease sexual capacities. Certain systemic diseases can produce chronic sexual problems, and local diseases of the genitourinary tracts may also interfere with sexual drive and performance. Sexual apathy is often seen in psychotic syndromes, especially in certain depressive conditions. Ellis (1961, p. 450) contends that certain cases of frigidity may be due to "innate or constitutional lack of sexual responsiveness."

The vast majority of impotent males and frigid females, however, do not suffer from any of the aforementioned conditions or any other organic lesions. In most cases of impotence and frigidity psychological factors play the major role. This implies that past experience or learning is usually responsible for the origin and maintenance of sexual inadequacy.

In broad neurophysiological terms, sexual arousal depends upon discharges of the autonomic nervous system. Erection in the male and clitoral enlargement and vaginal distension in the female are predominantly parasympathetic functions. Discharges of the sympathetic division exert an inhibitory effect on sexual arousal and performance. Thus, doubt, fear, guilt, shame, conflict, embarrassment, tension, disgust, irritation, resentment, grief, hostility, and most other "negative emotional reactions" will tend to undermine, diminish, or extinguish sexual capacities in men and women. In certain instances, however, negative emotions may heighten the sexual drive, akin to some compulsive eaters who use food to inhibit their anxieties. The sexual response is in fact a very delicate and vulnerable mechanism, perhaps more quickly and readily disturbed than any other aspect of behavior.

The "sexual drive" and its expression are often likened to the "hunger drive" and its ramifications. Despite obvious differences between so-called hunger pangs and a sexual appetite, both are stimulated by complex central and peripheral physiological processes, and both show wide individual differences in taste and appeal which, in turn, are a function of past experience and cultural conditioning. The crude and hurried ingestion of an ill-prepared meal and the gourmet's epicurean delights serve the same physiological purposes but occupy vastly different psychological planes. And so it is with sex where the flimsy division between ardor and obscenity can transform passion into an assault. The sexual anorexia of many a frigid female may be traced to formative encounters with insensitive men who provided crudeness and vulgarity in place of tenderness and consideration.

Simple and Complex Factors

In reviewing the life histories of impotent men and frigid women, diverse causative factors are evident. "I believe that I have damaged myself through excessive masturbation," said the twenty-year-old son of Calvinistic parents. A twenty-two-year-old frigid social worker stated, "The way my clients behave sexually doesn't offend me, but I personally have been raised to regard sex as an evil and degrading pastime." Frequent antecedents include fear of unwanted pregnancy (despite the advent of oral contraceptives), hostility toward the sexual partner, and various patterns of guilt and anxiety. Since the male's image of his own masculinity is so often dependent upon his sexual performance, he can readily develop a "fear of fear." The man, for instance, who enters sex with the thought, "Wouldn't it be awful if I became so tense or anxious during sex that I lost my erection!" may thereby engender sufficient anxiety to suppress all sexual feeling. Certain women these days also place such a premium on sexual adequacy that they inadvertently sabotage their sexual pleasures by becoming too concerned about their own level of performance. In some cases, sexual difficulties stem directly from doubts people have about the appearance and adequacy of their bodies in general and their sex organs in particular. Indeed, causal factors may range all the way from simple squeamishness to the complex personal philosophies concerned with the concept of pleasure.

I have observed a tendency among some psychologists and psychiatrists to view sexual difficulties with unnecessary pessimism. This stems from the habit of compounding sexual problems by insisting that nearly all cases of sexual inadequacy are deep-seated in origin and require extensive reconstructive therapy.

A case worth citing is that of a nineteen-year-old lad, seen at a psychiatric ward round, who mentioned his overriding fear of sexual intercourse and described how friends had informed him that in certain women the vagina was capable of such violent spasms and contractions as to endanger the male organ. The chief psychiatrist accordingly referred to "deep-seated castration anxieties" and predicted that even long-term analysis might not yield improvement. Yet, when one of the doctors simply corrected the lad's misconceptions and offered him factual information bolstered by the force of his own prestige, the problem was instantly resolved. In this age of psychological oversophistication, the search for complex answers to simple questions has become an international malady.

Pseudoinadequacies

A number of people who consult therapists for the treatment of frigidity or impotence suffer only from misinformation. It is extremely common, for instance, to find women who consider themselves frigid (or are regarded as such by their husbands) on the basis of being capable of achieving only manually induced clitoral orgasms. Freud (1938) is probably responsible for popularizing the myth that the woman who achieves a clitoral as opposed to a vaginal orgasm is immature and emotionally disturbed. Bergler and Kroger (1953, p. 711) exemplify this erroneous point of view: "Frigidity is the incapacity of a women to achieve a vaginal orgasm during intercourse. It is of no matter whether the woman is aroused during coitus or remains cold, whether excitement is weak or strong, whether it breaks off at the beginning or ends slowly or suddenly, whether it is dissipated in preliminary acts or has been lacking from the beginning. The only criterion of frigidity is absence of vaginal orgasm." Yet when reviewing the role of clitoral versus vaginal orgasms on the basis of experimental data, Masters and Johnson (1966, p. 66) arrive at very different conclusions: "Are clitoral and vaginal orgasms truly separate anatomic entities? From a biologic point of view, the answer to this question is an unequivocal No." Ellis (1962, p. 97) is equally explicit: "Penile–vaginal intercourse may abet orgasm through providing indirect stimulation for the clitoral situated genital corpuscles; or in some copulative positions, it may result in direct stimulation for the clitoris itself. No matter: the female orgasm is still mainly clitoral and not vaginal. So-called vaginal orgasm, therefore, is a myth." In *The Sexually Responsive Woman* (Kronhausen and Kronhausen, 1964, p. 26) the authors emphasize the following: "We now know, on the basis of such solid scientific research as is available, that there is no need for a shift or transfer of sensitivity from the clitoris to the vagina. On the contrary, it is not the vagina but the clitoris which remains throughout the woman's life the organ with the greatest potential for erotic stimulation." It is rather tragic to contemplate how many "man-years of analytic hours have been spent with presumably frigid women in exploring the causative psychological factors which prevented the clitoral–vaginal transfer" (Hastings, 1963, p. 35).

Another pseudoproblem involves the male who considers himself impotent because he is either sexually unresponsive to some women or incapable of immediate sexual arousal. Men's erotic boastings have led to a stereotype of the male as a most undiscriminating animal who desires to cohabit with almost every female, and in whom physical proximity with any woman will lead to immediate and sustained sexual arousal. Some men view any personal deviation from this putative norm with concern if not distress. Thus, a thirty-five-year-old man sought therapy after an unsuccessful encounter with a paid companion at a motel. He considered irrelevant the fact that he was somewhat fatigued after a long journey, had imbibed a fairly large quantity of alcohol, found the girl relatively unattractive, and was preoccupied with various business negotiations. "The way I see it is that if you're in bed with a woman, bombs could be bustin' up the joint and you shouldn't even notice it." This attitude typifies a widely prevalent contention that men worthy of the name should be capable of instant erections almost regardless of the prevailing circumstances. It is interesting that as one proceeds up the scale of refinement and sophistication, men, no less than women, pride themselves on their discernment, their discriminative selectivity, and their insistence that sexual intercourse is so much more enjoyable when it involves more than mutual friction of erogenous zones.

Marked individual differences in the need for sexual expression often occasion discord in marriage. If consistent discrepancies exist between the husband's and wife's respective potential for arousal and sexual gratification, attendant resentments may lead to specific impotence or frigidity (i.e., only with the marriage partner). This type of impasse is exceedingly difficult to remedy, especially in the case of highly sexed women married to sexually cold (but not necessarily impotent) men. Drugs, hormones, and other medical treatment are at best of limited value. The undersexed (but not necessarily frigid) female is usually capable of having intercourse even though she has no sexual desire or interest at the time. The male, of course, cannot have coitus unless he is sexually aroused. However, the sexually passive husband might be well advised to learn that many women prefer frequent digital stimulation combined with overt affection to infrequent coitus. Indeed, as will be discussed in the section on treatment, it is important to realize that sex need not be an all-or-none activity dependent upon adequate penile–vaginal stimulation.

A very common malady is the "frigid" woman who complains that her husband displays affection only in bed. Men who regard the expression of love and tenderness as vaguely, if not strongly, unmasculine not only abound but may even, regrettably, be in the majority. Yet many women find consideration and affection an essential precursor to sexual arousal. Verbal communication of an intimate and personal nature is almost nonexistent in many marriages in which time is absorbed by business and domestic chores, separate hobbies, sports, and other recreational pursuits. These and many additional dehumanizing forces can give rise to resentment where sexual withholding is ultimately used as a retaliatory weapon. However, it would be a misnomer to label this a form of impotence or frigidity.

Assessment Procedures

That therapy should always be based upon a comprehensive regime of problem identification and a thorough behavior analysis is an obvious but frequently neglected fact. Clearly, an individual whose sexual avoidance stems from irrational fears of contamination must proceed along a different therapeutic route from a patient who equates "carnal desire" with guilt and sin. The many and varied antecedent factors that can produce frigidity and impotence dictate the need for thorough and systematic assessment procedures. Apart from possible organic factors that have to be excluded whenever there is reason to suspect physiologic dysfunctioning, the therapist must acquire precise insights into the basic dimensions of each patient's problem.

The Presenting Complaint

The starting point is to focus upon the presenting complaint, using the following questions as a guide:

Is the patient engaging in some sort of marital "game" as described by Berne (1964)?
Does the difficulty stem from a distinct absence of feeling or attraction between the partners?

Does the problem stem, perhaps, from simple naïveté and inexperience?

Is the problem the result of simple or complex misconceptions?

Have there been specific traumata that have occasioned or reinforced a pattern of sexual withdrawal and avoidance?

Is there perhaps a latent homosexual preference?

Is the problem a manifestation of overgeneralized hostility toward the opposite sex?

Are the difficulties associated with human relationships in general rather than sexual contacts in particular?

To what extent is the problem compounded by superstitions and various inhibitions?

The Sexual History

When the ramifications of these nine questions have been explored, the history of the patient's sex life should be traced in detail:

When and how was knowledge of sex first acquired?

Was there any sex instruction in the home? (It is important to obtain precise information about parental attitudes, whether negative or positive to sex.)

At what age and under what circumstances did the patient first become aware of his or her sexual impulses?

Were there any developmental problems relating to menstruation, breast development, growth of pubic hair, voice change, etc?

Did masturbation arouse fear or guilt?

When did dating commence and what forms of petting occurred? (Information should be obtained about preadolescent sex play as well as subsequent sexual patterns.)

What were the details, circumstances, and repercussions of the first coital experience?

Is there relevant information about any other significant heterosexual (and/or homosexual) encounters?

What are the patient's prevailing attitudes and knowledge about sex? (Particular attention should be paid to the person's views on sexual morality.)

What are the patient's feelings about his or her own physical appearance?

What circumstances are inclined to result in sexual arousal and/or the achievement of orgasms (e.g., erotic literature, daydreams, masturbation)?

What is the patient's reaction to partial versus total nudity?

What information can be obtained regarding the patient's feelings about various coital techniques and positions?

Is there any preference for lovemaking in full light, in subdued light, or in the dark?

Are there any specific reactions to the absence or presence of sexual arousal in his/her partner?

It may also be necessary to explore various additional topics such as venereal disease, prostitution, contraception, abortion, perversions, and so forth.

It is important to remember that sexual disturbances may also emanate from nonsexual emotional sources. For instance, I treated a young man who achieved sexual potency after being desensitized to fears of blood. As a child he had felt acutely upset when seeing the slaughter of poultry, and had thereafter remained squeamish toward blood. His impotence clearly dated from a sexual experience with a woman who, unknown to him, had not quite completed menstruating.

Treatment

The preceding sections have stressed the fact that the terms *frigidity* and *impotence* refer to a wide range of sexual insufficiencies and inadequacies that stem from diverse causes. Therapeutic strategies differ according to both the type of problem and the antecedent conditions. The man, for instance, who cannot obtain an erection usually requires different therapeutic management from the patient who suffers from premature ejaculation. In women, techniques for overcoming orgasmic impotence differ markedly from those required in the treatment of vaginismus. Furthermore, two cases of sexual apathy will each require very different forms of treatment if the one is a manifestation of moralistic guilt and the other stems from homosexual inclinations. A number of specific therapeutic techniques will now be described.

The Correction of Misconceptions

Direct advice, guidance, information, reassurance, or instruction may suffice to overcome the milder, simpler, and more transient cases of impotence and frigidity. The correction of faulty attitudes and irrational beliefs is often an essential forerunner to specific techniques of lovemaking. One should endeavor to impart nonmoralistic insights into all matters pertaining to sex. It is often helpful to prescribe nontechnical but authoritative literature (e.g., Ellis, 1958, 1962, 1965; Kronhausen and Kronhausen, 1965; McCary, 1967). Patient and therapist may then exchange views on a variety of topics and examine sex in a rational, objective, and enlightened manner.

Graded Sexual Assignments

Wolpe (1958) evolved a simple but effective procedure for promoting sexual adequacy and responsiveness in those cases where anxiety partially inhibits sexual performance. Although it is intended primarily for the treatment of impotence, I have used this method in overcoming frigidity (Wolpe and Lazarus, 1966, pp. 110–111). A cooperative sexual partner is indispensable to the success of the technique. The patient is instructed not to make any sexual responses that engender feelings of tension or anxiety but to proceed only to the point where pleasurable reactions predominate. The partner is informed that she must never press him to go beyond this point, and that she must be prepared for several amorous and intimate encounters that will not culminate in coitus. The theory is that by maintaining sexual arousal in the ascendant over anxiety, the latter will decrease from one amorous session to the next. Thus, positive sexual feelings and responses will be facilitated and will, in turn, further inhibit residual anxieties. In this manner, conditioned inhibition of anxiety is presumed to increase until the anxiety reactions are completely eliminated.

An excerpt from a patient's letter should clarify the procedures:

> You will recall that both Julie and I were skeptical of the sexual program you advised. All the same we went through the paces. I think I went slower than anybody. The first few times we just sort of cuddled in the living room. In less than five minutes I became tense so we quit. A few nights after that we were, as the teenagers would put it, "making out," and I had my hand inside Julie's bra. I didn't feel tense but nor was I aroused. I don't remember exactly how soon afterwards—about a week I'd guess—we'd go through the motions of intercourse with our clothes on in the living room and I'd become semierect. It got to the point where we would masturbate each other in the living room to climax, but in the bedroom nothing would happen. I'm sure this was because the bedroom reminded me of all my past failures. In fact I think it had something to do with beds. It had gotten to the point where I could perform just fine on the living room rug when Julie surprised me by buying one of those sofa-bed arrangements. At first I was impotent until we moved back onto the floor. In fact one night we were in bed and kind of stroking each other. As usual nothing happened, so I suggested that we move onto the rug. There I was fine and we had intercourse. We used to kid each other about this floor angle, but it sort of bothered me. We overcame this problem in two ways. First, we would stimulate each other in bed, knowing full well that if nothing happened we could always move onto the floor. This was most reassuring. Secondly, we would make love in bed in the early morning when I tended to have an erection anyway.

When a man fails to obtain or maintain an erection, he often feels greatly embarrassed and somehow needs to "save face." It may be helpful for him to explain to his partner that ambivalance, or tension, or similar stressful factors can readily produce a state in which it becomes *physiologically* impossible for him to feel sexually aroused. He may wish to explain that the erotic needs of a sensitive, aesthetic, and cultured man can fairly easily be undermined even by subtle innuendos, whereas an uncouth male is probably incapable of having his sexual ardor dampened by anything less than a well-armed and irate husband. The refined and cultivated man could probably never perform rape!

Many impotent men require no formal treatment once they accept that penile–vaginal intercourse is but one way (not the only way, or the "proper" or "normal" way) of satisfying a woman. It is emphasized that a truly proficient lover should be so adept at manual, digital, and oral manipulations that he can induce multiple orgasms in most women without involving his penis at any stage of the proceedings. It is also stressed that when the onus of an expected level of performance is removed from the sufferer (i.e., by the knowledge that his partner need never emerge sexually frustrated whether or not he obtains or maintains an erection), adequate sexual adjustment usually ensues. When a man engages in oral and manual caresses, he will usually find that these actions not only arouse and satisfy the female but also arouse him, especially when he focuses on pleasure being bestowed on his partner instead of dwelling on his own genital problem. Some men may achieve "reflex erections" simply by relaxing while their partner manipulates, massages, or lubricates their genitals. If successful coitus then ensues, a generalization of sexual potency is often achieved without further treatment. Another helpful method is for the man to rub his flaccid penis on his partner's vulva and to use his fingers on her clitoris. If the woman achieves orgasms or very much enjoys this technique (and many women do), the man will often himself achieve a sufficient erection to enter her and thereby complete the sex act. The confidence that accrues from these maneuvers usually renders them redundant after a short while.

More serious sexual disorders usually necessitate the application of several procedures as exemplified by the case of Roy published in Ullmann and Krasner (1965, pp. 243–245). This patient required many discussions aimed at the correction of his misconceptions, as well as assertive training, specific advice, and desensitization, all within the context of a nonjudgmental therapeutic relationship.

The Role of Desensitization Procedures in Overcoming Frigidity

Treatment of chronic frigidity by systematic desensitization was first reported by Lazarus (1963). Therapeutic success was achieved with nine of sixteen recalcitrant cases after a mean of 28.7 sessions. Brady (1966) achieved marked improvement in four out of five chronic, severe cases of frigidity treated over an average of eleven sessions by desensitizing the patients after administering subanesthetic doses of methohexital sodium (Brevital) as a means of producing muscular relaxation. Desensitization has also been successfully applied to groups of impotent men and frigid women (Lazarus, 1961, 1968b, 1969). The preferred size of desensitization groups is between four and eight members. The sessions are conducted at the pace of the slowest (most anxious) individual. If one group member obviously delays the progress of the other patients, he is given a few individual sessions to expedite matters. The typical hierarchy applied to the frigid women consisted of the following progression: embracing, kissing, being fondled, mild petting, undressing, foreplay in the nude, awareness of husband's erection, moving into position for insertion, intromission, changing positions during coitus. Madsen and Ullmann (1967) have noted the advantages of enlisting the husband's assistance in the therapy room during the construction of hierarchies and in the presentation of hierarchy items.

Reference has already been made to the desensitization of nonsexual fears that may nevertheless impair sexual functioning (e.g., fear of blood, general squeamishness, fear of injury). Improvement in sexual functioning and responsiveness has been a fairly frequent by–product of desensitization programs directed at themes of criticism, rejection, disapproval, and ridicule. A frigid woman was unresponsive to many forms of treatment until she received desensitization along a dimension of "bodily criticism." A tactless, if not sadistic, husband from whom she was divorced had made numerous adverse comments about her body which had undermined her self-confidence over the years. Consequently, she avoided all sexual contacts. An eight-item hierarchy was constructed: You have gained weight; your thighs are flabby; your stomach sticks out; your breasts are drooping; your stretch marks will turn off any man; you have a masculine shape; your vagina has an odor; you have absolutely no sex appeal.

Only three desensitization sessions were required to lend her the courage finally to accept a boyfriend's sexual advances. Not only was the sexual experience per se successful, but she reported a newfound readiness and ability to believe that her lover genuinely considered her feminine and attractive.

In the treatment of vaginismus (as well as in those cases suffering from generalized fears of penetration), desensitization, first in imagination, followed at home by gradual dilation of the vaginal orifice, has proved highly successful. The patient, under conditions of deep relaxation, is asked to imagine herself inserting a graded series of objects into the vagina. When she is no longer anxious about the imagined situation, she is asked to use real objects. One might commence with the tip of a cotton bud, or the tip of the patient's little finger, followed by the gradual insertion of two or more fingers, internal sanitary pads, various lubricated cylinders, and eventually by the gradual introduction of the penis, culminating with vigorous coital movement. A detailed case study along these lines was presented several years ago by Rachman (1959). Masters and Johnson (1970) consider it necessary for husband and wife to cooperate in all phases of dilatation therapy.

Assertive Training for Impotent Men

Many impotent men appear to have servile attitudes toward women and respond to them with undue deference and humility. Their sexual passivity and timidity are often part of a generally nonassertive outlook, and their attendant inhibitions are usually not limited to their sex life. These men feel threatened when required to assume dominance in a male–female relationship.

Therapy is aimed at augmenting a wide range of expressive impulses, so that formerly inhibited sexual inclinations may find overt expression. This is achieved first by explaining to the patient how ineffectual forms of behavior produce many negative emotional repercussions. The unattractive and exceedingly distasteful features of obsequious behavior are also emphasized. The patient is then told how to apply principles of assertiveness to various interpersonal situations. For instance, he is requested to "express his true feelings; stand up for his rights," and to keep detailed notes of all his significant attempts (whether successful or unsuccessful) at assertive behavior. His feelings and responses are then fully discussed with the therapist, who endeavors to shape the patient's behavior by means of positive reinforcement and constructive criticism. Behavior rehearsal (Lazarus, 1966), a special form of role playing, is often an integral part of assertive training. This procedure enables the therapist to model desirable patterns of behavior and affords the patient a means of learning by imitation.

Case Illustration: The Use of a Prepared Script. A twenty-four-year-old lawyer, after 6½ months of marriage, was perplexed and distressed by his partial impotence. He was sexually adequate some of the time but was generally inclined to obtain only a semierection. His case history indicated that his domineering mother had taught him to fear and revere women, and that he was therefore unwilling, if not unable, to challenge or upbraid his wife on any terms whatsoever. Further inquiry revealed that he had accumulated considerable resentment toward his wife but felt, paradoxically, that giving vent to his feelings would be unmanly. Therapeutic attention was accordingly directed at his absurd and irrational attitudes, which led him to regard women as objects rather than as people. These topics were covered during the course of three interviews.

The patient was then required to memorize a carefully worded speech that he and the therapist composed together:

"Grace, I have something very important and very serious to discuss with you. It concerns you, me, our marriage, and life in general. I want you please to hear me out without interrupting me. I've spent a hell of a lot of time mulling over these points, and finally I think I've straightened out my ideas, and I want very much to share them with you.

"Let me put it as clearly as possible. I was raised by my mother to bottle up my feelings, especially in relation to women. In thinking over this attitude, I now realize that this is crazy and even dishonest. I feel, for instance, that if I resent the fact that you turn to your father for advice in matters about which I have more knowledge than he, I ought to express my resentment instead of hiding it from you. I feel that when you order me about and treat me like a child, I ought to tell you how I really feel about it instead of acting like an obedient puppy dog. And most important of all, when you go ahead and make plans for me without consulting me, and especially when you yell at me in front of your parents, maybe I should quit acting as if I didn't mind and let you know how strongly I really react inside.

"What I am getting at is simply that in spite of my love and affection for you, I would really rather be unmarried than be a henpecked husband like my father."

This little monologue was rehearsed several times during a one-hour session until playbacks on a tape recorder convinced the therapist that the client was ready to confront his wife and that he could do so in a forthright and sincere manner. His wife's most probable reactions to the various accusations and insinuations also received careful consideration. Rehearsal techniques were used in preparing the patient to cope with tears, interruptions, denials, counterallegations, etc. His assignment was then put into effect. The patient reported that his wife "heard me out without interruption... seemed a little upset, but agreed that I should not withhold or conceal my feelings, I felt incredibly close to her and that night we had very good sex."

The patient was seen once every two or three weeks to reinforce his newfound assertiveness. He also had a successful confrontation with his mother and reported therapeutic gains that extended beyond his original marital and sexual impasse.

Not all cases are so readily resolved. The passive man who marries a domineering woman may require more than mere assertive directives. Frequently both partners require conjoint therapy involving the exploration of attitudes and communication patterns, as well as complex desensitization regimes (Lazarus, 1968a).

Aversion-Relief Therapy in the Treatment of a Sexually Unresponsive Woman

It is well known that an unpleasant electric shock in the presence of a given object tends to produce an *avoidance* reaction to that object. Conversely, *approach* responses may be conditioned to a stimulus repeatedly presented at the moment of termination of an electric shock. Thrope, Schmidt, Brown, and Castell (1964) and Feldman and MacCulloch (1965) have successfully applied therapeutic procedures based upon these principles mainly to homosexuals and transvestites. The treatment of a sexually unresponsive woman by an aversion-relief method is outlined below.

Case Illustration. The patient, a twenty-six-year-old unmarried school teacher, complained that she was so repelled by male genitalia that sexual relations were impossible for her. A defloration experience some four years earlier had induced violent nausea, despite the fact that her lover had shown much skill and tenderness. Since that time she had abstained from sexual contacts except for several "platonic affairs," which involved activities "above the waist." She denied having any homosexual inclinations. Therapy was requested as she had become involved with a man whom she very much wished to marry "if I can get over my sexual hang-up."

Attempts to desensitize her failed because she experienced difficulty in visualizing the scenes. Accordingly, the following aversion-relief method was applied:

The leads of a faradic shock unit, powered by a 9-volt dry battery, were strapped to her left palm. The therapist said, "Shock!" and switched on the current. The patient was instructed to endure the pain and discomfort for as long as possible, while the current was gradually increased. When the electrical impulses became intolerable, she was required to turn her attention toward several photographs of nude men on the desk in front of her. Upon looking at the pictures, the shock was immediately terminated (producing definite signs of relief). She received intermittent shocks when averting her gaze from the pictures. After three separate twenty-minute sessions during the course of a week, she declared that "at least I now quite enjoy the penis in picture form." Various so-called pornographic photographs and drawings were used as relief stimuli during the next three sessions. Finally, a slightly modified method was employed during six additional interviews. The therapist said, "Shock!" and administered a very strong burst of electricity to the patient's palm if she did not proceed to look at the pictures within eight seconds. She was told that she could avoid the shock by looking at the pictures in good time.

After the tenth treatment she went home and had intercourse with her boyfriend. She described the encounter as "slightly successful." After the twelfth session she telephoned to report that during coitus she had achieved two orgasms in quick succession, stating rather coyly, "and that's the best form of anxiety relief on the market." Several months later she reported that she fully enjoyed most aspects of foreplay and coitus but that she was inclined to draw the line at oral–genital contact.

It should be noted that only the very naïve clinician would attribute change in the preceding instance to conditioning. The active variables at the very least involved a therapeutic relationship and an abundance of persuasion and suggestion. None of the foregoing may have sufficed, however, if not for the primary incentive derived from the patient's love for her boyfriend.

The Treatment of Premature Ejaculation

Premature ejaculation is sometimes a symptom of anxiety. The amelioration of anxiety by such techniques as relaxation, desensitization, and assertive training has therefore proved helpful in certain instances. In general, however, it should be noted that psychotherapeutic efforts have not proved especially effective in altering the premature response pattern. Nevertheless, some essentially simple tricks may occasionally meet with gratifying success. For instance, some individuals have managed to delay orgasm and ejaculation merely by dwelling on nonerotic thoughts and images while engaged in sexual intercourse. Others have found it more effective to indulge in self-inflicted pain during coitus (e.g., pinching one's leg, biting one's tongue). Masters and Johnson (1970), however, are not in favor of distraction techniques. The use of depressant drugs (e.g., alcohol or barbiturates) may also impede premature ejaculation in some individuals. The reduction of tactile stimulation (e.g., by wearing one or more condoms, or by applying anesthetic ointments to the glans penis) is also often recommended. All of the foregoing procedures are of limited value.

A fairly useful method of delaying orgasm is by means of a training program designed to increase the threshold of excitability. Extravaginal stimulation of the penis during erection is continued until a sensation premonitory to ejaculation is experienced by the patient. Semans (1956) states: "Stimulation is then interrupted until the sensation has disappeared. Penile stimulation is repeated until the premonitory sensation returns and then is again discontinued. . . . By repeating the procedure the response of ejaculation becomes no longer premature; that is, it can

finally be delayed indefinitely until female response has begun or is complete"
(p. 356).

A case illustration clarifying this procedure will now be outlined.

Case Illustration.   A twenty-two-year-old college student complained that he always ejaculated
a few moments after insertion. He was able to delay orgasm by masturbating with a dry hand, but use of a
lubricant, even during masturbation, resulted in rapid ejaculation. By means of the procedure described
by Semans (1956), he was soon able to delay ejaculation during masturbation with or without the use of
a bland cream. Next, his girl friend was instructed to stimulate him manually. Upon reaching a preorgasmic sensation, he was to remove her hand until the sensation disappeared. Stimulation was then
to be resumed and interrupted again when the preorgasmic sensation returned. Within three weeks the
patient reported that when he and his girl friend engaged in mutual masturbation (even with a lubricant)
she would invariably achieve an orgasm before him. Next, the patient was told to insert only the glans of
his penis into his girl friend's vagina and to avoid any movement. If ejaculation became imminent, he was
to withdraw immediately. In a gradual manner, he was to increase the depth and duration of insertion
and also the amount of movement. He was always to try and remain well within his capacity to avoid
ejaculation.

Approximately a month later, "after one or two mishaps," he reported a distinct breakthrough. A
few moments after intromission he nearly always felt like ejaculating, whereupon he would immediately
withdraw and wait for the impulse to subside. Upon resuming coitus, some thirty seconds afterwards, he
invariably found himself able to delay and control orgasm and ejaculation. A follow-up some ten months
later revealed that apart from a tendency to ejaculate prematurely when embarking on a sexual relationship for the very first time, he generally maintained excellent control and regarded his own level of
sexual performance as "far better than average."

The Squeeze Technique.   Masters and Johnson (1970) have found the
"squeeze technique" the most effective procedure for overcoming premature
ejaculation. When the man is about to ejaculate, instead of stopping stimulation as
in Semans's technique, the woman is instructed to squeeze her partner's penis for
about three seconds. Rather strong pressure is applied under and behind the glans
around the coronal ridge. During the first training session, four or five repetitions
of the pressure are applied each time the man feels an incipient ejaculatory urge.
After several manual sessions with the technique, the progression includes nondemanding and nonvigorous intromission, gradually introducing increasingly
powerful pelvic thrusts. Whenever the man feels a pending loss of ejaculatory
control, he withdraws and the woman applies the squeeze technique before reinserting the penis. It is of interest that in emphasizing dyadic factors in the genesis
and resolution of sexual problems, Masters and Johnson stress the fact that the
squeeze technique employed by the man in solitary masturbation does not produce
gains that transfer to the heterosexual situation. The main drawback to the squeeze
technique is that it sometimes produces temporary impotence. A urologist has
expressed the opinion that the procedure may produce prostatitis, but Masters and
Johnson make no reference to this possible side effect.

Walter Knopp, M.D., has drawn my attention to the following procedure for
the management of premature ejaculation which appeared in the *International
Drug Rx Newsletter*, September 1966, *1* (7):

Depending on the dose administered, a unique pharmacological action of the phenothiazine, thioridazine (Mellaril-Sandoz) is retardation or inhibition of ejaculation. To
relieve premature ejaculation prescribe 25 mg, two to four times daily (occasionally a
higher dose may be required). Some men respond immediately; others only after taking the
drug up to two months. After two months of symptomatic relief, reduce dosage by one-

half for another month. If relief is maintained, for this month, thioridazine should be discontinued. If premature ejaculation recurs, a second course of thioridazine therapy, with the same or slightly higher dosage, for two or three months, often produces lasting relief.

Addendum

The case histories and the various maneuvers described above may lend a deceptive aura of oversimplicity to the actual procedures involved. Some of the mechanistic procedures and precise clinical strategies may even suggest a computerized form of sex without love. Two points should therefore be emphasized: (1) It is hoped that persons who administer the techniques outlined in this chapter will be endowed with sufficient warmth, wit, and wisdom to operate within a context of empathy, sincerity, and flexibility. (2) It is erroneous to assume that spontaneity, affection, tenderness, and love are undermined by recognizing the existence and importance of various mechanisms. Scientific psychology is, in fact, only possible if lawful mechanisms of behavior can be identified.

In summary, the purpose of this chapter is to call attention to a variety of methods that have proved highly effective in overcoming many sexual inadequacies. The practitioner well versed in these procedures can, with confidence, offer a positive prognosis in most instances of frigidity and impotence.

References

Bandura, A., and Walters, R. H. *Social learning and personality development*. New York: Holt, 1963.

Bergler, E., and Kroger, W. S. The dynamic significance of vaginal lubrication to frigidity. *Western Journal of Surgery*, 1953, *61*, 711–719.

Berne, E. *Games people play*. New York: Grove Press, 1964.

Brady, J. P. Brevital-relaxation treatment of frigidity. *Behaviour Research and Therapy*, 1966, *4*, 71–78.

Ellis, A. *Sex without guilt*. New York: Grove Press, 1958.

Ellis, A. Frigidity. In A. Ellis and A. Abarbanel (Eds.), *The encyclopedia of sexual behavior*. New York: Hawthorn, 1961. Pp. 450–456.

Ellis, A. *The American sexual tragedy*. New York: Grove Press, 1962.

Ellis, A. *The case for sexual liberty*. Tucson: Seymour Press, 1965.

Feldman, M. P., and MacCulloch, M. J. The application of anticipatory avoidance learning to the treatment of homosexuality. I: Theory, technique and preliminary results. *Behaviour Research and Therapy*, 1965, *2*, 165–183.

Freud, S. Three contributions to the theory of sex. In A. A. Brill (Ed.), *The basic writings of Sigmund Freud*. New York: Modern Library, 1938. Pp. 553–629.

Fromme, A. *Understanding the sexual response in humans*. New York: Pocket Books, 1966.

Hastings, D. W. *Impotence and frigidity*. Boston: Little, Brown, 1963.

Kant, F. *Frigidity: Dynamics and treatment*. Springfield, Illinois: Charles C Thomas, 1969.

Kinsey, A. C., Pomeroy, W. B., Martin, C. E., and Gebhard, P. H. *Sexual behavior in the human male*. Philadelphia: Saunders, 1948.

Kronhausen, E., and Kronhausen, P. *The sexually responsive woman*. New York: Ballantine Books, 1965.

Lazarus, A. A. Group therapy of phobic disorders by systematic desensitization. *Journal of Abnormal and Social Psychology*, 1961, *63*, 505–510.

Lazarus, A. A. The treatment of chronic frigidity by systematic desensitization. *Journal of Nervous and Mental Disease*, 1963, *136*, 272–278.

Lazarus, A. A. Behavior rehearsal vs. non-directive therapy vs. advice in effecting behavior change. *Behaviour Research and Therapy*, 1966, *4*, 209–212.

Lazarus, A. A. Behavior therapy and marriage counseling. *Journal of the American Society of Psychosomatic Dentistry and Medicine*, 1968, *15*, 49–56. (a)

Lazarus, A. A. Behavior therapy in groups. In G. M. Gazda (Ed.), *Basic approaches to group psychotherapy and group counseling*. Springfield, Illinois: Charles C Thomas, 1968. Pp. 149–175. (b)

Lazarus, A. A. Group treatment for impotence and frigidity. *Sexology*, 1969, *36*, 22–25.

Madsen, C. H., and Ullmann, L. P. Innovations in the desensitization of frigidity. *Behaviour Research and Therapy*, 1967, *5*, 67–68.

Masters, W. H., and Johnson, V. E. *Human sexual response*. Boston: Little, Brown, 1966.

Masters, W. H., and Johnson, V. E. *Human sexual inadequacy*. Boston: Little, Brown, 1970.

McCary, J. L. *Human sexuality*. Princeton: Van Nostrand, 1967.

Rachman, S. The treatment of anxiety and phobic reactions by systematic desensitization psychotherapy. *Journal of Abnormal and Social Psychology*, 1959, *58*, 259–263.

Semans, J. H. Premature ejaculation: A new approach. *Southern Medical Journal*, 1956, *49*, 353–361.

Thorpe, J. G., Schmidt, E., Brown, P. T., and Castell, D. Aversion—relief therapy: A new method for general application. *Behaviour Research and Therapy*, 1964, *2*, 71–82.

Ullmann, L. P., and Krasner, L. (Eds). *Case studies in behavior modification*. New York: Holt, 1965.

Wolpe, J. *Psychotherapy by reciprocal inhibition*. Stanford, California: Stanford University Press, 1958.

Wolpe, J., and Lazarus, A. A. *Behavior therapy techniques*. New York: Pergamon, 1966.

This chapter presents a learning theory approach to sex therapy emphasizing the usefulness of observational or vicarious learning. The authors briefly discuss a rationale for the use of films, videotapes, books, and other media resources in the treatment of sexual problems. Indiscriminate use of these aids, however, can be countertherapeutic. Annon and Robinson have developed a conceptual scheme for determining the appropriateness of particular treatment strategies for particular patients at specific times, which they call the P-LI-SS-IT Model. The authors stress the importance of a thorough assessment to ensure effectiveness of treatment.

The issues raised in this article are especially timely. Therapists as well as the lay public seem to be succumbing to the rather naïve view that merely being exposed to sexually explicit films or other media is somehow inherently therapeutic. This chapter also cautions against the trend for sex therapy to become a rigid set of procedures and techniques, rather than an individualized program for each particular patient.

3

The Use of Vicarious Learning in the Treatment of Sexual Concerns

Jack S. Annon and Craig H. Robinson

During the past decade there has been a proliferation of therapeutic approaches for helping individuals with sexual concerns. The need for effective treatment strategies is only too obvious; however, the all too frequent theoretical and empirical shortcomings of many approaches are likewise sadly apparent.

This chapter attempts to describe how one process of facilitating change (i.e., vicarious learning) might be most effectively used in treating people with sexual concerns. First, a brief overview of the theoretical and empirical support for the concept of vicarious processes in learning will be given, followed by a description of the literature concerned with the clinical application of vicarious learning procedures. Next, a proposed conceptual scheme for the application of vicarious learning principles to treatment, research, and training in the sexual area will be described. This will then be followed by a discussion of the scheme's implications for future treatment and research.

This chapter is a condensation based on a paper presented at the Annual Meeting of the American Psychological Association, Chicago, September 1975.

Jack S. Annon and *Craig H. Robinson* • Department of Psychology, University of Hawaii, Honolulu, Hawaii

Theoretical and Empirical Overview

The process of vicarious learning, also referred to as observational learning, modeling, imitation, etc., is generally considered to occur when an organism performs an action similar to the action of another organism which the first has observed (Staats, 1975). In other words, vicarious learning is said to occur when a change of behavior is acquired as a result of observing the behavior of another person. Bandura, one of the leading social learning theorists in this area, considers vicarious processes to be a primary form of learning and seems to view the principles involved at the same basic level of theory as, say, the principles of classical conditioning (Staats, 1975).

While some authors attempt to distinguish between the various terms relating to vicarious learning (e.g., Rachman, 1972), Bandura (1971a) seems to regard most as essentially synonymous, particularly since it has not been demonstrated that different forms of vicarious learning are governed by separate determinants or mechanisms. Bandura maintains that observational learning produces three major effects: (1) Observers may acquire new behavior patterns not previously existing within their behavioral repertoires; (2) observers' behavior may be either inhibited or disinhibited as a result of viewing a model's behavior; and (3) the expression of already existing responses may be facilitated by watching a model emit those same responses.

Because vicarious learning refers directly to how an observer codes, and is later guided by, the response elements in that which is observed, there appears to be a wide variety of ways in which modeling stimuli can be presented. For example, modeling stimuli have the potential of effecting change even when occurring in symbolic forms, such as imaginal and verbal representational systems (Bandura, 1969). Bandura (1971a) points out that as long as the representation of actions serves a response guidance function, changes in behavior through vicarious learning can occur even though the desired behavior may be presented in such symbolic forms as pictures or words. Thus, many vicarious learning procedures have typically used symbolic (i.e., films, videotapes, pictures, etc.) as well as live models, and some support has been provided for the efficacy of covert modeling in which the desired change appears to be effected in the absence of any overt stimuli (e.g., Cautela, Flannery, and Hanley, 1974; Kazdin, 1974a,b).

The effects of observational learning have been demonstrated under many different conditions and across a wide range of problems. For reviews of the empirical support for vicarious learning, see Bandura (1962, 1965), Morrow (1971), Rachman (1972), and Robinson (1974b). Most of the empirical evidence regarding vicarious learning has been similar to the analogue studies used in the investigation of systematic desensitization (Rachman, 1972); however, more data have begun to appear regarding the direct clinical applications of vicarious learning procedures to client problems.

Nonsexual Problems.   While some analogue studies have demonstrated that vicarious learning can be effective as a technique for extinguishing fears and reducing avoidance behaviors (e.g., Bandura and Menlove, 1968; Bandura, Blanchard, and Ritter, 1969), and for teaching individuals the acquisition of novel responses not previously existing in their behavior repertoires (e.g., Bandura, 1965; Flanders, 1968), a number of studies have described the direct application of such procedures to clinical populations.

For example, some work with modeling has been done using adult psychotic or psychiatric inpatient populations (Goldstein, Martens, Hubben, van Belle, Schaaf, Wiersma, and Goedhart, 1973; Rachman, Hodgson, and Marks, 1971; Sherman, 1965).

As a medium for facilitating behavior and attitude change through vicarious learning, films and videotapes have recently been employed by several investigators (e.g., Fryrear and Werner, 1970; Mann, 1969, 1972; Muzekari and Kamis, 1973; Persons and Persons, 1973; Sarason and Ganzer, 1973).

These clinical studies indicate an increasing recognition that the process of vicarious learning may have profound therapeutic implications, and it is quite likely that this therapeutic tool will continue to receive much more attention from researchers regarding its clinical utility (Heller, 1971; Meichenbaum, 1973; Rachman, 1972).

Because the use of observational learning in the treatment of sexual problems obviously implies that behaviors may, it is hoped, be modified or learned by observing some form of sexual stimuli, it is relevant to examine briefly what effects such sexual stimuli (i.e., pornography) may have on behavior when observed in nontherapeutic settings.

Pornography. Exhaustive and detailed accounts of some behavior changes occurring as a result of observing sexually explicit material, presented both live and in symbolic fashion, have been described by a number of researchers in the area (e.g., Mann, Sidman, and Starr, 1971; Mosher, 1971; Kutschinsky, 1971; Robinson, 1974b). The findings from these studies, and others, seem to warrant the following conclusions:

1. No study has convincingly shown any long-term effects of pornography on sexual behavior and attitudes.
2. Attitudes regarding various sexual behaviors appear to be quite stable, despite exposure to erotic visual material.
3. Many males and females exposed to erotic films frequently report various degrees of short-term sexual arousal.
4. There tend to be increases in the frequency of coital activity (if the activity already exists in the individual's behavior repertoire) within twenty-four hours after viewing pornography; however, there still is no significant increase in the overall rates of intercourse.
5. It is relatively rare that novel sexual activities are tried, or that low-frequency sexual behaviors are increased, following exposure to erotica. The most reliable behavioral effect is an increase in masturbation during the twenty-four hours following exposure.
6. The majority of individuals who increase masturbation following exposure tend to be individuals with already established masturbatory patterns.
7. Viewing pornography often results in a temporary increase in sexual fantasy, dreams, and conversation about sex during the first twenty-four-hour period following exposure.

While there are numerous other tentative conclusions that may be drawn from the available literature, the preceding seem to have the most potential relevance for the present discussion. Since there are so many consistent "minimal" effects when pornography is viewed under natural or laboratory conditions, it would appear to justify the hypothesis that, given an appropriate therapeutic setting, coupled with therapeutic instructions, the minimal or nonexistent behavior and attitudinal changes currently displayed following exposure to sexually explicit stimuli might be greatly enhanced or instigated.

Sexual Problems. Considering the demonstrated effectiveness of vicarious learning procedures described previously, it is interesting to note that the extension of these procedures to the treatment of sexual problems has been relatively limited to a few clinical reports, with evaluative research being almost nonexistent. Wincze (1971) attempted to compare the effects of systematic desensitization with "vicarious extinction" in treating a twenty-nine-year-old woman who had no interest in sex and whose marriage was on the verge of a complete breakdown because of this. He first used a typical systematic desensitization approach, followed by vicarious extinction procedures where he had the woman observe films involving heterosexual petting and intercourse. This was then followed by reinstatement of systematic desensitization procedures. Improvement was only noted during the systematic desensitization procedures, and Wincze suggested that perhaps the films were too fear-provoking and inappropriate to the particular patient's experiences. In a subsequent study involving twenty-one females complaining of sexual frigidity, Wincze and Caird (1973) compared the relative effectiveness of systematic desensitization and "video desensitization" to an untreated control condition. Both groups showed significant decreases in heterosexual anxiety immediately after treatment. However, in follow-up, the video-treated group showed more overall positive changes than the group exposed to standard desensitization procedures. Recently, McMullan (1976) demonstrated the efficacy of some "automated" vicarious learning procedures for treating females concerned about lack of orgasm. A further report of evaluative research in this area (Robinson, 1974b) will be described in greater detail later.

Clinical reports are obviously more common than research studies, and one of the first descriptions of the use of vicarious learning principles in the treatment of sexually dysfunctional couples is that by Hartman and Fithian (1972). They utilize vicarious learning in a number of ways. First, they use a physical "sexological" examination of the client couple, which allows the male and female therapist to "model" for the male and female client in conducting physical client examinations. Once into treatment, the therapists direct the clients in giving and receiving a series of graded caresses, starting with the foot and the face and then extending to the body and the sexual areas. After the couple have practiced the caress they are shown a videotape of a research couple going through the caress that the client couple have just practiced. At later stages they provide client couples with further visual materials such as films and still shots of couples in different coital positions or videotapes of research couples using nondemand coital techniques. For working with nonorgasmic women, they also use an audiotape of a woman who describes how she became orgasmic and how she taught other women to function well sexually. This is later followed with a videotape of intercourse showing this formerly nonorgasmic woman, as well as a videotape of the woman that she emulated in becoming orgasmic.

A number of others have reported equal success in following the Hartman and Fithian approach to treatment. For example, More (1973) describes using videotapes and films in a similar fashion by showing the client couple videotapes of research couples engaging in the various activities that the clients have been asked to engage in. More stresses the importance of showing the couple the videotapes *after* the client couple has first engaged in the activity on their own so as not to induce "performance anxiety." On the other hand, Renick (1973) reports using very similar procedures except that he suggests showing the client couple the videotapes of research couples *before* the clients have engaged in a particular activity so as to provide a possible "model" for them. The two clinicians report equal success, and only systematic research will be able to evaluate which procedure might be most effective for what particular client with what presenting problem.

Serber (1974) reports using videotapes in treatment in a somewhat different manner. Couples are given homework assignments of sexual activity along with instructions on how to use a videotape recorder. The couples then make a videotaped recording of their homework assignment and subsequently bring the tape in with them to their interviews with the therapist, where all three view the tape and mutually discuss what they observe, followed by feedback and further directions from the therapist.

In addition to these approaches with videotapes, others have reported using vicarious learning procedures that employ a variety of audiovisual materials. For example, Lehman (1974) describes using slides in helping orgasmically dysfunctional women. Sayner and Durrell (1975), in order to reduce anxiety-related sexual functioning, ask couples to sit through hours of pornographic movies, or to read sexually explicit books together. Ellis (1975) uses a wide variety of materials such as pamphlets, books, readings, films, talks, and workshops in his "psychoeducative" procedures to help clients disabuse themselves of irrational ideas about sex. LoPiccolo and Miller (1975) incorporate some vicarious procedures into their program for enhancing the sexual relationship of normal couples, by having couples view a movie showing a wide variety of foreplay and intercourse techniques from which they can later select and enjoy some experimentation in sexual activity, free of pressure for any particular result.

The Sex Advisory and Counseling Unit of the Human Sexuality Program at the University of California Medical Center in San Francisco (Vandervoort and Blank, 1975) provides a broad range of educational and counseling services that, among other techniques, utilizes audiovisual and written materials, as well as charts and programmed home assignments. As part of their approach to the group treatment of preorgasmic women, they show a female masturbation movie to help "demystify" the process of orgasm, followed by an assignment to go home and masturbate, but not to the point of orgasm (Barbach, 1974). Mann (1975) further reports that they are in the process of carrying out a controlled study of vicarious group counseling of preorgasmic women. This combination of clinical treatment and research is certainly needed in order to evaluate the effectiveness of the wide variety of audio and visual materials now becoming available for use in the sexual area (e.g., see the catalogues of EDCOA Productions, Inc.; Enabling Systems, Inc.; Focus International; Multi Media Resource Center, Inc.; etc.). It is interesting to note that very few clinicians have appeared to take advantage of the powerful modeling effects that might be achieved by having the client view a "model" who successfully "learns" the desired behavior, rather than viewing a model who already possesses the desired behavior. Such attempts are usually limited to an occasional film such as *An Experiment in the Teaching Methodology of Sensate Focus* (Edcoa, 1974), which depicts a doctor directing an unrehearsed young couple in a series of sensate focus-type exercises that culminate in intromission; or the three recent films on *Becoming Orgasmic: A Sexual Growth Program for Women* (Focus International, 1976). The systematic use of such an approach in treatment will be described in detail later.

From this brief overview of the somewhat limited literature that describes the use of vicarious learning in the treatment of sexual problems, it can be seen that a number of promising results have been obtained even though the application of these principles has been relatively recent. On the other hand, there are some crucial questions that need to be answered. For example, what form of vicarious learning will be most helpful for what specific problem presented by what type of client to which therapist from what orientation? Should the therapist use films, videotapes, audio cassettes, slides, pictures, diagrams, and selected readings for each problem? How often and how many forms of symbolic learning would be most helpful? Indiscriminate use of a particular film or videotape just because it is available is obviously not therapeutically justified.

It should also be pointed out that the current stress by many learning-oriented therapists on a broad-spectrum approach to therapy has no virtue unless there is some plan for assisting clinicians in ordering and selecting appropriate treatment strategies. Without such a plan, broad-spectrum treatment is just as much a shotgun approach as is using the same one or two films or procedures for all problems.

What is needed is a flexible and comprehensive scheme that can be adapted to many settings and to whatever client or clinician time that is available. To be most effective such a plan should also be able to be used by a wide variety of people in the helping professions and allow for a range of vicarious treatment choices geared to the level of competence of the individual clinician. Ideally, the approach also needs to provide a framework for screening out and treating those problems that will be responsive to brief therapy approaches and those that may require intensive therapy. It would also be helpful for such a scheme to provide a framework for conducting evaluative research. Finally, for those who are involved in the teaching or training of sexual therapists, such a model should offer a method for providing training that can be geared to the level of competence of the individual trainee.

After several years of devising and testing a number of different plans in diverse settings with a variety of sexual problems, a conceptual scheme for treatment that looked promising was finally developed. This tentative scheme was then taught to others, and after further refinements, the final model emerged. Initially, this model was seen as only applicable to treatment in the sexual area. However, extensive use of this scheme by the Sexual Counseling Service of the Department of Obstetrics and Gynecology of the School of Medicine at the University of Hawaii has shown that it is equally applicable to research and training, and further develoment has demonstrated that it also offers an appropriate rationale for the use of vicarious learning principles in treatment. For the past several years this model has been passed on to others via lectures, courses, consultations, workshops, and training programs. It appears that many in the helping professions have found it to be useful, as it is currently being employed by a wide range of people such as clergymen, nurses, paraprofessionals within a range of disciplines, physicians from diverse specialties, practical nurses, psychiatrists, psychologists, school counselors, and social workers. This proposed scheme has been described extensively elsewhere (Annon, 1976); however, a brief overview of the model with particular emphasis on its application to vicarious learning procedures will be offered.

A Proposed Conceptual Scheme for the Use of Vicarious Learning in the Treatment of Sexual Concerns

The PLISSIT Model

As an aid to memory, this conceptual scheme is referred to as the PLISSIT model or, more accurately, P-LI-SS-IT. The model provides for four levels of approach, and each letter or pair of letters designates a suggested method for handling presenting sexual concerns. The four levels are: *P*ermission-*L*imited *I*nformation-*S*pecific *S*uggestions-*I*ntensive *T*herapy. A visual presentation of the proposed model may help clarify how it may be applied in a variety of clinical settings. Let each line in Figure 1 represent the different presenting sexual concerns that clinicians may encounter over time. Depending upon their setting, profession, and specialty, these problems may represent what they encounter in one day, one month, one year, or even one professional lifetime. It would obviously be inappropriate to attempt to assess and treat each presenting sexual concern in exactly the same way.

Figure 2 depicts the theoretical application of the P-LI-SS-IT model to these presenting sexual concerns. As Figure 2 further illustrates, the first three levels can be viewed as *brief therapy* as contrasted with the fourth level, *intensive therapy*.

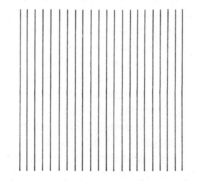

Fig. 1. A proposed conceptual scheme presenting sexual concerns over time.

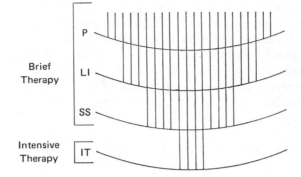

Fig. 2. Application of the P-LI-SS-IT model.

Utilization of this model has a number of distinct advantages. It may be used in a variety of settings and adapted to whatever client time is available. Theoretically, each descending level of approach requires increasing degrees of knowledge, training, and skill on the part of the clinician. Because each level requires increasing professional experience, the model thus allows individuals to gear their approach to their own particular level of competence. This also means that clinicians now have a plan that aids them in determining when referral elsewhere is appropriate. Most important, the model provides a framework for discriminating between those problems that require intensive therapy and those that are responsive to brief therapy.

How many levels of approach clinicians will feel competent to use will directly depend upon the amount of interest and time they are willing to devote to expanding their knowledge, training, and skill at each level. The following discussion will be devoted to brief practical suggestions on how to apply the model with suggestions for incorporating appropriate vicarious learning procedures.

The First Level of Treatment: Permission. Sometimes, all that people want to know is that they are normal, that they are okay, that they are not "perverted," "deviated," or "abnormal," and that there is nothing wrong with them. Mostly, they would like to find this out from someone with a professional background or from someone who is in a position of authority to know. Many times these people *are not* bothered by the specific behavior that they are engaging in, but they *are* bothered by the thought that there may be something "wrong" or "bad" with what they are doing. Frequently, clients just want an interested professional to act as a sounding board for checking out their concerns. In these cases, the clinician can let them know that they are not alone or unusual in their concerns and that many people share them. Reassurance that they are normal and permission to continue doing exactly what they have been doing is sufficient in some cases to resolve what might eventually become a major problem. (For a more detailed discussion of the application of permission to each of these areas, see Annon, 1976.)

Permission giving is most appropriate and helpful when it is used in direct relation to the client's goals. Keeping this in mind will make it easier for the clinician to decide what form of permission giving, if any, will be most beneficial for a particular client concern. Such permission giving by the clinician may be supplemented, or replaced, by the use of vicarious methods such as appropriate films, videotapes, audiotapes, slides, pictures, and other materials. For example, at the Sexual Counseling Service (SCS) a number of materials have been developed for this purpose, such as a "Sexual Satisfaction" audiotape (Pion, 1975b) that is available for clients to listen to either in the clinician's office or at home. The tape provides a "permission-giving" approach for engaging in a wide range of behaviors that clinicians may recognize as common and normal but that clients may not.

On the surface it may appear that the basic assumption underlying the permission-giving approach is that the clinician may sanction whatever sexual thought, fantasy, or behavior a consenting adult wishes to privately engage in, or engage in with other mutually consenting adults. In a very general sense this may be correct; however, there are some definite limitations to such an assumption. While it is ultimately up to the individual clients to choose whatever behavior that they wish to engage in, "blanket" permission giving by the clinician may not be appropriate if the client is not making an *informed* choice. It is the authors' definite belief that it is the clinician's responsibility to inform the unaware client of the possible adverse consequences that may result from engaging in certain thoughts, fantasies, or behaviors that the clinician knows may have negative consequences.

While further limitations of the permission-giving approach are obviously set by legal considerations (e.g., sexual activity with children, rape, etc.), most likely the major limitations will be set by the clinician. The extent to which clinicians feel comfortable with and are willing to use this level of treatment will generally depend upon their breadth of sexual knowledge, their theoretical orientation, and their value systems.

This approach will certainly not solve all sexual problems, or even many problems, but it may resolve some concerns for some people. If permission giving is not sufficient to resolve the client's concern and the clinician is not in the appropriate setting or does not have sufficient time or relevant knowledge, skills, or resources, then this is the time to refer the client elsewhere. On the other hand, if clinicians do have the appropriate setting, knowledge, and skills, then they can combine their permission giving with the second level of treatment.

The Second Level of Treatment: Limited Information. In contrast to permission giving, which is basically telling the client that it is all right to continue doing what he or she has been doing, limited information is seen as providing the client with specific factual information directly relevant to his or her particular sexual concern. It may result in his or her continuing to do what they have been doing, or it may result in his or her doing something different. For example, providing specific information for a young man concerned that his penis may be somewhat smaller than average may be all that is necessary to resolve his concern (e.g., the foreshortening effect of viewing his own penis, that there is no correlation between flaccid and erect penis size, that the average length of the vagina is usually three to four inches, that there are very few nerve endings inside the vagina, etc.).

It should be pointed out that limited information is usually given in conjunction with permission giving. While each can be conceptually viewed as a separate level, there obviously may be considerable overlap between the two.

Furthermore, both can also be used in conjunction with the remaining two levels of treatment. However, because each descending level of treatment usually requires more time, knowledge, experience, and skill on the part of the clinician for the most effective application, each level is presented and discussed separately.

In giving limited information, it is important for the clinician to do just that, provide "limited" information directly relevant to the client's concern. Robinson's (1974a,b) research at SCS has provided evidence indicating that even presenting three hours of a broad range of sexual information has little direct influence on changing a client's attitude or behavior associated with a specific sexual problem; however, presenting *limited information* directly related to the client's problem can effect a significant change in relevant attitudes and behavior.

Providing limited information is also an excellent method of dispelling sexual myths, whether they are specific ones such as those pertaining to genital size, or more general ones such as that, on the average, men and women differ markedly in their capacity to want and to enjoy sexual relations and in their fundamental capacity for responsiveness to sexual stimulation, or that men are more quickly aroused than women, etc.

There are many common areas where vicarious methods of providing limited information may be most helpful in treating sexual concerns. As an example, for women who may be overly concerned about their particular breasts or genitals, SCS has a number of pictorial books, slides, and videotapes of women available that illustrate the broad range of breast and genital shape, size, and configuration commonly found among women. For women concerned about their first pelvic or breast examination, learning models may be provided by having them view films and videotapes of women going through such procedures at SCS.

There are obviously many common areas of sexual concern where providing limited information through vicarious means may be most helpful. However, it is not within the scope of this discussion to provide extensive information for each of the many possible areas that may be handled by this level of treatment. Obtaining such knowledge is up to individual clinicians and how much interest, time, and effort they are willing to devote to such readings, which are available elsewhere (e.g., Annon, 1976).

As with permission giving, the degree to which clinicians feel comfortable with and are willing to use the second level, limited information giving, will generally depend upon their breadth of sexual and behavioral knowledge, their theoretical orientation, their skill and experience, and their value systems; and the limitations imposed by these factors discussed previously apply here as well.

As suggested in Figure 2, the additional use of this level of treatment may resolve some concerns that could not be handled by the application of the first level of treatment, permission, alone. On the other hand, if giving limited information is not sufficient to resolve the client's sexual concern, clinicians then have two options available to them at this point. They may either refer the client for treatment elsewhere, or, if they have the appropriate setting, knowledge, skills, and experiences, they may proceed to the third level of treatment.

The Third Level of Treatment: Specific Suggestions.   Before clinicians can give specific suggestions to clients, they must first obtain certain relevant information. The assumption here is that it would not be therapeutically appropriate or helpful to clients to offer specific suggestions, vicarious or otherwise, without first obtaining information about them and their unique set of circumstances. If clinicians were to immediately launch into a number of suggestions after hearing clients initially describe their problems (not their "labels" for their problems), not only might they waste the client's time (e.g., offering suggestions that the client has already tried) but they might further compound the problem.

What the clinician needs is a sexual *problem* history. This is not to be confused with a sexual history. If clinicians begin to take a sexual history, then they are heading into intensive therapy, not brief therapy. It is an assumption of the model proposed here that a comprehensive sexual history is not relevant or necessary at this level. As suggested in Figure 2, the application of the specific suggestion approach may resolve a number of problems that filtered through the first two levels of treatment; but, needless to say, it is not expected that it will successfully deal with all such problems. If the third level of approach is not helpful to the client, *then* a complete sexual history may be a necessary step for intensive therapy.

Guidelines for taking a sexual problem history that is deemed necessary for a brief therapy approach to treatment are:

1. Description of current problem.
2. Onset and course of problem.
   a. Onset (age, gradual or sudden, precipitating events, contingencies).
   b. Course (changes over time: increase, decrease, or fluctuation in severity, frequency, or intensity; functional relationships with other variables).
3. Client's concept of cause and maintenance of the problem.
4. Past treatment and outcome.
   a. Medical evaluation (specialty, date, form of treatment, results, currently on any medication for any reason).
   b. Professional help (specialty, date, form of treatment, results).
   c. Self-treatment (type and results).
5. Current expectancies and goals of treatment (concrete or ideal).

The taking of such a problem history will necessarily have to be adapted to the clinician's setting and the amount of time available. The proposed problem history is easily adapted to five minutes or five hours. Those interested in obtaining a more detailed explication of the taking of such a problem history along with illustrative case examples may refer to Annon (1976).

In contrast to permission and limited information giving, which generally do not necessarily require clients to take any active steps to change their behavior unless they choose to, specific suggestions are direct attempts to help clients to change their behavior in order to reach their stated goals. This is done from within a brief therapy framework, which means that the approach is time- and problem-limited. Most of the suggestions that may be given are those that can be used by a clinician who has only a relatively brief period, say ten to thirty minutes, for a client interview. Furthermore, they may also be used in those situations where the clinician is only able to see the client on one or several occasions, at the most. Obviously, these are minimum time limits that may be expanded and adapted to whatever time the clinician has available. However, this level of approach is mainly intended for use within the brief therapy framework proposed, and if the suggestions are not seen as helpful within a relatively brief period of time, then it is suggested that intensive therapy is probably more appropriate.

The application of this level of treatment is seen as providing clients with specific suggestions directly relevant to their particular sexual problem and designed to help them achieve their stated goals. This level of treatment is particularly effective for dealing with those heterosexual problems that are concerned with arousal, erection, ejaculation, orgasm, or painful intercourse. The specific suggestions given (e.g., redirection of attention, graded sexual responses, sensate focus techniques, dating sessions, alternate sessions, interrupted stimulation, squeeze technique, vaginal muscle training, etc.), or the method used (e.g., films, videotapes, pictures, etc.) will, of course, depend upon the information obtained in the sexual problem history. In general, it might be helpful to consider such suggestions as falling into three categories: suggestions to the male alone, suggestions to the female alone, and suggestions to the couple.

Quite often clinicians are seen by clients with heterosexual problems who have no immediate partners available. In such cases there are a number of suggestions that can be made using self-stimulation procedures (Annon, 1973) that may be helpful to the client until a partner is available. Often, too, clinicians may be faced with a situation where they are seen by a client who is in a relationship with a second person who has a problem, but the second person is not able, or willing, to come in for consultation. However, the most helpful suggestions are usually those that can be made to both partners together.

As with the levels previousy discussed, it is not within the scope of this chapter to offer extensive specific suggestions covering all possible sexual problems. For the interested clinician a detailed description of the application of such suggestions to the more prevelant heterosexual problems encountered by males and females is available elsewhere (Annon, 1976). However, it is within this level of treatment that many vicarious learning methods may be most advantageously used. An example might be a case where a woman has never learned to experience orgasm in any way, alone or with her partner. Suggesting that she learn to experience orgasm through self-exploration with the intention of teaching her partner what she has learned is often a helpful procedure. Providing her with appropriate film or videotape models of women successfully learning such procedures may be a more effective procedure than verbal instructions alone. Another method used by SCS is to provide the client with audiotapes and pictorial brochures that involve a female "model" relating how she has learned to engage in such activities with positive results. The use of pictorial pamphlets, brochures, magazines, and books may also be suggested by clinicians. They may use these symbolic forms of vicarious learning as another means of providing permission or limited information pertaining to a certain sexual area of client concern, or they may use them to supplement specific suggestions that they may have made, or to promote new client-initiated procedures. Finally, because of time limitations, either on them or on their clients' part, they may suggest them in lieu of any other specific suggestions. It is assumed that clinicians will not suggest any films, video- or audiotapes, or readings to clients until they are first well acquainted with their content and feel comfortable with recommending them.

Again, efficient use of this level of treatment will largely depend upon the clinicians' breadth of knowledge, skill and experience, and awareness of relevant therapeutic suggestions. The limitations discussed previously apply here as well.

As Figure 2 illustrates, this level of approach concludes the presentation of the brief therapy portion of the P-LI-SS-IT model. This brief therapy segment of the model has provided SCS with a framework for conducting the treatment of sexual concerns of individuals, couples, and groups, as well as for treatment-oriented research. For example, Morton and Pion (1976) report positive results in applying the P-LI-SS-IT model to female sexual enhancement groups. An example of a research treatment program for women with orgasm concerns, based on this brief therapy portion of the proposed scheme and utilizing modeling procedures, will be described shortly.

As Figure 2 further implies, a number of sexual concerns may be successfully treated by this brief therapy approach, but, on the other hand, a number of problems that cannot be solved by this approach will also filter through. This is the point at which clinicians may refer clients for appropriate treatment elsewhere, or if they have the requisite time, knowledge, experience, and skills, they may apply the fourth level of treatment.

The Fourth Level of Treatment: Intensive Therapy. Intensive therapy in the model proposed here does not mean an extended standardized program of treatment. In the P-LI-SS-IT model, intensive therapy is seen as highly individualized treatment that is necessary because standardized treatment was *not* successful in helping the client to reach his or her goals. Many learning-oriented therapists have decried the restrictive use of one or two standardized procedures and have advocated a broad-spectrum approach to therapy. However, there is no virtue in this approach to treatment unless there is some theoretically based plan for the ordering of their various interventions. The ideal relationship between the assessment of a problem and which vicarious learning procedure to use should be dictated by the client's unique circumstances and experiences rather than by the ready availability of a particular procedure or form of vicarious learning.

In other words, initial assessment should have a direct relationship to the treatment selected. Contrast this approach with that of many sex therapy clinics that do a comprehensive and exhaustive initial assessment only to have their clients all go through the identical expensive, long-term treatment program. In such programs it is difficult to see what purpose the initial intensive assessment serves.

Due to the prevalence of sexual problems and the difficulties associated with their resolution, it was considered of practical as well as of theoretical value to design and carry out a study to investigate methods of assessment and treatment in this area. Such an investigation was carried out (Annon, 1971) with the purpose of developing, testing, and refining a conceptual scheme for the ordering of sexual problems and their treatment from within a learning theory framework.

The major conclusion of the research was that an initial analysis of a client's sexual problem from within the A-R-D framework advanced by Staats (1968, 1970, 1975), followed by a careful evaluation of relevant behavioral repertoires, offered the most promising conceptual scheme for the ordering of sexual problems and the development of appropriate treatment procedures.

This conclusion is based upon a number of considerations. The use of this scheme offers a plan for the simultaneous consideration of the full range of the client's circumstances. Such an approach also allows for the ordering of priorities for intervention and provides guidance for the timing of multiple interventions. Finally, the use of such a conceptual scheme is not tied to any particular behavioral technique or procedure but fosters the development of appropriate procedures based upon theoretical analysis. A more comprehensive presentation of this approach along with its detailed application to those sexual problems that require intensive therapy may be found in Annon (1975a).

It is assumed that, before attempting intensive therapy, the clinician has first obtained a sexual problem history from the client and has attempted treatment from within the brief therapy model described earlier, and that now the clinician finds that this brief approach was not helpful, or appropriate, in assisting the person to reach his or her goals. In such a situation, the clinician may explain to the client that more detailed and extensive information is necessary in order to devise a tailor-made therapeutic program that is unique to the particular individual and to his or her life circumstances.

A number of forms and inventories such as the Sexual Fear Inventory (Annon, 1975b), the Sexual Pleasure Inventory (Annon, 1975c), the Sexual Response Profile (Pion, 1975a), the Heterosexual Attitude Scales (Robinson and Annon, 1975a), and the Heterosexual Behavior Inventory (Robinson and Annon, 1975b) have been developed at SCS in order to obtain such relevant initial assessment information for devising appropriate treatment modalities. In addition to such questionnaires and inventories, other methods for gathering relevant information may also be used. For example, when a brief therapy approach does not appear helpful or appropriate, Pion (see Pion and Annon, 1975) reports good results from providing clients with audiotape cassettes and recorders, along with written guidelines for making personal audiotapes at home that cover their description of the sexual problem history as well as their sexual learning history.

In addition to the above procedures a wide variety of other materials and procedures may be advantageously used during assessment and, particularly, during treatment, such as sexual diagrams, charts, pictures, and slides; anatomical models; mannequins; appropriate articles, magazines, and books; and audiotapes, films, and videotapes.

The extension of vicarious learning procedures to the treatment of sexual problems seems to be a potentially powerful therapeutic strategy. However, the delineation of those conditions under which such procedures might be expected to be most therapeutically effective can only be discovered by research and not by clinical intuition alone. To illustrate one approach to vicarious learning research in the sexual area, a brief description of one SCS research project that investigated the "successful learner" concept from within the P-LI-SS-IT framework follows.

Research

The genesis of this particular treatment research program came following numerous discussions by SCS staff speculating about the probable therapeutic efficacy of showing clients with sexual concerns various sexually explicit visual materials. Prior to this research, as well as currently, many therapists have reported using a variety of visual materials in helping people with sexual problems. With the proliferation of these visual "aids," produced by reputable companies for educational and treatment purposes, the researchers and clinicians at SCS began wondering just what specific effects, if any, such materials might have on clients' sexual behavior and attitudes. Therefore, a treatment program that attempted to rely as exclusively as possible on vicarious or observational learning as the therapeutic medium was designed and implemented (for a complete description of the investigation, see Robinson, 1974b).

The main purpose of the research was to assess the effects of a specially developed videotape treatment program on the sexual behaviors and attitudes of orgasmically dysfunctional women. The following experimental hypotheses were tested: In comparison to untreated control subjects, subjects exposed to a series of videotapes (i.e., vicarious learning) would experience (1) an increase in certain sexual behaviors (e.g., self-stimulation) discussed and/or modeled on the videotapes, (2) more favorable attitudes toward certain sexual activities presented on the videotapes, and (3) the occurrence of, or an increased frequency of, orgasm. The study further investigated, relative to each other and to an untreated control group, two variations of the videotape treatment program. Both segments of the brief therapy program consisted of three cassette videotapes ranging in length from twenty-nine to fifty-four minutes. The first three tapes constituted the A (or Attitudinal) series (i.e., A_1, A_2, and A_3) and was considered analogous to the Permission- and Information-giving levels of the P-I-SS-IT model. The remaining three tapes constituted the Specific Suggestions (or Behavior) portion or B series (i.e., B_1, B_2, and B_3). The basic format for all of the tapes involved a male therapist talking to a role-playing couple (successful learners) who had sought help for the female's difficulty in experiencing orgasm. In the A series the therapist presented a wide range of sexually related information to the modeling couple. In the B series, however, most of the information presented was limited to the area of self-stimulation and was accompanied by very specific suggestions given by the therapist to the female of the couple. No suggestions were ever given to clients to follow what was modeled on the tapes. They were merely asked just to "view the videotapes."

Results indicated that a variety of sexual behaviors could be acquired and/or increased in frequency by such observational learning procedures. Of particular importance was the finding that both videotape treatment conditions were highly effective in enabling client subjects to learn various methods of self-stimulation for the purpose of enhancing sexual arousal. Of the six who initially stated that they had never, or were not sure whether they had ever, masturbated, five began using self-stimulation after merely viewing the videotapes. Of the ten who at the outset stated they did not currently use self-stimulation for sexual arousal, nine subsequently began engaging in masturbatory activities. Of the fifteen who were exposed to either of the treatment group conditions, fourteen increased their frequency of masturbation. Results further suggested that both videotape conditions (i.e., A + B, or B only) were highly effective in promoting more positive attitudes toward self-stimulation activities. Although the data strongly supported the first two experimental hypotheses, hypothesis 3 was only partially supported in that the frequency of orgasm most reliably increased for just those client subjects who had experienced orgasm before. Only one client subject who had never experienced orgasm under any conditions was able to experience orgasm solely as a result of viewing the videotapes.

It should be remembered that the program was designed to see what effects, if any, a therapeutic program based almost solely on vicarious learning would have on certain sexual behaviors and attitudes of females concerned with sexual arousal and orgasm. The therapeutic package was never considered to be necessarily sufficient in and of itself to enable all client subjects to reach their individual goals. The treatment approach did, however, prove to be a major first step for most client subjects in establishing a foundation and later momentum for attaining their various goals concerning increased sexual responsiveness. In all but one case, individual treatment following the research program involved relatively few sessions and typically consisted of merely giving a few more specific suggestions logically following those that appeared on the videotapes. Furthermore, in each case except one, every female either eventually reported the occurrence of orgasm or markedly increased the frequency and conditions in which orgasm was experienced. The obvious financial and therapeutic benefits most client subjects received by being first exposed to this supplementary vicarious therapeutic approach certainly warrant further research attention.

Given the "success" of the program and considering the rigid conditions under which it was presented, it seems likely that there are several ways in which the effects of vicarious learning might be enhanced, such as: providing clear pretherapy instructions, providing the material in incremental order, using models who resemble the observer, viewing positive affective consequences accruing to the model, and observing models who provide verbalized guidance and reinforcement.

The data suggest that the frequent assumption that clients with sexual concerns must first develop more general positive sexual attitudes before significantly changing their sexual behaviors is questionable. The results also seem to have implications for the conceptual framework used. The reader may have noticed in the preceding summary reference to the "P-I-SS-IT" rather than "P-LI-SS-IT" model. Besides publication considerations, "Information" was changed to "Limited Information" to more accurately reflect what type of information giving was most likely to be effective. The research data suggested that the more global attitude changes client subjects showed following exposure to approximately three hours of videotaped material (A series) regarding a wide range of sexual topics had little if any relationship to subsequent behavior change in specific self-stimulation practices. Significant behavior changes only occurred following exposure to the B series, which involved limited information and specific suggestions directly related to the client subject's problem area. Based on this research, companies such as Edcoa Productions and Enabling Systems are producing short films, audio cassettes, and slides entirely within the P-LI-SS-IT framework and designed for the treatment of sexual concerns.

Training

For those who are involved in teaching or training sexual therapists, the P-LI-SS-IT model may offer a framework for providing training that can be geared to the level of competence of the individual trainee. For the past four years SCS has used the P-LI-SS-IT framework in offering training programs for professionals and paraprofessionals, both individually and in small groups, as well as in week-long workshops and seminars for organizations and interested clinicians in groups of a hundred or more. The programs themselves utilize a number of vicarious learning methods. For example, each level of treatment is introduced by the trainers "modeling" an example of how a particular level may be used with a client. After subsequent didactic presentation, a number of additional examples are again modeled by trainers for a number of different presenting concerns for a particular level of treatment. This is immediately followed by role-playing sessions where individual participants practice applying the suggested approaches to trainers who role-play clients with various sexual concerns.

In addition, a wide range of videotapes, films, and slides are presented in order to provide a model of how such vicarious procedures may be advantageously used in treatment. Thus, the P-LI-SS-IT framework appears to be a practical as well as flexible method for training clinicians in the treatment of sexual concerns, as it has been successfully used with a wide range of people from the helping professions possessing varying degrees of therapeutic competence. Finally, the model provides a framework within which clinicians can continue to develop and expand their own knowledge, experience, and skills.

Conclusion

The use of vicarious learning in the treatment of sexual concerns has been a relatively recent event, and a number of promising results have been obtained. However, there is a clear need for a planned systematic approach to treatment and research if the conditions under which such procedures might be expected to be most therapeutically effective are to be discovered and used on a wide scale. This chapter has attempted to provide a tentative scheme for such treatment and research.

The P-LI-SS-IT Model

Clinicians will naturally have to adapt their use of the P-LI-SS-IT model to their particular setting, the amount of time that they have available, their particular level of competence, and the vicarious materials available to them. It is also important to emphasize that while the brief therapy part of the model is not intended to resolve all sexual problems, it may handle many. It is the authors' firm opinion, based on an ever-increasing amount of clinical and research evidence, that it is now unethical to involve clients in an expensive, long-term treatment program of any type without first trying to resolve their problem from within a brief therapy approach. As the schematic presentation in Figure 2 implies, a number of sexual concerns may successfully be treated by such an approach if the clinician is willing to apply it. On the other hand, as the model also indicates, a number of problems that cannot be solved by this approach will filter through. There will be times when the specific suggestions, direct or vicarious, that may work for many others will not be effective for a particular client's problem, whether the clinician has provided one or a dozen. There will also be times when interpersonal conflict may prevent many of the suggestions from being carried through. When this happens, and when clinicians feel that they have done as much as they can from within the brief therapy approach, *then* it is time for intensive therapy.

However, the current stress by many therapists on a broad-spectrum approach to intensive treatment has no virtue unless there is some theoretically based plan for the ordering of their various interventions. Without such a plan broad-spectrum treatment is just as much a shotgun approach as is using the same one or two procedures for all client problems.

It should now be clear that intensive therapy does *not* mean an extended standardized program of treatment. By their very nature such standardized programs will not be of help to some people, or they may not even be necessary. It is the authors' belief that many of the essential elements of some of the current standardized programs now available can be successfully utilized within the brief therapy approach proposed here. In the P-LI-SS-IT model, intensive therapy is seen as highly individualized treatment that is necessary because standardized treatment was *not* successful in helping clients to reach their stated goals. In the present framework, intensive therapy means that a careful initial assessment of the client's special situation and experiences is necessary in order to devise a tailor-made therapeutic program that is unique to the particular individual and to his or her life circumstances. This is especially important, because what is available to the client beyond the fourth level of treatment?

The model proposed here suggests one possible conceptual framework for the ordering of sexual problems and their treatment through the use of vicarious learning principles and methods. Further clinical trials and systematic research will be necessary to determine whether this approach is equally applicable to other problem areas as well.

Future Research

That individuals can learn novel sexual behaviors or modify existing ones via a process labeled vicarious learning (or observational learning, modeling, imitation, etc.) seems to be well supported by a large amount of empirical data. While the precise theoretical underpinnings regarding why learning occurs through this process are still widely disputed (e.g., see Bandura, 1971b; Staats, 1975), the empirical operations involved are quite clearly specified and supported by a wealth of data. There is, however, a paucity of research that has made any systematic attempt to evaluate the effects of vicarious learning as a therapeutic modality for assisting persons with sexual concerns. Few attempts have been made to carefully evaluate what role these vicarious learning procedures actually have in client's sexual behaviors and attitudes. Even fewer attempts have been made to use the existing literature on vicarious learning as a guideline for maximizing its effectiveness.

Based on the research conducted at SCS, a number of suggestions can be offered to clinicians and researchers interested in this area. For example, one of the more obvious suggestions is to give clients clear pretherapy instructions regarding what they will be viewing, what they might be asked to do, and how the to-be-viewed material will be relevant to their goals. It might also be expected that a greater number of clients might attempt modeled activities if careful attention is given to presenting the vicarious material in incremental or hierarchial order. That is, the general format could involve having clients watch "successful learners" (i.e., role-players) following and successfully completing therapeutic instructions presented in a graduated manner. How rapidly clients progress (i.e., time intervals between vicarious learning sessions) could be set by clients themselves. After having met clearly specified ad hoc criteria at each level of such a program, clients could then be "eligible" to observe the next set of visual materials. Of course, failure or inability to meet criteria at any point would be closely monitored and dealt with accordingly with more individualized procedures. Data from the vicarious learning literature, and the results from SCS research, also suggest that the effects of observational learning may be enhanced by the use of models who resemble the observer, observing positive affective consequences accruing to the models, and observing models who provide verbalized attention and guidance to the more relevant aspects of the material being presented.

The extension of vicarious learning procedures to the treatment of sexual concerns does seem to be a potentially powerful therapeutic strategy; however, perhaps a statement made by Mowrer over ten years ago, and equally applicable today, offers a fitting conclusion to this chapter. In his discussion of modeling and imitation as a therapeutic procedure, he wrote: "How does it happen that this powerful methodology has been so neglected in that form of adult education known as psychotherapy? No attempt will be made here . . . to answer this question. Suffice it to say that efforts are now being made to correct this oversight of the past" (Mowrer, 1966, pp. 453–454).

References

Annon, J. S. The extension of learning principles to the analysis and treatment of sexual problems (Doctoral dissertation, University of Hawaii, 1971). *Dissertation Abstracts International*, 1971, *32* (6-B), 3627. (University Microfilms No. 72-290, 570)

Annon, J. S. The therapeutic use of masturbation in the treatment of sexual disorders. In R. D. Rubin, J. P. Brady, and J. D. Henderson (Eds.), *Advances in behavior therapy* (Vol. 4). New York: Academic Press, 1973. Pp. 199–215.

Annon, J. S. *The behavioral treatment of sexual problems: Intensive therapy.* Honolulu: Enabling Systems, Inc., P.O. Box 2813, Honolulu, Hawaii 96803, 1975. (a)

Annon, J. S. *The Sexual Fear Inventory—Male and Female Forms.* Honolulu: Enabling Systems, Inc., P.O. Box 2813, Honolulu, Hawaii, 96803, 1975. (b)

Annon, J. S. *The Sexual Pleasure Inventory—Male and Female Forms*. Honolulu: Enabling Systems, Inc., P.O. Box 2813, Honolulu, Hawaii, 96803, 1975. (c)

Annon, J. S. *The behavioral treatment of sexual problems: Brief therapy*. New York: Harper & Row, 1976.

Bandura, A. Social learning through imitation. In M. R. Jones (Ed.), *Nebraska symposium on motivation: 1962*. Lincoln: University of Nebraska Press, 1962.

Bandura, A. Behavioral modifications through modeling procedures. In L. Krasner and L. P. Ullmann (Eds.), *Research in behavior modification*. New York: Holt, Rinehart & Winston, 1965.

Bandura, A. *Principles of behavior modification*. New York: Holt, Rinehart & Winston, 1969.

Bandura, A. Analysis of modeling processes. In A. Bandura (Ed.), *Psychological modeling: Conflicting theories*. New York: Aldine-Atherton, 1971. (a)

Bandura, A. Psychotherapy based upon modeling principles. In A. E. Bergin and S. L. Garfield (Eds.), *Handbook of psychotherapy and behavior change*. New York: John Wiley & Sons, 1971. (b)

Bandura, A., Blanchard, E. B., and Ritter, B. Relative efficacy of desensitization and modeling approaches for inducing behavioral, affective, and attitudinal changes. *Journal of Personality and Social Psychology*, 1969, *13*, 173–199.

Bandura, A., and Menlove, F. L. Factors determining vicarious extinction of avoidance behavior through symbolic modeling. *Journal of Personality and Social Psychology*, 1968, *8*, 99–108.

Barbach, L. G. Group treatment of preorgasmic women. *Journal of Sex and Marital Therapy*, 1974, *1*, 139–145.

Cautela, J., Flannery, R., and Hanley, E. Covert modeling: An experimental test. *Behavior Therapy*, 1974, *5*, 494–502.

Edcoa Productions, Inc. An experiment in the teaching methodology of sensate focus, 1974, 12555 East 37th Ave., Denver, Colorado 80239.

Ellis, A. The rational–emotive approach to sex therapy. *The Counseling Psychologist*, 1975, *5*, 14–21.

Enabling Systems, Inc. P.O. Box 2813, Honolulu, Hawaii 96803.

Flanders, J. P. A review of research on imitative behavior. *Psychological Bulletin*, 1968, *69*, 316–337.

Focus International, Inc. Becoming orgasmic: A sexual growth program for women, 1976. 505 West End Avenue, New York, New York 10024.

Fryrear, J. L., and Werner, S. Treatment of a phobia by use of a videotaped modeling procedure: A case study. *Behavior Therapy*, 1970, *1*, 391–394.

Goldstein, A. P., Martens, J., Hubben, J., van Belle, H. A., Schaaf, W., Wiersma, H., and Goedhart, A. The use of modeling to increase independent behavior. *Behaviour Research and Therapy*, 1973, *11*, 31–42.

Hartman, W. E., and Fithian, M. A. *Treatment of sexual dysfunction*. Long Beach: Center for Marital and Sexual Studies, 1972.

Heller, K. Laboratory interview research as analogue to treatment. In A. E. Bergin and S. L. Garfield (Eds.), *Handbook of psychotherapy and behavior change*. New York: John Wiley & Sons, 1971.

Kazdin, A. E. The effect of model identity and fear-relevant similarity on covert modeling. *Behavior Therapy*, 1974, *5*, 624–635. (a)

Kazdin, A. E. Comparative effects of some variations of covert modeling. *Journal of Behavior Therapy and Experimental Psychiatry*, 1974, *5*, 225–231. (b)

Kutschinsky, B. The effects of pornography: A pilot experiment on perception, behavior, and attitudes. *Technical Reports of the Commission on Obscenity and Pornography* (Vol. 8). Washington, D.C.: U.S. Government Printing Office, 1971.

Lehman, R. E. The disinhibiting effects of visual material in treating orgasmically dysfunctional women. *Behavioral Engineering*, 1974, *1*, 1–3.

LoPiccolo, J., and Miller, V. H. A program for enhancing the sexual relationship of normal couples. *The Counseling Psychologist*, 1975, *5*, 41–45.

Mann, J. *A comparison of the effects of direct versus vicarious individual and group desensitization of test-anxious students*. Unpublished master's thesis, University of Arizona, 1969.

Mann, J. Vicarious desensitization of test anxiety through observation of videotaped treatment. *Journal of Counseling Psychology*, 1972, *9*, 1–7.

Mann. J. Is sex counseling here to stay? *The Counseling Psychologist*, 1975, *5*, 60–63.

Mann, J., Sidman, J., and Starr, S. Effects of erotic films on sexual behavior of married couples. *Technical Reports of the Commission on Obscenity and Pornography* (Vol. 8). Washington, D.C.: U.S. Government Printing Office, 1971.

McMullan, S. *Automated procedures for treatment of primary orgasmic dysfunction.* Unpublished doctoral dissertation, Rutgers University, New York, 1976.

Meichenbaum, D. H. Cognitive factors in behavior modification: Modifying what clients say to themselves. In R. D. Rubin, J. P. Brady, and J. D. Henderson (Eds.), *Advances in behavior therapy* (Vol. 4). New York: Academic Press, 1973.

More, J. *The use of videotape and film in sexual therapy.* Paper presented at the 81st Annual Convention of the American Psychological Association, Montreal, 1973.

Morrow, W. R. (Ed.). *Behavior therapy bibliography: 1950–1969.* Columbia: University of Missouri Press, 1971.

Morton, T., and Pion, G. A sexual enhancement group for women. *Journal of Sex Education and Therapy,* 1976, *2* (1), 35–38.

Mosher, D. L. Sex callousness toward women. *Technical Reports of the Commission on Obscenity and Pornography* (Vol. 8). Washington, D.C.: U.S. Government Printing Office, 1971.

Mowrer, O. H. The behavior therapies, with special reference to modeling and imitation. *American Journal of Psychotherapy,* 1966, *20,* 439–461.

Multi Media Resource Center, Inc. 540 Powell Street, San Francisco, California 94108.

Muzekari, L. H., and Kamis, E. The effects of videotape feedback and modeling on the behavior of chronic schizophrenics. *Journal of Clinical Psychology,* 1973, *29,* 313–316.

Persons, R. W., and Persons, M. K. Psychotherapy through media. *Psychotherapy: Theory, Research and Practice,* 1973, *10,* 234–235.

Pion, R. J. *The Sexual Response Profile.* Honolulu: Enabling Systems, Inc., P.O. Box 2813, Honolulu, Hawaii 96803, 1975. (a)

Pion, R. J. *Sexual satisfaction.* Honolulu: Enabling Systems, Inc., 1975. (b)

Pion, R. J., and Annon, J. S. The office management of sexual problems: Brief therapy approaches. *The Journal of Reproductive Medicine,* 1975, *15* (4), 127–144.

Rachman, S. Clinical applications of observational learning, imitation, and modeling. *Behavior Therapy,* 1972, *3,* 379–397.

Rachman, S., Hodgson, R., and Marks, I. The treatment of chronic obsessive–compulsive neurosis. *Behaviour Research and Therapy,* 1971, *9,* 237–247.

Renick, J. T. *The use of films and videotapes in the treatment of sexual dysfunction.* Paper presented at the 81st Annual Convention of the American Psychological Association, Montreal, 1973.

Robinson, C. H. *The effects of observational learning on the masturbation patterns of preorgasmic females.* Paper presented at the annual meeting of the Society for the Scientific Study of Sex, Las Vegas, November 1974. (a)

Robinson, C. H. The effects of observational learning on sexual behaviors and attitudes in orgasmic dysfunctional women (Doctoral dissertation, University of Hawaii, 1974). *Dissertation Abstracts International,* 1975, *35* (9-B). (University Microfilms No. 75-5040, 221) (b)

Robinson, C. H., and Annon, J. S. *The Heterosexual Attitude Scale—Male and Female Forms.* Honolulu: Enabling Systems, Inc., 1975. (a)

Robinson, C. H., and Annon, J. S. *The Heterosexual Behavior Inventory—Male and Female Forms.* Honolulu: Enabling Systems, Inc., 1975. (b)

Sarason, I. G., and Ganzer, V. J. Modeling and group discussion in the rehabilitation of juvenile delinquents. *Journal of Counseling Psychology,* 1973, *20,* 442–449.

Sayner, R., and Durrell, D. Multiple behavior therapy techniques in the treatment of sexual dysfunction. *The Counseling Psychologist,* 1975, *5,* 38–41.

Serber, M. Videotape feedback in the treatment of couples with sexual dysfunction. *Archives of Sexual Behavior,* 1974, *3,* 377–380.

Sherman, J. A. Use of reinforcement and imitation to reinstate verbal behavior in mute psychotics. *Journal of Abnormal Psychology,* 1965, *70,* 155–164.

Staats, A. W. Social behaviorism and human motivation: Principles of the attitude-reinforcer-discriminative system. In A. G. Greenwald, T. C. Brook, and T. M. Ostrom (Eds.), *Psychological foundations of attitudes.* New York: Academic Press, 1968. Pp. 33–68.

Staats, A. W. Social behaviorism, human motivation, and the conditioning therapies. In B. A. Maher (Ed.), *Progress in experimental personality research* (Vol. 5). New York: Academic Press, 1970. Pp. 111–168.

Staats, A. W. *Social behaviorism.* Homewood, Illinois: Dorsey Press, 1975.

Vandervoort, H. E., and Blank, J. E. A sex counseling program in a university medical center. *The Counseling Psychologist*, 1975, *5*, 64–67.

Wilson, F. S., and Walters, R. H. Modification of speech output of near-mute schizophrenics through social-learning procedures. *Behaviour Research and Therapy*, 1966, *4*, 59–67.

Wincze, J. P. A comparison of systematic desensitization and "vicarious extinction" in a case of frigidity, *Journal of Behavior Therapy and Experimental Psychiatry*, 1971, *2*, 285–289.

Wincze, J. P., and Caird, W. K. *A comparison of systematic desensitization and video desensitization in the treatment of sexual frigidity.* Paper presented at the meeting of the Association for the Advancement of Behavior Therapy, Miami, December 1973.

Sex therapy has never been a part of the mainstream of academic psychiatry and psychology. Rather, most sex therapists have been practicing clinicians with only tangential interest (or competence) in psychotherapy outcome research. In this chapter, an extremely thorough review of the clinical literature on sex therapy, Douglas Hogan offers a critique of the methodological problems inherent in much of the published literature. By closely examining this literature, the author identifies some consistent findings on both etiology and treatment that seem, therefore, to be firmly established. This article provides a framework against which many of the clinical chapters in later parts of this book can be better evaluated and understood.

4

The Effectiveness of Sex Therapy: A Review of the Literature

Douglas R. Hogan

Introduction

Two events in the late 1950s marked the beginning of a new, direct approach to the treatment of sexual dysfunctions. The first event was the publication of an article by Semans (1956) describing a simple technique for treating premature ejaculation. The second event was the publication of Wolpe's *Psychotherapy by Reciprocal Inhibition* (1958), which described the application of conditioning procedures to the treatment of various sexual dysfunctions. These techniques did not receive widespread attention until 1970, when Masters and Johnson's *Human Sexual Inadequacy* expanded these direct approaches into a comprehensive therapy program for sexual dysfunctions. Since that time, numerous articles have been published on sex therapy, sex therapy clinics have sprung up across the

The author thanks Joseph LoPiccolo and James Calhoun of the State University of New York at Stony Brook for their helpful ideas, comments, and suggestions.

Douglas R. Hogan • Department of Psychology, Sexual Dysfunction Clinic, and Department of Psychiatry and Behavioral Science, State University of New York, Stony Brook, New York

United States, and many additional techniques have been added to the repertoires of clinicians who treat sexual dysfunctions.

This chapter will examine the effectiveness of these techniques. In order to do so, three preliminary issues will be discussed: (1) definition and classification of sexual dysfunctions, (2) etiology of sexual dysfunctions, and (3) assessment of sexual dysfunctions. After these issues have been clarified, the available literature on the treatment of sexual dysfunctions will be examined.

Unfortunately, the lack of adequate research in the area precludes the possibility of forming definite conclusions about the effectiveness of many of these techniques. Investigations have been, for the most part, on a very primitive level. Specifically: (1) The interrelated issues of definition and classification of sexual dysfunctions have barely been discussed. (2) Discussions of the etiology of sexual dysfunctions are based almost entirely on uncontrolled, retrospective, patient self-reports that have been further distorted by the theoretical biases of the researchers. (3) Only a handful of researchers employ objective assessment instruments. Most researchers merely report their results in terms of global categories such as "improved" or "not improved," without providing any criteria for these judgments (LoPiccolo and Steger, 1974). (4) Despite the advent of many new treatment packages, few controlled studies have been conducted to evaluate their effectiveness (Cooper, 1971). The majority of papers published on the treatment of sexual dysfunctions merely report single case studies or series of case studies.

When the focus is shifted from the question of whether or not the new sex therapy packages work to the question of which of the components of the packages contribute to their effectiveness, the situation becomes even more dismal. Those researchers who have critically examined the issue all conclude that no firm knowledge exists (Annon, 1974; Franks and Wilson, 1974; Kaplan, 1974b; Prochaska and Marzilli, 1973). As LoPiccolo (1975, p. 5) writes, "At this point the 'active ingredients' and 'inert fillers' in the direct therapy package cannot be distinguished, and the explanations offered for the effectiveness of the approach are simply speculations rather than data-based interpretations." Paul and Bernstein (1973) point out that only the factorial group design with untreated and nonspecific treatment control groups can answer this question. To date, there have been no such studies published concerning the treatment of sexual dysfunction.

However, when uncontrolled studies repeatedly indicate a correlation between a particular therapeutic technique and a positive outcome, it can be assumed that this technique, rather than the numerous uncontrolled variables present in the various studies, was responsible for the improvement. Because of such correlations, it is possible to draw some tentative conclusions regarding the effectiveness of various techniques.

Definition and Classification

Sexual dysfunctions are cognitive, affective, and/or behavioral problems that prevent an individual or couple from engaging in and/or enjoying satisfactory intercourse and orgasm. Thus sexual dysfunctions are distinguished from sexual variations, in which the individual may successfully engage in intercourse in an unconventional way or with an unconventional object choice (Kaplan, 1974b).

Male sexual dysfunctions can be subdivided into erectile failure, premature ejaculation, retarded ejaculation, and dyspareunia. The term *impotence* has been used in the past to refer to the first three categories. However, the importance of distinguishing among these three disorders is emphasized both by Kaplan (1974b) and by Masters and Johnson (1970), since the three differ both physiologically and in their response to treatment. Kaplan (1974b) explains that both the male and female sexual responses are biphasic in nature. The first phase is the "genital vasocongestive reaction which produces penile erection in the male and vaginal lubrication and swelling in the female; . . ." and the second phase consists of "the reflex clonic muscular contractions which constitute orgasm in both genders" (Kaplan, 1974b, p. 13). The vasocongestive/erective phase in the male (and presumably the vaginal lubrication/swelling phase in the female) is mediated by the parasympathetic branch of the autonomic nervous system, while the ejaculatory response in the male (and possibly the orgasmic response in the female) is mediated by the sympathetic branch (Kaplan, 1974b; Wolpe, 1958). Because of the differing physiological bases of the two components, they are somewhat independent: Either phase can be affected separately in an individual, or both phases can be affected, giving rise to three different disorders in the male (erectile failure, premature ejaculation, and retarded ejaculation) and different combinations of these disorders. Different treatments are indicated for these disorders, so it is necessary to make clear distinctions between them.

Erectile failure (EF) refers to the inability of the male to achieve or maintain an erection to such an extent that he is unable to engage in satisfactory intercourse. Retarded ejaculation (RE), also termed "ejaculatory incompetence" (Masters and Johnson, 1970) and "ejaculative impotence" (Cooper, 1968a), is a disorder in which the male suffers from delayed intravaginal ejaculation or the inability to ejaculate intravaginally. Premature ejaculation (PE) is topographically the opposite of RE: The patient suffering from PE ejaculates prior to or soon after inserting his penis into his partner's vagina.* The final male dysfunction is dyspareunia, or painful intercourse. This disorder is usually caused by organic factors (Masters and Johnson, 1970), so it will be considered only briefly in the discussion of treatment techniques.

Female sexual dysfunctions have been divided into five categories: general sexual dysfunction, primary and secondary orgasmic dysfunction, dyspareunia, and vaginismus.

---

*Kinsey, Pomeroy, and Martin (1948) state that PE cannot be considered abnormal because most men reach orgasm within two minutes of penetration. [More recent data indicate that the median duration of intercourse is four to seven minutes (Gebhard, 1966).] They believe that the problem lies in the female partner's inhibited responding, and that PE is a "superior" biological trait. Kinsey and his colleagues employ a statistical model of abnormality: If a trait is common, it is normal, and if it is very infrequent, it is abnormal. Onto this statistical model they have superimposed some biological criteria by which they have judged PE to be superior.

The concepts of statistical normality and alleged biological superiority are not really relevant here. PE prevents satisfactory sexual intercourse and creates what Szasz (1969) terms "problems in living," and is therefore a sexual dysfunction.

General sexual dysfunction consists of the inhibition of the vasocongestive/ arousal stage of the sexual response, so that vaginal lubrication and swelling develop minimally or not at all. General sexual dysfunction is experienced subjectively by the female as a lack of erotic feelings. This dysfunction was first recognized as a discrete disorder in 1974 by Kaplan (1974a,b), and most investigators have not yet adopted the term. Patients presenting with this disorder are classified by other researchers as either inorgasmic or "frigid."

Orgasmic dysfunction consists of the inhibition of the orgasm phase of the female sexual response. It is subdivided into primary orgasmic dysfunction, which exists when the patient has never experienced an orgasm in any way, and secondary orgasmic dysfunction, a disorder in which the client has had an orgasm at least once through some form of sexual stimulation but currently experiences *coital* orgasms rarely or not at all.*

The term *frigidity* is often used in the literature on sexual dysfunctions as a catchall category for orgasmic dysfunction and general sexual dysfunction. The term has little utility, since it does not even inform one as to which of the two components of the sexual response has been inhibited, let alone finer details (e.g., whether the problem is primary or secondary). In addition, it has certain pejorative, sexist connotations. The term will be used only when a report does not provide enough detail to enable confident classification into one of the above categories.

Dyspareunia (painful intercourse) in the female can range from postcoital vaginal irritation to severe pain during penile thrusting. It is far more common in the female than in the male (Masters and Johnson, 1970), and female dyspareunia is more likely to involve psychological factors than is male dyspareunia. In the discussion below, "dyspareunia" will refer to female dyspareunia unless stated otherwise.

Vaginismus, the final female dysfunction to be discussed, is a condition in which the vaginal introitus closes tightly when intercourse is attempted, thus preventing penetration. It is caused by an involuntary spastic contraction of the sphincter vaginae and the levator ani, the muscles surrounding the vagina.

Etiology

An Interactional/Systems Approach

Traditional medical, psychoanalytical, and behavioral models of abnormal psychology have tended to conceptualize causation in a linear fashion: Events are seen as proceeding along a single temporal dimension of cause and effect. An interactional/systems model, however, views events as elements of systems: The different elements affect each other and are affected in turn via feedback loops. The concepts of cause and effect become completely relative, and the idea of linear causation is replaced by that of systems operating in a cyclical fashion. Event A

---

*The emphasis on coital orgasms is based purely on sociocultural factors and has no anatomical or physiological basis. See Kaplan (1974b) for a discussion of this point.

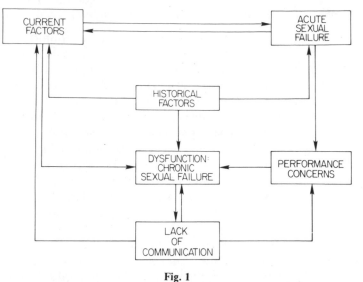

Fig. 1

*Table 1.   Historical and Current Factors Implicated in the
Etiology of Sexual Dysfunction*

Historical factors	Current factors
A. Psychological factors	A. Illness
1. Religious orthodoxy	B. Surgery
2. Homosexuality	C. Lack of sexual skill and
3. Hostility	knowledge
4. Other sexual dysfunctions	D. Misinformation about sex
B. Marital problems	E. Anxiety
C. Sexual trauma	F. Depression

may influence event B and in turn be influenced by B through a positive or negative feedback loop (Watzlawick, Weakland, and Fisch, 1974).

Figure 1* and Table 1 present a model of the interactional causation and
maintenance of sexual dysfunction. It can be seen from Figure 1 that a number of
different factors affect each other, resulting in a dysfunctional sexual system. This
model, based on the work of Ellis (1962, 1971), Kaplan (1974b), Lazarus (1974),
Masters and Johnson (1970), and Wolpe (1958, 1966, 1973), is a general one and
will have to be modified for any specific case. The concepts "historical factor" and
"current factor" are relative to each other, so the distinction between the two is
highly arbitrary.

A system can be altered by intervening at different points. This may explain
in part why many varied approaches to the treatment of sexual dysfunction have
been successful.

---

*The idea for the flowchart came from Davison and Neale (1974), p. 290.

Factors Implicated in the Etiology of Sexual Dysfunction

Sexual dysfunctions can result from many diverse etiological factors and from innumerable combinations of these factors. These factors include: (1) physical and physiological factors such as illness, surgery, irritation from contraceptive materials, and medication (Amelar and Dubin, 1968; Dengrove, 1968; Hastings, 1963; Kaplan, 1974b; Kaufman, 1967; Masters and Johnson, 1970; Twombly, 1968); (2) early environmental problems, for example, problems in the parents' relationship, rape, incest, traumatic experiences with prostitutes, religious orthodoxy, and homosexual experiences* (Masters and Johnson, 1970; Wallace and Barbach, 1974); (3) misinformation and lack of knowledge about sex (Ellison, 1972; Kaplan, 1974b; LoPiccolo and Lobitz, 1973); (4) lack of a skilled sexual partner (Annon, 1974; Kaplan, 1974b); (5) psychological factors, such as anxiety, guilt, depression, and a fear of losing control (Cooper, 1968b; D'Alessio, 1968; Kaplan, 1974b; Kiev and Hackett, 1968; Wolpe, 1971, 1973); (6) relationship problems, including hostility, marital conflicts, lack of communication, and lack of attraction toward one's partner (Cooper, 1968b,c; Gebhard, 1966; Kaplan, 1974b; Lazarus, 1963; McGovern, Stewart, and LoPiccolo, 1975; Snyder, LoPiccolo, and LoPiccolo, 1975; Masters and Johnson, 1970); and (7) other sexual dysfunctions (Masters and Johnson, 1970).

Certain etiological factors are more often associated with some types of dysfunctions than others. Physical and physiological factors, involved in only 3–20% of sexual dysfunctions (Kaplan, 1974b), are implicated most often in male and female dyspareunia, vaginismus, and erectile failure (Masters and Johnson, 1970). In general, arousal and orgasm appear to be more resistant to organic problems in the female than in the male (Kaplan, 1974b; Twombly, 1968).

Misinformation and lack of knowledge about sex and lack of a skilled sexual partner are often implicated in primary orgasmic dysfunction (Annon, 1974; Kaplan, 1974b). Secondary orgasmic dysfunction is associated with marital problems (McGovern et al., 1975), and secondary erectile failure† is most often caused by a pattern of premature ejaculation combined with the wife's complaints about her husband's inadequacy (Masters and Johnson, 1970).

Anxiety

Anxiety about sex and the possible consequences of sex (e.g., pregnancy and venereal disease) has been implicated in the etiology of most of the sexual dysfunctions. Wolpe (1973) believes that anxiety (which is a sympathetic response)

*Masters and Johnson (1970), who have done the most thorough investigation of the etiology of sexual dysfunctions, include homosexual experiences as an etiological factor. This inclusion reflects a bias that runs through the literature on sexual dysfunctions: Homosexuality is almost completely ignored, except when it seems to interfere with heterosexuality. Many sex therapists do not appear to accept homosexuality as a legitimate sexual orientation. Because of this, dysfunctions among gay couples have not been investigated or treated, and no one has mentioned heterosexual experiences or heterosexual conditioning as possible etiological factors leading to dysfunctions in homosexual couples.
†Secondary EF is a condition in which the male has had at least one successful instance of intromission, but who, on at least 25% of his coital attempts, is unable to achieve or maintain an erection sufficient for intromission (Masters and Johnson, 1970).

inhibits sexual arousal (a parasympathetic response) because the two are physiologically incompatible. This hypothesis would predict that erectile failure and general sexual dysfunction, the two dysfunctions involving the arousal/vasocongestive phase, would be especially associated with anxiety. Clinical experience has confirmed the importance of anxiety in the causation of erectile failure (e.g., Annon, 1974; Cooper, 1969a; Friedman, 1968), but the relationship between anxiety and general sexual dysfunction has not yet been examined.

Wolpe (1973) also discusses the role of anxiety in the development of premature ejaculation. Since ejaculation is mediated by the sympathetic branch of the autonomic nervous system, anxiety (which is also sympathetically mediated) facilitates ejaculation. Therefore, anxiety is likely to result in PE. Cooper's (1968a, 1969a) data demonstrate that, at least in some cases, anxiety does seem to be involved in the etiology of PE.

Kaplan (1974b) believes that anxiety does not play a major role in the genesis of PE. She does, however, state that it may play an indirect role: By preventing the man from focusing on the sensations prior to orgasm, it hinders him from learning to control his ejaculatory reflex.

At the present time, the relationship between anxiety and PE has not been established conclusively. Both Kaplan's and Wolpe's hypotheses are speculative, with little evidence supporting them. Cooper's (1969c) data indicate that the relationship is probably complex: Anxiety appears to play a role in some types of cases but not in others.

The role of anxiety is even more obscure in orgasmic dysfunction in women and retarded ejaculation in men. If Kaplan (1974b) is correct in her assumption that the two phases of the sexual response are largely independent, and that one can be inhibited without the other being affected, and if she is correct in her belief that the orgasmic phase is mediated by the sympathetic nervous system, it would appear that anxiety (since it is also sympathetically mediated) would *prevent* RE and orgasmic dysfunction rather than cause them. However, Masters and Johnson (1970) and Lazarus (1963) describe cases of female orgasmic dysfunction in which anxiety appears to be involved, and at least eight of the seventeen cases reported by Masters and Johnson (1970) appear to involve anxiety. Cooper (1969a) found a weak relationship between anxiety and onset of RE.

It is possible that anxiety inhibits orgasm indirectly by inhibiting the arousal/vasocongestive phase, so that patients do not get aroused enough to reach orgasm. If this is true, Kaplan's contention that the two phases are independent must be rejected. This hypothesis is supported by the fact that the orgasmic dysfunction cases cited by Lazarus (1963) also involved general sexual dysfunction, the inhibition of the arousal phase. Unfortunately, Masters and Johnson (1970) do not differentiate between orgasmic dysfunction and general sexual dysfunction, so it is difficult to analyze their cases. Therefore, at the present time, it is not possible to determine the precise relationship between anxiety and the male and female orgasmic dysfunctions.

Anxiety is often implicated in the etiology of vaginismus (Haslam, 1965; Kaplan, 1974b), and, since it interferes with lubrication, it can lead to burning, itching, and aching (dyspareunia) during and following intercourse (Annon, 1974; Masters and Johnson, 1970).

Performance Concerns

Masters and Johnson (1970) and Kaplan (1974b) believe that anxiety over sexual performance is the most important immediate cause of sexual dysfunction, since it can turn a single sexual failure, no matter what the original cause, into a chronic sexual dysfunction. Performance concerns have two components: (1) the affective component, termed "performance anxiety," and (2) the cognitive component, which Masters and Johnson (1970) call "spectatoring." This cognitive component involves thoughts in which the patient questions and evaluates his performance, then severely criticizes himself for failing.

Performance anxiety and spectatoring have been observed in cases of erectile failure by numerous clinicians (Annon, 1974; Cooper, 1969a; Friedman, 1968; Hastings, 1963; Salter, 1961), and also in cases of premature ejaculation (Cooper, 1969a), retarded ejaculation (Cooper, 1969a; Masters and Johnson, 1970), general sexual dysfunction (Kaplan, 1974b), and dyspareunia (Masters and Johnson, 1970).

Methodological Problems

It must be emphasized that these factors were derived almost exclusively from uncontrolled case reports. Researchers (with the exception of Cooper) have not examined nondysfunctional control groups, so it is entirely possible that many of these alleged etiological factors are present to the same degree in the histories of sexually functional people. If this proves to be the case, these factors can hardly be considered as etiological factors, unless they are involved in complex interactions.

Cooper (1968b,c) has examined the difference in incidence of certain factors between patients and controls, but even here, a statistical correlation between a factor and a dysfunction may not indicate a causal relationship. The dysfunction might have caused the "etiological" factor, or both might have been caused by a third variable (Neale and Liebert, 1973). Because of these considerations, one can at best assume a very tentative relationship between many of these factors and sexual dysfunctions.

Assessment

Treatment techniques cannot be evaluated adequately until sexual behavior can be assessed reliably and validly. Most clinicians currently use sexual history interviews (Annon, 1974; Masters and Johnson, 1970) or unstandardized paper-and-pencil questionnaires (Husted, 1972; Schneidman and McGuire, 1976) to diagnose cases. Although these instruments are useful for planning treatment, their utility as research instruments is limited.

Recently, however, a number of researchers have made significant contributions in this area. Caird and Wincze (1974; Wincze, 1971) have developed a series of four-minute cassettes depicting a series of sexual behaviors which they use for desensitization. In order to individualize the hierarchy for each client, they use fifty cards, each containing a synopsis of one of the cassettes. The client rates the amount of anxiety elicited by each of the cards. However, no research has been conducted to demonstrate the reliabilty or validity of this measure, and there are no norms available for nonclinical populations.

LoPiccolo and Steger (1974) have developed a questionnaire, the Sexual Interaction Inventory, that is more applicable to research. The questionnaire elicits quantitative information about the frequency of and the pleasure derived from seventeen heterosexual behaviors. This information can be transformed into eleven scales measuring various psychosexual concepts. LoPiccolo and Steger (1974) have demonstrated that all eleven scales possess significant test–retest reliability and are sensitive to treatment. Nine of the scales discriminate between client applicants and sexually adjusted couples.

Cooper (1969d) studied a number of prognostic indicators in a sample of forty-nine males suffering from erectile failure, premature ejaculation, and retarded ejaculation. He found that acute EF cases improved more than did PE or insidious onset EF cases and that younger patients responded better to treatment than did older patients. Other factors significantly related to positive outcome were: (1) short duration of the disorder, (2) heterosexuality, (3) intermittent rather than chronic failure, (4) love on the part of the patient for his wife, (5) marital happiness (as reported by the patient), (6) normal personality characteristics in the patient, (7) motivation for treatment, and (8) the wife's cooperation in treatment. Clinicians could increase their prognostic ability by including the assessment of these factors in sexual history interviews and questionnaires.

Several clinicians have employed direct or videotaped behavioral observation in the treatment of sexual dysfunctions (Hartman and Fithian, 1972; Serber, 1974). Although these methods may provide important information, the ethical issues involved have not yet been resolved.

Treatment

A Multitheoretical Approach

Behavior therapy and social learning theory have largely dominated the field of sex therapy, but other theories (e.g., general systems theory, psychodynamic approaches, rational emotive therapy, client-centered therapy, and Gestalt therapy) have contributed valuable conceptualizations and techniques. None of these theories, including social learning theory, is sufficient by itself to explain all of the phenomena involved in sexual dysfunctions and sex therapy.* Because of this, an empirical, multitheoretical approach will be taken here. The treatment techniques will be evaluated on the evidence of their effectiveness, regardless of the theoretical position from which they were originally developed. No attempt will be made to fit all of the data into a single theory: Elements from each of these theories are necessary to provide a complete description of the field of sex therapy.

---

*Davison and Neale (1974) make the same point in regard to the entire field of abnormal psychology.

Structured Sexual Experiences

Kaplan (1974b, p.xii) writes: "It is the integrated use of systematically structured sexual experiences with conjoint therapeutic sessions which is the main
innovation and distinctive feature of sex therapy."

Different hypotheses have been proposed to explain how and why structured
sexual experiences improve sexual functioning, but it is likely that their effectiveness is due to a number of different mechanisms whose relative importance is determined by the specific way in which treatment is applied.

Structured sexual experiences can vary along three independent dimensions:
type of involvement in the experience, method of overcoming anxiety, and
whether or not the experiences are graduated. The first factor, type of involvement, has three possible levels: (1) actual physical involvement, in which the experiences are engaged in at home with the partner, (2) imaginal involvement in the
experiences, and (3) vicarious involvement via films or videotapes of other people
engaged in the experiences. Four types of anxiety-inhibiting agents have been
used in conjunction with the sexual experiences: (1) the anxiety-inhibiting factors
inherent in the sexual activities themselves, (2) progressive relaxation training,
(3) chemical agents, and (4) hypnotically induced relaxation. The final dimension
along which the experiences can vary, extent of graduation, is theoretically a continuous variable but in actual practice is usually a dichotomous one: Either the
tasks are graduated or they are not. Most of the literature reporting on the use
of structured sexual activities consists of case studies, but a few theoretical and
experimental papers deal with the relative effectiveness of the levels of these
three factors.

Graduated and Nongraduated Experiences. The original theoretical basis
for the use of structured sexual activities was Wolpe's (1958) principle of "reciprocal inhibition." Wolpe (1958, p. 71) writes: "If a response antagonistic to anxiety can be made to occur in the presence of the anxiety-evoking stimuli so that
it is accompanied by a complete or partial suppression of the anxiety responses,
the bond between these stimuli and the anxiety responses will be weakened."

Since anxiety is mediated by the sympathetic division of the autonomic nervous system, any parasympathetically mediated response should be able to suppress the anxiety as long as the degree of anxiety elicited is kept at a low enough
level. Because of this, a hierarchy of sexual experiences is usually employed, starting with behaviors that elicit little anxiety and proceeding to behaviors that elicit
progressively more anxiety. As anxiety is deconditioned to the first behavior, the
anxiety-suppressing properties of the parasympathetically mediated response
generalize to the next step on the hierarchy, reducing the amount of anxiety
elicited by that behavior. Thus, the amount of anxiety elicited at any step on the
hierarchy is always kept at a minimum level (Wolpe, 1966).

However, Bandura (1969) points out that stimulus graduation is not a
necessary condition for the extinction of anxiety. Furthermore, two counter-
conditioning/extinction techniques, implosion and guided imagining, do not employ graduated experiences. Implosion involves the presentation of an imagined
scene to the client with the object of attaining a maximal level of anxiety at which
the patient is held until the anxiety is extinguished (Stampfl and Levis, 1967).

Frankel (1970) reports successfully employing implosion to treat a woman suffering from orgasmic dysfunction and general sexual dysfunction caused by her fear of sex.

Guided imagining (Wolpin, 1969) is an offshoot of Wolpe's reciprocal inhibition and Stampfl's implosion therapy. The therapist has the patient imagine a scene in which he is involved in anxiety-provoking behavior. Guided imagining is closer to Stampfl's procedure than to Wolpe's in that the scene is a continuous one rather than a series of discrete scenes, and no anxiety-inhibiting response is used,* so its effectiveness is thought to be due to extinction and positive reinforcement (for imagining the scenes) rather than to counterconditioning (although there may be elements of counterconditioning involved also, since the scene is presented in the relaxed atmosphere of the therapist's office). However, guided imagining is different from implosion in that it does not employ psychodynamic themes and unrealistic elements in the scenes. Guided imagining has been used successfully in the treatment of erectile failure, frigidity, vaginismus, and dyspareunia (Dittborn, 1957; Hussain, 1964; Leckie, 1964; Wolpin, 1969).

Nongraduated (and unsystematically graduated) experiences have also been presented via film, videotape, and still photographs in the treatment of various sexual dysfunctions (Annon, 1974; Barbach, 1974; Beigel, 1971; Hartman and Fithian, 1972; LoPiccolo, 1975; Schneidman and McGuire, 1976).

Although there is no solid experimentally obtained evidence demonstrating the superiority of graduated over nongraduated sexual experiences, Bandura (1969) suggests a number of reasons for preferring graduated activities: (1) Nongraduated experiences provoking high levels of anxiety may increase the client's anxiety instead of extinguishing it; (2) even if the nongraduated approach is effective, it unnecessarily entails exposing the client to subjectively uncomfortable levels of anxiety; and (3) graduated experiences provide the clinician and client greater control over the change process.

Wincze (1971) reports a case that supports Bandura's theorizing. In the course of treating a patient for general sexual dysfunction with systematic desensitization, Wincze showed her two (pornographic) films depicting heterosexual petting and intercourse. The films made the client emotionally upset and produced change in the negative direction. Wincze believes the adverse effects were due to two factors: (1) The client was not in control of the presentation of the scenes and was forced to view scenes that were too anxiety-provoking, and (2) the films lacked any logical hierarchy, and many important behaviors were not depicted.

In summary, although there is little evidence on which to decide the issue, theoretical reasons and some empirical evidence indicate that graduated sexual experiences are preferable to nongraduated experiences.

Type of Involvement in the Experiences. As discussed above, the client can participate in the sexual experiences directly, in imagination, or vicariously (via films or tapes). Imaginal involvement has been used extensively in the treatment of sexual dysfunctions with both graduated and nongraduated experiences and employing a variety of anxiety-inhibiting agents.

*Leckie (1964), however, employs hypnotic suggestions to relax the patient.

In systematic desensitization, imaginal exposure to sexual activities is combined with progressive muscle relaxation. This technique has been used successfully in the treatment of all the sexual dysfunctions (e.g., Annon, 1974; Dengrove, 1967, 1971; Ince, 1973; Lazarus, 1961, 1965, 1968; Rachman, 1959; Razani, 1972; Wincze, 1971; Wolpe, 1958, 1973).

Imaginal exposure has also been employed in conjunction with chemical agents (Brady, 1966, 1971; Dengrove, 1967; Friedman, 1968; Kraft, 1969a,b; Kraft and Al-Issa, 1968), hypnotic relaxation (Dittborn, 1957; Fuchs, Hoch, Abramovici, Timor-Tritsch, and Kleinhaus, 1975; Fuchs, Hoch, Paldi, Abramovici, Brandes, Timor-Tritsch, and Kleinhaus, 1973; Hussain, 1964; Kroger, 1969; Lazarus, 1973; Leckie, 1964; Schneck, 1965), and sexual responses (Frankel, 1970; Wolpin, 1969) as anxiety inhibitors.

Direct involvement in graded experiences has been employed even more frequently than imaginal exposure for the treatment of sexual dysfunctions (Kaplan, 1974b; Lazarus, 1971a; LoPiccolo, 1975; Masters and Johnson, 1970; Wolpe, 1958, 1973). The most common variant of this procedure, which uses sexual arousal as the anxiety-inhibiting agent, has been used successfully in the treatment of the majority of sexual dysfunctions (Annon, 1974; Kaplan, 1974b; Lazarus, 1971b; LoPiccolo and Lobitz, 1973; Masters and Johnson, 1970; Sharpe and Meyer, 1973; Wolpe, 1958, 1966, 1973; Wolpe and Lazarus, 1966). Progressive relaxation (Wolpe, 1958, 1966) and hypnotic relaxation (Fuchs et al., 1973, 1975; Hartman and Fithian, 1972; Lazarus and Rachman, 1960; Salzman, 1969; Schneck, 1965; Tinling, 1969) have also been used successfully with direct involvement in sexual activities.

Chemical relaxation agents have been used rarely in combination with direct sexual experiences. Dengrove (1971), however, reports a case of erectile failure in which he suggested that the patient drink a cocktail before engaging in the sexual activities. Dengrove also prescribes mild sedatives in the treatment of EF.

The final mode of involvement in sexual experiences is vicarious experience. The use of nongraduated activities in films and tapes has been discussed above (see section on graduated and nongraduated experiences). In addition to these cases, vicarious exposure has been used with systematically graduated activities. McVaugh (cited by Wolpe, 1973) reports a 90% success rate in the treatment of primary orgasmic dysfunction using a graded series of slides of a couple making love. Caird and Wincze (1974) have successfully used a graduated, individualized hierarchy of sexual activities presented via videotape in the treatment of general sexual dysfunction and primary orgasmic dysfunction.

A number of investigators have tried to determine experimentally which of the three modes of involvement is the most effective. Wincze and Caird (1976) found that a graduated series of videotaped sexual experiences combined with relaxation training was slightly more effective than (imaginal) systematic desensitization in reducing anxiety in women suffering from general sexual dysfunction and orgasmic dysfunction. Husted (1972) found that imaginal and in vivo desensitization were equally effective in treating general sexual dysfunction, but imaginal desensitization required significantly fewer sessions to reduce anxiety than did in vivo desensitization. On the basis of these experiments, it would appear that vicarious desensitization is the treatment of choice, followed by imaginal and then in vivo desensitization.

However, the situation is in reality more complicated than this. First, only one of Husted's (1972) dependent variables (the number of sessions required to reduce anxiety) showed any differences between the two treatment groups: Coital frequency and enjoyment, orgasmic frequency, and self-ratings of improvement were not significantly different for the two groups. Husted (1972) observes that even complete reduction of anxiety did not automatically lead to the achievement of orgasm, indicating that anxiety may not even be the most important variable to be studied. Wincze and Caird (1976) report similar results: Only 25% of the women in the study who were inorgasmic prior to treatment became orgasmic during treatment. The ambiguity of these results makes it difficult to evaluate the relative effectiveness of the three modes of exposure.

Secondly, although exposure to sexual activities via all three modes produces change in part through the processes of counterconditioning, extinction, and positive reinforcement, a number of the underlying mechanisms are specific to certain modes. For example, only direct involvement includes shaping of skills through practice with and feedback from the partner. Vicarious involvement (modeling) produces clinical change through: (1) teaching clients novel response patterns, (2) response facilitation (Bandura, 1969), (3) sex education, and (4) legitimizing the activities depicted (Austin and Liberman, 1973).

Because these techniques produce changes through different mechanisms, they probably interact with client variables such as amount of sexual anxiety, skill, and knowledge. Therefore, a thorough assessment of these variables must be conducted in order to decide upon the best combination of the three modes of exposure.

Most sex therapy programs include direct involvement in sexual experiences, because the partners can learn through actual practice with partner feedback. Kaplan (1974b) and Lazarus (1968) suggest the use of imaginal exposure prior to direct exposure if the client experiences high degrees of anxiety in relation to the activities. Imaginal exposure to sexual experiences can be conceptualized as the early (low-anxiety) items on a hierarchy that will later include direct exposure. Husted's (1972) finding that imaginal desensitization takes fewer sessions to reduce anxiety supports this approach. Imaginal exposure is also useful when treating a client without a partner, since he cannot participate directly in the experience (Bass, 1974).

Vicarious exposure to sexual experiences is particularly useful when treating clients with low levels of sexual skills and knowledge, since it is the most efficient method of showing the client exactly what to do. Most programs use films or tapes as adjunct procedures when the client has a skill deficit in a particular area (e.g., masturbation). If the graduated videotapes produced by Caird and Wincze (1974) become available to clinicians, vicarious desensitization may eventually replace the less efficient imaginary desensitization when treating clients with high levels of anxiety.

Anxiety-Inhibiting Agents. As discussed previously, sexual responses, progressive relaxation training, hypnotic relaxation, and chemical agents have been used to inhibit anxiety during sexual activities. When treating clients with low levels of anxiety, sexual arousal by itself is usually sufficient to overcome anxiety as long as the sexual experiences are systematically graduated. If clients suffer from high levels of anxiety, it is often necessary to use an additional anxiety-inhibiting agent.

If an anxious client is involved in direct exposure to sexual experiences, a simple way to reduce the anxiety is to have the client drink a small amount of alcohol prior to engaging in the activity (Dengrove, 1971). If this is not sufficient, the client can be instructed in progressive relaxation or self-hypnotic relaxation. These two methods are probably safer than the use of prescription drugs because of the possibility of misusing the drugs when there is no physician present.

There is considerable controversy over the relative effectiveness of progressive relaxation and hypnotic relaxation. Bernstein and Borkovec (1973) state that progressive relaxation is preferable because hypnosis has undesirable connotations for clients, progressive relaxation can be used in everyday life, and some research indicates that progressive relaxation is more effective in decreasing physiological activity. Paul (cited by Bernstein and Borkovec, 1973) found that progressive relaxation was more effective and faster in reducing heart rate and muscle tension.

However, others have reached opposite conclusions. Dengrove (1973) states that hypnotism can be used to intensify imagery when imaginary exposure is used, and posthypnotic suggestions can be given to the client instructing him to relax in a shorter time at the next session. Dengrove (1973) quotes Wolpe as saying that he believes hypnotism has an accelerating effect in producing relaxation.

Lazarus (1973) believes that the client's attitude toward hypnotism is the major variable in determining its relative effectiveness. He found that subjects who requested hypnotism improved more when hypnotic relaxation was used than when progressive relaxation was used, but subjects who did not request hypnotism did equally well in both conditions.

When imaginal exposure to sexual experiences is used (in the therapist's office), methohexital sodium is preferable to progressive or hypnotic relaxation. Brady (1966, 1971) points out that not only is methohexital sodium more reliable than these other techniques but it is quicker, since no training is needed. However, it is probably wise to ask the client which mode of relaxation he desires, in order to capitalize on placebo effects and to eliminate any problems caused by fear of injections.

Clinicians are not in complete agreement as to which chemical agent is the most effective in producing relaxation. One study in which imaginal exposure and methohexital sodium were used in the treatment of premature ejaculation resulted in only three cures out of six (Friedman, 1968), and Ahmed (1968) claims that this drug causes pain, anxiety, and distraction in the majority of cases. Because of this, Ahmed uses thiopentone sodium in the treatment of PE. However, methohexital sodium has been used successfully in the treatment of many cases of sexual dysfunction (Brady, 1966, 1971; Friedman, 1968; Kraft, 1969a,b; Kraft and Al-Issa, 1968). It has been found to be safer than thiopentone (Eyres and Kernkamp, 1965, cited by Brady, 1966; Pitts et al., 1965, cited by Brady, 1966 and Kraft and Al-Issa, 1968), and the recovery time for methohexital is quicker than that for thiopentone (Jolly, 1960, cited by Brady, 1966 and Kraft and Al-Issa,

1968). The weight of empirical evidence thus favors the use of methohexital sodium.

In summary, anxiety-inhibiting agents interact with mode of involvement and client variables. The decision as to which agent to use in any particular case depends on both of these other factors.

Masturbation Therapy. Masturbation has been included in a number of treatment packages using structured sexual experiences. It is useful for a number of reasons: (1) It is not as anxiety-provoking as heterosexual behavior for some clients, so it is useful as an initial step in the hierarchy of activities (Kaplan, 1974b); (2) it enables the client to find out what types of stimulation are most arousing for her so that she can then teach her partner these methods of stimulation (Annon, 1973; LoPiccolo and Lobitz, 1972); (3) Kinsey et al. (cited by LoPiccolo and Lobitz, 1972) found that women are more likely to reach orgasm through masturbation than through any other technique; (4) Masters and Johnson (1966) found that masturbation leads to more intense orgasms than intercourse or manual stimulation by the partner; (5) it is useful for clients who do not have partners (Annon, 1974); (6) it is a good way for a male to practice the squeeze or pause technique for premature ejaculation without any performance demands from his partner (LoPiccolo and Lobitz, 1973); and (7) it can be used to increase the frequency of orgasm, leading to a longer ejaculation latency in men suffering from premature ejaculation (Annon, 1974).

Masturbation has been used in the treatment of erectile failure (Annon, 1971, 1974), premature ejaculation (Annon, 1971, 1974; LoPiccolo and Lobitz, 1973), retarded ejaculation (Annon, 1974), frigidity (Annon, 1971), general sexual dysfunction (Annon, 1973), primary orgasmic dysfunction (Annon, 1973, 1974; Hastings, 1963, 1966; Kaplan, 1974b; Wright, 1969, cited by Annon, 1974), and secondary orgasmic dysfunction (Annon, 1973).

LoPiccolo and Lobitz (1972) have developed a nine-step masturbation program for primary orgasmic dysfunction in which the client explores her body (including her genitals) visually and tactually, locates sensitive areas that produce feelings of pleasure, stimulates these areas manually and then with an electric vibrator, teaches her husband how to stimulate her, and engages in intercourse with concurrent manual or vibrator stimulation. LoPiccolo and Lobitz (1973) have used this technique in eleven cases of primary orgasmic dysfunction: All eleven women became orgasmic through manual stimulation, and nine were orgasmic through intercourse following therapy (apparently the majority of this latter group required concurrent manual stimulation). LoPiccolo and his colleagues (McGovern et al., 1975) report on six more women treated with this procedure who all became orgasmic in intercourse. Other investigators have included the LoPiccolo and Lobitz procedure in various types of treatment packages with considerable success (Barbach, 1974; Bruni, 1974; Kohlenberg, 1974; Reisinger, 1974; Schneidman and McGuire, 1976; Wallace and Barbach, 1974).

Annon (1973) has developed a successive approximation masturbatory treatment for women who are able to achieve orgasm only via masturbation. Annon instructs them to gradually change their style of masturbation to progressively approximate intercourse. Wolpe (1971) reports the successful use of a similar technique. LoPiccolo and his colleagues have attempted to use their nine-step program with secondary inorgasmic women with little success (McGovern et al., 1975), but they were able to treat three cases successfully when they employed marriage therapy in addition to their program (Snyder et al., 1975).

Use of Dilators in the Treatment of Vaginismus. An interesting variation of the graded sexual experiences technique is the use of dilators of graduated size in the treatment of vaginismus and psychogenic dyspareunia. The technique consists of having the patient relax and then insert lubricated dilators of increasing size into her vagina. This technique, which has been in use since 1916 (Hühner, 1916), has been employed in a variety of ways. The dilators can be inserted by a physician in his office (Ellison, 1972) using progressive relaxation (Cooper, 1969b; Haslam, 1965) or hypnotism (Fuchs et al., 1973) to relax the patient, or the patient can insert the dilators herself (Cooper, 1969b). In addition, the dilators can be used at home, with either the patient (Annon, 1974; DeMoor, 1972; Fuchs et al., 1973, 1975; Hastings, 1963, 1966; Hussain, 1964) or her husband (DeMoor, 1972; Fuchs et al., 1975; Masters and Johnson, 1970) inserting them. Other variations include using either the patient's or her husband's finger instead of dilators (Kaplan, 1974b), systematic desensitization with imaginal dilators (Wolpe, 1973), and pairing imaginal and actual finger insertion with orgasms achieved via manual stimulation of the clitoris (Wilson, 1973). Fuchs et al. (1973) report success in six out of nine cases treated in the office, and thirty-one out of thirty-four cases treated at home, while Masters and Johnson (1970) report success in all twenty-nine of the vaginismus cases they have treated.

Cognitive/Attentional Techniques

A number of cognitive/attentional techniques have been developed to treat sexual dysfunctions. Many clinicians instruct their clients to direct their attention to their own physical sensations instead of worrying about their performances or trying to control orgasms. This technique has been used in the treatment of erectile failure (Annon, 1974; Ellis, 1962; Kaplan, 1974b; Lazarus, 1968; Masters and Johnson, 1970), frigidity (Annon, 1974; Ellis, 1962), general sexual dysfunction (Kaplan, 1974b), and primary and secondary orgasmic dysfunction (Ellis, 1962; Kaplan, 1974b).

Jemail (1973) and Kaplan, Kohl, Pomeroy, Offit, and Hogan (1974) believe that the squeeze and pause procedures for the treatment of premature ejaculation (see section below) are effective because they direct the client's attention to the physical sensations preceding orgasm, thus enabling him to learn to develop ejaculatory control.

Fantasy and pornography have been used to enhance sexual arousal and also to stop obsessive cognitions in the treatment of erectile failure, retarded ejaculation, general sexual dysfunction, and primary orgasmic dysfunction (Kaplan, 1974b), and to distract a patient from his "cognitive pain" in a case of psychogenic male dyspareunia (Sharpe and Meyer, 1973).

Thought stopping has been used to stop obsessions over performance and partners' orgasms in the treatment of erectile failure (Garfield, McBrearty, and

Dichter, 1969; Kaplan, 1974b) and to directly stop ejaculation in one case of premature ejaculation (Ince, 1973).

Ellis (1962, 1971) teaches clients to stop their irrational thoughts about their performance by challenging these thoughts on logical and empirical grounds and by replacing these irrational thoughts with rational ones. Ellis (1971) claims that this technique, called "rational emotive therapy," is successful in 75–80% of the erectile failure and frigidity cases that he treats, but he presents no quantitative evidence to support this assertion.

Finally, some clinicians teach their clients to relabel anxiety, tension, or coldness as "sexual arousal" when they have been mislabeling their sensations (Lobitz, LoPiccolo, Lobitz, and Brockway, 1974; LoPiccolo, 1975). This technique has been used in cases of frigidity (Annon, 1974) and orgasmic dysfunction (LoPiccolo, 1975).

The Pause and Squeeze Procedures

Two very effective techniques for the treatment of premature ejaculation are the pause (Semans, 1956) and the squeeze (Masters and Johnson, 1970) procedures. The pause technique consists of the female stimulating the male manually until he feels the physical sensations immediately preceding orgasm. At this point, the wife stops stimulating him until the sensations subside, then begins stimulating the penis again, and stops just before ejaculation. As this procedure is repeated, the male begins to develop ejaculatory control. The next step consists of repeating the procedure with the penis lubricated, so that the intravaginal environment is more closely approximated.

Masters and Johnson (1970) have developed a modification of this procedure in which the wife manually stimulates the penis until it becomes erect. She then squeezes the penis at the coronal ridge for three to four seconds, which causes the man to lose the urge to ejaculate and to lose 10–30% of his erection. The wife waits fifteen to thirty seconds, then repeats the procedure. After practicing for a few days, the couple repeats the procedure with intravaginal containment of the penis, but no thrusting, to produce stimulation. The next steps are intravaginal containment with slow movement, and than fast movement, using the squeeze as before.

LoPiccolo (1975) has added a preliminary step to these two techniques. He instructs the male to first practice the pause or squeeze during masturbation in order to reduce anxiety. The client then proceeds through the steps outlined by Semans and Masters and Johnson.

Researchers do not agree on the mechanism by which these two techniques work. LoPiccolo (1975) believes that they work on the basis of Guthrie's principle of "crowding the threshold," by which s-r connections between minimal stimulation and ejaculation are extinguished. Jemail (1973) and Kaplan (1974b) believe that the active ingredient involves focusing the client's attention on his physical sensations prior to orgasm. Tanner (1973) believes the techniques work via operant shaping and time out for reinforcement. No data have been presented to support any of these hypotheses.

Many sex therapists advocate the use of the pause (Annon, 1974; Dengrove, 1971; Kaplan, 1974b; LoPiccolo, 1975; Wolpe, 1973) and the squeeze technique (Annon, 1974; Dengrove, 1971; Hartman and Fithian, 1972; Kaplan, 1974b; LoPiccolo, 1975; Wolpe, 1973), and individual case studies have been reported in which the pause (Lazarus, 1971b; Razani, 1972) and squeeze (Tanner, 1973) have been used successfully. Kaplan et al. (1974) treated thirty-two couples conjointly using the pause technique, and all of the couples who completed the program were cured. In addition, they have treated four couples in a group, with a 50% success rate at posttreatment and a 100% success rate at the four-month follow-up. Semans (1956) used the pause technique in eight cases, with a 100% success rate. Cooper, however, had less success with this technique. He included the pause as a component in his treatment package in two studies. In one study (Cooper, 1968a) only one patient out of nine improved, and in a second series of sixty clients (Cooper, 1969c) only 43% improved, while 7% actually got worse.

The squeeze technique has also been shown to be very effective. LoPiccolo and Lobitz (1973) treated 6 cases with a 100% success rate, and Masters and Johnson (1970) treated 186 cases with only 4 failures. Finally, Mikulas and Lowe (1974) treated 10 cases of PE via bibliotherapy, in which the squeeze was one component. The mean ejaculation latency for the treatment group increased from 1.8 to 37.2 minutes, while that for the waiting list control group remained at 1.4 minutes. However, after the clients in the control group were given the bibliotherapy, their mean latency increased to 18.6 minutes. The subject with the least improvement had a latency of 4.5 minutes after treatment, which is within the normal range.

The success rate for both the squeeze and the pause techniques has been excellent, with the exception of Cooper's studies. It is unclear why his results were so much worse, but possible factors include client variables and slightly different methods of treatment.

Group Therapy

Group therapy has a number of advantages over individual therapy: (1) Patients are exposed to a variety of models (Lazarus, 1968; Stone and Levine, 1950) and can receive positive social reinforcement and support from a number of people; (2) patients are able to share their problems with each other and learn that they are not the only ones suffering from a particular problem, which in turn reduces their feelings of isolation (Stone and Levine, 1950); (3) patients are exposed to a wider range of opinions (Lazarus, 1968), which maximizes the generalization of behavior change, since new behaviors are more likely to fit societal norms; and (4) group therapy is more economical. Because of these factors, a number of clinicians have used group therapy in the treatment of various sexual dysfunctions.

A variety of techniques have been utilized in conjunction with group treatment, including systematic desensitization, graded sexual activities, support and empathy, instruction in sexual technique (Lazarus, 1961, 1968), the pause technique (Kaplan et al., 1974), masturbation therapy, readings, movies, and explanations of sexual anatomy and physiology (Barbach, 1974). Group treatment has been successful for erectile failure (Lazarus, 1961, 1968), premature ejaculation (Kaplan et al., 1974), and primary orgasmic dysfunction (Barbach, 1974; Lazarus, 1968; Schneidman and McGuire, 1976).

Group therapy appears to be effective in the treatment of various sexual dysfunctions. However, none of these studies compared group therapy to conjoint therapy, so their relative effectiveness is not known. It is possible that group therapy, which can capitalize on a number of factors such as consciousness-raising techniques, would be more effective for primary orgasmic dysfunction, while conjoint therapy would be more effective for patients suffering from psychological problems in addition to their sexual problems. This question can only be answered through research.

Another interesting question involves the relative effectiveness of couples' groups and same-sex groups. It is possible that this factor interacts with diagnosis and other factors, but no data at all are available on this issue.

Communication Training and Marital Therapy

Many people suffering from sexual dysfunction are unable to discuss sexual topics openly with their partners. This lack of communication prevents them from solving their sexual problems and often causes the couple to perceive the problem in a grossly distorted manner. For example, wives of men suffering from erectile failure caused by anxiety often believe the erectile problems indicate that their husbands do not love them. In addition to communication problems in the sexual area, dysfunctional couples are sometimes unable to communicate adequately in nonsexual areas. Because of this, sexual and nonsexual communication training is often used as an adjunct therapeutic technique.

Therapists have discussed with clients the need to communicate about sex in general (Tanner, 1973); sexual feelings, sensations, and fears (Kaplan, 1974b; Prochaska and Marzilli, 1973); specific sexual stimulation techniques and other sexual behaviors that they enjoy (Fodor, 1974; Kaplan, 1974b; Lobitz and LoPiccolo, 1972; LoPiccolo, 1975; Masters and Johnson, 1970); sexual behaviors that they dislike (Fodor, 1974; Lobitz and LoPiccolo, 1972; LoPiccolo, 1975); sexual fantasies (LoPiccolo, 1975; Prochaska and Marzilli, 1973); and ways to initiate sex and to gently refuse sexual advances made by their partners (Lobitz and LoPiccolo, 1972; LoPiccolo, 1975). Masters and Johnson (1970) and Hartman and Fithian (1972) teach clients to use physical touch to communicate feelings to their partners, and Masters and Johnson (1970) emphasize the importance of clients giving feedback to their partners during a sexual activity. Finally, a number of therapists teach couples to express nonsexual feelings to each other (Lobitz and LoPiccolo, 1972; Prochaska and Marzilli, 1973; Snyder et al., 1975).

Only one experimental study has been reported in which sexual communication training was investigated. Husted (1972) compared desensitization techniques alone and in combination with sexual communiation training. The addition of communication training did not increase the effectiveness of therapy for any of the dependent variables, which included sexual anxiety, coital frequency and enjoyment, and coital and noncoital orgasmic frequency, nor did it decrease the number of sessions needed to treat the clients.

The beliefs of many clinicians are thus in direct conflict with what little experimental evidence is available. At this point, it is impossible to determine whether communication training is actually ineffective, or if Husted's techniques were not powerful enough or her dependent variables too insensitive. Her study should be replicated using more powerful therapy techniques and different dependent variables (e.g., the Sexual Interaction Inventory), therapists, client populations, and dysfunctions before definite conclusions are drawn.

Some couples may need marital therapy in addition or prior to sex therapy if their marital problems are involved in the etiology of the sexual dysfunction or if their marital problems are so severe that they would prevent the couple from carrying out the tasks required by sex therapy (Kaplan, 1974b). LoPiccolo (1975) lists the changing of destructive sex roles as a basic principle of sex therapy, and clinicians have reported the use of marital therapy in the treatment of erectile failure, premature ejaculation (Dengrove, 1971), and secondary orgasmic dysfunction (McGovern et al., 1975; Wolpe, 1971).

Information Giving, Correcting Misconceptions, and Instruction in Technique

The majority of clients presenting with sexual dysfunctions are ignorant about many aspects of sex, have certain misconceptions about sexual functioning, and/or are deficient in techniques of sexual stimulation. Lazarus (1971b), for example, reports the case of a man who feared sexual intercourse because a friend had told him that the vagina was capable of such violent contractions and spasms that it could harm the penis, and Leckie (1964) reports that many women suffering from sexual dysfunctions believe that intercourse necessarily involves pain. Because of this lack of information and skill, many therapists include sex education (facts on sexual anatomy, physiology, psychology, and "normality"), correcting misconceptions, and instruction in sexual technique as part of their programs.

These three factors have been used by themselves to successfully change attitudes, and to a much lesser extent, behavior, in the treatment of erectile failure (Roen, 1965; Stone and Levine, 1950), general sexual dysfunction (Stone and Levine, 1950), and orgasmic dysfunction (Robinson, 1974; Stone and Levine, 1950). However, Lazarus (1961) found sex education combined with insight therapy to be less effective than systematic desensitization in the treatment of erectile failure. Education and instruction are useful by themselves in the treatment of what Lazarus (1971b) terms "pseudoinadequacies"—sexual problems due entirely to ignorance or misinformation, when no real psychopathology exists. In more severe cases, they serve as useful components in treatment packages.

Assertive Training

Sexual behavior does not take place in an interpersonal vacuum, as the section on communication training and marital therapy indicates. Before engaging in sex, a person must have certain social skills and be able to overcome inhibitions about making social contacts, forming interpersonal relationships, and maintaining these relationships. Assertiveness is an important element in this process. It is also important in the area of communicating about sexual needs and preferences.

Assertive training has been used as a component in the treatment of erectile failure (Dengrove, 1967; Garfield et al., 1969; Lazarus, 1965, 1971b; Salter, 1961; Wolpe, 1958; Wolpe and Lazarus, 1966), premature ejaculation (Yulis, 1976), frigidity (Dengrove, 1967; Gelder and Marks, cited by Paul, 1969), general sexual dysfunction (Goldstein, 1971; Wolpe, 1973), primary orgasmic dysfunction (Fodor, 1974), and secondary orgasmic dysfunction (Salter, 1961).

Cotherapy

Masters and Johnson (1970, p. 4) write: "Definitive laboratory experience supports the concept that a more successful clinical approach to the problems of sexual dysfunction can be made by the dual-sex teams of therapists than by an individual male or female therapist. Certainly, controlled laboratory experimentation in human physiology has supported unequivocally the initial investigative premise that no man will ever fully understand a woman's sexual function or dysfunction. . . . The exact converse applies to any woman."

Masters and Johnson (1970) further state that having two opposite-sexed therapists gives each of the client's a "friend in court" who presents the client's view to the spouse and the other therapist, and who interprets what the client is trying to say. In addition, while one therapist is talking, the other one can sit back and observe the patients' reactions, and the presence of two therapists increases the reliability of the therapists' observations, conceptualizations, and interpretations. Finally, having opposite-sexed therapists reduces the probability that the clients and therapists will be become emotionally or sexually involved with each other. Reding and Ennis (1964) add another point in favor of a dual-sex therapy team: The cotherapists model a positive relationship for the couple, which facilitates communication between the husband and wife.

However, Masters and Johnson (1970) do not present any details of the "controlled laboratory experimentation in human physiology" that allegedly demonstrates that men cannot understand women's sexual functioning and vice versa. In fact, in their comprehensive book on sexual physiology, Masters and Johnson (1966, p. 285) write: "The parallels in reaction to effective sexual stimulation emphasized the physiologic similarities in male and female responses rather than the differences. Aside from the obvious anatomic variants, men and women are homogeneous in their physiologic responses to sexual stimuli."

Other clinicians argue that cotherapy is not necessary. Kaplan (1974b) states that therapists can be trained to understand the sexuality of opposite-sexed patients, and McCarthy (1973) presents a similar viewpoint. Furthermore, cotherapy is expensive in terms of time and money (McCarthy, 1973).

While Masters and Johnson's (1970) arguments all have a certain amount of validity to them, the counterarguments presented by other therapists are also plausible. The issue is an empirical one. Does the use of coptherapy teams increase the effectiveness of sex therapy enough to offset the additional costs? No controlled research has been conducted to answer this question conclusively, but the available evidence suggests that the answer is no. Prochaska and Marzilli (1973) point out that Masters and Johnson (1970) used no control groups, so it is impossible to determine whether or not the dual team is an effective component in their package. Franks and Wilson (1974) state that no research supports Masters and Johnson's claim that the teams are essential, and that the clinical evidence suggests that single male therapists can successfully treat female dysfunctions (Brady, 1969; Lazarus, 1963; Wolpe, 1969, all cited by Franks and Wilson, 1974). Prochaska and Marzilli (1973) treated nineteen couples with a modified Masters and Johnson program using single therapists, and report improvement in fifteen cases. McCarthy (1973) reports improvement in twelve out of fourteen cases in a similar program. Kohlenberg (1974) reports no difference in success rates between couples treated by single therapists or cotherapists. (However, couples were apparently not randomly assigned to treatment conditions, and no information is presented on the criteria used in assigning them.) Thus, the evidence does not support Masters and Johnson's assertion that coptherapy teams are a vital component in the treatment package.

Kaplan (1974b) mentions that cotherapy *is* useful as a training procedure. An experienced therapist can be paired with an inexperienced one, so that the trainee receives experience without harming the patient.

Conjoint Therapy

Another Masters and Johnson (1970) dictum is that the relationship, rather than either of the partners, is the patient. Because of this, they treat couples and not individual patients. Kaplan (1974b) and LoPiccolo (1975) echo this view. LoPiccolo (1975) emphasizes to the husband and wife that they are both responsible for future change, and Kaplan (1974b) believes that conjoint therapy is more effective than individual therapy because the shared sexual experiences are the crucial factor in therapy.

There is some empirical evidence that supports this view. Cooper (1969d) treated forty-nine patients presenting with erectile failure, premature ejaculation, or retarded ejaculation. Cases in which the wife cooperated with therapy responded significantly better than those in which the wife did not cooperate. Prochaska and Marzilli (1973) report only minimal success with eight patients seen individually.

However, Masters and Johnson's belief that a sexual problem is *always* a problem with the relationship is questionable. This belief is based on the view that "sexual response represents . . . interaction between two people" (Masters and Johnson, 1970, p. 2). This assumption is a bias rather than a fact: Masturbation is no less of a sexual response than intercourse.

Just as sexual response can involve only one person, sexual dysfunction in some cases is localized in one person. For example, a person might have had a traumatic sexual experience as a child or been brought up in a severely moralistic home, so that he or she is unable to function sexually with any partner as an adult. It would be unjustifiable to claim in either of these cases that the problem was due to an interaction between husband and wife. Although the majority of cases probably does involve an interaction of two people, there do exist cases where an individual's dysfunction is so severe that the partner's behavior is not involved in the etiology of the dysfunction and is only minimally involved in its maintenance.

Even where dysfunctions involve an interaction between the two partners, it is sometimes possible to produce a cure without treating both partners. Systematic desensitization and rational emotive therapy have been used successfully with a variety of dysfunctions, and masturbation therapy has been used successfully to treat inorgasmic women in all-women groups (see sections above).

Husted (1972) treated inorgasmic women with systematic desensitization or in vivo desensitization. Half of the women in each group were randomly assigned to joint treatment with their husbands, while half of the women received individual therapy. On all of the dependent measures, which included reduction in sexual anxiety, increase in coital frequency and enjoyment, and increase in frequency of orgasm through coital and noncoital stimulation, there were no differences between the group treated individually and the group treated conjointly.

This evidence demonstrates that the real issue is much more complex than simply: "Is conjoint therapy more effective than individual therapy?" Presence of the spouse probably interacts with many factors such as the type of problem, the quality of the relationship between the husband and wife, and the type of treatment employed. For example, primary orgasmic dysfunction may respond best to group treatment with partners absent, while secondary orgasmic dysfunction and erectile failure probably respond better to conjoint therapy. In addition, rational emotive therapy and systematic desensitization may work equally well with single patients or couples, while Masters and Johnson's package treatment may work better with couples. Only future research will be able to unravel these complex interactions.

Conclusion

Future research in the area of sexual dysfunctions should be carried out within a broad framework in which etiology is viewed from an interactional approach and treatment techniques are derived from a multitheoretical approach. These approaches will prevent a simplistic conceptualization of etiology in which one or two factors are given undue prominence, or a narrow treatment approach based on one theory and unable to effectively modify the diverse components involved in sexual dysfunctions.

Due to the lack of controlled research in the area, there is little definitive knowledge concerning the etiology, assessment, or treatment of sexual dysfunctions. In the area of etiology, studies utilizing control groups of normals and psychiatric outpatients not suffering from sexual problems must be conducted. Once the factors involved in etiology are delineated, educational programs aimed at preventing sexual dysfunctions can be devised and tested.

In the area of assessment, Cooper's (1969d) list of prognostic indicators should be included in paper-and-pencil inventories. Standardized video cassettes depicting specific sexual behaviors, such as those of Caird and Wincze (1974), should be made available to clinicians. Researchers should agree on a standard assessment battery so that studies conducted by different investigators can be compared.

Finally, treatment outcome studies utilizing factorial designs should be carried out. The three main factors to be examined are client variables (e.g., type of dysfunction, type of onset, type of marital or psychological problems present), treatment components (e.g., different variations of structured sexual experiences, cognitive/attentional techniques, and marital therapy), and mode of therapy (e.g., individual, conjoint, group, cotherapy, single therapist, and bibliotherapy).

References

Ahmed, S. H. Treatment of premature ejaculation. *British Journal of Psychiatry*, 1968, *114*, 1197–1198.

Amelar, R. D., and Dubin, L. Sex after major urologic surgery. *Journal of Sex Research*, 1968, *4*, 265–274.

Annon, J. S. *The extension of learning principles to the analysis and treatment of sexual problems.* Unpublished doctoral dissertation, University of Hawaii, 1971. (Abstract)

Annon, J. S. The therapeutic use of masturbation in the treatment of sexual disorders. In R. D. Rubin, J. P. Brady, and J. D. Henserson (Eds.), *Advances in behavior therapy* (Vol. 4). New York: Academic Press, 1973. Pp. 199–215.

Annon, J. S. *The behavioral treatment of sexual problems.* Honolulu: Mercantile Publishing Company, 1974.

Austin, N., and Liberman, R. Relax and enjoy it (review). *Behavior Therapy*, 1973, *4*, 715–717.

Bandura, A. *Principles of behavior modification.* New York: Holt, Rinehart & Winston, 1969.

Barbach, L. G. Group treatment of preorgasmic women. *Journal of Sex and Marital Therapy*, 1974, *1*, 139–145.

Bass, B. A. Sexual arousal as an anxiety inhibitor. *Journal of Behavior Therapy and Experimental Psychiatry*, 1974, *5*, 151–152.

Beigel, H. G. The hypnotherapeutic approach to male impotence. *Journal of Sex Research*, 1971, *7*, 168–176.

Bernstein, D. A., and Borkovec, T. D. *Progressive relaxation training: A manual for the helping professions.* Champaign, Illinois: Research Press, 1973.

Brady, J. P. Brevital-relaxation treatment of frigidity. *Behaviour Research and Therapy*, 1966, *4*, 71–77.

Brady, J. P. Brevital-aided systematic desensitization. In R. D. Rubin, H. Fensterheim, A. A. Lazarus, and C. M. Franks (Eds.), *Advances in behavior therapy: Proceedings of the third conference of the association for advancement of behavior therapy.* New York: Academic Press, 1971. Pp. 77–83.

Bruni, E. Psychotherapists as sex therapists. *Psychotherapy: Theory, Research and Practice*, 1974, *11*, 277–281.

Caird, W. K., and Wincze, J. P. Videotaped desensitization of frigidity. *Journal of Behavior Therapy and Experimental Psychiatry*, 1974, *5*, 175–178.

Cooper, A. J. A factual study of male potency disorders. *British Journal of Psychiatry*, 1968, *114*, 719–731. (a)

Cooper, A. J. Hostility and male potency disorders. *Comprehensive Psychiatry*, 1968, *9*, 621–626. (b)

Cooper, A. J. "Neurosis" and disorders of sexual potency in the male. *Journal of Psychosomatic Research*, 1968, *12*, 141–144. (c)

Cooper, A. J. A clinical study of "coital anxiety" in male potency disorders. *Journal of Psychosomatic Research*, 1969, *13*, 143–147. (a)

Cooper, A. J. An innovation in the "behavioral" treatment of a case of non-consummation due to vaginismus. *British Journal of Psychiatry*, 1969, *115*, 721–722. (b)

Cooper, A. J. Clinical and therapeutic studies in premature ejaculation. *Comprehensive Psychiatry*, 1969, *10*, 285–295. (c)

Cooper, A. J. Disorders of sexual potency in the male: A clinical and statistical study of some factors related to short-term prognosis. *British Journal of Psychiatry*, 1969, *115*, 709–719. (d)

Cooper, A. J. Treatment of male potency disorders: The present status. *Psychosomatics*, 1971, *12*, 235–244.

D'Alessio, G. R. The concurrent use of behavior modification and psychotherapy. *Psychotherapy: Theory, Research and Practice*, 1968, *5*, 154–159.

Davison, G. C., and Neale, J. M. *Abnormal Psychology: An experimental clinical approach*. New York: Wiley, 1974.

DeMoor, W. Vaginismus: Etiology and treatment. *American Journal of Psychotherapy*, 1972, *26*, 207–215.

Dengrove, E. Behavior therapy of the sexual disorders. *Journal of Sex Research*, 1967, *3*, 49–61.

Dengrove, E. Sexual responses to disease processes. *Journal of Sex Research*, 1968, *4*, 257–264.

Dengrove, E. Behavior therapy of impotence. *Journal of Sex Research*, 1971, *7*, 177–183.

Dengrove, E. The uses of hypnosis in behavior therapy. *International Journal of Clinical and Experimental Hypnosis*, 1973, *21*, 13–17.

Dittborn, J. Hypnotherapy of sexual impotence. *International Journal of Clinical and Experimental Hypnosis*, 1957, *5*, 181–192.

Ellis, A. *Reason and emotion in psychotherapy*. New York: Lyle Stuart, 1962.

Ellis, A. Rational-emotive treatment of impotence, frigidity and other sexual problems. *Professional Psychology*, 1971, *2*, 346–349.

Ellison, C. Vaginismus. *Medical Aspects of Human Sexuality*, August 1972, pp. 34–54.

Fodor, I. E. Sex role conflict and symptom formation in women: Can behavior therapy help? *Psychotherapy: Theory, Research and Practice*, 1974, *11*, 22–29.

Frankel, A. S. Treatment of multisymptomatic phobia by a self-directed, self-reinforced technique. *Journal of Abnormal Psychology*, 1970, *76*, 496–499.

Franks, C. M., and Wilson, G. T. (Eds.). *Annual review of behavior therapy: Theory and practice*. New York: Brunner/Mazel, 1974.

Friedman, D. The treatment of impotence by Brietal relaxation therapy, *Behaviour Research and Therapy*, 1968, *6*, 257–261.

Fuchs, K., Hoch, Z., Abramovici, H., Timor-Tritsch, I., and Kleinhaus, M. Vaginismus—The hypnotherapeutic approach. *Journal of Sex Research*, 1975, *11*, 39–45.

Fuchs, K., Hoch, Z., Paldi, E., Abramovici, H., Brandes, J. M., Timor-Tritsch, I., and Kleinhaus, M. Hypno-desensitization therapy of vaginismus: Part I, "In vitro" method. Part II, "In vivo" method. *International Journal of Clinical Experimental Hypnosis*, 1973, *21*, 144–156.

Garfield, Z. H., McBrearty, J. F., and Dichter, M. A case of impotence successfully treated with desensitization combined with in vivo operant training and thought substitution. In R. D. Rubin and C. M. Franks (Eds.), *Advances in behavior therapy, 1968*. New York: Academic Press, 1969. Pp. 97–103.

Gebhard, P. H. Factors in marital orgasm. *Journal of Social Issues*, 1966, *22*, 88–95.

Goldstein, A. Case conference: Conflict in a case of frigidity. *Journal of Behavior Therapy and Experimental Psychiatry*, 1971, *2*, 51–59.

Hartman, W. E., and Fithian, M. A. *The treatment of sexual dysfunction*. Long Beach, California: Center for Marital and Sexual Studies, 1972.

Haslam, M. T. The treatment of psychogenic dyspareunia by reciprocal inhibition. *British Journal of Psychiatry*, 1965, *111*, 280–282.

Hastings, D. W. *Impotence and frigidity*. Boston: Little, Brown, 1963.

Hastings, D. W. Can specific training procedures overcome sexual inadequacy? In R. Brecher and E. Brecher (Eds.), *An analysis of human sexual response*. New York: The New American Library, 1966. Pp. 221–237.

Hühner, M. *A practical treatise on disorders of the sexual function in the male and female*. Philadelphia: F. A. Davis, 1916.

Hussain, A. Behavior therapy using hypnosis. In J. Wolpe, A. Salter, and L. Reyna (Eds.), *The conditioning therapies: The challenge in psychotherapy*. New York: Holt, Rinehart & Winston, 1964. Pp. 54–61.

Husted, J. R. Effect of method of systematic desensitization and presence of sexual communication in the treatment of sexual anxiety by counterconditioning. *Proceedings of the 80th Annual Convention of the American Psychological Association, Honoluli, Hawaii*, 1972, *7*, 325–326.

Ince, L. P. Behavior modification of sexual disorders. *American Journal of Psychotherapy*, 1973, *27*, 446–451.

Jemail, J. A. *Behavior modification and human sexual inadequacy.* Unpublished manuscript, State University of New York at Stony Brook, 1973.

Kaplan, H. S. The classification of the female sexual dysfunctions. *Journal of Sex and Marital Therapy*, 1974, *1*, 124–138. (a)

Kaplan, H. S. *The new sex therapy.* New York: Brunner/ Mazel, 1974. (b)

Kaplan, H. S., Kohl, R. N., Pomeroy, W. B., Offit, A. K., and Hogan, B. Group treatment of premature ejaculation. *Archives of Sexual Behavior*, 1974, *3*, 443–452.

Kaufman, J. Organic and psychological factors in the genesis of impotence and premature ejaculation. In C. W. Wahl (Ed.), *Sexual problems: Diagnosis and treatment in medical practice.* New York: Free Press, 1967. Pp. 133–148.

Kiev, A., and Hackett, E. The chemotherapy of impotence and frigidity. *Journal of Sex Research*, 1968, *4*, 220–224.

Kinsey, A. C., Pomeroy, W. B., and Martin, C. E. *Sexual behavior in the human male.* Philadelphia: W. B. Saunders, 1948.

Kohlenberg, R. J. Directed masturbation and the treatment of primary orgasmic dysfunction. *Archives of Sexual Behavior*, 1974, *3*, 349–356.

Kraft, T. Behavior therapy and target symptoms. *Journal of Clinical Psychology*, 1969, *25*, 105–109. (a)

Kraft, T. Desensitization and the treatment of sexual disorders. *Journal of Sex Research*, 1969, *5*, 130–134. (b)

Kraft, T., and Al-Issa, I. The use of methohexitone sodium in the systematic desensitization of premature ejaculation. *British Journal of Psychiatry*, 1968, *114*, 351–352. (Abstract)

Kroger, W. S. Comprehensive approach to ecclesiogenic neuroses. *Journal of Sex Research*, 1969, *5*, 2–11.

Lazarus, A. A. Group therapy in phobic disorders by systematic desensitization. *Journal of Abnormal and Social Psychology*, 1961, *63*, 504–510.

Lazarus, A. A. The treatment of chronic frigidity by systematic desensitization. *Journal of Nervous and Mental Disease*, 1963, *136*, 272–278.

Lazarus, A. A. The treatment of a sexually inadequate man. In L. P. Ullman and L. Krasner (Eds.), *Case studies in behavior modification.* New York: Holt, Rinehart & Winston, 1965. Pp. 243–245.

Lazarus, A. A. Behavior therapy in groups. In G. M. Gazda (Ed.), *Basic approaches to group psychotherapy and group counseling.* Springfield, Illinois: Charles C Thomas, 1968. Pp. 149–175.

Lazarus, A. A. Behavior therapy of sexual problems. *Professional Psychology*, 1971, *2*, 349–353. (a)

Lazarus, A. A. *Behavior therapy and beyond.* New York: McGraw-Hill, 1971. (b)

Lazarus, A. A. "Hypnosis" as a facilitator in behavior therapy. *International Journal of Clinical and Experimental Hypnosis*, 1973, *21*, 25–31.

Lazarus, A. A. Multimodal behavior therapy: Treating the "BASIC ID." In C. M. Franks and G. T. Wilson (Eds.), *Annual review of behavior therapy: Theory and practice.* New York: Brunner/ Mazel, 1974. Pp. 679–690.

Lazarus, A. A., and Rachman, S. The use of systematic desensitization in psychotherapy. In H. J. Eysenck (Ed.), *Behavior therapy and the neuroses: Readings in modern methods of treatment derived from learning theory.* New York: Pergamon Press, 1960. Pp. 181–187.

Leckie, F. H. Hypnotherapy in gynecological disorders. *International Journal of Clinical and Experimental Hypnosis*, 1964, *12*, 121–146.

Lobitz, W. C., and LoPiccolo, J. New methods in the behavioral treatment of sexual dysfunction. *Journal of Behavior Therapy and Experimental Psychiatry*, 1972, *3*, 265–271.

Lobitz, W. C., LoPiccolo, J., Lobitz, G., and Brockway, J. A closer look at simplistic behavior therapy for sexual dysfunction: Two case studies. Preprint of a chapter in H. J. Eysenck (Ed.), *Case studies in behavior therapy.* London: Routledge and Kegan Paul, 1974.

LoPiccolo, J. Direct treatment of sexual dysfunction. Preprint of a chapter in J. Money and H. Musaph (Eds.), *Handbook of sexology.* Amsterdam: Elsevier/ North Holland Biomedical Press, 1975.

LoPiccolo, J., and Lobitz, W. C. The role of masturbation in the treatment of orgasmic dysfunction. *Archives of Sexual Behavior*, 1972, *2*, 163–172.

LoPiccolo, J., and Lobitz, W. C. Behavior therapy of sexual dysfunction. In L. A. Hamerlynck, L. C. Handy, and E. J. Mash (Eds.), *Behavior change: Methodology, concepts, and practice.* Champaign, Illinois: Research Press, 1973. Pp. 343–358.

LoPiccolo, J., and Steger, J. C. The sexual interaction inventory: A new instrument for assessment of sexual dysfunction. *Archives of Sexual Behavior*, 1974, *3*, 585–595.

Masters, W. H., and Johnson, V. E. *Human sexual response.* Boston: Little, Brown, 1966.

Masters, W. H., and Johnson, V. E. *Human sexual inadequacy.* Boston: Little, Brown, 1970.

McCarthy, B. W. A modification of Masters and Johnson sex therapy model in a clinical setting. *Psychotherapy: Theory, Research and Practice*, 1973, *10*, 290–293.

McGovern, K., Stewart, R., and LoPiccolo, J. Secondary orgasmic dysfunction I: Analysis and strategies for treatment. *Archives of Sexual Behavior*, 1975, *4*, 265–275.

Mikulas, W. C., and Lowe, J. C. *Self-control of premature ejaculation.* Paper presented at the Rocky Mountain Psychological Association, Denver, 1974.

Neale, J. M., and Liebert, R. M. *Science and behavior: An introduction to methods of research.* Englewood Cliffs, New Jersey: Prentice-Hall, 1973.

Paul, G. L. Outcome of systematic desensitization I: Background, procedures, and uncontrolled reports of individual treatment. In C. M. Franks (Ed.), *Behavior therapy: Appraisal and status.* New York: McGraw-Hill, 1969. Pp. 63–104.

Paul, G. L., and Bernstein, D. A. *Anxiety and clinical problems: Systematic desensitization and related techniques.* Morristown, New Jersey: General Learning Press, 1973.

Prochaska, J. O., and Marzilli, R. Modifications of the Masters and Johnson approach to sexual problems. *Psychotherapy: Theory, Research and Practice*, 1973, *10*, 294–296.

Rachman, S. The treatment of anxiety and phobic reactions by systematic desensitization psychotherapy. *Journal of Abnormal and Social Psychology*, 1959, *58*, 259–263.

Razani, J. Ejaculatory incompetence treated by deconditioning anxiety. *Journal of Behavior Therapy and Experimental Psychiatry*, 1972, *3*, 65–67.

Reding, G. R., and Ennis, B. Treatment of the couple by the couple. *British Journal of Medical Psychology*, 1964, *37*, 325–330.

Reisinger, J. J. Masturbatory training in the treatment of primary orgasmic dysfunction. *Journal of Behavior Therapy and Experimental Psychiatry*, 1974, *5*, 179–183.

Robinson, C. H. *The effects of observational learning on sexual behavior and attitudes in orgasmic dysfunctional women.* Unpublished doctoral dissertation, University of Hawaii, 1974. (Abstract)

Roen, P. R. Impotence: A concise review. *New York State Journal of Medicine*, 1965, *56*, 2576–2582.

Salter, A. *Conditioned reflex therapy, the direct approach to the reconstruction of personality* (2nd ed.). New York: Creative Press, 1961.

Salzman, L. F. Systematic desensitization of a patient with chronic total impotence. In R. D. Rubin and C. M. Franks (Eds.) *Advances in behavior therapy, 1968.* New York: Academic Press, 1969. Pp. 131–137.

Schneck, J. M. Hypnotherapy for vaginismus. *International Journal of Clinical and Experimental Hypnosis*, 1965, *13*, 92–95.

Schneidman, B., and McGuire, L. Group therapy for nonorgasmic women: Two age levels. *Archives of Sexual Behavior*, 1976, *5*, 239–247.

Semans, J. H. Premature ejaculation: A new approach. *Southern Medical Journal*, 1956, *49*, 353–357.

Serber, M. Videotape feedback in the treatment of couples with sexual dysfunction. *Archives of Sexual Behavior*, 1974, *3*, 377–380.

Sharpe, R., and Meyer, V. Modification of "cognitive sexual pain" by the spouse under supervision. *Behavior Therapy*, 1973, *4*, 285–287.

Snyder, A., LoPiccolo, L., and LoPiccolo, J. Secondary orgasmic dysfunction II: Case study. *Archives of Sexual Behavior*, 1975, *4*, 277–283.

Stampfl, T. G., and Levis, D. J. Essentials of implosive therapy: A learning theory based psychodynamic behavioral therapy. *Journal of Abnormal Psychology*, 1967, *72*, 495–503.

Stone, A., and Levine, J. Group therapy in sexual maladjustment. *American Journal of Psychiatry*, 1950, *107*, 195–202.

Szasz, T. S. Mental illness is not a disease. In E. A. Southwell and H. Feldman (Eds.), *Abnormal psychology: Readings in theory and research.* Belmont, California: Brooks/Cole, 1969. Pp. 5–11.

Tanner, B. A. Two case reports on the modification of the ejaculatory response with the squeeze technique. *Psychotherapy: Theory, Research and Practice*, 1973, *10*, 297–300.

Tinling, D. C. Auto-desensitization to phobic fears with an audio-visual instructional aid. In R. D. Rubin and C. M. Franks (Eds.) *Advances in behavior therapy, 1968.* New York: Academic Press, 1969. Pp. 11–15.

Twombly, G. H. Sex after radical gynecological surgery. *Journal of Sex Research*, 1968, *4*, 275–281.

Wallace, D. H., and Barbach, L. G. Preorgasmic group treatment. *Journal of Sex and Marital Therapy*, 1974, *1*, 146–154.

Watzlawick, P., Weakland, J. H., and Fisch, R. *Change: Principles of problem formation and problem resolution.* New York: Norton, 1974.

Wilson, G. T. Innovations in the modification of phobic behaviors in two clinical cases. *Behavior Therapy*, 1973, *4*, 426–430.

Wincze, J. P. A comparison of systematic desensitization and "vicarious extinction" in a case of frigidity. *Journal of Behavior Therapy and Experimental Psychiatry*, 1971, *2*, 285–289.

Wincze, J. P., and Caird, W. K. The effects of systematic desensitization and video desensitization in the treatment of essential sexual dysfunction in women. *Behavior Therapy*, 1976, *7*, 335–342.

Wolpe, J. *Psychotherapy by reciprocal inhibition.* Stanford, California: Stanford University Press, 1958.

Wolpe, J. *The practice of behavior therapy.* (1st ed.). New York: Pergamon Press, 1966.

Wolpe, J. Reciprocal inhibition as the main basis of psychotherapeutic effects. In H. J. Eysenck (Ed.), *Behaviour therapy and the neuroses: Readings in modern methods of treatment derived from learning theory.* New York: Pergamon Press, 1960. Pp. 88–113.

Wolpe, J. Correcting misconceptions in a case of frigidity: A transcript. *Journal of Behavior Therapy and Experimental Psychiatry*, 1971, *2*, 251–258.

Wolpe, J. *The practice of behavior therapy* (2nd ed.). New York: Pergamon Press, 1973.

Wolpe, J., and Lazarus, A. A. *Behavior therapy techniques.* New York: Pergamon Press, 1966.

Wolpin, M. Guided imagining to reduce avoidance behavior. *Psychotherapy: Theory, Research and Practice*, 1969, *6*, 122–124.

Yulis, S. Generalization of therapeutic gain in the treatment of premature ejaculation. *Behavior Therapy*, 1976, *7*, 355–358.

The development of brief forms of psychotherapy such as behavior therapy and sex therapy has been relatively recent. As opposed to more traditional forms of long-term open-ended therapy, these therapies are often symptom-focused and time-limited.

As outlined in LoPiccolo's survey article in Part I, brief sex therapy is usually oriented in the here and now, and involves some direct intervention in the couple's or individual's sexual behavior patterns. Because of this orientation, effective assessment of the couple's or individual's ability to benefit from such a therapy program is essential. For some patients, marriage therapy or individual psychotherapy, rather than sex therapy, might be the treatment of choice.

Once sex therapy has been decided upon, clinical assessment can be used to gather information necessary for understanding the etiology and maintenance of a particular sexual dysfunction. This assessment is essential in order to determine the most appropriate and effective treatment interventions.

5

Clinical Assessment in the Treatment of Sexual Dysfunctions

W. Charles Lobitz and Gretchen K. Lobitz

Since Masters and Johnson first published their definitive work on the treatment of human sexual inadequacy (Masters and Johnson, 1970), sex therapy has become the choice topic for neighborhood cocktail parties, popular magazines, and recently even television soap operas. As a result of this popularity, many more people are defining their problems as sexual and seeking sexual dysfunction treatment than did six years ago. People who might have been reluctant to consult a mental health professional for fear of being labeled "crazy" or in dread of spending costly hours exploring their past relationship with their mother are now willing to seek treatment. They anticipate that sex therapists will work with their sexual problem directly rather than viewing it as a symptom of underlying psychopathology. This upsurge in the popularity of sexual dysfunction treatment and the resulting increase in treatment centers and training facilities across the country have saved many couples from a life of sexual misery and ignorance. At the same time they have increased the need for a more careful assessment of couples, many of whom refer

W. Charles Lobitz • Division of Clinical Psychology, Department of Psychiatry, University of Colorado School of Medicine, Denver, Colorado   *Gretchen K. Lobitz* • Department of Psychology, University of Denver, Denver, Colorado

themselves for sex therapy. It is the task of the professional to determine if a couple, who often have their own minds made up, is appropriate for sex therapy or might benefit more from another approach. It is also the task of the professional to determine what factors are contributing to the couple's sexual problems so that appropriate treatment interventions can be tailored to the couple's specific situation. This assessment process is what differentiates the *professional* practice of psychosocial therapy from therapy as a *trade* where treatments are applied without recognition of the individual differences in patients' problems (Peterson, 1976). This chapter is addressed to that process.

As in all forms of psychosocial therapy, sex therapy necessitates a thorough assessment of the patients' problems, including their strengths and weaknesses, before the appropriate treatment interventions can be initiated. In sex therapy the assessment process consists of three phases: first, the evaluation of the patients' appropriateness for sex therapy; second, the development of the patients' sexual histories and problem lists, including goals for treatment; and third, the ongoing evaluation of the patients' progress, including follow-up assessment after treatment. This chapter describes the use of the clinical interview in the first two phases. In addition, supplementary diagnostic testing of both personality factors (e.g., Minnesota Multiphasic Personality Inventory—Dahlstrom, Welsh, and Dahlstrom, 1972) and sexual behavior (e.g., Sexual Interaction Inventory—LoPiccolo and Steger, 1974) are important aspects of the assessment process and are covered elsewhere in this book. The third phase of the assessment is an integral part of the treatment process and is beyond the scope of this chapter. It is discussed elsewhere as part of treatment interventions (e.g., Lobitz and LoPiccolo, 1972; Lobitz, LoPiccolo, Lobitz, and Brockway, 1976).

In the present chapter we are making several assumptions about the format of sex therapy. Because the Masters and Johnson (1970) format is the most common, we are basing our discussion on the model of a dual-sex therapy team treating a dual-sex patient couple. Our assessment of sexual dysfunction patients who do not have regular partners and are treated through individual or group therapy differs in format, but not in principle, from the assessment process we are discussing. We are also assuming that the treatment is short-term (twelve–twenty hours), intensive (two–fifteen weeks), and directive in orientation (LoPiccolo, 1975). Although patients who seek out sex therapy frequently do so at a sexual dysfunction clinic where the treatment is separate from individual or conjoint therapy, the assessment issues discussed here apply equally well to treatment that is conducted as part of a patient's ongoing psychotherapy.

The Initial Evaluation

The first phase of the assessment process typically includes one and sometimes two one-hour interviews. Although one therapist can easily suffice, particularly for the initial evaluation, it is useful to have a dual-sex therapy team so that each patient has an "ally," especially if one partner is known to be resistant to treatment or marital problems are anticipated to be intense. The purpose of the evaluation session is made clear to the couple at the very beginning, that is, "to give us a chance to determine if this kind of treatment would be most useful for you right now and for you to decide whether or not what we have to offer is what you want." The bilateral nature of this decision usually works to decrease the couple's initial anxiety and, if accepted, to increase their commitment to treatment since they had a major role in the decision.

Once the purpose is clear, we begin talking about sex directly by focusing on the current sexual problem and its development over time. Although we are sensitive to couples' inhibitions about discussing sex openly, we believe it is more important to obtain the information necessary for a well-educated decision than to spend the hour exploring their inhibitions. If we perceive some hesitation on the couple's part, we will explore its meaning. We acknowledge to the couple that many people find talking about sex difficult at first, given the taboos that have surrounded sexuality in our culture. In addition, we stress that we do not expect them to agree with each other's perceptions: Sex is a very sensitive, individual concern for each person and we state that we can be most useful if we understand their different perspectives from the beginning.

Although the style varies from therapist to therapist, the content of the initial interview is relatively standard. Keeping in mind that the goal of the session is to determine if a couple is appropriate for sex therapy, we cover the following topics, emphasizing some more than others depending on a particular couple and their responses to our questions: (1) demographic information such as occupations, length of relationship, previous marriages; (2) the nature and development of the sexual difficulty, including what hypotheses the couple has generated as to its etiology and what attempts they have made to resolve the difficulty; (3) a description of their current sex life, including questions regarding the frequency of intercourse, specific noncoital activities, male's latency to ejaculation, and female's orgasmic potential; (4) a brief psychosexual history from each partner, focusing on what sexual messages each has learned, as well as past and present psychological difficulties and traumas, particularly those involving previous or current psychotherapy; (5) each partner's impressions of the quality of their relationship; (6) their individual and cooperative motivation for treatment; (7) their physical health, medical history, and physicians' names; and (8) their method of birth control. Over the years we have found that a variety of paper-and-pencil assessment devices (e.g., Sexual Interaction Inventory—LoPiccolo and Steger, 1974) are extremely helpful in collecting specific factual information such as the frequency of orgasm. Thus, we can spend more time in the initial session focusing on those areas that are more difficult to assess, such as the quality of the couple's relationship.

We gather the preceding information in order to evaluate certain individual factors as well as certain factors in their relationship. Individual factors that we assess in making a decision about a couple's appropriateness for sex therapy include (1) the possible presence of organic pathology that might affect a person's sexual performance, (2) the degree of psychopathology in one or both partners, and (3) each partner's motivation for treatment including commitment to the relationship and willingness to participate in treatment. Those relationship factors that we ask about and also observe during the session include the level of hostility between the partners and the level of intimacy between them. Given the brevity of this first phase of assessment, definitive statements regarding each of these factors are impossible; however, serious problems in any one of these areas are usually apparent in the initial evaluation.

Reports on the extent of organic involvement in sexual dysfunction vary from 3% to 20%, with cases of erectile dysfunction, vaginismus, dyspareunia, and sudden loss of sexual interest or arousal having a greater probability of organic involvement than other dysfunctions (Kaplan, 1974). Thus, as part of the initial evaluation we refer our patients to a physician to rule out the possibility that the dysfunction has an organic basis. Unfortunately, not all physicians are sensitive to both the psychological and medical issues in cases of sexual dysfunction. We have found it advisable to choose medical consultants with care. Until recently most medical schools did not teach anything about sexual behavior (Vincent, 1968). Female patients have received advice from physicians such as "Don't worry about it, just pretend you enjoy sex" and "Your childhood masturbation is what made you frigid" (LoPiccolo and Lobitz, 1973). In a case of erectile dysfunction, one of our male patients had been told by an older physician, "So join the club. It happens to all of us sooner or later," Where there is an organic basis for the dysfunction, such as female dyspareunia caused by broad ligament tears during childbirth (Masters and Johnson, 1970), we refer the couple for the appropriate medical treatment. However, the existence of an organic factor in the dysfunction does not always rule out the need for psychosocial sex therapy, particularly in cases where the organic factor caused but does not appear to be maintaining the dysfunction, for example, a central nervous system trauma, which caused temporary erectile dysfunction but which, after recovery, does not interfere with the erectile reflex. If organic factors are involved but some sexual responsiveness is still possible, we want to talk with the physician to understand the physical limitations a couple must face in adapting to a changed sexual relationship.

A second individual factor that we assess is the degree of individual psychopathology in each partner. Sometimes a person, feeling a need for therapy, finds it easier to simplify his depression or anxiety by labeling it a sexual dysfunction. Or one spouse, recognizing a need for help in the other, finds it easier to get his or her partner in for treatment in the guise of sex therapy. Patients presenting with a sexual complaint as their target problem are not always accurate in their self-diagnoses. If we perceive that a psychological problem exists in addition to the sexual dysfunction, we assess the cause–effect relationship between the two, particularly in terms of predicting what effect improving the sexual dysfunction would have on the additional problem(s). If we decide that the sexual dysfunction is secondary to other psychological problems, we will not accept the couple until the other problems have been treated. We base our decision to accept or reject patients with observed psychopathology on two primary criteria: (1) The problem should not interfere greatly with the person's everyday functioning and (2) the problem should not be likely to interfere with treatment. For example, if a female presenting with primary inorgasmia was depressed to the degree that she was having difficulty functioning in several areas of her life, we would recommend treatment focusing on her depression rather than her inorgasmia. First, we see alleviating her depression as immediately more important in terms of her total life functioning. Second, it is likely that her depression would interefere with the treatment program. She would have less motivation and energy to get involved in self-exploration exercises and sensate-pleasuring with her partner than if she were not depressed. Alcoholism is another example. Because of the adverse effects of alcohol on sexual response (e.g., Briddel and Wilson, 1976), alcoholics frequently develop erectile dysfunctions. Although performance anxiety may have developed in response to initial episodes of erectile dysfunction due to alcohol, patients rarely associate their sexual problem with their drinking (Masters and Johnson, 1966). Sex therapy is contraindicated for alcoholics unless they have been able to control their drinking for at least six months.

Where a patient has a psychotic disorder and seeks sex therapy, the decision to accept for treatment is more complex. Many sex therapists advise against treating psychotic patients for sexual dysfunctions or accept these patients only under narrowly defined conditions. We have successfully treated selected couples where one or both partners had a chronic major psychosis. We accept psychotic patients for sex therapy under the following conditions: The psychosis is not acute, and the patient can be seen concurrently by a psychiatrist who will maintain the patient on antipsychotic medication and/or provide individual therapy to support the patient's functioning. In addition, treatment is structured so that the patient's defenses are not threatened. In particular, we are careful not to force increased intimacy on the couple, steps toward change are more gradual, and treatment extends beyond the usual fifteen to twenty sessions. We also make the "homework" assignments concrete so as to minimize the opportunity for psychotic distortion of the patient's own responses or the partner's behavior.

The final individual factor that we assess is motivation, that is, each partner's reason in seeking sex therapy at this particular time, his or her commitment to the relationship, and the degree of willingness to participate in treatment. Reasons for seeking treatment vary; often people come in for their own sake, sometimes for their partners' benefit. The danger in a person's agreeing to treatment solely to benefit the partner is that he or she has no goals in treatment other than changing the partner and may attempt to be a third therapist, making the identified patient feel even more inadequate and pressured. We challenge this position in the initial interview and attempt to redefine the difficulty as a problem belonging to the relationship and not just to one partner (Masters and Johnson, 1970; LoPiccolo, 1975). In other situations one partner may willingly seek treatment only to facilitate a separation. If we have any questions regarding a couple's commitment, we will talk with the partners individually during the initial interview. If one partner is not committed to the relationship, we will not see them in conjoint sex therapy. For example, we interviewed a couple in which the wife seemed ambivalent about the relationship. When we spoke with her individually, she admitted that she wanted to help correct her husband's premature ejaculation so that she could then leave the marriage without feeling guilty. In this case we recommended divorce counseling for the couple and treated the male's ejaculatory problem in individual therapy.

The final issue in assessing motivation is each partner's willingness to cooperate in the treatment program. We emphasize that treatment will take a great deal of time outside the actual clinic visits. This is often surprising to patients who are accustomed to traditional psychotherapy where homework assignments are not given. These couples discover that undertaking sex therapy will require a reordering of their daily priorities. In order to make time to complete their assignments for verbal and nonverbal interactions, they must put sex before relatives, sports, social engagements, and visitors, at least for the duration of treatment. Often one partner expresses concern about the time or money involved. This concern is sometimes an indirect way of saying that he or she is not really interested in treatment; sometimes it is an expression of fear or anxiety about therapy itself. We usually interpret these resistances, but we never push or persuade the couple to get involved in treatment. The couple must make the decision, and each partner must be somewhat motivated in order for treatment to work; if it is not a mutual decision, we run the danger of one partner sabotaging treatment.

Deciding whether or not to treat a couple in a sexual dysfunction framework involves more than just evaluating them as two individuals. We also evaluate the relationship—how they work, play, and fight together. Recent evidence (Frank, Anderson, and Kupfer, 1976; Sager, 1976) suggests that couples referring themselves for sex therapy are also experiencing considerable marital discord. It is impossible to clearly separate sexual dysfunction from other problems in the relationship, but we do find it possible to evaluate whether (1) other relationship problems are so salient that they would interfere with sex therapy, (2) the couple's needs would be better met by being seen in a more broadly defined marital therapy program, and (3) the equilibrium in their relationship would be severely upset if sex therapy were begun. We attempt to answer these questions by evaluating the level of hostility and the degree of intimacy in the couple's relationship.

Sager (1974, 1976) focused on marital discord as a major relationship factor in determining whether a couple would be more appropriate for sex therapy or for marriage therapy. Severe marital discord and the accompanying hostility make sex therapy almost impossible. It is hard to imagine a couple who spend most of their days and nights arguing being able to take time out to get involved in a sensate-focus exercise. However, as Sager emphasized, we also find it useful to assess whether the discord resulted in the dysfunction or the dysfunction preceded the discord.

In assessing the degree of discord in the relationship, we again use the couple's verbal report, paper-and-pencil assessment devices (e.g., The Marital Adjustment Test—Locke and Wallace, 1959; the Areas of Change Questionnaire—Weiss and Margolin, 1975), and our clinical observations. We ask questions that generate a history of the relationship, for example, "When did the sexual difficulty begin?" "Was anything else happening at that time?" "How was the relationship before?" "How has it been since?" "How did the two of you meet?" "What attracted you to each other?" "Has the difficulty been a problem with previous partners?" "What changes would you like to see in your partner—both sexual and otherwise?" In addition to collecting a relationship history we also focus on how the patients resolve conflicts by asking such questions as "What do you fight about?" "How do you fight?" "How do fights get resolved?" In a case in which the husband was having erectile problems, he typically responded to fighting by passively withdrawing. This pattern of fighting told us something important about one function that his erectile problem might be serving in the relationship. *What* the couple says in response to our questions is less important than *how* they say it. If there is so much hostility that they are continually interrupting or derogating each other, arguing about who is right and who is wrong, and blaming the other person, sex therapy would be contraindicated and marriage therapy recommended. Treatment of the relationship is an important aspect of sex therapy, but in cases where generalized hostility is a central problem, the relationship is more easily treated in a broadly defined marriage therapy.

A second relationship factor that we consider is their level of intimacy, that is, the couple's willingness to be open with each other and to share feelings, opinions, and moments together. Although we are still speculating at this point, we hypothesize that a high degree of intimacy indicates a positive prognosis; sex is an extremely sensitive, vulnerable area in an interpersonal relationship and is more easily dealt with if the couple is able to trust each other. Thus, we ask questions such as "How much do you disclose to your partner?" "What kinds of concerns and feelings?" "How much time do you spend together?" "Has it always been this way?" "Was it different in other relationships?" Sometimes when we find that there is no apparent hostility between the couple, we discover that they have established themselves at a comfortable distance, rarely expressing feelings to each other or spending time together. It is likely that sex therapy will upset this equilibrium. Although we probably would not reject a seemingly motivated couple on this basis, we would predict that resistance to assignments that require intimacy might become a problem as treatment progressed. We would be alert to such signals and cautious about forcing intimacy upon them. Also, prior to treatment, we would warn the couple that treatment is likely to put a great deal of stress on each of them and their relationship, and they might discover problems that they had not been aware of previously.

At the end of the initial interview we explain the treatment program to the couple and give them an opportunity to ask us questions. Occasionally, we will set up a second interview if we want to talk with each partner individually or have concerns that we have not resolved in the first interview. We encourage them to talk with each other about their feelings and questions regarding treatment and tell them we want to do likewise. We delay a decision on whether sex therapy is appropriate at this time until we have reviewed their paper-and-pencil assessment forms and have shared our impressions with each other. If we feel that sex therapy would not be appropriate or that one partner is strongly resistant to treatment, we set up a second interview for the feedback. Couples who are not accepted for sex therapy are sometimes disappointed or angry. They have heard about the high success rates and have imagined sex therapy as *the* answer to their problems. However, we have found that if we explain our reasoning in words they can understand and have another therapy available, they work through their feelings quickly and usually follow our recommendations. In addition, we always leave the opportunity for sex therapy open to them once the more pressing individual or relationship issues have been resolved.

Sexual History Interviews

Once a couple has been accepted for treatment of the sexual dysfunction, the second phase of the assessment process begins. The purpose of the first phase of the assessment process was to identify those problems that were not treatable by the techniques and approaches of what has become known as "traditional" sex therapy (cf. Masters and Johnson, 1970; Lobitz and LoPiccolo, 1972; LoPiccolo and Lobitz, 1973; Kaplan, 1974) or that would interfere with the treatment process. In the second phase, the purpose is to identify psychosocial problems that are contributing to the couple's sexual dysfunction, whether directly or indirectly. At the end of this phase, we formulate the case in terms of those factors that contribute to the dysfunction. Alleviating these problems becomes a primary treatment goal and the focus of our interventions. Our approach is to share these observations and goals with the treatment couple at the end of this phase.

The method and format of the second phase of assessment vary from clinician to clinician. The most common approach is the individual interview of each patient by each therapist (Masters and Johnson, 1970). The format typically consists of the male therapist interviewing the male patient while the female therapist interviews the female patient. Each interview usually lasts from 1½ to 2 hours. Following these interviews, the cotherapists compare impressions and identify discrepancies or missing information that the opposite-sex therapist can pursue in the next interview. The female therapist subsequently interviews the male patient and vice versa.

The interview information is obtained largely through patient self-report. In addition, some therapists observe semisexual aspects of the couple's physical interaction. For example, occasionally we have asked partners to massage each other's hands in our consulting room in order to observe their nonverbal behavior with each other. Although these observations are useful in understanding how the partners approach each other physically, this method is replete with the problems of subject reactivity to being observed (Johnson and Bolstad, 1973; Wiggins, 1973). As part of their assessment, other therapists observe and record the couple engaging in overtly sexual behaviors, including intercourse (Serber, 1974; Hartman and Fithian, 1972). This approach is generally not used by most therapists. Not only are the problems of subject reactivity magnified but also the method raises questions about the ethics of patient privacy as well as possible complications in the patient–therapist relationship.

In the individual patient–therapist interview, the therapist attempts to elicit information about the patient's current and past sexual behaviors, attitudes, and feelings. The style of this interview depends on the clinician's own therapeutic manner. However, it is important to note that even though the therapist is comfortable discussing the specifics of human sexuality, this may be the first time the patient has ever discussed the details of his or her sex life. He or she is probably feeling nervous or embarrassed. This response is often more pronounced during the interview with a therapist of the opposite sex. These emotions may be manifest or they may be disguised behind a shield of unresponsiveness, thinly veiled anger, or forced frivolity. The therapist's task is to facilitate the patient's comfort in talking so that an accurate and thorough picture of the patient's sexual background and current situation can be developed. Statements like "I know this is difficult to talk about but it gets easier as we go along" help to ease the patient's discomfort. Unlike some treatment situations where the therapist awaits the patient's disclosures with infinite patience, the sex therapist must inquire directly about specific details of the patient's history. Yet, he or she must be careful not to turn the interview into an inquisition. The therapist needs to strike a balance between directness, which may run the danger of being intimidating, and passivity, which permits the patient to avoid specific information altogether. We have found "ubiquity statements" (Wahl, 1967) to be useful in eliciting information by informing the patient about the universality of various sexual experiences. An example of a ubiquity statement to introduce the topic of masturbation is "People sometimes hear strange stories about masturbation, as they grow up. How did you first learn about it?"

Throughout the assessment interview, the therapist is trying to elicit information in two general areas: (1) those conditions or situations that may have *predisposed* the individual or couple to develop the dysfunction, and (2) those conditions or situations that may be *maintaining* the dysfunction. Although these two areas of inquiry are closely related, the former calls for historical information, whereas the latter depends on information about the couple's current behaviors, thoughts, and feelings. The therapist's inquiry about historical events does not need to be a detailed personal history. It is an attempt to delineate the development of the patient's sexual beliefs and behaviors and to understand how they are related to the dysfunction. Although the interview format varies from therapist to therapist and patient to patient, we cover the following topic areas: (1) sexual attitudes and behaviors of parents or other significant authority figures; (2) source and content of early sexual information, e.g., parents, peers, siblings, church, school, self; (3) early sex play, same or opposite sex, with peers, siblings, adults; (4) self-discovery of one's own sexuality, e.g., erection, orgasm, menstruation, noctural emission; (5) masturbation; (6) social–sexual experience in adolescence, e.g., dating, petting, intercourse; (7) social–sexual values and any changes that occurred in them, particularly sexual responsivity, virginity, contraception, and male versus female role; (8) first intercourse; (9) first and subsequent social–sexual involvement with present partner; (10) significant other social–sexual relationships; (11) onset and course of specific sexual dysfunction(s); (12) attempts to change the dysfunction(s) either by self or by others.

Despite the focus of sex therapy on "here-and-now" issues and interventions, it is important for both the therapists and patients to understand the etiology of the dysfunction in light of the patient's sexual development. On seeking help for a sexual dysfunction, patients are often confused about their problem. They may fear that they are "sick," particularly that they have "a mental disease" or "abnormality." While insight about their development does not always directly lead to a change in the patient's behaviors, it helps to reduce the patient's confusion and anxiety by putting the dysfunction in a rational pespective. For example, a common factor in the development of premature ejaculation is a long history of rapid masturbation (LoPiccolo and Lobitz, 1973). Where a client believes that his dysfunction represents a defect in his character, he can be reassured that the problem was something he learned and that it can be unlearned. Similarly, childhood or adolescent masturbation seems to be an important developmental step in learning about one's sexual responses (Lassen, 1976). It is valuable for therapist and patient alike to recognize the powerful effect of parental proscriptions against masturbation in the case of preorgasmic women who have never masturbated.

Although a developmental sexual history is useful in understanding those factors which predispose a patient to *develop* a sexual dysfunction, it is more important to collect historical as well as current information about those factors which *maintain* the problem. Following the multimodal approach described by Lazarus (1973), the purpose of the assessment interview is to identify deficits in the following areas which currently contribute to the couple's dysfunction: behavior, cognition, affect, sensation, imagery, interpersonal relations, biology, and personality. Obviously, problems in each of these can affect the other areas. Nevertheless, we have found it useful to identify deficits in each area separately before formulating their interaction. This facilitates the process of problem identification and goal setting, as well as the evaluation of treatment outcome (Grant and Lewis, 1974). As part of the assessment interview we also identify the couple's strengths in each of these areas. These strengths are the resources on which the therapists rely for the success of their interventions.

One of the most common factors in a couple's dysfunction is a repertoire of inappropriate or ineffective sexual *behaviors* (LoPiccolo, 1975). The couple may engage in a limited amount of physical caressing before attempting intercourse or they may focus their caressing exclusively on the genitals when other parts of the body are equally sensitive. The male may be rough and aggressive when his partner prefers a gentle touch or he may be too passive when she wants him to "take her" forcefully. In addition, the couple may engage in appropriate behaviors but may do so at an inappropriate time. For example, one of our patients was always able to reach orgasm through manual stimulation of her genitals by her husband, but only if she were previously aroused by nongenital stimulation. Without sufficient arousal she found direct genital stimulation aversive and sometimes physically painful. Yet, her husband persisted in "making a dash for my clitoris," as she put it, as soon as sexual play began. Although the assessment of deficits in a couple's sexual behaviors is aided by pencil-and-paper instruments such as the Sexual Interaction Inventory (LoPiccolo and Steger, 1974), we also inquire directly about their specific behaviors in the individual interview. Asking each partner to describe step-by-step what they do sexually is necessary to get a complete picture of the behavior problems that may exist. We find that such an inquiry during the individual interview by the same-sex therapist facilitates the disclosure of more detailed information than if the partner or opposite-sex therapist were present.

Many of the behavior problems that a couple experiences are a function of deficits in other areas. Thus, our assessment of other factors is equally important. The importance of covert or mental behavior has recently been emphasized by directive therapists (e.g., Mahoney, 1974; Meichenbaum, 1974; Ellis, 1962). Individuals with sexual dysfunctions are apt to have inappropriate *cognitions*, which contribute to their problems. These fall generally into three categories. First, many clients are ignorant about the biology of human sexual response (LoPiccolo, 1975). Consequently, their sexual behaviors are inappropriate, not as a result of a behavioral deficit per se but because of beliefs based on ignorance. For example, one of our recent couples believed that female orgasm during intercourse was produced primarily through deep vaginal stimulation by the penis, rather than by any stimulation of the clitoris. Although the woman was easily orgasmic through direct clitoral stimulation, neither she nor her partner made any attempt to manipulate her clitoris during intercourse, thus depriving her of coital orgasm. The belief that it is unnecessary or inappropriate to provide concurrent clitoral stimulation during intercourse is so prevalent among dysfunctional couples and so often responsible for a woman's secondary orgasmic dysfunction that we have identified it as the "Look Ma, no hands" syndrome.

A second category of inappropriate cognitions are destructive attitudes that inhibit sexual arousal. The most common of these is the "good girl–bad girl" dichotomy. Despite a liberalization of our culture's attitudes toward female sexuality, many of our patients maintain the belief that there are two mutually exclusive kinds of women: those who are sexually responsive and sexually active and those who are good wives, mothers, and citizens. Whether this belief is held consciously or unconsciously, it results in the woman subtly being reinforced by her partner and herself for being responsible, conscientious, and *un*sexy. If a woman's self-image includes this dichotomy, she will always be in conflict about her sexual arousal. Furthermore, if her partner also holds this belief, not only will he unwittingly discourage her sexual responsiveness but also he may be in conflict about *his* arousal in response to her. This belief on the part of the man is frequently most manifest by his arousal to erotic literature, magazines, movies, and fantasies, but not to his partner. In this example, one clue to the existence of sexually destructive attitudes is the patient's sexual developmental history. For example, a recent patient was taught by his parents that "nice girls" are not interested in sex. Although he might have had an opportunity to prove this untrue with girls in his peer group, in early adolescence his family moved to a more upper-middle-class community where he did not have a peer group that immediately accepted him. Desiring social acceptance and cognizant of his parents teachings, he restrained himself from any behavior that might be termed sexually aggressive with all girls whom he dated. This included anything more than hand-holding. Prior to meeting and marrying his wife, his sexual behavior consisted exclusively of masturbation to erotic literature and fantasies and, occasionally, intercourse with prostitutes.

The third category of inappropriate cognitions are the self-defeating thoughts, called "self-statements" (Meichenbaum, 1974), that patients make about their sexual behavior. A common monologue that patients with erectile dysfunction have with themselves goes like this: "Oh damn! My penis isn't hard anymore. I'm sure she wants to have intercourse now. Come on, damn it! I just can't get it up. It's no use, once I lose it I can never get it back. I'll bet she's thinking I'm a homosexual. She'll never want to make love with me again. I'm such a failure!" A man with premature ejaculation engages in another kind of covert monologue: "Uh-oh! I'm pretty excited. I'm going to ejaculate too soon. Quick, don't think of sex. Shut your eyes. Count backwards by sevens. 93-86-79-72—uh—let's see, 65, uh. Oh, no! I'm going to come now!—Damn it. I did it again. I'll bet she's angry with me. I feel so awful. I'm such a failure." Not only are these cognitions self-defeating but also they obviously take all the fun out of sex. Instead of enjoying his arousal and orgasm, the patient is preoccupied with arithmetic. These cognitions present an added liability if they are practiced over time. The patient progressively reduces the threshold of arousal to which he will ejaculate (LoPiccolo and Lobitz, 1973).

In addition to evaluating the patient's behaviors and cognitions, we assess the contribution that their *affects* make to the dysfunction. Specifically, we ask patients about their subjective feelings when they engage in or think about sex. The prevailing affect in cases of sexual dysfunction is almost always anxiety, usually over one's performance (Masters and Johnson, 1970). Regardless of what factors may have originally produced a dysfunction, anxiety is usually central to the maintenance of the problem (LoPiccolo and Lobitz, 1973). In both men and women, significant levels of anxiety interfere with genital vasocongestion, the physiological substrate of sexual arousal (Kaplan, 1974). Although many patients readily admit to feelings of anxiety either during or in anticipation of lovemaking, other patients may deny these feelings but manifest performance anxiety in other ways. One common indicator of underlying performance anxiety is an intense focus on "goals" in lovemaking, such as reaching orgasm or maintaining an erection, rather than an enjoyment of the "process" of giving and receiving sensual pleasure.

Depression, although less central than anxiety, can also contribute to sexual dysfunctions, as mentioned in the previous section. Where the problem is low self-esteem, lovemaking may be used to counteract these feelings to the detriment of the sexual relationship. For example, one of our patients, a woman with chronic low self-esteem, constantly pressured her husband to have frequent intercourse with her as proof that he still loved her. This pressure resulted in his developing severe erectile dysfunction, which further deepened her depression and led her to pressure him more.

In order for a couple to enjoy the process of making love, they need to be able to focus on *sensations* rather than goals or behaviors. We regularly inquire which senses are assets and liabilities to their lovemaking. For some individuals sight and hearing are positive aspects of sex; they are particularly aroused by the sight of their partner's body and the sounds he or she makes while making love. Others find the smell of sex most arousing but are not so excited by sight or sound. Acute sensitivities can also have a negative influence on a couple's sexual relationship. For example, one of our patients, a nonsmoker, found kissing his wife to be extremely aversive because of the tobacco smell on her breath. In contrast to those individuals who are acutely conscious of the sensations of sex, some patients are so focused on their performance that they are unaware of the pleasures of touch, sight, smell, taste, and sound during lovemaking. An extreme example of this was a patient of ours who complained of "anesthetic orgasms." During lovemaking he was so preoccupied with the goal of his partner's orgasm that he was oblivious to his own. Because his primary deficit was in the area of sensation, treatment focused on sensory awareness training (Gunther, 1968).

Closely related to the area of sensation is the contribution of *imagery* to sexual function and dysfunction. A common deficit for inorgasmic women is their inability to fantasize sexually arousing images. Similarly, men with erectile difficulties are often deficient in their ability to enhance their arousal through fantasy. In contrast to those forms of therapy where assessing the fantasy content per se is important, in sex therapy we assess the patient's capacity to fantasize. Where this capacity is low, treatment needs to include imagery training.

The most important area of assessment, which we also consider carefully in the initial phase of evaluation, is the couple's *interpersonal relationship.* Because sexual function and dysfunction typically involves at least two people, we focus especially on the interaction between the partners. LoPiccolo (1975) has outlined several interpersonal factors that maintain sexual dysfunctions. The first of these is the degree to which the couple takes mutual responsibility for resolving the dysfunction. If one partner insists that he or she is in treatment merely to help the "sick spouse," treatment needs to engage the resistant partner by emphasizing that he or she also needs to profit personally from treatment for it to work.

A second interpersonal factor is the life-style of the couple. Not only do we evaluate the degree to which the couple shares responsibility for their life but also we assess the degree of mutuality in their relationship as a whole. If the sex roles are divided strictly along stereotypic lines where the husband is responsible only for the family's financial support while the wife handles all the domestic duties (child care, cooking, cleaning), she may be feeling some resentment toward her husband, not only for not having a career of her own but also for having a work day that extends well beyond her husband's nine-to-five schedule. We have found this to be a consistent pattern in cases of secondary female orgasmic dysfunction. Although the woman has given herself permission to be sexually responsive and orgasmic, e.g., through masturbation, she is not willing to share her response with a man from whom she feels little emotional or practical support. This finding is consistent with the results of McGovern, Stewart, and LoPiccolo (1975), who stressed the importance of marital-relationship therapy in cases of secondary female orgasmic dysfunction.

For some dysfunctional couples the problem with the life-style is not the lack of mutuality. Rather, the problem is the way they have ordered their priorities (LoPiccolo, 1975). Pleasurable sex is a leisure activity. Couples who always place job, children, dinner, house, lawn, sports, pets, neighbors, and television before their sex life are setting up their lovemaking for failure. By the time they are "ready" to make love, usually about 12:30 a.m., they are physically tired, mentally exhausted, and emotionally drained. Yet, they are generally puzzled that their sex life is disappointing and frustrating.

The most important interpersonal factor is the degree of communication in the couple's relationship. Not only is this crucial in cases of sexual dysfunction but also it is a major variable in relationships that have minor sexual problems but do not require a full course of sex therapy (Lobitz, 1976; LoPiccolo and Miller, 1975). Difficulties in communication may manifest themselves in the way a couple initiates and refuses sex or in the way they tell each other what activities are arousing or aversive. We have found it useful to ask each patient separately to describe how his or her partner typically initiates and refuses lovemaking. In addition, we ask the patient to list those things that are particularly sexually stimulating or annoying to his or her partner. Among dysfunctional couples the most common response is "Gosh, I don't know. I've never asked and he/she has never told me. We don't talk about sex." It is also important to ascertain whether the couple's communication problems occur only in the sexual area or whether they pervade their entire relationship. We ask our patients how they resolve disagreements about sex and how they resolve disagreements in other areas such as child-rearing, household duties, and leisure-time activities. Where their difficulties in communication pervade the relationship, the couple needs general training in communication and problem resolution skills as part of their sex therapy. Where the deficit is isolated to their sexual relationship, they need to learn how to transfer the skills they already possess to the more emotionally laden area of sex.

Biological factors are less important in this phase of the assessment than in the initial evaluation. Nevertheless, there are many patients whose dysfunctions are caused in part by biological deficits but who can benefit from sex therapy. For example, we have successfully completed treatment with patients whose erectile dysfunction was originally caused by neurological damage, in one case by meningoencephalitis and subsequent craniotomy, which resulted in a chronic organic brain syndrome, and in another case by chemotherapy for Hodgkin's disease. In both cases it was important to collaborate with the patient's physicians to assess how much of the dysfunction was attributable to organic causes and how much was a function of behavioral, cognitive, affective, sensory, imagery, and interpersonal deficits.

Personality factors are also relevant to this phase of the assessment process. For example, Lassen (1976) has described how the personality characteristics of many men with erectile problems contribute to their dysfunction. We have found that many of these men are hard-driving, achievement-oriented successes in their professional life. Their typical style of handling problems is to "try harder," what we have dubbed the "Avis response." Although this style has been effective in most other aspects of their life, it is both physiologically and emotionally counterproductive when applied to sexual function. For example, the male erectile response is facilitated by physical and emotional relaxation and inhibited by anxiety, including "trying" (Masters and Johnson, 1970). The purpose of sex therapy is not to change the patient's personality or biology. Yet, as we have shown elsewhere, assessment of personality factors helps determine the tactics of therapeutic intervention (Lobitz et al., 1976). In addition, knowledge of the patient's personality and biology provides a framework within which to set treatment goals and evaluate its success.

Formulation and Feedback

Once the clinical assessment interviews are completed, we formulate a list of problems for treatment intervention, using the areas of behavior, cognition, affect, sensation, imagery, interpersonal relations, biology, and personality as a guide. The patients are always aware of some of these problems, for example, "We don't talk about sex" or "I get anxious every time I think about having intercourse." Other problems evolve during the interviews without the couple's conscious awareness of their importance, for example, a total lack of mutuality in the couple's life-style, which causes one partner to resent the other. Following the identification of specific problems, we formulate the interaction between them and hypothesize about their historical development. Hypotheses about development are particularly important in giving the patients the sense that they "learned" their problems and therefore can "unlearn" them (LoPiccolo and Lobitz, 1973).

Formulations about the interaction of problems are important in clarifying the usually complex relationships between various factors and the specific dysfunction. Figure 1 schematically represents the interaction of various factors in a hypothetical case of erectile dysfunction. The factors are drawn from actual cases where this symptom was the presenting complaint. Each factor is identified in parentheses. Excessive expectations, ignorance, and a sexually destructive life-style combine to produce performance anxiety on the part of the male. This anxiety, combined with an achievement-oriented personality, cause him to "try" to get an erection and to attempt intercourse while he is tense. This prevents him from being able to "receive" sensual pleasure. This physiological "unreceptivity" to sensual pleasure (i.e., the sympathetic nervous system dominance from anxiety) prevents his erection from occurring. In addition, a lack of communication between partners obscures his need for direct genital caressing by the female. This lack also makes it less likely that his penis will become erect. Being aware of his lack of erection, he labels himself a "failure," which enhances his anxiety as well as causing him to be depressed. These feelings continue to lower his receptivity to sexual stimulation, which further reduces the likelihood that he will get an erection.

These factors interact so as to form a process that not only precipitates the dysfunction but also maintains it in the absence of therapeutic intervention. Treatment of performance anxiety alone will not resolve the dysfunction in that a variety of factors produce conditions that will continue to precipitate and maintain the primary symptom. As Lazarus (1973) has stated, the success of treatment is directly related to the *different* areas of intervention. Of course, multiple factor interventions are not possible if the various problem areas have not been assessed prior to treatment.

Identification of the couple's strengths also becomes important in formulating the case and planning the treatment interventions. To continue the example of the hypothetical case in Figure 1, let us assume that the couple has a high degree of mutuality both in terms of their responsibility for resolving the sexual dysfunction and in terms of their sex roles (interpersonal). In addition, they derive pleasure and joy from each other's company outside of their sexual relationship (affect). Contrary to his beliefs, she does not expect him always to have an erection (cognition) because she is able to reach orgasm by noncoital stimulation (behavior) as well as through intercourse. He has a vivid imagination and is able to obtain an erection through fantasy (imagery), provided he is not overwhelmed by anxiety. These positive factors provide avenues through which the therapists can intervene in the problem areas. Obviously, if the therapists are unable to identify strengths in *any* area, treatment will be more difficult, if not impossible.

Once we have formulated the interaction of factors which has precipitated and maintained the dysfunction, we meet with the patient couple to give them feedback on our observations and to establish goals for treatment. This meeting is similar to the "round table" described by Masters and Johnson (1970). Providing detailed feedback differs from "traditional" psychotherapy where the therapist's observations and formulations may be withheld until later in treatment or until the patient develops the "insight" on his or her own. In some therapies this is seen as the end point of treatment. In sex therapy the focus is on helping the

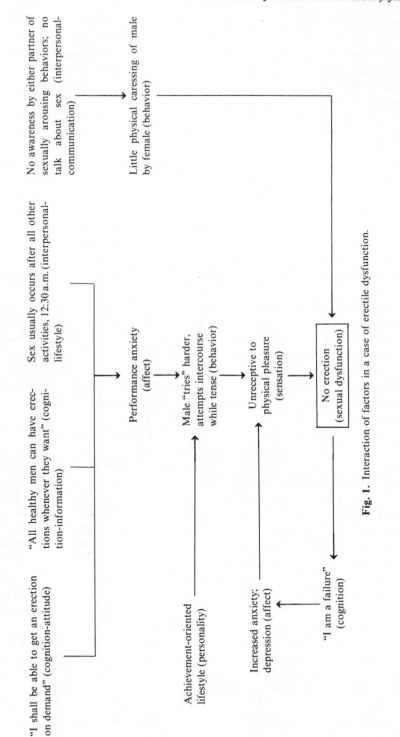

Fig. 1. Interaction of factors in a case of erectile dysfunction.

patients (1) increase their awareness of their behavior and (2) change the behavior if it inhibits their sexual function. Since this is achieved in a relatively short time frame (twelve to twenty sessions), we believe it is more efficacious to *begin* with the therapists' observations and formulation than to end with them.

In presenting the feedback, we label our formulations as impressions, not as facts. This is to encourage the patients to respond with their own impressions based on the information we have shared. Usually they concur with our formulations. However, they may also disagree and offer additional data or alternative explanations. Our involving the patients as "colleagues" is one of the ways we increase the likelihood that the positive effects of treatment will be maintained (Lobitz and LoPiccolo, 1972; Wyatt, Strayer, and Lobitz, 1976). Although this type of participation reaches a peak in the latter part of treatment, it begins with the sharing of the therapists' formulations during the feedback session.

Out of this discussion we arrive at mutually agreeable goals for treatment. These goals are typically reflections of the problem areas that we have identified as contributing to the dysfunction. Thus, the goals are more extensive than a unitary behavior such as "reach an orgasm" or "last longer." They include changes in cognitions, affect, sensation, imagery, and the couple's relationship as well. This feedback session and mutual goal sharing mark the end of the formal, circumscribed assessment process. It also marks the beginning of the third and final phase of assessment. This stage, i.e., the ongoing evaluation of treatment progress, is as critical as the first two in effecting change. However, measured success in treatment depends on the effectiveness of the pretreatment evaluation. The more thorough the therapists are in the first two stages of assessment, the more likely they will be to find that their treatment has been successful and that their results are maintained after therapy has ended.

References

Briddel, D. W., and Wilson, G. J. Effects of alcohol and expectancy set on male sexual arousal. *Journal of Abnormal Psychology*, 1976, *85*, 225–234.

Dahlstrom, W. G., Welsh, G. J., and Dahlstrom, L. E. *An MMPI handbook. Volume I. Clinical interpretaton.* Minneapolis: University of Minnesota Press, 1972.

Ellis, A. *Reason and emotion in psychotherapy.* New York: Lyle Stuart, 1962.

Frank, E., Anderson, C., and Kupfer, D. J. Profiles of couples seeking sex therapy and marital therapy. *American Journal of Psychiatry*, 1976, *133*, 559–562.

Grant, R. L., and Lewis, R. *Use of the problem-oriented system in assessment of learning: Problem definition skills.* Paper presented at the Conference on the Assessment of Clinical Learning in the Psychiatric Education of Medical Students, Medical University of South Carolina, November 1974.

Gunther, B. *Sense relaxation.* New York: Collier Books, 1968.

Hartman, W. E., and Fithian, M. A. *Treatment of sexual dysfunction.* Long Beach, California: California Center for Medical and Sexual Studies, 1972.

Johnson, S. M., and Bolstad, O. D. Methological issues in naturalistic observation: Some problems and solutions for field research. In L. A. Hamerlynck, L. C. Handy, and E. J. Mash (Eds.), *Behavior change: Methodology, concepts, and practice.* Champaign, Illinois: Research Press, 1973.

Kaplan, H. S. *The new sex therapy.* New York: Brunner/Mazel, 1974.

Lassen, C. L. Issues and dilemmas in the treatment of sexual dysfunction. *Journal of Sex and Marital Therapy*, 1976, *2*, 32–39.

Lazarus, A. A. Multimodal behavior therapy: Treating the "basic id." *Journal of Nervous and Mental Disease*, 1973, *156*, 404–411.

Lobitz, W. C. Clinical recognition and treatment of sexual dysfunction. In F. J. Cozzetto and H. R. Brettell (Eds.), *Topics in family practice*. New York: Stratton, 1976.

Lobitz, W. C., and LoPiccolo, J. New methods in the behavioral treatment of sexual dysfunction. *Journal of Behavior Therapy and Experimental Psychiatry*, 1972, *3*, 265–271.

Lobitz, W. C., LoPiccolo, J., Lobitz, G. K., and Brockway, J. A closer look at "simplistic" behavior therapy for sexual dysfunction. In H. J. Eysenck (Ed.), *Case studies in behavior therapy*. London: Routledge & Kegan Paul, 1976.

Locke, H. J., and Wallace, K. M. Short marital adjustment and prediction tests: Their reliability and prediction. *Marriage and Family Living*, 1959, *21*, 251–255.

LoPiccolo, J. Direct treatment of sexual dysfunction. In J. Money and H. Musaph (Eds.), *Handbook of sexology*. Amsterdam, Holland: ASP Biological and Medical Press, 1975.

LoPiccolo, J., and Lobitz, W. C. Behavior therapy of sexual dysfunction. In L. A. Hamerlynck, L. C. Handy, and E. J. Mash (Eds.), *Behavior change: Methodology, concepts, and practice*. Champaign, Illinois: Research Press, 1973.

LoPiccolo, J., and Miller, V. A program for enhancing the sexual relationships of normal couples. *The Counseling Psychologist*, 1975, *5*, 41–45.

LoPiccolo, J., and Steger, J. The Sexual Interaction Inventory. A new instrument for assessment of sexual dysfunction. *Archives of Sexual Behavior*, 1974, *3*, 585–595.

Mahoney, M. *Cognition and behavior modification*. Cambridge, Massachusetts: Bollinger, 1974.

Masters, W. H., and Johnson, V. E. *Human sexual response*. Boston: Little, Brown, 1966.

Masters, W. H., and Johnson, V. E. *Human sexual inadequacy*. Boston: Little Brown, 1970.

McGovern, K. B., Stewart, R. C., and LoPiccolo, J. Secondary orgasmic dysfunction. I. Analysis and strategies for treatment. *Archives of Sexual Behavior*, 1975, *4*, 265–276.

Meichenbaum, D. Self-instructional methods. In F. H. Kanfer and A. P. Goldstein (Eds.), *Helping people change*. New York: Pergamon, 1974.

Peterson, D. R. Is psychology a profession? *American Psychologist*, 1976, *31*, 572–581.

Sager, C. J. Sexual dysfunctions and marital discord. In H. S. Kaplan, *The new sex therapy*. New York: Brunner/Mazel, 1974.

Sager, C. J. The role of sex therapy in marital therapy. *American Journal of Psychiatry*, 1976, *133*, 555–559.

Serber, M. Videotape feedback in the treatment of couples with sexual dysfunction. *Archives of Sexual Behavior*, 1974, *3*, 377–380.

Vincent, C. E. *Human sexuality in medical education and practice*. Springfield, Illinois: Charles C Thomas, 1968.

Wahl, C. W. Psychiatric techniques in the taking of a sexual history. In C. W. Wahl (Ed.), *Sexual problems: Diagnosis and treatment in medical practice*. New York: The Free Press, 1967.

Weiss, R. L., and Margolin, G. Marital conflict and accord. In A. R. Ciminero, K. S. Calhoun, and H. E. Adams (Eds.), *Handbook for behavioral assessment*. New York: John Wiley & Sons, 1975.

Wiggins, J. S. *Personality and prediction: Principles of personality assessment*. Reading, Massachusetts: Addison-Wesley, 1973.

Wyatt, G., Strayer, R., and Lobitz, W. C. Issues in the treatment of sexually dysfunctioning couples of Afro-American descent. *Psychotherapy: Theory, Research, and Practice*, 1976, *13*, 44–50.

The necessity of doing an in-depth history on clients entering sex therapy is still open to debate. Some clinicians such as Dr. William H. Masters and Virginia Johnson advocate extensive interviews lasting a total of around seven hours, while others do no history-taking beyond the initial evaluation interview. It is probably safe to say, however, that most clinicians spend some time reviewing the past history of their clients.

History-taking can serve many functions. Perhaps the three most important are: (1) to get a frame of reference for understanding the etiology and maintenance of the sexual difficulties of the particular individuals; (2) to afford the opportunity to build rapport with the clients; and (3) to provide a basis on which to begin formulating treatment interventions.

6

Sexual Assessment and History Interview

Leslie LoPiccolo and Julia R. Heiman

This is an outline of content areas that are to be covered with a client before an informed treatment program can be planned. Without getting a thorough picture of the couple's current sexual attitudes and behaviors, as well as relevant historical information, the therapist can be very badly mistaken about just what problems are to be treated. For example, some cases of identified female dysfunction turn out to actually be cases of male premature ejaculation.

The structure of the interview can vary. If a male–female cotherapy team is involved, the majority of the time is usually spent on same-sexed therapist–client interviews, with a much smaller amount of time devoted to conjoint and cross-sexed assessment. However, same-sexed interviews are not necessarily the most comfortable or advantageous in terms of equal rapport among clients and therapists. Alternatives exist such as equally splitting the amount of time between interviewing the male and female separately and together. Certainly a single therapist working alone will want to divide the history time proportionately among individual and couple interviews.

Leslie LoPiccolo • Department of Psychiatry and Behavioral Science, School of Medicine, State University of New York, Stony Brook, New York   *Julia R. Heiman* • Long Island Research Institute; Department of Psychiatry and Behavioral Science, School of Medicine, State University of New York, Stony Brook, New York

In conducting this assessment, don't be an inquisitor. Briefly explain the purpose of the interview and take some time to build a rapport with the client. It is useful to begin with less loaded, more general content areas before moving to the more explicitly sexual information. Ask your questions in an open-ended manner that encourages the client to explain their situation rather than merely answer yes or no. Be very straightforward about the use of sexual terms—model for the client that there is nothing to be ashamed of in talking about sex. It seems best to avoid use of slang words—most clients perceive this as inappropriate in a professional helping context. Give the client an opportunity to ask *you* questions about sex. Clients often have a good deal of misinformation about sex, and you should provide correct information whenever you hear mistaken beliefs. Use this outline as a guide. You do not need to ask every question.

The therapist's main goals are to try and understand the nature of the sexual problem and how it functions, both positively and negatively, as part of the couple's relationship. This is an occasion to develop some working hypotheses about the development and maintenance of sexual dissatisfaction, hypotheses that will be "tested" as therapeutic interventions are made. The focus should be on the couple as a system, with each person's needs, attitudes, and behaviors helping to create and maintain that system.

Historical Information

I. Background and Early Childhood

The purpose here is to develop an understanding of the client's early affectionate and interpersonal experiences and his or her feelings about those experiences. Of special concern are early attitudes and feelings about affection, closeness, trust, male–female relationships, and sex that might have been fostered while the person grew up.

A. Family Background
   1. Place of birth? Did your family travel around much during your childhood?
   2. How old were your parents when you were born?
   3. Do you have any brothers or sisters?
   4. Are your parents still living?
      a. Are they still married?
      b. Had either had a previous marriage?
   5. What were your parents' occupations?
   6. Quality of relationships with family while growing up?
      a. One or both parents emotionally distant, close, warm, binding, seductive?
      b. More attached to one parent than the other?
      c. Closer to same-sexed or opposite-sexed brother or sister?
B. Religious Influences
   1. In what religion were you raised?
   2. Were both of your parents of the same faith?
   3. How religious were your parents?

4. Was religion an active factor in your early life (Sunday school, parochial school, etc.)?

C. Attitudes toward Sex in the Home
   1. Were you allowed to ask questions about or discuss sexual topics?
      a. How did your parents usually respond to questions?
      b. Did you ever turn to siblings for information?
      c. Can you remember any examples?
      d. Did you get the feeling that one or both parents would be uncomfortable if you had tried to ask them questions about sex?
   2. Was affection shown between your parents?
      a. How were your parents affectionate with each other (was affection usually expressed verbally or physically)?
      b. Did you get the feeling that your parents cared a lot about each other, whether or not they were visibly affectionate?
      c. Was one parent more affectionate than the other?
   3. Were your parents affectionate with you?
      a. Describe the kind of affection you received (verbal, physical) and who was more affectionate.
      b. Would you have liked more, less, or the same amount of affection from your parents?
   4. What was the attitude toward nudity (or modesty) in your home?
   5. What do you think your parents' attitudes toward sex were?
      a. With each other?
      b. Toward your own developing sexuality?
   6. What kinds of sexual comments were made around the house by your parents either about other people, each other, or in terms of jokes?
   7. What influence did your siblings or friends have on how you thought about sex at this time?
      a. Did you ever discuss sex with friends or siblings?
      b. Was sex the subject of jokes and embarrassment?
      c. Did you consider sex dirty, frightening, curious, interesting?
   8. Do you recall playing any games with sexual content as a child (i.e., "Doctor")?

D. Emerging Sexuality
   1. At about what age do you recall first having pleasurable genital feelings?
      a. Were these in connection with any particular thoughts, activities, or situations?
      b. Did you define these activities as good or bad feelings at the time?
   2. At what age did you first experiment with masturbation (or any other solitary activity that produced genital feelings of pleasure)?
      a. Describe how and where you did this.
      b. How often did you engage in this?
      c. How did you feel about doing this?
      d. Were you ever discovered at this?
   3. Do you remember any upsetting experiences that occurred during childhood with regard to sex?

II. Puberty and Adolescence

    A. Sexual Education

        1. Toward which parent/sibling did you feel closest? To whom did you take your problems?

        2. Did you have many friends, a few close friends, or were you a "loner"? Were they mostly the same sex or opposite sex? Have you had many, a few, or almost no close friends of the opposite sex?

        3. When did you first learn about conception and reproduction?

          a. How did you learn?

          b. How did you react to this?

(Females) 4. At what age did you start to menstruate?

          a. Had menstruation been explained to you in advance? How and by whom?

          b. Was the subject discussed among your friends? What term(s) did you use to refer to it?

          c. What were your feelings in anticipation of menstruation?

          d. How did you feel after it had begun?

            (1) Do you recall it influencing your life-style in any way?

            (2) Did you feel any differently about yourself and your body?

          e. Have you ever had any menstrual difficulties?

          f. Have you ever had sex during your period? How do you feel about this idea?

        5. Have you ever had sexual dreams where you felt you were aroused in your sleep? Have you ever had an orgasm during sleep?

(Males)   6. How old were you when you had your first nocturnal emisson (or "wet dream")?

          a. Had you been told about these in advance? How and by whom?

          b. How did you react?

        7. How did you feel when you first heard about the fact that women menstruate?

    B. Dating Behavior

        1. At what age did you start to date?

          a. In groups?

          b. On single dates?

        2. Were most of your friends at this time male or female?

        3. Did you date many different people or did you usually have a steady relationship with one person at a time?

    C. Petting Behavior

        1. What kinds of petting did you engage in?

        2. Where did petting behavior usually occur? Under what circumstances?

        3. What kind of emotional relationship did you have to have with someone before you would become involved in petting?

        4. Was there any touching or manipulation of genitals involved?

        5. How did you respond sexually to these behaviors?

        6. How did you feel about engaging in these behaviors?

7. How would your parents have responded if they knew? What were their attitudes about petting or other nongenital sexual contact?
8. Any negative petting experiences?
D. Coital Experiences
   1. Did you ever engage in intercourse premaritally? If so, describe the first time.
   2. Under what circumstances and how frequently did intercourse usually occur?
   3. How did you respond sexually? (Were you orgasmic? Or were there any problems with erection or premature ejaculation?)
   4. What were the emotional conditions that you needed to have intercourse with someone? For instance, was it important that you were in love with each other, emotionally involved in some way, committed to a long-term relationship, engaged, or married? Could you have sex with someone without being emotionally involved with them?
   5. What feelings usually accompanied intercourse (satisfaction, guilt, pleasure, embarrassment, anxiety, etc.)?
   6. Were you ever "walked in on" while you were having sex with someone?
   7. Have you ever had any problems with VD? Pain during sex? Herpes?
   8. What form of contraception did you use? Whose responsibility was this?
   9. Did your parents ever discuss intercourse with you? Contraception?
E. Other Experiences
   1. Did you read erotic material? Go to pornographic movies?
   2. How frequently did you have sexual fantasies with masturbation, petting, or intercourse?
   3. How often were you masturbating during these years?
   4. Do you remember any sexual encounters with a member of the same sex? If so, how did you feel about this?
   5. Do you remember ever seeing a person expose himself or masturbate in public?
   6. Did you have any unpleasant experiences with undue physical intimacy by strangers or a family member or friend?
   7. Any other unusual or unpleasant sexual experiences during these years?
(Females) 8. Do you remember any discussions about homosexuals? Or the possibility of assault or rape? Describe.
(Males)   9. What did you think of the women who would have intercourse with you? What about the women who refused?
F. Premarital Behavior and Feelings
   1. Have you ever been in love before?
      a. What does being in love mean to you?
      b. Do you easily become emotionally involved with people? Do you easily fall in love?
   2. Were you ever engaged, married, or seriously involved in another relationship(s) before meeting your spouse? If so, describe.

3. Describe the different sexual behaviors engaged in with spouse before marriage.
4. Describe the quality of these sexual experiences.
   a. How did you respond sexually (orgasmic, etc.)?
   b. How did you feel about these?

Current Information

I. *Current Attitudes and Beliefs*

A. The purpose of this section is to find out:
   1. Current sexual values and behaviors
   2. The degree of integration or segregation of sex from other aspects of the client's life
   3. What areas might be particularly difficult for him/her to change
B. Current Attitudes toward Sex
   1. What is your attitude toward sex in general? What specific activities are enjoyable? Do you ever feel dirty or guilty about any aspects of sex? Or thinking about sex?
   2. Do you feel positive, negative, or neutral about:
      a. Your genital area
      b. Menstruation
      c. Vaginal secretions and semen
      d. Masturbation
      e. Oral–genital contacts
      f. Foreplay
      g. Intercourse
      h. Manual orgasms
      i. Sexual fantasy
   3. What do you think are your partner's perceptions of (1) and (2) above?
   4. Do you feel that men and women should have distinct and different roles in nonsexual activities? In sexual activities? How does your current situation agree or disagree with views on sex-specific roles?
   5. What sort of conflicts do you have between your own attitudes about sex and those of:
      a. Peer groups
      b. Religion
      c. Your partner
   6. How do you see the place of sex in marriage? Is it very important to you or not?

II. *Current Behavior*

A. Some of this is redundant. Pursue according to nature of problem and clarity of information already derived from other questions. Some repetition is useful to check reliability and to allow clients to share some information that they might not have recalled earlier.

B. Types of Noncoital Activity
   1. What are the more pleasurable physical contacts between you and your partner that are not followed by intercourse? Do these activities occur frequently enough for you?
   2. What are the more pleasurable contacts between you and your partner that do precede intercourse? How would you change them (duration, frequency, emphasis on manual or oral)?
C. Homosexuality
   1. How would you describe your sexual identity? Are you comfortable with it?
   2. Have you ever thought you would like to experience a sexual activity with someone of the same sex? How do you feel about this?
D. Extrarelationship Coitus
   1. What kinds of social relationships do you have with people of the opposite sex (close friendships, frequent socializing, etc.)?
   2. During your marriage or current relationship, have you had any noncoital affectionate relationships with opposite-sexed friends? What sort of behaviors were involved? How intimate do you view the contacts? Was and is your partner aware of them?
   3. Have you experienced coitus outside of your marriage relationship? How many times? Was it pleasurable? How did you feel about it? Were you orgasmic? Would you repeat the experience? Did/does your partner know?
E. Communication
   1. Are you and your partner able to talk about most things? What are subjects that you avoid, find difficult, or often fight about?
   2. Would you like to change the ways in which you communicate? How would you like to see your communication patterns change?
   3. Is it difficult to tell your partner what you like about him/her? What you don't like?
   4. Do you tell your partner what you do and do not like *during sex*? Do you feel comfortable expressing your preferences about what is going on when you are having sex? Do you feel comfortable sometimes being the initiator of sexual activity? How do you feel when your partner initiates sexual activity or refuses a sexual advance that you make?
F. Relationship
   1. How do you feel about your relationship? Are you getting the things you want from it? What are some good things?
   2. Do you feel satisfied with the amount and type of physical affection you have with your spouse? How often is he/she affectionate without necessarily expecting sex to follow? How about nonphysical affection—things that show consideration or caring?
   3. What happens when you argue? What do you argue about? Have you ever separated or considered divorce?
   4. How do you see your sexual difficulties affecting other aspects of your relationship?

5. What other areas in your marriage, in addition to sex, are currently causing trouble for you?

G. Life-Style

1. Are you working or unemployed? How do you feel about this? Any plans to go back to school or work, or to retire? How does your work (or your spouse's) affect your marital and sexual relationship? Do you feel you have enough time together? Are worries about work a problem? Is fatigue a problem?

2. If there are children: How do you feel your children affect your over-all relationship with your spouse? Do you feel they affect your sexual relationship in any way? For example, do you feel concerned about a lack of privacy with the children around?

H. Nature of Sexual Difficulty

1. How would you describe the sexual problem(s) you've been experiencing?

2. How long has this been a problem? Do you recall the circumstances under which it first occurred or you became aware of the problem?

3. What are your ideas on how or why this problem developed? If dysfunction is present for both partners: Which do you recall as having developed first?

4. If dysfunction centers in one partner: In what way do you feel the problem affects your own or your partner's sexual functioning?

5. How have you both handled this difficulty in the past? What have you tried to remedy this problem (read books, tried different techniques, sought marital or sexual counseling)?

6. Information on specific dysfunctions.

Below are some of the questions that should be asked in order to get a clear picture of the sexual problem. It is a good idea to inquire about all aspects of the sexual relationship since clients may not recognize all the problem areas. It is important to get the clients' feelings about the problem as well as the relevant facts. The spouse should also be asked for his/her perceptions of the problem in order to clarify any discrepancies and to evaluate the interactional factors that may be involved. Words such as *intromission* and *foreplay* should be defined for the client to ensure accuracy of information.

a. Premature ejaculation

(1) How often do you have intercourse? How does this compare with your frequency in the past? Have you noticed any relationship between recency of intercourse and premature ejaculation?

(2) When did you begin to notice this as a problem? After stimulation begins, how long does it usually take for you to have an orgasm? Does ejaculation occur inside or outside of the vagina?

(3) What kinds of stimulation do you usually receive during foreplay? Do you usually enjoy foreplay (too long, too short, too predictable)?

       (4) What do you do after ejaculation (manually stimulate wife, try for second erection, etc.)?

       (5) What about masturbation—how often do you masturbate? How quickly do you ejaculate?

       (6) Have you found anything that influences how quickly you ejaculate (alcohol, drugs, the use of a condom, etc.)?

       (7) What have you tried to delay ejaculation?

       (8) Have you ever seen a medical doctor for this? When? Any previous therapy experiences?

       (9) Are you on any medication? Have you noticed any relationship between taking the medication and the problem of premature ejaculation?

     (10) Inquire about any upsetting experiences that may relate—psychiatric problems, other medical problems.

  b. Erectile problems

       (1) Has this ever been a problem for you? When did this problem start? Under what circumstances does it usually occur? What influence does your relationship with your spouse have on this problem? What percentage of time is this a problem?

       (2) When do you have a problem with erections—during foreplay? during intromission? during intercourse?

       (3) Have you ever experienced pain with intromission or ejaculation?

       (4) If you have a problem getting an erection, how do you as a couple handle this? What have you tried to remedy this problem? Any previous therapy?

       (5) Do you have a history of diabetes? Heart or circulatory problems? Kidney or prostate problems?

       (6) Are you or have you ever been a heavy drinker?

       (7) Are you on any medication? For what? For how long? Have you noticed any relationship between the medication and the problem of erectile difficulties?

       (8) Do you have nocturnal emissions? Morning erections? Are you often fatigued when you begin sexual activities?

       (9) Have you seen a medical doctor about this problem? How recently?

     (10) How often do you masturbate? Do you have any erectile problems during masturbation?

     (11) Are there upsetting experiences that may relate? Psychiatric problems? Other medical problems?

     (12) What kinds of contraception do you use? Are you concerned about your spouse becoming pregnant?

  c. Orgasmic dysfunction

       (1) Do you get aroused during foreplay? Intercourse?

       (2) Have you ever had an orgasm during foreplay? What percentage of time? During intercourse? What percentage of time? What kind of stimulation do you receive during fore-

play? During intercourse? What positions do you use for intercourse?

(3) When did you first start experiencing problems? What seems to influence your ability to become aroused? Are you often tired when you begin sexual activities?

(4) Are you orgasmic during masturbation? What percentage of time? If female seems uncertain about whether she's orgasmic or not, or to find out if orgasm is pleasant to each female client: How would you describe your sensations during arousal? orgasm?

(5) What arouses you? Do you have sexual dreams or fantasies? How does your relationship with your spouse affect the problem?

(6) How much time is spent in foreplay? In intercourse?

(7) Do you ever experience any discomfort or pain? (If yes, get client to specify where, when.) Do you have problems with vaginal or bladder infections? How often?

(8) Does sexual contact usually lead to intercourse? What percentage of time?

(9) Do you take any medication? Any problems with alcohol, diabetes?

(10) What kind of contraception (if any) do you use? For how long? Any problems? Are you concerned about getting pregnant?

(11) If age indicates, inquire about menopause.

(12) Do you have any menstrual difficulties?

(13) Have you seen a medical doctor about your sexual concerns?

(14) What have you tried to do about this problem? Any previous therapy?

(15) Are there any other upsetting experiences that may relate? Psychiatric problems? Other medical problems?

Questions about other sexual problems such as vaginismus, dyspareunia, or low sex drive should follow the same type of format: When did the problem start; what influences the occurrence of the problem; any relevant medical information and the couple's or individual's attempts to solve the problem. Usually a thorough medical exam is advised as a matter of course to rule out any physical causes of dysfunction.

III. Summary Question

Is there anything else that you would like to tell me about your background that you feel bears on your sexual life?

IV. Goals

A. Why did you decide to come for sex therapy at this time?

B. How would you like things to be different sexually and nonsexually after therapy? (Ask for specifics from both partners.)

A major problem in research on the effectiveness of sex therapy procedures has been the lack of a valid and reliable measure of sexual functioning. In many other types of direct, behavioral therapy (e.g., assertiveness training) the patients can be directly observed while engaging in the target behavior. In the area of sexual behavior, ethical and social considerations obviously make direct observation impossible. Consequently, many clinicians have relied on the patients' unsystematic verbal report as the measure of treatment outcome. This chapter offers a structured behavioral self-report inventory as an alternative to such informal assessment.

Many of the other chapters in this volume include data from this inventory as a measure of treatment effectiveness. This chapter will familiarize the reader with the inventory and make the clinical chapters to follow more easily understood.

7

The Sexual Interaction Inventory: A New Instrument for Assessment of Sexual Dysfunction

Joseph LoPiccolo and Jeffrey C. Steger

Introduction

Since the publication of Masters and Johnson's *Human Sexual Inadequacy* in 1970, interest in treatment of sexual dysfunctions has become widespread among mental health professionals. Unfortunately, it seems that research methodology has not kept pace with advances in clinical treatment techniques. Specifically, research on clinical treatment of sexual dysfunction has been greatly hampered by the lack of objective, valid, and reliable outcome measures. In case reports and technique papers, it is not uncommon to find therapists simply listing case outcomes in terms of categories such as "much improved," "improved," "somewhat improved,"

Joseph LoPiccolo • Department of Psychiatry and Behavioral Science, School of Medicine, State University of New York, Stony Brook, New York   *Jeffrey C. Steger* • Department of Rehabilitation Medicine, University of Washington, Seattle, Washington. When this chapter was originally published, Jeffrey C. Steger was a postdoctoral fellow at the University of Oregon Medical School, Portland, Oregon.

and "no change." In most papers, the basis for these global judgments is not specified (see, e.g., Lazarus, 1963; Marquis, 1970).

Masters and Johnson (1970, p. 113) attempted to deal with the outcome assessment issue through the use of simple and objective criteria of treatment success. One was the presence or absence of female orgasm on 50% of coital opportunities following treatment for premature ejaculation. While an improvement over global ratings, this measure has numerous problems: (1) It is an "after-only" measure rather than a "pretreatment versus posttreatment" change measure; (2) it is arbitrary (why 50% instead of, for example, 73%, which is the average frequency with which women reach orgasm in coitus?) (Kinsey, Pomeroy, Martin, and Gebhard, 1953); and (3) sexual adequacy is defined in terms of a one-item test, female orgasm, which neglects other aspects of the sexual relationship (including subjective satisfaction).

Currently, there do not seem to be any assessment devices that focus on the actual sexual functioning and sexual satisfaction of heterosexual couples. There are a number of simple behavioral checklists (Podell and Perkins, 1957; Brady and Levitt, 1965; Bentler, 1968) that assess the range of sexual behaviors a person engages in, but this information is obviously a very incomplete assessment of sexual functioning and satisfaction. There are a number of psychodynamically oriented sex questionnaries, which do not focus on actual sexual functioning but rather on postulated intrapsychic traits such as castration anxiety (Blum, 1949), sex guilt (Mosher, 1968), and masculinity–femininity (see Goldberg, 1971, for a review of various M–F scales). No relationship between scores on such trait-oriented measures and actual sexual functioning and sexual satisfaction has been established.

There are also a number of tests for assessing heterosexual–homosexual orientation (Zamansky, 1956; Feldman and MacCulloch, 1971) or sexual preference for specific body types (Wiggins, Wiggins, and Conger, 1968). Again, the relevance of such procedures in assessing sexual dysfunction is minimal.

Perhaps the nearest approach to a relevant measure is provided by the Thorne Sex Inventory (Thorne, 1966). This questionnaire, designed to screen potential sex offenders, measures such traits as "neurotic conflict associated with sex" and "repression of sexuality," and hence may be at least indirectly related to a person's actual sexual behavior and satisfaction.

For the past three years, a clinical research project has been treating client couples with a variety of sexual dysfunctions. Various aspects of the project have been reported elsewhere (LoPiccolo and Lobitz, 1972, 1973; Lobitz and LoPiccolo, 1972; LoPiccolo, Stewart, and Watkins, 1972; McGovern, Stewart, and LoPiccolo, 1975; Snyder, LoPiccolo, and LoPiccolo, 1975). Because of the lack of treatment outcome measures, one of the research goals of this project has been to develop a paper-and-pencil inventory that would accurately reflect the nature of a couple's sexual relationship, in terms of both sexual functioning and sexual satisfaction. This chapter reports the results of three years of development of such an instrument—the Sexual Interaction Inventory (SII).*

---

*A scoring and interpretation manual is available from the authors.

Materials and Methods

Rationale

In designing the SII, three basic principles were followed: (1) The SII should focus on the actual sexual behaviors performed by a couple and the enjoyment and satisfaction from these behaviors, so as to be a direct measure of treatment outcome. (2) Since there are no objective standards for what is "normal," "adequate," or "functional" sexual behavior, dysfunction should be assessed in terms of a couple's satisfaction with themselves and with each other as sexual partners, rather than by comparing each partner separately to some arbitrary external standard. (3) Items in the SII should be "obvious and direct" rather than "subtle and projective," for previous research has demonstrated that obvious-direct items have higher discriminant validity and factorial purity (Thorne, 1966).

Test Format

The SII consists of a list of seventeen heterosexual behaviors. This list, adapted from Bentler's (1968) Guttman scaling of sexual behavior, covers fairly comprehensively the range of marital heterosexual behaviors, and is shown in Table 1. For each behavior, both husband and wife separately answer six questions using a response format of a 6-point rating scale with verbal labels. A sample page of the SII is shown in Fig. 1. Responses from each member of a couple are summed across all seventeen behaviors, and these totals are used to derive an eleven-scale profile, as is shown in Fig. 2. The standard score means of 50 and SDs of 10 for each scale

Table 1.   Sexual Interaction Inventory Item List

SII page number	
1.	The male seeing the female when she is nude.
2.	The female seeing the male when he is nude.
3.	The male and female kissing for one minute continuously.
4.	The male giving the female a body massage, not touching her breasts or genitals.
5.	The female giving the male a body massage, not touching his genitals.
6.	The male caressing the female's breasts with his hands.
7.	The male caressing the female's breasts with his mouth (lips or tongue).
8.	The male caressing the female's genitals with his hands.
9.	The male caressing the female's genitals with his hands until she reaches orgasm (climax).
10.	The female caressing the male's genitals with her hands.
11.	The female caressing the male's genitals with her hands until he ejaculates (has a climax).
12.	The male caressing the female's genitals with his mouth (lips or tongue).
13.	The male caressing the female's genitals with his mouth until she reaches orgasm (climax).
14.	The female caressing the male's genitals with her mouth (lips or tongue).
15.	The female caressing the male's genitals with her mouth until he ejaculates (has a climax).
16.	The male and female having intercourse.
17.	The male and female having intercourse with both of them having an orgasm (climax).

The male caressing the female's breasts with his mouth (lips or tongue).

When you and your mate engage in sexual behavior, does this particular activity usually occur? How often would you like this activity to occur?

1. Currently occurs: 2. I would like it to occur:

    1._____ Never   1._____ Never

    2._____ Rarely (10% of the time)   2._____ Rarely (10% of the time)

    3._____ Occasionally (25% of the time)   3._____ Occasionally (25% of the time)

    4._____ Fairly often (50% of the time)   4._____ Fairly often (50% of the time)

    5._____ Usually (75% of the time)   5._____ Usually (75% of the time)

    6._____ Always   6._____ Always

How pleasant do you currently find this activity to be? How pleasant do you think your mate finds this activity to be?

3. I find this activity: 4. I think my mate finds this activity:

    1._____ Extremely unpleasant   1._____ Extremely unpleasant

    2._____ Moderately unpleasant   2._____ Moderately unpleasant

    3._____ Slightly unpleasant   3._____ Slightly unpleasant

    4._____ Slightly pleasant   4._____ Slightly pleasant

    5._____ Moderately pleasant   5._____ Moderately pleasant

    6._____ Extremely pleasant   6._____ Extremely pleasant

How would you like to respond to this activity? How would you like your mate to respond? (In other words, how pleasant do you think this activity ideally should be, for you and for your mate?)

5. I would like to find this activity: 6. I would like my mate to find this
                                              activity:

    1._____ Extremely unpleasant   1._____ Extremely unpleasant

    2._____ Moderately unpleasant   2._____ Moderately unpleasant

    3._____ Slightly unpleasant   3._____ Slightly unpleasant

    4._____ Slightly pleasant   4._____ Slightly pleasant

    5._____ Moderately pleasant   5._____ Moderately pleasant

    6._____ Extremely pleasant   6._____ Extremely pleasant

Fig. 1. Sample page of the SII.

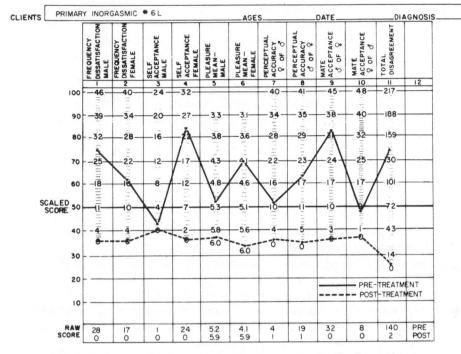

Fig. 2. Pre- and posttreatment profiles in a case of primary orgasmic dysfunction.

are based on the scores obtained by two samples totaling 124 couples who volunteered to participate in a study of marital sexuality and who reported a satisfactory sexual relationship, as described below. For illustrative purposes, the pre- and posttreatment scores for a case of primary orgasmic dysfunction are plotted in Fig. 2.

These eleven scales were chosen on the basis of clinical experience in treating dysfunctional couples. This experience indicated that issues of dissatisfaction with frequency and range of sexual behaviors engaged in, self-acceptance, pleasure obtained from sexual activity, accurate knowledge of partners' preferred sexual activities, and acceptance of partner were all crucial in determining sexual satisfaction.

Scales 1 and 2 (frequency dissatisfaction) are difference scores, derived by totaling, across all seventeen items, the differences between responses to questions 1 and 2. A high score on either of these scales, then, indicates that the person is quite dissatisfied with the range and/or frequency with which he or she engages in sexual behavior and activities.

Scales 3 and 4 (self-acceptance) are also difference scores, derived by totaling differences between responses to questions 3 and 5. High scores here indicate that the person would like to experience much more pleasure from engaging in sexual activities. In other words, this scale measures "real self–ideal self" congruence or self-acceptance.

Scales 5 and 6 (pleasure mean) are simple means of responses to question 3, across all seventeen items, and thus give a global measure of how much pleasure a person is obtaining from sexual activity. This is compared with the reference group of 124 adjusted individuals of the same sex.

Scales 7 and 8 (perceptual accuracy) measure just how accurately each person knows which particular sexual activities are pleasurable for his sexual partner. Again, these are difference scores derived by summating differences in responses to questions 3 and 4. To clarify, in scale 8, for example, the female's responses to question 3 (female's self-report of pleasure) are compared with the male's matching responses to question 4 (male's perception of female's pleasure). Obviously, high scores on these scales indicate that the sexual partners do not effectively communicate, and are likely to be quite unsatisfying to each other as sexual partners.

Scales 9 and 10 (mate acceptance) are difference scores derived from summing differences in responses to questions 4 and 6. High scores here indicate that the respondent sees his sexual partner as unresponsive or not deriving very much pleasure from sexual activity. In one sense, it measures "real partner–ideal partner" congruence. Of course, scales 9 and 10 must be interpreted configurally with scales 8 and 7, respectively. Being dissatisfied with a partner's perceived responsiveness means one thing if the perception is accurate and another if the perception is inaccurate.

Scale 11 is a summary scale, derived by totaling all the raw difference scores on the other scales. (This excludes scales 5 and 6, which are means, not difference scores.) This scale was included as a measure of the total disharmony and dissatisfaction in the sexual relationship being assessed.

When a test and its scales have been constructed on an intuitive or logical basis, as the SII was, obviously there is no a priori reason to believe it will be a reliable and valid measure. Therefore, after construction of the SII, a series of empirical investigations of its reliability and validity were undertaken.

Subjects

The sexual adjustment of four samples of married couples was assessed with the SII. Sample I ($N = 28$ couples) consisted of all clients applying to the university clinic for treatment of sexual dysfunction. Sixteen of these couples completed treatment and were again assessed with the SII at the close of treatment. Sample II ($N = 70$ couples) was obtained by depositing letters soliciting participation in a study of marital sexuality at 300 addresses scattered widely and systematically through the town of Eugene, Oregon. Sample III ($N = 78$ couples) was obtained by mailing solicitation letters to some 300 couples listed in official Eugene city records as having been married at least two but not more than six years. Sample IV ($N = 15$ couples) was obtained by advertising for subjects through notices placed on university bulletin boards. All subjects were unpaid volunteers, with the exception of subjects in sample IV, who were paid $5 for participation.

All subjects filled out the SII in the privacy of their homes, and mailed back their responses anonymously. Demographic characteristics of the subjects indicated that all of these samples were biased in the directions of being young (mean age of twenty-seven for men, twenty-six for women), well educated (mean of slightly less than four years of college), married recently (mean of four years), and having few children (mean of .7). There were no statistically significant differences between the samples on these demographic variables.

Results

Test–Retest Reliability

Subjects in sample IV were administered the SII on two occasions, separated by a two-week interval. Pearson product–moment correlations were computed for each of the eleven SII scale scores derived from this test–retest sample and are shown in Table 2. All of these correlations are significant at the .05 level or better with a sample size of fifteen.

Absolute magnitude of these correlations is not as large as one might wish. Subjects who participated in this research frequently reported that after taking the SII the first time they had perhaps their most detailed and frank discussion of their sexual relationship. Obviously, this exchange of information seems quite likely to have an effect both on the couple's sexual relationship and on their responses to a second administration of the SII. While the SII is reliable in a statistical sense, it appears to be a rather reactive test. This result is consistent with other research, indicating that merely having people keep records of their sexual activity leads to marked changes in sexual behavior (Mann, 1973).

Internal Consistency

Cronbach's α coefficient (Cronbach, 1951) for measuring internal consistency or homogeneity of a scale was computed for the SII scores obtained from sample III. These coefficients are also shown in Table 2 and indicate good internal consistency for the SII scales.

Table 2.   Test Construction Statistics

SII scale	Test–retest r	Cronbach α coefficient	Correlation with self-report of sexual satisfaction
1	.893	.886	−.296[a]
2	.652	.852	−.188[b]
3	.857	.853	−.204[b]
4	.713	.895	−.254[b]
5	.804	.920	+.207[b]
6	.891	.933	+.238[b]
7	.533	.854	+.004
8	.667	.795	−.176[b]
9	.902	.921	−.336[a]
10	.690	.901	−.127
11	.818	.881	−.350[a]

[a] $p < .01$.
[b] $p < .05$.

Convergent Validity

If the SII is a valid measure of sexual functioning, scale scores should correlate with a couple's simple self-report of sexual satisfaction. Such correlations might be expected to be rather low, however, since each scale alone measures only one of many variables that presumably all contribute to overall sexual satisfaction. Subjects in sample II were therefore asked to separately rate their overall sexual satisfaction in their marriage, on a scale from 1 (extremely unsatisfactory) to 6 (extremely satisfactory). Husbands' and wives' scores were then summed to form sexual satisfaction scores for each couple. Correlations between this sexual satisfaction score and each SII scale score were then computed and are shown in Table 2. It is to be expected, of course, that since all SII scales (except 5 and 6) are difference scores, these correlations will be negative. All correlations in Table 2 are in the predicted direction, and nine of them are significant at the .05 level or better. However, the absolute magnitude of these correlations is low, with the exception of scale 11, indicating that the traits measured by each scale separately do not bear a strong relationship to global self-rating of sexual satisfaction.

Discriminant Validity

Scores obtained by the twenty-eight sexually dysfunctional client couples (sample I) were compared with the scores obtained by the "normal," nondysfunctional couples in Sample III.* To ensure that this comparison was truly between a dysfunctional group and a "normal" group, subjects in sample III were asked to self-rate their sexual satisfaction on a scale from 1 to 6. If either the husband or the wife rated their sexual relationship as being less than 4 (slightly satisfactory), the couple was not included in this discriminant validity analysis. This procedure eliminated fifteen of the seventy-eight couples in sample III. As Table 3 indicates, nine of the eleven SII scales do discriminate client applicants from sexually satisfied couples.

Reactivity to Treatment

Sixteen of the twenty-eight client applicant couples completed a full fifteen-session course of treatment at the university clinic and were again administered the SII. Comparison of the pre- and posttreatment SII scores, as shown in Table 3, indicates that all eleven of the SII scales are reactive to treatment.

Discussion

Statistical Considerations

This research has demonstrated generally good reliability and validity for the SII. The SII scales are generally internally consistent, reliable on retest, able to

---

*Sample II is also a "normal" sample; *t*-tests indicated no significant differences between samples I and II on any of the eleven SII scales.

Table 3.   SII Validity Statistics

SII scale	1 Clients, pretreatment Mean	SD	2 Clients, posttreatment Mean	SD	3 Satisfied normals Mean	SD	4 T 1 vs. 2	5 T 1 vs. 3
1	21.11	8.03	9.88	8.73	10.87	6.73	3.57^b	6.30^c
2	20.07	6.71	8.56	7.05	10.46	6.25	5.06^c	6.82^c
3	7.19	7.48	2.00	2.13	3.89	4.27	2.65^b	2.66^b
4	15.74	9.15	7.56	7.59	6.79	5.09	2.80^b	5.98^c
5	5.16	.68	5.56	.33	5.28	.54	1.94^a	<1.00
6	4.69	.70	5.36	.43	5.11	.54	3.12^b	3.11^b
7	12.13	6.59	6.88	3.69	9.59	6.08	3.49^b	1.80^a
8	15.31	5.75	8.38	5.49	10.58	5.65	3.26^b	3.66^c
9	21.25	12.77	8.81	8.81	10.00	7.29	2.77^b	5.32^c
10	8.98	6.47	4.00	4.98	8.56	7.65	3.05^b	<1.00
11	120.79	30.08	56.07	26.39	70.57	29.26	8.64^c	6.97^c

$^a p < .05.$
$^b p < .01.$
$^c p < .001.$

discriminate clients from nonclients, reactive to treatment, and correlated with self-report of sexual adjustment.

There are a number of factors that indicate, however, that these results should be interpreted cautiously at present. Samples are relatively small, consist only of Eugene residents, and are all either volunteers for sex research or applicants for sex therapy. While ethical considerations of "informed consent" make it impossible to obtain data from a more representative sample, there are other data to suggest that volunteers for sex research are *not* a representative sample of the general populace (Kaats and Davis, 1971).

Furthermore, some of the statistical results obtained may be partially inflated by the fact that there is some partial item overlap between the various scales. There are, indeed, moderate nonsignificant correlations between most of the scales, reflecting this item overlap. Further analysis, with the goal of producing factorially pure scales, is indicated.

Clinical Utility

In addition to serving as a measure of treatment outcome, the SII has considerable diagnostic utility. The pattern of scale elevations tells the therapist just which aspects of a couple's sexual relationship are most disturbed, and thus aids in planning treatment strategy. Changes in these scale elevations following treatment function as a relevant, symptom-specific treatment-outcome measure.

Research and treatment in the area of human sexual behavior are greatly hampered by the researcher's inability to directly observe the phenomena being studied. Obviously, social mores, personal values, and ethical considerations generally make it impossible to observe people actually engaging in sexual behavior. Structured self-report inventories, such as the SII, may be the best approximation to actual behavioral observation available at the present time. It is hoped that the Sexual Interaction Inventory will aid sex researchers in obtaining meaningful, quantified data on the sexual behavior of heterosexual couples.

References

Bentler, P. M. Heterosexual behavior assessment. *Behaviour Research and Therapy*, 1968, *6*, 21–30.

Blum, G. S. A study of the psychoanalytic theory of psychosexual development. *Genetic Psychology Monographs*, 1949, *39*, 3–99.

Brady, J. P., and Levitt, E. E. The relationship of sexual preferences to sexual experience. *Psychological Record*, 1965, *15*, 377–384.

Cronbach, L. J. Coefficient alpha and the internal structure of tests. *Psychometrika*, 1951, *16*, 297–334.

Feldman, M. P., and MacCulloch, M. J. *Homosexual behavior: therapy and assessment*. New York: Pergamon, 1971.

Goldberg, L. R. A historical survey of personality scales and inventories. In McReynolds, P. (Ed.), *Advances in psychological assessment*. Palo Alto, California: Science and Behavior Books, 1971.

Kaats, G. A., and Davis, K. E. Effects of volunteer biases in studies of sexual behavior and attitudes. *Journal of Sex Research*, 1971, *7*, 26–34.

Kinsey, A. C., Pomeroy, W. B., Martin, C. E., and Gebhard, P. H. *Sexual behavior in the human female*. Philadelphia: Saunders, 1953.

Lazarus, A. A. The treatment of chronic frigidity by systematic desensitizaton. *Journal of Nervous and Mental Disease*, 1963, *136*, 272–278.

Lobitz, W. C., and LoPiccolo, J. New methods in the behavioral treatment of sexual dysfunction. *Journal of Behavior Therapy and Experimental Psychiatry*, 1972, *3*, 265–271.

LoPiccolo, J., and Lobitz, W. C. The role of masturbation in the treatment of orgasmic dysfunction. *Archives of Sexual Behavior*, 1972, *2*, 163–171.

LoPiccolo, J., and Lobitz, W. C. Behavior therapy of sexual dysfunction. In L. A. Hammerlynck, L. C. Handy, and E. J. Mash (Eds.), *Behavior change: Methodology, Concepts, and Practice*. Champaign, Illinois: Research Press, 1973. Chapter 13.

LoPiccolo, J., Stewart, R. C., and Watkins, B. Treatment of erectile failure and ejaculatory incompetence of homosexual etiology. *Journal of Behavior Therapy and Experimental Psychiatry*, 1972, *3*, 233–236.

Mann, J. The effects of erotica. *Sexual Behavior*, 1973, *3*, 23–29.

Marquis, J. N. Orgasmic reconditioning: Changing sexual object choice through controlling masturbation fantasies. *Journal of Behavior Therapy and Experimental Psychiatry*, 1970, *1*, 263–271.

Masters, W. H., and Johnson, V. E. *Human sexual inadequacy*. Boston: Little, Brown, 1970.

McGovern, K. B., Stewart, R. C., and LoPiccolo, J. Secondary orgasmic dysfunction. I. Analysis and strategies for treatment. *Archives of Sexual Behavior*, 1975, *4*(3), 265–275.

Mosher, D. L. Measurement of guilt in females by self-report inventories. *Journal of Consulting and Clinical Psychology*, 1968, *32*, 690–695.

Podell, L., and Perkins, J. C. A Guttman scale for sexual experience: A methodological note. *Journal of Abnormal Psychology*, 1957, *54*, 420–422.

Snyder, A., LoPiccolo, L., and LoPiccolo, J. Secondary orgasmic dysfunction. II. Case study. *Archives of Sexual Behavior*, 1975, *4*(3), 277–283.

Thorne, F. C. A factorial study of sexuality in adult males. *Journal of Clinical Psychology*, 1966, *22*, 378–386.

Wiggins, J. S., Wiggins, N., and Conger, J. C. Correlates of heterosexual somatic preferences. *Journal of Personality and Social Psychology*, 1968, *10*, 83–90.

Zamansky, H. S. A technique for assessing homosexual tendencies. *Journal of Personality*, 1956, *24*, 436–448.

Clinical interviews and self-report questionnaires, the focus of the two preceding chapters, both involve the patient's subjective psychological report. In contrast, this chapter reports on objective physiological measurement of sexual arousal, through plethysmographic measurement of genital blood flow. The potential utility of this psychophysiological measure in both research and treatment is examined in this chapter, and some cautionary remarks about potential misuse of such psychophysiological data are offered.

8

Uses of Psychophysiology in the Assessment and Treatment of Sexual Dysfunction

Julia R. Heiman

Sex therapists repeatedly acknowledge the extent to which an individual's thoughts and feelings facilitate or hinder physiological sexual responses (Annon, 1974, 1975; Kaplan, 1974; Masters and Johnson, 1970). A substantial amount of therapeutic time is devoted to teaching clients various forms of cognitive control. Techniques for enhancing responsiveness vary from using sensate focus to diminish the phallocentric concerns of a man experiencing erectile problems, to using fantasy to expand the erotic repertoire of a nonorgasmic woman. The central concept of such techniques is the same: to replace antisexual anxiety with sexual pleasure.

It appears that the facilitation and maintenance of sexual arousal and the thought processes associated therewith are vital, if not central, ingredients for the treatment of sexual dysfunctions. While Masters and Johnson's (1966) early work

This chapter is an expanded version of a paper presented at the American Psychological Association Meetings, Chicago, 1975. The author would like to thank Joseph LoPiccolo for his generous support and James Geer for laboratory space made available for this research. Part of this research was funded by NIMH Research Grant 5 R01 MH26631-02.

Julia R. Heiman • Long Island Research Institute; Department of Psychiatry and Behavioral Science, School of Medicine, State University of New York, Stony Brook, New York was intended to carefully specify the physiological progression of sexual arousal, *Human Sexual Response* offered only perfunctory and casual references to the subjective experiences that accompanied the 10,000 sexual cycles. As a result, we have numerically precise idea regarding the range of changes in blood pressure, heart rate, genital vasocongestion, respiration, and orgasmic contractions—but almost no idea of the range of subjective emotional experiences that accompany various phases of sexual response. While not denying the importance of physiological data, the omission of psychological correlates obviates any thorough attempt to understand the personal and shared meaning of sexuality. Given the importance of cognitive elements for successful sex therapy, research into subjective correlates of the physical experience of sex would be a contribution toward clarifying the differences between functional and dysfunctional sexuality as well as making more explicit some of the ingredients of therapeutic change.

One area of research that holds promise in this regard is psychophysiology. Psychophysiology offers a convenient method for studying sexual arousal in that both physiological and subjective responses are recorded. The physiological responses of interest include heart rate, blood pressure, temperature, muscle tension, skin conductance, and, of particular importance, penile or vaginal vasocongestion. Penile vasocongestion is typically measured with a mercury-filled or mechanical strain gauge, both of which are simple, relatively unobtrusive measures of changes in penile tumescence (Barlow, Becker, Leitenberg, and Agras, 1970; Bancroft, Jones, and Pullan, 1966). Vaginal vasocongestion can be reliably measured with a vaginal photoplethysmograph, a tamponlike acrylic tube that uses a photocell and light source to measure blood volume and pressure pulse changes in the vagina (Sintchak and Geer, 1975; Geer, Morokoff, and Greenwood, 1974). The value of genital measures is that they provide a reliable indicant of specifically sexual arousal and they can be correlated with other measures of the autonomic nervous system. In turn, all of these physiological measures can be compared with subjective responses during various erotic conditions presented in a controlled experimental setting. Such an approach provides an avenue for (a) evaluating the conditions under which a person will perceive low levels of sexual arousal, (b) discriminating the individuals and conditions that demonstrate a contradiction between subjective perceptions and physiological measures of sexual arousal, (c) identifying other affective states that correlate with an individual's feelings of how sexual a situation is for him or her, and (d) comparing functional and dysfunctional subjects on their general sexual arousability and concomitant subjective correlations.

However, the use of psychophysiology has been, at best, an isolated method in sex research. Almost exclusively a psychophysiological approach has been used to assess sexual preferences. Thus, with the penile strain gauge heterosexuals have been discriminated from homosexuals (e.g., Bancroft, 1971; Marks, Gelder, and Bancroft, 1970; Marks and Gelder, 1967; McConaghy, 1967) and from pedophiliacs (e.g., Freund, 1963, 1965, 1967), but not always with diagnostic certainty (Abel, Barlow, Blanchard, and Mavissakalian, 1975; Rosen, 1972; Henson and Rubin, 1971; Laws and Rubin, 1969). Barlow and his associates refined the genital assessment procedure into a pre–posttherapy measure for a variety of sexual preferences

(Barlow and Agras, 1973; Barlow, Reynolds, and Agras, 1973; Barlow, 1973). Barlow's work goes beyond straight physiological assessment (Barlow, 1974) and remains the most extensive psychophysiological work in clinical sex research.

Yet from the point of view of applying a psychophysiological approach to diagnosis and treatment in sex therapy, there remains a tremendous void. Only one study (Wincze, Hoon, and Hoon, 1976) has attempted to examine variables affecting sexual arousability in a dysfunctional female sample, and no research has compared arousal patterns prior to and following treatment. Though it is only recently that a female genital measure has been developed (Sintchak and Geer, 1975), a reliable male genital measure has been available for several years since sex therapy has been in vogue (Barlow et al., 1970; Bancroft et al., 1966). The following three sections discuss a rationale and procedure for exploring the potential usefulness of psychophysiology in sex therapy, with singular attention to female sexuality. A discussion of the kinds of questions appropriate for this framework is followed by a few remarks on possible uses and misuses of psychophysiological measures. Finally, some preliminary data will be presented from an ongoing study in which this author and a colleague, Patricia Morokoff, are pursuing several hypotheses regarding female sexual dysfunction.

Direction of Inquiry

It is perhaps not surprising that there has been little research to date on the mechanisms of sexual arousal among dysfunctional individuals. Certainly the overall 80–85% success rate of Masters and Johnson (1970) and others suggests that, in many cases, the treatment is effective enough to obviate the practical necessity for a more detailed examination of sexual response patterns. Nonetheless, one cannot help but be intrigued by clinical cases such as a thirty-year-old woman who has had intercourse an average of twice a week for ten years but who reports having been sexually aroused only once in her life. There is also the somewhat less frequent situation of a woman entering therapy complaining of an inability to become sexually aroused *except* through one idiosyncratic masturbatory pattern (LoPiccolo, 1977; Snyder, LoPiccolo, and LoPiccolo, 1975). Furthermore, certain dysfunctions such as secondary inorgasmic dysfunction and erectile difficulty have higher failure rates (LoPiccolo, 1977; Masters and Johnson, 1970), a fact that has engendered more armchair speculation than research investigation.

One series of questions that psychophysiology can deal with has to do with assessment of arousability. For instance, if we compare orgasmic and nonorgasmic women on their ability to become sexually aroused during fantasy and erotic films or audiotapes, are their arousal patterns different? Do nonorgasmic women show longer latency to a maximum or criterion arousal, or lower overall magnitude of arousal, or less time above a criterion response level than orgasmic women? We have no reason necessarily to expect a diminished response pattern during arousal since a number of nonorgasmic women report they can get aroused but not go beyond a certain level of high arousal. The recent Wincze et al. (1976) study deserves mention for the one attempt along these lines. Wincze and his colleagues found that women who were having difficulty experiencing orgasm did show significantly less vaginal vasocongestion, measured by a vaginal photoplethysmograph, during an erotic film than did a sexually nondysfunctional group of women. Also during the erotic stimulus, diastolic blood pressure was a discriminating measure of the two groups; the clinical sample showed increases and the nonclinical sample showed decreases on this measure. As potentially interesting as these results are, it is unfortunate that the sample size was so small ($N = 6$ for each group). A far more serious difficulty that obscures the results is the fact that the experimental design differed for the clinical and the normal subjects: The normal sample was exposed to a counterbalanced order of a neutral and a dysphoric film in addition to the erotic film, while the clinical sample saw only the erotic film. This latter point is of particular concern because of (a) the possible generalized physiological activation effect of the dysphoric stimulus and (b) the likelihood that increased time (which the normal group had) in a sex laboratory that includes genital measures may very well decrease inhibition or reduce performance anxiety, a factor of considerable importance for a sexually dysfunctional sample. Nevertheless, the Wincze et al. effort is a beginning at trying to combine psychophysiology and assessment of sexual dysfunction.

In addition to physiological arousal it is necessary to assess the degree of agreement between subjective and objective measures of sexual arousal. For instance, if a woman's vaginal vasocongestion shows a 25% increase from baseline during erotic stimulus A and a 150% increase during erotic stimulus B, yet she subjectively reports that the two stimuli were equally arousing, it is possible that she has difficulty labeling or distinguishing between different levels of sexual arousal. This would seem to support the frequent clinical observations that certain women enter therapy very unaware of their own physical responses during sexual arousal. It is also possible that a 125% change in vaginal vasocongestion is not a subjectively discernible one, a point to be illustrated later.

Generally, subjective measures of arousal have been ignored in psychophysiological studies of sex. Studying heterosexual and homosexual males, Bancroft (1971) found that correlations between erections and subjective rating of arousal were inconsistent, but the degree of correlation was clearly a function of the degree of tumescence. Greater increases in erection were associated with greater agreement between subjective and physiological sexual arousal. No comparable work with sexually dysfunctional females has been done, although Heiman's (1977) study on functional college females demonstrated that subjective rating of arousal to erotic tapes was highly correlated with one measure of vaginal vasocongestion (pulse amplitudes) but not well correlated with a second measure (blood volume). The Wincze et al. (1976) study did take subjective arousal measure on dysfunctional subjects but did not correlate them with physiological arousal. It is unfortunate that subjective correlates of physiological sexual arousal have been so neglected since it is an important area dealt with in sex therapy. By searching for patterns that show some consistent relationship between subjective and physiological sexual activity, or more generally between affective states and sexual functioning, therapists might more precisely identify and thus more effectively treat sexual problems.

An additional use of psychophysiology in assessment is to compare pre–posttreatment changes, not unlike the methodology of the work by Barlow (e.g., Barlow et al., 1973) and Bancroft (e.g., Bancroft, 1971). Applying this approach to the nonorgasmic woman would offer information about whether posttherapy sexual arousal is elevated above pretherapy arousal and, if so, whether the increase is correlated with the experience of achieving orgasm per se. Equally important, one could explore the degree to which posttherapy changes measured psychophysiologically correlate with maintenance of therapeutic improvements and sexual satisfaction in general. The presence or absence of pre–post changes in arousal patterns can be an important contribution toward understanding the effect of becoming orgasmic on the sexual response cycle, as well as providing clues to variables important to the ease of sexual arousal and the relationship between levels of sexual arousal and of sexual enjoyment.

Psychophysiology can also be directly involved in the therapeutic process. The most obvious example is that of biofeedback. For a nonorgasmic woman who claims she cannot become sexually aroused, even though her objective vaginal response to erotica indicates she does respond sexually, a feedback procedure has therapeutic potential. Just giving such a woman the information that her body is responding can be a useful beginning since she may have strong doubts about her sexual capacity. Elaborate biofeedback procedures that provide a continuous signal are also promising as adjunctive therapeutic aids. However, the generalizability of such a procedure to situations outside the experimental setting, if we take heed of earlier biofeedback work on other human physical systems (e.g., Shapiro, Tursky, Gershorn, and Stern, 1969, 1970), may depend on cognitive mediation (Weiss and Engel, 1971; Bergman and Johnson, 1971). What appears to be a conditioned involuntary response may actually be a response controlled by changes in an individual's thoughts. The best use of external monitoring of sexual arousal would seem to be as an aid in developing the individual client's own psychological–physiological feedback loop. Thus, rather than teach a woman to become sexually aroused, a psychophysiological method might teach her to be more subjectively aware of the physical changes that occur during arousal, and to label those changes "sexual."

Hoon, Wincze, and Hoon (in press) have looked at biofeedback of vaginal vasocongestion in two sexually functional women. They found that biofeedback, using a continuous visual feedback signal plus fantasy, and the knowledge of the target response (vaginal vasocongestion) produced vaginal blood volume (VBV) increases in both subjects. Fantasy without biofeedback or knowledge of the target response produced VBV in one subject. Interestingly, this subject also showed greater response during fantasy alone than during the biofeedback condition. This suggests what may be obvious: that for some women, biofeedback (and/or knowledge of the target response) does not optimize but instead detracts from maximum sexual arousal. Many sex therapists would predict just that, since the tendencies to watch and continuously monitor arousal are believed to be contributors to several male and female sexual dysfunctions (Annon, 1975; Kaplan, 1974; Masters and Johnson, 1970). Further exploration of this and other clinical assumptions could be made by a psychophysiological study that varied the modality of feedback since visual feedback may be especially distracting. Fantasies and erotica could be studied under biofeedback and no biofeedback conditions, to examine the extent to which biofeedback (self-monitoring) might enhance or detract from sexual arousal and enjoyment.

Limitations of Psychophysiology

An assessment of treatment program on sexual dysfunction which relied exclusively on laboratory psychophysiological procedures would clearly be in-adequate. This is true for several reasons: (a) The extent to which any pre–post-therapy plethysmographic changes have external validity to patterns outside of the laboratory has not yet been tested. The laboratory is an admittedly artificial and restricted setting. Recent modifications of the vaginal photoplethysmograph system (Sarrel, Foddy, and McKinnon, 1977) hold some promise of reducing the external validity problem. Sarrel et al. have developed the use of a small portable cassette recorder to take continuous measurement of vaginal blood volume while a woman is in her own home. A comparable degree of privacy should be possible for measurement of men's genital vasocongestion but as yet no such alternative has been developed. (b) There are obviously important issues in sex therapy that in-fluence and extend beyond a person's specific sexual response pattern. Relationship problems are a prime and frequent example (McGovern, Stewart, and LoPiccolo, 1975; Kaplan, 1974). Individual attitudes about sex and sex roles can also be important to therapeutic progress. (c) Further cautions regarding the use of psychophysiology concern the assumptions surrounding the genital devices. It seems to be both an advantage and a disadvantage that we can label a vaginal photoplethysmograph "an objective measure." Physiological measurement is advantageous because it is a valid, reliable indicant of a specifically sexual re-sponse (vaginal vasocongestion) that allows an investigator to go beyond exclusive reliance on subjective report. The major disadvantage is that the genital measures are often regarded as the only source of "truth" about sexual response. As tempting as this assumption might be, there is no a priori reason to assume that a disagree-ment between levels of subjective and physiological arousal necessarily means that the individual's subjective perception is incorrect. It may indicate that the arousal level is actually too low to detect for a particular individual. It is quite likely that sexual arousal thresholds differ from person to person and that, as Bancroft (1971) found, below a certain level of physical response almost everyone will have difficulty labeling his/her own arousal. Alternatively, subjective and objective measures may disagree because subjects choose not to subjectively acknowlege physical arousal to an erotic stimulus that she/he does not like or enjoy. Just as humans intentionally ignore other physiological events, such as pain or discomfort, individuals are likely to do the same thing, under certain conditions, with sexual arousal.

In spite of the above limitations, psychophysiology offers a viable methodology for dealing with cases where the facilitation and maintenance of sexual arousal is a major therapeutic issue. Psychophysiology permits one of the few controlled settings in which sexual arousal to a variety of sexual contents and stimulus modes can be assessed, without the person being directly observed during sexual activities. It is also a unique opportunity to study correlations between the cognitive and physiological responses in sexually functional versus sexually dysfunctional individuals.

One Approach and Some Preliminary Data

Out of interest in which variables might discriminate between orgasmic and nonorgasmic women, psychophysiological study is currently in progress which is directed at several questions about sexual arousal patterns, three of which are relevant here: (1) Do women who are orgasmic show different sexual arousal patterns than infrequently orgasmic women in response to erotic stimuli in a laboratory setting? (2) Are there consistent differences in subjective correlates of sexual arousal between orgasmic and infrequently orgasmic women? (3) If primary inorgasmic women are tested before and after successful therapy, and thus before and after their first orgasm experience, will these women demonstrate increased sexual responsiveness on the posttest?

To investigate these questions, volunteer subjects were selected from Long Island communities to make up a sexually functional sample of forty women, and a sexually dysfunctional sample was gathered from those women who were prospective clients at the Sex Therapy Clinic at the State University of New York at Stony Brook. The entire procedure was explained to each woman before she decided to participate.

Subjects were asked to fill out a 200-question sexual history questionnaire and to participate in two one-hour experimental sessions in which they would be exposed to tapes and films with explicitly sexual content. The design of the experimental sessions was as follows: Following a five-minute baseline, subjects were asked to fantasize ("imagine a sexual scene"); they then listened to an erotic tape, fantasized again, saw an erotic film, and fantasized a final time. The entire procedure lasted approximately forty-five minutes, with three three-minute fantasies, a seven-to-nine-minute tape and film, and five-minute periods after each tape, film, and fantasy condition. A vaginal photoplethysmograph monitored vaginal pressure pulse and blood volume continuously. Subjective response forms were completed immediately following each fantasy, tape, and film. The two experimental sessions were fifteen weeks apart and were identical in content. However, after the second session was completed a second film was shown to test responses to a novel erotic stimulus.

The dependent measure was vaginal pulse amplitude rather than vaginal blood volume. Recent work by this author has strongly suggested that pulse amplitude is a more valid indicator of sexual arousal, demonstrating better correlations to the subjective reports of sexually functional females (Heiman, 1976, 1977).

A preliminary analysis has been done on the first portion of the data. The dysfunctional (clinical) sample at this point is small ($N = 6$) so any statements regarding this group are of a very tentative nature. Forty percent of the data on the sexually functional (nonclinical) subjects has also been analyzed. This sample will be discussed in more detail because of a more substantial N (16), and because it is this group against whom the clinical data will be compared.

The median age was 30.6 years (range: 27–38) for the clinical sample and 30.1 years (range: 20–44) for the nonclinical sample. All of the nonclinical sample was orgasmic. The clinical sample was equally divided between primary and secondary inorgasmic dysfunction.

Looking at the vaginal pulse amplitude response for the *nonclinical* subjects, there were several interesting patterns (Figure 1). A repeated measures analysis of variance, which statistically compared physiological response during the tape, film, and fantasy conditions, was highly significant across both sessions [$F(5, 75) =$ 19.69, $p < .001$]. Figure 1 suggests that the film was the most effective arousal facilitator with tapes being somewhat more effective than fantasy. This result is not conclusive, since the tape always preceded the film and the counterbalanced subjects were not included in this preliminary analysis. However, women in both groups rated the film as more arousing than the tape, a finding that agrees with the Abel et al. (1975) study already mentioned. Fantasy itself seemed to be strongly affected by the external audio or visual erotic stimuli; a one-way analysis of variance on fantasy alone showed a significant difference among the fantasies, with a post hoc comparison that showed vaginal pulse amplitude during the third (postfilm) fantasy to be significantly greater than during the other two fantasies. Additionally, even though the absolute level of fantasy arousal decreased slightly during Session II, the Fantasy factor was still significant [$F(2, 30) = 8.36, p = .022$]; in fact, it accounted for a greater percentage of the variance (21% vs. 13%) during Session II than during Session I (ω^2, Hays, 1963).

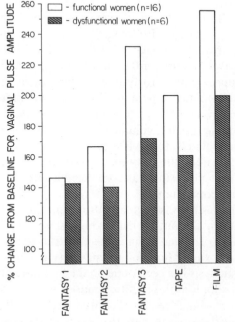

Fig. 1. Vaginal pulse amplitude response during fantasies, tape, and film for sexually functional and dysfunctional subjects (Session I).

The *clinical* subjects showed physiological response patterns that were similar to nonclinical subjects during each of the conditions of Session I (Figure 1). An ANOVA testing the effects of the tape, film, and fantasies was significant [$F(4, 20) = 7.83, p < .001$], with greater arousal occurring during the film. Though the third fantasy appears to show a stronger response, testing for a Fantasy effect showed significance only at the .06 level. In general, the pattern of physiological sexual arousal during the various conditions was more similar than dissimilar when clinical and nonclinical subjects were compared. However, the absolute level of arousal across all conditions was somewhat lower in the clinical sample. As more dysfunctional subjects are added to the clinical sample, it will be more interesting to see if this difference becomes a significant one, and if primary inorgasmic women show lower maximum arousal than secondary inorgasmic women.

The degree of agreement between subjective report of sexual arousal and physiological arousal was also examined. It was expected that clinical subjects would show lower correlations during all conditions, particularly during fantasy, in which a subject has no external stimulus to possibly help verify her arousal level (see Heiman, 1977). Surprisingly, clinical and nonclinical subjects demonstrated a similar lack of subjective–physiological agreement during the fantasies of Session I. The only exception to this finding was also contrary to our expectations: For nonclinical subjects, verbal and genital responses were significantly *negatively* correlated on the second fantasy ($r = -.50, p < .05$). Two possible explanations for this lack of agreement are that (a) it may be more difficult to get strong correlations when physical response is comparatively low-level (cf. Bancroft, 1971), and (b) verbal responses were restricted to a small 5-point range. However, there was significant positive subjective–physiological agreement for nonclinical subjects during the tape ($r = .68, p < .01$) and film ($r = .54, p < .05$) of Session I. Although the correlations for the clinical group were of comparable magnitude and direction, ($r = .63, r = .57$, respectively) they were not significant, probably because of the limited sample size. Apparently, higher levels of arousal and the presence of an external erotic stimulus were more likely to result in agreement between physiological and subjective ratings of sexual arousal. This so far seems to be the case for both the clinical and the nonclinical women.

Looking at Figure 1, it is unclear whether higher arousal levels or the presence of an erotic stimulus might be the more important variable in contributing to better agreement between subjective and physiological sexual arousal. Generally higher arousal levels occurred during the tape or film. However, the fact that there was greater physical arousal during the third fantasy than during the tape suggests that an external erotic stimulus may have the greater influence on the subjective labeling of how aroused a woman feels. This supports other research that concluded that women may require some form of external validation in order to acknowledge or perhaps admit to sexual arousal (Heiman, 1977).

Alternatively, there may be a third variable outweighing the other two: The physical arousal during *all* conditions may have been essentially too low to perceive. Subjects may then evaluate their arousal on a purely cognitive dimension (i.e., how aroused their thoughts are or should be) rather than evaluate themselves on a physical dimension. Under such conditions, more sexual arousal would be reported during the presentation of erotic materials than during a self-generated fantasy primarily because sustained attention to obviously explicit materials makes it easier to define the experience as sexual.

Finally, Figure 2 illustrates the kind of results possible in the pre–post therapy design. One of the dysfunctional subjects, a twenty-eight-year-old woman, married with two children, reported that she could remember being sexually aroused on only two occasions. She had never experienced orgasm nor attempted masturbation. During Session I of the experimental procedure, her physiological response was notably lower than the normal sample during the tape, film, and fantasy conditions (Figure 2). During fifteen weeks of therapy she became orgasmic in masturbation. At posttest, her vaginal response during the first two fantasies was much stronger, roughly an additional 80% above baseline, as was her response to the tape, an additional 42% above baseline. Her subjective responses during the various conditions showed little relationship to her vaginal response. She rated the tape and film as equally arousing on Session I even though her physiological data showed 70% more response from baseline during the film than during the tape. More perplexing, on Session II (after therapy), she rated Film 2 as most arousing, whereas her genital response showed less arousal on this film than on all other conditions.

It should be noted that this case is not necessarily typical of all primary inorgasmic women, either in pre- or posttherapy sexual arousal patterns. For this

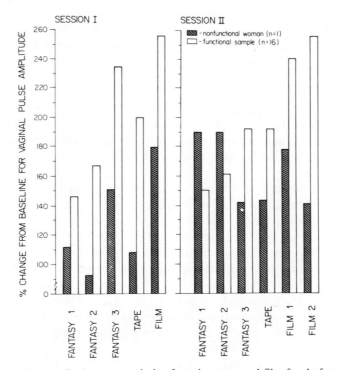

Fig. 2. Vaginal pulse amplitude response during fantasies, tape, and film for dysfunctional subject and functional sample (Sessions I and II).

particular person, however, it appears that she was more physically responsive, particularly during fantasy, following therapy. This increased arousal during the second exposure to erotica is a notable contrast with the decreased arousal for the sexually functional sample. Decreased arousal was expected, given the fact the erotic materials were presented twice, and a certain amount of habituation was predicted. However, this woman's subjective labels still contradicted her physiological arousal. Exploring possible factors involved in this discrepancy is a fascinating area for future research. One wonders, for instance, if personal criteria of sexual arousal vary across stimuli conditions and/or across individuals. A more continuous measure of subjective arousal would better identify at what levels of sexual arousal subjective–physiological correlations are strongest, and what percentage increases in physical arousal are subjectively discriminable.

Conclusion

Certainly, results from psychophysiology give new meaning to Hayakawa's (1973) remark that the "erotic is inextricably bound up with the semantic" (p. 407). The erotic is also bound up with affective and imaginal experience. By sorting out relationships that describe the physical manifestations of cognitive processes, a substantial contribution to understanding functional and dysfunctional sexuality might be made. At this point we have no clear idea of the extent to which the cognitive–affective experience is independent from the physiological experience of sexual arousal. It is imperative not to rush into a therapeutic approach such as genital biofeedback before we have a better grasp of patterns and individual perceptions of sexual arousal. Teaching a woman to "correctly" label vaginal response seems to be at best shortsighted, at worst clinically and scientifically negligent, if we have no idea which factors influence the lack of subjective–physiological agreement. Exploring this discrepancy, rather than racing to change it, could very possibly give us the greater amount of insight about human sexuality.

In addition, as Kaplan (1974) has pointed out, certain sexual dysfunctions can be classified as a category of psychosomatic disorders. It is thus reasonable to expect that studying the variables involved in the facilitation of sexual arousal will contribute to psychosomatic areas beyond that of sexual response.

References

Abel, G., Barlow, D., Blanchard, E., and Mavissakalian, M. Measurement of sexual arousal in male homosexuals: Effects of instructions and stimulus modality. *Archives of Sexual Behavior*, 1975, *4*, 623–630.

Annon, J. *The behavioral treatment of sexual problems, Vols. 1 and 2: Brief therapy*. Honolulu: Kapiolani Health Services, 1974, 1975.

Bancroft, J. The application of psychophysiological measures to the assessment-modification of sexual behavior. *Behaviour Research and Therapy*, 1971, *8*, 119–130.

Bancroft, J., Jones, H. G., and Pullan, B. T. A simple transducer for measuring penile erection with comments on its use in the treatment of sexual disorders. *Behaviour Research and Therapy*, 1966, *4*, 239–241.

Barlow, D. Increasing heterosexual responsiveness in the treatment of sexual deviation: A review of the clinical and experimental evidence. *Behavior Therapy*, 1973, *4*, 665–671.

Barlow, D. The treatment of sexual deviation: Toward a comprehensive behavioral approach. In K. Calhoun, H. Adams, and K. Mitchell (Eds.), *Innovative treatment methods in psychopathology.* New York: John Wiley & Sons, 1974.

Barlow, D., and Agras, W. Failing to increase heterosexual responsiveness in homosexuals. *Journal of Applied Behavior Analysis*, 1973, *6*, 355–366.

Barlow, D, Becker, R., Leitenberg, and Agras, W. A mechanical strain gauge for recording penile circumference change. *Journal of Applied Behavior Analysis*, 1970, *3*, 73–76.

Barlow, D., Reynolds, J., and Agras, W. Gender identity change in a transsexual. *Archives of General Psychiatry*, 1973, *28*, 569–576.

Bergman, J., and Johnson, H. The effects of instructional set and autonomic perception on cardiac control. *Psychophysiology*, 1971, *8*, 180–190.

Freund, K. A laboratory method for diagnosing predominance of homo- and hetero-erotic interest in the male. *Behaviour Research and Therapy*, 1963, *1*, 85–93.

Freund, K. Diagnosing heterosexual pedophilia by means of a test for sexual interest. *Behaviour Research and Therapy*, 1965, *3*, 229–234.

Freund, K. Diagnosing homo- and heterosexuality and erotic age preference by means of a psycho-physiological test. *Behavior Research and Therapy*, 1967, *5*, 209–228.

Geer, J., Morokoff, P., and Greenwood P. Sexual arousal in women: The development of a measurement device for vaginal blood volume. *Archives of Sexual Behavior*, 1974, *3*, 559–564.

Hayakawa, S. I. Semantics and sexuality. In E. Morrison and V. Borosage (Eds.), *Human sexuality: Contemporary perspectives.* Palo Alto: National Press Books, 1973.

Hays, W. L. *Statistics.* New York: Holt, Rinehart & Winston, 1963.

Heiman, J. R. Issues in the use of psychophysiology to assess female sexual dysfunction. *Journal of Sex and Marital Therapy*, 1976, *2*, 197–204.

Heiman, J. R. A psychophysiological exploration of sexual arousal patterns in females and males. *Psychophysiology*, 1977, *14*, 266–274.

Henson, D., and Rubin, H. Voluntary control of eroticism. *Journal of Applied Behavior Analysis*, 1971, *4*, 37–44.

Hoon, P., Wincze, J. and Hoon, E. The effects of biofeedback and cognitive mediation upon vaginal blood volume. *Behavior Therapy*, in press.

Kaplan, H. *The new sex therapy.* New York: Brunner/Mazel, 1974.

Laws, D., and Rubin, H. Instructional control of an autonomic sexual response. *Journal of Applied Behavioral Analysis*, 1969, *2*, 93–99.

LoPiccolo, J. Direct treatment of sexual dysfunction in the couple. In J. Money and H. Musaph (Eds.), *Handbook of sexology.* Amsterdam: Excerpta Medica, 1977.

Marks, I. M., and Gelder, M. G. Transvestism and fetishism: Clinical and psychological changes during faradic aversion. *British Journal of Psychiatry*, 1967, *113*, 711–729.

Marks, I. M., Gelder, M. G., and Bancroft, J. Sexual deviance two years after elective aversion. *British Journal of Psychiatry*, 1970, *117*, 173–185.

Masters, W. H., and Johnson, V. E. *Human sexual response.* Boston: Little, Brown, 1966.

Masters, W. H., and Johnson, V. E. *Human sexual inadequacy.* Boston: Little, Brown, 1970.

McConaghy, N. Penile volume change to moving pictures of male and female nudes in heterosexual and homosexual males. *Behaviour Research and Therapy*, 1967, *5*, 43–48.

McGovern, K., Stewart, R., and LoPiccolo, J. Secondary orgasmic dysfunction. I. Analysis and strategies for treatment. *Archives of Sexual Behavior*, 1975, *4* (3), 265–275.

Rosen, R. *Feedback effects on the suppression of an elicited autonomic response: Penile tumescence.* Unpublished doctoral dissertation, Stony Brook, 1972.

Sarrel, P., Foddy, J., and McKinnon, J. Investigation of human sexual response using a cassette recorder. *Archives of Sexual Behavior*, 1977, *6*, 341–348.

Shapiro, D., Tursky, B., Gershorn, E., and Stern, M. Effects of feedback and reinforcement on the control of human systolic blood pressure. *Science*, 1969, *163*, 588–590.

Shapiro, D., Tursky, B., Gershorn, E., and Stern, M. Differentiation of heart rate and systolic blood pressure in man by operant conditioning. *Psychosomatic Medicine*, 1970, *32*, 417–432.

Sintchak, G., and Geer, J. A vaginal photoplethysmograph system. *Psychophysiology*, 1975, *12* (1), 113–115.

Snyder, A., LoPiccolo, L., and LoPiccolo, J. Secondary orgasmic dysfunction. II. Case study. *Archives of Sexual Behavior*, 1975, *4* (3), 277–283.

Weiss, T., and Engel, B. Operant conditioning of heart rate in patients with premature ventricular contractions. *Psychosomatic Medicine*, 1971, *23*, 301–321.

Wincze, V., Hoon, E., and Hoon, P. A comparison of the physiological responsivity of normal and sexually dysfunctional women during exposure to erotic stimulus. *Journal of Psychosomatic Research*, 1976, *20*, 44–50.

In any case of sexual dysfunction, a major assessment issue is the evaluation of a possible physiological basis for the dysfunction. Obviously, the psychological procedures of sex therapy cannot be expected to reverse actual physical pathology. One very common assessment issue is the question of whether a man with erectile impotence is physiologically capable of achieving an erection. Until very recently, sex therapists had to rely on indirect assessment of erectile capability. Typically, neurological, hormonal, and blood studies would be performed, but the results were often ambiguous. Psychological screening also has not been able to differentiate functional and organic impotence with certainty. Recently, however, it has been discovered that penile erection is one component of rapid-eye-movement (REM) sleep in physiologically intact males. Subsequently, monitoring of nocturnal penile tumescence has been shown to be a means of accurately evaluating erectile capability. In this article, Karacan describes the use of techniques to measure nocturnal penile tumescence in order to make the differential diagnosis of functional and organic erectile impotence.

9

Advances in the Psychophysiological Evaluation of Male Erectile Impotence

Ismet Karacan

Introduction

The diagnosis of male erectile impotence (a persistent inability to effect satisfactory vaginal penetration) has until recently remained one of the less advanced aspects of the study and treatment of sexual dysfunction. In fact, it has essentially remained an art, and methods of treating impotence have now surpassed methods of diagnosis in sophistication and specificity. The major purpose of this chapter is to describe an updated diagnostic procedure for male impotence. This procedure is recommended for its comprehensiveness and for its inclusion of both an *objective* technique of differential diagnosis and evaluations designed to determine the pathogenesis of erectile failure.

The Traditional Diagnostic Procedure and Its Limitations

Most authorities on impotence have recommended a two-phased procedure for differentially diagnosing psychogenic and organogenic impotence: (1) physical

Ismet Karacan • Sleep Disorders Center, Department of Psychiatry, Baylor College of Medicine, Houston, Texas

examination for evidence of conditions known to be associated with impotence, and (2) examination of the history for signs of psychogenic impotence—rapid onset, transitory occurrence, selective occurrence (i.e., with one but not with another partner), occurrence of some sexual response (spontaneous, masturbatory, or morning erections).

There are a number of limitations to this procedure:

1. It is systematically and comprehensively implemented only rarely. The component examinations, if they are performed at all, are often superficial at best. The "halo effect" is frequently the primary basis for diagnosis. For example, the patient who has a condition in which the prevalence of impotence is high (e.g., diabetes, multiple sclerosis, spinal cord injury) is usually assumed to have organogenic impotence that is related to that condition and little is done to obtain definitive support for this hypothesis.

2. The accuracy of diagnosis for organogenic impotence is questionable because direct scientific information on the pathophysiology of organogenic impotence is very limited and the physician must rely on information that has been derived largely from unsystematic clinical studies or observations.

3. The accuracy of diagnosis for psychogenic impotence is questionable because in practice any patient who has no gross physical disorder or injury typically receives that diagnosis (diagnosis by exclusion); because, although the so-called historical signs of psychogenic impotence make intuitive and theoretical sense, they have not been tested against independent criteria; and because the historical data that form the basis for the diagnosis are subjective and therefore potentially inaccurate.

4. There is no provision for direct observation of the patient's erections, so structural abnormalities or inaccurate descriptions of erectile capacity cannot be detected.

5. Although a "cause" of impotence may be stated, there is usually no systematic attempt to isolate the pathogenesis of the complaint.

When methods of managing and treating impotence were limited in variety and effectiveness, inaccurate differential diagnosis and the failure to investigate pathogenesis had relatively few serious repercussions. But now, the availability of various medical, surgical, psychiatric, psychological, and behavioral methods of treatment creates compelling ethical and medicolegal reasons for systematic use of a more comprehensive and reliable diagnostic procedure.

Objective Differential Diagnosis of Impotence

The first step in a comprehensive diagnostic evaluation is differential diagnosis by assessment of nocturnal penile tumescence (NPT). NPT occurs in all healthy boys and men, but its characteristics vary somewhat as a function of age (Karacan, Williams, Thornby, and Salis, 1975; Karacan, Salis, Thornby, and Williams, 1976). In adults, nocturnal erectile episodes typically occur every 90–100 minutes during sleep, last an average of 20–40 minutes, and are closely associated with rapid-eye-movement (REM) sleep, the phase of sleep that is characterized by autonomic activation and dreaming. Although NPT and dreams often occur at the same time, there is no evidence that NPT is consistently related to sexual dreams. Both REM sleep and NPT are more prominent in the later than in the earlier portion of a normal night of sleep. Men may notice erections on awakening in the morning because they have awakened from REM-related NPT, *not* because bladder pressure stimulates erection.

The working assumptions in the use of NPT for differential diagnosis are that in a man who complains of impotence but who has normal NPT for his age, impotence is psychogenic, whereas in a man who complains of impotence and who has abnormal NPT for his age (reduced total amount and especially reduced amount of full NPT), impotence is organogenic. These assumptions have been derived from study of the NPT characteristics of over 2,000 healthy men and 300 impotent patients (Karacan, Scott, Salis, Attia, Ware, Altinel, and Williams, 1977; Fisher, Schiavi, Lear, Edwards, Davis, and Witkins, 1975). Follow-up evaluations to locate the pathology have been performed in many of the patients and so far there has been no evidence that the working assumptions are incorrect.

Comprehensive NPT Differential Diagnosis Procedure

A full NPT evaluation is most easily performed in a sleep laboratory or clinic.* At our facility, the patient is required to spend three consecutive nights in the Sleep Disorders Center. On his initial visit, a complete medical history is taken and the patient receives a thorough general physical examination. Throughout each evaluation night, three EEG channels (frontal, central, parietal), two eye-movement channels (EOG), and two erection channels are monitored on a polygraph. The EEG and EOG channels provide information that allows assessment of both the quantity and the quality of the patient's sleep: If sleep is abnormally brief or poorly organized in terms of the different sleep stages, the NPT data cannot be confidently interpreted because the probability of false negative results (i.e., little NPT because of poor sleep) is high.

Changes in penile circumference are monitored by means of two mercury-filled strain gauges (Karacan, 1959) that are positioned around the penis. One gauge is placed at the base of the penis and one at the tip, just caudal to the glans. Changes in penile circumference are reflected directly by calibrated baseline deflections on the polygraph tracing. In Figure 1, A and B show schematic representations of the two types of NPT episodes, full and partial. In these episodes, circumference change is typically larger (up to three times) at the base of the penis than at the tip. C and D illustrate why two gauges are always used. In C, there is too great a discrepancy between base and tip circumference changes and although erection is sufficient at the base it is insufficient at the tip. In D, the tip is sufficiently erect but the base is not. Both anomalies may indicate structural defects or disease processes, and both may hamper satisfactory vaginal penetration.

On the third evaluation night, three special procedures are performed for patients who have exhibited at least some erectile response on the first two nights.

---

*Addresses available from William C. Dement, M.D., Ph.D., President, Association of Sleep Disorders Centers, Stanford University, 780 Welch Road, Suite 203, Palo Alto, California 94304.

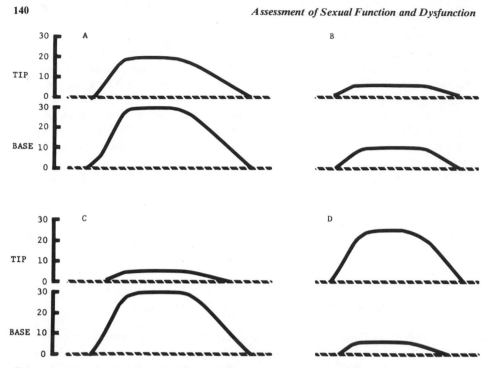

Fig. 1. Schematic representations of penis tip and base circumference changes for normal full (A), normal partial (B), and anomalous (C, D) NPT episodes. Vertical deflections from baseline (flaccid circumference; broken line) represent calibrated changes (mm) in penile circumference. Abscissa represents time.

Before monitoring begins, data from the first two nights are inspected so that we have an estimate of the circumference change that characterizes the patient's largest erection and the time during the night when this erection occurs. Because these values are relatively stable from night to night, we can predict with reasonable accuracy when on the third night the patient will experience his fullest erection. When this erection occurs, the patient is awakened. He and the examiner first estimate the fullness of the erection on a scale of 0–100%; for the patient, this estimate is made with reference to his premorbid experience. Next, a specially designed pressure device is used to measure the force required to make the patient's erect penis buckle. Finally, the erect penis is photographed with a special camera that allows exact measurement of penile dimensions from the photograph.

The measurement of buckling pressure is a method of estimating penile rigidity and is the most important of the third-night procedures. Degree of rigidity is obviously the characteristic of an erection that most directly determines whether or not the erection is effective for vaginal penetration. Until recently, there was no satisfactory means of measuring degree of rigidity. When we were studying healthy men, this limitation was relatively minor because in such men there is generally a very close relation between rigidity and circumference. But in impotent patients, whose main complaint concerns defective rigidity, it is imperative to measure this characteristic directly. The present method is still not ideal, for only a few isolated measurements are possible and the patient must be awakened to make them. Nevertheless, the rigidity measure becomes an integral part of the final decision-making process. Several devices that measure rigidity continuously and without disturbing the sleeping patient are now being developed. When they prove to be reliable and valid, then the continuous measure of rigidity will in all probability supplant the measure of circumference change in importance.

The estimate of degree of erection is helpful because it indicates the accuracy of the patient's perception of his erectile response. An estimate that varies greatly from that of the examiner is a signal that psychological factors may cause the patient to under- or overestimate his degree of erection and may thereby contribute in various ways to his complaint.

The photograph provides permanent information on the appearance of the patient's erect penis. Sometimes it reveals structural defects or disease processes that may not be detected in examination of the flaccid penis. In addition, if the patient ultimately undergoes surgery for implantation of a penile prosthesis, the photograph provides information to the surgeon both about such abnormalities and about the size of the required prosthesis.

At the completion of the NPT evaluation, the objective in assessing the data is to categorize the patient as having normal, abnormally diminished, or absent NPT. First, the circumference change value that corresponds to a penile rigidity measure of 100 mm Hg is estimated by considering the actual rigidity reading in ratio with the circumference change that characterized the penis when the reading was made. Our research indicates that erections that resist buckling with pressures greater than 100 mm Hg can definitely be effective erections, whereas erections that buckle with pressures up to that amount can be ineffective. The circumference change value that is so estimated becomes, in the classification of the patient's NPT episodes, the division point between full erections and partial erections. Once the episodes have been classified, further computations produce the total amounts, average lengths, and frequencies of the two types of episodes. Data from the second evaluation night receive the greatest weight at this stage. Data from the first night are given less weight because atypical sleep and NPT patterns often occur as part of a "first-night effect"; data from the third night are not used because of the disturbing effect of the deliberate awakenings. The second-night data are compared to normative data from persons of ages comparable to that of the patient and the final categorization is made.

NPT Screening Procedure

The development of a portable unit* that monitors changes in penile circumference makes it possible for any physician to perform an NPT screen in an office, hospital, or patient's home. Although this NPT screen cannot include every aspect of the clinic evaluation (e.g., monitoring of sleep patterns, systematic measurement of penile rigidity), it can, if performed with care, be a fast and efficient way of ob-

*Available from American Medical Systems, Inc., 6500 Olson Memorial Highway, Golden Valley, Minnesota 55427.

taining information on the probable nature of the patient's complaint (psychogenic or organogenic) and guide further explorations of the problem. Ideally, monitoring should be performed throughout several nights. If at all possible, some attempt should be made to assess penile rigidity during an NPT episode and to obtain the patient's estimate of the degree of erection and a photograph of the erect penis. Certain precautions must be taken to assure that the NPT data are reliable. For monitoring in an office or a hospital, the physician should be sure that the patient's sleep is not induced by drugs and that it is reasonably satisfactory in terms of quantity and quality. Attention to the drugs is especially necessary in a hospital, where hypnotics are routinely given to many patients. Most hypnotics and other psychoactive medications suppress REM sleep to at least some degree and this effect might also generalize to REM-related NPT. Particularly for patients with spinal cord injuries, the physician should determine whether or not NPT episodes are related to spasms; if all NPT episodes are related to spasms, it is likely that the patient can experience only reflex erections. Monitoring in the patient's home is the least satisfactory method because there is little or no control over the placement of the strain gauges, the calibration of the NPT monitor, the drug status of the patient, or the quantity and quality of the patient's sleep. If home monitoring is to be done, the physician must first be sure that the patient has no reason to consciously or unconsciously sabotage the recording and has been fully instructed in the recording procedures.

Use of the circumference change data from the portable unit necessitates the assumption that the circumference of the penis is a reliable index of its degree of rigidity. This assumption is valid for about 90% of patients, but the physician should make the assessment of penile rigidity so that its validity for the patient under study can be established. In evaluating the circumference change data, the first step is to determine whether or not NPT is present. If it is not present, the patient is classified as having absent NPT. If it is present, the physician should next evaluate the total amount of NPT and the relative amounts of full and partial NPT. A reliable rule of thumb for the typical patient is as follows: A circumference change on the penis tip of 1 cm or more indicates a full erection, while a circumference change of up to 1 cm indicates partial (i.e., insufficiently rigid) erection. Finally, the cyclicity of the NPT episodes should be evaluated. A patient is classified as having abnormally diminished NPT if his NPT is exclusively or predominantly partial or if the total amount of NPT is abnormally low for his age. An irregular NPT cycle suggests the operation during the recording period of some extraneous factor that has rendered the data invalid. Among the most likely possibilities are drugs that affect REM sleep and abnormal or disturbed sleep patterns. If NPT cycles are irregular, additional recordings should be made under more controlled conditions.

Other Components of the Diagnostic Procedure

The admission medical history and physical examination are, of course, important aspects of the diagnostic procedure and should be very carefully done. In our experience, they are often superficial. For example, we have found obvious deposits of Peyronie's plaque in several patients; these deposits had not been discovered by the numerous urologists that the patients had previously consulted.

The results of the NPT evaluation serve as a guide for the types of evaluations that constitute the remainder of the diagnostic procedure. If NPT is abnormal, then each of the procedures listed below should be performed. If NPT is normal, then the medical procedures may be deleted.

Medical

1. Urological examination (external genitalia, bladder function).
2. Neurological examination (especially for signs of trauma and neuropathy).
3. Endocrinological examination (especially for testosterone levels).
4. Vascular examination of pelvic area (especially for penile blood pressure and pulse).

Psychiatric/Psychological

1. Social and sexual history (sexual history independently from patient and his sexual partner).
2. Evaluation for psychopathology.
3. Evaluation for psychological causes of or contributors to impotence.
4. Assessment of prognosis for psychological and social adjustment if treatment is successful.

Assessment of bladder function in the urological examination is important for the information it provides on the integrity of lumbar and sacral neural function. The neurological examination should also focus on these two regions. Testosterone is often routinely administered to impotent men, despite the fact that most have normal testosterone levels and the efficacy of the treatment for such patients has not been unequivocally demonstrated. The endocrine examination should be performed so that the rare patient with endocrine dysfunction can be identified. The vascular examination is performed because pelvic vascular insufficiency may contribute to erectile dysfunction; it should include systemic and penile readings. Penile arterial pressures can be measured with a special ultrasonic device and should be taken on the dorsum, at the base and tip of the flaccid penis, along the midline, and on the right and left sides. Pressures that are consistently less than brachial pressure suggest vascular insufficiency (Abelson, 1975).

The psychiatric/psychological examination is recommended for every patient, regardless of the suspected type of impotence. It is important to recognize that the existence of identifiable psychopathology does not necessarily indicate the existence of a psychological cause of impotence (Beutler, Karacan, Anch, Salis, Scott, and Williams, 1975; Beutler, Scott, and Karacan, 1976; Cooper, 1969; Derogotis, 1976). Therefore, these two aspects of the clinical picture should receive separate consideration. The derivation of a prognosis for psychological and social adjustment should focus on the effects on both the patient and his sexual partner of the restoration of potency. It may be that either or both people have too great an investment in the patient's impotence for a satisfactory relationship ever to be fully restored. When surgical implantation of a prosthesis is a potential mode of treatment, special attention should be paid to the effect on the patient's self-concept of restoration of potency by artificial means and of at least some irrevocable destruction of physiological potential for a normal erection. For some patients, implantation of a prosthesis damages the body image too much for successful adjustment to be achieved.

These various evaluations have the primary function of uncovering evidence of the pathogenesis of impotence. If one of the routine examinations produces suggestive evidence, it should be followed by a detailed examination that is designed to further isolate the locus of the pathology. For example, if the routine neurological examination suggests that neural dysfunction in lumbar or sacral regions may be contributory, electrophysiological evaluations of lumbar and sacral function should be performed. Of particular interest to us are the possibilities offered by monitoring activity in the bulbocavernosus and ischiocavernosus muscles during NPT. In practice, we monitor this activity during any differential diagnostic evaluation. We suspect that these muscles play a role in pumping blood into the penis at the onset of erection, and we have preliminary evidence that defective neuromuscular function may contribute to impotence in some patients.

A second NPT evaluation may be advisable for some patients. Alcohol and drugs such as tranquilizing, antidepressant, antihypertensive, and anticholinergic agents are suspected of inhibiting erectile response (although systematic studies have yet to be performed). If it is concluded that one of these agents may contribute to the problem, the patient should be reevaluated after a two- to four-week period when he has not taken the drug or when he has taken a substitute that is more benign with respect to the side effect of impotence.

Conclusion

The monitoring of nocturnal penile tumescence is a method for systematic, objective differential diagnosis of psychogenic and organogenic impotence. This method should be employed in the diagnostic evaluation of *every* patient who complains of and seeks treatment for impotence. Furthermore, the growing availability of treatment methods of various types makes it mandatory to isolate, whenever possible and by whatever means, the pathogenesis of the complaint. If the diagnostic procedure herein described is implemented, the physician will be in a strong position to *rationally* select the appropriate treatment for each patient.

References

Abelson, D. Diagnostic value of the penile pulse and blood pressure: A Doppler study of impotence in diabetics. *Journal of Urology*, 1975, *113*, 636–639.

Beutler, L. E., Karacan, I., Anch, A. M., Salis, P. J., Scott, F. B., and Williams, R. L. MMPI and MIT discriminators of biogenic and psychogenic impotence. *Journal of Consulting and Clinical Psychology*, 1975, *43*, 899–903.

Beutler, L. E., Scott, F. B., and Karacan, I. Psychological screening of impotent men. *Journal of Urology*, 1976, *116*, 193–197.

Cooper, A. J. Factors in male sexual inadequacy: A review. *Journal of Nervous and Mental Disease*, 1969, *149*, 337–359.

Derogotis, L. R. Psychological assessment of sexual disorders. In J. K. Meyer (Ed.), *Clinical management of sexual disorders*. Baltimore: Williams and Wilkins, 1976. Pp. 35–73.

Fisher, C., Schiavi, R., Lear, H., Edwards, A., Davis, D. M., and Witkin, A. P. The assessment of nocturnal REM erection in the differential diagnosis of sexual impotence. *Journal of Sex and Marital Therapy*, 1975, *1*, 277–289.

Karacan, I. A simple and inexpensive transducer for quantitative measurements of penile erection during sleep. *Behavior Research Methods and Instrumentation*, 1969, *1*, 251–252.

Karacan, I., Salis, P. J., Thornby, J. I., and Williams, R. L. The ontogeny of nocturnal penile tumescence. *Waking and Sleeping*, 1976, *1*, 27–44.

Karacan, I., Scott, F. B., Salis, P. J., Attia, S. L., Ware, J. C., Altinel, A., and Williams, R. L. Nocturnal erections, differential diagnosis of impotence, and diabetes. *Biological Psychiatry*, 1977, *12*, 373–380.

Karacan, I., Williams, R. L., Thornby, J. I., and Salis, P. J. Sleep-related tumescence as a function of age. *American Journal of Psychiatry*, 1975, *132*, 932–937.

The subject of orgasm in women has always been a topic of great interest to sex researchers. Although orgasmic dysfunction is quite rare in men (under 1%) it is the most common dysfunction in women (Kinsey reported about 11% of women are totally inorgasmic even after ten years of marriage).

In this chapter, Morokoff analyzes the masses of data that have been collected on women's orgasm. Beginning with an overview of the different definitions of female orgasm, she goes on to evaluate studies that attempt to correlate orgasm with other factors in the woman's life.

10

Determinants of Female Orgasm

Patricia Morokoff

This chapter is an exploration of factors relating to women's orgasm. Although orgasm is only one facet of the total sexual experience, it remains the most easily quantifiable index of satisfaction during sex. As such, a great deal of research and theory has been directed toward elucidating those variables relevant to the experience of orgasm. The basic questions to be examined here are: (1) What is an orgasm, from both subjective and physiological points of view? (2) What factors, physiological, sociological, and psychological, contribute to a woman's ability to experience orgasm? (3) In what way do cultural values influence women's potential for orgasm?

What Is an Orgasm?

This is the most intuitive question to be explored, and most women reading this will have their own personal answer. Yet those investigators who have taken the time to record descriptions of orgasm have offered us insight into the variety of

Patricia Morokoff • Department of Psychology, State University of New York, Stony Brook, New York

subjective experiences resulting from the physiological reflex. Fisher (1973), in his ambitious investigation of female orgasm, asked women to give a detailed description of sensations experienced as they attain orgasm. One woman wrote, "Orgasm comes with a dizziness, a loss of self—almost as if I didn't exist as a body but I exist as a sensation. After orgasm my body completely relaxes—goes limp for a few seconds until I am conscious of what has really happened and how much my partner means to me." Another woman wrote, "The sensation of the orgasm is one of mounting tension and warmth followed by a desire for more (whatever is happening at the moment) until finally a release and satisfaction is attained." Hite (1976) also asked women to describe their physical sensations during orgasm. One woman responded, "There are a few faint sparks, coming up to orgasm, and then I suddenly realize that it is going to catch fire and then I concentrate all my energies, both physical and mental, to quickly bring on the climax—which turns out to be a moment suspended in time, a hot rush—a sudden breathtaking dousing of all the nerves of my body in pleasure. . . ."

The most precise and thorough description of physiological changes that occur during orgasm is afforded by Masters and Johnson's (1966) observations of thousands of sexual response cycles in 382 women. In contrast to the variety of ways in which women describe their subjective experience, one of the most surprising findings of this study was the similarity of physiological response across women. During buildup of sexual tension, an intense vasocongestion occurs in the entire pelvic area. This congestion creates what is called the orgasmic platform—a "platform" of the engorged tissues of the outer third of the vagina and surrounding tissues. Orgasm is signaled by a series of rhythmic contractions of the orgasmic platform. The contractions are set off by a reflex stretch mechanism in the responding muscles when vasocongestion and myotonia reach a critical point (Sherfey, 1973). The contractions occur at intervals of .8 seconds for the first three to six contractions. Intervals between contractions become longer as contractions continue. There is a direct correlation between the number and intensity of contractions and the perceived intensity of orgasm, a mild orgasm having only three to five contractions and an intense orgasm perhaps eight to twelve or more. The sensations of orgasm result from the expulsion of blood produced by these contractions (Sherfey, 1973). The contractions of the female's orgasmic platform involve the same muscles that produce ejaculation and orgasm in males, although men additionally experience contraction of the musculature surrounding the prostate gland, seminal vesicles, and ejaculatory bulb. Furthermore, the interval between initial contractions is identical for men and women. A significant difference between male and female sexual response cycles is that many women do not seem to have a refractory phase following orgasm. That is, if effective sexual stimulation is continued, the potential exists for another orgasm to be reached immediately. This phenomenon is referred to as a capacity for multiple orgasm.

One of the most socially significant observations made by Masters and Johnson was that the physiological response of orgasm is identical regardless of the type of stimulation used to produce the orgasm. Study subjects were observed engaging in natural intercourse with a male partner, artificial coition, and manual and mechanical manipulation of their external genitals. In all cases the orgasm response was identical. Masters and Johnson state unequivocally that "from an anatomical point of view, there is absolutely no difference in the responses of the pelvic viscera to effective sexual stimulation, regardless of whether the stimulation occurs as a result of clitoral–body or mons area manipulation, natural or artifical coition, or for that matter, specific stimulation of any other erogenous area of the female body" (1966, pp. 65–66). These findings have bearing on the Freudian theories of clitoral versus vaginal orgasm, as will be discussed later.

Also of import to clitoral versus vaginal orgasm theories is Masters and Johnson's explication of secondary stimulation to the clitoris during intercourse. Contrary to the claims of many marriage manuals, Masters and Johnson state that consistent direct clitoral glans stimulation during coition is impossible. Nevertheless, the clitoris is indirectly stimulated during intercourse. As the clitoris becomes erect during arousal, it retracts into the vasodilated clitoral hood. During penile thrusting, traction exerted on the clitoral hood causes the clitoris to be rhythmically pulled forward and backward, thus receiving stimulation. Sherfey (1973) has elaborated on the significance of this phenomenon, which she terms the *preputial–glandular mechanism*. This mechanism occurs regardless of what position is used for intercourse. Since stimulation of the clitoris and the vagina does not occur independently, it is impossible to say orgasms resulting from intercourse are exclusively vaginal, even though no external manual stimulation of the clitoris is employed.

Masters and Johnson's data have not, however, laid to rest speculations about different kinds of physiological orgasm. On the basis of reports by various clinicians that some women claim to experience a highly pleasurable and satisfying form of release, which does not, however, include perceived vulval contractions, Singer and Singer (1972) have postulated three types of orgasm. Their first type, which they call the "vulval orgasm," is identical to that described by Masters and Johnson. The second type, the uterine orgasm, involves no contractions of the orgasmic platform and is typified by emotional changes, the most marked of which is a "gasping type of breathing leading to diaphragmatic tension and apnea." They describe the orgasm as occurring at the moment when the breath is explosively exhaled, with the pleasurable effects depending on uterine displacement. This type of orgasm is said to occur only in coitus, and results from deep thrusting with repeated penis–cervix contact. The third type of orgasm is a combination of the first two types, which they refer to as a blended orgasm. Fox and Fox (1969) provide data substantiating the occurrence of apnea during orgasm. They further indicate (Fox and Fox, 1967) that a pressure differential is created within the uterus before and after orgasm, causing the uterus to contract in such a way that semen is sucked in and transported toward the fallopian tubes. Singer and Singer suggest that this uterine suction (not observed by Masters and Johnson) is consistent with the blended and probably the uterine orgasm. The Singers' objective here is to quantify subjective orgasm experiences that women describe. They speculate that it would be interesting to investigate factors such as foreplay technique which might correlate with the different types of orgasm.

Physiological Factors

There is a paucity of data on physiological factors that relate to orgasmic capacity. Masters and Johnson found no support for the contention that variations in clitoral size or location influence sexual response. This finding contradicts earlier data cited by Landis, Bolles, and D'Esopo (1940) indicating that sexual adjustment is negatively correlated with the distance from the urinary meatus to the clitoris.

Kegel (1953) has suggested a relationship between the strength and tone of the pubococcygeus muscle and vaginal sexual response. This muscle encircles the vagina and urinary bladder to form a sphincter with additional fibers converging on the lateral walls of the lower third of the vagina. Kegel reports that approximately one-third of all women have a weak and atrophic pubococcygeus muscle, which he relates to lack of vaginal sensation and poor sexual response. He indicates that as this muscle is strengthened through voluntary contractions, vaginal sensations return and patients become less interested in clitoral stimulation. According to Kegel, the poor tone of this muscle in so many women can be accounted for by the fact that phylogenetically it is an old muscle, which lost its primary source of exercise when humans adopted an upright position. Good muscle tone is associated with greater ease in reaching orgasm. According to Kline-Graber and Graber (1975), if the pubococcygeus muscle is in good condition, orgasm will be more likely to occur and will be experienced as more intense.

Hormones play an intricate role in maintaining sexual functioning in women, and a possible relationship between concentration of the gonadal hormones and ability to reach orgasm has been examined in various ways. One method has been to determine whether frequency of sexual activity and orgasm is greater during one phase of the menstrual cycle versus another. Estrogen is the predominant hormone of the first half of the cycle, reaching a peak one or two days before ovulation. In the second half of the cycle, both estrogen and progesterone are secreted, but progesterone predominates. Prior to the onset of menstruation there is a sharp drop in levels of both hormones. A number of studies have been conducted correlating sexual desire with phase of the menstrual cycle. Results are not particularly clear-cut, although peaks of desire are typically reported before and after menstruation and less frequently around the time of ovulation. Udry and Morris (1968) provide data relating frequency of orgasm to cycle phase. They found a sharp rise in frequency of both intercourse and orgasm at mid-cycle. Because peaks of sexual activity have been correlated with high estrogen levels (mid-cycle) as well as low levels of estrogen (immediately before menstruation) no clear statement can be taken from these data on the significance of estrogen in facilitating sexual response. Furthermore, studies of libido in women who have undergone menopause or ovariectomy show that a high level of estrogen is not necessary to maintain either sexual desire or capacity to reach orgasm (Filler and Drezner, 1944; Kinsey, Pomeroy, Martin, and Gebhard 1953). Testosterone, which is primarily secreted from the adrenal glands in women, is the only hormone that has positively been associated with increased capacity for orgasm. When large amounts of testosterone are administered to women for medical reasons, the clitoris becomes enlarged and orgasm is more easily reached. Women who had never experienced sexual desire reported their first sexual cravings while receiving this treatment (Wilson, 1940;

Loeser, 1940; Salmon and Geist, 1943; Greenblatt, 1943; Greenblatt, Mortara, and Torpin, 1942).

Fisher (1973) made physiological recordings of heart rate and vaginal temperature under a range of conditions including rest, stress, and erotic stimulation. He found these indices unrelated to women's orgasmic capacity.

Thus, few positive statements can be made relating physiological variables to capacity for orgasm. The supposition that anatomical differences in size and/or position of the clitoris are related to orgasmic responsivity has not been substantiated. Also, differences in physiological response during arousal do not predict likelihood of orgasm. Despite the fact that exogenously administered testosterone increases the probability of orgasm, no data currently exist indicating that women with high endogenous testosterone levels reach orgasm more frequently than women having lower levels. The most promising physiological variable is condition of the pubococcygeus muscle; however, rigorous studies correlating condition of this muscle to orgasm potential have not been undertaken.

Let us now turn to sociological and psychological factors that have been found to correlate with women's orgasm.

Sociological Factors

Over the course of the twentieth century, attitudes toward female sexual responsivity have undergone marked change. Marie Robinson (1959) writes, "The prevailing attitude toward woman and her sexuality throughout the nineteenth century and up to the end of World War I was that sex, as we understand it today, did not exist for her." She quotes medical authorities of that day who believed that sexual feelings among women were highly unusual and indeed pathological. Brown (1966), in a thorough review of early writings on female sexuality, concludes that "until recent times it was taken for granted, at least in most of the Western world, that the majority of females had neither the desire nor the capacity for sexual gratification—and in the minority who did, it was a defect that should be denied or somehow eliminated." Female sexuality was reclaimed as a legitimate topic for serious consideration under such influences as Freud (1905/1963), Ellis (1922), and Van de Velde (1926), author of one of the first books exploring the sexual relationship within marriage.

Beginning in the 1920s, empirical investigations of women's (and men's) attitudes toward sex were undertaken. These studies have attempted in a variety of ways to determine what factors are related to the sexual satisfaction of women and how sexual satisfaction relates to marital happiness. Before exploring specific correlates, it may be of interest to review the incidence of orgasmic inadequacy reported in studies over the course of this century. One of the earliest investigations was undertaken by Hamilton (1929), who administered a structured interview to 100 men and 100 women. Hamilton found that 54% of the women interviewed were "relatively normal, or adequate, as to capacity for experiencing the orgasm in the sex act." This broke down to 33% experiencing orgasm always or usually, and 21% having orgasm between 20% and 75% of the time. Thus, 46% of his sample had had orgasm infrequently or never. He included in this group 5% who experienced multiple orgasm, following the Freudian notion that multiple orgasms are clitoral and therefore not true orgasms. By current standards we would recategorize these women as sexually normal, thus leaving 41% in the "inadequate category." A full 20% of these women reported never having reached orgasm and another 11% were doubtful. Dickinson and Beam (1931) found that of 164 married women, 61% usually reached orgasm. Terman (1938) conducted a large-scale study of factors relating to sexual and marital happiness. In all, 792 middle-class couples were administered an intensive questionnaire including two personality inventories, the Bernreuter Personality Inventory and the Strong Interest Test. This study and a subsequent replication (Terman, 1951) constitute the first systematic large-scale investigation of personality correlates of sexual adequacy in women. Overall, Terman found that 66.6% of the 760 women who replied to the question always or usually reached orgasm. Of the sample, 25.1% "sometimes" reached orgasm and 8.3% never reached orgasm.

Kinsey et al. (1953) reported the most extensive and thorough investigation to date of women's sexual patterns. A total of 2,480 women who were currently or had been married were studied. Kinsey reports that 90% of women will have coital orgasm at least once during marriage, leaving 10% who never experience orgasm. Percentages of women reaching orgasm all or almost all of the time (90–100% of coital attempts) range from 39 to 47%, depending on years of marriage. The proportion of women who never reach orgasm drops from a high of 25% in the first year of marriage to 11% in the twentieth year.

Chesser (1956) conducted a large-scale investigation of the sexuality of British women. Questionnaires were distributed to the patients of general practitioners in the National Health Service. In this way data were collected on a total of 3,705 married women. In this sample, 59% of women reported "always" or "frequently" experiencing coital orgasm, while 10% of the sample "rarely" and 5% "never" experienced coital orgasm.

Fisher (1973) has more recently explored a variety of life history, personality, and physiological correlates of orgasmic consistency in women. He studied seven samples of married middle-class women (each sample included approximately forty women). Across samples, Fisher found that 39% of the women were achieving orgasm "always" or "nearly always." About 5 or 6% had never experienced orgasm.

Hunt (1974) reported the results of an extensive survey of sexual attitudes and behaviors commissioned by the Playboy Foundation. The survey was conducted by the Research Guild, Inc., an independent organization that conducts market surveys and behavioral research. Respondents to the questionnaire constitute the most truly representative sample yet to be studied with respect to sexuality. The sample included 1,044 women, 75% of whom were or had been married, and was a cross section of educational, occupational, and racial groups. Hunt found that 53% of the married women experience coital orgasm all or almost all of the time, 40% reach coital orgasm between one-quarter and three-quarters of the time, and 7% reach coital orgasm none or almost none of the time.

The studies described are not an exhaustive review of surveys of sexual satisfaction but are representative of the kind of research that has been done. From them we may examine the correlations between orgasmic ability and such variables as age, education, social class, religion, decade of birth, and previous experience.

Age, Length of Marriage, and Decade of Birth

Do women reach orgasm with greater or lesser consistency as they grow older? Kinsey et al. (1953) found that between the ages of thirty-one and forty-two, 90% of all women studied had reached orgasm, at least on occasion. Of women in their early fifties, only 78% were reaching orgasm, and only 65% of those women in their late fifties were reaching orgasm. Hunt's (1974) data substantiate these findings: His younger married women were less orgasmic than women in their mid-thirties to mid-fifties. He also found that orgasmic frequency decreases in women over fifty-five. Chesser's (1956) data also show an association between age and frequency of orgasm. The group she found to be most consistently orgasmic (twenty-one- to thirty-year-olds) was, however, younger than that reported by Kinsey. Chesser reports a steady decrease with age in the percent of women reporting that they always or frequently reach orgasm, and a steady increase with age in percent of women reporting that they rarely or never reach orgasm (up to 20% in her women fifty-one and older). The age variable is closely associated with length of marriage. Consistent with her findings of a decrease in orgasm frequency with age, Chesser finds a decrease in orgasm frequency with increased length of marriage. These findings are contradicted by Kinsey's data, which show a steady *increase* in coital orgasm with years of marriage. Terman (1938), however, found no correlation. He reports, "It is significant that the wife's ability to experience orgasm does not improve with increasing length of marriage . . . if orgasm is not established within the first year of marriage it is likely to never appear." Clearly, age as a variable is hopelessly entwined with experience as represented in length of marriage. Two other variables, however, are also confounded. One is husband's performance or interest. Kinsey et al. (1953) emphasize that declines in frequency of coital orgasm "do not provide any evidence that the female ages in her sexual capacities" (p. 353). Because frequency in and enjoyment of masturbation do not decline for older women, Kinsey implicates the aging process in the male as an explanation of coital decreases. A second difficulty in drawing conclusions relates to changing societal expectations over the course of this century. Kinsey found a marked association between the decade of the woman's birth and her orgasmic consistency, those women born before 1900 having much lower incidence of coital orgasm than women born in the 1920s. The cultural variables will be discussed more thoroughly later.

Education and Social Class

Do college-educated women or women from upper- or middle-class backgrounds differ in orgasmic potential from working-class women? Kinsey et al. (1953) found some correlation with both of these variables. He found that coital orgasm frequency was higher among women from upper educational backgrounds. He also found that for marriages of all lengths, a larger number of women with limited education had never reached coital orgasm. His data on social class are based on the woman's parental occupational class. He found that more women from "upper-white-collar" or "professional" homes reached orgasm consistently in coitus (90–100% of the time) than from backgrounds of unskilled or semiskilled labor. These differences, however, were not great. Terman (1938, 1951) found education to be totally unrelated to orgasm adequacy; however, his sample included smaller percentages of women at either educational extreme than Kinsey's. He did find a slightly larger proportion of "adequates" (meaning women who reach orgasm "usually" or "always") among those women whose husbands were in the professional group. This difference is reported as not being reliable. Chesser (1956) found a similar pattern: Women whose husbands were semiskilled or unskilled tended to have less frequent orgasm than women whose husbands were in professional, clerical, or skilled manual labor groups. She also found that the higher the husband's income, the more frequently women experienced coital orgasm.

Hunt's (1974) more recent study does not support these education and social class differences. Hunt found that a slightly greater percent of high-school-educated women are consistently orgasmic (and fewer not orgasmic) than higher educational groups. The same trend was found among blue-collar wives compared to white-collar wives in the younger half of his sample. Hunt hypothesizes that these differences may reflect the fact that college-educated and white-collar women marry later and thus have had less marital experience. He concludes that the differences evident in earlier studies between occupational classes or educational levels and orgasm frequency have ceased to exist.

Religion

Strict religious upbringing has often been implicated as a cause of frigidity or lack of enjoyment in sex. In *Human Sexual Inadequacy*, Masters and Johnson (1970) state, "While the multiplicity of etiological influences is acknowledged, the factor of religious orthodoxy still remains of major import in primary orgasmic dysfunction as in almost every form of human sexual inadequacy." Of 193 women referred for treatment who had never experienced orgasm (primary orgasmic dysfunction), 41 came from devoutly religious backgrounds. Despite the intuitive appeal of this explanation, survey data have not upheld a strong correlation between religious devoutness and orgasmic inadequacy. Kinsey et al. (1953) found that dividing his sample into devout, moderate, and inactive groups did not predict frequency of coital orgasm. He did find that a relatively high proportion of moderate and devout Catholic women in their first year of marriage (approximately one-third) fail to reach orgasm entirely. It should be noted that no data are provided for Catholic women past the first year of marriage, so that it cannot be determined whether or not this trend continues. Futhermore, data are not available on Orthodox Jewish women, making a true comparison between Catholic and Jewish women impossible.

Terman (1938) found no correlation between a woman's religious training and her orgasmic adequacy but did find a correlation between the husband's religious training and his wife's orgasmic adequacy. Terman points out that two interpretations are possible: Either men obtaining strict religious training are less able to elicit orgasm in their wives or they tend to select as a wife the type of woman who becomes sexually inadequate. For Hunt's (1974) sample as a whole, no relation between devoutness and orgasm frequency was found. However, when the sample was split in two, devout women in the younger half experienced more orgasms, while in the older half, the nondevout were more orgasmic. Hunt suggests that devout women may marry earlier than their nonreligious counterparts, and again calls upon longer marital experience to explain the higher orgasm frequencies.

Less frequent coital orgasm among devout Catholic and Jewish women is substantiated in two studies. Hamblin and Blood (1956) found that devout Catholics had a lower rate of coital orgasm than "inactive" Catholics, a distinction that did not appear between devout and inactive Protestants. Goshen-Gottstein (1966) furthermore found that coital orgasm was rarely or never attained in an Orthodox Jewish group living in Israel. It is important to bear in mind differences between data from the general population and clinical data (derived from women seeking sexual treatment, as in Masters and Johnson's sample). As will be seen shortly, low frequency of coital orgasm does not necessarily imply sexual dissatisfaction. It is theoretically possible that a covariance exists among religious devoutness, orgasm frequency, and degree of sexual satisfaction. Chesser's (1956) data do not contradict this possibility. She found that a higher proportion of those women who attend church regularly or occasionally experience consistent orgasm than of those women who never attend church. The same difference was found with respect to sexual satisfaction. Chesser interprets this association as reflecting a higher degree of marital happiness among her sample of regular churchgoers. It is also interesting that she found no correlation between strength of religious background and orgasm frequency or sexual satisfaction. Fisher (1973) could find no correlation between orgasm consistency and a variety of indices of religiosity (church attendance, measures of religious values, devoutness of parents, etc.).

Sexual Satisfaction and Marital Happiness

How does orgasm frequency relate to sexual satisfaction and marital happiness? Terman (1951) reported that 60% of his "sexually inadequate" group reported complete or fairly complete sexual satisfaction. Chesser (1956) reports a fairly close connection between sexual satisfaction and achievement of orgasm, but notes that a "higher proportion of women stated that they obtained a lot of satisfaction from sexual intercourse than the proportion who stated they always or frequently achieved orgasm" (p. 422). Fisher (1973) found that women who often had difficulty attaining orgasm nevertheless valued sexual stimulation and felt sex was very important in their lives. Hunt's (1974) data further substantiate the finding that orgasm need not be experienced for the woman to find sex very pleasurable.

Terman (1938, 1951), Chesser (1956), and Gebhard (1966) found orgasm adequacy and marital happiness (as rated by women) to be highly correlated. Marital happiness was the single factor most strongly associated with orgasm consistency in Chesser's study. As she points out, however, sexual satisfaction may be either a result or a cause of marital happiness.

Summary

In reviewing these findings it is obvious that no definitive sociological determinants emerge. Women maintain their biological capacity for orgasm as they age, but may experience orgasm in a smaller percentage of coital contacts.

Contradictions are found across studies as to whether frequency of orgasm increases the longer one is married. Fairly consistent differences in orgasm frequency related to education and social class were found in the older studies but have disappeared among younger women in the most recent survey (Hunt, 1974). Except in the more devout subgroups, religion seems either to have no influence on orgasmic responsiveness or possibly to have a positive influence. Among these mixed and/or weak results, one association is clearly uncontested: Birth later in the century is related to higher frequency of orgasm. Whatever cultural changes in attitude toward female sexuality are at work, it seems possible that women who are better educated, have higher social standing, and/or do not have rigid religious morals have been more easily influenced. This observation could account for the more recent erasure of differences based on educational and social standing. It has often been observed that Victorianism lingers more in the lower middle class (Rainwater, 1965). If these observations are true, it becomes crucial to unravel what attitudes are socially communicated that make it more or less likely that women will attain sexual fulfillment.

Psychological and Interpersonal Factors

Childhood Experiences

Before looking to our culture as a whole, however, let us look at the individual woman within her own family to determine what childhood experiences or personality characteristics have been found associated with sexual adequacy and inadequacy. Various childhood experiences, such as the occurrence of sexual trauma or the way in which parents discuss sexuality with the child, may intuitively appear to be determinants of a woman's ability to enjoy a sexual relationship as an adult. It is important to realize, however, that emphasis on early childhood experiences in determining adult sexuality is in large part a derivative of Freud's theory of sexuality. A knowledge of this theory is thus important in order to understand much of the subsequent research on personality and experiential correlates of orgasmic adequacy. In simplified form, Freud (1959) believed that females have two sex organs, one male (the clitoris) and one female (the vagina). Two changes must occur in the female child on her way toward sexual maturity. She must renounce the clitoris as her primary genital zone in favor of the vagina, and the original mother object must be exchanged for the father. Freud envisioned both male and female children as attached to the mother in the first years of life because of the mother's role in feeding and caring for the child. However, the mother cannot completely fulfill the child's demand for love and so the child becomes dissatisfied. During this period (through the fourth or fifth year) the female child's sexuality is focused around the clitoris and she may further resent her mother for prohibiting masturbation. Somewhere around this time the little girl has an opportunity to discover that she does not possess a penis, realizes her biological inferiority, and accepts that this is the fate of womanhood. With this realization, her mother suffers a loss in her eyes for not having given her a proper genital. The little girl thus turns to her father as a love object. With this transition, a diminution of active sexual impulses and an increase in passive sexual impulses occurs, thus opening the way for development of femininity. Two other courses were also considered possible, however. The girl might denounce all sexuality (because she possesses an inferior organ) or she might cling to her threatened masculinity and continue to hope for a penis. Both of these paths lead to frigidity in the adult woman, according to Freudian conceptualization.

As defined by Bergler (1944), frigidity is the inability to reach a vaginal orgasm. It is easily apparent that the clitoral-versus-vaginal-orgasm debate, with emphasis on a vaginal orgasm as the only true and mature orgasm, stems from Freud's initial conceptualization of the clitoris as masculine and the vagina as feminine. Based on this developmental theory, several predictions can be made. First, a woman's early relationships with her mother and father should influence her adult sexuality. This should be particularly true within the areas of sexual training and discipline. Second, the organization of the personality should be demonstrably different for sexually adequate and inadequate women. Third, inorgasmic women should be less mature or more neurotic than their orgasmic counterparts. The first two of these predictions have been addressed in depth by Terman in his 1938 and 1951 studies. Both studies employ the same questionnaire and personality inventories and thus serve to cross-validate findings.

The major result of the two studies is that very little difference can be reliably demonstrated between adequate wives (those who experience orgasm always or usually) and inadequate wives (who reach orgasm sometimes or never). In the 1938 study, Terman concludes, "Our search for correlates of orgasm adequacy, so hopefully begun, has been disappointing. Why one woman out of three fails to achieve orgasm, or achieves it only rarely, is still a mystery." In the 1938 study, Terman found the following factors unrelated to orgasm adequacy: degree of attachment to father or mother, conflict with mother or father, resemblance of spouse to opposite-sex parent, childhood happiness, type of childhood discipline or amount of punishment. On the positive side, adequate wives (and husbands of adequate women) more often rated the happiness of their parents as extremely high. The inadequate wives and husbands both rated opposite-sex parents as below "average" on attractiveness. Inadequate wives reported that they had received little or no sex instruction and tended to get their information from other children rather than from parents, teachers, or physicians. Terman further found developing sexual attitudes unrelated to adult sexual adequacy. Thus, a premarital attitude of disgust toward sex was unrelated to orgasm adequacy. With reference to Freudian developmental theory, Terman writes, "We find nowhere in our data any clear trace of Oedipus or Electra influences upon the wife's experience of orgasm." The results of the 1951 study were in the same direction as the earlier study, although significant items were not necessarily the same. There was some indication in this sample that the wife's adequacy might be related to her own childhood happiness. Adequate wives and their husbands tended not to have had a favorite parent, were more than "moderately" attached to both parents, and had little conflict with either. There was also some positive correlation between orgasm adequacy and quality of sex instruction, as in the first study.

Personality

With regard to personality, again positive finding were overshadowed by a far larger number of negative findings. Furthermore, since orgasm tends to be related to happiness, many of the correlations between adequacy and personality variables are spurious in that they merely reflect this association. The positive differences found were that (1) inadequates tended to give indifferent or indecisive responses, which Terman interprets as difficulty in making decisions; (2) inadequates tended more to be conformists while adequates were more individualistic; (3) the adequates preferred player roles while the inadequates preferred the audience role. In the 1951 study Terman summarized a trend for inadequate wives to be less happy, less self-confident, less secure, less persistent, less well-integrated, more sensitive, more moody, more exclusive in friendships, and more apt to conform to authority and conventions. In a review of the two studies, Fisher (1973) points out that only five items from the Bernreuter scale consistently differentiated adequates and inadequates in both of Terman's studies. These items indicate that adequates view themselves as less miserable, lonely, or grouchy, and more optimistic. They also do not drive themselves as "steadily" in their work. In his own study, Fisher (1973) did not find that a score based on these items was able to differentiate adequates and inadequates. It is thus apparent that personality traits may be weakly associated at best with difficulty in reaching orgasm, although the tendency exists, where differences are found, for orgasmic women to have the more socially desirable personality characteristics.

Terman (1938) found the husbands of inadequate women to be more docile, more conformist, less self-sufficient, and less socially competent. In the 1951 study, husbands were described as less well integrated toward a definite goal. Interestingly, the inadequate wives rated their husbands more harshly on this dimension than the husbands themselves. Also, the inadequate wives viewed their husbands as less happy, less easy to get along with, and less emotional than the adequate wives viewed their husbands.

Other studies of background and personality variables have similarly failed to show large differences. Chesser's (1956) questionnaire included a variety of items on childhood experiences. Only two factors were significant: happiness of the parent's marriage (consistent with Terman's findings) and a view of sex as unpleasant (negatively correlated with orgasm). Hamilton (1929) interprets his results as supporting parental attitude (or what Terman calls the inhibition theory) as a determinant of orgasm adequacy. However, Ferguson (1938) analyzed Hamilton's data and found that none of the items pertaining to parental attitude toward sex reached statistical significance. Hamilton's data thus provide only weak support for this theory.

The most recent intensive investigation of background and personality variables is Fisher's 1973 study. Fisher utilized a combination of background experience questionnaires, projective and personality tests, behavioral samples, and physiological recordings of responsivity. He obtained a variety of negative results similar to other investigators. He found no correlation between orgasm and the amount of information given about sex, whether parents were permissive or repressive concerning sex, parents' attitude to nudity, openness in displaying affection, reaction to onset of menstruation, or attitude toward mother. Furthermore, personality traits such as degree of femininity, aggressiveness, passivity, guilt, impulsivity, and narcissism were unrelated to orgasm consistency. Fisher writes, "One cannot glibly speak of orgasm as more likely to occur in women with certain personality traits as compared to others" (p. 400). The factor that he found most predictive was a trend for women lacking orgasm consistency to feel that love objects are not dependable. The data source for this finding is projective test themes and frequency of actual losses in the woman's life (such as death or absence of father). The theory that Fisher derives from this observation is that women who have experienced their love objects (particularly their fathers) as undependable will have an increased need to maintain control over object relations and will avoid situations such as high arousal in which such control tends to be lost. "It was theorized that the woman who feels that objects are undependable and who fears their loss finds the blurring of her relationships with objects that is produced by sexual excitement so threatening that she has to 'turn it off.'" Fisher emphasizes that this feeling that love objects are not dependable is not a personality disturbance and may be associated with a variety of different personality traits. He illustrates this by suggesting that schizophrenic women who have frequently experienced this blurring of consciousness may be less threatened by the phenomenon (due to its increased familiarity) and thus experience an unusually high orgasmic ability. Clinical reports of schizophrenic women do sometimes suggest such abilities.

Let us return now to the three predictions from Freudian theory made earlier in this section. The notion that specific aspects of the early parental relationships determine adult sexuality has not held up very well. Other than a weak trend for consistently orgasmic women to have had happily married parents and to have obtained sexual information from an adult, few specifics have emerged. Fisher's findings lend the most support to Freudian theory in that they validate the importance of one kind of childhood experience in determining orgasm consistency. Fisher writes, "Although the empirical findings support psychoanalytic theory in its *general* emphasis on the importance of early socialization influences, they rarely fit with more specific psychoanalytic formulations" (p. 426). Congruently, no personality dimensions other than "happiness" seem consistently related to orgasm adequacy. The third prediction, that orgasmic women will be less neurotic or more mature, has also not been borne out in research. Winokur, Guze, and Pfeiffer (1959) compared the sexual functioning of neurotic, psychotic, and normal women. The three groups were not siginificantly different with respect to orgasm rate and the authors concluded that the groups did not signifiantly differ in sexual responsivity. Cooper (1969) set out to determine personality factors in frigidity, particularly whether or not frigid women were elevated in neuroticism. Using the Neuroticism Scale Questionnaire (Scheier and Cattell, 1961) he found that his entire sample, including component subgroups, was within normal limits. Cooper concludes that "frigidity is not generally a neurotic response." Such findings are in direct contrast to clinical observations of psychoanalytic writers. Hitschmann and Bergler (1949) write that "many neurotic women, producing a variety of neurotic symptoms, achieve no orgasm at all in sexual practices with men. . . . On the other hand, only exceptional cases achieving vaginal orgasm suffer from neurotic difficulties." Bergler (1944) categorically states, "Frigidity is a symptom of a neurosis, a disease of the unconscious." Such impressions are clearly not borne out empirically.

Sexual Technique

To this point we have examined factors relating to the female as determinants of her orgasm capacity. Another intuitive approach, however, ascribes great power to the male's sexual technique in determining whether or not his partner will reach orgasm. This theory receives popular support from both men and women: Some women search for years for the right man who will make them orgasmic, while men may boast that their own sexual prowess is the best cure for frigidity. The theory receives further support in marriage manuals that tell men to concentrate on the clitoris to obtain maximum arousal in their partners, and in current sex therapy programs that train men in methods to delay their ejaculation, stimulate their partners during intercourse, and obtain feedback about what kinds of stimulation are most arousing. The data suggest that sexual technique used by men is not as important in determining women's orgasms as is popularly believed. Terman (1938) found that duration of intercourse did not differ greatly between adequate and inadequate women. Approximately the same proportion of women had difficulty reaching orgasm in the total sample as in a subset for whom intercourse lasted more than fifteen minutes. Terman concludes that theories of orgasm inadequacy based on sex technique are unsupported. Hamilton's (1929) data also support this contention: Of the women who felt their partner's orgasm occurred too quickly, half were in his adequate orgasm-capacity group, half in the inadequate group. Furthermore, women who described themselves as "indulging in sex play" were evenly divided between the adequate and inadequate groups. He further found that a change in sex partner did not typically lead to greater orgasmic adequacy. Kinsey is in agreement with these findings. He states, "Our data even suggest that the use of extended and varied techniques may, in not a few cases, interfere with the female's attainment of orgasm" (p. 385).

Gebhard (1966) analyzed data from interviews conducted by the Institute for Sex Research to look specifically at correlations among amount of foreplay, length of intromission, and orgasm. The data show that only a small percentage of wives who consistently reach orgasm fall in the category of couples who employ brief foreplay (one to ten minutes). Many more of these wives engage in foreplay lasting fifteen to twenty minutes or longer. It was also true that women who rarely reach orgasm generally engage in brief foreplay. A similar set of correlations was found with respect to length of intromission. Women who consistently reached orgasm usually engaged in intercourse of longer duration than women who reached orgasm less frequently. Gebhard postulates that lengthy foreplay with brief intromission and brief foreplay with lengthy intromission may be equally effective in producing female orgasm.

Characteristics of the male other than sexual technique also play a role in determining his partner's orgasmic ability. These include, according to Terman's data, some personality characteristics and, according to Fisher, his ability to allay his wife's fears of his lack of dependability as a love object. It should be borne in mind that the weak correlation between sex technique and orgasm ability do not show that an improvement in sex technique *cannot* lead to greater frequency of orgasms.

Cultural Influences

In Terman's 1938 study the age of the woman was not a significant correlate of orgasm ability. This fact was remarkable to Terman in the light of major changes in societal attitude toward sexuality. Terman wrote, "Between the 1890s and the 1920s the cultural patterns affecting attitudes toward sex underwent a tremendous change. . . . But the proportion experiencing orgasm remains almost at a dead level regardless of date of birth." By the time of publication of the results of Kinsey et al. (1953), the woman's decade of birth was one of the strongest predictive factors. Kinsey writes, "This is evidence that the attitudes and publicly accepted mores of the group to which a female belongs may influence her attitudes and sexual performance." Also in Kinsey's study, correlations between orgasmic responsivity and the socioeconomic variables of education and parental occupational class became evident. Such differences were not apparent in Terman's data, which had been collected earlier and on a more constricted sample of women. Twenty-one years following publication of Kinsey's data, Hunt (1974) again delineated further societal shifts: Education and socioeconomic class no longer predicted differences in orgasmic regularity. Differences could still be found by dividing the sample into older and younger halves, but this time among the younger women (most recent generations), it was the less educated, blue-collar wives and, surprisingly, the more devout ("surprisingly" since religion has not in the past been a reliable correlate of orgasm adequacy), who have more frequent orgasms. Hunt attributes the increase in orgasm regularity found in his survey to the social revolution of the past generation. In a field of enquiry where negative results and lack of correlations prevail, such changes stand out as worthy of note. We have already seen that few specific elements of early training predict whether a woman will be able to consistently reach orgasm. Few personality traits distinguish the orgasmic from the nonorgasmic woman. No measurable indices of physiological responsivity discriminate, and nothing in particular about the husband's sexual technique will ensure orgasm. Let us look more closely, then, at the meaning of societal attitudes and mores in the psychosexual development of the female.

It is obvious to anyone who reads, goes to movies, watches television, or listens to the radio that women are capable of sexual enjoyment. It would be next to impossible, should parents so desire, to prevent their daughters from learning of the female's sexual potential, regardless of their social class, educational level, or degree of religious devotion. In her sensitive cross-cultural treatise on sex roles, Margaret Mead (1949) underscores the capacity of human societies "to build cultural systems that are extraordinarily detached from any biological base." She points out that should a society devise methods of child-rearing resulting in total inhibition of arousal and orgasm capabilities in the male, it would necessarily not reproduce itself. No such biological injunction precludes comparable societal training for the female. Some have even argued that such inhibitory training was essential to the evolution of modern society. Sherfey (1973) postulates that primitive woman's strong sexual drives were incompatible with the rigid demands of structured family life in which it is important that paternity be clearly identified and energies be directed to child care. She states that "not until these drives were gradually brought under control by rigidly enforcing social codes could family life become the stabilizing and creative crucible from which modern civilized man emerges" (p. 139).

Yet societies differ greatly in their expectations of sexual responsivity on the part of the female. Mead (1949) contrasts the Mundugumor and the Arapesh, two primitive South Seas societies in which the former expect women to derive the same satisfaction from sex that men do, and the latter in which female orgasm is unrecognized, not reported, and has no name. She remarks, "The human female's capacity for orgasm is to be viewed, much more as a potentiality that may or may not be developed by a given culture, or in a specific life history of an individual, than as an inherent part of her full humanity" (p. 217).

Mead further suggests that "the capacity to learn a total orgasmic response is present differentially in all women" (p. 218) and that those cultures that impose rigid styles of foreplay or proscribe sexual activity except under certain stylized circumstances (under the covers at night with the lights out) may fail to evoke the orgasmic potentiality in large subsets of women.

Substantiation for this notion is provided by comparison of two cultures having markedly different expectations of female sexuality. The inhabitants of Inis Beag, an island off the coast of Ireland, were studied by Messenger (1971), who reports that the female orgasm is unknown there. The cultural expectation is that women will receive no pleasure from sexual activity. In fact, sexual activity is extremely limited on this island: Premarital coitus is unknown, and marital foreplay is limited. Intercourse is performed only in the male superior position with underclothes left on. The average age for women to marry is twenty-five. It is evident that sexual activity is severely circumscribed in this culture with a negative expectation of arousal in women. This pattern is in direct contrast to that found in the Polynesian island of Mangiai, as described by Marshall (1971). As far as could be determined, all Mangiain women reach orgasm. The islanders believe that women must be taught to have orgasms. In former times this task was allotted to older women, but now the function is performed by the young girls' initial lovers. The cultural goal is for the women to have two or three orgasms to her partner's one, and for coitus to culminate in simultaneous mutual orgasm. Sexual activity begins at puberty and premarital coitus is expected with different partners. Liking or feeling affection toward a person is not a prerequisite for his choice as a sexual partner. In this culture, many and varied sexual experiences are the norm, with social disapproval extended to the male who does not bring his partner to multiple climax.

It is clear in our own society that the expectation for female orgasm has undergone major reversal since the turn of the century. It is also clear that this expectation is not taught primarily by parents but rather by media. From this point of view it is not surprising that studies evaluating specific child-rearing practices have found these practices to be unrelated to orgasm capability. It is also true that in our culture sexual arousal and orgasm in the female are associated with a letting go, a loosening. This achieves literal meaning in terms of letting go of previously held prohibitions against arousal in women. As surely as girls are taught their biological ability to be orgasmic (if they are sexually "free" enough), they are taught that straight-laced, prudish, or Victorian women (of a bygone era) do not let go sexually. Thus, in our time of change, "letting go" is the metaphor for arousal and orgasm. (It is relevant to note that achievement of erection and ejaculation in men is not associated with "letting go" sexually.) Thus Fisher's theory that the orgasmically inadequate women are those who have personal reason to fear losing control can be seen in a larger cultural perspective. These are the women who, for reasons based in their individual life histories, find difficulty in taking up the new cultural directive to "let go."

In a sophisticated society such as our own, the way in which persons of learning discuss sex can be seen as a reflection of deeper cultural values. It is interesting to examine in this context the half-century-long debate over clitoral versus vaginal orgasms. When women were not expected to experience pleasure in sex, such questions were of no import. But with the reemergence of female sexual drive as a cultural expectation, it suddenly became of major concern to establish what was the right, or most mature, or best expression of this sexuality. Enjoyment of clitoral stimulation and hence clitoral orgasm was established by Freud as representing the active and masculine. Vaginal orgasm in his theory depended on a switch to acceptance of feminine passivity. Thus, in simplest terms, this debate symbolizes a cultural conflict between women taking an active versus a passive role in sex. Masters and Johnson's (1966) data showing that an orgasm is an orgasm have been frequently cited as laying the vaginal versus clitoral orgasm controversy to rest. In truth, this finding really does not address the basic issue for it has little to say about what sexual role women should play in our culture. Yet it is of interest that it has been latched onto as an eagerly awaited scientific indication of which way things should be. Female activists such as Shulman (1971) cite Masters and Johnson's data in support of the political position that the clitoris should receive acceptance as the primary sexual organ in women. The vaginal orgasm, now a cultural symbol of female passivity, has been relegated by activists to the status of myth. Shulman writes, with reference to woman's experience of the vaginal orgasm, that "she cannot know what such an orgasm is supposed to feel like because there is no such thing." That sexual enjoyment through female passivity has not been culturally renounced is evident in articles such as Singer and Singer (1972), in which the authors argue for the validity of an orgasm not based on the "sharp violence" of a clitoral orgasm, but which is characterized by "sensations that are indistinguishable from emotion."

Physiological and psychological factors affecting a woman's ability to reach orgasm cannot be separated from the cultural expectations for ways in which orgasm will occur, if indeed it is expected to occur at all. Although orgasm regularity is not necessary for experienced satisfaction with sex, it may societally become necessary. It is probable that until our society settles into a comfortable conceptualization of how men and women should relate to one another, particularly on a sexual level, a sizable percentage of women will experience dissatisfaction with their sex lives.

References

Bergler, E. Problem of frigidity. *Psychiatric Quarterly*, 1944, *18*, 374–390.

Brown, D. G. Female orgasm and sexual inadequacy. In R. Brecher and E. Brecher (Eds.), *Analysis of human sexual response*. New York: Signet, 1966.

Chesser, E. *The sexual marital and family relationships of the English woman*. London: Hutchinson's Medical Publications, 1956.

Cooper, A. J. Some personality factors in frigidity. *Journal of Psychosomatic Research*, 1969, *13*, 149–155.

Dickinson, R. L., and Beam, L. *A thousand marriages. A medical study of sex adjustment*. Baltimore, Maryland: Williams and Wilkins, 1931.

Ellis, H. *Little essays of love and virtue*. New York: Doran, 1922.

Ferguson, L. W. Correlates of woman's orgasm. *Journal of Psychology*, 1938, *6*, 295–302.

Filler, W., and Drezner, N. The results of surgical castration in women under forty. *American Journal of Obstetrics and Gynecology*, 1944, *47*, 122–124.

Fisher, S. *The female orgasm*. New York: Basic Books, 1973.

Fox, C. A. and Fox, B. Uterine suction during orgasm. *British Medical Journal*, 1967, *1*, 300–301.

Fox, C. A., and Fox, B. Blood pressure and respiratory patterns during human coitus. *Journal of Reproduction and Fertility*, 1969, *19*, 405–415.

Freud, S. [Three essays on the theory of sexuality] (J. Strachey, Ed. and trans.). New York: Basic Books, 1963. (Originally published, 1905.)

Freud, S. *Collected papers* (Vol. 5). (J. Strachey, Ed.). New York: Basic Books, 1959.

Gebhard, P. H. Factors in marital orgasm. *Journal of Social Issues*, 1966, *22*, 88–95.

Goshen-Gottstein, E. R. Courtship, marriage and pregnancy in "Geula." A study of an ultra-orthodox Jerusalem group. *Israel Annals of Psychiatry and Related Disciplines*, 1966, *4*, 43–66.

Greenblatt, R. B. Testosterone propionate pellet implantation in gynecic disorders. *Journal of the American Medical Association*, 1943, *121*, 17–24.

Greenblatt, R. B., Mortara, F., and Torpin, R. Sexual libido in the female. *American Journal of Obstetrics and Gynecology*, 1942, *44*, 658–663.

Hamblin, R. L., and Blood, R. O., Jr. Premarital experience and the wife's sexual adjustment. *Social Problems*, 1956, *4*, 122–130.

Hamilton, G. V. *A research in marriage*. New York: Albert and Charles Boni, 1929.

Hite, S. *The Hite report*. New York: MacMillan, 1976.

Hitschmann, E., and Bergler, E. Frigidity in women—restatement and renewed experiences. *Psychoanalytic Review*, 1949, *36*, 45–53.

Hunt, M. *Sexual behavior in the 70's*. Chicago: Playboy Press, 1974.

Kegel, A. H. Sexual functions of the pubococcygeus muscle. *Western Journal of Surgery*, 1952, *60*, 521–524.

Kinsey, A. C., Pomeroy, W., Martin, C., and Gebhard, P. *Sexual behavior in the human female*. Philadelphia: W. B. Saunders, 1953.

Kline-Graber, G., and Graber, B. *Woman's orgasm: A guide to sexual satisfaction*. Indianapolis: Bobbs-Merrill, 1975.

Landis, C., Bolles, M. M., and D'Esopo, D. A. Psychological and physical concomitants of adjustment in marriage. *Human Biology*, 1940, *12*, 559–565.

Loeser, A. Subcutaneous implantation of female and male hormone in tablet form in women. *British Medical Journal*, 1940, *1*, 479–482.

Marshall, D. S. Sexual behavior on Mangiai. In D. S. Marshall and R. C. Suggs (Eds.), *Human sexual behavior. Variations in the ethnographic spectrum*. New York: Basic Books, 1971.

Masters, W. H., and Johnson, V. E. *Human sexual response*. Boston: Little, Brown, 1966.

Masters, W. H., and Johnson, V. E. *Human sexual inadequacy.* Boston: Little, Brown, 1970.

Mead, M. *Male and female.* New York: William Morrow, 1949.

Messenger, J. C. Sex and repression in an Irish folk community. In D. S. Marshall and R. C. Suggs (Eds.), *Human sexual behavior. Variations in the ethnographic spectrum.* New York: Basic Books, 1971.

Rainwater, L. *Family design. Marital sexuality, family size and contraception.* Chicago: Aldine, 1965.

Robinson, M. N. *The power of sexual surrender.* Garden City: Doubleday, 1959.

Salmon, U. J., and Geist, S. H. Effects of androgens on libido in women. *Journal of Clinical Endocrinology,* 1943, *3,* 235–238.

Scheier, I. H., and Cattell, R. A. *Handbook for the neuroticism scale questionnaire.* 1961.

Sherfey, M. J. *The nature and evolution of female sexuality.* New York: Vintage Books, 1973.

Shulman, A. Organs and orgasms. In V. Gornick and B. K. Moran (Eds.), *Women in sexist society. Studies in power and powerlessness.* New York: Basic Books, 1971.

Singer, J., and Singer, I. Types of female orgasm. *Journal of Sex Research,* 1972, *8,* 255–267.

Terman, L. M. *Psychological factors in marital happiness.* New York: McGraw-Hill, 1938.

Terman, L. M. Correlates of orgasm adequacy in a group of 556 wives. *Journal of Psychology,* 1951, *32,* 115–172.

Van de Velde, T. H. *Ideal marriage.* New York: Random House, 1926.

Udry, J. R., and Morris, N. M. Distribution of coitus in the menstrual cycle. *Nature,* 1968, *220,* 593–596.

Wilson, L. Action of testosterone propionate in a case of endometriosis. *Endocrinology,* 1940, *27,* 29–32.

Winokur, G., Guze, S. B., and Pfeiffer, E. Developmental and sexual factors in women: A comparison between control, neurotic and psychotic groups. *American Journal of Psychiatry,* 1958–59, *115,* 1097–1100.

The search for successful strategies for the treatment of female orgasmic dysfunction has led to an investigation of the factors that correlate with orgasm in women. In this chapter Gebhard goes back to some data collected by Kinsey and his co-workers on the frequency of marital orgasm. Gebhard focuses on three variables: the woman's self-report of marital happiness, the duration of foreplay, and the duration of coitus. The findings show that women who are very unhappy in their marriages are unlikely to reach orgasm during coitus. It is doubtful that those briefer forms of sex therapy that largely focus on the sexual aspect of a couple's relationship would affect the coital orgasm rate of such women. As was suggested by Lobitz in Part II, Chapter 5, assessment of such cases is extremely important and referral for marriage therapy might be suggested. Some cases will need marital therapy, while in those cases where the sexual problem is the major cause of marital unhappiness, sex therapy is indicated.

The findings on duration of foreplay and coitus suggest that increasing the amount of time spent in these activities results in an increased probability that the woman will reach orgasm. However, there is a great deal of variability among women on these dimensions; some women are orgasmic with little or no foreplay and short coitus, while others are inorgasmic despite twenty or more minutes of foreplay and lengthy coitus. This seems to indicate that failure to reach orgasm is often a complex problem that is not likely to respond to simplistic "marriage manual" approaches of more foreplay, prolonged coitus, and so on.

11

Factors in Marital Orgasm

Paul H. Gebhard

The Institute for Sex Research has in its standard schedule of questions asked of every interviewee a large number devoted to marriage and marital sexual behavior. The answers to these questions provide us with too large a body of data to be compressed into any one chapter; consequently, I have chosen to select one aspect of sexuality in marriage to serve as an illustration of our studies. This aspect is one that has received much attention in marriage manuals but that has never been subjected to any large-scale empirical testing: the matter of the wife's orgasm in marital coitus.

Background

From the Victorian middle- and upper-class unconcern with female orgasm, we have, through the emancipation of women and the emergence of sex as a discussable subject, reached a point of intense concern with orgasm. It has become to no small degree a symbol of woman's being accepted as a human of equal stature and with her own sexual needs. Orgasm in marital coitus has become not only her goal but her due, and inability to achieve it frequently engenders feel-

Paul H. Gebhard • Institute for Sex Research, Indiana University, Bloomington, Indiana

ings of personal inadequacy and failure in both the husband and the wife. The pendulum has swung from unconcern to overconcern in less than a century.

In our culture, enchanted with technology and with a mechanistic conception of the body, the emphasis on female orgasm has produced a veritable flood of marriage manuals and similar publications that say, in essence, that the key to female orgasm is in the length of precoital foreplay and the duration of penile intromission once coitus has begun.

Reacting against this preoccupation with foreplay and intromission Kinsey, Pomeroy, Martin, and Gebhard (1953, p. 364) stated, "We are not convinced that the data demonstrate that any limitations or extensions of pre-coital petting are of primary importance in establishing the effectiveness or satisfactoriness of coitus." However, we presented no data supporting this statement. Nevertheless, the decade-of-birth data did clearly show an increase in the orgasm rates of wives and a growing use of more elaborate precoital and coital techniques. All of this could be construed to indicate that more elaborate and protracted foreplay was, after all, conducive to increased female orgasm. No data were presented on duration of penile intromission.

Considering the emphasis in literature and clinical practice on the importance of female orgasm, the omissions in our prior volumes call for rectification, and this was undertaken in the study now reported in this article.

Sample

The data in this chapter derive from some of the interviews conducted in the United States by the Institute for Sex Research between 1939 and 1960. The interview consists of a lengthy series of questions designed to give a comprehensive account of the individual's overt sexual behavior and some of his or her responses and attitudes from childhood to the time of the interview. The respondent's answers are recorded in code at the time and any confusion or ambiguity can be dealt with then. The interview of an adult with one marriage requires on the average about 1½ hours. The information is, of course, subject to the reservations that accompany any recollected reported data, but by reinterviewing a number of individuals after an interim of years, we have demonstrated that the reliability of such reported data is high.

In order to minimize selective bias the Institute ordinarily chose target groups (e.g., a parent–teacher group, a classroom, a business office) where a complete list of group members could be made so that all could be solicited for interview. Where interviewing all members proved impossible, the group was not abandoned until at least three-quarters of the members had been interviewed. A study of reluctant interviewees demonstrated that persons resist being interviewed for a great diversity of reasons and, therefore, they do not constitute a sexually homogeneous unit; hence the refusal rate may have little bias effect. The portion within a group who were not interviewed did not consist wholly of refusals but included persons not solicited and persons who had agreed to an interview but with whom mutually satisfactory appointments could not be made.

Table 1.   Female Orgasm Rate and Marital Happiness in Intact Marriages

Percent of coitus resulting in orgasm	Marital happiness rating						
	1 Very happy	1–2	2 Moderately happy	2–3	3 Moderately unhappy	3–4[a]	4 Very unhappy
	Percent						
0	4.4	3.2	9.0	16.1	15.8	—	19.0
1–9	3.6	9.5	4.5	12.9	8.8	—	19.0
10–39	6.5	20.6	11.3	3.2	10.5	—	9.5
40–59	9.5	12.7	17.1	12.9	15.8	—	4.8
60–89	16.5	17.5	17.1	16.1	14.0	—	9.5
90–100	59.4	36.5	41.0	38.7	35.1	—	38.1
Cases	587	63	222	31	57	4	21

[a]—, Too few to calculate.

The Institute staff has interviewed roughly 8,000 females and a sample from these case histories was selected for this discussion.

Originally the sample was to have consisted of white U.S. females with some college education who had been married for one year or more, and in the case of multiple marriage the data were to derive only from the first marriage. The data obtained from this original sample were confusing, and it became evident that this was due to an uncontrolled variable, which proved to be unhappy marriage terminating in separation or divorce. A series of tabulations revealed that greater marital happiness was associated with a higher percentage of coitus resulting in orgasm for the wife (Table 1). This was not an unexpected finding since our clinical impression has always been that separation or divorce is frequently presaged by a decline in female orgasm rate. It was also found that marriages in our original sample that terminated in separation or divorce tended to be shorter than those marriages that were intact at the time of interview (Table 2). Since we know

Table 2.   Female Orgasm Rate and Duration of Marriage in Intact Marriages and Marriages Broken by Separation or Divorce[a]

Percent of coitus resulting in orgasm	Intact marriages		Broken marriages	
	Median years duration	Cases	Median years duration	Cases
0	7.0	74	4.9	76
1–9	7.0	54	5.0	36
10–39	7.6	87	5.5	46
40–59	8.5	119	6.3	32
60–89	8.3	168	5.3	30
90–100	8.8	524	7.6	94

[a]There were too few widows to merit a category.

from our prior studies that female orgasm rates increase with length of marriage (Kinsey et al., 1953, pp. 383–384), this difference in marriage duration was clearly another analytical problem to be overcome.

Since the number of marriages that terminated in separation or divorce were not equal in the various analytical categories used in this study, one could never be sure whether or not variation was due to this fact rather than to items presumably being tested.

The simple, albeit somewhat painful, solution was to confine the sample to women whose marriages were intact at the time of interview and who expressed no intention of terminating their marriages.* This reduced the sample to 1,026 women. The sample size in some tables totals less than this due to interviewer failure to obtain, or to properly record, usable data.

Marital Happiness

Table 1 clearly illustrates that wives who reach orgasm in 90 to 100% of their marital coitus are found more commonly (59%) in very happy marriages than in any other marriages. Curiously, the five other categories of marital happiness do not differ much in terms of female orgasm: the figures for wives who reach orgasm with 90–100% frequency remain within six percentage points of one another (35 to 41%) even when happy marriages are compared to very unhappy marriages, and no trend is visible. If all six of the categories had roughly the same percentages of women experiencing orgasm in all or nearly all of their coitus, one could postulate that a sexually responsive female can reach orgasm from sexual activity alone, independent of her customary feeling toward her spouse. However, this is not the case. Rather than abandon the hypothesis, perhaps one should add to it a statement that in the very happy marriages, in addition to the sexually responsive wives who would reach orgasm under most circumstances, there are a number of other women who are less responsive and who would not reach orgasm so often were it not for the happiness of the marriage.

This modified hypothesis fits well with the figures concerning wives who never reach orgasm in marital coitus: here we see a clear negative correlation between the number of such women and happiness. There are but 4% of the very happy marriages wherein the wives fail to reach orgasm, but this figure gradually increases as marital happiness decreases until in the very unhappy marriages it reaches 19%.

With wives who reach orgasm rarely (1–9%) this correlaton is still visible; in the central categories (orgasm rates of 10–39% and 40–59%) it disappears; and in the 60 to 89% orgasm category the small N in the very unhappy marriages prevents our assuming that the correlation reappears.

One is left with the impression that marital happiness and female orgasm do correlate but only in the extreme categories: at both ends of the orgasm scale

---

*Tables 1, 3, and 4 were controlled by duration of marriage (one to three years; four to ten years; eleven years) to see if this variable was causally related to the results found. No alteration occurred and thus duration of marriage does not qualify any of the relations reported in these tables.

(0 and 90–100%) and at both ends of the happiness scale (very happy and very unhappy). Perhaps the correlation is elsewhere simply obscured by other factors, including the physiological.

Duration of Marriage

As Kinsey et al. (1953, pp. 383–384) demonstrated, the percentage of coitus resulting in the wife's orgasm rises steadily with increased length of marriage. Consequently, it is not surprising to see in Table 2 that there is a distinct tendency for women with higher orgasm rates to have been married longer than women with lower orgasm rates. The differences, however, are not great: the wives without orgasm having been married an average (median) of 7 years while the wives who almost always experienced orgasm had the longest marriages, the average being 8.8 years. This same trend was noted among the marriages that ended in separation or divorce, and which were briefer than the intact marriages.

Duration of Precoital Foreplay

The sample for Table 3 was considerably reduced in size because many wives reported duration of foreplay in terms of ranges rather than averages, and time considerations prevented our converting these ranges into averages. In connection with a later study, we intend to program the computer so as to make these conversions. No substantial change in the findings is anticipated since the majority of ranges appear to center about the averages reported here. In order to increase the sample size within categories, several categories were combined. Despite these handicaps it is clear from Table 3 that there is a positive correlation between duration of foreplay and wife's orgasm rate.

Where one to ten minutes of foreplay were involved, two-fifths of the wives reached orgasm nearly always; fifteen to twenty minutes foreplay raised this percentage to half; and still longer foreplay resulted in nearly three-fifths of the

Table 3.   Female Orgasm Rate and Duration of Precoital Foreplay in
Intact Marriages

Percent of coitus resulting in orgasm	Average duration of foreplay in minutes			
	0	1–10	15–20	21 plus
	Percent			
0	(2 cases)	3.9	7.6	7.7
1–39	(1 case)	19.5	12.6	7.7
40–89	(1 case)	34.6	28.9	25.6
90–100	(2 cases)	41.9	50.6	58.9
Cases	6	179	79	78

women achieving this high orgasm rate. Conversely, wives with lesser orgasm rates received shorter periods of foreplay, the one-to-ten-minutes category having the most cases.

The women who never experienced orgasm in marital coitus constitute a separate phenomenon. While their number in Table 3 is small, it appears that many of their husbands (most of whom were also college-educated) were protracting foreplay with the hope of inducing orgasm. The number of cases in the fifteen-to-twenty-minute and twenty-one-plus-minute categories are nearly twice the number in the one-to-ten-minute category.

One may legitimately raise the possibility that the women were unconsciously giving the interviewers biased data: that the women with lesser orgasm rates were minimizing the amount of foreplay. This possibility seems quite remote in view of the smallness of some of the differences and particularly in view of the fact that the wives without orgasm reported lengthy foreplay.

Duration of Intromission

The length of time the penis is in the vagina prior to ejaculation—after which most males soon cease pelvic movements and withdraw—is a matter accorded great importance in our folklore as well as in our marriage manuals. All females with coital experience were questioned as to duration of intromission. Their responses appear to be reasonably accurate since they agree with the time measurements from a small but growing number of cases of observed coitus. Our data here are not easy to interpret: it seems that the effect of duration of intromission is masked by other variables. It is not unlikely that lengthy foreplay with brief intromission may be as effective for female orgasm as brief foreplay and lengthy intromission; this has yet to be tested.* Also, the lack of strong distinctions in Table 4 may reflect the fact that most males of this upper- and upper-middle socioeconomic level can delay ejaculation for two minutes but seldom can delay for over seven, and hence most cases fall in our 2–3.9-minute and 4–7-minute categories. Yet another complication is the probability of the husband's adjusting himself to the speed of his wife's response, a man with a highly responsive wife being less inclined to delay ejaculation.

Nevertheless, one can see a tendency for higher orgasm rates to be associated with lengthier duration of intromission. Note that where intromission is under one minute only slightly over one-quarter of the wives achieved orgasm always or nearly always, while lengthier intromission (one to eleven minutes) raises this proportion to roughly half, and where intromission is protracted beyond eleven

---

*A check was made on the interrelation of foreplay and intromission with the finding that there generally was little relationship except at the higher orgasm rates (90–100% orgasm), wherein some synergistic effect was found, and when duration of intromission was held constant, a greater amount of foreplay was conducive to a higher orgasm rate. Similarly, if foreplay was held constant, longer intromission resulted in more orgasm. But in general this control worked only in a minority of cells in the table, so that Tables 3 and 4 may stand by and large as they are.

Table 4.   Female Orgasm Rate and Duration of Penile Intromission in
Intact Marriages

Percent of coitus resulting in orgasm	Average duration of intromission in minutes						
	−.9	1–1.9	2–3.9	4–7	8–11	12–15	16 plus
	Percent						
0	12.5	6.9	7.0	4.5	12.4	2.7	5.1
1–9	10.0	5.6	5.1	4.5	5.6	2.7	5.1
10–39	20.0	11.2	9.4	6.5	6.7	6.8	7.7
40–59	12.5	9.4	12.9	13.6	14.6	4.1	7.7
60–89	17.5	15.6	15.2	19.2	12.4	21.9	7.7
90–100	27.5	51.2	50.2	51.6	48.3	61.6	66.7
Cases	40	160	255	308	89	73	39

minutes three-fifths to two-thirds of the wives reach this high orgasm rate. Conversely, the women with low orgasm rates (none, 1–9%, and 10–39%) tend to have experienced brief intromission.

The same correlation was seen, though less clearly, in calculations based on broken marriages. An unexpected fact emerged from these calculations: there was a general tendency for lesser duration of intromission in the marriages that ended in separation or divorce, and considerably fewer wives in any duration-category reached orgasm nine or more times out of ten acts of coitus. In categories 1–1.9, 2–3.9, and 4–7 minutes roughly one-third of the women reached orgasm 90 to 100% of the time; in these same categories based on intact marriages (as Table 4 shows) half of the wives had orgasm rates of 90 to 100%.

Examination of Table 4 permits some interesting inferences. First, it is clear that penile intromission of less than one minute is insufficient to cause regular orgasm in most women. Second, it appears that about half of the wives are capable of high (90–100%) orgasm rate with intromission ranging from one to eleven minutes. This uniformity, regardless of whether intromission is 1–1.9, 2–3.9, 4–7, or 8–11 minutes, is puzzling and one is tempted to hypothesize that, except for extremely brief or extremely prolonged intromission, some physiological or psychological constant is maintaining this plateau. Perhaps about half of the women are capable of this high orgasm rate, although some require but one minute while others require eleven.

Extremely prolonged (i.e., about the upper 10% in terms of duration) intromission evidently can raise another 10 to 15% of the wives to the high orgasm rate. We see that intromission of sixteen minutes or more results in (the causal implication is intentional) high orgasm rate for two-thirds of the wives. The remaining third are scattered so evenly throughout the other orgasm rate categories one gains the impression that these women, too, have reached their physiological ceiling. In brief, sixteen or more minutes of intromission suffices to bring essentially all women to the limits of their orgasmic capacities.

Concluding Comment

There are certain neurophysiological and unconscious psychological factors that prevent female orgasm in coitus, but the degree of their influence cannot be accurately ascertained by means of the data currently available. However, there are several reasons for believing this influence is of the magnitude of five to ten percentage points:

1. In extremely happy marriages only 4.4% of the wives have not experienced orgasm in marital coitus.
2. In marital coitus preceded by lengthy (twenty-one or more minutes) foreplay only 7.7% of the wives have not experienced orgasm.
3. Where penile intromission lasts sixteen minutes or more only 5.1% of the wives have failed to experience orgasm.

Aside from the limitations imposed by physiological and unconscious psychological factors, it is clear that there is a strong correlation between female orgasm and marital happiness (presumably causal in both directions); a definite correlation between female orgasm rate and duration of precoital foreplay; and a moderate (and complex) correlation between female orgasm rate and duration of penile intromission.

Reference

Kinsey, A. C., Pomeroy, W. B., Martin, C. E., and Gebhard, P. H. *Sexual behavior in the human female.* Philadelphia: W. B. Saunders, 1953.

The controversy about clitoral versus vaginal orgasms was discussed in Chapter 10. In this article, the Singers offer a new typology of orgasm, which tries to integrate recent physiological research with women's subjective experience of orgasm. While the authors' typology has not gained widespread acceptance, this article is valuable for its careful description of the various subjective and physiological components of orgasm. The authors also make the point that description of what orgasm is can cause distress in women who discover that their orgasm does not meet some criteria. Orgasms are indeed different for different women, and for the same women on different occasions.

12

Types of Female Orgasm

Josephine Singer and Irving Singer

Since erotic consummations are so diverse among themselves, many people have wondered whether orgasms are basically alike or whether they can be analyzed into different types. In the male, problems about orgasm are related to the nature of ejaculation and the circumstances under which it occurs. In the female, the criteria for orgasm are less obvious. Recent writers often employ what is virtually an arbitrary definition of the term and then assume that others always mean the same. The result has been a great deal of vagueness and unnecessary confusion. As a way of approaching the problem, we shall seek to reawaken a controversy that was only temporarily laid to rest by the laboratory research of the 1960s. The issue is whether or not convulsive contractions in the muscles of the outer third of the vagina, or in general those forming the pelvic floor, are a necessary element in the female orgasm.

The most succinct statement of the controversy occurs in the Levine–Malleson exchange in 1948, published under the heading, "A criterion for orgasm in the female" (Levine, 1948; Malleson, 1948). In routine history-taking at the Margaret Sanger Research Bureau, Dr. Lena Levine noticed that some women attain "satisfaction and resulting complete relaxation with no description of involuntary,

Josephine Singer • Boston, Massachusetts   *Irving Singer* • Department of Linguistics and Philosophy, Massachusetts Institute of Technology, Cambridge, Massachusetts

perineal contractions." Levine uses the phrase *perineal contractions*, whereas Malleson (as we shall soon see) prefers the term *vulval contractions*. They both are referring to contractions in the outer third of the vagina which Masters and Johnson refer to as "contractions of the orgasmic platform." In these pages we shall use "vulval contractions" interchangeably with "contractions of the orgasmic platform."

In describing her observations, Levine goes on to say:

> The description of the general reaction was so varied and depended so much upon the emotional type and personality of the individual, that it was extremely difficult to make a definite classification of the woman's response. Where the involuntary, perineal contractions occur, they are definite and are observable by the woman, if her attention is directed to them. . . . And once observed, it follows that every time orgasm is reached, the contractions occur. But what about those women who have not experienced these involuntary, muscular contractions and yet who describe an intense general reaction, which seems to reach a peak and then subsides? Our impression is that these women have not really reached a peak but a point in the rise of tension just short of it, with subsequent slow release. That this reaction is satisfactory to the patient, is unquestionable, and the patient can be reassured that this reaction is adequate for her. But it cannot be described as an orgasm. . . . By accepting involuntary, perineal contractions as the criterion for the female orgasm, we would have a definite standard for evaluation of the reaction of the female, which can be used in diagnosis and in treatment. . . .

With respect to orgasms that involve vulval contractions, Masters has pointed out that "irritability, emotional instability, restlessness, pelvic discomfort, lack of sleep" are the usual aftermaths of orgasmic frustration (Masters, 1971, p. 144). This being so, it is surprising that Levine should think that women can be excited to a point "just short of" orgasm of this sort and yet find the experience satisfying. But since the patients do report satisfaction that is "intense" and "unquestionable," satisfaction that seems "to reach a peak and then subsides," one wonders by what authority Levine or anyone else can inform these women that they have not *really* had an orgasm. It would seem more plausible to believe that female orgasms are not always the same, in fact that they vary significantly in their behavioral manifestations.

Dr. Joan Malleson, a London gynecologist (1900–1956), explicitly asserts that not all orgasms involve vulval contractions. She replies to Levine's suggestion as follows:

> Dr. Levine writes as though the observable contractions at the vulva (not confusing voluntary ones which could be simulated) is a proof of orgasm. It is only a proof of clitoral orgasm, but even then, that must not be taken as being proof of satisfactory clitoral orgasm. Women can have this and experience no satisfaction whatever; it is the exact equivalent of the male who has an emission without erection. It is most important, I consider, that false criteria of this sort should not be accepted.
>
> I wish I could be more specific about vaginal orgasm. I do not myself believe that there are "measurements" that can be observed *always*, and assessed; and I do not think that these vulval contractions are necessarily found with a true vaginal orgasm. Such movement as there is, I should say, is confined much more to the levator and the upper vaginal musculature. . . .
>
> I certainly have one patient, who had an unsuccessful analysis, and whose husband is deceived by the fact of these vulval contractions, which are perfectly genuine in her case. She gets them with clitoral orgasm, but the orgasm gives no pleasure whatever, although she is glad to feel that there is some muscular response. This woman has a total vaginal

anesthesia, and is certain that she has never had vulval contractions of this sort of any spontaneous nature at any time, other than during clitoral stimulation. But as I say, it is as valueless as ejaculation in the male without an erection (1948, her italics).

Apparently the Masters and Johnson laboratory research of the 1960s has not resolved the basic issue since many gynecologists still believe that not all orgasms involve the contractions. Eustace Chesser, for example, writing in 1969, states:

Another popular fallacy is that an orgasm is not real without powerful contractions of the vagina. Those women who do not experience these contractions worry about their inability to attain orgasm. They vainly pursue an imaginary ideal. When closely questioned they admit they find intercourse intensely enjoyable. They have, in fact, experienced the release from tension which is what constitutes orgasm. All they miss are certain aftereffects which do not necessarily add to the pleasure because they happen to be so striking (p. 190).

Prior to Chesser, Kinsey had also distinguished between the orgasm and its aftereffects: "This explosive discharge of neuromuscular tensions at the peak of sexual response is what we identify as orgasm. The spasms into which the individual is thrown as a result of that release, we consider the aftereffects of that orgasm" (Kinsey, Pomeroy, Martin, and Gebhard, 1953, p. 627). In talking of spasms in general, Kinsey says only that they are "the usual product" of orgasmic release; and with respect to vulval or perineal spasms, he is even more tentative. "Some women" experience them, he says, but it is difficult "to determine whether the lack of vaginal spasms represents any loss of pleasure for a female" (p. 633). At the same time, Kinsey does maintain that "orgasm in the female matches the orgasm of the male in every physiologic detail except for the fact that it occurs without ejaculation" (p. 635). How this can be the case if the female orgasm need not be accompanied by contractions comparable to the male's, Kinsey does not tell us, and one can only speculate about the effect of this ambiguity upon the data he collected.

One can see why Masters and Johnson would have sided with Levine. As descendants of the behaviorist tradition, they were undoubtedly attracted by the fact that contractions of the orgasmic platform *can* be considered "a definite standard." When asked at a symposium for his definition of female orgasm, Masters stated: "For our anatomic and physiologic purposes, if the orgasmic platform contracts, the woman is having an orgasm. This phenomenon happens in the outer third of the vagina" (Masters, 1965, p. 531). Such contractions are verifiable by the woman herself, by her partner, and by the laboratory scientist. Moreover, these contractions are consistently accompanied by physiological changes such as generalized vasocongestion, increased muscle tension, rhythmic contractions of the uterus, heavy and rapid respiration, increased heart rate, and high blood pressure. Masters and Johnson chose to concentrate upon measuring these and other events that occur in this kind of orgasm and that can be induced in almost all women.

But in focusing on orgasms that *do* involve vulval contractions, Masters and Johnson have neglected every other kind of climax that many women would be likely to call an "orgasm." Should a woman turn to Masters and Johnson for enlightenment, they can, by means of a vibrator if all else fails, show her what "the" orgasm is supposed to be. But more often, women who are truly satisfied by a habit of climactic release from tension *without* the contractions do not present themselves for clinical counseling. Thus, it is easy for sexologists to ignore their type of sexuality.

Paul J. Fink, in a study that tries to resolve some of the differences between the Freudians and Masters and Johnson, reports that "Masters has collected a large amount of psychological information from his subjects. For instance, he has indicated that some women may show an intense vaginal response in orgasm from masturbatory activity only to report that subjectively it was not very exciting. In coition, such women may exhibit a minimal orgastic response but may find it exceedingly pleasurable subjectively" (1969, p. 9). But if an orgasm is a release of sexual tension due to vulval contractions, how can a strong contractile response be less exciting than a minimal one? When a woman finds the lesser response so "exceedingly pleasurable," the reason may well be more than merely "psychological."

This brings up an important methodological point. Women keep talking about the "emotional satisfaction" of the so-called vaginal orgasm. This emotional satisfaction is assumed to be subjective or psychological by Masters and Johnson, and hence outside the realm of physiological investigation. But emotions are not merely mental. They have physiological components, and most of these have been studied by reputable physiologists for many years. If there are emotional differences between different kinds of orgasm, then the physiological differences ought to be measurable. It is possible that some of the emotional aspects of orgasm may disappear when the sex partners know they are being observed in a laboratory. And if this is so, there would be a tendency for all orgasms to look alike despite their normal diversity. The fact that Masters and Johnson never report data from women who distinguish between their own "clitoral" and "vaginal" responses may itself indicate a major limitation in their findings. They seem to ignore a population of women represented by one who wrote the following in a letter to Masters and Johnson: "I just know that if someone would watch me copulate with a partner, the best I could do would be a little outer clitoral climax, as fast as possible to get the silly situation over with. I do not call that an orgasm" (Lowen, 1967, p. 238). What it is that this woman would call an orgasm we do not know, but the quantitative reports now available that *do* distinguish between types of orgasms have been made by a pair of physiologists, C. A. and B. Fox, who assembled laboratory equipment in their own bedroom, thereby avoiding all human observers (Fox, Wolff, and Baker, 1970; Fox and Fox, 1969). Their research will be discussed presently.

With these methodological considerations in mind, we may now reformulate our original question: If a woman can have a highly pleasurable experience with a "minimal orgastic response," might she not have a climactic and wholly satisfying sexual release with *no* vulval contractions whatever? And in such a case, is it not probable that an untutored woman would naturally call such a climax an "orgasm"? Lee Rainwater, the sociologist, complains of the difficulty in ascertaining what women actually mean when they refer to orgasm: "Women, and their husbands, were asked specifically about whether and how often the wife achieved orgasm (or 'came' or reached a 'climax' or some other synonym). Most of the respondents understood the question and were able to give a response that sounded reasonable. However, over a third of the women answered in ways that left the analyst unsure of whether they actually referred to orgasm" (1965, p. 63fn.). By sorting out the different types of sexual climax, perhaps a certain amount of confusion can be eliminated.

Three new terms will be introduced that, it is hoped, will avoid all normative significance:

1. The *vulval orgasm* is characterized by involuntary, rhythmic contractions of the orgasmic platform, as well as by the other physiological changes that have been measured in the laboratory by Masters and Johnson, and to which we have already referred. This kind of orgasm does not depend upon coitus since it can be produced by a variety of other procedures, for instance clitoral masturbation.

2. The *uterine orgasm* does not involve any contractions of the orgasmic platform, but it does involve emotional changes that can be measured. The most notable of these is apnea caused by laryngeal displacement. Apnea is an interruption of breathing, which in this case results from a strong contraction of the cricopharyngeus muscle in the throat. This muscle, which draws the larynx down and back, is linked with the abdominal viscera by a circuit involving the vagus nerve. The cricopharyngeus muscle tenses under many circumstances—for example, sobbing, laughing, yawning, screaming. One can contract it voluntarily by "swallowing" the back of the tongue. In the uterine orgasm its contraction and the resulting apnea follow upon a gasping, cumulative type of breathing. After considerable diaphragmatic tension has been achieved, the apnea occurs as an involuntary breath-holding response. The orgasm results when the breath is explosively exhaled; it is immediately succeeded by a feeling of relaxation and sexual satiation. This kind of orgasm occurs in coitus alone, and it largely depends upon the pleasurable effects of uterine and visceral buffeting by the thrusting penis. Subjectively the orgasm is felt to be "deep," i.e., dependent on repeated penis–cervix contact. In the sexological literature, its respiratory and emotional effects were outlined by Roubaud, whose description of the female orgasm Kinsey much admired, maintaining that it had not been surpassed by later authors (Kinsey et al., 1953, p. 631fn.): "In cases of intense exaltation . . . [the breathing may be] temporarily suspended, in consequence of laryngeal spasm, and the air, after being pent up for a time in the lungs, is finally forcibly expelled, and they utter incoherent and incomprehensible words" (Roubaud, 1855/1969).

3. The *blended orgasm* combines elements of the previous two kinds. As with the uterine orgasm, it depends upon the female's desire for intromission and is followed by a terminative feeling of satisfaction and fulfillment. It is characterized by contractions of the orgasmic platform, but the orgasm is subjectively regarded as *deeper* than a vulval orgasm. Some women report a sensation of vaginal "heaving" or, as one put it: "My vagina swallows one or two times and I have an orgasm" (Heiman, 1969, p. 43). From the reports to which the present writers have access, apnea would seem always to occur in blended orgasms. It occurs repetitively for about five seconds at a time in the moments preceding the climax (Fox and Fox, 1969). In her description of what is (in effect) the blended orgasm, Robinson says: "With the approach of orgasm the breathing becomes interrupted; inspiration comes in forced gasps and expiration occurs with a heavy collapse of the lungs" (1962, p. 23). The data of the Foxes (1969) provide quantitative corroboration of this account.

In giving this analysis, we have intentionally ignored the common distinction between "clitoral orgasm" and "vaginal orgasm." These words have taken on so many confusing and value-laden connotations that surely they ought to be avoided in scientific discourse wherever possible. For one thing, all types of coitus entail *some* clitoral stimulation. As Masters says in an interview, "it is physically impossible *not* to stimulate the clitoris during intercourse. . . . You see, with each thrust the minor labia are pulled down toward the rectum and, in the process, stimulate the shaft of the clitoris" (Masters, 1971, p. 147). The mere fact of clitoral involvement in no way indicates how or how much the clitoris functions in various orgasms. But since all orgasms are "clitoral" to *some* extent, this terminology is hardly useful for distinguishing one kind from another. For another thing, the term *clitoral orgasm* gives the misleading impression that *only* the clitoris is involved in some orgasmic responses. Prior to Masters and Johnson, Robinson made the following blunder: "The clitoral orgasm takes place on the clitoris only. It excludes the vagina from sensual participation" (1962, p. 69). There is, however, no such thing as an orgasm taking place on the clitoris alone. Even mild or superficial vulval orgasms involve the following muscles: bilateral bulbocavernosi, transverse perineals, external anal sphincter, and rectus abdominus, with secondary involvement of the levator ani and the ischiocavernosi. Since these are all muscles in the vulval region, most of which have no direct effect on the clitoris, it is clearly preferable to talk of a vulval rather than a clitoral orgasm. Finally, the words *clitoral orgasm* have acquired a pejorative sense. They have traditionally been used for the sake of contrasting vulval orgasms unfavorably with the more desirable phenomenon called "vaginal orgasm." There is no reason, however, to disparage the vulval orgasm or to consider it inferior. For a variety of sexual opportunities it is optimal and even ideal; many women have no need for anything else.

The term *vaginal orgasm* is worth abandoning not only because it implies a unique superiority that has never been proved but also because it too has acquired a welter of different meanings. It has been used to signify any of the following: a coital vulval orgasm, called "vaginal" because the penis stimulates the vagina during intercourse even though the response differs in no physiological way from non-coital vulval orgasms; a blended orgasm, sometimes referred to as deep and characterized by an emotional satisfaction that is absent from many vulval orgasms; a uterine orgasm, which is both deep and emotionally satisfying. In short, the term has been applied to almost any kind of coital experience that a woman would consider climactic and desirable. It is too ambiguous to be of much use.

The term *uterine orgasm* is problematic in one sense. As Masters and Johnson (1966) show, every vulval orgasm is accompanied by uterine contractions, and therefore to a certain extent all orgasms might be considered "uterine." But it is not the uterine *contractions* that prompt the label, but rather the fact that the uterus is repetitively displaced by the penis, thereby causing stimulation of the peritoneum, a highly sensitive organ. The peritoneum is the membranous lining that surrounds the intestines, uterus, and other abdominal viscera. One may also speculate that the uterus contracts more *strongly* in a uterine orgasm than in others. Heiman writes: "Observations of large farm animals (mare and cow) indicate that . . . uterine contractions are not only present during mating, but that they start when the female sights the male, increase as the male approaches and mounts, and reach a climax at the ejaculation of the male. Ejaculation is accompanied by tetanic contractions of the uterus" (1963).

A tetanic contraction is one in which the clenching of the womb persists for several seconds—in the case of the cow, sometimes for nearly a minute (Van-Demark and Hays, 1952). If a uterine orgasm is comparable to what a mare or cow experiences, then one would expect it to be accompanied by tetanic contractions. Even if it were, however, the woman undergoing the experience would be oblivious to the tetanic contractions as such. They undoubtedly would augment her peritoneal stimulation; but since no woman can be sure what her uterus is doing at the moment of climax, we must leave this measurement for future physiologists. One would especially like to know whether there are different kinds or patterns of uterine contractions, different ways in which the waves of muscular tension and relaxation are coordinated.

If the Fox data are typical, blended orgasms entail a pressure differential within the uterus before and after orgasm in such fashion that the uterus acts like a rubber squeeze-bulb that is first squeezed and then released, enabling the semen to be sucked in and transported toward the fallopian tubes (Fox et al., 1970; Fox and Fox, 1967). It is likely that the uterine suction response measured by the Foxes is also a consistent element in what we are calling the uterine orgasm, but measurements for this phenomenon have not yet been made in the context of the uterine orgasm. The experiments of the Foxes contradict Masters and Johnson's findings with respect to uterine suction; but as Masters and Johnson also point out, investigation of the uterus is still in its infancy.

Before presenting a more detailed phenomenological description of the uterine orgasm, one should emphasize the fact that involuntary laryngeal displacement is characteristic of a variety of emotions. Grief, surprise, fear and joy—all of these often involve laryngeal displacement with concomitant diaphragmatic tension. This fact may help to explain what some women mean when they describe a "vaginal" orgasm as "nothing but emotion." For example, Doris Lessing in *The Golden Notebook* (1964) writes the following: "A vaginal orgasm is emotion and nothing else, felt as emotion and expressed in sensations that are indistinguishable from emotion. The vaginal orgasm is a dissolving in a vague, dark generalized sensation like being swirled in a warm whirlpool" (p. 213). Lessing contrasts this more satisfying experience with the "sharp violence" of a "clitoral" orgasm. The following description of the uterine orgasm is more precise:

> The stimulus is uterine jostling. That is what produces the response. But the response is a kind of laryngeal spasm in the throat, accompanied by tension of the diaphragm. The breath is inhaled cumulatively, each gasp adding to the amount of breath contained previously in the lungs. When the diaphragm is sufficiently tense, the breath is involuntarily held in the lungs, and the crico-pharyngeus muscle tenses, drawing the larynx down and back. The feeling is one of "strangling in ecstasy." Finally the crico-pharyngeus snaps back to a resting position, and the breath, simultaneously, is exhaled. The suddenness with which this occurs produces the explosiveness without which the term "orgasm" would hardly apply. For a day or two following an orgasm, I sense a pronounced tonic state of the deep vaginal muscles. The satisfaction is so complete that subsequent climaxes are quite impossible for at least a day. For me, the relief from sexual tension which this crico-pharyngeal orgasm brings is analogous to the relief from pent-up nervous tension which an acute sobbing spell may bring. Both involve crico-pharyngeal action. Perhaps ethologists would care to know that my facial expressions are different in my two types of

orgasm. In a clitoral orgasm, my teeth are bared and my brow is furrowed with "anger" lines. In this other kind of orgasm, my brow is smooth and the corners of my parted lips are drawn back, although my teeth are not bared: i.e., a typical "fear" expression. The significance of this is not clear to me.

Masters and Johnson make no mention whatsoever of any kind of apnea or laryngeal displacement. Indeed there is reason to think that neither of these occurs with the simple hyperventilation typical of a vulval orgasm. Hyperventilation is a heavy, panting type of breathing, generally regular, quite rapid, and free of interruptions. It is characteristic of breathing in the male during coitus, and in fact, most males manifest no other pattern of breathing whether or not they are active or passive prior to ejaculation. The Foxes' measurements of breathing patterns in the blended orgasm indicate that, at least for this one woman, repetitive brief apnea is a consistent precursor of her terminative orgasm. Mrs. Fox's normal response is to have two sets of contractions of the orgasmic platform during intercourse. The second, while far more satisfying subjectively, was shown to be less intense according to blood pressure readings. This is in keeping with the psychological reports mentioned earlier of women whose "minimal" coital orgasms are more exciting than preliminary stronger ones.

The blended orgasm's pattern of brief, repetitive apnea, while differing from the panting type of hyperventilation of the vulval orgasm, also differs from the apnea of the uterine orgasm. In a uterine orgasm a cumulative amount of breath is held in the lungs and the apnea may be total for twenty or thirty seconds just prior to the sexual climax. It is not improbable that such prolonged apnea is inconsistent with contractions of the orgasmic platform and that this is why it contributes to a different kind of orgasmic peak. Perhaps the fact that contractions of the orgasmic platform in coitus seem to depend on more or less strenuous pelvic movement by the female may help to explain the incompatibility between the contractions and prolonged apnea. Such activity would very likely cause a woman to become "out of breath," thereby requiring her to inhale periodically and so precluding the possibility of prolonged apnea. In the typical uterine orgasm, the pelvis stays motionless, although muscles in the limbs and face are tensed, as are the diaphragm and the cricopharyngeus.

Behavioral differences between stimuli leading to the three types of orgasm include the kind of thrusting involved. For a uterine orgasm, the thrusting is strong, accelerating, deep, and relatively brief—of the kind that Masters and Johnson (1970) would condemn as being too "demanding" (pp. 229, 308–309). Masters and Johnson repeatedly advise men to be gentle and slow in order to elicit the woman's orgasm. The blended orgasm, on the other hand, seems to result from thrusting that starts out slow and then, within three to twenty minutes, becomes strong and deep. The same timing is also mentioned by Lowen (1967, p. 212). That this time period is not statistically normal is indicated by Kinsey's finding that 75% of all males in his sample ejaculate within two minutes after intromission (Kinsey, Pomeroy, and Martin, 1948, p. 580). The two-minute period of time—brief as it may seem—is entirely consistent with the requirements of the uterine orgasm; but obviously it is not conducive to vulval and blended orgasms. The question of how long, in minutes, intromission should last is one that Masters and Johnson avoid. To define *premature ejaculation* as they do, in terms of the duration required to elicit vulval contractions, is misleading in view of the fact that some women reach this kind of orgasm either very slowly or never.

The effect of cervical contact is also relevant, and it too is never formally treated in the Masters and Johnson study. This is surprising, since Kinsey et al. (1953) are clear on this point:

> [The cervix] has been identified by some of our subjects, as well as by many of the patients who go to gynecologists, as an area which must be stimulated by the penetrating male organ before they can achieve full and complete satisfaction in orgasm. (p. 584)

> Many females, and perhaps a majority of them, find that when coitus involves deep vaginal penetrations, they secure a type of satisfaction which differs from that provided by the stimulation of the labia or clitoris alone. (p. 581)

Recently LeMon Clark's (1970) experiments gave substance to the reports of these women. He had women stimulate themselves first with a clitoral vibrator alone, and subsequently with two vibrators at once, one giving a continuous, mild jostling to the uterus, and the other providing the usual clitoral stimulation. Nearly all of his subjects reported far greater satisfaction resulting from the simultaneous joint stimulation. Clark suggests that the enhanced satisfaction results from pleasurable peritoneal stimulation. If this hypothesis is correct, it answers all the questions about how a vagina can be neurally so impoverished and yet capable of transmitting sexual sensations.

Women who have uterine and blended orgasms report that they are fully satisfied, wholly satiated, on each occasion of their occurrence (Fox and Fox, 1969; Lessing, 1964; Lowen, 1967; McDermott, 1970; Robertiello, 1970; Robinson, 1962). What Sherfey (1966) says about the inherent insatiability of the female and her consequent multiorgasmic needs would seem to be applicable only to women who experience nothing but vulval orgasms. From this one may conclude that different kinds of orgasm provide different kinds of satisfaction. A priori, none of them—whether terminative or nonterminative—is necessarily preferable to any other.

In these pages we have attempted to raise questions for investigation. By clarifying what women *might* mean when they talk about "an orgasm," it is hoped that ultimately sexologists will become aware of the multiplicity of what they *do* mean. A simple, inoffensive question such as "Do you ever hold your breath during an orgasm?" or "Is your breathing repeatedly interrupted just before the peak?" could help future investigators to identify the type of climax that one or another woman might have. One must recognize, however, that few people are able to analyze their own response at the moment of orgasm. Prior to their respiratory measurements, neither of the Foxes was aware of the repetitive apnea that their experiments showed to be characteristic of Mrs. Fox's preorgasmic breathing pattern. Apparently this is one area of human experience in which even trained physiologists have limited powers of self-observation.

Despite this problem, however, improved questionnaires might reveal many of the orgasmic differences that have thus far been neglected. Most questionnaires now in existence are limited by vagueness in their definition of *orgasm*. For example, Wallin and Clark (1963) define the word as "a climax of intense feeling which is followed by a pretty sudden feeling of relief and relaxation." Since this kind of definition applies indiscriminately to all three types of orgasm, many of the results of such studies are cloudy and confusing. New studies are needed to analyze coital enjoyment in the light of the different types of orgasm that we have been discussing.

Equally fascinating would be a statistical analysis of the varieties of foreplay techniques correlated with the types of orgasm. It may well be that the brief, relatively "impoverished" techniques of certain working-class males may be such as to elicit uterine orgasms more frequently than the elaborate foreplay rituals prescribed by current best sellers on sensuous sexuality. Studies of women who exprience more than one type of orgasm are needed. And correlations of interpersonal attitudes required for satisfactory lovemaking would also be useful. Malleson quotes one two-type patient who says: "The inside climax comes from loving, but the outside one is just animal feeling" (1949). Would other two-type women agree with such a statement, and if so, cannot the word *loving* be analyzed further?

Clearly there is a great need for more physiological data acquired by couples in domestic surroundings with only machines as "observers." The Foxes' experiment on intrauterine pressure needs repeating until data are available from many women for the different types of orgasm. *If* the squeeze-bulb kind of uterine behavior should turn out to be typical for uterine and blended orgasms, and not for the vulval orgasm, then Freud's original clitoral–vaginal distinction—freed, if possible, of its normative overtones—might reappear in a physiologically sophisticated form. Freudian analysis of female sexuality needs radical revision; but given the evidence currently available, it seems premature to assert (as Masters and Johnson do) that "clitoral and vaginal orgasms are not separate biologic entities" (1966, p. 67).

By approaching the definition of orgasm in a pluralistic way, one can hope to alleviate some of the sexual strictures that recent "how-to" books impose on their public. There is no single correct, definitive, or supremely normal kind of female orgasm. Since people differ in so many aspects of their being, one should expect variability in their modes of sexual satisfaction as well. But obvious as this might seem, psychiatrists and family physicians report that already there are many cases of couples seeking counseling and even divorce because the wife is unable to achieve contractions of the orgasmic platform, even though she responds with great emotional enjoyment to coitus. Many of the young are also confused. The psychiatrist Judianne Densen-Gerber (1972) has recently remarked: "The teen-age girl hung up on the idea of female orgasm ends up by humiliating her masculinity-obsessed but usually inexperienced partner. This syndrome is the major route to youthful drug addiction."

Perhaps the most misunderstood women of all are those who enjoy coitus without an orgasm of any kind. Helene Deutsch (1961) believes that these women are the most "typical" and the most "feminine." Malleson (1962) also defends these women:

> For a great many married couples, this doctrine of the over-valuation of orgasm is disturbing, since it puts a false emphasis on one limited factor in the whole sexual relationship. Such teaching tacitly implies that the mere presence or absence of orgasm should be the criterion of successful intimacy. Apart from the fact that orgasm is by no means possible for many women, people cannot measure their deepest feeling by a physical response. No

one would dream of saying that a person could not really be happy unless he were heard to laugh, nor feel sorrow unless his tears could be seen. (p. 97)

It seems reasonable to believe that there are many different patterns of healthy sexual adjustment, some orgasmic and others not. To insist that women should mold their responses to any one pattern does an injustice to the multiplicity of human nature.

References

Chesser, E. *Love and the married woman,* New York: G. P. Putnam's Sons, 1969.

Clark, L. Is there a difference between a clitoral and a vaginal orgasm? *Journal of Sex Research,* 1970, *6,* 25–28.

Densen-Gerber, J. quoted in *Time,* March 20, 1972, p. 32.

Deutsch, H. quoted in Panel report: frigidity in women (B. E. Moore reporting). *Journal of the American Psychoanalytic Association,* 1961, *9,* 571–584.

Fink, P. J. A review of the investigations of Masters and Johnson. In P. J. Fink and Van B. O. Hammett, (Eds.), *Sexual function and dysfunction.* Philadelphia: F. A. Davis, 1969.

Fox, C. A., Wolff, H. S., and Baker, J. A. Measurement of intra-vaginal and intra-uterine pressures during human coitus by radio-telemetry. *Journal of Reproduction and Fertility,* 1970, *22,* 243–251.

Fox, C. A., and Fox B., Uterine suction during orgasm. *British Medical Journal,* 1967, *1,* 300.

Fox, C. A., and Fox, B., Blood pressure and respiratory patterns during human coitus. *Journal of Reproduction and Fertility,* 1969, *19,* 405–415.

Heiman, M. Psychoanalytic interpretations of Masters' and Johnson's research. In P. J. Fink and Van B. O. Hammett (Eds.), *Sexual function and dysfunction.* Philadelphia: F. A. Davis, 1969.

Heiman, M. Sexual response in women, *Journal of the American Psychoanalytic Association,* 1963, *2,* 360–385.

Kinsey, A. C., Pomeroy, W. B., Martin, C. E., and Gebhard, P. H. *Sexual behavior in the human female.* Philadelphia: W. B. Saunders, 1953.

Kinsey, A. C., Pomeroy, W. B., and Martin, C. E. *Sexual behavior in the human male.* Philadelphia: W. B. Saunders, 1948.

Lessing, D. *The Golden Notebook.* Harmondsworth: Penguin Books, 1964.

Levine, L. A criterion for orgasm in the female. *Marriage Hygiene* (later *International Journal of Sexology*), 1948, *1,* 173–174.

Lowen, A. *Love and orgasm.* New York: Signet Books, 1967.

Malleson, J. *Any wife or any husband.* Baltimore: Penguin Books, 1962.

Malleson, J. Notes and comments. *International Journal of Sexology,* 1949, *2,* 255.

Malleson, J. A criterion for orgasm in the female. *Marriage Hygiene* (later *International Journal of Sexology*), 1948, *1,* 174.

Masters, W. H. quoted in Lehrman, N., *The nature of sex.* London: Sphere Books, 1971.

Masters, W. H. Questions and group discussion. Appended to Masters, W. H., and Johnson, V. E. The sexual response cycles of the human male and female: Comparative anatomy and physiology. In F. A. Beach (Ed.), *Sex and behavior.* New York: John Wiley & Sons, 1965.

Masters, W. H., and Johnson, V. E. *Human sexual response.* Boston: Little, Brown, 1966.

Masters, W. H., and Johnson, V. E. *Human sexual inadequacy.* Boston: Little, Brown, 1970.

McDermott, S. *Studies in female sexuality.* London: Odyssey Press, 1970.

Rainwater, L. *Family design: Marital sexuality, family size, and contraception.* Chicago: Aldine, 1965.

Robertiello, R. C. The "clitoral versus vaginal orgasm" controversy and some of its ramifications. *Journal of Sex Research,* 1970, *6,* 307–311.

Robinson, M. N. *The power of sexual surrender.* New York: Signet Books, 1962.

Roubaud, F. Traité de l'impuissance et de la sterilité chez l'homme et chez la femme. 1855. Quoted in Brecher, E. M., *The sex researchers.* Boston: Little, Brown, 1969. Pp. 288–289.

Sherfey, M. J. The evolution and nature of female sexuality in relation to psychoanalytic theory. *Journal of the American Psychoanalytic Association*, 1966, *9*, 28–128.

VanDemark, N. L., and Hays, R. L. Uterine motility responses to mating. *American Journal of Physiology*, 1952, *170*, 518–521.

Wallin, P., and Clark, A. L. A study of orgasm as a condition of women's enjoyment of coitus in the middle years of marriage. *Human Biology*, 1963, *35*, 131–139.

This chapter reports on the use of masturbation in the treatment of women who have never experienced orgasm (primary orgasmic dysfunction). A nine-step program was developed by the authors that includes directed masturbation in conjunction with sensate pleasuring and other therapy procedures.

A study done by Kohlenberg [Directed Masturbation and the Treatment of Primary Orgasmic Dysfunction, Archives of Sexual Behavior, 1974, 3 (4), 349–356] attempted to test the effectiveness of using masturbation as an adjunct to treatment. The subjects were three couples who had not benefited from a treatment program modeled after that of Masters and Johnson, which did not include masturbation. In all three cases the women became orgasmic at some point after masturbation training was begun.

In spite of the demonstrated effectiveness of masturbation training, some clinicians do not include masturbation as part of their treatment program. It is possible to achieve reasonably good outcome with some primary orgasmic patients using a program that does not include masturbation. However, for those patients who do not do well, referral to a program that included masturbation would be indicated.

13

The Role of Masturbation in the Treatment of Orgasmic Dysfunction

Joseph LoPiccolo and W. Charles Lobitz

Introduction

"No other form of sexual activity has been more frequently discussed, more roundly condemned, and more universally practiced than masturbation" (Dearborn, 1967). In contrast to this general condemnation of masturbation, we feel that masturbation is not only a normal, healthy activity but an extremely effective aid in the treatment of primary orgasmic dysfunction in women. This chapter will describe the role directed masturbation plays in therapy at the University of Oregon Psychology Clinic Sexual Research Program.

Greenbank (1961) studied the attitude toward masturbation of graduating medical students and the faculty in five Philadelphia area medical schools. His research indicated that "half of the students have a feeling that mental illness was

Joseph LoPiccolo • Department of Psychiatry and Behavioral Science, School of Medicine, State University of New York, Stony Brook, New York   ***W. Charles Lobitz*** • Division of Clinical Psychology, Department of Psychiatry, University of Colorado School of Medicine, Denver, Colorado. When this chapter was originally published, Joseph LoPiccolo and W. Charles Lobitz were with the Department of Psychology, University of Oregon, Eugene, Oregon.

frequently caused by masturbation. Even one faculty member in five still believes in this old, and now discredited idea." Because of the apparently still widespread misconceptions about masturbation, even among health professionals, a note on its normality is in order.

Among subhuman primates, masturbation occurs in many species even when ample opportunity to copulate with receptive partners exists (Ford and Beach, 1951). Although masturbation is more common in male than in female animals, it has been observed in female dogs, chinchillas, rats, porcupines, elephants, and dolphins, among other species (Ford and Beach, 1951; Kinsey, Pomeroy, Martin, and Gebhard, 1953). The phylogenetic evidence, then, is that masturbation is a "natural" rather than an "unnatural" act and is seemingly an inherent part of our biological endowment.

Other cultures vary considerably in their attitudes toward masturbation (Ford and Beach, 1951). In some cultures, the Lesu in Melanesia, for example, masturbation is acceptable and is practiced casually in public. In other cultures, it is severely prohibited. Such prohibitions seem to have only the effect of causing people to masturbate in secret rather than actually reducing the occurrence of masturbation. For example, Apinaye boys and girls masturbate frequently, even though such activity is punished if detected and despite the fact that at a ceremony conducted when they are half-grown, their genitals are examined and they are severely beaten if there is any "evidence" of masturbation (Ford and Beach, 1951).

Masturbation is culturally prohibited in American society, despite the total lack of any scientific evidence that it has any psychologically or physiologically harmful effects (Johnson, 1968; Dearborn, 1967). This prohibition seems to have arisen from religious doctrine rather than from any rational scientific basis (Johnson, 1968).

In spite of this cultural prohibition, masturbation is more common in our society than many parents, therapists, and clients realize. The Kinsey data (Kinsey, Pomeroy, and Martin, 1948; Kinsey et al., 1953), now over 20 years old, indicate that 94% of men and 58% of women masturbate to orgasm at some point in their lives. Other more recent studies have obtained higher figures, up to virtually 100% of men and 85% of women (Dearborn, 1967). These incidence figures can be useful in reassuring clients (and therapists) about the "normality" of masturbation.

Theoretical Basis for the Use of Masturbation in Treatment

Although the high incidence of masturbation is useful information for encouraging its acceptance by clients, the ability of masturbation to produce orgasm has more therapeutic importance. Masturbation is especially therapeutic for the primary inorgasmic woman, i.e., one who has never experienced an orgasm from any source of physical stimulation. For this problem, it seems most sensible to begin treatment with the technique most likely to produce an orgasm. Kinsey et al. (1953) reported that the average woman reached orgasm in 95% or more of her masturbatory attempts. This figure considerably exceeds the probability of reaching orgasm through coitus (about .73 for average married women).

Not only is masturbation the most probable way of producing an orgasm, it also produces the most intense orgasm. In a now famous study, subjects' subjective reports as well as recordings of their physiological responses (heart rate and vaginal contractions) indicated that masturbation produced a more intense orgasm than either coitus or manipulation of the genitals by a partner (Masters and Johnson, 1966). It has been suggested that an intense orgasm leads to increased vascularity in the vagina, labia, and clitoris (Bardwick, 1971). In turn, there seems to be evidence that this increased vascularity will enhance the potential for future orgasms. "Frequent orgasms will effect an increase in vascularity, which in turn enhance the orgasmic potential. Nothing succeeds like success, and the increased number of orgasms will lead to the psychological anticipation of pleasure in sex" (Bardwick, 1971). This notion that increased vascularity enhances orgasmic potential is supported by the findings of Kegel (1952). He discovered that patients who strengthened the pubococcygeus muscle through his prescribed exercises experienced an increase in their frequency of orgasm. Since exercising a muscle leads to increased vascularity, it is possible that the increased vascularity in the pubococcygeus was responsible for the increased orgasmic frequency. An increase in pelvic vascularity has also been suggested to explain the effectiveness of androgen therapy in facilitating orgasm (Bardwick, 1971).

To summarize, since masturbation is the most probable method of producing an orgasm and since it produces the most intense orgasm, it logically seems to be the preferred treatment for enhancing orgasmic potential in inorgasmic women.

Although masturbation has been noted in the past to facilitate orgasmic potential, it apparently has not been a systematic part of a therapy program. Hastings (1963) reported that some of his patients increased their sexual responsiveness by increased masturbation. Similarly, sex authorities from Albert Ellis (1960) to "J" (1969) have recommended masturbation with an electric vibrator to facilitate an orgasm. We have developed such a systematic masturbation program for treating primary orgasmic dysfunction.

The Masturbation Program

The masturbation program does not form the totality of our treatment program for inorgasmic women but is an adjunct to a behavioral, time-limited (fifteen sessions) treatment program involving both the husband and wife. The general program involving both husband and wife and a male–female cotherapy team is modeled very directly after the procedure developed by Masters and Johnson (1970) for treating inorgasmic women. The masturbation component of our program is unique to our own work, however, and has been developed by us.

In prescribing a masturbation program, the therapist must obviously deal with both the woman's and her husband's attitudes toward masturbation. It is typical of our clients to have learned very negative attitudes toward masturbation. Several of our clients were directly instructed by their parents that masturbation would have dire consequences ranging from acne to cancer to insanity and were severely punished for masturbating as adolescents. One of our clients was forced, as a child, to bathe wearing her underpants, so that she would never directly see or touch her own genitals. In such cases, it would be extremely naïve to expect a simple order to "go home and masturbate" to have any therapeutic effect if these negative attitudes, fears, and simple errors of fact were not dealt with.

There are several techniques that can be used to help overcome the client's negative attitudes toward masturbation. One such technique is to ask the client to estimate what percentage of people masturbate, before and after marriage. Even well-educated clients typically grossly underestimate these figures (i.e., estimates of 20 to 30% premaritally and 5 to 10% postmaritally are common). The client can be given the correct information, with the therapist also correcting other misconceptions about the normality and universality of masturbation at this point.

However, a lecture by the therapist on the true facts about masturbation does not always deal with the client's irrational emotional reaction to masturbation. In cases where resistance to masturbation is not based so much on ignorance and misinformation as on emotional conditioning, therapist self-disclosure is often useful in changing the client's attitude. That is, given that the client has had time to develop some regard and respect for the therapist, the therapist's calmly and unashamedly discussing his or her own masturbation can be extremely effective in changing the client's negative attitude. The therapist, of course, must be truly unconflicted and comfortable about revealing this information for it to be effective.

When prescribing masturbation for an inorgasmic woman, it is crucial to enlist the cooperation and support of her husband. That is, if the woman has to sneak off to masturbate and feels her husband disapproves, there is little chance that masturbation will be effective in producing orgasm. The husband should be made fully aware of what is wife is doing and the reasons for it, and he should be instructed by the therapists to fully support his wife's masturbation. In our treatment program, we typically split up initially. The female cotherapist discusses masturbation with the female client, while the male cotherapist does the same with the male client. In these individual sessions, the male therapist explains to the husband the rationale for a masturbation program for the wife and deals with any negative reactions the client has. The therapist then directly trains the husband to support his wife's masturbation. With modeling and role-play techniques, we train the husband to make convincingly supportive statements. Our male clients typically take to this procedure well, since they are highly motivated to help their wives become sexually responsive.

In this individual session, the male therapist also suggests to the husband that he should masturbate or, if the husband does masturbate, that he tell his wife about it. We advocate this for two reasons. First, for the wife to feel truly guilt-free about her masturbation, she needs to know not only that her husband approves but that he masturbates as well. In addition, masturbation by the husband is useful in keeping him cooperative, in that the early phases of the Masters and Johnson (1970) treatment for inorgasmic women involve abstinence from intercourse. While the male cotherapist is following this procedure with the husband, the female therapist is similarly explaining the necessity of masturbation to the wife and dealing with any negative reactions she has.

Following these individual sessions, the therapy team rejoins, and the masturbation program is explained in detail to husband and wife.

This program usually consists of nine steps, with the client typically working on one step per week. These steps will be described, with case history data to exemplify the principles involved.

Step 1

In step 1, the client is told that she is "out of touch" with her own body, that indeed she has never really known her own body nor learned to appreciate the beauty of her sexual organs. Accordingly, she is given the assignment to increase her self-awareness. She is told to examine her nude body carefully and try to appreciate its beauty. The client is to use a hand mirror to examine her genitals closely, identifying the various areas with the aid of the diagrams in Hasting's book *Sexual Expression in Marriage* (1966). We recommend this genital exploration be done just after bathing, for reasons of cleanliness and to capitalize on the relaxing qualities of a warm bath. Many of our clients express amazement after following this step. Typical statements are "I never really knew what was down there" and "I was amazed at how little I knew about myself."

At this time, the client is also started on a program of Kegel's (1952) exercises for increasing the tone and vascularity of the pelvic musculature, which presumably will increase her orgasmic potential. We advocate having the client tense and relax her pelvic muscles ten times, repeating this exercise three times daily.

Step 2

Next the client is instructed to explore her genitals tactually as well as visually. She is instructed to explore through touch the various parts of her genitals. To avoid putting her under any performance anxiety to arouse herself sexually, the client is not given any expectation that she should be aroused at this point. In these first two steps, we merely want to the client to become desensitized to the sight and feel of her genitals and to become used to the idea of masturbation. Interestingly enough, it is in these first two steps that we get most resistance from clients. Not uncommonly, the woman reports that she tried but could not bring herself to look at or touch herself. Additional support from the therapists and the husband will usually overcome this problem. It is also useful for the therapist to tell the client that we expect her to feel some apprehension or aversion at this point but that these feelings usually disappear once she begins actually following the program.

Step 3

Next, the client is instructed to continue visual and tactual exploration of her genitals, but with an emphasis on locating sensitive areas that produce feelings of pleasure. She is not to focus on any area in particular but to thoroughly explore the clitoral shaft and hood, the major and minor labia, the vaginal opening, and the whole perineum, especially that area immediately adjacent to the clitoris. In line with the findings of Kinsey et al. (1953) and Masters and Johnson (1966), we have yet to have a client locate the vagina as a strong source of sexual pleasure; most of our clients focus on the clitoral area as the most pleasurable.

Step 4

With the pleasure-producing areas located, the client is now told to concentrate on manual stimulation of these areas. The female cotherapist at this time discusses techniques of masturbation with the client. As most of our clients locate the clitoris as the most pleasurable area, this is usually a discussion of techniques of clitoral manipulation; topics covered include variations of stroking and pressure and the use of a sterile lubricant jelly to enhance pleasure and prevent soreness.

Step 5

If orgasm does not occur in step 4, the client is told to increase the intensity and duration of her masturbation. She is told to masturbate until "something happens" or until she becomes tired or sore. We think of thirty to forty-five minutes as a reasonable upper limit for duration of masturbation and indeed have had clients achieve their first orgasm after as much as forty-five minutes of continuous, intense masturbation. We also recommend the use of pornographic reading material or pictures to enhance arousal. In addition, we suggest the use of erotic fantasies to further increase arousal. Interestingly, the concept of fantasizing during masturbation does not seem to occur spontaneously to our female clients. This is consistent with the data of Kinsey et al. (1953) that a much smaller proportion of women than men fantasize during masturbation.

Step 6

If orgasm is not reached in step 5, we instruct the client to purchase a vibrator of the type sold in pharmacies for facial massage. These can be purchased for as little as five dollars and, as the classified ads in any underground newspaper will attest, are extremely effective in producing sexual arousal. There are two general types of vibrators available: those that strap on the hand and cause the fingers to vibrate and those that are applied directly to the object to be massaged. Both types are effective, but individual preference varies. We have prepared a fact sheet for our clients which lists the various types of vibrators available in town, the price, and where they may be purchased. The client is instructed to masturbate, using the vibrator, lubricant jelly, and pornographic materials. In our most difficult case to date, three weeks of vibrator masturbation, with daily forty-five-minute vibrator sessions, was required to produce orgasm.

We have found a technique of use in cases where orgasm does not occur after some time in step 6. A woman may simply be embarrassed or afraid to have an orgasm, fearing an undignified loss of control with muscular convulsions, inarticulate screaming, and involuntary defecation or urination. To desensitize them to their fears of loss of control, we have such clients role-play the experience of orgasm in their own homes.

Step 7

Once a woman has achieved orgasm through masturbation, our focus shifts to enabling her to experience orgasm through stimulation by her husbasnd. As the first step in this process, we instruct the woman to masturbate with her husband observing her. This desensitizes her to visibly displaying arousal and orgasm in his presence and also functions as an excellent learning experience for her husband. He learns just what techniques of genital stimulation are effective and pleasurable for his wife, from the only person who is truly expert in this subject. Some clients are initially reluctant to masturbate in front of their husbands, but the same techniques of therapist's verbal self-disclosure and coequal involvement of the husband that are used to overcome initial reluctance have also proven effective here.

Step 8

Step 8 simply involves having the husband do for his wife what she has been doing for herself. If she has been using a vibrator, he now uses it on her. If she has been manually manipulating her genitals, he now begins to do this for her.

Step 9

Once orgasm has occurred in step 8, we instruct the couple to engage in intercourse while the husband concurrently stimulates the wife's genitals, either manually or with a vibrator. We recommend the female superior sitting, lateral, or rear-entry coital positions for this activity, as all three positions allow the male easy access to the female's genitals during intromission. Once orgasm has occurred at this step, the client should logically be considered "cured," since the clitoris and not the vagina is now known to be the major locus of sexuality and orgasm in the normal woman (Masters and Johnson, 1966; Kinsey et al., 1953; Lydon, 1971; Weisstein, 1971; Ellis, 1962). Some clients, however, especially those who have been exposed to psychoanalytic theory and its specious distinction between "clitoral" and "vaginal" orgasm, express a wish to achieve orgasm without the necessity for concurrent manual stimulation during coitus. For such clients, we emphasize the importance of achieving adequate clitoral stimulation from some source (e.g., the husband's symphysis) during coitus and point out that this stimulation is most effectively achieved through direct manual manipulation.

In assessing the effectiveness of this program, two questions arise: How successful is the program in producing an orgasm for the totally inorgasmic woman, and how regularly does this woman become orgasmic in sexual activity with her husband?

We have completed treatment (fifteen therapy sessions) with eight women who had never previously experienced orgasm. In all eight cases, these women have gained the ability to achieve orgasm.

In regard to the second effectiveness question, two of these women are now orgasmic with clitoral manipulation by their husbands, but not yet during intercourse. The other six women have achieved orgasm through intercourse with their husbands and continue to experience orgasm in this way. Four of the six no longer require direct manual manipulation of the genitals during intercourse to reach orgasm. The regularity of coital orgasm varies—one client reports orgasm on about 25% of coital opportunities, one on about 50% of coital opportunities, and the other four on nearly every occasion. We are continuing to gather follow-up data on these clients, to assess the stability of change. So far, our follow-up (up to six months) indicates no relapses but rather further gains in the enjoyment of sexual relations.

It is also of interest to note that the crucial first orgasm may occur seemingly at almost any step in this program or indeed in response to nonmasturbatory stimulation following exposure to the program. Of our eight clients, one client first experienced orgasm at step 2, one client at step 3, two clients at step 4, and two clients at step 6. The other two clients experienced first orgasm not through masturbating but in sexual activity with their husbands. One woman experienced first orgasm in clitoral manipulation by the husband, which was temporally concurrent with step 4. The other client achieved first orgasm in intercourse with her husband, which followed several weeks on step 6. While it cannot be proven, it is our feeling that neither of these women would have achieved orgasm without having first experienced our masturbation program.

Although our sample is as yet small, we feel that this masturbation program offers considerable promise in the treatment of primary orgasmic dysfunction.

References

Bardwick, J. M. *Psychology of women: A study of bio-cultural conflicts.* New York: Harper & Row, 1971.

Dearborn, L. W. Autoeroticism. In A. Ellis and A. Abarbanel (Eds.), *The encyclopedia of sexual behavior.* New York: Hawthorn Books, 1967.

Ellis, A. *The art and science of love.* New York: Lyle Stuart, 1960.

Ellis, A. *The American sexual tragedy.* New York: Lyle Stuart, 1962.

Ford, C. S., and Beach, F. A. *Patterns of sexual behavior.* New York: Harper & Bros., 1951.

Greenbank, R. K. Are medical students learning psychiatry? *Medical Journal,* 1961, *64,* 989–992.

Hastings, D. W. *Impotence and frigidity.* Boston: Little, Brown, 1963.

Hastings, D. W. *Sexual expression in marriage.* New York: Bantam, 1966.

"J". *The sensuous woman.* New York: Dell, 1969.

Johnson, W. R. *Masturbation.* SIECUS Study Guide No. 3, Sex Information and Education Council of the United States, 1968.

Kegel, A. H. Sexual functions of the pubococcygeus muscle. *Western Journal of Surgery, Obstetrics and Gynecology,* 1952, *60,* 521.

Kinsey, A. C., Pomeroy, W. B., and Martin, C. E. *Sexual behavior in the human male.* Philadelphia: W. B. Saunders, 1948.

Kinsey, A. C., Pomeroy, W. B., Martin, C. E., and Gebhard, P. H. *Sexual behavior in the human female.* Philadelphia: W. B. Saunders, 1953.

Lydon, S. The politics of orgasm. In M. Garskof (Ed.), *Roles women play.* Belmont, California: Brooks/Cole, 1971.

Masters, W. H., and Johnson, V. E. *Human sexual response.* Boston: Little, Brown, 1966.

Masters, W. H., and Johnson, V. E. *Human sexual inadequacy.* Boston: Little, Brown, 1970.

Weisstein, N. Psychology constructs the female, or the fantasy life of the male psychologist. In M. Garskof (Ed.), *Roles women play.* Belmont, California: Brooks/Cole, 1971.

Systematic desensitization of anxiety responses is a common element of many behavior therapies. In this chapter Husted discusses the use of desensitization in cases of female sexual dysfunction involving anxiety as a factor.

 Husted reports on the results of a study she conducted comparing systematic desensitization through imagery with desensitization in a real-life situation (in vivo). The results are of interest because although she found the imaginal desensitization to be more rapidly completed, there was no significant difference between the two in reducing anxiety in sexual situations. Also, it is important to note that neither therapy program was particularly effective in increasing the rate of coital orgasm for primary inorgasmic women.

 A recent study by Wincze and Caird (The effects of systematic desensitization in the treatment of essential sexual dysfunction in women, Behavior Therapy, *1976, 7, 335–342) compared the standard imaginal desensitization procedure with a procedure using relaxation plus the viewing of a videotaped hierarchy. Their findings suggest that the video desensitization procedure is more effective in reducing anxiety to heterosexual situations. However, only 25% of the women who were inorgasmic at the beginning of the study were able to achieve orgasm at the end of treatment, regardless of whether they received the standard or video desensitization. Both this study and Husted's research seem to suggest that while desensitization may be effective in lowering anxiety in sexual situations, it is not a very effective means of increasing orgasmic capacity. It seems likely that addition of a directed masturbation training program to desensitization would increase effectiveness in producing orgasm, as discussed in other chapters of this volume.*

14

Desensitization Procedures in Dealing with Female Sexual Dysfunction

June R. Husted

A therapist who works with many cases involving marital or sexual difficulties may encounter some cases of sexual dysfunction that appear to be less amenable to treatment using current popular methods. Not infrequently, a client requests therapy for sexual dysfunction but does not have a sexual partner. Indeed, the anxiety a client experiences at the thought of intimate contact with a member of the opposite sex may be so great as to prevent him or her from developing a sexual relationship. In other cases, a sexual partner may be available but unable to attend therapy sessions. Still other clients reveal such a deep and pervasive neurosis that behavioral approaches to treatment appear to be inadequate.

 Consider the following example of an actual case. A woman applied for treatment in a clinic with a complaint of chronic vaginismus. She reported that she had sexual intercourse about once a year in seven years of marriage. Because of the strong contractions of the vaginal opening that occurred with any contact in the genital area, her husband was rarely able to penetrate for intercourse, despite the fact that she had become pregnant on one occasion and had delivered a baby two years before. Her gynecologist had tried to stretch the muscles sur-

June R. Husted • Veterans Administration Hospital, Long Beach, California

rounding the vaginal opening through a series of physical exercises, with no success. For this and no other reasons, her marriage had disintegrated and she was getting a divorce.

She revealed a history that would have given a psychoanalyst material for prolonged therapy. She hated the female figures with whom she identified, a stepmother and an older stepsister. The stepsister had forced her to perform oral–genital stimulation when she was six or seven. A strange man had exposed himself to her at age nine, which frightened her and made her feel guilty and ashamed. She cringed at all physical contact and had felt an aversion to petting and sexual activities since her first experiences with them. In addition, she saw herself as ugly, with an unattractive figure, and she had not worn a bathing suit for five years because of this self-image. In reality, she was quite attractive, although she dressed in a very austere manner, apparently so as to avoid attracting men. She panicked if a male even started a friendly conversation with her. She didn't have a sexual partner, and didn't *want* one, although she felt upset and "abnormal" that this was true.

Despite her psychodynamics and her lack of a sexual partner, the limited amount of time available for treatment prompted a decision to begin systematic desensitization, using imagery. Two hierarchies were constructed. One of these included items concerned with evaluation, such as entering a room full of men, going to the beach in a bathing suit, showering nude in the presence of other women, and swimming nude in mixed company. The second hierarchy included sexual items, such as situations of foreplay and intercourse, as well as scenes in which men made suggestive comments, or in which she entered a man's apartment. She was first presented items from the evaluation hierarchy, since she estimated these elicited less anxiety than items from the sexual hierarchy. By the time she had completed half of the evaluation items, she arrived at the next therapy session, reporting she had bought a bathing suit, tried it on in front of a mirror, and concluded she didn't look bad. At each subsequent session, her skirts became shorter, her hairstyle became softer, and her style of dress became sexier. After she began the sexual hierarchy and had finished some of the earlier items including kissing and light petting, she came to the following session describing in enthusiastic detail how she had accepted a lunch date with a man from work. Somehow they ended up necking in the car—and she experienced considerable pleasure, and no anxiety. Two weeks later, after five desensitization sessions, and the completion of three-fifths of the sexual hierarchy, including an item describing sexual intercourse, she arrived at her appointment with a look of amazed satisfaction. She reported that she had sexual intercourse repeatedly the previous evening with a new boyfriend, the first successful and emotionally satisfying experience of her life. One year later, she reported continued sexual adjustment, and no recurrence of anxiety.

Like any technique, systematic desensitization is not always so remarkably successful, and not always the best method to use. It can be an effective means of treating many types of sexual dysfunction, both with and without adjunctive treatment methods. Because it can be such an efficient technique, this chapter will describe what it is, when and how it can be used, and what results can be expected from its use. The present focus will be on the treatment of female sexual dysfunction, and some related research findings. However, desensitization is also widely used in the treatment of impotency.

Systematic desensitization is not a new technique. It was developed by Dr. Wolpe and described in his book on behavior therapy in 1958, and it has been used in the treatment of a wide variety of phobias, as well as sexual fears, since that time (Wolpe, 1958). Wolpe states: "If a response antagonistic to anxiety can be made to occur in the presence of anxiety-evoking stimuli so that it is accompanied by a complete or partial suppression of the anxiety responses, the bond between these stimuli and the anxiety responses will be weakened" (p. 71).

Wolpe considers the most effective responses for counterconditioning in human adults to be relaxation responses, sexual responses, and assertive responses. Deep muscle relaxation is the response most widely selected as antagonistic to anxiety for use of the technique. From this theoretical framework, systematic desensitization will be most effective in treating sexual dysfunction where anxiety is a major component. An anxiety response involves the widespread discharge of the sympathetic division of the autonomic nervous system. In contrast, penile erection and preorgasmic arousal are assumed to be a function of the parasympathetic nervous system, and consequently inhibited by discharges of the sympathetic nervous system that are produced in response to anxiety. As a result, anxiety inhibits sexual arousal.

We know there are different varieties of sexual dysfunction in women, and this approach might not be indicated for all, since anxiety is not always involved. (1) Among these types of dysfunction is vaginismus, in which an involuntary reflex that occurs in response to attempted vaginal penetration causes a spastic contraction of the vaginal opening, so that penile penetration is either painful or impossible. This condition may or may not include the presence of negative or aversive emotional reactions to other sexual behaviors. (2) There are women who report negative or aversive emotional reactions to coitus (e.g., anxiety or repugnance). (3) There are women who report a lack of interest in sexual arousal and intercourse, which is considered a neutral experience. (4) There are many women who report varying amounts of sexual arousal and pleasure, sometimes with a high level of sexual tension that does not culminate in the achievement of orgasm. We might add a fifth category, since because of the historic psychoanalytic distinction between orgasms experienced through clitoral stimulation and those experienced with vaginal penetration, the term *frigidity* has been extended by some authors to refer to women who achieve orgasmic release only through extra-coital stimulation. Although we now know there is no physiological difference between these two types of orgasm, there are women who fall in this category who would prefer to reach orgasm during penetration.

Systematic desensitization is probably not the treatment of choice for women in the last two categories, where anxiety is not a component of the problem. The woman who enjoys all sexual interactions, and experiences varying levels of arousal without reaching orgasm, is not likely to respond differently after treatment directed at anxiety reduction. Since anxiety is not apparently present to inhibit her responsiveness, what is needed is a technique to build up or increase her sexual tension. This may be more efficiently provided by masturbation training, use of a vibrator, or possibly use of the Kegel exercises for increasing the muscle tone of the pubococcygeus muscle (Deutsch, 1968; LoPiccolo, 1971). For women in the last tentative category, who enjoy sex but reach orgasm through noncoital stimulation, what would appear to be needed is some method of shaping response, such that penetration occurs at the point of most intense arousal initially or is combined with noncoital methods of direct stimulation, so that arousal cues become associated with penetration. In addition, educational methods and Kegel exercises may be appropriate, so that the woman learns to obtain peak levels of stimulation.

Desensitization is most effectively used with women in the first two groups: those with vaginismus, and those with aversive and anxiety reactions to sexual situations. The initial source of these negative reactions is not necessarily important. We're not dealing with the initial cause of anxiety unless it still exists, which is rarely the case. What is important is that the laws of conditioning apply and generalization occurs, so that anxiety as well as arousal is elicited by a wide variety of sexual cues. A colorful example of the effects of conditioning is seen in a study in which the slide of a woman's boot was shown to a group of male subjects immediately following the presentation of a slide of an attractive nude female (Rachman, 1966). After several such presentations, the slide of the boot was shown alone, and sensitive measures of penile erection indicated that arousal responses occurred in response to the slide of the boots alone, as a result of classical conditioning. In addition, when other slides of boots and shoes were shown, the arousal response followed a normal generalization curve.

The same generalization occurs when anxiety responses are involved. For example, one client showed considerable anxiety when her breasts were touched in foreplay, and panicked when her breasts were orally stimulated by her husband. After repeated presentation of an item describing breast stimulation in the desensitization procedures, with considerable anxiety, she recalled that she had breast-fed her child, and the nipples had become dry and cracked, eliciting extreme pain with any contact. This had occurred years before and had been forgotten. Yet now she avoided any breast contact in sexual foreplay, and tension was elicited in other sexual situations. Although breast feeding may have been the cause of the anxiety, there was no need to include memories of this scene in the treatment; it was the *present* sexual scenes that had to be desensitized. It was notable that the majority of women who participated in a research project for reduction of sexual anxiety had reported that considerable pain occurred with penetration during many of their initial sexual experiences. Two of them were so traumatized that they avoided all coitus during the first several months of their marriages. Even though pain was no longer present, they continued to have more anxiety and usually anesthesia during situations involving penetration, with a resultant drop in sexual arousal at this point. At the time of penetration, then, not only were they losing the direct stimulation that they may have had during foreplay, but arousal was also being inhibited by the anxiety conditioned to these penetration cues. Systematic desensitization is appropriate for this group of clients because it inhibits the anxiety elicited by such sexual cues, allowing them to be naturally arousing.

Desensitization is probably also effective for many women in the third group, for whom sex is a neutral experience, even though they report no anxiety. Some recent research shows that most subjects having sexual dysfunction show greater autonomic reactivity in response to sexual cues than do subjects without any dysfunction, even when they do *not* verbally report anxiety. It is possible that such women are less aware of anxiety and tension, and therefore merely experience a lack of sexual arousal. As a result, they become apathetic about sexual experiences. Through desensitization, such tension as is not consciously experienced may be reduced, and greater sexual arousal may result.

One research study was designed to learn the effects of two forms of systematic desensitization on anxiety and the results of anxiety reduction on sexual behavior (Husted, 1972). Only those subjects were selected who reported anxiety or negative emotional reactions in sexual situations, despite their ability to reach orgasm. Most of the women who finally participated rarely or never achieved orgasm at the present time, although some had been orgasmic in the past. Despite advertisements and referral requests which clearly stated the requirements, about two of every three referrals and inquiries received stated that the women did not experience any noticeable anxiety and that they enjoyed sex. They were simply unable to reach orgasm. This suggests that women who are aware of anxiety or negative emotional reactions in sexual situations are only a small proportion of those experiencing sexual dysfunction. Cooper (1970) found this type of patient was most resistant to treatment. He found only 25% of women in this category showed any improvement after one year of therapy, which consisted of a variety of behavioral and counseling techniques. For this group of clients, then, some form of treatment to reduce anxiety seems essential.

How to Use Systematic Desensitization

Having decided that systematic desensitization should be used, where does one start? The first step is to develop a rather complete list of all sexual situations that would generally be relevant to the individual's experience. This should include items that represent real experiences in which the woman has been involved or expects to be involved in the future. For example, for women who do not have an ongoing relationship, situations of initial dating or entering a man's apartment, as in the first example, may be relevant. For someone who is married or involved in a more regular relationship, more idiosyncratic cues may be included. The item should be described in sufficient detail for the patient to clearly picture the scene, and preferably in the kinds of words that are familiar and comfortable to the individual. Items should be included from all levels of anxiety, from complete relaxation (0 subjective units of distress, or "suds") to complete panic (100 suds), and from the full range of situations in which anxiety may be present. Generally, a hierarchy might include from ten to twenty-five items, although longer hierarchies are reported in the literature.

Traditionally, Wolpe has stressed the importance of minimal distance between items (5 to 10 suds), with very careful development of a hierarchy such that each item elicits only slightly more anxiety than the item before. This could create some difficulty, since in sexual situations more than one patient reports the greatest anxiety when her partner makes some verbal or physical overtures, and claims that actual intercourse doesn't cause as much anxiety if things have progressed that far. If a client is to perform behaviors as they are desensitized, one can see the obvious difficulties in setting up a hierarchy such that she can have intercourse (if it elicits low anxiety) but no foreplay or interactions that normally precede intercourse. This is a bigger problem where in vivo (live) methods of desensitization are used. Fortunately, research has shown that standardized hierarchies can be as effectively used as individualized ones in many cases, and desensitization can be successfully accomplished even when the items on the hierarchy are not specifically arranged in gradually increasing order. Therefore, the hierarchy can be arranged in a more logical order, of gradually increasing intimacy.

Hierarchy items were selected from clients previously treated for sexual dysfunction and were arranged in order of increasing intimacy. Thirty women with sexual anxiety then estimated the amount of anxiety elicited by each of these sexual situations, using the suds scale of 0 to 100. On the basis of their estimates, the results obtained are shown in Table 1, showing the average suds rating, and the hierarchy rank for each item.

You'll notice that the hardest item for these women was using a new position during coitus (63 suds); and that both items involving penetration were ranked very high. Penetration of the vagina manually by the partner, during foreplay, was the second most difficult item, while penetration for the initiation of coitus was fourth most difficult. Surprisingly, seven women ranked oral stimulation of their breasts by partners as causing the greatest amount of anxiety, perhaps suggestive of considerable inhibition during foreplay. Other results worth noting included: (1) Having sex somewhere other than in the bedroom, with its sexual cues, elicited less anxiety; (2) intercourse itself produced less anxiety than the genital contact that usually precedes it; and (3) situations in which the woman was in control, i.e., she was stimulating the male, were a source of less anxiety than situations in which she was receiving stimulation. These results may not hold true for all clients, and it requires a careful interview to be sure all relevant cues are taken into account in developing an individualized hierarchy. Though none of these women referred to any additional relevant cues, it might be advisable for some women to add items concerned with contact with semen and vaginal fluids, when these are aversive, or to include scenes depicting loss of control during orgasm if relevant.

If relaxation responses are to be used in the counterconditioning process, there are three main steps involved. First, the client is trained in relaxation exercises similar to those developed by Jacobson (1938), so as to achieve increasingly deep levels of complete muscular relaxation. These relaxation exercises have been abbreviated to allow training within six or fewer sessions, and the client is instructed to practice them at home daily for a total of thirty minutes (Wolpe and Lazarus, 1966). Other techniques for developing progressive relaxation can also be used. Second, the list of anxiety-producing events or situations is developed, with careful identification of all sources of anxiety. The important situations are ranked according to increasing amounts of subjective anxiety, or modified to

Table 1. Sexual Hierarchy, Showing Average Suds Rating and Rank of Items

Suds	Rank	Item	
15.9	3	1.	You are dancing with your husband/boyfriend while fully clothed.
11.3	1	2.	You are sitting on your husband's lap, fully clothed.
13.1	2	3.	He kisses your cheeks and forehead tenderly.
18.4	4	4.	He kisses and caresses your face and hair.
25.9	6	5.	You are at home alone with him and he gives you a warm, suggestive look or comment.
27.8	7	6.	He kisses you in a warm, suggestive way on your lips.
24.5	5	7.	He caresses your shoulders and back (vice versa).
42.1	10	8.	He caresses your buttocks and thighs (v.v.).
33.5	8	9.	He French-kisses you, with tongue contact.
43.3	12	10.	You embrace and hug while clothed, and are aware of your partner's desire for sexual relations.
38.5	9	11.	You caress your partner's genitals while you are clothed.
42.2	11	12.	He caresses your breasts while you are clothed.
52.6	22	13.	He caresses your genital area while you are clothed.
45.5	14	14.	You are lying in bed clothed, are hugging and cuddling, and are aware of your partner's erection and desire for intercourse.
50.3	16	15.	You are lying in bed unclothed, hugging and holding your partner prior to his arousal, and aware of the feeling of his body against yours, and of his desire for sex.
51.2	19	16.	You are lying in bed unclothed, hugging him, and aware of his erection as you feel his body against yours.
50.5	17	17.	He caresses your breasts while you are naked.
59.5	28	18.	He orally stimulates your breasts and nipples.
51.6	21	19.	You are lying in bed unclothed, and he runs his hands over your nude body (v.v.).
44.8	13	20.	You caress your partner's genitals while he is nude, prior to his arousal.
51.4	20	21.	You caress his genitals while he is nude, and he has an erection.
55.9	26	22.	He manually stimulates your clitoral area.
59.7	29	23.	He inserts his finger into your vagina during foreplay.
56.9	27	24.	He penetrates you for the initiation of intercourse, with you in the superior position.
53.6	23	25.	You encompass his penis in your vagina while in the female-superior position, and begin slow pelvic movements.
51.0	18	26.	You are engaged in active sexual intercourse.
62.9	30	27.	You are engaged in sexual intercourse, using a new position.
49.1	15	28.	You are having sexual intercourse in the living room or some other location.
	Optional		
53.9	24	29.	Your husband is stimulating your genitals with his lips and tongue.
55.9	25	30.	You are stimulating your husband's genitals with your lips and tongue.

approximate increasing intimacy as described above. Third, the events that are least anxiety-provoking are verbally presented to the client when she is deeply relaxed. If visualization of the described scene elicits any anxiety, the patient signals, she is told to stop imagining the scene, and suggestions are given to reinstate relaxation. The scene is presented repeatedly until there is no indication of anxiety on two successive occasions, at which time the next item in the hierarchy is presented. This procedure continues until the entire hierarchy of events has been neutralized and fails to elicit anxiety. Only a few scenes are usually presented in any session, the progress dependent upon the rate at which anxiety-producing scenes are neutralized, according to the client's subjective report.

During this process, the client's actual sexual encounters are curtailed so as to parallel the process of desensitization, eliminating the fears that may be associated with final performance. He or she may then engage in any of the behaviors she enjoys and wishes to try only *after* the behaviors have been neutralized through desensitization using imagery. If a behavior still elicits some residual anxiety when performed in real life, it is repeated in the next session with explicit description of the important cues that relate to the anxiety. This may be necessary as the client discovers new cues that are present in the described situations or, if transfer is not complete, as may occur.

As mentioned earlier, Wolpe proposes that sexual responses themselves can be used in counterconditioning procedures when anxiety has produced a partial, rather than a complete, inhibition of sexual responsiveness. He reports successful treatment of many cases of impotence using such in vivo systematic desensitization, without the use of relaxation responses. There are almost no reports of successful treatment of female sexual dysfunction using such in vivo desensitization prior to the work of Masters and Johnson. One exception is the treatment of two cases of vaginismus reported by Haslam (1965). By introducing glass rods of gradually increasing diameter into the vagina of the women, spasms that were preventing intercourse were eliminated.

It is stated *prior* to the work of Masters and Johnson, because in vivo desensitization appears to be one important component of their treatment. As Wolpe describes his procedures, the client is firmly admonished not to engage in any sexual activity until it can be done with complete confidence and without anxiety. He or she is advised initially to merely lie next to the partner and to enjoy contact, with no attempt at sexual intercourse. The couple proceeds no further than non-genital caressing for the first one or two occasions. As anxiety decreases in these sessions, sexual arousal is expected to emerge automatically and to increasingly inhibit any remaining anxiety. Intimate contact continues through initial contact and foreplay, to varying degrees and duration of penile insertion, and increasing amounts of movement (Wolpe and Lazarus, 1966). A hierarchy may be developed by the procedures described above, but the obvious constraints exist for the order of behaviors tried. Therefore, the client follows a schedule of gradual approach to increasingly more intimate behaviors. Each early behavior is repeated until additional anxiety is eliminated through inhibition or extinction. When the elimination of anxiety permits the inherently pleasurable aspects of these behaviors to become more potent, sexual responsiveness occurs automatically and acts to further inhibit anxiety through counterconditioning. This form of desensitization eliminates the need for training in relaxation and may be necessary for those clients who cannot learn deep muscle relaxation or cannot visualize. On the other hand, the earlier described form of systematic desensitization with relaxation and imagery provides an ideal method of treatment for clients without a sexual partner, or with too much anxiety or inhibition to seek one.

Another variation of desensitization is seen in the masturbation theory of LoPiccolo and Lobitz (1971). They report that they don't usually use relaxation in treatment but do have clients work through a hierarchy of situations at home. As with the other forms of desensitization, the clients discontinue intercourse and other anxiety-arousing behaviors. His hierarchy centers around masturbation techniques, on the premise that masturbation is the most probable method of producing orgasm in the primarily inorgasmic woman. His hierarchy begins with initial self-exploration of the woman's genital area visually, then to manual exploration, increasingly intense self-stimulation alone—often with the use of a vibrator—followed by self-stimulation with the husband observing, and then stimulation of the genital area by the husband. As with all desensitization procedures, the individual starts with the easiest situations and repeats each until it can be comfortably performed with no anxiety. The usual result of this is that arousal occurs.

The Effects of These Forms of Desensitization in Treatment

It was suggested that the more successful work that has been reported for the treatment of sexual problems has had as a common factor the use of one of these forms of systematic desensitization. We also noted that the original theory proposes that both relaxation responses and sexual responses would be effective for counterconditioning, since they are both predominantly a function of the parasympathetic nervous system, and thus antagonistic to the sympathetic nervous system dominance associated with anxiety. In contrast to Wolpe's suggestion that sexual responses might be directly used only when sexual responsiveness has been partially and not completely inhibited by anxiety, Masters and Johnson did all of their work with "sensate focus" and show very good results. While this is a variety of in vivo desensitization, we do not have any measure of the level of anxiety of the clients. In addition, their treatment involves more than sensate focus alone, so there is still little evidence that in vivo desensitization alone might be effective. In addition to counseling and sensate focus exercises, at least three other therapy measures are routinely included in the Masters and Johnson treatment of the nonorgasmic female. First, the Kegel exercises are introduced to strengthen the muscle tone of the pubococcygeus muscle. Deutsch (1968) reported that these exercises alone produced improvement of sexual responsiveness in 65% of nonorgasmic women. Second, the nonorgasmic woman is taught to masturbate and is instructed to do so daily during treatment. Third, the use of a vibrator is introduced to increase sexual tension where needed. While such adjunctive measures are not mentioned in their book, they may be a very important part of treatment and certainly need to be objectively evaluated if we are to understand the process of reversal of sexual dysfunction and to continue to make improvements.

To more clearly learn the comparative effects of these two forms of desensitization, with and without the participation of a partner in therapy, a research study was designed which carefully excluded all of the extra techniques that might normally be added in typical sexual counseling and therapy. There were no attempts to reeducate the patients; even their requests for book referrals were postponed until the end of the project. There were no attempts to change the woman's attitudes or "sexual value system." There were no instructions to masturbate or to use other auxilliary means of stimulation, although women were allowed to use any means of stimulation that were a normal part of behavior. There were no instructions for use of the Kegel exercises. For half of the subjects, there was no partner involved in therapy, although they all had a partner who agreed to participate and cooperate with the instructions. Half of the women were treated through imaginal systematic desensitization, in which relaxation responses were paired with visualization of increasingly more intimate sexual behaviors; and half of the women were treated using in vivo sexual responses, introduced in a progressively more intimate order, similar to sensate focus exercises. All the women used the same hierarchy of sexual situations and completed them in the same order. Each subject progressed to the next hierarchy item only after completing the earlier items on two successive occasions with no reported anxiety. The duration of the sessions and the limitations on progress were structured so that all women could complete the hierarchy in the same period of time. The therapy sessions continued until all items on the hierarchy had been neutralized, for a maximum of fifteen sessions. An explicit description of the instructions is available in the original manuscript (Husted, 1972).

To understand the contributions of increased sexual communication to each of these forms of desensitization, the partners of half of the subjects were excluded from the therapy sessions. These husbands were interviewed initially, and each was told what the therapy would involve. His cooperation was assured, and he was invited to call the therapist if any problems or questions developed. It was then possible to determine statistically whether there were any significant effects of including the partner in therapy, as well as any differences in the two basic treatment techniques.

Differences in Efficiency

The most important and significant difference between treatment groups, as shown in the research results, was a difference in efficiency. The number of sessions required to neutralize all items on the Sexual Hierarchy was compared for the two forms of desensitization, and for the presence/absence of the partner in therapy with attempts to increase "sexual communication." The statistical analysis revealed a highly significant difference in the number of sessions required by the two methods of desensitization ($p < .001$). Inspection of the means for the two levels of desensitization showed that subjects treated by imaginal desensitization required an average of 7.8 sessions, while those treated by in vivo desensitization required an average of 13.3 sessions, almost twice as many to achieve the same level of anxiety reduction. The participation of the partner in therapy did not have a significant effect on the number of sessions.

Two factors appeared to contribute to treatment differences. First, since the treatment didn't remove women from their normal environment, such events as house guests, marital arguments, overtime work, or school pressures provided distractions for the in vivo groups, who would then not complete their home assignments. The same distractions would not interfere with progress during a session of imaginal desensitization, whether or not the behaviors were then engaged in at home. Second, for women who were treated by desensitization using relaxation and visualization, attempts to engage in the neutralized behaviors in real life were frequently made with no residual anxiety, suggesting that the anxiety reduction that had been accomplished in the sessions had transferred or generalized to the actual situations. For women treated by in vivo methods, the same behavior might have to be repeated several times before sufficient anxiety reduction had been accomplished to allow progress to the next behavior on the hierarchy. The women kept daily checklists of the behaviors they engaged in at home, and the amount of anxiety reported in response to at-home behaviors, and the results showed there were more than twice as many anxiety points reported by women in the in vivo treatment. This suggests that for outpatient treatment, the type of desensitization that used the deep muscle relaxation and visualization is the fastest, most efficient method of reducing sexual anxiety, with the lowest amount of distress produced during the progress of treatment. This reduces the number of sessions needed for treatment.

That these results are so clear-cut, in contrast to studies comparing the two forms of desensitization for treatment of other types of phobias, may be due to a third factor. Most phobias follow an avoidance paradigm, such that the subject is never or rarely actually exposed to the feared object or situation, and anxiety reduction reinforces the avoidance response. In contrast, despite her general aversion to sexual encounters, a woman with sexual anxiety must frequently overcome her emotional reactions and expose herself to the feared situation in order to please her husband. She therefore has a history of many encounters with the source of her anxiety, without any reduction in the amount of anxiety. The effectiveness of in vivo methods may be reduced because of this, resulting in the superiority of relaxation as a counterconditioning response.

Attitude Change

In reviewing the many approaches to treatment of sexual dysfunction, we see they overlap in some ways and complement each other in other ways. Some of the therapies are directed toward emotions, some toward attitudes, and some toward behaviors, all with some positive effect. This probably illustrates how these three aspects—attitude, emotion, and behavior—interact with one another, such that a change in any one of the three produces changes in the others. Much of the research in social psychology on "cognitive dissonance" demonstrates the way changes in behavior cause changes in attitudes. The research described above included no attempt to change the client's attitude or "sexual value system" through education, counseling, or other means. The women were asked to record the frequency of certain attitudes that are commonly expressed, positive ones such as "I looked forward to expressing affection to my husband today," and negative ones such as "male sexuality seems too physical and demanding." The maximum score that could be tallied on either scale was 16. A statistical trend analysis showed surprisingly clear results. It demonstrated a reciprocal relationship between anxiety and subjective reports of sexual interest and arousal, with a highly significant linear trend in attitude change as the hierarchy items were completed. Arousal and positive sexual attitudes increased, while negative attitudes decreased in a linear fashion with therapeutic progress. There were no significant differences between treatment groups on either of these changes, although the imaginal groups showed somewhat smoother progress. Thus, much attitude change appeared to be a result of anxiety reduction, directly related to the progress of counterconditioning, even when attitude was not directly dealt with in the therapy.

Effect of Treatment

Since desensitization procedures are directed toward anxiety reduction, changes in ratings of anxiety were of major interest. The subjects rated the amount of anxiety they felt in each of the sexual situations on the hierarchy, using the "suds" ratings, and these were totaled to provide an anxiety score. The women repeated these ratings when half the items had been completed, again at the end of treatment, and finally six weeks after treatment had been finished. The reduction in anxiety for experimental subjects, shown by this change score, was highly significant when compared with the control subjects. Anxiety scores dropped 60% by mid-treatment, and 80% by the end of treatment and at follow-up. In comparisons between treatment groups, however, statistical analysis showed no significant differences resulting from either type of desensitization used, or from the participation of the husband in therapy with efforts to increase sexual communication.

This reduction in sexual anxiety was seen to be accompanied by increases in coital frequency ($p < .05$), increases in extracoital orgasmic responsiveness ($p < .01$), and higher self-ratings of improvement ($p < .01$) compared with control subjects, on both posttreatment and follow-up measures. Ratings of coital enjoyment increased also, though this just missed significance. When we compared the changes in frequency of orgasm with coitus for the different groups across time, it looked as though the groups without husbands in therapy were signficantly better. A careful look at the data, however, indicated that the differences were not due to treatment effects. Rather, subjects in the communication groups were, through chance distribution, all primary nonorgasmic women; four subjects in the noncommunication groups had been at least occasionally orgasmic in the past. The frequency of orgasmic response increased for these latter women following treatment, producing the statistical difference. Similar significant increases were seen in the frequency of noncoital orgasms for some treatment groups as therapy progressed. A close look revealed the results were largely due to the fact that two subjects in one group had purchased a vibrator during the course of treatment (without telling the therapist) and began to use it with their partners when the appropriate point was reached—with success. It's quite possible that the reduction in anxiety and focus on sexual enjoyment may have enabled the women to try some of these techniques. One of the women claimed she had *never* experienced any feelings of sexual arousal previously and had considered herself incurably "frigid" prior to treatment. With anxiety and inhibitions reduced she became more innovative.

The fact that frequency of orgasmic response increased when anxiety was reduced for all subjects having an orgasmic history but rarely for others demonstrates that the presence of anxiety can inhibit responsiveness; but lack of anxiety does not ensure completion of the response cycle. Two subjects who reported a complete absence of any sexual anxiety following treatment (a total hierarchy score of 0, and ratings of 0 anxiety for all behaviors at home), and who reported greater sexual pleasure than was ever previously experienced, with intense levels of arousal, nonetheless remained nonorgasmic. For such women, adjunctive measures that increase sexual tension, such as the use of vibrators, training in masturbation techniques, or muscular exercises, appear to be necessary for complete reversal of orgasmic impairment.

Because of the restrictions on therapy techniques required for a controlled investigation of these two components of treatment, there are still more questions to be answered by other research. There are nonetheless some relevant conclusions to be seen from the results, and some strong suggestions for approaches to treatment.

First, systematic desensitization using relaxation responses with images appears to be the fastest method of reducing anxiety and inhibitions regarding sexual behaviors for women in whom such anxiety is a factor. In addition, this technique reduces the amount of tension and distress during the actual sensate focus exercises at home. Thus it is an efficient method of bringing the client to a stage of enjoyment where other methods of treatment can be introduced.

Second, since the presence of the partner in therapy sessions had no significant effect on the results of treatment, providing, of course, he cooperates in the progress of therapy, it isn't essential that he participate. If the partner absolutely cannot come to therapy for some reason, the therapist doesn't need to refuse treatment. In addition, for clients who do not have a sexual partner, use of imaginal desensitization methods may reduce sexual anxiety and inhibitions so as to allow them to develop the desired relationships. Sexual communication appears to act more like a dependent variable, in that it increases automatically with the progress of therapy and the focus on sexual exercises, even when direct attempts to increase such communication are not made in therapy.

Third, this type of client tends to label herself as neurotic, and as having some deep psychological problem, even though her personality profile shows most scales are within the normal range of the MMPI. She is very much reassured to learn that the problem is psychological only in the sense that *learning* is psychological; and through relearning, the problem can be reversed. Most therapists have seen the tension that develops when the clients start to worry about why they are not "normal." To stress the role of conditioning elicits their active cooperation in a problem-solving approach to recondition their sexual responsiveness.

Finally, for the primary nonorgasmic woman, physical and "mechanical" methods appear to be a very important adjunct in treatment. We're apparently faced with two levels of treatment. One is focused on the reduction of anxiety and inhibitions; the second is focused on the increase of sexual tension for those women who do not have a predisposition for easy orgasmic release, for reversal of orgasmic impairment. We don't need to apologize for such mechanical measures; they need to be given objective appraisal. For the woman with high levels of arousal and no anxiety or inhibition, training in methods to build up sexual tension may be all that is required. She does not need systematic desensitization techniques. For those women who do experience sexual anxiety, systematic desensitization appears to be the highly effective method for reducing such anxiety and thereby increasing sexual responsiveness.

References

Cooper, A. J. Frigidity, treatment and short-term prognosis. *Journal of Psychosomatic Research*, 1970, *14*, 133.

Deutsch, R. M. *The key to feminine response in marriage*. New York: Random House, 1968.

Haslam, M. T. The treatment of psychogenic dyspareunia by reciprocal inhibition. *British Journal of Psychiatry*, 1965, *111*, 280–282.

Husted, J. R. *The effect of method of systematic desensitization and presence of sexual communication in the treatment of female sexual anxiety by counterconditioning*. Unpublished doctoral dissertation, University of California, Los Angeles, 1972.

Jacobson, E. *Progressive relaxation*. Chicago: University of Chicago Press, 1938.

LoPiccolo, J., and Lobitz, W. C. *The role of masturbation in the treatment of orgasmic dysfunction*. Unpublished manuscript, University of Oregon, 1971.

Masters, W. H., and Johnson, V. E. *Human sexual inadequacy*. Boston: Little, Brown, 1970.

Rachman, S. Sexual fetishism: An experimental analogue. *Psychological Record*, 1966, *16*, 293–296.

Wolpe, J. *Psychotherapy by reciprocal inhibition*. Stanford: Stanford University Press, 1958.

Wolpe, J., and Lazarus, A. A. *Behavior therapy techniques: A guide to the treatment of neuroses*. New York: Pergamon Press, 1966.

*As clinicians continue to treat sexual dysfunctioning, our diagnostic categories are be-
coming more refined and specific. "Frigidity" has been replaced by a number of diagnostic categories including primary and secondary orgasmic dysfunction. This article notes
that these two disorders differ in a number of ways: Primary orgasmic dysfunction, in
contrast to secondary orgasmic dysfunction, is not necessarily associated with marital
distress and responds much better to focused sex therapy. While these differences have
potentially important implications for differential treatment of these two disorders, the
small size of the patient sample in this article suggests caution in generalizing the authors'
conclusions.*

15

Secondary Orgasmic Dysfunction.
I. Analysis and Strategies for Treatment

Kevin B. McGovern, Rita Stewart McMullen, and Joseph LoPiccolo

Introduction

Over the last five years, we have developed a behavioral treatment program for
clients with a variety of sexual dysfunctions. Various aspects of this program have
been described (LoPiccolo and Lobitz, 1972; Lobitz and LoPiccolo, 1972; LoPiccolo, Stewart, and Watkins, 1972). Basically, it focuses on anxiety reduction,
sexual skill training, and improving communication between sexual partners.
Clients also complete an extensive assessment battery (LoPiccolo and Steger,
(1974) before and after treatment.

    A major percentage of the client couples treated complain about female
orgasmic dysfunctions. Current thinking divides female orgasmic dysfunction

Kevin B. McGovern • Columbia Psychiatric Clinic, Portland, Oregon   ***Rita Stewart McMullen*** •
Desert Counseling Clinic, Inc., Ridgecrest, California   ***Joseph LoPiccolo*** • Department of Psy-
chiatry and Behavioral Science, School of Medicine, State University of New York, Stony Brook,
New York

into two major categories (Masters and Johnson, 1970). Primary orgasmic dysfunction is the condition of a female who has never experienced an orgasm through any mode of physical stimulation. In contrast, a woman with secondary orgasmic dysfunction has experienced at least one orgasm through some mode of sexual stimulation but is dissatisfied because of a low frequency of orgasmic response, the type of sexual stimulation required for orgasm, or the stimulus conditions under which orgasm occurs. The most typical characteristic of secondary orgasmic dysfunction is a low frequency of coital orgasms.

After six primary and six secondary orgasmic dysfunctional women and their spouses had completed therapy, an analysis of their assessment data revealed that (1) both women with primary and women with secondary orgasmic dysfunction reported increased satisfaction with their sexual and marital relationships after treatment and (2) all of the primary inorgasmic women became orgasmic in coitus, whereas the majority of the secondary inorgasmic women did not. In contrast, the Marriage Council of Philadelphia has reported a higher rate of success with secondary dysfunction than with primary dysfunction (Brenton, 1972).

The purpose of this article is to examine possible reasons for the differential results obtained in the treatment of these two client groups. In order to adequately portray the similarities and differences between couples with primary and secondary orgasmic dysfunction, a comprehensive description of their assessment scores will be provided. In addition, strategies for the future treatment of secondary orgasmic dysfunction will be discussed.

Description of Clients

General Information

The majority of the couples were referred by local physicians or through local mental health facilities. Prior to treatment, all the women were required to obtain a thorough gynecological examination. The physicians' reports indicated no medical basis for their dysfunction. The treated couples had been married an average of 4.75 years (primary couples 4.83 years and secondary couples 4.67 years). The average ages of the primary and secondary couples were 27.7 and 26.6 years, respectively.

Each client couple completed a Background Information Inventory (Steger, 1972), the Sexual Interaction Inventory (LoPiccolo and Steger, 1974), and the Locke–Wallace Marital Adjustment Test (Locke and Wallace, 1959) before and after treatment. Client responses to each of these three types of self-report questionnaires are described below.

Background Information Inventory

The Background Information Inventory consists of questions pertaining to (1) demographic characteristics of the client (e.g., age, education, occupation), (2) actual and desired frequency of occurrence of various specific sexual behaviors

Table 1. Background Information Inventory Pre- and Posttreatment Scores: Frequency of Orgasms Through Masturbation, Genital Caressing by Mate, and Coitus

	Client	Masturbation (%)		Caressing (%)		Intercourse (%)	
		Pre	Post	Pre	Post	Pre	Post
Primary	P_1	0	0	0	0	0	25
	P_2	0	75	0	50	0	50
	P_3	0	100	0	25	0	75
	P_4	0	100	0	100	0	25
	P_5	0	25	0	0	0^a	25
	P_6	0	75	0	100	0	75
Secondary	S_1	0	0	25	0	50	50
	S_2	0	25	50	50	50	25
	S_3	100	100	100	100	0	0
	S_4	100	100	0	0	0	25
	S_5	100	100	0	0	0	0
	S_6	100	100	no data	100	0^a	0

^{a}While completing the preassessment inventories, clients P_5 and S_6 mislabeled a high state of sexual arousal as an orgasm.

(e.g., frequency of orgasm through masturbation), and (3) self-ratings of sexual satisfaction. The data in Table 1, from the inventory, illustrate the orgasmic frequency of dysfunctional women prior to and after treatment in masturbation, genital caressing by mate, and coitus.

The pretreatment data presented in Table 1 indicate that, in accordance with the definition of this disorder, none of the primary dysfunctional women had ever experienced orgasm through any mode of physical stimulation prior to treatment. In contrast, all of the secondary dysfunctional women had experienced orgasm through one or more types of physical stimulation. Also, the majority of secondary dysfunctional women experienced a high frequency of orgasm through masturbation but were unable to reach orgasm in coitus with any degree of regularity.

The posttreatment data in Table 1 demonstrate that the treatment program was highly effective in changing the orgasmic responses of the six primary inorgasmic women. At termination, all of the primary inorgasmic women were experiencing orgasms through one or more modes of physical stimulation: Five were orgasmic during masturbation and four in genital caressing by mate, and all six were able to experience orgasm in coitus. It should be underscored that prior to treatment none of these women had experienced an orgasm through any mode of physical stimulation.

In contrast, the secondary dysfunctional women demonstrated minimal pre–post masturbatory orgasmic response changes.* In addition, none of these clients improved their frequency of orgasm via genital caressing by their partners.

*It is important to note, however, that prior to treatment the majority of the secondary dysfunctional women reported reaching masturbatory orgasm 100% of the time.

Regarding coitus, only one of the clients reported an increased frequency of orgasm, four indicated no change, and one reported a decrease in frequency. These data illustrate, then, that the sexual treatment program was highly successful in altering the orgasmic responses of primary but not of secondary dysfunctional women.

Sexual Interaction Inventory (SII)

The Sexual Interaction Inventory was designed to provide both a diagnostic device and a treatment outcome measure for therapists treating heterosexual couples with a sexual dysfunction (LoPiccolo and Steger, 1974). The SII format consists of seventeen items that comprehensively cover a variety of typical heterosexual behaviors ranging from kissing to coitus. Each client is instructed to answer the following six questions about each of the seventeen sexual behaviors. The questions ask (1) how regularly the client engages in a particular sexual behavior, (2) how regularly the client would like the sexual behavior to occur, (3) how pleasurable the client finds this activity to be, (4) how pleasurable the client thinks his or her mate finds this activity to be, (5) how pleasurable the client would like this activity to be, and (6) how pleasurable the client would like this activity to be for his or her mate.

The client's scores are combined into eleven scales and plotted on a profile sheet in reference to the scores obtained by a control sample of 133 married couples with a satisfactory sexual adjustment. The scale titles shown in Figures 1 and 2 indicate how the raw scores were combined into scales that measure distinct aspects of a sexual relationship. For example, scale 4, labeled "perceptual accuracy" (male's accuracy for the female), is the summed difference between the female's rating of how pleasurable she finds each sexual activity and the male's rating of how pleasurable he thinks she finds each activity. LoPiccolo and Steger (1974) have demonstrated that the SII discriminates between client applicants and a sexually satisfied control group, has acceptable levels of internal consistency and test–retest reliability, and is reactive to treatment effects.

Pretreatment SII scores indicated no significant differences between the primary and secondary couples ($p \geqslant .05$, two-tailed t test). More specifically, the pretreatment client profiles revealed that (1) the twelve couples desired to engage in sexual activities more frequently (scales 1 and 7), (2) the dysfunctional women wanted their sexual interactions to be more pleasurable (scale 8), (3) the clients often misperceived their partner's sexual preferences (scales 4, 5, 10, 11).

Figure 2 shows that following treatment both primary and secondary couples were very satisfied with most aspects of their sexual relationship. In fact, the primary couples demonstrated statistically significant ($p \leqslant .05$, one-tailed t test) signs of improvement on ten of the eleven scales. In addition, the secondary couples showed statistically significant ($p \leqslant .05$, one-tailed t test) signs of improvement on seven of the eleven scales. As was the case with the pretreatment SII scores, there were no statistically significant differences between the primary and secondary couples with respect to the posttreatment SII scores ($p \geqslant .05$, two-tailed t test).

SEXUAL INTERACTION INVENTORY
Joseph LoPiccolo, Ph.D. and Jeffrey C. Steger, Ph.D.

CLIENTS _____ AGES ____ DATE ___ DIAGNOSIS_____

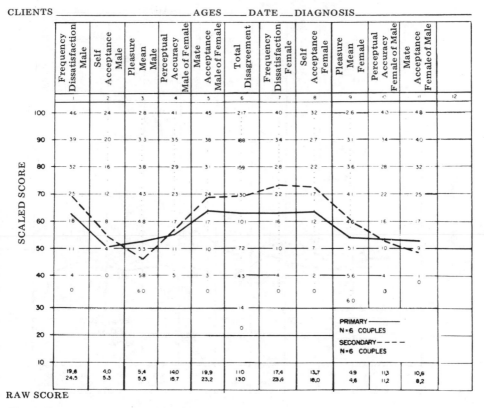

Fig. 1. Pretreatment profiles for couples diagnosed as having primary or secondary orgasmic dysfunction.

In summary, prior to treatment the primary and secondary couples had similar maladaptive SII sexual profiles. By the end of treatment, however, both types of dysfunctional couples demonstrated therapeutic improvement on the eleven scales. These data demonstrate that although the therapeutic program was not powerful enough to change the orgasmic response patterns of the secondary dysfunctional females, *it did successfully improve the sexual compatibility of these couples* (e.g., perceptions, acceptance of spouse's sexual identity, increased frequency and enjoyment of sexual activities).

Locke–Wallace Marital Adjustment Test

To determine whether primary and secondary couples differed with respect to marital happiness, their pretreatment Locke–Wallace Marital Adjustment scores were compared. Locke and Wallace (1959) have reported that a score of 100 or

SEXUAL INTERACTION INVENTORY

Joseph LoPiccolo, Ph.D. and Jeffrey C. Steger, Ph.D.

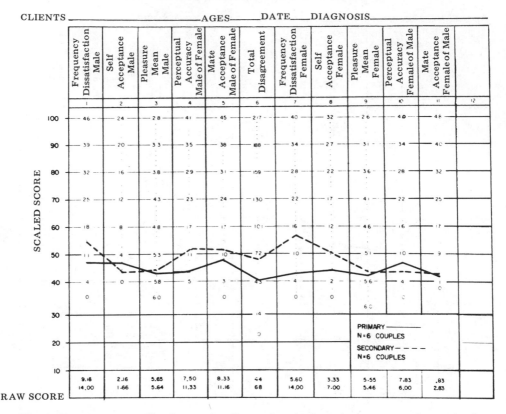

Fig. 2. Posttreatment profiles for couples diagnosed as having primary or secondary orgasmic dysfunction.

above is an indicator of marital happiness and satisfaction, whereas a score below 100 reflects marital discord and disharmony.

The pretreatment means, standard deviations, ranges, and *t* scores for the Locke–Wallace test are displayed in Table 2. Although the 13.50 pretreatment mean difference score between primary and secondary dysfunctional women did not reach statistical significance, the individual client scores reflect some important differences. Five of the six primary dysfunctional women scored above 100, whereas four of the six secondary dysfunctional women scored 93 or below. This suggests that the majority of the secondary dysfunctional women were more dissatisfied with their marital relationships prior to treatment.

The six male partners of the primary dysfunctional women obtained a mean Locke–Wallace score of 104.33 prior to treatment, whereas the six male partners of the secondary dysfunctional women obtained a mean score of 86.91. The 17.42 mean score difference was statistically significant at the .05 level. Furthermore, five of the six primary male partners scored above 100 on the Locke–Wallace, whereas four of the six secondary male partners obtained a score of 95 or below.

Table 2. *Locke–Wallace Pretreatment Scores: Primary and Secondary Orgasmic Dysfunctional Couples*

	Primary	Secondary
Females		
$\overline{X}$	103.83	90.33
SD	15.31	21.54
Range	76–128	64–128
N	6	6
	$t = 1.14$	
Males		
$\overline{X}$	104.33	86.91
SD	10.40	18.28
Range	84–118	69–110
N	6	6
	$t = 1.85^a$	

[a] $p < .05.$

These data indicate that the male partners of the secondary dysfunctional women were also more dissatisfied with their marital relationships prior to treatment.

The Locke–Wallace posttreatment means, standard deviations, ranges, and t scores reveal that the secondary dysfunctional women, the male partners of the secondary women, and the primary dysfunctional women were all much more satisfied with their marital relationships after treatment (Table 3). However, the

Table 3. *Locke–Wallace Posttreatment Scores: Primary and Secondary Orgasmic Dysfunctional Couples*

	Primary	Secondary
Females		
$\overline{X}$	120.5	122.1
SD	18.44	7.03
Range	89–145	111–133
N	6	6
Pre–post difference, t	2.91^a	2.96^a
Males		
$\overline{X}$	103.3	107.1
SD	23.7	12.35
Range	61–131	86.5–122.0
N	6	6
Pre–post difference, t	.09	2.68^a

[a] $p < .05.$

male partners of the primary dysfunctional women did not demonstrate significant improvement. This result may be related to the fact that in treating primary dysfunctional couples the therapists usually focus on the specific fears, concerns, and maladaptive behaviors of the dysfunctional woman.

In summary, the Locke–Wallace Marital Adjustment scores reveal that most of the secondary dysfunctional couples were more dissatisfied with their marital relationship prior to treatment than were the primary dysfunctional couples. However, at the end of treatment, both the primary dysfunctional women and the secondary dysfunctional couples reported a statistically significant degree of improvement in their marital relationships.

Discussion and Implications for Treatment

The preceding data indicate that the sexual satisfaction and marital happiness of both the primary and the secondary couples improved significantly by the end of treatment. However, in contrast to the primary dysfunctional women, the secondary females were unable to increase their frequency of orgasmic response to genital caressing and coitus.

What factors may be responsible for this differential treatment effect? The fact that most secondary couples enter treatment with more disturbed marital relationships than primary couples is one possible explanation for the less successful treatment results with secondary couples. All couples in this treatment program were seen for fifteen therapy sessions lasting one hour each. Since the secondary couples were more dissatisfied with their marital relationships prior to treatment, it was necessary for the therapist to devote a large percentage of therapy time working through nonsexual marital problems. Responses to an informal questionnaire administered to the therapists who treated these clients indicated that several sessions were spent teaching the secondary couples fundamental communication skills and/or functional methods for resolving marital conflict. As a result, the therapist may have lacked sufficient therapy time in which to focus on specific sexual behaviors designed to alter the orgasmic responses of the secondary dysfunctional females. A speculation arises: The reversal in treatment success rates with primary and secondary cases between those reported here and those of the Philadelphia Marriage Council may reflect a difference in the percentage of time devoted to sexual versus marital interventions. In general, it appears that primary inorgasmic women respond best to therapy focused specifically on sexual matters, whereas secondary inorgasmic women may respond better when traditional marital therapy is combined with sex treatment.

On the basis of these findings, it is recommended that either most secondary dysfunctional couples should be referred to another agency for short-term marital therapy prior to beginning a sexual treatment program or the therapists should extend the number of therapy hours to allow sufficient time to treat the marital problems within the context of the sexual treatment program.

In addition to the more disturbed marital relationship in the case of the secondary couples, there is another factor that may help account for the differential results obtained in treating these two client groups. While the primary dysfunctional female has never experienced an orgasm, the secondary dysfunctional woman has already established a pattern of orgasmic release that often interferes with her ability to experience orgasm during intercourse. What seems to occur is that the majority of secondary dysfunctional women have a long history of masturbating in one very constrained way. One of these clients, for example, was orgasmic only when she was lying on her stomach with her legs pressed together, with a bedsheet between her genitals and her hands, and stimulating herself by cupping her hands over her genital area. This long history of an exclusive reliance on one particular and narrow technique of self-stimulation tends to bring orgasm under very tight stimulus control. In these cases, the therapist should teach the secondary inorgasmic client how to extinguish these maladaptive narrow stimulus-response links and learn new self-stimulation techniques that can be generalized to intercourse. In a sense, then, the primary inorgasmic client can simply be taught an adaptive response pattern, while the secondary inorgasmic female must first unlearn maladaptive habits.

There are two therapy approaches that would seem to have promise in helping the woman with a constrained masturbation pattern extinguish her previous pattern and transfer orgasmic response from masturbation to sexual intercourse. The first approach involves prohibiting her from employing her previous method of achieving orgasmic release, allowing her sexual tension to build up over a period of a few weeks, and then having her begin to learn a new way of masturbating to orgasm by following a nine-step program of directed masturbation shown to be effective in producing coital orgasms (LoPiccolo and Lobitz, 1972).

During the first phase of this program (steps 1–3), the client is instructed to visually and tactually explore her genitals, locating sensitive areas that produce feelings of pleasure. In addition, she is advised to practice Kegel's (1952) exercise to increase the tone and vascularity of the pelvic musculature. As the program progresses (steps 4–6), the woman stimulates the pleasure-producing areas (e.g., the clitoral area) by hand or vibrator. In the final stage (steps 7–9), the client teaches her mate how to stimulate her to orgasm during foreplay and/or coitus.

The second therapy approach is an adaptation of Annon's (1971) method of successive approximations. This procedure involves instructing the woman to gradually shift her locus of self-stimulation from the clitoris downward to the vulva, and eventually to the vaginal opening. Each new downward movement is first attempted at the point of orgasm. Annon also recommends having the woman gradually change her body position and body movements during self-stimulation to those more closely approximating sexual intercourse. This method, in contrast to the first approach, does not rely on high levels of sexual tension and/or the learning of entirely new methods of self-stimulation. Instead, women are instructed to gradually change their focal point of self-stimulation so that their masturbatory manipulations closely parallel coital behaviors (e.g., body movement, positions, focal point of stimulation). There are no data at this point to indicate which of these two approaches would be more effective.

Summary

The pretreatment data clearly illustrated that both the primary and secondary dysfunctional couples (1) were dissatisfied with their sexual relationships, (2) had similar misperceptions about their sexual roles, and (3) had dysfunctional sexual behavior. In contrast to the primary couples, the majority of the secondary partners were dissatisfied with their marital relationship and most of the secondary women could reach orgasm only through one rigid and narrowly constrained method of masturbation.

The posttreatment data revealed that the primary and secondary couples reported increased satisfaction with their sexual and marital relationships after treatment. Also, the treatment program was extremely effective in increasing the orgasmic responses of primary but not of secondary dysfunctional women.

In general, it appears that primary inorgasmic couples respond best to therapy focused specifically on sexual matters. In contrast, secondary dysfunctional couples may respond more effectively if marital therapy is combined with a sexual treatment program. For the majority of secondary dysfunctional couples, therapists should closely examine and treat the existing marital problems. Once the major marital obstacles have been removed, treatment can then focus on teaching the secondary orgasmic woman to extinguish her rigid, constrained technique of masturbation and to learn new, functional techniques of sexual arousal that can be generalized to lead to orgasm in intercourse.

References

Annon, J. *The therapeutic use of masturbation in the treatment of sexual disorders.* Paper presented at the Fifth Annual Meeting of the Association for the Advancement of Behavior Therapy, Washington, D.C., September 1971.

Brenton, M. Profile of a sex and marriage clinic. *Sexual Behavior*, 1972, *2*, 28–32.

Kegel, A. H. Sexual functions of the pubococcygeus muscle. *Western Journal of Surgery, Obstetrics, and Gynecology*, 1952, *50*, 521.

Lobitz, W. C., and LoPiccolo, J. New methods in the behavioral treatment of sexual dysfunction. *Journal of Behavior Therapy and Experimental Psychology*, 1972, *3* (4), 265–271.

Locke, H. J., and Wallace, K. Short marital adjustment and prediction tests: Their reliability and prediction. *Marriage and Family Living*, 1959, *21*, 251–255.

LoPiccolo, J., and Lobitz, W. C. The role of masturbation in the treatment of primary orgasmic dysfunction. *Archives of Sexual Behavior*, 1972, *2*, 163–171.

LoPiccolo, J., and Steger, J. C. The Sexual Interaction Inventory: A new instrument for assessment of sexual dysfunction. *Archives of Sexual Behavior*, 1974, *3*, 585–595.

LoPiccolo, J., Stewart, R., and Watkins, B. Case study: Treatment of erectile failure and ejaculatory incompetence in a case with homosexual etiology. *Journal of Behavior Therapy and Experimental Psychology*, 1972, *3*, 233–236.

Masters, W. H., and Johnson, V. E. *Human sexual inadequacy.* Boston: Little, Brown, 1970.

Steger, J. *The assessment of sexual function and dysfunction.* Paper presented at the Western Psychological Association Meeting, Portland, Oregon, 1972.

As noted in previous chapters, there is disagreement about whether a woman who can reach orgasm during masturbation or partner manipulation but not during coitus should be considered dysfunctional. Adding to this controversy has been the fact that most sex therapy programs have reported mediocre success in achieving coital orgasm with such patients. This chapter accepts coital orgasm as a legitimate goal and offers a conditioning program of pairing vaginal insertion with clitoral stimulation to achieve coital orgasm. As is the case with many of the clinical articles in this volume, the small number of patients treated suggests caution in accepting this procedure as uniformly effective.

Such small sample studies, however, represent the way in which new treatment procedures are developed. Large-sample clinical trials, the next step in the validation process, are just now beginning to be undertaken in the sex therapy field.

16

Orgasm during Intercourse: A Treatment Strategy for Women

Antonette M. Zeiss, Gerald M. Rosen, and Robert A. Zeiss

Current reports suggest that as many as 20–80% of females with situational orgasmic dysfunctions remain inorgasmic during intercourse at the conclusion of their treatment (Lobitz and LoPiccolo, 1972; Masters and Johnson, 1970; McGovern, Stewart, and LoPiccolo, 1975). However, sex therapists have recently encouraged women who are inorgasmic during intercourse not to consider themselves sexually dysfunctional if they are able to attain orgasm through manual stimulation of the clitoris or some other method. This orientation may be part of a general emphasis for women to be self-sufficient and independent from male demands for performance. Additionally, since female orgasms resulting from masturbation, oral stimulation, manual stimulation by a partner, or intercourse are

The authors are grateful to Elizabeth A. Steinbock, Susan Phillips, Dr. Susan Gilmore (Eugene, Oregon), and Dr. Herbert Orenstein (Seattle, Washington) for their comments on this chapter. Appreciation is also extended to Ricks Warren, who served as cotherapist on the second case.

Antonette M. Zeiss • Department of Psychology, Arizona State University, Tempe, Arizona *Gerald M. Rosen* • Providence Family Medical Center, Seattle, Washington *Robert A. Zeiss* • Valle del Sol, Phoenix, Arizona and Department of Psychology, Arizona State University, Tempe, Arizona. When this chapter was written, the authors were at the University of Oregon.

all physiologically similar (Masters and Johnson, 1966), sex therapists have encouraged women not to overevaluate the importance of coital orgasm. We agree with most aspects of the above argument, but we feel that it should not be imposed on women who seek assistance for orgasmic dysfunctions. A woman's desire for coital orgasm is a justifiable behavioral goal, especially when it does not involve increased performance demands or suggestions that only one "right way" for sexual expression exists.

This chapter presents two case studies to illustrate a therapy technique for coital orgasmic problems that was originated by Rosen and described by Rosen, Zeiss, and Zeiss (unpublished). The program was suggested by earlier work in which orgasm brought about by masturbation was paired with new stimuli (Davison, 1968; Marquis, 1970; Annon, 1971). In the technique presented, fantasies of insertion, vaginal insertion of a dildo, and the presence of a male partner are gradually incorporated into the masturbatory behavior of female clients. Once these procedural steps are strongly associated with arousal and orgasm, sexual activity with a male partner can be assigned; these activities are planned to maximize transfer of feelings learned in masturbation with the dildo to feelings obtained from penile insertion, containment, and thrusting.

Procedures

The therapy program consists of three conceptual stages subdivided into six steps that clarify the progression of therapy. The program generally requires twelve to sixteen therapy sessions, depending on a couple's rate of progress and initial orgasmic patterns. Prerequisites for this program include the ability to manually masturbate to orgasm and a constant male partner.

Stage 1: Fantasy

Step 1. Just prior to and during orgasm brought on by manual masturbation, the woman fantasizes intercourse (specifically, vaginal insertion of her partner's erect penis). If a woman habitually masturbates to a fantasy other than intercourse with her current partner, she should switch that fantasy just prior to orgasm and imagine penile insertion and intercourse with her current partner. With continued practice, fantasies of insertion and vaginal containment of the partner's penis should be started earlier in the masturbation sequence.

Step 2. The male partner is brought into the woman's masturbation practice sessions as a learner–observer, primarily to increase the woman's comfort while reaching orgasm in his presence. If the woman is already comfortable with the man's presence, this step will proceed quickly or may not be necessary. If the woman is uncomfortable, gradual introduction of the male is recommended.

Stage 2: Dildo

Step 3. For several practice sessions, the woman by herself experiences the sensations associated with vaginal containment of a dildo or another safe phallus-like object. The choice of the specific object may be left with the woman, but the remainder of the program will probably benefit more if the chosen object approximates in size the partner's erect penis. Gradual movement of the dildo is introduced during this practice to familiarize the woman with sensations of vaginal containment and thrusting. Orgasm need not occur in these practice sessions; the woman's goal is to become accustomed to the sensations associated with vaginal stimulation.

Step 4. The woman fantasizes having intercourse with her partner while she masturbates. As she approaches orgasm, she inserts the dildo and fantasizes insertion of her partner's penis.

Step 5. The male partner is again brought into the program to allow the female to feel comfortable while reaching orgasm with the dildo in his presence. This step also allows the partner to become familiar with the types of stimulation and thrusting that arouse her and bring her to orgasm. When the male's presence does not interfere with her arousal and orgasm, she should begin to insert the dildo earlier in her arousal sequence while using manual clitoral or other stimulation to maintain and increase arousal to the point of orgasm. With continued practice, the woman fades out other stimulation and relies more on the dildo to bring about orgasm.

To learn the types of thrusting that are likely to bring the woman to orgasm, the male can gradually assume control over dildo movement, with extensive verbal coaching from the female.

Stage 3: Intercourse

Step 6. To the extent that the male partner is able to control his arousal and ejaculatory processes, the preferred next step is to replicate, with the man's erect penis, the same procedure used with the dildo. Thus the female, (a) first (with no pressures for arousal or orgasm) experiences the sensations associated with vaginal containment of the penis and gradual thrusting movements. (b) Next, the woman fantasizes intercourse with her partner during foreplay involving clitoral stimulation, and as she approaches orgasm, the partner inserts his penis. (c) Subsequently, insertion of the penis begins earlier in the arousal sequence in conjunction with stimulation to maintain and increase arousal to the point of orgasm. As a couple becomes successful at this step, other stimulation is decreased and the couple relies more on penile stimulation to bring the woman to orgasm. If the male has less than desired control over his ejaculatory processes, part (a) of this step would be omitted and more reliance would be placed on parts (b) and (c).

Case 1

The first couple, Mr. and Mrs. A, were seen by the first author, without a co-therapist, for fifteen sessions over a period of eight months. Mrs. A came alone to ten of the sessions; both Mr. and Mrs. A were present at the others. Assessment at the beginning and end of therapy consisted of the Locke–Wallace marital inventory (Locke and Wallace, 1959), the Sexual Interaction Inventory (SII)

(LoPiccolo and Steger, 1974), and a sexual information form routinely used at the University of Oregon Psychology Clinic.

Mr. and Mrs. A, an upper-middle-class Caucasian couple aged forty-one and thirty-one, respectively, had been married for about a year with a sexual relationship for two to three years. Shortly before treatment, Mrs. A had become orgasmic through self-initiated manual stimulation of the clitoris. Her husband remained unable to stimulate her to orgasm by any means. Both partners appeared to enjoy sex, and at no time did they express a dislike for their encounters. Pretreatment Locke–Wallace scores reflected an adequate, but not excellent, marital relationship; Mrs. A's score was high (125), and Mr. A's was moderately low (96). The SII profile indicated a large frequency dissatisfaction for Mrs. A. This reflected Mrs. A's desire for orgasm during sexual activity with Mr. A and her desire for more sexual behaviors in foreplay. Other scales on the SII profile were not significantly elevated. As reported on the sexual information form, Mrs. A's acceptance of sexual initiations was *reluctant*, and her rated satisfaction with their sexual relationship was *slight*. Her husband reported accepting *with pleasure*, and his satisfaction was *moderate*.* Mrs. A reported that she was orgasmic in masturbation *90% of the time*.

Because Mrs. A was originally orgasmic with only one stereotyped pattern of masturbation, she was first assigned masturbatory practice sessions in which she explored diverse patterns of self-stimulation. Once she was able to reach orgasm with diverse types of stimulation, the six-step program began. During the first step in the procedure, Mrs. A needed coaching in sexual fantasy, and *My Secret Garden* (Friday, 1974) was assigned. As Mrs. A was most aroused by romantic fantasies, she was instructed to masturbate while imagining a romantic evening, followed by erotic love play. Just before attaining orgasm, she was to switch to fantasies involving vaginal insertion of her partner's penis during intercourse. Mrs. A rapidly eroticized her thoughts regarding intercourse and moved easily through Step 1 of the program.

Step 2 was somewhat difficult, and a fading procedure was used to introduce her husband to the masturbation sessions. Mrs. A first masturbated while her husband was asleep beside her, then while he was drowsy but awake. She next masturbated while her husband stimulated himself at the same time. After this graduated sequence, Mrs. A could comfortably masturbate to orgasm in her husband's presence.

In Steps 3 and 4, Mrs. A used a penis-shaped vibrator (which was not turned on) as a dildo. She was eager to try this procedural step and quickly learned to enjoy the sensations of dildo containment and various styles of thrusting. She became orgasmic with dildo thrusting after first stimulating herself manually to the plateau phase of arousal.

Mrs. A developed a mild case of pneumonia at this point in treatment, causing a one-month delay. Following her recovery, Steps 3 and 4 were repeated to reacquaint her with the procedures. When the next step was discussed, Mrs. A felt uncomfortable about using the dildo while her husband was present, and the couple

---

*In reporting preassessment and postassessment for both cases, the italicized words present the description checked on the sexual information form.

skipped to Step 6. They also introduced a procedural variation of their own in which initial arousal with penile thrusting was followed by vaginal containment of the penis without thrusting while Mrs. A manually stimulated herself to the point of orgasm. At that point, Mr. A resumed thrusting, and his wife experienced her first orgasm during intercourse. Thereafter, they faded out her interim manual stimulation and relied more on his thrusting.

Posttreatment assessment measures suggest that treatment effects were specific to the couple's goal of achieving orgasm in intercourse. Mrs. A's Locke–Wallace score remained high (129) and Mr. A's score increased considerably (125). Duration of foreplay and intercourse remained at pretest levels, intercourse frequency continued at *three to four times per week*, and Mr. A's satisfaction continued to be *moderate*. However, Mrs. A was orgasmic (without manual stimulation) during intercourse *25% of the time;* her acceptance of sexual initiations had changed from *reluctant* to *with pleasure;* and she now reported *extreme satisfaction* with their sexual relationship. On the SII her frequency dissatisfaction score decreased substantially while other scores remained within a normal range.

Case 2

Mr. and Mrs. B were seen by the first author with a male cotherapist for fifteen sessions over a period of five months; Mr. and Mrs. B both came to all sessions. Assessment at the beginning and end of therapy was identical to that of the first case.

Mr. and Mrs. B were both 27-year-old middle-class Caucasians. Prior to treatment, Mrs. B was able to achieve orgasm through either her own or her partner's manual stimulation of her clitoris, but she had never experienced orgasm during intercourse. Mr. and Mrs. B reported feeling tense and anxious about their sexual relations together, although Mrs. B enjoyed masturbation. Initial Locke–Wallace scores were moderately high for Mrs. B (112) and low for her husband (82). The SII showed elevated scores on female self-acceptance ($t = 73$) and male acceptance of the female ($t = 72$). Mr. and Mrs. B reported an intercourse frequency of *once each week;* Mrs. B *often refused* her husband's initiations. He reported *moderate* satisfaction with their sexual relationship; she reported only *slight* satisfaction.

Because of the couple's tension and avoidance of sexual encounters, the first phase of treatment involved body-pleasuring (sensate-focus) assignments devoid of performance demands. The B's were also asked to spend time together sharing nonsexual concerns in a relaxed and supportive atmosphere. After four therapy sessions focused on these procedures, the B's reported enjoying their sexual activities together. They then began the six-step program for attaining orgasm in intercourse.

Because Mrs. B used only one stereotyped pattern of self-stimulation, she followed the same initial procedures as Mrs. A, including the use of *My Secret Garden* (Friday, 1974) to facilitate sexual fantasy. Since Mr. B was already observing his wife masturbate to orgasm, Step 2 was unnecessary for this couple. At Step 3, Mrs. B preferred not to buy a dildo and instead used various organic vegetables. She became orgasmic with the use of her dildo substitutes almost immediately. Mrs. B was creative in her use of fantasies and choice of dildos, and she was uninhibited about demonstrating stimulation techniques to her husband. During this phase of treatment, Mrs. B reported a change from thinking of herself as a sexually inhibited, cold woman to seeing herself as a sexually creative, uninhibited woman.

The transition to sexual intercourse for this couple was nonproblematic. Mr. B had sufficient ejaculatory control to use the kinds of penile stimulation that his wife had most preferred during stimulation with her dildos. Mrs. B became regularly orgasmic during the first intercourse experience and by the end of treatment had achieved a satisfactory pattern of being multiply orgasmic during at least 50% of her intercourse experiences without concomitant manual stimulation during intercourse.

In addition to her ability to attain orgasm during intercourse, Mrs. and Mr. B reported an increase in the frequency of their sexual activity (*twice a week*), and both partners now said they accepted sexual initiations *with pleasure*. Mrs. B's satisfaction ratings also increased from *slight* to *moderate*. The SII at posttest had no elevated scores, and Mr. B's Locke–Wallace score had substantially increased (117). Other relevant points of data remained unchanged.

Discussion

The two case studies presented in this chapter provide initial support for a six-step treatment program for achieving orgasm during intercourse. In both cases, the women became orgasmic during intercourse without the need for continued direct clitoral stimulation.

Although the findings are strongly suggestive, the percentage of coital orgasmic dysfunctions that respond to this six-step program remains unspecified, as do the clinical subtypes that might best respond. As with any new treatment, critical process factors also require further investigation. In the present two cases, use of a dildo seemed extremely useful and was comfortably accepted by both couples. It seems likely that clients will accept the procedures when they are presented with an appropriate rationale. However, it can be argued that some women could progress directly from masturbatory practice sessions to insertion of the partner's erect penis without the intermediate steps involving a dildo. Even though this is feasible, we believe that the majority of cases should benefit from the additional procedural steps. The use of a dildo allows the woman to conduct practice sessions alone, during which time she can become familiar with feelings of vaginal containment and thrusting. By pairing the use of a dildo with arousal and orgasm brought on by manual masturbation, the woman can learn to achieve high levels of arousal from thrusting. She can learn this while maintaining total control over thrusting movements and in the absence of a partner whose presence could evoke anxiety or create performance demands. After these initial success experiences, the woman can fade her partner into the procedures.

It should be noted that procedural variations occured with the two reported cases. As with any behavioral treatment, it is best to think of the sequencing of procedures as flexible. It should also be noted that procedures common to other sex therapies were used in the present cases. For example, the couples spent intimate but nonsexual time together; they engaged in sensate-focus exercises (Masters and Johnson, 1970), and the wives practiced Kegel (1952) exercises. Unlike traditional approaches to sexual dysfunction, it was not always necessary to meet with both partners during therapy sessions, and one case was seen by a single therapist rather than by a cotherapy team.

When using the present treatment program, clinicians should remain sensitive to marital and reeducational issues. For example, couples so distressed or argumentative that they will not conduct practice sessions are probably poor candidates for this (or any other) behavioral sexual dysfunction program until they can begin to work more cooperatively. Women whose self-esteem or marriage appears to be dependent on achieving coital orgasms are certainly in need of exploring their definitions of the problem. The present program does not alleviate the need for clinicians to evaluate such issues. It merely demonstrates that a direct behavioral approach can help women achieve orgasm during intercourse.

References

Annon, J. *The therapeutic use of masturbation in the treatment of sexual disorders.* Paper presented at the Fifth Annual Meeting of the Association for Advancement of Behavior Therapy, Washington, D.C., September 1971.

Davison, G. Elimination of a sadistic fantasy by a client-controlled counter-conditioning technique: A case study. *Journal of Abnormal Psychology,* 1968, *73,* 84–90.

Friday, N. *My secret garden.* New York: Pocket Books, 1974.

Kegel, A. H. Sexual functions of the pubococcygeus muscle. *Western Journal of Surgery,* 1952, *60,* 521–524.

Lobitz, W. C., and LoPiccolo, J. New methods in the behavioral treatment of sexual dysfunction. *Journal of Behavior Therapy and Experimental Psychiatry,* 1972, *3,* 265–271.

Locke, H. J., and Wallace, K. M. Short marital adjustment and prediction tests: Their reliability and validity. *Marriage and Family Living,* 1959, *21,* 251–255.

LoPiccolo, J., and Steger, J. C. The Sexual Interaction Inventory: A new instrument for assessment of sexual dysfunction. *Archives of Sexual Behavior,* 1974, *3,* 585–595.

Marquis, J. N. Orgasmic reconditioning: Changing sexual object choice through controlled masturbatory fantasies. *Journal of Behavior Therapy and Experimental Psychiatry,* 1970, *1,* 263–271.

Masters, W. H., and Johnson, V. E. *Human sexual response.* Boston: Little, Brown, 1966.

Masters, W. H., and Johnson, V. E. *Human sexual inadequacy.* Boston: Little, Brown, 1970.

McGovern, K. B., Stewart, R. C., and LoPiccolo, J. Secondary orgasmic dysfunction. I. Analysis and strategies for treatment. *Archives of Sexual Behavior,* 1975, *4,* 265–275.

Rosen, G. M., Zeiss, A. M., and Zeiss, R. A. *Orgasm in intercourse program for secondary inorgasmic women.* Unpublished manuscript, University of Oregon, 1974.

The use of the exercises developed by Arnold Kegel to strengthen vaginal musculature is a common element in many sex therapy programs for inorgasmic women. This chapter describes a very thorough approach to using the Kegel exercises with inorgasmic patients. While the authors emphasize the role of vaginal musculature in producing orgasm considerably more than do most sex therapists, their approach is certainly one that can be used in modified form by most clinicians. It seems clear that such a program of Kegel exercises adds to the effectiveness of treatment programs for inorgasmic women. It is interesting to note, however, that actual empirical data on the correlation of vaginal muscle tone with orgasmic capability are lacking at this point.

17

Diagnosis and Treatment Procedures of Pubococcygeal Deficiencies in Women

Georgia Kline-Graber and Benjamin Graber

Interest in the problem of physiological deficiencies of the vaginal musculature began in the 1940s with the late gynecologist Arnold Kegel's work treating urinary stress incontinence secondary to weakness of the supporting musculature of the pelvic organs (Kegel, 1948a,b, 1949, 1951, 1952a,b,c, 1956a,b; Kegel and Powell, 1950). Although "Kegel's exercises" to strengthen the pubococcygeus muscle, the most important muscle for supporting the urinary bladder, are prescribed worldwide by gynecologists, the sexual aspects of this musculature have received surprisingly little medical attention.

In 1952, Kegel (1952c) published an article in which he discussed an accidental finding of his work. He presented the case history of a forty-two-year-old woman who had been married for twenty-one years. When first seen, she had been suffering for seven years from a frequent loss of urine. A physical examination revealed poor condition of the vaginal muscle and the patient did not know how to contract it. She was placed on an exercise program that was successful in treating her urinary problem. Kegel related that at the final visit the patient said that the exercise

Georgia Kline-Graber and *Benjamin Graber* • Department of Psychiatry, University of Wisconsin Medical School, Madison, Wisconsin

program had dramatically improved her and her husband's sex life together. A further history showed that although both had wanted to engage in more sex, intercourse had not been enjoyable for the woman and so had occurred infrequently. Following restoration of her muscle—undertaken because of the urinary problem—the couple had intercourse several times a week and the patient was able to achieve orgasm, which previously she had not been able to do. Reportedly, two years later the couple were still having good sexual relations.

Kegel (1952c) made the following generalization from his clinical population of several thousand women:

> Wherever the perivaginal musculature is well developed . . . sexual complaints are few or transient. On the other hand, in women with a thin, weak, pubococcygeus muscle . . . expressions of indifference or dissatisfaction regarding sexual activity were frequently encountered. When a more careful history was taken, the symptoms revealed a definite pattern . . . In the patients' own words: "I just don't feel anything"; or "I don't like the feeling"; or "The feeling is disagreeable." . . . Following restoration of the pubococcygeus muscle, numerous patients incidentally volunteered the information: "I can feel more sexually"; and some experienced orgasm for the first time.

The diagnosis of pathophysiological deficiencies in the pubococcygeus is accomplished by using two diagnostic techniques—the perineometer, a device developed by Kegel, as well as a digital examination.

Perineometer readings should be obtained with the patient lying supine on the examining table with the legs in a "frog" position; digital examination should be performed with the patient in the standard lithotomy position. Only a small amount of lubricant such as K-Y jelly should be used on the perineometer, as additional lubricant significantly reduces friction and lowers the reading obtained by contraction of the muscle. In our clinical practice the evaluation of the pubococcygeus is included as a part of the complete gynecological examination given to each female patient as part of the diagnostic process.

Although evidently Kegel used only perineometer readings in following his treatment progress, we have found it necesssary to assess and follow six separate factors: control, atrophy, tone, vaginal displacement, initial strength, and sustained strength.

Control is simply a measure of whether or not the patient is able to voluntarily contract and relax the muscle at will and is assessed by use of the perineometer.

Control is given a good or 3 rating if the patient can depress the pressure-sensitive bulb inserted in the vagina at least 2 mm of Hg, which is the smallest increment the instrument measures. To receive a 3, she must move the needle without the assistance of accessory muscles such as the abdomen, buttocks, or thighs. If the patient can move it the 2 mm but uses these accessory muscles, she is rated fair or 2. If the patient is unable to move the needle with or without accessory muscles, then she is rated poor or 1.

The degree of *atrophy* is assessed by doing a clinical mapping of the muscle with the index finger to evaluate areas that may be missing or atrophied, and includes evaluation of any scar tissue present. This is done first with the muscle in a contracted state, then in a relaxed state. If there is any measurable atrophy present, the muscle is evaluated as poor for this factor; if the muscle is entirely intact, it is evaluated as good.

Tone provides a measure of the consistency or degree of resistance of the muscle to the examining finger, and it is evaluated first with the muscle in a relaxed condition, then in a contracted state. Tone is evaluated as poor when the muscle offers little or no degree of resistance to the examining finger in either the relaxed or the contracted state, but rather feels soft as a wet sponge would be if depressed. Tone is evaluated as moderate when the muscle in the contracted state offers a high degree of resistance to the examining finger, but no resistance in the relaxed state. Tone is evaluated as good when the muscle in both the relaxed and contracted states is firm and unyielding to the pressure of the examining finger.

Vaginal displacement is assessed by a combination of digital examination and the perineometer. With the index finger an assessment is made as to whether the vagina continues back in a straight, narrow line from the introitus, or whether there is a deviation to one or both sides. This is done with the pubococcygeus muscle in a relaxed state and is subjectively assessed as poor (severe deviation, of right, left, or both), moderate deviation, mild deviation, or no deviation. In addition, the initial perineometer resting reading is used to evaluate this factor.

Initial strength is evaluated by using the perineometer and having the patient contract and maintain the contraction for a period of one second. Initial, contracting, and displacement (difference between relaxed and contracting) readings are recorded. The gauge is calibrated from 0 to 100.

Sustained strength is again measured by use of the perineometer, with the patient holding the contraction or attempting to hold it for a count of ten seconds. Initial, contracting, and displacement readings are recorded.

A resistive exercise program must be implemented using the perineometer, which is available only by prescription.* Restoration always occurs in a fixed sequence of stepwise progression, starting with control, then atrophy, then tone, then vaginal displacement, then initial strength, then sustained strength. Depending on the diagnostic classification of the pubococcygeus upon initial examination, treatment can take up to several months, and many treatment failures have resulted from lack of patient preparation as to the potential difficulties and longevity involved.

Although it is not necessary to give each patient printed instructions that include all the general information included in the following "Patient Instructions," if this is not done then time should be taken to explain the information. We have found that well-informed patients have a much higher tendency to comply and follow through with the therapeutic exercise program because they understand why and what they are doing and this greatly improves motivation. Motivation is the single greatest factor that interferes with a patient's follow-through—the exercises are tedious, time-consuming, and without immediate positive gratification, and they require a great deal of self-discipline and frequently family cooperation as well (to arrange such things as child care during the exercise period). Since treatment can take several months to restore the muscle to full health, these women deserve all the help they can get to encourage and

---

*Information as to ordering and price of perineometers may be obtained from Perineometer Research Laboratory, P.O. Box 1273, Tustin, California 92680.

sustain their motivation, which must remain high in order to carry through with the treatment program.

Following are the *therapeutic* exercise instructions we have developed from clinical practice with hundreds of female patients; these differ from *maintenance* exercises (Kline-Graber and Graber, 1975), which are prescribed for patients with physiologically healthy pubococcygeus muscles.

Patient's Exercise Instructions—General—For All Muscle Deficiencies

What and Where Is the PC Muscle? The pubococcygeus muscle gets its name from its attachments—the pubic bone in front (under the pubic hair region) and the coccyx or end of the spine (tailbone) in back. Since both of these bones are immobile, the pubococcygeus gets no exercise (does not move) during the course of the day as most other muscles in the body do, except in two situations—when it is consciously contracted, as you are being taught to do, and involuntarily during orgasm.

The pubococcygeus is a band of muscle that runs like a thick rubber band from the pubic bone to either side of the urethra and part of the bladder, to either side of the middle of the vagina, and to either side of the rectum to the coccyx. It can be felt about 1½ inches inside the entrance to the vagina. Each time you hold back on urinating, it is the pubococcygeus muscle you are contracting. And each time you squeeze your vagina together, you contract the same pubococcygeus muscle. An important function of this muscle is to aid in holding the pelvic organs in the proper position.

How Do I Know What Condition My Muscle Is In? There are six factors that are evaluated during physical examination to determine this.

1. *Control*, measured with the perineometer, is the ability to contract and relax the muscle at will.

2. *Atrophy*, measured by physical exam, is the degree to which segments of the muscle are diminished in size or missing.

3. *Tone*, measured by physical exam, is the degree of resistance.

4. *Vaginal displacement*, measured with both the perineometer and physical exam, is the distance between the vaginal walls.

5. *Initial strength*, measured with the perineometer, is the degree to which you can contract the muscle without holding the contraction.

6. *Sustained strength*, measured with the perineometer, is the degree to which you can contract and hold the muscle for a count of ten seconds.

How Do These Factors Relate to One Another? Progressive change always occurs in a predictable manner.

Control is necessary as a prerequisite to doing the exercises, so that it is the first goal to accomplish.

With control properly learned, *atrophy*, if it is present, begins to fill in next as a natural consequence of the therapeutic process.

When the muscle is fully intact, i.e., atrophy is gone, *tone* improves.

When tone is good, *vaginal displacement*, if any, will disappear, leaving a tight, narrow canal for the entire length of the vagina.

When vaginal displacement is gone, *initial strength* increases.

When initial strength is good, *sustained strength* becomes good, leaving you with a muscle that is not only tight and narrow but that has the ability to contract against the penis during intercourse, producing increased sensation for both you and your partner.

Improvement does not occur in the strict sense of only one category at a time—there is some overlapping of improvement from one category to the next, i.e., initial strength and sustained strength may both show some improvement at the same time. However, in general, improvement occurs in a stepwise fashion, with each factor required to be healthy before the next can improve.

How Long Does It Take to Restore My Muscle to Health? The answer to this question is highly individualized. Naturally, the more factors that are already healthy to begin with, the less time it will take to restore health to the muscle, because the less there is left to do. For instance, a woman who had no control of the muscle, and severe atrophy, would be required to repair all six factors of the muscle before she would be finished. On the other hand, a woman who had good control, no atrophy, good tone, no vaginal displacement, but whose muscle was simply not as strong as it should be, would require much less time to bring her muscle back to full health.

To further explain, if there is significant atrophy present, tone is never good. As atrophy begins to disappear (fill in), the woman ends up with an intact muscle but one with poor tone. As tone improves, then vaginal displacement disappears, and then initial strength becomes better, and so on.

So the length of time required to bring the muscle to full health is very much dependent on which of the six factors are already evaluated as good and which are not. Two other factors that affect how long the exercises must continue are whether or not the woman is doing the exercises correctly, and how frequently and regularly she does them.

How Often Do I Need to Be Examined? Unfortunately, it is impossible to evaluate the condition of your own muscle even with the aid of the perineometer. This is because the first changes in the muscle are always internal ones and don't alter the perineometer readings. This can lead to the false impression that no improvement is taking place. In addition, many women need constant supervision and correction in the proper exercise technique as they go through the therapeutic process. For these reasons you should return to your physician at regular intervals to be checked (with your own perineometer if you are using one, to make sure it's working correctly).

These examinations usually occur once every one or two weeks.

Patient's Exercise Instructions to Correct Poor Control

These exercises are to be done during urination. Go to the bathroom when you normally would, when you have the desire to urinate. Sit on the toilet with your legs separated and your forearms resting on your thighs so that your weight is supported by your thighs. This is done to relax the abdominal muscles; otherwise they are tensed in the process of holding you in an upright position and will contract along with the pubococcygeus.

Begin to let the urine out, but only let out about one teaspoon and then cut off the flow of urine completely. When it is fully stopped, let out another teaspoon and then cut it off again. Continue doing this until your bladder is completely emptied.

These exercises must be done by any woman who cannot move the needle on the manometer of the perineometer at least one notch, or two points, at will back and forth between a relaxed and contracting reading. They should also be done by every woman doing therapeutic exercises with a perineometer. In both instances, they should be done each time the woman urinates until she can do them perfectly.

For the woman with good control who is beginning to use the perineometer, this may require only doing these urination exercises once or twice—enough only to assure her that her control cannot benefit from doing them. Once good control is accomplished, the exercises may be discontinued, as the only effect of doing them is to increase control of the muscle—there is no effect on atrophy, tone, vaginal displacement, or strength. When control is gained, it will be exercised by correct use of the perineometer at the same time that the other factors mentioned above will be affected.

Occasionally, a woman will be able to do the urination exercises without difficulty but will be unable to perform the exercises correctly with the perineometer. Such women are not ready to begin the exercise program detailed below for correction of atrophy, tone, vaginal displacement, and strength, but need modified and individualized instruction on furthering control until they are able to use the perineometer correctly.

An attempt should be made to determine if there is muscle mass present which is either not being contracted or is being contracted sporadically. Sometimes a woman has a fairly intact muscle, but when she attempts to contract, only a portion of it responds in movement. This is easily diagnosed when there is sporadic or intermittent movement of the muscle, as some of the time muscle can be felt contracting and at other times it cannot. If all or a portion of the muscle is not contracting at all even though it is intact, it is not always possible to be certain of this until sufficient control is gained to assess the amount of muscle present in a contracted state. However, in women with no control of the muscle, this is frequently the case, and complete diagnostic classification of the pubococcygeus muscle must be deferred until control is sufficiently learned to further evaluate the other five factors.

Instruction should consist of assisting the woman to begin to identify movement in the pubococcygeus, and can be accomplished by several methods.

Firm pressure with the tip of the finger can be applied against a portion of the muscle while asking the patient to try and squeeze the vagina together in such a way as to move the finger, or to simply try and move the finger. This should be done with every part of the muscle.

Another method is to insert two separated fingers, the index and the middle one, into the vagina, and to ask the patient to squeeze against them as if she were closing a pair of scissors. This is done with slight resistance of the fingers against the vaginal walls, causing the patient to exert a somewhat greater effort than normal to contract the muscle. The fingers are placed at the top of the vagina with palm up, at the bottom of the vagina with palm down, and in the mid-vaginal area, to help the patient identify different portions of the muscle that need to be moved. A woman can be instructed to practice this herself at home in a sitting position with knees drawn up and legs spread.

The perineometer is also useful as an aid in control. The patient is instructed to do fast flicks of five in a row, without any attempt to hold the contraction, for five to ten minutes a day. As success is gained, the time can be increased, and she can be taught to hold the contraction first for a count of one, then two, then three. At this point, she can be put on the regular corrective exercise program with the perineometer, outlined below.

Some patients will need modifications of these basic suggestions to begin to learn control, but if instruction begins by using whatever ability of control the patient already has, then this can be increased with positive reinforcement, leading to eventual success with the exercises and full restoration of pubococcygeal health.

Patient's Exercise Instructions to Correct Atrophy, Poor Tone, Vaginal Displacement, Initial Strength, and Sustained Strength

General Information

What Is the Perineometer Used For? The perineometer is a medical instrument available only by prescription from your physician. It functions both as a measuring device to evaluate the condition of your muscle and as a therapeutic device to correct muscle pathology.

Although it is physically possible to perform the exercises without the perineometer, it plays a very important function in the therapeutic process. The rubber cot portion that is inserted into the vagina is filled with air; when you contract your muscle against this cot, the air is deflated and causes the needle on the attached gauge to rise according to the degree of the exertion.

When you contract your muscle against the perineometer, your muscle has to work harder to perform the contraction than if the perineometer were not inserted in the vagina. In other words, contracting the muscle by itself is an *exertion* of the muscle, but contracting against the perineometer is an *overexertion*. It is this extra amount of exertion that is needed to actually change the muscle from an unhealthy state to a healthy one, although once the muscle is healthy a normal amount of exertion without the perineometer is useful for *maintaining* the healthy state. In effect, the perineometer functions as a passive resistant device, i.e., resistant because it is there in the vagina (in the way of the muscle contracting) but passive because it gives way beneath the exertion of the muscle, causing the muscle to work harder in the process. This is similar to barbells or weights that the athlete might use to strengthen and build up the biceps in the arms.

The perineometer also has a biofeedback device in the form of the gauge that measures the amount of the exertion accomplished. This is necessary because once something is inserted in the vagina the sensation of contracting is greatly diminished. Since you can no longer accurately perceive the degree to which you are contracting with the perineometer in place, the gauge allows you to perceive it by seeing the measurement.

How Often Should I Do the Exercises? There is a cumulative effect from doing the exercises. A woman doing them three times a day will correct the pathology more than three times faster than the woman doing them once a day, and a woman doing them twice a day will correct the pathology more than twice as fast as the woman doing them once a day. This makes it desirable to do them three times a day if it can be arranged. More than three times a day is not effective, as it creates too much muscle fatigue to be beneficial.

There should be at least a three-hour span between exercise periods to allow for recovery of strength. Exercises may be done during the menstrual cycle unless severe cramping creates discomfort. Most women do not find this to be a problem.

How Should I Time Myself When Exercising? Do not look at a watch or clock during the exercise period. Instead, buy an inexpensive kitchen timer and set it for twenty minutes. The "countdown" from the timer is a much more positive feedback than the "count-up" from a clock, and is significantly more encouraging. Many women feel quite depressed to find when looking at a clock that only five minutes have passed instead of what felt to them like twenty minutes. The timer does not have this effect, and for that reason is much preferred over a clock or watch.

Can I Do Anything Else During the Exercises? Without a distraction, the exercises can seem long and tedious. Therefore, it is strongly suggested that some form of entertainment be provided.

A radio talk show is ideal if it is of some interest to you; it allows you to focus your eyes entirely on the perineometer gauge and yet provides constant diversion. Television can be used in a similar way if the television is situated in a direct line of vision from where the gauge will be held by your hand, so that you are not required to be constantly turning your head from looking at the gauge to looking at the television screen.

Perhaps one of the nicest forms of entertainment can be provided by your partner if time allows. This is in the form of his reading aloud something of interest to you both, preferably a book that can be continued each day only when you do these exercises. This provides not only diversion but also a great deal of positive reinforcement in the form of attention from him, his commitment to helping you with the exercises, and anticipation and interest in the continuing story. In this situation, the exercises become almost incidental and a positive reinforcement, because by doing them you earn this other activity (reading a story together) that you look forward to and enjoy.

Should I Keep a Record of My Exercises? A simple log should be kept of your progress. This is helpful in keeping an account of how many times you have done the exercises in a given period of time and is necessary to properly evaluate your progress and the effectiveness of the exercises as you are doing them. In addition, it provides a record of the effort actually achieved, which can be compared with the measurements obtained in the office.

List the date, length of exercise period (i.e., twenty minutes), and the *average* reading for that exercise session. Put three numbers for the reading—relaxed reading/contracted reading at the *end* of the three-second holding period*/extra contracted reading. An example would be 20/40/50. Do this each time you do the exercises, so that if you do them twice a day you would have two entries in your log for that date.

How Do I Take Care of My Perineometer? The perineometer requires very little care. After use it can simply be wiped with a damp washcloth and put away in its box for storage. Since you will be the only one using it, it does not require hot water, soap, or disinfectants.

The only exception to this is if you should get a vaginal infection. In this case, the cot should be washed with hot water and soap (carefully, so as to avoid getting water under the disc and into the internal workings of the device, which can destroy it), dried, and set in a glass jar that has been washed with hot water and soap, dried, and filled almost to the top with rubbing alcohol so that the alcohol comes almost to the top of the cot. The rim of the jar should be somewhat smaller in diameter than the outside of the disc on the perineometer so that the disc will rest on the jar and keep it from falling in (a peanut butter or jam jar works well). Leave it in the alcohol for fifteen minutes, remove, dry, and put away for the next use. This is an effective method of sterilization and will prevent you from reinfecting yourself while you are being treated for the vaginal infection.

Specific Exercise Instructions

Lie Flat. Lie flat on your back with a small pillow under your head for comfort. The more of a sitting position you assume, the more the abdominal muscles will tense along with the pubococcygeus; this is to be avoided, as the goal is to isolate the pubococcygeus for specific exercise.

Legs in "Frog." Bring your legs into a "frog" position, i.e., knees bent, legs spread somewhat, soles of feet facing each other. If this is not completely comfortable, a pillow of moderate size may be placed under the outside portion of each knee area for support. This position renders it difficult to contract the auxiliary muscles (abdomen, buttocks, thighs) and allows for greater isolation of the pubococcygeus.

Should I Use a Lubricant with the Perineometer? You may use only a small amount of a medical lubricant (such as K-Y jelly, available in pharmacies without prescription), water, or even saliva, applied directly to the cot portion, which is inserted into the vagina. As you increase the amount of lubricant, friction decreases and the exercises are not as effective as the muscle does not have to work as hard. So keep lubricant to a minimum. Do not use anything else such as petroleum jelly or baby oil, as these will damage the rubber cot in one use, requiring

*See the next main section, "Specific Exercise Instructions."

you to replace it. Most women find that partially inserting the cot, removing it part way, and reinserting it will accomplish full insertion with a minimum of discomfort, avoiding the need for any other lubricant.

Insert Cot Properly.   Insert the cot of the perineometer so that the disc rests snugly against the outside of the vagina. This will ensure a consistent relaxed reading from one exercise period to the next.

"Clap" Vagina Together.   Visualize in your mind that the vagina is composed of two sides, a left and a right, or two little boards of wood. When you contract the muscle, bring those two little boards together as if you are clapping your hands. This will encourage the entire length of the muscle to move and is especially helpful for moving the smaller, upper part of the muscle.

If you were to think of the vagina as a tunnel, or as a donut, and tried to contract by closing the middle of the tunnel or donut, the top of the muscle and perhaps the sides as well would not actually move as much as they should.

Therefore, it is very important to keep this visual concept in mind when doing the exercises, especially because you will not be able to feel exactly how the muscle is moving with the perineometer in place.

Six-Second Count.   The exercises are to be done to a count of six seconds and can be timed by counting aloud in the following manner: one thousand *one*, one thousand *two*, etc.

Contract, Hold, Hold, Hold, Extra Squeeze, Relax.   One is a slow, steady, deliberate contraction of the muscle.

Two, three, four is maintain, or attempt to maintain, the original contraction *without* letting the needle on the gauge drop. This is to be held for a full three seconds.

Five is an extra contraction, using auxiliary muscles, trying to get the needle to rise as high as possible.

Six is to fully relax the muscle back to the original relaxed reading. When this is accomplished, begin the six-second set again, and continue this for twenty minutes.

Twenty Minutes Twice a Day.   The exercises should be done for a period of twenty minutes each time. The ideal format is three exercise periods a day, but this is simply not possible for many women. Twice a day is necessary, however, unless the degree of pathology is slight. Only in instances where there is little pathology to correct should they be done as little as once a day, and never less than that except under special circumstances such as illness.

Don't Underestimate Your Progress.   Most women, when beginning the therapeutic exercise program, are not able to do the exercises perfectly. For instance, they may not be able to hold the original contraction for the full three seconds, or perhaps they cannot hold it at all. Nonetheless, the attempt should be made regardless of the fact that the perineometer is registering otherwise. This continued attempt will eventually have the same effect as if they were being done correctly, because they will lead to the ability to do them.

Although it is possible to duplicate these exercises without a perineometer, our research indicates that this does not produce reversal of any physiologic pathology of the pubococcygeus. However, exercises without the perineometer are valuable to a woman with a physiologically intact pubococcygeus muscle because they increase sexual awareness and *maintain* strength and condition of this muscle. These maintenance exercises can be prescribed to a patient who already has a healthy muscle or at the completion of a therapeutic regime; they should be the same as the exercises to correct poor control, done with urination once a day, or simply twenty-five contractions a day without the perineometer.

There have been many articles in women's magazines and popular books, as well as a marketed device, that essentially advocate the utilization of "Kegel's exercises" without the perineometer. There are as yet no published data to support these recommendations, and our research and clinical experience demonstrate that this would only be helpful to a woman possessing an already healthy muscle (Kline-Graber and Graber, 1975). An analogy would be to suggest that a deficiency in the biceps muscle could be corrected by simply contracting the arm muscles, rather than the accepted procedure, which is contracting against passive resistance, such as weight lifting.

Continuing work on the study of the function and restoration of the pubococcygeus may shed light on the mechanism of female orgasmic response in general and specifically female coital orgasm. Currently, treatment techniques as developed by LoPiccolo and modified by others, utilizing clitoral masturbation, have been successful in teaching patients to achieve noncoital orgasm but have not been uniformly successful in generalizing to coitus independent of concurrent direct clitoral stimulation (LoPiccolo and Lobitz, 1972; Barbach, 1975).

This dilemma can be understood by looking at orgasm in a reflex model (Kaplan, 1974). A reflex requires an afferent or sensory stimulus and an efferent or muscular response. The patellar knee jerk is a simple example. The knee tap is the stimulus, the knee jerk is the response. In terms of orgasm, the muscular response in the male is well documented, with its sequela, the ejaculate, an observable phenomenon of that response.

This has been more obscure in regard to female orgasm, leading to much confusion. Masters and Johnson (1966) have described contractions of the "orgasmic platform" as occurring simultaneously with subjective and objective signs of orgasm in the female. Deutsch (1968) has shown that drawings of this orgasmic platform correspond precisely to the anatomical position of the pubococcygeus muscle. This, together with the fact that the orgasmic platform is described as vascularly engorged mucosa—a tissue devoid of contractile properties— suggests the pubococcygeus as the efferent or muscular responder in female orgasm.

It is, however, the afferent or sensory side of the loop that is mired in even deeper controversy. Is orgasm triggered by clitoral or vaginal stimulation? Most professionals are in agreement as to how noncoital orgasm occurs, but the controversy surrounding coital orgasm has led to the argument about clitoral versus vaginal orgasm. Masters and Johnson's evidence was used to suggest a labial-preputial mechanism in which the clitoris is implicated as the trigger for coital orgasmic response (Sherfey, 1966). However, data we have accumulated about a condition in which the foreskin adheres to the clitoris provided us with suspicion as to the validity of this mechanism. Some of the women examined with this condition, known as clitoral foreskin adhesions, were orgasmic with coitus. This evidence, together with clinical difficulties in generalizing to coitus success with a clitoral masturbation program, suggests another possible mechanism for triggering female coital orgasm—coital stimulation of the pubococcygeus muscle.

The widespread deficiencies in the condition of the pubococcygeus observed in large clinical populations by ourselves and Kegel correlate with the epidemiological evidence of coital orgasmic difficulties in women (Kinsey, Pomeroy, Martin and Gebhard, 1953; Hunt, 1974).

We have just completed a retrospective (Graber and Kline-Graber, submitted) review of 281 female patients who were seen at a sexual dysfunction clinic. These patients were divided into three groups based on orgasmic capacity. Statistically significant differences were found between these groups on measures of atrophy and sustained strength of the pubococcygeus muscle. Women who were totally incapable of achieving orgasm—either coitally or noncoitally—had the worst muscles; those women able to achieve only noncoital orgasm had somewhat better muscles; and women able to achieve both noncoital and coital orgasm had the muscles that were anatomically and physiologically in the best condition.

This data supports a significant role for the pubococcygeus in female orgasmic dysfunction but does not delineate if its role is efferent, afferent, or both.

We have discussed diagnostic and treatment procedures related to physiological deficiencies of the pubococcygeus muscle and have suggested its possible role as both afferent trigger and efferent responder in female coital orgasm. The evidence is strong enough to warrant the questioning of current theories and increased scientific investigation into the role of the pubococcygeus in female sexual response. Further research in this area may produce a definitive understanding of the clitoral-versus-vaginal controversy, providing a sound basis for clinical treatment of female coital anorgasmia.

References

Barbach, L. G. *For yourself: The fulfillment of female sexuality.* Garden City: Doubleday, 1975.

Deutsch, R. *The key to feminine response in marriage.* New York: Ballantine Books, 1968.

Graber, B., and Kline-Graber, G. Pathophysiology of female orgasm. Submitted for publication.

Hunt, M. *Sexual behavior in the seventies.* Chicago: Playboy Press, 1974.

Kaplan, H. K. *The new sex therapy.* New York: Brunner/Mazel, 1974.

Kegel, A. The non-surgical treatment of genital relaxation. *Annals of Western Medicine and Surgery,* 1948, *2,* 213–216. (a)

Kegel, A. Progressive resistance exercise in the functional restoration of the perineal muscles. *American Journal of Obstetrics and Gynecology,* 1948, *56,* 238–248. (b)

Kegel, A. The physiologic treatment of poor tone and function of the genital muscles and of urinary stress incontinence. *Western Journal of Surgery, Obstetrics and Gynecology,* 1949, *56,* 527–535.

Kegel, A. Physiologic therapy for urinary stress incontinence. *Journal of the American Medical Association,* 1951, *146,* 915–917.

Kegel, A. Stress incontinence and genital relaxation. *Ciba Clinical Symposia,* February–March 1952, *4*(2), 35–51. (a)

Kegel, A. Physiologic therapy of urinary stress incontinence. In B. N. Carter (Ed.), *Monographs on surgery 1952.* Baltimore: Williams and Wilkins, 1952. (b)

Kegel, A. Sexual functions of the pubococcygeus muscle. *Western Journal of Surgery, Obstetrics and Gynecology*, 1952, *60*, 521–524. (c)

Kegel, A. Stress incontinence of urine in women: Physiologic treatment. *Journal of International College of Surgeons*, 1956, *25*, 487–499. (a)

Kegel, A. Early genital relaxation. *Obstetrics and Gynecology*, 1956, *8*, 545–550. (b)

Kegel, A., and Powell, T. The physiologic treatment of urinary stress incontinence. *Journal of Urology*, 1950, *63*, 808–813.

Kinsey, A. C., Pomeroy, W. B., Martin, C. E., and Gebhard, P. H. *Sexual behavior in the human female*. Philadelphia: W. B. Saunders, 1953.

Kline-Graber, G., and Graber, B. *Woman's orgasm: A guide to sexual satisfaction*. New York: Bobbs-Merrill, 1975.

LoPiccolo, J., and Lobitz, M. A. The role of masturbation in the treatment of orgasmic dysfunction. *Archives of Sexual Behavior*, 1972, *2*, 163–171.

Masters, W. H., and Johnson, V. E. *Human sexual response*. Boston: Little, Brown, 1966.

Sherfey, M. J. *The nature and evolution of female sexuality*. New York: Random House, 1966.

Frequently, women who experience painful intercourse will seek out sex therapy. These women may be self-referred or referred by a physician after a medical examination failed to disclose a physical basis for the complaint.

In this chapter, Abarbanel outlines the possible etiological factors that can account for coital discomfort. He also includes a guide for history taking that enables the physician or clinician to gather the relevant information that is necessary for accurate diagnosis and successful treatment. A description of the steps involved in the medical evaluation of problems of coital discomfort as well as treatment approaches is included.

Although this article covers some purely medical procedures, it is of interest and value to the psychotherapist as well. Often, a clinician must assess the need for a medical consultation on a patient requesting sex therapy. Abarbanel's chapter is useful as a guide in making this assessment.

18

Diagnosis and Treatment of Coital Discomfort

A. R. Abarbanel

Nature of the Problem

Coital discomfort is indeed a most distressing event to both partners. It may be perceived as a momentary sharp pain of varying intensity, intermittent twinges of hurting to repeated intense discomfort, or it may be present during coitus as an aching sensation. Combinations of these may also occur before, during, or after coitus.

Coital discomfort is often called *dyspareunia*, a rather inadequate term for this condition. Pareunia comes from the Greek, meaning "lying beside in bed," while the prefix *dys* is a combining one that may mean difficult, painful, bad, disordered. *Coitalgia* probably is the better term, signifying algesic coitus.

Clinically, if an individual has a sore, swollen finger that becomes painfully unpleasant when touched or used, that individual will avoid any such stimulus. Clearly, then, if a sufficiently unpleasant ache or pain derives from sexual activity— before, during or after—then that individual's defense mechanisms will avoid

---

A. R. Abarbanel • Medical Director, Fertility Institute, and Independent Practice, Obstetrics and Gynecology, Los Angeles, California.

the stress of coitus, or be on guard throughout the act, to prevent unpleasant aches or pains.

Basically, there always has to be a stimulus that activates a tissue to respond with a sensation of discomfort or pain. The stimulus may be real or imaginary. Fear of recurrence of the injury, by repetition of the same or similar stimulus, may set up a reflex of fear of possible hurt. Alternatively, fear alone of discomfort or pain may be sufficient to cause real or apparent discomfort in the absence of any physical damage.

In such a situation, anxiety replaces enjoyment, thus detracting from or displacing the concept of sexual intercourse being pleasurable for both partners. The possible syndrome of "fright-fight-flight" replaces full and joyous participation in the sexual act.

Factors Relating to Coital Discomfort

Basically, there are four main categories that may lead to coital discomfort, singly or in combination: (1) anatomic factors, (2) pathological factors, (3) psychosomatic factors, and (4) iatrogenic factors.

Anatomic factors are fundamentally either congenital or developmental in origin, affecting primarily the introitus (the opening into the vagina) and the vagina itself.

Pathologic factors are acute and chronic infections of the genital tract such as trichomoniasis, fungus and yeast infections, nonspecific vaginitis, irritations, and skin diseases of varying etiology; residua of pelvic inflammatory diseases involving the adnexae and broad ligaments; endometriosis; constitutional diseases affecting the genital tract; malignant and nonmalignant growths; and disorders or diseases of the adjacent viscera. These involve (1) the urethra and bladder, (2) the anus and the anal canal and lower sigmoid, and (3) orthopedic problems such as subluxation of the symphysis pubis in pregnancy as well as problems of the sacroiliac area, the lumbosacral area, and the hips. Also, there might be skeletal muscle disturbances such as psoas and obturator muscle injuries and arthritis. Other causes are acute and chronic illnesses, which produce sufficient malaise and upset both physically and mentally and which may reduce or erase libido. The lessening of libido contributes to failure of arousal, which in turn results in inadequate precoital lubrication. Postoperative or postpartum scarring of the genital tract or adjacent viscera may also lead to coital discomfort. Abdominal scars are frequently a source of postcoital pain in the female.

Psychological factors fall into two main categories. In some cases there are imagined fears of pain and injury associated with coitus—at times to such an extent that the act is not consummated. In other cases fear is precipitated by actual experience with a previously painful coital episode that was sufficiently disturbing that the female avoids coitus on future occasions. Examples of psychological factors are feelings of guilt or shame in sexual situations and tension occasioned by new situations. New situations can be coitus with a new partner, the use of a new position for intercourse, or new techniques such as the use of a vibrator. Insufficient foreplay or inept precoital techniques may contribute to a lack of arousal in the female, which results in insufficient lubrication for comfortable intercourse. Situational problems may also play a role. For example, anxiety that children may wander into the bedroom may create a response of anxiety, fear, and tension, which can lead to loss of desire or arousal. Ignorance of the anatomy and physiology of sexual response and the life cycle may also serve to perpetuate fears that can occasion coital discomfort—for example, fears of sexual activity during pregnancy or fears about becoming pregnant. Another situational problem may be physical or mental fatigue, which may be sufficiently strong to inhibit arousal.

Iatrogenic factors, which may be physical or psychological, are those induced by the physician. Most common are those surgically induced. For example, a shortened vagina, especially with a painful scar at the vaginal vault, is common. A painful episiotomy scar is also common.

In addition, the attitude of the physician in discussing sexual problems may induce such feelings of shame or guilt that secondary coital discomfort may result.

Another factor is the influence of drugs and medications. Anorectics, tranquilizers, antihypertensive medications, sedatives, and hypnotics are the most common precipitating causes of loss of libido, arousal, and response.

Obtaining a History of Coital Discomfort

The clinician must recognize that coital discomfort rarely is the primary reason for which the woman has come to the office. Most commonly, the physician learns of it in the course of obtaining an adequate history from the patient. On the other hand, the presence of coital discomfort may so alter the sexual activities of a couple that the sexual harmony of the relationship is disrupted. The physician must learn not only to hear what the woman is actually saying but to "hear" what she is not saying or is failing to clarify.

Clearly, then, the physician must have an adequate psychosocial perspective, with full understanding of the basic significance of the family unit in the development of the mature human person. This includes a basic knowledge of the psychology of personality development and the sociology of marriage. In addition, an expertise in the anatomy and physiology of human sexuality is essential.

The physician's attitude must be calmly objective with absolutely no personal bias based on his or her own conflicts or emotional problems. This concept cannot be emphasized too strongly. The patient is only interested in resolving her own problems and attaining her own personal goals. The physician's attitude, then, must be warm and friendly, objectively interested in the woman as an adult individual striving to be her own person in resolving *her* problem and achieving *her* goals.

The first step is to obtain a routine medical history in the usual manner. Remember, the chief complaints may actually appear to be unrelated to the real problem. As her story unfolds, a clue here and there may become evident, but do not jump to any tentative conclusions until a fairly definitive pattern begins to evolve.

The following outline may be utilized in addition to taking the usual medical history. It represents a methodology the author has developed to bring forth evidence of psychosocial and sexual problems. This approach very frequently brings forth verbalizations of many conflictual areas, most of which the doctor can help clarify for the patient. (Let the patient "lead" the conversation as much as is feasible.)

A. *Menstrual History*
1. Age of onset. What were her reactions to it? Was she prepared for it? What does menstruation mean to her? When did she first use tampons?
2. Cycles. Regularity? Irregularity? Changes with birth control pills, if used.
3. Duration and amount of flow.
4. Discomfort and pain. If present, at what age did it first start? Has it changed since then? Exactly how disabling is it? Does she have to remain in bed? How long does it last? Is the degree of discomfort related to activity, diet, urination, defecation, etc.? What medications are necessary to relieve it? Is emotional tension likely to make it worse? Does sexual activity cause any change before or during menses?
5. First day of onset of last regular menses and the one before that.
6. Evaluation of premenstrual tension.
   a. Psychosocial significance. This syndrome is of the utmost significance in the psychosocial evaluation of the woman. (There is some evidence that suggests premenstrual tension may be a factor in suicides of women and in "crimes of passion" by women.)
   b. Common signs and symptoms that may occur in the premenstrual phase.
      (1) Breasts. Do your breasts swell up or hurt before your period? If so, for how long?
      (2) Gums. Do your gums have a tendency to bleed (pink tooth brush)?
      (3) Headache. Is it only premenstrual or at other times? Show me with your fingers where it occurs. Does it get better during flow or after? (The most common premenstrual tension headache occurs at the back of the neck. Next most common is a sense of fullness over the frontal area.) What relieves it?
      (4) Skin. Do you get pimples on your face? Do they disturb you? How? (Patient's self-image may reveal itself.) Do you bruise easily?
      (5) Irritability. Do you become nervous, jumpy, moody premenstrually? Is this when both of you have most of your disagreements and fights? Do little things bother you that you would ordinarily overlook or not even notice?
      (6) Bloat. Degree and duration.
      (7) Depression. Duration, degree, how manifested.
      (8) Cry. Easily? What seems to start it off?
      (9) Suicide. Ever think about it or try it? If so, why and when?
      (10) Desire for sweets. Do you have a tendency to eat more or seek out sweets at this time? Have you ever noticed that if you have lunch at noon that you *must* nibble some candy or sweets about three hours later?

(11) Salt. Do you add salt to your food? If so, why? Do you look for salty foods during this time?

(12) Weight gain. How much weight do you gain before a period or lose after it starts? (Average norm is two to three pounds.)

(13) Low backache. Do you ever get it? At what time of the cycle? Have you ever noticed that it is most likely to occur when you stand on your feet for two or more hours? Is it relieved by lying down?

(14) Leukorrhea. Have you ever had a vaginal discharge? If so, when? Do you have one now? Color? Odor? Does it burn or itch?

(15) Douching. If so, why? What do you use? How often?

(16) Itching. If so, where? At vaginal opening? About lips? In the pubic hair? Always? Occasionally? Relationship to sexual activity? to coitus? oral stimulation?

The approach to the patient's sexuality, patterns, and responses is easily made at this time: Do you enjoy your sexual activities and get along well with your partner(s)? Do you achieve an orgasm? (Be sure she understands the term. One may use the word *climax* or the phrase "do you come?") Single or multiple? With each encounter? Frequently? Occasionally? Or not at all? Do you reach a climax with intercourse? Manual stimulation? Oral stimulation? Can you reach a climax by self-manipulation (masturbation)?

Further investigation can be decided on the basis of her answers or by her avoidance of certain topics. If she seems reluctant to discuss any or all phases of her sexuality, one may explain that the sexual aspects of her life-style are just as important in understanding her as a mature person as knowledge of her respiratory system or any other system. If this fails, stop the inquiry.

If a history of coital discomfort is obtained, a systematic approach is utilized. This involves elucidating with the patient the "when" and the "where" of the discomfort. How the woman reacts to the discomfort is also significant. The "why" is discovered by systematic physical examination. The "what" is the indicated therapeutic approach for the clinical management of the cause(s) of the discomfort (see Tables 1–5).

The woman is encouraged to present her problem of coital discomfort. Then the presenting data are systematically reviewed. It is important to assess the influence of the four factors relating to coital discomfort mentioned earlier: anatomic, pathological, psychosomatic, and iatrogenic factors.

A. *The "When"*
1. Onset. Sudden or gradually increasing in severity.
2. Description. Discomfort, twinges of pain, or a persistent ache.
3. Frequency. Only with first coitus, rarely, occasionally, frequently or always.
4. Does the discomfort occur:
   a. In the arousal phase. Before or during precoital maneuvers, including manual and oral–genital arousal activities?
   b. At intromission. As penis enters the vagina?
   c. On deeper penetration. As the penis proceeds deeper into the vagina?
   d. On thrusting. With full penetration?

Table 1.   Diseases and Disorders of External Genitalia That May Produce Coital
Discomfort and Pain

Site	Diseases and disorders of external genitalia
Labia majora	1. Skin lesions—may be local or local manifestation of a generalized skin disease or of various constitutional diseases, especially diabetes mellitus. May also represent drug reactions, allergy. 2. Local irritants—clothing, medication, excessive local sprays, nylon underwear. 3. Venereal diseases—chancroid, granuloma inguinale, lymphopathia venereum, chancre, herpes progenitalis. 4. Hidradenoma 5. Varicosities 6. Carcinoma—especially postradiation dermatitis. 7. Congenital and developmental anomalies are very rare.
Labia minora	1. Local irritants—clothing, medications. 2. Infections—local or from vaginitis. 3. Trauma—(a) from lack of coital lubrication. (b) from oral–genital action—too vigorous insucking, biting, unshaven chin of male. 4. Varicosities—especially in pregnancy. 5. Synechiae—rare in adult, usually results from poor hygiene. 6. Postradiation
Clitoris	1. Synechiae—of frenulum (prepuce). 2. Balanitis—rare. 3. Improper hygiene—very common. 4. Hypertrophy—rare. 5. Inept or excessive stimulation—common
Posterior commissure (Below and caudad to fossa navicularis)	1. Hypertrophied—rare. 2. May rise high enough up to block introitus when woman spreads drawn-up thighs. 3. Easily traumatized—if high. 4. Local irritants
Perineal body	1. Chronic irritation—most common from repeated attacks of herpes progenitalis of fossa navicularis (relatively rare). 2. Iatrogenic—after vaginal surgery.
Fossa navicularis (fourchette) Area between hymen and frenulum labiorum pudendi (posterior commissure) (Actually posterior aspect of area just before vaginal opening)	1. Congenital—very rare. 2. Developmental—very rare. 3. Infections—(a) primary—herpes progenitalis. (b) secondary—to vulvovaginitis of monilia or trichomoniasis: systemic diseases. 4. Postoperative—vaginal repair—painful scar. 5. Postpartum—episiotomy—painful scar. 6. Traumatic—(a) injury—lack of precoital lubrication. 7. Chronic irritation 8. Postradiation

Table 2.   Diseases and Disorders of Areas about Introitus That May Cause Coital Discomfort

Site	Disease and disorder

Hymen	1. Congenital and developmental
	    (a) Imperforate
	    (b) Cribiform
	    (c) Bipartite
	    (d) Absent—associated with absent vagina
	2. Hymeneal scars
	    (a) After rupture at first coitus
	    (b) After episiotomy repair
	    (c) After posterior vaginal repair
	    (d) May be secondary to repeated attacks of herpes provaginalis.
	    (e) Posttrauma—postirradiation

Urethra	1. Urethral caruncle
	2. Urethritis
	    (a) Primary
	    (b) Secondary to prolonged cunnilingus
	3. Urethral diverticulum
	4. Scar tissue—secondary to anterior vaginal repair

Anorectal area	1. Fissures 2. External hemorrhoids 3. Cryptitis 4. Postoperative—scars 5. Ischiorectal abscess 6. Pinworms

Perineal body and levator ani muscles	1. Vaginismus
	    (a) Psychosomatic—primary or secondary
	    (b) Secondary to (1) hymeneal scars
	                          (2) chronic herpes provaginalis
	2. Chronic vulvovaginitis
	3. Postoperative scars
	4. Endometriosis

Vaginal opening (Introitus)	1. Marked regression
	    (a) Postmenopausal
	    (b) Postradiation
	2. Congenital and developmental anomalies
	3. Inadequate precoital lubrication

Symphysis pubis	1. Subluxation in pregnancy 2. Postfracture
Skene's and Bartholin glands	1. Acute infection 2. Cysts—rarely unless large

*Table 3.   Diseases and Disorders of the Areas about the Vaginal Tract and
            Adjacent Viscera That May Cause Coital Discomfort*

Site	Disease and disorder

Vagina	1. Congenital
	   (a) Absence
	   (b) Mid-canal stenosis
	   (c) Gartner's cyst
	   (d) Dermoid cyst
	2. Postoperative
	   (a) Narrowing
	   (b) Scars—including vault
	   (c) Shortening
	   (d) Stenosis—(especially after transsexual operation)
	3. Infections
	   (a) Monilia
	   (b) Trichomoniasis
	   (c) Mixed
	4. Postmenopausal regression
	5. Postradiation
	6. Endometriosis
	7. Postpartum—scarring of fornices–cervical tears
	8. Disproportion—excessive penile size
	9. Coccydynia

Urethra and bladder	1. Infections—urethritis, cystitis, trigonitis 2. Urethral caruncle 3. Urethral diverticulum 4. Scar tissue—after vaginal surgery 5. Postradiation
Anorectal area	1. Internal hemorrhoids 2. Cryptitis 3. Diverticulitis 4. Marked constipation 5. Postradiation 6. Pinworms 7. Coccydynia

    e. During orgasm?

    f. After coitus completed?

    g. Combination of two or more of above?

    h. Body activity associated with coitus. Does movement of hips or legs aggravate the discomfort?

    i. Position. Is she on top—sitting up? or bending over? If she is on bottom, position of her legs?

B. *The "Where"*—In what specific areas is the discomfort noted? What is its intensity? How long does it last? Does it occur with each coitus? Is discomfort always noted in the same place?

C. *The "Why"*—Relationship of discomfort to sexual activity.

    1. Coital position. Is the discomfort induced or made worse by any specific position?

Table 4. *Diseases and Disorders of Cervix, Uterus, and Adjacent Viscera That May Cause Coital Discomfort and Pain*

Site	Disease and disorder
Cervix	1. Infection—especially with: (a) lymphangitis of uterosacral ligaments (b) parametritis 2. Hypertrophy
Fornices	1. Scars after difficult delivery 2. Varicosities of broad ligament 3. Metastatic tumors
Uterosacral ligaments	1. Endometriosis 2. Post-P.I.D. 3. Lymphangitis 4. Adnexal tumors
Uterus	1. Adenomyosis 2. Fixed retroversion
Lumbosacral area Obturator and psoas muscles	1. Usually follows trauma— Muscles become tender and spastic Obturator neuritis
Low back Hips	1. Any disease or disorder that produces discomfort, pain, or aching on motion or in certain positions: Congenital and developmental Posttrauma Arthritides

2. Alteration of discomfort. Outside of coital abstinence, what factors may make discomfort worse or better?
3. Precipitating factors
    a. Did symptoms arise after use of a new douche preparation, a different soap, powder, cosmetic, or feminine hygiene spray; or following the wearing of tight pants, especially nylon?
    b. Influence of any of the four main factors: anatomic, pathological, psychosomatic, and iatrogenic.
4. Physical examination for possible causes of coital discomfort. This involves a routine systematic evaluation of each system with particular reference to its possible influence on the sexual response of the woman.

Table 5. *Diseases and Disorders of Adnexae and Broad Ligaments That May Cause Coital Discomfort and Pain*

Site	Disease and disorder
Broad ligaments and adnexae	1. Varicosities 2. P.I.D.[a] with residual adhesions 3. Prolapsed ovary in cul-de-sac 4. Endometriosis 5. Postoperative scar tissue at vault or in cul-de-sac

[a]P.I.D., pelvic inflammatory disease.

a. Skin. Note pimples, rashes, dryness, etc.
b. Tongue and teeth. Possible source of disturbing odors.
c. Breasts. Adenosis, fullness, nipples. Examine for possible secretion. Examine breasts with patient lying down and sitting up. (If the time permits, teach her how to examine her own breasts.)
d. Pelvic examination. Full thighs and lower abdomen exposed. (It is wise to permit patient to watch with the aid of an adequate hand mirror.)
　(1) Inspection and palpation. External genitalia.
　　(a) Prepuce and clitoris. Does prepuce retract easily so that corona is easily exposed?
　　(b) Labia majora. Skin lesions, varices, fullness especially with obesity. Unilateral skin thickening. Observe evidence of perspiration laterally at juncture of thighs. Varices?
　　(c) Labia minora. Full, pendulous, scant.
　　(d) Hymen. Intact? Note areas where hymeneal rupture may have occurred. Also check carefully for episiotomy and postoperative scars. Press firmly down with one finger and note if painful at that site. Repeat with two fingers spread apart in vagina.
　　(e) Urethra. Note meatus. Does it protrude forward or does it recede under symphysis? Search for evidence of inflammation, irritation, urethral caruncle. Pass one finger into vagina to level of bladder neck and then firmly but gently strip urethra down against symphysis. Observe for any secretions. If so, make a slide and also culture. Search for Skene's glands.
　　(f) Fourchette (Vestibule—Fossa navicularis). Is it smooth and glistening? or irritated? Look for evidence of "friction burn" if coitus in previous twenty-four hours. Search carefully for evidence of small blebs or blisterlike cystic areas if menses due in two or three days, or during or just after menses. Use magnifying glass for best results. (The latter should also be used in a search for scabies, especially in mons pubis area.)
　　(g) Frenulum pudendi (Posterior commissure). Place a finger on each end, ask the patient to spread her knees wide apart, then press each finger laterally. If a high ridge of tense, taut tissue develops, it may be a factor in discomfort and occasionally causes difficulty in intromission.
　　　　Press on juncture of fourchette with frenulum. Normally, tissue should be yielding and somewhat pulpy. If firm, hard, or rigid, may be a cause of intromission discomfort.
　(2) Bimanual examination. One hand on lower abdomen and two fingers in introitus. (N.B.: Speculum examination may precede this. See below.)
　　(a) Symphysis pubis. Palpate mons with particular reference to area where pubic bones join. In pregnancy, these interpubic surfaces may separate slightly (called subluxation) and be a cause of coital discomfort. Occasionally, the subluxation may persist after delivery. Rarely, direct trauma to the area may result in a prolonged healing process or leave a painful scar.

(b) Reevaluate possible painful areas about hymeneal ring by spreading fingers apart and gently but firmly pressing down her vaginal muscles.

(c) Levator muscle (Sphincter cunni) evaluation. As she tightens her muscles, usually two and occasionally three separate bands can be palpated. The.ı ask patient to relax and again ask her to gently tighten them once more.

(d) Evaluation of coital angle of vaginal axis in relationship to clitoris. Extend both vaginal fingers firmly along with wrist. As patient again tightens her muscles, note whether gentle in-and-out motion of fingers causes the labia minora to draw into the vaginal tube. This should then bring the clitoris downward to make contact with the hand or fingers.

(e) Evaluation of cervix. Size. Location. Does it feel smooth? Is there evidence of fibrous healed lacerations? Is it freely movable? Painlessly so? Then press on cervix so as to push it deeper into the pelvis. Is it painless?

(f) Corpus uteri. Location. Size. Tender to motion?

(g) Fornices. Are adnexae palpable? Tender? Search for fullness, doughiness, thickening, foreshortening on one side; if parous, also look for scar tissue. (For further investigation, see under rectovaginal examination.)

(h) Uterosacral area. Note the area of convergence of uterosacral ligaments on posterior surface of cervix. Press fingers up, first on one side, then the other. Observe for nodularity, thickening, tenderness, or discomfort as cervix and uterosacral area are lifted toward the anterior abdominal wall. (For further details see rectovaginal examination.)

(i) Bladder and urethra. Now press tips of fingers upward and with firm but gentle pressure sweep fingers downward. Note any areas of tenderness. (Cystitis is a rather common cause of coital discomfort.) If discomfort present, note whether discomfort lessens or disappears if angle at which fingers enter vagina is changed.

(j) Posterior vaginal wall. Turn fingers so as to press down on rectovaginal septum. Then press gently but firmly down as fingers are brought to outside. Search for any areas of tenderness or increased sensitivity. Internal hemorrhoids, cryptitis, and other lesions of the anal canal may cause coital discomfort. Check coccyx for evidence of previous fracture or tenderness.

(3) Speculum examination. Warm if possible. (Lubrication is usually not needed.)

(a) Evaluation for relaxation. Before inserting, ask patient to cough or bear down if she is parous. Then place two fingers about two inches past the hymeneal ring and press down. Repeat request for cough or bearing down.

(b) Evaluation for vaginal and cervical pathology. Insert speculum to its full length and fit snugly into place. Observe vaginal secretions. Study cervix for evidence of lacerations, cervicitis, and endocervicitis. Size. Location. Place cotton swab in endocervix; observe for pain and/or bleeding. Make Pap smear and hanging drop preparation. Grasp with tenaculum. Sound uterine canal for depth. Search for discomfort at level of internal os.

(4) Rectovaginal examination:

(a) External evaluation. Observe for hemorrhoids, fissures, evidence of local irritation. Note condition of perianal skin.

(b) Evaluation of anal canal. Place lubricating cream or jelly on middle finger of examining hand. Then gently insert into anal canal. Press for areas of tenderness by pressing up against posterior vaginal wall.

(c) Evaluation of uterosacral and broad ligaments. Place index finger in vaginal canal. Both fingers are then allowed to progress inward. Each ovary may be palpable. The junction of the uterosacral ligaments on the cervix is carefully noted for nodularity, tenderness, and discomfort or achiness.

Particular attention is also directed at the base of the broad ligaments. A fullness or doughiness should make one suspicious of varicosities of the broad ligament, the anatomical basis of the syndrome of chronic pelvic congestion.

The rectal finger is then swept over each obturator notch and over the obturator muscle searching for tender areas. The coccyx is also checked.

The levator muscle group may also be reevaluated by asking her to contract these muscles repeatedly but slowly. Defects are quite easily ascertained.

(d) Further evaluation of uterosacral and broad ligaments. One finger remains in the anal canal and the other in the vagina. The woman is asked to flex first one leg then the other on her abdomen. Then she is asked to extend one leg then the other and stand upon the base of the examining table with her legs apart. As she rises to a standing position, if varicosities are present, the broad ligaments will become fuller, tauter, and often uncomfortable, especially if she is premenstrual. The base of the uterosacral ligaments becomes easier to evaluate; the fingers may then be swept laterally, carefully checking each side. The examining hand is then removed at this time or after the patient sits down. The anal area is carefully wiped clean and dry.

The rectovaginal examination, especially with the woman in the standing position, is an extremely valuable procedure in clarifying the cause of the vast majority of deep pelvic aches and pains associated with deep pelvic thrusting of the penis. Clearly, then, it should become a part of the routine gynecological examination. Where there is a history of deep pelvic discomfort or pain on deep penile penetration, it should be mandatory.

Once the "when," the "where," and the "why" of coital discomfort have been determined the next step, the "what," is the therapeutic approach required to resolve the discomfort.

Clinical Management of the More Common Causes of Coital Discomfort (Table 6)

Precoital Discomfort/Vaginismus (Tables 1-5)

The most common causes of precoital discomfort are psychosomatic—fear of pain, fear of the erotic stimulus, fear of failure to respond, fear of rejection, religious conflicts, persistence of various beliefs or myths based on fantasy rather than fact.

In all of these factors, the common denominator is the fear of the fantasied event—be it of pain or shame or guilt. The end result is fear–tension–avoidance, the so-called fright–fight–flight syndrome. For some woman, however, these fears are based on actual discomfort on a previous occasion. Fear of repetition of such discomfort can become real in the mind of the individual.

In the first group, education is the goal of therapy. Usually, an adequate explanation of the anatomy and physiology of sexual responsiveness will relieve anxieties and help resolve the basic problems.

In the group who have experienced discomfort on more than one occasion, a diligent search for the etiology of the discomfort is basic to the initiation of a therapeutic regime to resolve it. Once the physician is certain that there is no organic pathology present, referral of the woman to an experienced psychotherapist is indicated.

Vaginismus. This is a condition in which the vaginal levator ani muscles go into such clonic spasm as to prevent penile entry. It is usually a "learned" response: to avoid penile penetration of the vagina.

In the primary type, the basic cause may be fantasy associated with a fear of possible great pain from vaginal entrance of the penis or a fear of pregnancy. It may also be secondary to previously painful coitus. To avoid such coital pains the perineal muscles become clonically spastic at the very thought of penile–vaginal penetration.

Basic approach entails (1) a careful, detailed history of the precipitating events leading to the condition. This is *the* significant factor in the unraveling of the psychosomatic element; (2) a thorough physical examination by a competent gynecologist for organic pathology that may produce intense discomfort or actual sharp pain. If necessary, urological and anorectal consultants may be utilized. Hypnotherapy is a valuable adjunct.

Treatment includes (1) correction of all organic causes of coital discomfort and pain, (2) dissipation of anxiety-provoking myths and fears as they arise, (3) insertion of Hegar dilators at home by the woman herself and then by the husband or lover, (4) intravaginal containment of larger and larger objects for longer and longer periods of time, and (5) coitus tried when fear–tension–pain syndrome is sufficiently reduced.

Discomfort as Penis Enters Vagina (Tables 1, 2, and 6)

Inadequate or Absent Precoital Lubrication. This is one of the commonest causes of discomfort on entrance. If a sufficient "friction burn" develops, the labia minora may be sore and uncomfortable for several days.

Table 6. Coital Discomfort (Painful Pareunia)—Summary Outline of Systematic Approach to the "When," the "Where," the "Why," and the "What" of the More Common Problems in Clinical Practice[a]

The When	The Where	The Why	The What
Precoital foreplay (Table 1)	External genitalia	1. Active skin diseases 2. Chronic vulvovaginitis 3. Inept male techniques 4. Psychosomatic 5. Climacteric regression 6. Adjacent structures—arthritis	1. Proper treatment 2. Proper treatment 3. Education and communication 4. Information and reeducation 5. Proper treatment 6. Proper treatment
As penis enters (Table 2)	Introitus	1. Lack of lubrication 2. Fourchette—infection irritation 3. Position—"angle-of-dangle" syndrome 4. Urethritis 5. Postmenopausal regression 6. Scars—iatrogenic, previous trauma 7. Subluxation—symphysis (pregnancy)	1. Education of partner 2. Proper treatment 3. Education 4. Proper treatment 5. Proper treatment 6. Medical or surgical 7. Education
Penis in mid-vagina (Table 3)	Vaginal canal and adjacent viscera	1. Cystitis 2. Vaginitis 3. Postmenopausal regression 4. Iatrogenic—scars 5. Position—"angle-of-dangle" syndrome 6. Anorectal disease	1. Proper treatment 2. Proper treatment 3. Proper treatment 4. Medical or surgical 5. Education 6. Medical or surgical

Deep penetration with thrusting (Table 4)	Cervix-fornices Cul-de-sac Broad ligament, adnexae Anorectal canal Obturator muscles Lower back, hips Lower abdomen	1. Varices of broad ligament 2. Endometriosis—cul-de-sac 3. Cystitis 4. Iatrogenic—scars and adhesions 5. Postmenopausal regression 6. Position—"angle-of-dangle" 7. Anorectal diseases 8. Orthopedic problems 9. Residua of P.I.D. 10. Fixed retroversion uterus 11. Subluxation-sacroileac (pregnancy)	1. Medical or surgical 2. Hormonal–surgical 3. Proper treatment 4. Medical or surgical 5. Proper treatment 6. Education 7. Medical–surgical 8. Medical–surgical 9. Medical–surgical 10. Medical–surgical 11. Education

Orgasmic (Table 5)	Deep pelvis
	Lower back
	Lower abdomen
		1. Varices of broad ligament
		2. Endometriosis
		3. Iatrogenic—scars
		   Vaginal vault
		   Abdominal wall
			1. Medical–surgical
			2. Hormonal–surgical
			3. Medical–surgical

Postcoitus	Deep pelvis Abdominal wall Lower back	1. Varices of broad ligament 2. Endometriosis 3. Abdominal scars—hernia 4. Vaginal scars	1. Surgical–medical 2. Hormonal–surgical 3. Medical–surgical 4. Medical–surgical

a The "When," the "Where," and the "Why" result from combining a systematic, carefully taken history and a meticulous systematic physical examination. The "What" represents the rational remedial measures to resolve the problem of coital discomfort in line with the patient's goals. From A. R. Abarbanel and Daniel G. Zarowitz (unpublished data).

Most frequently, precoital lubrication in the female is inadequate because (1) male partner was inept in stimulating her, (2) her libido was low, (3) she responded slowly, or (4) the situation was not conducive, e.g., fear of children coming into the bedroom. There are also two special causes of inadequate precoital lubrication—developmental, and the special needs of the climacteric woman.

Developmental factors include inadequate lubrication due to a lack of androgenoid steroids, a lack of testosterone receptors, a deficiency of certain enzymes or, most likely, a combination of all three. In these women, libido is normal but the amount of lubrication is very slight and on rare occasions absent.

Treatment consists of two approaches: (1) Artificial lubrication—she is advised to keep a tube of water-soluble lubricating jelly at the bedside. Just before coitus begins, she places a small amount about the vaginal opening and spreads it with her finger. (2) Stimulation with methyl testosterone—the woman is given a prescription for thirty tablets of buccal methyl testosterone, 10 mg each. She is instructed to place the 10-mg tablet between her gum and cheek and let it dissolve there, usually in twenty to thirty minutes. She alternates the site each day. After two weeks, she takes half a tablet, or 5 mg, buccally. By the end of six weeks, over 90% will note that precoital lubrication is adequate. The other 10% may require an additional six to eight weeks of buccal methyl testosterone, 5 mg daily. To the category of the climacteric woman should be added many posthysterectomy women, especially those in whom both ovaries were also removed. These women are treated with buccal methyl testosterone, as outlined above, for six weeks. If response is not adequate, then 100 mg of testosterone propionate is given by injection. It may need to be repeated in two to three weeks. In the older women, usually over fifty years of age, the best method is subcutaneous implantation of a pellet of estradiol 25 mg and a pellet of testosterone 75 mg. As a rule, these pellets will last about six months to two years. About 75% will require these pellets for two to ten years. One patient returned for pellets over a span of twenty-two years. (On the above doses of androgen, hirsutism will not increase. On rare occasions mild acne may appear.)

Painful Scars at the Vaginal Opening.   The most common are those occurring following vaginal surgery for repair of a rectocele or an episiotomy. These are handled by inserting a medium-sized Grave's speculum, then gently widening the valves, then slowly rotating them forty-five degrees. As a rule, three or four treatments, a week apart, are sufficient to stretch the opening adequately so that discomfort does not occur on intromission. Persisting hymeneal scars resulting from her first coital experience usually have to be surgically excised.

"Tight Britches" Syndrome.   In these women, the combination of nylon panties and tight pants of the Levi's type causes an increased amount of perspiration. The nylon panties then act as an irritating force upon the labia minora, the fourchette, and even the perineal skin as it rubs back and forth as she moves about.

For these women, the use of cotton panties is advised. In addition, it is suggested that she pin a Kleenex in her panties over the area of the vulva. If she tends to perspire a good deal in the crotch, she is advised to rub an antiperspirant cream in the angle where the thigh impinges in the labia majora. A spray should never be used for fear of intensely irritating the labia. The locally inflamed and irritated areas are treated with a hydrocortisone cream or ointment.

Coital Discomfort in Mid-Vaginal Area (Tables 3 and 6)

By far the most common causes are urethritis, trigonitis, and cystitis. These are treated with appropriate antibiotics. If the coital discomfort persists, then an appropriate consultation with a knowledgeable urologist is recommended.

Anorectal diseases, such as cryptitis or internal hemorrhoids, should be discovered on vaginal and rectovaginal examinations.

Coital Discomfort on Deep Penetration, Especially on Thrusting (Tables 4 and 6)

The most common causes of pelvic discomfort are (1) pelvic congestion syndrome with varicosities of the broad ligament, (2) endometriosis involving the uterosacral ligaments and the lower portion of the broad ligaments, (3) residua of a previous pelvic inflammatory disease, and (4) prolapsed ovary.

Another common cause of discomfort is in the obstetrical patient who had a long and difficult labor with a resultant cervical tear at delivery that was not repaired at that time. Scar tissue may develop in the healing. This scar tissue in either fornix may become painfully sensitive to the thrusting of the penis on deep penetration. Not infrequently, hysterectomy may be required to resolve this problem of discomfort.

Posthysterectomy scars at the vaginal vault are a frequent cause of coital discomfort. The reason for this is that the vault is closed at right angles to the vaginal axis. All too often the transverse scar is in the line of penile thrusting. If the patient has had a vaginal hysterectomy, the vagina may also be shortened, compounding the problem of coital discomfort.

In my own experience, I have found that suturing the vaginal vault in the sagittal direction—that is, parallel with the vaginal axis—is the best way of avoiding this problem. Additionally, the uterosacral ligaments should also be approximated to the midline. The Moschowitz type of enterocele repair is the best way of keeping the vaginal vault out of the line of fire.

The "Angle-of-the-Dangle" Syndrome (Tables 3, 4, and 6).   Originally, this syndrome dealt with the angle at which the male inserted his penis into the vagina so as to make the best possible contact with the clitoris during coital activity, expecting that such optimal contact would expedite orgastic response in the female. It did prove helpful, in many instances, in aiding the fulfillment of this pleasurable goal.

We have extended the use of this term to include those positions and coital activities that may precipitate coital discomfort. The more common conditions are noted and the management outlined.

Cystitis and trigonitis cause discomfort especially when the female lies on her back with her knees drawn up halfway—the so-called missionary position. By bringing her knees all the way back toward her abdomen, the penis enters at a more downward angle and so avoids hitting the bladder neck, preventing discomfort in the female.

The best position, however, is with the female astride the male and bending forward so that she rests on her elbows or supports herself on her hands. If she sits up at right angles to her lover, she will have discomfort.

Discomfort or pain in deep thrusting—be the cause endometriosis, pelvic adhesions from a previous pelvic inflammatory disease, pelvic varicosities, or even scar tissue in the lateral fornix from a previous tear at the time of delivery— may best be avoided with the female on top bending over at 75 degrees or so. Some women find that, when they are on the bottom, if they bring their thighs closer together the penis cannot penetrate as deeply. Unfortunately, many males feel that they must be on top to establish their "machismo" and prove they are the master or superior one. These men feel that if the female is on top during coitus, she is rendering him her slave or is so usurping his male dominance as to castrate him symbolically. Proper education, preferably with actual pictures or drawings, will ease his mind.

Some couples find that coitus "doggie fashion" prevents discomfort.

If the penis is unusually long, seven to eight inches (18 to 20 cm), most women avoid discomfort by the female-on-top position, bending over. In this way depth of penetration may be controlled by her. With the female on the bottom, bringing the knees closer together controls the depth of penile penetration.

Postcoital Discomfort (*Tables 4, 5, and 6*)

Abdominal Scars. In the coitally active woman, exuberantly participating in the act, a full orgastic response involves the abdominal muscles. Frequently these muscles may go into spasm for a short while. These muscle spasms can become very painful, especially if she has a vertical midline scar. Painful muscle spasm is infrequent with a low transverse scar.

Occasionally, an umbilical hernia may become symptomatic under these conditions.

Hyperventilation may also occur, adding to the discomfort.

Careful education of the patient may help her utilize other positions. By trial and error most women learn to modify their coital activities and responses so as to avoid the postcoital aches and pains.

Medication

It is essential in taking the history that each and every prescription medication be detailed, as well as any over-the-counter drugs and "home" remedies.

Hypertensive women, especially if they have a total body orgasmic response, may experience a painful throbbing, pulsating headache. This is more likely to occur if the woman is on top. Two primary precipitating factors should be carefully elucidated: Did she take her antihypertensive medication that day? If so, when? The usual story is that she took it in the morning. If so, she is encouraged to take it at night. In one out of three hypertensive females, noncompliance with medical regimens is the rule. Most often these are women who have discovered that medication serves to depress their libido and that their precoital lubrication is diminished or absent. Unless women and their husbands are alerted to possible side effects, misunderstandings can result. The husband may begin to think his wife is no longer sexually aroused by him or does not care about coitus any more.

In turn, any fears he may have about his ability to perform sexually are compounded and he may then begin to avoid coitus. This may result in the wife feeling rejected, guilty, or resentful.

The precipitating factor is iatrogenic in that the physician, when prescribing the antihypertensive medication, fails to warn the patient of the possible side effects of the drug(s).

Vaginismus (spastic contractions of the vaginal musculature that make intercourse impossible) has long been considered difficult, if not impossible, to treat with traditional psychotherapy. Surgical removal of the hymen is also ineffective, as the problem is a muscle spasm, not an imperforate hymen. In this article, the use of systematic desensitization with sexual imagery is described, as is actual (in vivo) use of a series of graduated dilators. Note that although the authors do not emphasize it, the use of dilators was much more effective. All thirty-one patients who completed dilator therapy (out of thirty-four who began therapy) were cured, while only six of nine desensitization patients were cured. Other clinical work has indicated that use of dilators—with or without the hypnosis these therapists used—is indeed the treatment of choice for vaginismus.

On a minor point, the authors' statement that gynecological examination is impossible for these patients is not always correct. The examination situation is very different from the sexual situation, and some patients have vaginismus only in response to one of these situations and not to the other.

19

Hypnodesensitization Therapy of Vaginismus: In Vitro and in Vivo Methods

K. Fuchs, Z. Hoch, E. Paldi, H. Abramovici, J. M. Brandes, I. Timor-Tritsch, and M. Kleinhaus

Vaginismus, one of the most disabling symptoms in a woman's life, may be compared to impotence in a man. It is clinically characterized by spastic contractions of the vaginal and pelvic floor muscles and adduction of the thighs as a reaction to attempted sexual intercourse, or even to the very thought of it. As a consequence, vaginal penetration becomes impossible. Many couples are ashamed to admit failure of coitus, and, therefore, the marriage often ends in divorce, which could have been prevented by proper treatment.

There are a series of theoretical speculations regarding the etiology of vaginismus which seemed rather irrelevant to us. Malleson (1942) saw the vaginal con-

We are very grateful to Professor A. Peretz for his generous help and encouragement and for reviewing our article.

K. Fuchs, Z. Hoch, E. Paldi, H. Abramovici, J. M. Brandes, I. Timor-Tritsch, and *M. Kleinhaus* ● Rambam University Hospital, Aba Khoushy School of Medicine, Haifa, Israel; and Assaf Harofeh Hospital, Tel-Aviv University Medical School, Tel-Aviv, Israel

tractions as a defense mechanism identical to the blinking of the eye before touching it, or as a result of repeated use of rectal suppositories or enemas during childhood. Frank (1948) viewed them as a defense mechanism against pregnancy, denial of womanhood, or violation of incest taboo with the husband symbolizing the father. We believe that vaginismus is a symptom of faulty psychosexual development which generates a phobia process: i.e., phobia to the penetration of a foreign body into the vagina. (As is well known, gynecological examination is also impossible in these patients.)

Masters and Johnson's (1970) observations that vaginismus is related to psychosexual inhibiting influences of excessively severe control of social conduct inherent in religious orthodoxy, as well as a possible homosexual orientation of the female partner, may explain some cases. According to them, physical assault, organic dyspareunia, or husband's impotence may also generate this symptom. Dawkins and Taylor (1961) relate vaginismus to a weak and overconsiderate husband who often suffers from premature ejaculation or impotence. Different kinds of treatment of this condition have been proposed, their roots originating from the various theoretical points of view about its pathogenesis as outlined below.

Surgical Defloration.   This was, in the past, the most frequent treatment, based on the assumption that the symptom was an expression of the fear of defloration. This kind of treatment is unsuccessful in the majority of cases. However, in some specific cases, its validity may always be reconsidered. Its use may eventually be of value in women who think in a very concrete way and where other techniques have failed. Generally, the application of surgical treatment is useless and can produce an intensification of the symptomatology, because of the traumatic situation involved and the disappointment caused by lack of therapeutic results.

Psychoanalysis and Analytically Oriented Psychotherapy.   Taking into consideration the theoretical premises of psychoanalysis, one must consider vaginismus as a symptom of faulty psychosexual development. Therapy should, therefore, be aimed at uncovering the inner conflicts and dynamic processes—vaginismus being their somatic translation. Undoubtedly the analytical treatment of vaginismus can be successful; however, it is an enormously time-consuming procedure.

According to our point of view, the therapy of vaginismus should be managed as a medical emergency, this in order to avoid the following negative implications: (a) danger of fixation of the symptom, which can bring the patient to a situation where the establishment of mature heterosexual relationships will not become possible; (b) conditioning of the partner to faulty sexual intercourse; (c) disruption of the marital relationship and danger of dissolution of the marriage; and (d) development of pathologic reactions in patients involved, such as guilt feelings or a depressive state (frustrated by their failure to achieve what "every simple animal is able to do," as stated by one of our patients). It is for these reasons that we decided to use *systematic desensitization during the hypnotic state.*

Systematic desensitization may proceed in two main ways (Wolpe, 1969): in vitro or in vivo. Both methods use a basic state of relaxation and feeling of safety in order to confront the patient with the lowest item on a hierarchy of anxiety-evoking stimuli. This continues until anxiety is no longer evoked, as reported by the patient. The next higher item on the list is then prescribed, until the anxiety response to it is extinguished. The procedure is continued until eventually even the strongest of the anxiety-evoking stimuli fails to evoke any stir of anxiety in the patient. In the in vitro technique, the patient is asked to imagine the stimuli. In the in vivo technique, real stimuli take the place of imaginary ones.

In order to strengthen the above-mentioned desensitization process, we decided to use hypnotic techniques for two reasons: because it is an easy and smooth method of achieving a deep state of relaxation, and because imagery and visualization of suggested content under hypnosis is much more vivid and plastic. In some cases, hallucinations for the suggested scenes and situations can be produced. The patients who applied to the psychiatric department were treated by the in vitro method; those who applied to the department of obstetrics and gynecology were treated by the in vivo technique. There was a close and continuous contact between the two departments.

Part I: In Vitro Method

Material and Method

During the period of 1968–1970, nine women suffering from severe vaginismus of two to five years' duration were treated by a method of in vitro hypnodesensitization.

The first session with the couple was devoted to obtaining the history and establishing an adequate therapeutic relationship. The patient and her husband were consequently encouraged to discuss freely their sexual problems and sexual matters, followed by an explanation (in general terms) of hypnosis and desensitization. Usually this took one or two sessions.

The next two sessions with the wife were dedicated to the induction and deepening of hypnosis until deep relaxation and, if possible, hallucinations were obtained. At this point, we instructed the patient to let us know (a) when she felt fully relaxed and (b) when she felt anxious. In order not to disturb the process by spoken words, we asked her to signal these two feelings by raising one hand or the other, similar to the procedures of Wolpe (1958). From here we proceeded with the building of the anxiety hierarchy (a scale of 1 to 12): The weakest stimulus was to be with the partner in some pleasurable, noncommitting situation, and the strongest was full sexual intercourse. Generally, this took about six to eight sessions. At the end of every session of one-half to one hour, we asked the patient to reproduce the above-mentioned situation with the partner at home, and in this way we reinforced the achievements.

Case Report

A woman, aged twenty-three, had been married for two years without consummation of marriage due to her active resistance to any attempt at sexual intercourse, because of "fear of pain." She was born and brought up in a *kibbutz* (an agricultural settlement) and had received a liberal sexual education. No traumatic sexual experiences in the past were reported. She denied any difficulties in the family setting (parents and three sisters) and spoke warmly about the close family relationship. After one year of marriage, she decided to consult a gynecologist, and surgical defloration under anesthesia was performed with no results but further disappointment and frustration. Under the pressure of the gynecologist and her family, she finally agreed to a psychiatric examination and was then referred to a psychiatric consultant who succeeded in lowering her resistance and fears of psychiatric treatment and hypnosis. The patient was then referred to us. It should be mentioned that she reported claustrophobia, a phobia to dissection of chicken and fish, and a phobia to childbirth pictures.

First Session. In the first session we obtained a detailed history, with special focus regarding the patient's psychosexual education and knowledge, and the emotional insecurities and fears regarding sexual relationship, pregnancy, and childbirth. Attention was concentrated on supporting and reinforcing any positive motivation toward a normal sexual life. We discussed, as freely as possible, the patient's knowledge of the technique of intercourse, giving her appropriate information, when necessary. All of this was done in an understanding and warm atmosphere and with a noncritical approach.

Second Session. In this session we explained the technique of the treatment along general lines. We stressed our views on hypnosis as a learning process and clarified any possible misconceptions the patient might have regarding hypnosis. We also tried to explain again in general terms the process of desensitization and its rationale (just as a child who is afraid of water should be taught to go into the sea in a slow, progressive way).

Third Session. The technique of induction of relaxation and hypnosis is variable and adapted to the patient's individual needs (dynamic methods). We tried to achieve deep relaxation in the hypnotic state within the range of light hypnosis to a deep hallucinatory state. This depended, of course, on the aptitudes of the patient, the focus being not on depth but on relaxation. If we achieved only relaxation we used imagery only as the medium of stimuli; if in deep hypnosis, we used hallucinations of the suggested situations. We also taught the patient to signal to us the feeling of relaxation (raising of the right arm) or anxiety (raising of the left arm).

Fourth Session. At this time we presented the stimulus hierachy under hypnosis. We asked the patient to visualize herself at the beach in the company of her husband. After she complied we suggested she visualize a pleasant and relaxing situation. Then we asked her to visualize herself with her husband, going back home and resting with her husband and talking. As a next step, we suggested visualization of a tired feeling and herself retiring with her husband in the bedroom (still without sexual situation).

Fifth Session. Suggestions given during this session were the same as those presented in session 4 but were carried further. The purpose of this session was to have the patient achieve erotic excitement. The suggestions were as follows: (a) Imagine yourself caressing, petting, and embracing your husband; (b) imagine yourself in a love-play situation with your husband; (c) imagine yourself undressing in the presence of your husband; (d) imagine yourself going to bed with your husband, without feeling threatened by intercourse. Between the suggestions we left enough time for the patient to work herself into the suggested situation. We again asked the patient to signal to us the feeling of relaxation or anxiety by raising the appropriate arm.

Sixth Session. In this session the patient received suggestions of further erotic feelings, yet without threat of penetration. The patient was asked to imagine the following: (a) being in bed with her husband, (b) her husband's body and sexual organs, and (c) friction of sexual organs with husband.

Seventh Session. Procedures of previous sessions were repeated, with the following additional suggestions: (a) imagery of patient with husband in bed, undressed, with love-play, (b) friction of sexual organs, and (c) penetration of the head of penis.

Eighth Session. After repeating the last few sessions, we tried to give the patient, for the first time, suggestions for the anticipation of actual intercourse. This was repeated several times until the patient responded to the last suggestion without any signs of anxiety.

Ninth Session. The suggestions in this session are similar to the ones in the last session.

After the ninth session, the patient informed us that she succeeded in having full sexual intercourse with satisfaction. She also informed us of the complete disappearance of her other phobias (claustrophobia, phobia to the dissection of chicken and fish, and phobia of childbirth pictures).

Part II: In Vivo Method

Material and Method

During a five-year period, 1965–1970, we treated thirty-four women suffering from severe vaginismus. Most of these patients had been suffering for more than two years, and a few for five to seven years. All had been treated previously by gynecologists and psychiatrists for long periods of time without results. A large portion had undergone surgical dilatation of the hymen and vagina, and several had undergone plastic surgery.

During our first consultation with a couple, we allowed them to speak freely about their problems, without adopting any attitude. We subsequently requested strict cooperation from the husband and asked him to refrain from any further attempts at intercourse until allowed to do so by us.

During the second meeting we explained to the patient that her suffering was due to the contraction of involuntary muscles, which she could learn to relax under hypnosis. She then received an explanation of the meaning of hypnosis and the technique we were using. At the end of this consultation, the patient was asked to decide in her own time whether she would like to undergo treatment. If she agreed, she was brought to a hypnotic trance according to a passive–permissive approach, although it was sometimes necessary to resort to an active–authoritative one. The patient was then taught the technique of autohypnosis, which she was instructed to practice at home.

At the end of the third or fourth consultation, we mentioned for the first time that she would soon have to undergo a gynecological examination to rule out the possibility of anatomical disorders. The suggestion of gynecological examination had purposely been avoided until we had gained the patient's full confidence. It is interesting to note that after a few more sessions, the majority of the patients voluntarily requested examination. A special technique was devised for these examinations. The patient lay on the examination table and reached a state of autohypnosis. After only an external examination had been made, she was informed that a gynecological examination had been carried out, without specifying the details of the examination. The patient was thus reassured that there was no pain, and we then asked her to carry out a self-examination by the use of her finger. In most cases she succeeded. She was then asked to choose, from a set of Hegar dilators, one which approximated the size of her examining finger and to insert it in the vagina. Having done this, the patient took the dilator home with instructions to insert it twice daily after self-inducing hypnosis. We then asked for her permission to insert the Hegar dilator ourselves. While doing this, we managed to switch to a larger dilator. She then repeated the self-insertion without noticing the change in size. The patient was asked to report every other day for the purpose of changing her dilator for a larger one. Within a week or ten days, she was able to insert a Hegar 27–28 mm.

Having reached this stage, we asked her to sit on the dilator while holding it in a vertical position. This she also managed to do without any difficulty. At this time she was told that she was ready to have intercourse with her husband in the female superior position. The husband was interviewed separately, and the desired technique of intercourse was explained to him. It was impressed upon him that he must adopt a passive role at the beginning and leave all the initiative to his wife.

Case Report

A couple of new immigrants from North Africa who had been married for 2½ years were referred to us by their family doctor. The husband, a twenty-eight-year-old technician, made a good impression and displayed a quiet character and a high intellectual level. He was most cooperative and obviously very much in love with his wife. The wife was a pretty, nineteen-year-old professional model, with a normal medical and gynecological history. Since their marriage, they had not experienced real coitus. After several attempts, the husband abandoned further trials because of the pain it caused his wife. From their history we learned that the husband came from a rather religious family, though he, himself, was only moderately religious. The wife's parents showed low affective reciprocal communication and denied their children any sexual education. The patient remembered being both surprised and scared by her first menstruation. She had had a number of dates in her earlier teens but never permitted more than slight petting. Her husband had limited premarital sexual experience with two girls, without emotional involvement. During their six months of courtship they had little opportunity for being alone and did not attempt an intimate sexual encounter. As mentioned before, after 2½ years of marriage they still had not experienced coitus.

At the first interview, the wife displayed anger and resentment at being considered the partner at fault. Her husband showed more readiness for cooperation and self-control. Nevertheless, both were interested in succeeding and were motivated by a good general relationship. After having evaluated the history and their present situation, we explained our treatment procedure to them. The meaning of medical hypnosis was made as clear as possible in order to prevent, insofar as possible, any hint of frightening magical ideas. Anatomical diagrams were shown and the mechanism of vaginal spasm was explained. It became clear to them that we had to achieve relaxation and that we used hypnosis to arrive at this goal. Husband and wife were instructed to completely avoid any further attempts at coitus until otherwise notified by us.

For the first working session, the patient was invited to attend a class of pregnant women being prepared for natural childbirth by means of auto-hypnosis. We started with a permissive–passive kind of induction. Later it was felt that a more authoritative method was needed. The patient was taught auto-hypnosis, together with the pregnant women, and was instructed to practice this technique at home. At the end of her second session, we expressed the hope that gynecological examination would take place at the next or subsequent visit. The patient canceled the next visit, but she did eventually come and request examination.

After lying in gynecologic position, she was told to proceed to auto-hypnosis in which we helped by deepening her trance somewhat. After several minutes, we informed her that we were going to perform the examination and she was asked whether she agreed to what we were going to do. After touching and exerting light pressure, both on her lower abdomen and on the vulvar region, we told her that the examination was over. She readily agreed to insert one of her own fingers into the vagina and was further reassured of the lack of pain. Still in slight hypnotic trance, she was shown a prelubricated set of Hegars and was asked to choose the one similar to her finger's width and to insert it in the vagina, in order to find out her depth. She had to repeatedly extract and reinsert the instrument after looking at the depth she reached. We then asked for the patient's permission to introduce the dilator ourselves, once or twice. While doing this, we managed to switch to a larger instrument (no. 9) and then to an additional one (no. 10). In between, she repeated the self-insertion without noticing the change in size. The patient was instructed to practice at home, after inducing self-hypnosis. Every second day she returned for a session in our clinic, during which we gradually increased the size of the Hegar. After eight sessions she was able to insert a no. 28 Hegar without any difficulty, both under hypnosis and without it. She was then instructed to introduce the dilator in a position similar to the female superior position and to practice this for two more days.

During this interval we had a personal meeting with her husband and informed him that his wife would be ready to proceed to intercourse in the female superior position. His only task was to lie passively on his back and provide her with an erect penis. The wife was instructed to lubricate and use her husband's penis in the same manner she did with the Hegar no. 28. As the couple reported complete success, they were advised to continue their sexual contact in the same position for the next two weeks. They had not only to perform but to start feeling sexually for the first time in their lives. At a follow-up session the couple reported increasing sexual enjoyment and orgasm. Twelve months later, they had their first baby.

Results

By the in vitro systematic desensitization method under hypnosis, we were able to deal successfully with six out of nine patients in a relatively short time. One patient, who did not achieve full penetration, was referred to a gynecologist for a further treatment by the in vivo technique. Out of the nine patients treated by the in vitro technique, we did a follow-up on six patients, for a period of one to three years.

In our series of thirty-four patients treated by the in vivo technique, thirty-one were successfully treated (three discontinued treatment after the first few sessions). Out of the thirty-four patients treated by this technique, it was possible to do a follow-up on twenty-nine patients, for a period of one to five years.

On follow-up, all successfully treated patients (in terms of both the in vitro and the in vivo techniques) maintained a normal sexual adjustment, and none showed evidence of symptom substitution. Further, the patients reported having orgasm in most of their sexual intercourse.

Discussion

We should emphasize here Wolpe's (1958, 1969; Wolpe, Salter, and Reyna, 1965) contribution to the importance of the role of fear and anxiety in the production and maintenance of a symptom. Vaginismus may be viewed as an avoidance reaction to an anxiety-producing situation. Systematic desensitization then becomes the treatment method of choice for these patients. This kind of treatment has proved particularly successful in dealing with specific phobias (Chesser, 1970; Cooper, 1969; Frazier and Carr, 1967; Leckie, 1964; Lief, 1967). Similarly, Haslam (1965) has used deconditioning with relaxation responses and sexual responses in treating severe dyspareunia with the aid of increasingly large glass bougies. He reported good results, although progress was somewhat slow for some of his patients.

Friedman (1966), Brady (1966, 1971), and others (Kraft, 1967; Reed, 1966) have used Brevital-aided systematic desensitization for the treatment of phobic symptoms (frigidity, stuttering, insomnia) as a facilitator of profound relaxation. Their drug-induced hypnoidal state helped reduce the number of sessions and undoubtedly played a similar role as that of hypnosis in the treatment of our patients. One difference, however, is that our patients, who learned self-hypnosis, took an active part in their desensitization process and by so doing had a better chance to maintain their self-achieved therapeutic results.

The importance of the doctor–patient–husband relationship cannot be overemphasized. The doctor's gentle approach to the problem can be a model example of sexual communication between the couple. The husband has to be understanding and supportive during the treatment period, becoming a sharing part of the wife's progress. Masters and Johnson (1970) even actively involve the husband in the treatment process by instructing him in the use of Hegar dilators in the privacy of the marital bedroom with the wife's physical cooperation, at first with her manual control and then by verbal directions.

Some technical points should be further emphasized: (a) Although for the in vitro method a light trance is perfectly adequate, more rapid results are obtained by deeper trance with hallucinations. It is not necessary for the patients treated by the in vivo method to develop deep trance. (b) The "gynecological examination" without insertion of examining fingers in the vagina (but only by pressing them on the vulvar region) and the rather rapid change to larger Hegars during the sessions, without verbally informing the patient, who is asked only to note the depth (rather than the size) reached by the instrument, prevent any possible triggering of the phobic symptom. (c) The female superior position provides the wife with a similar situation as practiced during the last stage of therapy; she continues to be active and by so doing prevents her previously formed image of an "attacking" husband. Her self-esteem and self-confidence gained during therapy will be further reinforced by her successful insertion of the husband's penis.

We believe that hypnodensensitization is the treatment of choice in women suffering from vaginismus. We suggest treatment along the following lines:

1. Treatment may be performed by a psychiatrist, a gynecologist, or a general practitioner.

2. We suggest hypnosis (a) as a method for relaxation, (b) as a method for imagery and visualization of the suggested material, and (c) as an aid for desensitization.

3. The first step should be done in vitro. If this step is not fully successful in relieving symptoms, the in vivo technique should be a natural continuation of the in vitro method, though this can be used as the first and only method by gynecologists trained in medical hypnosis.

References

Brady, J. P. Brevital relaxation treatment of frigidity. *Behaviour Research and Therapy*, 1966, *4*, 71–77.

Brady, J. P. Brevital-aided systematic desensitization. In R. D. Rubin, H. Fensterheim, A. A. Lazarus, and C. M. Franks (Eds.), *Advances in behavior therapy: Proceedings of the 3rd Conference of the Association for Advancement of Behavior Therapy.* New York: Academic Press, 1971. Pp. 77–83.

Chesser, E. S. Behaviour therapy. *Practitioner*, 1970, *205*, 296–306.

Cooper, A. J. An innovation in the "behavioural" treatment of a case of non-consummation due to vaginismus. *British Journal of Psychiatry*, 1969, *115*, 721–725.

Dawkins, S., and Taylor, R. Non-consummation of marriage: A survey of seventy cases. *Lancet*, 1961, *280*, 1029–1033.

Frank, R. T. Dyspareunia: A problem for the general practitioner. *Journal of the American Medical Association*, 1948, *136*, 361–365.

Frazier, S. H., and Carr, A. C. Phobic reaction. In A. M. Freedman and H. I. Kaplan (Eds.), *Comprehensive textbook of psychiatry.* Baltimore: Williams and Wilkins, 1967. Pp. 899–911.

Friedman, D. A new technique for the systematic desensitization of phobic symptoms. *Behaviour Research and Therapy*, 1966, *4*, 139–140.

Haslam, M. T. The treatment of psychogenic dyspareunia by reciprocal inhibition. *British Journal of Psychiatry*, 1965, *111*, 280–282.

Kraft, T. The use of methohexitone sodium in behaviour therapy. *Behaviour Research and Therapy*, 1967, *5*, 257.

Leckie, F. H. Hypnotherapy in gynecological disorders. *International Journal of Clinical and Experimental Hypnosis*, 1964, *12*, 121–146.

Lief, H. I. Anxiety reaction. In A. M. Freedman and H. I. Kaplan (Eds.), *Comprehensive textbook of psychiatry*. Baltimore: Williams and Wilkins, 1967. Pp. 857–870.

Malleson, J. Vaginismus: Its management and psychogenesis. *British Medical Journal*, 1942, *2*, 213–216.

Masters, W. H., and Johnson, V. E. *Human sexual inadequacy*. Boston: Little, Brown, 1970.

Reed, J. L. Comments on the use of methohexitone sodium as a means of inducing relaxation. *Behaviour Research and Therapy*, 1966, *4*, 323.

Wolpe, J. *Psychotherapy by reciprocal inhibition*. Stanford: Stanford University Press, 1958.

Wolpe, J. Basic principles and practices of behavior therapy of neuroses. *American Journal of Psychiatry*, 1969, *125*, 1242–1247.

Wolpe, J., Salter, A., and Reyna, L. J. *The conditioning therapies: The challenge in psychotherapy*. New York: Holt, Rinehart & Winston, 1965.

Premature ejaculation is usually considered the easiest of the sexual dysfunctions to treat. Contrary to psychoanalytic theories of the etiology and psychological significance of premature ejaculation, this dysfunction responds readily to a program based on simple physical retraining of the ejaculatory response.

In this article, the authors report on a study designed to test the ability of couples to treat premature ejaculation on their own, with the help of a written treatment guide. In essence, this article describes a self-help program that involves minimal contact (if any) with a therapist.

Although the results were good and have probably contributed to a trend toward self-help programs in other areas of sexual dysfunction, some reservations might be noted. All patients who participated in this program were in a nondistressed relationship and had a female partner who was willing to cooperate with the program.

This patient selection procedure raises the question of whether such couples are typical of the majority of couples who seek sex therapy for the treatment of premature ejaculation. If not, what Lowe and Mikulas have developed is a program that is effective for a certain select population of individuals. Indeed, this criticism may be relevant for all such self-help programs, and research is needed to ascertain just which types of individuals or couples can benefit from these programs.

20

Use of Written Material in Learning Self-Control of Premature Ejaculation

John C. Lowe and William L. Mikulas

Premature ejaculation is a common problem for many men whose ejaculatory reflex occurs very rapidly during sexual activities. Because the partner of the premature ejaculator is often not sexually satisfied, premature ejaculation may lead to sexual incompatibility and interpersonal problems. In addition, it may result in secondary impotence in the male and/or orgasmic dysfunction in his partner.

There are many forms of treatment for premature ejaculation. Psychotherapeutic approaches generally focus on assumed underlying causes such as fear of women, castration fears, and interrelational conflicts (Rowan and Howley, 1963; Saltzman, 1972). However, most approaches view the problem as the male having too low a threshold of sensitivity. Treatment then consists of reducing sexual arousal or raising the excitability threshold of the ejaculatory reflex. Sexual arousal during coitus may be reduced by the male's focusing his attention on nonerotic stimuli such as the pain produced by biting his lip or thinking about business activities (Hastings, 1966, p. 131). Sexually arousing input may be reduced

John C. Lowe and *William L. Mikulas* • Department of Psychology, University of West Florida, Pensacola, Florida

by putting several layers of gauze and a condom over the penis (Hastings, 1966, p. 133) or applying anesthetics to the glans (Damrau, 1963).

The most effective treatment involves raising the excitatory threshold of the ejaculatory reflex. In Semans's (1956) procedure the penis is stimulated extravaginally until the male feels premonitory sensations of ejaculation. Stimulation is then discontinued until the sensations subside. This procedure is continued until penile stimulation can be tolerated for longer periods of time without ejaculation. To this procedure Masters and Johnson (1970, p. 103) added the "squeeze technique." When the male signals oncoming ejaculation, the female squeezes around the coronal ridge of the penis in a way that is not painful but stops the urge to ejaculate. This stimulation-plus-squeeze technique is continued until the male has fairly good extravaginal control. Then the male is gradually taught intravaginal ejaculatory control.

Premature ejaculators treated by Masters and Johnson are also exposed to educative counseling and sensate focus. In sensate focus the male and his partner take turns touching and exploring each other's body, while the person being touched provides feedback about how he feels, what is most pleasurable, and so forth.

The purpose of the present study was to determine whether couples could eliminate for themselves the problem of premature ejaculation using only a written program as a guide. The program was modeled after the procedures of Masters and Johnson including sensate focus and the squeezing technique.

Method

Subjects

Ten heterosexual couples chosen as subjects met the following criteria: (1) The male ejaculated anteportal, upon penile–vaginal contact, or within three minutes after intromission; (2) the female agreed to cooperate with the treatment program; and (3) there were no apparent interpersonal problems with the couple that should be treated first. Four of the couples came via referral and were treated in Pensacola by one therapist, while the other six couples responded to a newspaper ad in Los Angeles and were treated there by a second therapist.* The couples were alternatively assigned to an experimental or control group.

Materials

All males were given a questionnaire covering various aspects of their ejaculatory tendencies, including estimates of the length of time between the onset of sexual stimulation and the completion of the ejaculatory reflex. These estimates were compared with corresponding posttreatment estimates by the subjects as a measure of the effectiveness of the treatment.

Treatment utilized an eighty-page program written for this study. The pro-

*We appreciate the help of Harvey M. Lowe, who served as the second therapist.

gram included the following sections: (1) the problem and proposed treatment of premature ejaculation, (2) instruction in sensate focus, (3) use of the squeeze technique and related body positions, (4) intravaginal ejaculatory control and the female-superior coital position, and (5) use of the lateral coital position. Quizzes at the end of each section helped the subject determine his comprehension of that section before attempting to follow the instructions. Depending on the subject's experiences with any section, he was either instructed to continue on to the next section or was sent back through the same section with additional instructions. The program ended with some preventative measures to maintain ejaculatory control, e.g., regular sexual activity and occasional use of the squeeze technique.

Procedure

After determining if the couple met the criteria, all males were given the questionnaire. Then the experimental couples were given the program and told to complete it at their own rate. The control couples were put on a waiting list. After three weeks, the average amount of time for use of the program, the control couples were given the program and became a second experimental group. All couples, including those on the waiting list, were contacted by phone twice per week to check and encourage their progress. The couples could also call their therapist at any time they encountered problems.

When the couple completed the program, the male again estimated the time of ejaculatory control. If the male reported unlimited control, he was assigned a value of sixty minutes.

Results and Discussion

Pretreatment the first experimental males had a mean of 1.8 minutes of ejaculatory control. Posttreatment their mean increase of control was 37.2 minutes. (Individual pre–post changes were: 2 to 60, .5 to 15, 3 to 45, 1 to 60, and 2.5 to 15 min.) Control males began at a mean of 1.4 minutes and reported no change while on the waiting list. However, after they became the second group their mean increase in control was 18.6 minutes. (Individual pre–post changes were: .5 to 5, 1 to 30, 2 to 20, .5 to 15, and 3 to 30.) Nine of the ten males (five from the first group) increased their ejaculatory control from 12.5 to 59 minutes. The tenth male gained only 4.5 minutes. Compared with the control males on the waiting list, the mean differences in pre–post scores for both the first group ($t = 3.67$, $df = 4$, $p < .05$) and the second group ($t = 4.19$, $df = 4$, $p < .02$) were significant.

Masters and Johnson (1970) often conceptualize their impressive treatment program for sexual dysfunctions as primarily a form of psychotherapy. Viewing their procedures from a behavioral orientation suggests possible improvements (Murphy and Mikulas, 1974). The present study is a case in point. Many cases of premature ejaculation appear to be simple behavioral deficits unrelated to any interpersonal problems, pathology, or underlying causes. For such people psychotherapy or two weeks with Masters and Johnson seems unnecessary. Rather, simply training ejaculatory control, as with the present program, seems sufficient and efficient. This is supported by the fact that to minimize interpersonal interpretations the therapists kept their interactions with the subjects strictly on an instructive level. For other cases, training in ejaculatory control might be coupled with such things as sexual education, desensitization, or marriage counseling.

All subjects of this study were volunteers. A programmed self-control approach might not work as well with nonvolunteers, perhaps due to differences in motivation. Similarly, contacting the subjects twice per week may have improved motivation and cooperation.

The educational level of the subjects was fairly high: Two couples had completed high school, six had completed college, and two were graduate students. Perhaps educational level affects how well a person does with a written program. However, in this study the improvement in ejaculatory control for the male high school graduates (27 to 58 minutes) was quite good compared to the over-all group mean improvement of 27.9 minutes. The subject with only slight improvement (4.5 minutes) was a graduate student in psychology who was previously familiar with the treatment procedure. He followed the program only through the section on the squeeze technique. Then, after reading through the rest of the program once, he continued on his own.

A limitation of the study was the reliance on the subjects' estimates of time of ejaculatory control. Such approximations could be influenced by demand variables and biases of the experiment. For example, the subjects' estimates or reports of these estimates might be biased by the expectancy of change or a desire to please the therapist. But this study was merely to demonstrate the possibility of using a written program for control of premature ejaculation. Use of a more accurate measure, although desirable in further research, would probably impair the effectiveness of the program to the extent that it distracts from the sexual activity. There is also a need for long-range follow-ups and assessment of the effectiveness of preventative measures.

Only one couple reported that sensate focus was useful; the other nine considered it a hindrance. This may be because this part of the program was poorly written or because our particular subjects were already relatively skilled and knowledgeable in this area. Two of the subjects reported that the program seemed too mechanical. But this was a minor problem they quickly overcame. Overall, then, at least for some subjects, use of a written program appears to be a fast, efficient, and inexpensive way to treat premature ejaculation.

References

Damrau, F. Premature ejaculation: Use of ethyl aminobenzoate to prolong coitus. *Journal of Urology*, 1963, *89*, 936–939.
Hastings, D. W. *A doctor speaks on sexual expression in marriage.* Boston: Little, Brown, 1966.
Masters, W. H., and Johnson, V. E. *Human sexual inadequacy.* Boston: Little, Brown, 1970.

Murphy, C. V., and Mikulas, W. L. Behavioral features and deficiencies of the Masters and Johnson program. *Psychological Record*, 1974, *24*, 221–227.

Rowan, R. L., and Howley, T. F. Premature ejaculation. *Fertility and Sterility*, 1963, *14*, 437–440.

Saltzman, L. Interesting sexual cases: Premature ejaculation. *Medical Aspects of Human Sexuality*, 1972, *6*, 119–127.

Semans, J. H. Premature ejaculation: A new approach. *Southern Medical Journal*, 1956, *49*, 353–358.

Although the success rates reported for the treatment of premature ejaculation are consistently high (usually better than 95%), the reason why some men are premature ejaculators remains a mystery. A number of hypotheses have been suggested, and in this article the theory of etiology and treatment program developed at Cornell Medical Center are presented.

Group treatment for sexual dysfunction is a relatively new phenomenon that is rapidly gaining acceptance (see articles in Part 8). Early work developed out of the Encounter Group research and generally involved an unstructured exposure to experiences designed to enhance one's sexuality.

This chapter reports on a group treatment program for premature ejaculation that incorporates a structured sex therapy format into a group setting. The case reports illustrate some of the patient characteristics and treatment issues that often must be dealt with in sex therapy.

One criticism that may be made of this study is the lack of actual numerical data on the latency to ejaculation of the patients both before and after treatment. This is a common flaw in many clinical case reports where global judgments of improvement are often used to evaluate treatment outcome.

21

Group Treatment of Premature Ejaculation

Helen S. Kaplan, Richard N. Kohl, Wardell B. Pomeroy, Avodah K. Offit, and Barbara Hogan

Introduction

A pilot study of the group treatment of premature ejaculation is being undertaken as part of the Sex Therapy and Education Program of the Payne Whitney Psychiatric Clinic of the New York Hospital–Cornell Medical Center. The following is a report of the first group, which consisted of four couples. Premature ejaculation of the male was the chief complaint of each couple. The goal of the treatment was limited to the attainment of ejaculatory control.

Helen S. Kaplan • Department of Psychiatry, Cornell University Medical College, and Payne Whitney Psychiatric Clinic, New York Hospital Medical Center, New York, New York   *Richard N. Kohl* • Department of Psychiatry, Cornell University Medical College, and Payne Whitney Psychiatric Clinic, New York Hospital Medical Center, New York, New York   *Wardell B. Pomeroy* • Independent Practice, Psychology, San Francisco, California   *Avodah K. Offit* • Payne Whitney Psychiatric Clinic, New York Hospital Medical Center, New York, New York   *Barbara Hogan* • Department of Psychiatry, Cornell University Medical College, and Payne Whitney Psychiatric Clinic, New York Hospital Medical Center, New York, New York. When this chapter was originally published, Wardell B. Pomeroy was at Cornell University Medical College, New York, New York.

Definition of Premature Ejaculation

Premature ejaculation is probably the most common sexual dysfunction of American males, occurring in the psychiatrically healthy as well as in patients exhibiting various forms of psychopathology. It is a condition wherein a man reaches orgasm very quickly. Definitions of premature ejaculation have varied. They have been given in terms of length of coital time prior to ejaculation, number of strokes prior to ejaculation, and, by Masters and Johnson (1970), percentage of times in which the man reaches orgasm before the woman (more than 50% equals premature ejaculation). In contrast, at the Cornell Medical Center, we believe that the essential parameter of premature ejaculation consists of the failure of the man to attain control over the ejaculatory reflex once an intense level of sexual arousal has been attained, with the result that once excited, he reaches orgasm rapidly. Hence, we define prematurity as the inability of a man to tolerate high (plateau) levels of sexual excitement without ejaculating reflexly.

Types of Treatment

Various forms of therapy have been tried to cure prematurity with varying degrees of success. These have included psychoanalytic methods, "commonsense" and behavioral approaches, and, more recently, a highly effective "sensory training" technique.

Psychoanalytic treatment is based on the premise that premature ejaculation is an expression of the unconscious conflicts regarding women which derive from developmental problems in the patient's childhood. The analytic methods have been employed to uncover and resolve the patient's postulated unconscious conflicts and hostilities toward females, with the expectation that such a resolution would be accompanied by an automatic improvement in sexual functioning. Although no systematic study has been performed, the general impression is that results of insight therapy alone, at least for the relief of premature ejaculation, have been disappointing.

The commonsense approach, which is widely espoused by the medical profession and laity alike, is based on the supposition that premature ejaculation is caused by excessive erotic sensation and that the remedy lies in diminishing this sensation. Specific techniques prescribed by physicians include the use of condoms, anesthetic ointments applied to the penis, distraction from the sexual experience in progress by nonerotic imagery, and the use of alcohol, sedatives, and tranquilizers. All of these have been unsuccessful.

Behavioral approaches have also been applied to the therapy of prematurity. These have mainly employed desensitization, on the theory that anxiety is a cause of premature ejaculation. Behavioral treatment has not been very effective.

Various pharmacological treatments have also been tried. The use of tricyclic and hydrazine antidepressants has some success while the patient uses those drugs. However, when medication is discontinued, the man again is unable to exert voluntary control over ejaculation and reaches climax quickly.

Marital therapy treats prematurity by attempting to resolve the alleged transactional roots of the symptom. Again, to date there are no reports of success of this approach.

The most successful, however, and the foundation of the Masters and Johnson approach, was reported in 1956 by the urologist James Semans, who based his treatment on "prolonging the localized neuromuscular reflex mechanism of ejaculation," which he felt was "extremely rapid" in premature ejaculation. His technique was exceedingly simple. It consisted of extravaginal stimulation of the man by his wife, until the sensation premonitory to ejaculation was attained, then interruption of the stimulation until the man could tolerate this stimulation indefinitely without ejaculating. At this point, in the eight patients who made up his study population prematurity was permanently relieved.

The Masters–Johnson approach is essentially the same. It differs primarily in substituting a "squeeze" of the penis (just below the rim of the glans) at the time of ejaculatory premonition, rather than a simple cessation of stimulation. The Masters–Johnson treatment also involves a complex, intensive format wherein the couple under treatment is seen every day for two weeks by a mixed-gender cotherapy team. In addition to the squeeze technique, various other exercises, including sensate focus, are included in the treatment regimen. A 98% success rate is reported by Masters and Johnson with this approach.

A Working Concept of Premature Ejaculation

One implication of the success of the Semans type of approach is that an understanding of the original motivation roots of premature ejaculation is irrelevant for the purpose of treatment: The underlying dynamics do not have to be resolved in order for the patient to achieve ejaculatory control. Perhaps there are many remote factors that play a role in the etiology of prematurity. However, the multiple remote causes of the condition may be bypassed. It is only the immediate antecedents of the man's failure to acquire ejaculatory continence that have to be modified to cure the patient. What are these immediate antecedents? The final answer to this question is not clear. However, we postulate that for some reason, because of unconscious conflict or perhaps some other cause, the premature ejaculator has not focused his attention on the sensation of sexual arousal. He virtually does not perceive the sensations premonitory to orgasm and has therefore failed to learn control of his ejaculatory reflex. This is analogous to a child's failure to learn urinary continence because he has not perceived the sensations of a full bladder. The essential aim of treatment then becomes the clear-cut one of supplying previously deficient perceptual links to encourage the patient to be aware of and experience his sexual sensations.

Approach of the Cornell Program

The approach to the therapy of prematurity in our program is based on these principles. As is true of the treatment of all sexual dysfunctions, the format employs exercises to be carried out by the patient and his wife in the privacy of their home which are integrated with conjoint psychotherapeutic sessions in the clinic. The primary aim of the exercises used in the therapy of prematurity is to help the man focus his attention and concentrate on, and fully experience, the sensations premonitory to orgasm. This experience must occur together with his partner because it is anxiety engendered by the sexual and marital transactions which often seems to distract the husband from abandoning himself to his sexual sensations.

Treatment begins with an evaluation session, attended by the couple, during which a detailed history is obtained of the sexual functioning of both partners. All motivated couples are accepted for treatment except those in which *either* partner exhibits active, severe psychopathology or in which the sexual symptom appears to be employed as a major defense against pathology.

The couple is given an explanation of the rationale behind the treatment, and it is made clear to the wife that, initially at least, there may be little reward for her. If she can defer her immediate gratification, a therapeutic "contract" is entered into with the couple, whereby they agree to cooperate in the recommended treatment. They are also made aware that they themselves are responsible for the success of the treatment. Finally, they are told that the prognosis for rapid relief is excellent, provided that they adhere to the treatment.

Couples are seen conjointly, usually twice a week for three to six weeks, for a total of six to twelve times, and are encouraged to telephone their therapist should questions arise. The exercises themselves, carried out in the home, follow a two-part sequence: extravaginal stimulation, and stimulation during coitus. The exercises are based on the Semans approach. Initially, the man is stimulated manually by his wife, with four premonitory "ceases" prescribed before ejaculation is to be allowed. When improvement in control is seen, the exercises are repeated, with the penis first lubricated by vaseline, as this more closely simulates the vaginal environment. After three to six extravaginal sessions, sufficient improvement is usually attained to permit the beginning of intercourse. Intercourse is first attempted in the female-superior position, as being less stimulating to the man; with success, the lateral and then the male-superior position is attempted. The stop-short technique is used during the early intercourse sessions and is suggested for occasional use after treatment is terminated. As stated, the prognosis is excellent in that, if the couple follows the instructions and performs the exercises, the man will reach his goal of being able to choose when to ejaculate. In fact, we have treated thirty-two premature-ejaculation couples with this approach, and of the couples who have completed therapy none has failed to attain ejaculatory continence. However, since these trials were not done under controlled conditions these promising results must be regarded with caution. Nonetheless, we were encouraged by this apparent success to hypothesize that the essential ingredients in the therapy of prematurity have been identified. Moreover, the therapy was exceedingly simple and might be more economically applied in a group setting in which several couples could be treated simultaneously.

Group Treatment

Our first group treatment for prematurely ejaculating men was undertaken with four couples, all having stable marriages, all without severe psychopathology in either partner, all previously screened and evaluated. Group sessions were forty-five minutes long, and the group was seen once a week for six weeks. The group was directed by Drs. Kaplan, Pomeroy, Offit, and Mrs. Hogan* as a task-oriented, theme-centered group, with the group process used to enhance the sex treatment. Specifically, it was the objective of the group sessions to convey instructions for the exercises that the couples were to carry out at home and also to deal with obstacles to sexual functioning and resistances to treatment that almost invariably emerge during the course of therapy. The group met once a week and the session began with the review of each couple's experiences during the previous week. The therapists worked with intrapsychic and transactional resistances to treatment as they emerged. As is usual in group therapy, the group dynamics were employed in the service of revealing and resolving conflicts. However, in this setting our objective was limited to the treatment of prematurity. Therefore, in contrast to the usual group therapy, where transactions between the members are employed to reveal and resolve all manner of problems, here interpretations were made only to implement sex therapy. For this reason, competition among couples was bypassed; emphasis was on mutual support and encouragement. Perhaps the group process can best be understood by describing the results obtained by each couple individually.

First Couple

In couple 1, the man, a twenty-five-year-old carpenter, was married to a woman of the same age. They had been married to each other for 1½ years, and it was the second marriage for each. The wife had two children from her former marriage and was four months pregnant when the treatment began. She was attractive, intelligent, and easily multiorgastic. Her husband, whose early sexual experience had been with prostitutes, had been a premature ejaculator since he commenced sexual activity. On his first manual stop/start session, the husband twice successfully controlled his ejaculatory reflex. However, resistances emerged during the next session. He had had too much to drink, and when they began to exercise again he was unable to concentrate on his sensations and thus failed to stop in time, and ejaculated. The wife also presented obstacles. For the third exercise session, the couple did not practice the extravaginal sequence as recommended, but, with the wife's urging, the man proceeded directly to intercourse, in the female-superior position. Not surprisingly, he was unable to concentrate on the penile sensations and ejaculated immediately on insertion.

During a group discussion of these events, the wife of another couple pointed out that this man seemed to have a fear of failure that was distracting him from focusing on his sensations and that his wife also seemed fearful and was pressuring her husband. Clarification of the resistances of this couple helped the rest in getting in touch with their own previously unconscious fears of sexuality. The mutual discussion of this material was extremely helpful to all. However, the

*The use of four therapists was motivated primarily by staff interest in the project. Subsequently, we have been using single therapists, which is, of course, far more economical and seems to be equally effective.

couple did not attend the third group session. They came to the fourth. A new resistance was revealed. Describing the exercises they had performed in the meantime, they reported waiting for the man's sexual sensation to cease completely before resuming manual stimulation, instead of resuming stimulation after a few seconds, per instructions. Again, resistances and anxieties were dealt with in the group. The man's sense of inadequacy and some of its roots were discussed during the session. In addition to psychodynamically oriented interpretations, it was pointed out that they were waiting too long and losing the benefit of experience with high plateau levels of excitement. It was suggested by the therapists that they have some additional extravaginal experience and then move to intravaginal stop/start. This was the couple's last session in the group. They canceled the final meeting and were rescheduled four months later for follow-up. Surprisingly, this resistant couple had a successful outcome. At the follow-up meeting, they reported having followed the recommended exercise sequence, after they left the group, with the husband moving to the lateral and then the male-superior position with increasing success. The husband described a sense of control and awareness of his penile sensations. They declared that intercourse now lasted as long as they liked. She was multiorgastic on coitus, which was now a positive experience for both of them.

Second Couple

In couple 2, the man, a forty-four-year-old writer, had been married for eight years to a thirty-seven-year-old woman, the second marriage for both. They were a very sensitive, intelligent couple. The woman had been in analysis a number of years previously; she had great insight and freely communicated her knowledge and impressions to other group members in a helpful way. She was sexually responsive but coitally inorgastic. The man seemed to have an essentially normal history of sexual and psychological development. His prematurity had its onset with sexual activity. The couple had read Masters and Johnson and had tried, without success, to deal with the prematurity problem by themselves. Although the marriage was basically a healthy one, the man was obsessive and constantly worried about his inability to control his ejaculation and his wife's inability to have orgasm during coitus. For this couple, treatment proceeded without the dramatic resistances demonstrated by couple 1.

The husband learned to concentrate on his sensations, which he had previously failed to do. He was very impressed with the sexual abandonment that was described by the multiorgastic wife of the first couple. He compared this with his own constricted attitudes. He was delighted with the improvement of his sexual enjoyment and ejaculatory control, when he too was able to abandon himself "selfishly" to the sexual experience. The other women in the group vociferously confronted the husband with the pressure he was placing on his wife for coital orgasm. The couple discussed this openly between themselves in the group. Two sessions later, she reported that, free from having to worry about her husband's concern for her, she was able to concentrate on her own sexual feelings and was able to experience coital orgasm. He gained satisfactory ejaculatory continence by the fifth group session. The couple could not be reached for follow-up.

Third Couple

Couple 3 had been married for seven years and had one child. The man was a stockbroker, thirty-five years old; the woman was a teacher and social worker, thirty-two years old. This also appeared to be a good marriage. The man suffered from premature ejaculation. The wife, who had been in therapy for a short time, had been orgastic in the past, but not within a year of treatment. The man was suffering from a mild depression.

The treatment for this couple also progressed easily to a successful conclusion. The husband was able to participate in the exercises and concentrate on his sensation without resistance as soon as it became clear that his wife had no objections to such "selfishness." On the contrary, she was too eager to be generous. It was pointed out in group sessions that she was neglecting her own pleasures and that she too permitted overconcern for her partner to impair her sexual abandonment. During the sessions, it became clear that both partners were governed by unconscious fears that the other would abandon them. The remoter causes of this dynamic were not dealt with in the group sessions because it did not present direct obstacles to improved sexual functioning. This couple was seen four months later. At that time, they reported that success had continued; in addition, the wife had become orgastic again and was no longer worried about sex. The husband reported that his mild depression had lifted.

Fourth Couple

Couple 4 were two college-educated people married to each other for twenty years. The man was forty-seven years old, the woman two years his junior and easily orgastic. To find a cure for his premature ejaculation, the man had previously spent ten years in therapy, going two or three times a week. Although he felt that he had benefited in general from the experience, his ejaculatory control had not improved. The goal that brought this couple to the clinic was not only increased ejaculatory control for the man but also an increase in the frequency of intercourse; at the time of treatment, they had intercourse about once every three to four weeks.

This couple began the Semans exercises along with the others. At first there was no difficulty. The man was easily aroused in his erotic feelings, approached the exercises eagerly, and experienced a number of initial successes. Then, quite suddenly, he began to have trouble achieving and maintaining an erection.

He revealed to the group that he had encountered this problem previously and that it had been related to a feeling of pressure to perform and consequent anxiety that he might fail. The treatment regimen was modified for this couple to accommodate for his erectile difficulty. They were advised that, if necessary, additional sessions could be scheduled with them in the fall but that in the meantime they should resume the exercises in a nondemand context, that is, at the husband's discretion, with no demand for coital stimulation.

During the group sessions, it became apparent that the wife was placing obstacles in the way of her husband's progress. As his functioning began to improve, her anxiety about losing control over him seemed to motivate her to place on him excessive demands for sexual performance. Not surprisingly, this vulnerable man began to experience erectile difficulties. His wife's demands, their destructive effects, and some of their underlying sources were discussed during group sessions. Consequently, she was able to control her behavior. Relieved of the demands for performance, the man was able to respond, to obtain an erection and carry through the start/stop sequences. Soon his ability to control ejaculations extravaginally improved, and a little later, when he proceeded to insertion, he also quickly attained intravaginal control. He discovered that he was capable of having intercourse two or three times a week, and even claimed that he had had more sexual experiences in the six weeks of group treatment than in the past ten years.

The alleviation of this man's symptoms required more than the modification of the immediate obstacles to sexual functioning which sufficed to help the other couples. It was necessary to deal with some of the remote roots of the problem. Both transactional and intrapsychic determinants were dealt with in the group. It emerged that he was unconsciously continuing his struggle against a controlling "mother" (i.e., his wife) via the use of sex. He had already dealt with his relationship with his mother in his previous psychotherapy; however, he had heretofore failed to make the necessary connection between this genetic material and his current sexual functioning. This was done in group. This couple was later rescheduled and seen in four months, by which time the man had achieved complete ejaculatory control. There were no further erectile problems, and frequency of sexual contact was once per week.

Discussion

Our pilot experiment with the group treatment of premature ejaculation is gratifying on many levels. First, experience has supported our hypothesis that we have developed a useful working concept of the pathogenesis and essential treatment parameters of this condition. The hypothesis that the immediate obstacle to ejaculatory control lies in the man's failure, for multiple reasons, to perceive sensations premonitory to ejaculation requires experimental validation before it can be regarded as established. However, on an empirical level, the concept is useful. Similarly, it appears that the active ingredient of the successful therapy methods consists of overcoming the immediate obstacle to ejaculatory continence by inducing the man to experience the previously avoided perception of high levels of erotic arousal while he is with his sexual partner. This procedure may be thought of as supplying the perception necessary for learning ejaculatory continence.

From a technical standpoint, it seems that the group process can be employed to implement this treatment goal. Specifically, in the group sessions we gave directions for the stop/start exercises that are designed to overcome the alleged immediate cause of prematurity. In addition, the group process was employed to deal with obstacles and resistances that were motivated by deeper causes. How far we had to go to resolve these varied with each couple. Thus, in one instance, couple 2, very little deeper transactional and intrapsychic material was interpreted.

In contrast, the problems presented by couple 4 necessitated explicit work with more complex marital interactions as well as with interpretation of the husband's unconscious conflicts and explorations of some of their genetic roots.

This treatment of premature ejaculation was based on a theme-centered target-symptom-removal group. Success was defined as the husband's attainment of voluntary ejaculatory control with consequently prolonged coitus. The attainment of such control was indicated only if both spouses agreed that this had happened. According to this criterion, of the four couples in the pilot study, two were treated with success in the six group sessions, and the other two had gained ejaculatory continence successfully two months later. All four couples reported continued and improved sexual functioning at four months follow-up.

Results obtained in only one program involving only four couples cannot of course be definitive, but they are consonant with the results obtained with the single-couple treatment provided in the program, which is based on the same concept of pathogenesis and treatment. The group format seems well suited to implement the treatment procedure.

At the present time, we are seeing additional groups of premature ejaculators and their wives, using only single therapists, and the results continue to be excellent. It may be inferred that other types of sexual dysfunction may be similarly amenable to such treatment provided that the essential principles of treatment for these syndromes are also clearly delineated.

It is worth noting also that the actual amount of therapist time spent in helping four couples achieve success amounted to about 7 hours, or about 1½ hours per couple. This represents a significant reduction in therapist time from the already rapid treatment format for individual couples that is used at the Payne Whitney Clinic, where a couple is seen for an average of 7 hours. Four couples would thus have required 28 hours of therapist time.

References

Kaplan, H. *The new sex therapy*. New York: Brunner/Mazel, 1973.

Masters, W., and Johnson, V. *Human sexual inadequacy*. Boston: Little, Brown, 1970.

Semans, J. Premature ejaculation: A new approach. *Southern Medical Journal*, 1956, *49*, 353–358.

In contrast with the excellent results in treatment of premature ejaculation reported by most sex therapists, ejaculatory incompetence has usually been found to be very difficult to treat. In this chapter, Razani describes the use of systematic desensitization in treatment of one case of ejaculatory incompetence. While this case was successfully treated, the sexual inexperience of this patient is not necessarily typical of ejaculatory incompetence patients, many of whom have been married and having intercourse for years. Sexual anxiety seems to be a less central element in such cases, which suggests that desensitization would not be as effective as Razani reports it was with this patient. Even in this case, it is difficult to attribute the success to systematic desensitization, as a number of other procedures were used concurrently, including training the sexual partner in providing penile stimulation for the patient. Given, however, the lack of success that characterizes treatment of ejaculatory incompetence, even single case reports of successful treatment are valuable.

22

Ejaculatory Incompetence Treated by Deconditioning Anxiety

Javad Razani

An association between sexual dysfunctions and coital anxiety has frequently been noted (Allen, 1962; Stekel, 1927; Wolpe, 1958). Cooper (1969a,b) reported a 94% correlation between coital anxiety and male potency disorders in a study of forty-nine patients. Ejaculatory incompetence (inability to ejaculate intravaginally) is an infrequent form of male sexual dysfunction. Masters and Johnson (1970) found only seventeen cases in an eleven-year period.

The case described below is that of a twenty-four-year-old male with ejaculatory incompetence associated with coital anxiety. It had persisted for six years. It resolved rapidly with systematic desensitization in the office and in vivo techniques at home.

The author thanks Dr. Neil B. Edwards for his critical evaluation of this article and Dr. Alan Goldstein for his advice in the treatment of the case.

Javad Razani • Department of Psychiatry, University of Southern California, School of Medicine, Los Angeles, California. When this chapter was originally published, Javad Razani was with the Department of Psychiatry, Temple University Health Sciences Center, Philadelphia, Pennsylvania.

Case History

B.M., a twenty-four-year-old, engaged, postgraduate student, referred himself to the Behavior Therapy Unit with the complaint of never having been able to ejaculate intravaginally satisfactorily since his first attempt at coitus six years previously. Although able to achieve and maintain erection sufficient for intercourse, both before and during intercourse he would have doubts about his ability to perform, and at the same time become anxious about the possibility that he might impregnate his partner. As a result, even though he was able to maintain his erection intravaginally for several minutes, he would gradually lose his erection, eventually withdrawing without ejaculation. This, understandably, left him and his partner disappointed and frustrated.

Since the age of fourteen he had masturbated regularly an average of three times a week with no premature emissions. He dated infrequently during his high school years, the extent of his sexual activity being kissing and light petting. Since the onset of his sexual difficulty, he had retained a normal desire for intercourse as evidenced by his use of fantasies of women during masturbation.

Six years before his coming to the clinic, while a freshman in college, he had taken a girl friend to a motel after a dance with the intention of having intercourse (his first-ever attempt). The girl expressed fear of becoming pregnant even though she had had a hysterectomy, and he became apprehensive about this possibility. He attained a firm erection, but in attempting penetration, aimed inaccurately, which resulted in an increase in his anxiety and premature ejaculation. Thereafter, he became reluctant to have intercourse, and even though he dated off and on, did not try again until four years later when he became engaged for the first time.

He attempted intercourse with his first fiancée a total of seven times, but each experience ended with partial loss of erection and withdrawal without ejaculation. His first engagement lasted thirteen months and ended because of the sexual dysfunction. After a three-month period, he became engaged a second time. Four months later he came for treatment. With his second fiancée he had attempted intercourse a total of thirteen times. On three occasions he was able to ejaculate intravaginally, but with much apprehension and anxiety. On eight occasions he had suffered partial loss of erection and on two occasions lost his erection before penetration. He was clearly on a path toward secondary impotence (Masters and Johnson, 1970) when he came to us. His fiancée was understanding and eager to cooperate and he was highly motivated for treatment.

His initial clinical evaluation and psychological testings (Fear Survey Schedule, Eysenck Personality Inventory, EPAT Self-Analysis Form, and MMPI) revealed a somewhat shy, passive, and introspective young man who suffered from a lack of confidence in his sexual performance. He was well adjusted in his occupational and social environment and there was no evidence of any overt interpersonal anxiety or of phobic or obsessional symptoms. His acquaintances perceived him as a warm and sensitive person and he had been able to establish several close interpersonal contacts.

He was born in a middle-class Jewish family, who were not religiously devout. His past history did not reveal any significant neurotic symptoms and he described his childhood as a happy one. There had been no discussions dealing with sexual matters at home. His one brother, twenty-nine years old, is apparently functioning well sexually and otherwise.

Treatment

He was seen for five sessions each lasting fifty minutes. His first session was directed to clinical evaluation. A urological examination after this session showed no genitourinary pathology. During his second session, he was seen with his fiancée and a discussion about normal human sexual response ensued. He was then instructed in deep muscle relaxation. In order to decondition his fear of sexual contact he and his fiancée were taught Semans's (1956) technique, according to which she was manually to stimulate his erect penis to the point premonitory of ejaculation and then to desist so as to allow the sensations to dissipate. The sexual arousal was expected to inhibit the fear. She was to repeat this two or three times before allowing him to go on to ejaculation. In the second and third sessions they carried out this technique several times, with the result that he no longer felt threatened by sexual contact with his fiancée. At the third session systematic desensitization was applied to the image of intravaginal ejaculation. He was able to practice coitus successfully at home with his fiancée in the female superior position described by Masters and Johnson (1970). At the fifth session he reported many successful intravaginal ejaculations after an average of two to three minutes of containment. At this time a switch was made to the male superior position without any difficulty. Thereafter, he was able successfully to ejaculate intravaginally with no recurrences of erective inadequacy and with mutual satisfaction. He married his fiancée shortly afterward.

Monthly follow-ups (six months until now) show continuation of satisfactory sexual performance. He has reported an increase in confidence in thinking about his performance and is able to regard sex as natural and physiological. As before, he continues to do well in other spheres of life.

Discussion

Masters and Johnson state that a man with ejaculatory incompetence rarely has difficulty in achieving or maintaining the erection necessary for successful coitus. The problem usually arises during the first coital experience and continues unresolved by subsequent attempts. Pressure to succeed can become so acute that secondary impotence may develop. Masters and Johnson had a cure rate of 83–84% in their seventeen treated cases. Seven of the cases described by Cooper (1969a,b) would appear to fit Masters and Johnson's description of ejaculatory incompetence. Six of these responded rapidly to treatment that consisted of deep muscle relaxation, Semans's technique, sexual education, and "psychotherapy." It may be presumed that anxiety reduction was central to Cooper's successes. In the case described here, recovery followed specific deconditioning of the anxiety evoked by the coital situation.

References

Allen, C. *A textbook of psychosexual disorders.* London: Oxford University Press, 1962.

Cooper, A. J. A clinical study of "coital anxiety" in male potency disorders. *Journal of Psychosomatic Research*, 1969, *13*, 143–147. (a)

Cooper, A. J. Clinical and therapeutic studies in premature ejaculation. *Comprehensive Psychiatry*, 1969, *10*, 4. (b)

Masters, W. H., and Johnson, V. E. *Human sexual inadequacy.* Boston: Little, Brown, 1970.

Semans, J. H. Premature ejaculation: A new approach. *Journal of Urology*, 1956, *49*, 353–357.

Stekel, W. *Impotence in the male.* New York: Liveright, 1927.

Wolpe, J. *Psychotherapy by reciprocal inhibition.* Stanford: Stanford University Press, 1958.

Wolpe, J. *The practice of behavior therapy.* New York: Pergamon Press, 1969.

In the introduction to the preceding chapter, the role of providing intensive penile stimulation as an element in treatment of ejaculatory incompetence was mentioned. In this chapter, Newell reports on the use of an electric vibrator to induce ejaculation. Note that in both this case and the case in the preceding article, fear of pregnancy is mentioned. Such fear is a factor in many cases of ejaculatory incompetence, but not in all of them.

This article is also interesting in that a successful outcome was obtained even though the wife refused to participate in treatment. Such a result is not typical and contradicts the frequently stated assertion that both partners must be treated if therapy is to succeed.

23

A Case of Ejaculatory Incompetence Treated with a Mechanical Aid

Adrian G. Newell

Ejaculatory incompetence is the inability to ejaculate into the vagina. Some patients can ejaculate (usually by means of masturbation) outside but not into the vagina; others cannot ejaculate in response to any type of sexual stimulation. The presence in the latter of nocturnal emissions (Kaplan and Abrams, 1958) indicates a physiological ability to ejaculate.

The condition is apparently infrequent. Masters and Johnson (1970) state that over eleven years, of 448 males requesting treatment for sexual problems only 17 had ejaculatory incompetence; of these, only three were unable to masturbate to climax. No data are given on nocturnal emissions. Masters and Johnson reported treating their patients by the "sensate focus" method with attempts to force ejaculation.

Case History

The patient was a twenty-nine-year-old male of average intelligence. He was a police constable who at the time of referral had been married for 6 years. He

Adrian G. Newell • Department of Clinical Psychology, St. James's Hospital, Leeds, England

reported being able to maintain an erection for long periods and that he could continue masturbation or intercourse until he made a conscious decision to stop. He could not recall ejaculating after any form of sexual stimulation in the waking state. He had started to masturbate at thirteen but ceased the activity when he realized he did not climax. Nocturnal emissions had begun at fifteen and had continued about once a week. Since he had married he had no difficulty in obtaining an erection, and had sexual intercourse once or twice a week without ejaculation.

The patient had been investigated by physicians for possible organic causes of his complaint and no abnormality had been detected. The initial interviews did not elicit a clear etiology. However, there were two potentially important facts. The patient reported that he did not get particularly aroused in the sexual situation but had intercourse out of a sense of duty rather than for pleasure. Second, he appeared to be reducing the impact of any sexual stimulation by constantly watching for signs of ejaculation—i.e., by adopting "the spectator role" (Masters and Johnson, 1970).

Treatment

Initially it was decided to try and increase the amount of sexual stimulation by treating him in conjunction with his wife using a Masters and Johnson (1970) sensate focus program. This program had to be discontinued after a few sessions because of the wife's refusal to cooperate. She did this on two grounds: (a) she felt that the program was modifying her own sexual response—she was nonorgasmic and did not want to experience orgasm; (b) she feared pregnancy and was unwilling to use contraceptives.

In spite of his wife's attitude the patient continued to request help in achieving ejaculation. It was, therefore, decided to try and produce an ejaculation by other means.

Reports of induction of ejaculation in the literature are of two types, (a) electroejaculation, (b) mechanical stimulation. Rowan, Howley, and Nova (1962) reported a study on thirty-five patients treated by electrical stimulation. Unfortunately, none of these patients ejaculated, and pain limited the stimulation that could be given. Sobrero, Stearns, and Blair (1965) described a stimulating device consisting of a vibrator with a rubber cap to stimulate the glans of the penis. They reported that of one hundred chronic schizophrenics eighty achieved successful ejaculation. Schellen (1968) reports work with eleven patients, nine of whom reported ejaculation following electrovibration.

The patient was therefore induced to obtain a male vibrator from a sexual aids center. This device consists of a phallus-shaped vibrator (for female use) to which is attached a stiff extension sheath to contain the penis and transmit the vibration to the glans. He used this device regularly at home while looking at erotic photographs. He was told to enjoy any stimulation present without expecting or attempting to produce any ejaculation, i.e., he was encouraged to abandon the "spectator role."

Following three weeks' solitary use of the device the patient reported that he had experienced ejaculation. He was subsequently able to ejaculate during intercourse with his wife. The patient reported that ejaculation was accompanied by a pleasant sensation.

Initially he was followed up monthly for six months. During this period he stopped using the mechanical aid and continued to ejaculate during intercourse on about 50% of occasions. A follow-up one year later indicated that he had maintained this frequency of ejaculation in sexual intercourse one to three times per week. He also reported that the occasions on which he ejaculated were usually during what is described as the "safe period" even when he started to use contraceptives.

As stated above, a contributing etiological factor was that the patient's wife did not want to become pregnant and was unwilling to use contraceptives. The patient showed some collusion with this wish in that after treatment he ejaculated only during the "safe period." Of course, this did not explain his inability to ejaculate since adolescence. The patient's wife reacted to the successful treatment by refusing to discuss her husband's ability to ejaculate either with her husband or with the therapist. Otherwise the marital relationship appeared unaffected.

References

Kaplan, A. H., and Abrams, M. Ejaculatory impotence. *Journal of Urology*, 1958, *79*, 964–968.

Masters, W. H., and Johnson, V. E. *Human sexual inadequacy*. London: Churchill, 1970.

Rowan, R. L., Howley, T. F., and Nova, H. R. Electro-ejaculation. *Journal of Urology*, 1962, *87*, 726–729.

Schellen, T. M. C. M. Induction of ejaculation by electrovibration. *Fertility and Sterility*, 1968, *19*, 566–569.

Sobrero, A. J., Stearns, H. E., and Blair, J. H. Technic for the induction of ejaculation in humans. *Fertility and Sterility*, 1965, *16*, 765–767.

This chapter provides, in brief form, a very thorough review of the anatomy and physiology of penile erection, the organic factors that can lead to erectile dysfunction, and the functional (psychogenic) causes of erectile dysfunction. The authors' integration of biological and psychodynamic causative factors with directive, symptomatic treatment is an especially valuable part of this article.

Many traditional clinicians have resisted the directive techniques of sex therapy, on the grounds that complex psychodynamic factors are involved in the etiology of some cases of erectile dysfunction. Reckless and Geiger point out that while such dynamic etiology factors may be related to the cause of the dysfunction, it is not always necessary to focus on them to produce treatment gains.

24

Impotence as a Practical Problem

John Reckless and Nancy Geiger

The dictionary defines impotence as "a lack of strength; a physically or psychologically abnormal state usually of a male characterized by the inability to copulate." Medical diagnosis of impotence depends on the criteria used—whether erection is entirely absent or whether erection when accomplished provides no emission or only inadequate emission.

We adhere to the definitions used by Masters and Johnson (1970), who classify as primary impotence the condition of the man who has never been able to achieve or maintain an erection of sufficient strength to accomplish coital connection successfully. The man who has experienced successful intromission, either heterosexual or homosexual, is described as having secondary rather than primary impotence when he fails in subsequent experience. Equally valid distinctions may be made between failures caused by physiologic conditions and those in which an unimpaired organism is made unable to perform by psychologic distress, whether conscious or unconscious. Even primary impotence can result, for example, from an early, harsh indoctrination against sexual activity on grounds of religious morality and control. And secondary impotence may appear in the mature years because of the gradual—and perhaps unacknowledged—realization that a marriage

John Reckless • John Reckless Clinic, P. A., and School of Nursing, Duke University Medical Center, Durham, North Carolina   *Nancy Geiger* • Trouro Infirmary, New Orleans, Louisiana

has over the years become stiflingly dull. Disappointment and recriminations over career limitations, disagreements over rearing the children, the lack of personal privacy, and the fading of romance can bring a man to a state of depression likely not only to cause secondary impotence but to perpetuate it, at least with the usual partner. Treatment must deal with the interpersonal aspects of the marriage rather than sexual responsiveness in such cases, just as in primary impotence caused by overrigid moral views treatment must concentrate on intrapsychic rather than organic difficulties. Indeed, the secondarily impotent male may be cured spontaneously if he finds a partner who persuades him that affection and good humor matter more to her than sexual prowess, since this attitude will relieve performance anxiety, which is at the root of so much failure.

The man who ejaculates prematurely or whose ejaculation does not take place intravaginally is not considered impotent. Nevertheless, premature ejaculation can be a severe problem, particularly in view of recent changes in the expectations and life-style of women. Although, in the past, men were conditioned to think only of achieving sexual satisfaction for themselves, young women today expect and even demand sexual satisfaction and orgasm; their often candid appraisal is difficult for men and intensifies the often self-fulfilling fear of failure.

The prevalence of impotence has not been statistically established. Stafford-Clark (1954) worked with a group of American husbands before the publication of Kinsey's work and found 45% dissatisfied with their sexual capacity. Impotence has been a complaint over the centuries, and many reasons for it have been suggested. It was attributed during the Middle Ages to curses, witchcraft, sorcery, and the like; the *Malleus Maleficarum** made mention of it in 1486. More recently it became usual to blame masturbation or excessive sexual activity. We now know that it may be caused by a number of physical or psychologic circumstances, and that there are a number of variables in its occurrence that may involve different phases of sexual union or different responses with different partners or in different environments; also, it may be transient or long-lasting. In any case, the problem is a distressing one that suggests a deficit in masculinity and is not only precipitated but reinforced by the fear it evokes.

The Physiology of the Male Sexual Response

The male sexual response has four physiologic stages: erection, emission, ejaculation, and detumescence. An intact neuromuscular system and an adequate blood supply to the lower genitourinary region are required for the achievement and maintenance of an erection that will culminate in orgasm.

Erection is initiated by either psychic or physical stimulation. Sexual excitement may spontaneously result from impulses conveyed from the diencephalon to the spinal area after the brain has received appropriate impulses from the sense organs. Erections are also a reflex response to direct tactile stimulation of the external genitalia.

---

*A text published in the reign of Pope Innocent VIII (1488) on the malignant influences abroad in the world. It is considered a manual on witchcraft. English text published by Dover Books (1973).

Nervous Control of Penile Erections

Sympathetic and parasympathetic activity affects the vessels of the penis (Fig. 1). Nervous impulses from L_2, L_3, and L_4 inhibit vasoconstriction, with resultant vasodilation leading to increased filling of the cavernous tissues. Parasympathetic outflow, S_2, S_3, and S_4 via the nervi erigentes and presacral plexus, produces vasodilation by relaxing the muscle coat of the arterioles and the spongiosa and of the spongy tissue of the corpora cavernosa while concomitantly the dorsal vein of the penis is compressed. Blood from the profunda artery is channeled to the spaces of the corpora cavernosa as the muscle pillars occlude the A–V shunts.

Sympathetic activity via L_1 and L_2 triggers contraction of the muscular coat of the epididymis, ejaculatory ducts, seminal vesicles, and prostate, resulting in the emission of semen into the posterior urethra. Ejaculation occurs immediately after emission as a reflex stimulated by the presence of semen in the urethra. At this point, ejaculation is inevitable. Sympathetic stimuli close off the internal vesical sphincter to prevent semen from entering the bladder. Somatic stimulation from S_2, S_3, and S_4 via the pudendal nerves contracts the bulbocavernosus and ischiocavernosus muscles, which eject semen from the posterior urethra by rhythmic spurts that cause a pleasurable sensation.

After ejaculation, the blood in the profunda artery passes to the efferent vein through A–V shunts as the pillar occludes the vessels of the corpora cavernosa. There is decreased sympathetic stimulation after orgasm; the arterioles in the penis contract and erection subsides (Morales, Ducrez, Delgado, and Whitehead, 1973). The sacral area of the cord is primarily responsible for tumescence; ejaculation is a function of the lumbar cord. During initial arousal, parasympathetic activity increases and, as orgasm approaches, the sympathetic system takes over, with parasympathetic dominance returning once again after its completion. The pelvic response depends on the sacrolumbar area of the cord and on intact efferent nerves and organs. However, for sexual "satisfaction," a functioning cord between the stimulus and the brain is required. The upper areas of the cord are necessary to transmit psychologic stimulation from the cerebrum to the genital and pelvic areas.

Male potency depends on endocrine function. Adrenarche in the male begins before biologic change is indicated by the increase in secretion of adrenal androgen. During puberty, the hypothalamus produces releasing factors (RF) that initiate and regulate the secretion of pituitary gonadotropins (FSH) and luteinizing hormone (LH) or interstitial cell-stimulating hormone (ICSH). FSH is responsible for the secretion of testosterone by Leydig cells. One of the earliest effects of androgen is to differentiate the hypothalamus as being "masculine." FSH-RF is

Sympathetic Nervous System	Parasympathetic Nervous System
$L_{2, 3,}$ and $_4$	$S_{2, 3,}$ and $_4$
↓	↓
Inhibition of vasoconstriction	Vasodilation effect
↓	↓
Vasodilation and increased filling of cavernous spaces	Vasodilation and increased filling of cavernous spaces

Fig. 1. Nervous control of penile erections.

secreted in the anterior part of the hypothalamus in the male and LH-RF in the posterior part. This occurs during puberty and provides a relatively constant rate of secretion of testicular hormones. Testosterone, the primary androgen, is responsible for the development and functioning of the male reproductive organs and the appearance of secondary sexual characteristics. It may also influence spermatogenesis. Some recent work indicates that testosterone is a prehormone that is converted in the cytoplasm to other androgens by 5-J alpha reductions (Wilson and Gloyna, 1970). Testosterone blood levels regulate the secretion of pituitary gonadotropins by inhibiting LH-RF. It is less effective in the regulation of ICSH-RF, in which estrogens play a role.

Secretion of hypothalamic-releasing factor is determined by activities in other areas of the brain. The efferent tract that controls the anterior hypothalamus also relays impulses from the limbic system. The reticular formation of the midbrain sends a nerve tract to the posterior hypothalamus and communicates directly with the limbic system, which is affected by sex hormones. Gonadotropin-RF may be inhibited by the pituitary hormone melatonin, which also inhibits maturation of gonads. Oxytocin is a neurohormone produced by the paraventricular nuclei and released by the posterior pituitary under the influence of the hypothalamus. It stimulates the smooth muscle in the male reproductive organs and thus facilitates erection and ejaculation. Its secretion is stimulated during sexual arousal, possibly due to activation of hypothalamic nerve impulses to the genital tract.

Man's libido is regulated by the brain and sex hormones. Dingman's hypothesis is that there is a "sex center" deep in the temporal lobe, probably part of the hypothalamus, which has an important role in the production and release of the trophic hormones from the anterior pituitary (Dingman, 1969). These hormones then influence the testicular synthesis, the secretion of testosterone and other ketosteroids and, ultimately, sexual behavior. Cooper (1972b) compared the testosterone levels of two groups of impotent men. They were lower in the first group, in which impotence had appeared early and persisted for more than two years, and in which the members had experienced no orgasm by any means. The group with higher levels was composed of men whose problems were late in onset and the duration was less than two years; this latter group had a relatively stronger sex drive and had used alternative sexual outlets.

The neurologic pathways of erection and ejaculation are similar to those of micturition. The major ascending pathway to the thalamic region is the lateral spinal thalamic tract, which passes through the anterior hypothalamus, the septum, the mamillary bodies, and the medial dorsal nucleus of the thalamus. The descending pathways pass through the ansa lenticularis to the hypothalamus, then descend in the medial forebrain bundle to the dorsal aspect of the substantia nigra to the pons. From there, they go to the ventrolateral aspect of the superior olive and the lateral side of the pyramids, where they meet the spinal thalamic paths. This sugests that the neural basis of the sexual response lies in the limbic system (Dingman, 1969).

The male's sexual arousal can be divided into four phases (Masters and Johnson, 1963). The first phase, *excitement*, is initiated by physical or psychic stimuli. Anxiety or apprehension can inhibit this stage, the duration of which varies with the type and intensity of the stimulus. Phase two marks a *plateau* during which there is vasoconstriction of both the superficial and the deep vessels of the pelvic viscera. As sexual tension rises, receptivity to minor stimuli is reduced. If the stimulation is interrupted at this point, the male may resolve slowly without ejaculating. Phase three is the *orgasmic phase*, which begins with the contraction of organs of the reproductive system and lasts until the final expulsive contraction of the periurethral musculature. The length of this phase depends on the volume of ejaculate, the intensity of contractions and the muscular tension. *Resolution* constitutes the fourth phase; this is the retracting period, during which the man is resistant to stimulation immediately following ejaculation.

Sexual excitement brings about predictable reactions in the male body. Penile response to stimulation is erection, which develops rapidly, with the penis becoming fully engorged within from three to five seconds in an involuntary reaction. At the approach of orgasm, the penis may change color to a darker hue; its circumference always increases. Detumescence follows the expulsion of seminal fluid. The entire length of the penile urethra is involved. The urethral and bulbocavernosus muscles contract and the testes respond by elevation toward the perineum, brought about by a shortening of the spermatic axis and anterior rotation of the testes. This continues into the plateau phase and often is accompanied by an increase in size due to vasocongestion. In resolution, the testes descend and decongestion takes place. The external sphincter of the rectum contracts both voluntarily and involuntarily with direct stimulation during the excitement and plateau phases, and there are regular involuntary contractions during orgasm itself. The urethra expands to two or three times its diameter in the distention that immediately precedes orgasm and contracts with the penile body. The urethral meatus constricts to normal size immediately after ejaculation. The scrotum is tense and thick during the excitement phase; resolution may be rapid or slow. A vasocongestive flush may appear over the anterior chest wall, the neck, face, forehead, shoulders, upper arms, and thighs during the plateau phase and last until resolution. The male breasts are not always responsive but some nipple erection may be evident in the excitement phase and disappear after orgasm.

Physiologic Causes of Impotence

In our culture, men with sexual dysfunction find it considerably more acceptable to blame it on physical disability than on psychologic difficulty and, indeed, anything that affects the neuromuscular, vascular or hormonal components of the male sexual response can produce functional and sometimes even structural impotence. Such impairment will be evident in every attempt at coitus whatever the situation. Although the physiologic nature of impotence can be established by the patient's response to electrically induced pain (Rowan and Hanley, 1965), it is well to remember that early experience may influence even the sexual dysfunction due to physical causes.

Various physical deformities of the genitalia can cause impotence. The penis seldom is congenitally absent, but this sometimes is the case in the individual with multiple congenital anomalies. A penis concealed beneath scrotal or perineal skin can be released by plastic surgery. In the condition of adherent penis, the scrotum is attached by a band to its lower surface. Diphallus (double penis) is seen occasionally in a variety of forms and invariably causes impotence. Hypoplasia of the penis diminishes its size significantly. In hypospadias, the anterior urethra terminates on the undersurface of the penis, often causing impotence, especially when the hypospadic opening is at the junction of the penis and the scrotum and the penis is small and curved; the degree of deformity is the determinant here.

In Peyronie's disease there is a fibrous induration of the penis. The pathologic process begins with vasculitis of the areolar connective tissue sleeve below the tunica albuginea and continues to the adjacent structures. The inflammation is followed by fibrosis associated with collar formation due to perivascular fibrosis and the production of elastic fibers. The cause is not known and the onset is insidious. The disease runs a limited course regardless of treatment and, although surgery may be considered if Buck's fascia has not become involved, it may result in loss of erective ability. A few patients are left by this disease with curvature of the penis and pain on erection.

In monorchism, impotence can arise from fear of failure and shame over having but one testicle. Anorchism, the congenital absence of testes, is accompanied by femininity of voice and habitus, a lack of sexual desire and the absence of erection and emission. Occasionally, one sees the combined absence of spermatic cord, seminal vesicles, epididymis, testes, and prostate. Cryptorchidism (the failure of testicles to descend) may cause impotence because of attendant deficiencies in secondary sexual characteristics and the psychologic influence this deviation exerts. In orchialgia, for which no cause is know, testicles and epididymis are extremely sensitive.

Phimosis is a small opening of the prepuce that makes it difficult to draw back the foreskin; this causes pain connected with voiding and erection. Elephantiasis is the hypertrophy and swelling of the penis and scrotum. Hydrocele is the abnormal accumulation of serous fluid along the spermatic cord because of overproduction or underabsorption of lymphatic transudate. Varicocele may be due to chronic congestion of the pelvic area and cause elongation, dilation, and tortuosity of the veins of the pampiniform plexus.

Priapism is a pathologic erection unassociated with sexual desire and occasioned either psychogenically or by damage of the valvelike structures in the corpus cavernosum, abnormal stimulation by efferent nerves, blood dyscrasia, infection, or lesions of the spinal cord. The defect is in the mechanism that releases blood to the corpus cavernosum. The resultant ischemia causes fibrosis; it has been treated by surgery, anticoagulant therapy and massage with anesthesia. Whatever the treatment, impotence is a common outcome. Lesions, growths or tumors of the genital area can cause impotence by being painful, by causing deformity or by making the individual self-conscious.

Impotence can be caused neurologically by the disruption of anatomic pathways by surgery, infection, the growth of a tumor, or degeneration. Contributory conditions are amyotrophic lateral sclerosis, tumor or transsection of the cord, multiple sclerosis, nutritional deficiency, parkinsonism, peripheral neuropathies, spina bifida, sympathectomy, tabes dorsalis, and temporal lobe lesions (Jackson,

1968). Also, lesions may occur in the hypothalamus, limbic system, or spinal cord. A sympathectomy can cause ejaculatory failure by its interruption of orgasm; emission is made into the bladder because the sphincter is relaxed and spermatozoa are fewer because of decreased peristalsis in the vas deferens. Erection fails because the remaining sympathetic fibers develop increased tonus that produces vasoconstriction and reduces blood flow to the penis. When the ganglia that give rise to the fibers supplying the pelvic viscera are removed, sensitization to circulatory adrenin is accomplished and increased vasoconstriction of penile vessels results.

A wide variety of conditions with endocrine involvement cause impotence: Addison's disease, adrenal neoplasms, chromophobe adenoma, craniopharyngioma, diabetes mellitus, acromegaly, pituitary insufficiency, feminizing interstitial cell tumor, infantilism, castration, eunuchoidism, the ingestion of feminine hormones, myxedema, obesity, and thyrotoxicosis. Testicular failure causes hormone deficiency in the male because the testicles are responsible for the production of androgens, especially testosterone, which are secreted by Leydig cells after stimulation by LH from the anterior pituitary. Primary testicular failure may appear in pubescence or as early as prepuberty. The amount of urinary gonadotropins increases and the urinary ketosteroids and estrogens diminish because of testicular atrophy following mumps, traumatic lesions, surgery, X-rays, or castration. Secondary testicular failure is due to a failure of the pituitary and may be occasioned by vitamin deficiency, malnutrition, diabetes mellitus, tumor, injury, trauma, or X-rays. The urinary gonadotropins as well as urinary ketosteroids are low. Stress can also lower the testosterone concentration because of the effects of epinephrine on the hypothalamus.

Klinefelter's syndrome presents a spectrum of deficiencies in masculinization. Individuals with this problem are genetically XXY or XXXY and have degeneration of the seminiferous tubules, small testicles, gynecomastia, and a high urinary FSH titer. They have the potential for normal libido but all are aspermatic. Exogenous testosterone may be used to correct this disorder.

In hyperthyroidism, the following may occur: gynecomastia, atrophy of the seminiferous tubules, and low sperm count. Hormonal deficiency is treated by replacement therapy; orally administered methyltestosterone (5–25 mg per day) and fluoxymesterone (Ora-Testryl) (2.5 mg per day) often are advocated. Only that impotence caused by hormonal deficiency will yield to treatment with hormones.

Although there is not enough evidence to infer that the diabetic male is predisposed to impotence, diabetes is implicated. Cooper (1972b) found that from 30% to 60% of all diabetic males eventually become impotent, and Masters and Johnson (1970) found a 200—300% higher incidence of a diabetic or prediabetic curve in the male symptoms of secondary impotence than in a cross section of the population according to results of a five-hour glucose tolerance test. Impotence in diabetes may occur only periodically or may progressively worsen. Erections may start to get flaccid or be suddenly lost. The problem increases with the age of the diabetic rather than the duration of his illness and is not caused by the agent used for control of diabetes. Impotence appearing late in long-established diabetes is not likely to be reversible; the outlook is equally bleak when it appears among the early signs of the disease at a time when hypoglycemia may have gone undetected for some time and the diagnosis of maturity-onset diabetes is not yet suggested. Kancz and Bdodims (1970) found no correlation between potency and the control of diabetes, although impotence may accompany diabetic relapse and vanish when the disease once again is under control, unless the transient problem has evoked unfavorable psychologic reaction. This is the only circumstance in which control of diabetes can restore potency, but good control of the disease can help to prevent it.

In diabetes, three mechanisms—neurologic, endocrine, and vascular—are implicated. Schoffling, Federlin, Ditschuniet, and Pfeiffer (1963) found that the excretion of 17-ketosteroids was slightly elevated in the impotent male diabetic, with estrogen excretion higher than in diabetics who were potent. Such changes are evidence of impaired testicular function. However, more recent investigation indicates that the testicular abnormalities may be secondary to lesions of the autonomic nervous system, since diabetic neuropathy may impair sensation or weaken certain muscle groups and thus cause impotence. There is considerable evidence for this (Faerman et al., 1972). Androgens usually are not given in treatment, since they can increase desire without increasing functional efficiency. Norris and Yunis (1964) found greater calcification in the regional arteries of the seminal vesicles and vas deferens of impotent diabetic males than in those of controls. They believed that obliteration of penile arteries and microangiopathy of the small vessels to the corpora cavernosa could reduce blood flow and induce impotence. Whatever the mechanism involved, it is important that the patient understand that his problem is not psychologic but due to a disease process; also, it is incumbent on the physician to weigh the possibility of any other pathologic condition that might be responsible.

Many kinds of drugs can cause impotence (Table 1): addictive drugs, alcohol, alpha-methyldopa, amphetamines, atropine, chlordiazepoxide, chlorprothixene, guanethidine, imipramine hydrochloride, methantheline bromide, monoamine-oxidase inhibitors, phenothiazines, reserpine, thioridazine hydrochloride, nicotine, and digitalis. The addicting drugs, including barbiturates, morphine, heroin, cocaine, and alcohol, cause chronic depression in the central nervous system and thus decrease libidinal drive. The psychodynamics of the drug-dependent man must also be considered. Phenothiazines can decrease libido and erectile ability and inhibit ejaculation. So may chlorpromazine, by adrenergic blocking of the hypogastric plexus of the thoracolumbar sympathetic system with decreased peristalsis of the vas deferens, seminal vesicles, and ejaculatory ducts, with the possibility of some hypothalamic endocrine involvement. The ability to sustain an erection and to ejaculate seems at risk. Chlorpromazine, although not affecting excitement or erec-

Table 1.   Drugs That May Lead to Impotence

Drugs of addiction	Barbiturates, morphine, heroin, cocaine, alcohol, amphetamine, and bromide
Tranquilizers and antidepressants	Chlordiazepoxide, chlorprothixene, imipramine, certain phenothiazines, such as chlorpromaxine and thioridazine, and drugs of the monoamineoxidase inhibitors
Drugs of the vascular system	Reserpine, nicotine, digitalis, guanethidine, and methantheline

tion, may prevent ejaculation. Antidepressants of the imipramine–amitriptyline group can cause impotence by interfering with cholinergically mediated systems and potentiate the sympathomimetic amines, especially norepinephrine, increasing sympathetic action (Simpson, Blane, and Amoso, 1965). The monoamine-oxidase inhibitors have direct sympathomimetic effects. Several antihypertensives are known to produce impotence as a side effect, although the method of this is not clear. Benthanidine, guanethidine, and spironolactone may cause impotence by affecting the endocrine system through their steroid configuration (Greenblatt and Koch-Weser, 1973). Any of the anticholinergic agents can produce impotence by partially paralyzing the parasympathetic system. A report (Espir, Hall, Shirreffs, and Stevens, 1970) concerning five farm workers who used various herbicides and pesticides indicates that four of them became impotent; the chemicals used were organiferous compounds, substituted phenols, carbamates, and others. The workers' potency returned as soon as their contact with these chemicals ceased and hormone therapy was given.

Any vascular problem (see Table 2) that impairs the flow of blood to the pelvis can cause impotence, as in occlusive aortoiliac disease, aneurysm, arthritis, sclerosis, and thromboembolic obstruction of the bifurcation (Masters and Johnson, 1970). If the penile pressure is close to or greater than mean brachial pressure, it is not likely that obstruction of the main arteries to the penis is the cause of impotence (Gaskell, 1971).

Impotence may be a complication in several kinds of surgery. An aortofemoral

Table 2. *Physiopathologic Conditions That May Cause Impotence*

Anatomic defects	Congenital absence of the penis, diphallus, hypoplasia of the penis, hypospadias, cryptorchidism, and anorchism
Endocrinologic	Addison's disease, adrenal neoplasms, chromophobe adenoma, craniopharyngioma, diabetes mellitus, acromegaly, pituitary insufficiency, feminizing interstitial cell tumor, infantilism, castration, eunuchoidism, the ingestion of feminine hormones, myxedema, thyrotoxicosis, testicular failure, Fröhlich's syndrome, Laurence–Moon–Biedl syndrome
Neurologic	Amyotrophic lateral sclerosis, cord compression, tumors of the spinal cord, Parkinson's disease, multiple sclerosis, peripheral neuropathies, tabes dorsalis, and general paresis
Inflammatory	Prostatis, seminal vesiculitis
Vascular	Aortic obstruction (Leriche's syndrome), calcific obliteration or thrombosis of the vessels supplying the penis
Other	Trauma, side effects of surgery, Klinefelter's syndrome, Peyronie's disease, lead and herbicide poisoning
Psychogenic	Religious orthodoxy, negative early sexual education and experience, plus situations that lead to shame, fear, guilt, and demand for performance, also, lack of confidence in sexual performance

bypass for correction of aortofemoral occlusion may produce or aggravate it, and the surgeon aware of this possibility may prefer an endarterectomy of intact iliac vesicles. Since hypogastric nerves innervate the prostate, the seminal vesicles, ejaculatory ducts, and internal sphincters, dissection of the aorta that interferes with the hypogastric plexus can cause impotence because of the section of sensory axons in the hypogastric nerves, decreasing the power of emission into the urethra and decreasing the pressure in the urethra itself in such a way that the internal sphincter fails to close and permits retrograde ejaculation to occur (Hallbook and Holmquist, 1970).

Thirty-nine percent of the patients studied by Gold and Hotchkiss (1969) reported problems with impotence after a prostatectomy. The type of prostatectomy is less significant than the patient's age in this outcome. Although radical perineal or pelvic surgery for the removal of malignant growth may cause impotence, a vasectomy does not affect male performance unless the female partner has had serious objections to the procedure and the relationship is troubled.

Pelvic or penile trauma can cause impotence, especially when it causes such deformation as deviation of the penis or damages the corpora cavernosa. A fracture of the pelvis along with urethral rupture is very likely to cause impotence. The reason for this is not altogether clear, but it seems probable that vascular damage accounts for it. As in most other cases of impotence, the patient's own anxiety about performance after an injury can compound the problem.

The occult herniated intervertebral disk, which often impairs bladder function, may produce impotence. Relief is obtained when the disk is corrected, provided that the man has not lost confidence in his sexual capacity during the period of distress with his back.

"It is a general rule that all men show a decline in sexual activity with aging" (Dingman, 1969). The effects of aging differ among individuals but must be anticipated. The decline is manifested in different ways; some men simply engage less frequently in sexual activity, whereas others lose the ability to complete the act. Although unreliable performance may reflect the actual fluctuation of supply of the sex hormones, psychologic deterrents may appear after the initial difficulty.

The Duke University Center for the Study of Aging and Human Development has been conducting and is continuing a longitudinal study of behavior health changes in senescence. The project began with Study I in 1955–57 with 260 participants. Study II took place in 1959–61 with 190 volunteers and Study III was carried out in 1964 with 126 participants. At the time of the first study, the ages of the subjects ranged from 60 to 94 years. The number of participants declined over the years due to deaths or serious illness.

From their medical histories, data were gained about their sexual behaviors. It was decided that many variables entered into sexual functioning in the aging male. Among these factors were genetic biologic endowment and such sociocultural factors as occupation, education, religion and ethnic background, physical illness as noted in Table 2, and reduced sexual behavior; such other factors as boredom, monotony, and degree of sexual interest were influential in the rate of sexual activity.

The data revealed that age and degree of sexual activity are not related. The incidence of sexual activity declines to approximately 50% during the sixth decade of life and to 10–20% after 80 years of age (Pfeiffer, Verwoerdt, and Wang, 1969).

Masters and Johnson note that with aging it takes the male longer to reach a full erection and climax, so the erection may be maintained for longer periods without the need for ejaculatory demand. Seminal fluid may seep rather than be expelled, and intensity and duration of the process of vasocongestion are diminished. The male experiences fewer genital spasms and there is a slowing of the development of a full penile erection. There is a reduction in both the amount and force of his ejaculation and it takes a longer time to achieve another erection. These changes may add to the female sexual pleasure, because the erection can be maintained for a longer period before climaxing (Masters and Johnson, 1963).

These changes in the aging male are described in detail, for the patient and the uninformed physician may incorrectly interpret these as precursors of the symptom of impotence.

Psychologic Causes of Impotence

Situational impotence is selective and transient, occurring in special situations only. Morning erections are a good indication that the impotence experienced is psychogenic in origin. Strauss (1950) estimated that 90% of all impotence is psychogenic in origin. Anxiety and fears of three different types are involved. They may be only indirectly associated with the immediate situation and reflect a childhood fear of being punished for spying on the sexual activity of adults in the family, especially parents. They may be evoked by the possibility of giving or receiving bodily harm in intercourse or by the implied vulnerability of intimacy. Behavior-conditioning theorists hold that fear becomes a conditioned response associated with the initiation of the sex act (Freud, 1950). Freud connected fears with the knowledge that the mother lacks a penis. The male may attach his sexual feelings to his oedipal conflict and may fear castration. The dread, however, may focus on the sex act itself and misgivings about performance. In honeymoon impotence, for example, the man may be tired, excited, or inexperienced, or he may be so worried about being impotent that his anxiety is self-fulfilling. An apprehensive concentration on performance not only leads to failure but begins a vicious circle. Cooper (1968a,b, 1969) uses the term *coital anxiety* to describe this specific but often temporary problem; in one study, he learned that a large number of the men involved had some anxiety during coitus. The fear of failure, however, may be part of a generalized feeling of inadequacy and anticipated rejection by the female partner. The fear of such consequences as pregnancy, injury, disease, discovery, or simply a loss of independence may be equally cogent.

Some men feel deep resentment toward women as a result of frustrated oedipal desires and some suspect entrapment and perceive the partner as manipulative, domineering, and opportunistic. The hostility may arise from feelings of disgust, possibly engendered early by encounters with prostitutes. The man may unconsciously long for revenge for present or past experience, or his hostility may be a cover for fear. Hostility and resentment usually impair sexual performance; Hastings (1963) found that men whose wives are consistently critical of them often suffer impotence on that account. Interestingly, treatment for this kind of impotence has been more successful when it was himself rather than his wife that the man blamed for his hostile feelings.

The unilateral dominance of either mother or father in a family can undermine a son's confidence in his masculinity and increase the possibility of his feeling inadequate (Masters and Johnson, 1970). The absence of one parent seems to make less difference than the overriding of one parent by the other. The son whose mother controls and belittles her spouse lacks a strong male figure with whom to identify. When the home culture does little to honor the mother, the overwhelming masculine emphasis encourages the young boy to compare himself with his father and assess his own manly potential harshly.

Homosexuality is also an issue, usually after the awakening of homosexual interest in the mid-teens before there has been any heterosexual experience. The boy is left with a homosexual orientation and has male-oriented fantasies as he masturbates. Although he may marry, after an untroubled period, homosexual desires may return and heterosexual interests diminish. When the wife becomes demanding, such a man can experience erective failure.

As indicated earlier, sexual taboos based on early religious and moral teachings can foster psychogenic impotence in the man who, having reached maturity, denies the natural sexual component in himself and others and is convinced of the degrading nature of any sexual manifestation. This type of flight and negation requires readjustment of personal values and attitudes if normal sexual adequacy is to be established.

Unwise counseling can similarly promote impotence by planting seeds of doubt (Masters and Johnson, 1970) in the mind of the patient or intimations that impotence is a punishment or represents a hopeless situation. The counselor who discusses a variety of possible causes and makes a prognosis without giving adequate attention to either physiologic or psychologic concomitants of the sexual dysfunction is also less than helpful.

Although there is no direct cause-and-effect relationship between psychiatric disorder and impotence, the latter condition may in fact be a presenting symptom of any one of a number of neurotic states or sexual perversions. It is not clear whether in such cases neurosis precedes or follows the sexual failure, but they are known to exacerbate each other. Impotence often appears in the functional psychoses, especially in endogenous depression and schizophrenia.

One may anticipate any one of five interactional patterns in the life of the impotent man (Lewis, 1969). The first involves a passive male and an aggressive female; although this balance may meet some of the man's needs, it evokes hostility, which is expressed in withdrawal. Impotence then may occur during periods of heightened unconscious hostility. The partner's aggressive manner may recall childhood feelings of helplessness attended by resentment. The second pattern concerns the male who is aggressive outside the male–female relationship and who lacks satisfaction for his dependency needs to such an extent that he unconsciously encourages his wife to be more self-assertive. If she tolerates this poorly, a conflict may result. The third situation appears when a daughter who is allied with a very passive father against the wife and mother begins to grow up. The father's incestuous feelings produce in him guilt and impotence. When there has been instead a strong mother–son alliance, the husband may feel abandoned and use impotence as a retreat from competition. The fourth design centers around castration anxiety; oedipal feelings and incestuous fantasies fuse when a man marries a "good" partner "just like his mother." The fifth depends on visualization of parental intercourse, perceived as aggression and recalled as conflictual.

Although we have noted the great variety of causes of impotence, we also know that many men have in fact not become impotent under these conditions. And we know that men have recovered potency without specific therapy. We must consider the combined effect of psychosocial and biophysical factors on innate characteristics of each individual in question. Imprinting may determine the effects of a given situation (Johnson, 1968) and certain patterns can be learned only during limited periods of sensitivity by systems capable of responding. Such variables explain in part why one set of circumstances will render one man impotent but not another.

Treatment of Impotence

At the outset of any medical consideration of sexual behavior, it is important to realize that only since 1960 have human sexual function and dysfunction been studied extensively in the core curriculum required of all medical students. Thus, the physician who now is over forty years of age may not have been taught how to treat the sexual dysfunction of his patients. Indeed, many physicians confess to embarrassment at even being questioned by patients concerning sexual behavior and the particulars of intercourse.

Attempts now are being made to provide postgraduate education in such matters for physicians from a variety of specialties. The Institute for Sex Research, Inc., in Bloomington, Indiana, where Kinsey did his earlier work, has held summer classes for the past several years; and in 1973 Masters and the staff of his Reproductive Biology Foundation in St. Louis began courses to acquaint the professional with what is involved in human sexual response and to provide him with an understanding of sexual dysfunction. These are not being offered to train therapists in the use of Masters and Johnson treatment methods, although in 1971 seven teams of cotherapists were so trained. The senior author was a member of one of these teams and can, therefore, appreciate the technical difficulties involved as well as the high cost in time and money. A number of universities have set up clinics for the treatment of sexual problems. Those who provide treatment in such clinics should have had highly specialized training.

A poll of thirty-nine recognized specialists in the treatment of sexual dysfunction was undertaken by Arvidson (1973) in order to assess the components of competence. Her report is cited here because an understanding of what training and attitudes the therapist must have to be successful provides an ideal base for a discussion of treatment methods, especially since the majority of cases of impotence reported are psychologic in origin. A significant number of the sex experts polled pointed to the following technical requirements for the effective treatment of sexual disorders:

1. A knowledge of the physiology of sexual function and of the organic pathology that can interfere with such function.

2. A knowledge and understanding of interpersonal relationships as they affect sexual function.
3. A knowledge of personality formation and psychiatric disorders.
4. Familiarity with the research and methodology of Masters and Johnson and with methods developed by other authorities in the field of sexual research and treatment.
5. A working knowledge of methods used in behavior modification.

We hold that whatever method may be used to treat sexual dysfunction, the therapist must be able to discuss sexual function with the patient empathically; such capability rests on the therapist's confidence in his or her own sexual identity and sexual competence. Moreover, the therapist should understand not only his own value system in respect to sex but his patient's (which may be quite different), be aware of cultural taboos, and recognize that the society in which we live has promoted a number of false beliefs that can cause considerable anxiety and misgiving. Among these are the following masculine notions:

1. It is the function of the male to satisfy the female partner.
2. A real man can achieve an erection rapidly under any circumstances, even in a casual male–female encounter.
3. The size and firmness of the erection are necessary determinants of the female partner's satisfaction, and any deficit in either automatically causes failure in sexual intercourse.
4. The number of ejaculations of which a man will be capable during his lifetime is limited, and excessive masturbation can exhaust a man's potential by his early middle age.

Unfortunately, many women reinforce their partner's sense of inadequacy because of their own value systems and attitudes, which often are based on the following feminine notions:

1. It is a man's duty to be available for sex and to manage to give his partner orgasm in intercourse.
2. A man's failure to achieve an erection indicates not only a diminution of affection for his partner but in all probability his involvement with another woman.
3. A man should know instinctively how to please a woman despite the fact that during sexual activity her pleasure in different kinds of caresses may change from moment to moment.

The distress of the impotent man can be understood against the background of such commonly accepted ideas. Inasmuch as our culture reinforces the view that adequate sexual performance is an index of manhood, sexual impotence seriously reduces self-confidence and self-esteem. Since his feeling of inadequacy may deter the impotent man from seeking treatment—or even prevent his acknowledging to his physician that he is sexually dysfunctional—it is important to include questions about sexual activity in the taking of any medical history, whether in connection with a routine physical examination or any other type of medical consultation. It is likely that the impotent male will respond to such questions with shame, fear, guilt, anger, bitterness, or resentment; he may, however, achieve a veneer of apparent disinterest and acceptance that serves to conceal such feelings.

The physician who takes time to probe into the sexual experience of his male patients is likely to uncover cases of impotence that otherwise would go unreported. Much depends on his skill and acumen. The physician disinclined to pursue such matters, either because he lacks the necessary special training or is personally inhibited, will do well to make referral to an appropriate treatment agency, where reversal of the dysfunction may be accomplished by others.

The physician treating an impotent patient must guard the confidentiality of the relationship. Such treatment should not be attempted by a physician who is himself struggling with sexual difficulty or who is uncomfortable in such concerns, since a nonjudgmental attitude, a desire to help, and the ability to listen patiently and alertly are crucial in the eliciting of the patient's history.

No treatment should be initiated until the cause is determined (Cooper, 1972b). One is well advised to consider physiopathology until the possibility of this has been ruled out. Too often it is the case that organic causes are not searched for relentlessly enough. We do not suggest that every impotent male undergo a full endocrine work-up at great cost of time, energy, and money, but painstaking care in obtaining the history and conducting the physical examination may arouse the suspicion of metabolic dysfunction. Screening tests such as the "SMA 12"* can be extremely useful in exposing gross pathology and may provide subtle clues that suggest the need for referral to experts in endocrinology, urology, or neurology. A clinic for sexual disorders, if medically oriented, should provide the skills necessary to determine whether the patient's dysfunction has a medical or psychologic basis. In some cases, a trial of psychologic treatment will be necessary to test the possibility of psychologic causation.

Who Should Treat Impotence?

The primary physician is the logical therapist, particularly when the onset has been acute, connected possibly with an alcoholic binge, or the acute trauma of honeymoon failure. A simple, brief explanation, given by a trusted physician already known to the patient, may be all that is required if the impotence was occasioned by the man's feeling required to perform while overcome by anxiety or stress, for example.

Since the partner of an impotent male may ask her gynecologist for advice about how and where to refer him for treatment, he has both a special responsibility and opportunity, and the urologist or internist who can afford the time to do so may treat acute cases of impotence successfully. Chronicity of the symptom, however, usually demands referral to specialists in sexual dysfunction.

---

*SMA 12 Screening Test: Calcium, inorganic phosphate, glucose (two-hour postprandial), blood urea nitrogen, uric acid, cholesterol, total protein, albumin, globulin and A/G ratio, total bilirubin, alkaline phosphatase, lactic dehydrogenase, and serum glutamic oxaloacetic transaminase. A four-hour glucose tolerance test is indicated for all impotent males.

Strategies of Therapy

Since this discussion has noted the importance of physical disease, we will discuss under initial treatments the reversal of a correctable illness whose presence is the prime determinant of the impotence.

Endocrinologic illnesses, such as hypothyroidism, which do not have irreversible chemical or structural change, provide a model for the illness where replacement therapy reverses the general symptoms and the specific complaint of impotence. Attention is directed to Table 2. Where there is structural damage such as neuropathy, as with advanced diabetes mellitus, bringing the patient under chemical balance will not reverse this structural damage. Consequently, the symptom of impotence will persist with these two models of acute and chronic illness. The reader can determine those conditions that may remit with appropriate treatment of the primary disease.

Drug-Induced Impotence

Antihypertensives, diuretics, phenothiazines, and certain other tricyclic antidepressants can lead to erective failures (Bulpitt and Dollery, 1973. Appropriate substitution of other drugs with different pharmacologic bases but providing equally good symptom relief can produce good correction of impotence.

Impotence as a Sequel to Medical Illnesses

The cardiac patient exemplifies the damage ignorance can do to sexual happiness. It is important that he understand his physiologic capacity lest fear of a heart attack render him impotent. "Heart rate, blood pressure and minute ventilation increase progressively during arousal and intromission, peak rapidly during orgasm and decrease to control levels just as rapidly during resolution" (Eliot and Miles, 1973). Angina, which occurs most frequently during resolution, may be prevented by the prophylactic use of nitroglycerin. Propranolol can be taken to lower the heart rate and the systemic pressure. Eliot and Miles (1973) found that if the cardiac patient can walk on a treadmill at three to four miles per hour, climb stairs, or complete a single Master 2-step test without symptoms of undue elevation of blood pressure, heart rate, or electrocardiographic changes, his exercise capacity is equal to the energy demands of sexual intercourse. It is advised that intercourse take place in familiar surroundings and without prolonged use of arms and legs. It is not recommended after a heavy meal or when the patient is intoxicated. Since any circumstance about which an involved individual lacks working information can produce so much fear and anxiety that he is unable to perform, the man with heart problems, in particular, is entitled to sound sex advice.

One may also consider here the effect on the man of the surgical mutilation made necessary for his partner by malignant or other disease. When a man shuns intercourse with a wife who has a colostomy, for example, individual therapy often is less helpful than therapy for both partners in a group. The expression by each within a sympathetic group of guilt, shame, fear, and embarrassment can, with appropriately supportive therapy, often reverse the situation.

The spouse's libido must be taken into account in providing treatment for the aging patient, since it is scarcely beneficial to increase a man's desire if his partner is unable to meet his needs. Although hormone therapy may be used to improve male hormonal levels, prudence is required in prescribing hormones, since excessive stimulation could produce an artificial rejuvenation that would have social consequences. Moreover, the administration of hormones in unwise amounts can cause benign prostatic hypertrophy and coronary artery disease.

Where organic causes have been identified and these are surgically reversible or amenable to medication for the correction of chemical imbalance, the choice of treatment is obvious. For example, chromophobe adenoma of the pituitary may reveal itself by reduction of sexual drive accompanied by ejaculatory incompetence and inability to sustain erection. The treatment of choice here would be treating the primary lesion and then appropriate testosterone replacement therapy. Brief psychologic counseling also may be indicated whenever a process of reeducation in active sexual behavior is taking place.

Where tactile stimulation is needed in excess of that produced by manual stimulation of the penis, an electrical vibrator such as is commercially available at many drugstores may be used to increase the level of stimulation. The novelty and increased vibration, if used on the penis by a female partner, may lead to an increased rigidity of the penis. If the vibrator is applied at the perineum between the base of the scrotum and the anus simultaneously while the penis is masturbated, the speed of ejaculation is increased. Any gains, however, usually are transitory and this method is described for the purpose of completeness only.

Prosthetic implants may be used when organic treatment holds out no hope and psychotherapy has failed. They do not produce ejaculations but facilitate intromission with a flaccid penis. Polyethylene implants securely covered with soft tissue (Morales et al., 1973) are well tolerated. Their semirigidity permits slight lateral and cephalad mobility. They function and look better placed between the tunica albuginea and corpora cavernosa rather than between the Buck's fascia and tunica albuginea.

Candidates for implant should have good sexual desire, normal sensation in the phallus, and a capacity for some type of orgasm, since the prosthesis only assists copulation. Valuable in impotence due to diabetes mellitus, priapism, Peyronie's disease, penile trauma, pelvic surgery, and in some instances of neurologic disease and idiopathic impotence, the prosthesis occasionally causes complications, such as aseptic necrosis, lymphatic edema, hemorrhage, herniation of the lip of the tunica albuginea because of an inappropriate length, or ulceration of the corona of the glans. It is inconspicuous and bulging need not be feared.

A training device for coitus, a metal splint held in place by elastic bands, has been used to permit intromission with a flaccid penis. Resort to this will serve the patient with intractable impotence if he has a sympathetic partner.

Treatment with One Therapist

Cooper (1968c) works with impotence by trying to remove whatever factors prevent the patient from reaching normal sexual capacity. His approach provides an environment made optimally favorable for sexual success by combining physical and psychologic stimuli; sex education to correct false information and to acquaint the patient with the anatomy, physiology, psychology, and technique; psychotherapy to reassure the man and encourage him to become aware of and able to express his feelings; and exercises in progressive muscle relaxation to promote equilibrium between the sympathetic and parasympathetic systems. Using this type of treatment, he was able to effect improvement in nearly half his patients. Success was correlated with cooperation from the spouse, heterosexual drive, and the recency of symptomatology (Cooper, 1972a).

Another way of treating impotence, though not one we recommend, is to blame some physical condition and allay fear and anxiety about "inadequacy" by this means. The patient may be told he has prostatitis and that he should abstain from liquor, spicy foods, sex, and undue anxiety and should drink more than the usual amount of liquids. When he returns a week later, he is advised that he may have intercourse in relaxed circumstances with extended precoital play but that intromission should not be attempted immediately on erection. It is emphasized that a "failure" does not indicate a problem in the erectile mechanism. Treating the patient this way temporarily removes the pressure for performance and, by attributing failure to something other than his own "inadequacy," removes much of the fear and anxiety he has experienced. This technique utilizes the power of suggestion but also reduces the performance fear of the male and, as such, may have an initial success. The major objection is that the scientific explanation is untrue, and the later correct explanation may reduce the patient's faith in the physician's integrity and so deny the doctor–patient relationship.

Hormone Therapy Alone

Although hormones have been used for many years to treat impotence, if they are given when impotence is not due to hormone deficiency, they can increase libido without improving performance and thus worsen the patient's plight. Androgen treatment increases the risk of atherosclerosis, coronary thrombosis, and cancer of the prostate. Testosterone or testosterone derivatives should be used only when testosterone levels are low or FSH levels are high. Testosterone cyclopentylpropionate may be given parenterally 150-200 mg at intervals of from two to three weeks (Johnson, 1968). Methyltestosterone can be associated with severe toxic effects. Clomiphene, a nonsteroid triethylene derivative, significantly increases urinary steroid metabolites in males (Cooper, Ismail, Harding, and Love, 1972). Mesterolone, a synthetic androgen, is effective when given orally and is virtually nontoxic in therapeutic dosage. Its androgenic effect is like that of methyltestosterone, but it does not inhibit exogenous testosterone formation or spermatogenesis. Afrodex, an extremely controversial drug, contains 5 mg methyltestosterone, 5 mg yohimbine HCl, and 5 mg nux vomica per capsule (*Medical Letter on Drugs and Therapeutics*, 1968). Although some believe that it is without clinical effect in impotence and serves only as a placebo, others maintain that peak effects appear from two to three weeks after treatment with it is initiated and that it is significantly beneficial. However, it seems that absolute androgen levels are not important to the potency of the male as long as there is a crucial minimum at the receptor site. A recent study revealed that the mean testosterone-binding affinities (as measured by the reciprocal of the quantity of plasma needed to bind 50% of the [^{3}H] testosterone tracer) were similar for impotent, normal, and oligospermic men (Lawrence and Swyer, 1974). In our opinion, this presumption that androgen therapy usually is useless in the treatment of impotence is correct.

A Method Using Hormones and Psychotherapy

Fellman (1974) has been particularly resourceful in developing in his urologic practice a method appropriate for use by any physician willing to examine the patient physically and to prescribe drugs by injection. A reversal rate of 80% was achieved for a specially selected group of patients from which those with physically caused impotence, deeply rooted psychosexual problems, and profound depression or severe marital conflict were excluded. Such exclusions typically leave a large patient population whose impotence has had a reasonably acute onset and classifies as what Fellman calls "reactive impotence"—that condition in which anxiety has compounded the demonstrated inadequacy in a succession of recent failures and the patient has failed to take into account such precipitating factors as debilitating acute illness, physical fatigue following emotional or physical overexertion, alcohol excess, acute and self-limiting emotional depression, or guilt over sexual behavior.

Fellman's method requires a thorough social, physical, and sexual history and, to exclude the possibility of physical cause, a physical examination that includes urinalysis. The physician is advised to exclude, in addition to the various illnesses already mentioned, feminization and generalized atherosclerosis. The integrity of the sacral cord is checked by perineal examination, the bulbocavernosus reflex is tested, and the prostate gland is examined to exclude the possibility of prostatitis or neoplasm, the presence of which would preclude androgen therapy.

The next stage in treatment involves giving the patient a thorough explanation of the absence of physical causality of his impotence and information about the delicacy of the erectile mechanism. The therapist indicates the destructive effects of anxiety regarding the reversibility of the symptom on the actual sexual performance. Eight weekly injections of chorionic gonadotropin are given by the therapist. Acknowledging that the impotent male is not hypogonadal, Fellman states that androgenic agents effect a mood elevation and provide a feeling of well-being often accompanied by an increase in libidinal drive and improvement in sexual performance. The patient is cautioned not to expect response in less than five weeks' time, since it takes that long for the injected hormones to stimulate his testicles to produce male hormones.

This combination of education, reassurance, and hormonal treatment—possibly with placebo effect—along with the support of an authority figure effects significantly greater reversibility than does the usual insight-oriented psychotherapy, according to Fellman.

Behavior Therapy and Behavior Modification

In treating impotence, "the indication for behavior therapy alone appears to be the presence of learned maladaptive behavior without apparent interpersonal stress, and the absence of marked personality disorder or secondary gain" (Friedman and Lipsedge, 1971). In the absence of physical pathology, sexual dysfunction can be regarded as learned. It is maintained internally by anxiety over performance and externally by a nonreinforcing environment (Lobitz and LoPiccolo, 1972). Aversion conditioning, desensitization based on relaxation and reciprocal inhibition, and training in assertive behavior have all been used to treat impotence. Desensitization is accomplished by the systematic evocation of anxiety and the teaching of a relaxed response to it. As the patient learns to tolerate anxiety-producing stimuli, more disturbing ones are presented; the number of desensitization sessions required depends on the complexity of the problem. Deep muscle relaxation may be induced by sodium methohexital. No behavior is incorporated into the patient's repertoire until it can be performed without anxiety during the deconditioning sessions. When homosexuality is a contributory factor, the patient is instructed to masturbate with a male fantasy, replacing it earlier and earlier with a female fantasy until the latter dominates. Pictures may be used if the patient has difficulty with fantasy (LoPiccolo, Stewart, and Watkins, 1972). Training the patient to be assertive in social situations helps him overcome anxiety and social inhibitions.

Obler (1973) working alone with the impotent male, used similar conditions in forty-five-minute weekly sessions. During the first session, a complete sexual history was taken, with special emphasis on social and sexual anxiety-provoking situations. From this history, a hierarchy of anxiety-producing events was catalogued from the least to the greatest anxiety-producing activities. Each patient was asked to abstain from actual sexual events in which he experienced sexual anxiety.

Total body muscular relaxation was taught at the second session, after which, in subsequent sessions, individual items in the hierarchy were imagined for thirty to sixty seconds and repeated twice, at one-minute intervals. Usually eight to ten items were presented at each session, from the least to the most disturbing. The items in the hierarchy at the outset were in the order of twelve per patient, but new items were added from the subject's own sexual experience as treatment progressed. Hierarchies never exceeded twenty-five items and the patients avoided the feared sexual activity until anxiety was not perceived under desensitization. If the imagined sexual activities did not evoke sufficient fear, visual aids of a male failing in intercourse were projected and the patient learned to extinguish this fear by the desensitization technique.

Subsequent sessions were used to develop assertive and social training in relationship to self and the opposite sex by use of further hierarchies, and the patient was asked to report weekly on his improvement in actual social situations outside therapy. Obler (1973) reports that this technique obtained very favorable success rates for impotent men.

Psychotherapy and Psychoanalysis

The impotence of some men reflects deep-rooted personality disorder, psychoneurosis, or psychotic state. In appropriate hands, psychotherapy and psychoanalysis provide the treatment of choice for such men, particularly those with a predisposition to homosexuality. It can also be recommended when a man who enjoys a good relationship with his spouse suffers sufficiently severe intra-psychic difficulty to require psychiatric intervention for relief from inner stress.

Should Therapy Be Given by One Therapist or Two?

Psychologic treatment for impotence traditionally has been given by one therapist, usually a man. Masters and Johnson (1970), however, have stressed the value of using both a male and a female therapist, and treating the "marital unit" of the man and his partner rather than the impotent male by himself. Fifteen of the specialists queried by Arvidson (1973) reported working as sole therapist with their patients, whereas seven others customarily worked with another, usually one of the opposite sex.

The senior author, in another paper, has discussed the advantages of dual therapy in the treatment of sexual dysfunction (Reckless and Fauntleroy, 1974). In establishing such a male–female therapy team, it is essential that each member of the team have a personal experience in the meaning of an enriched sexual life. The team members should have a similar and comparable sexual value system. A sexual value system is defined as the composite of all the learned and experienced sexual values and taboos acquired during biologic and social maturation.

At least one member of the team should be a physician so that as treatment progresses for the impotent male any evidence of underlying physical pathology can be treated. Not all of the apparent cases of psychogenic impotence have only a psychogenic etiology. Neurosis may mask and be concurrent with the emergence of any of the physical illnesses noted in Table 2.

A comparable professional philosophy with respect to each patient must be shown by the two therapists. A cornerstone of the therapy is that both male and female are equal although not necessarily similar in the eyes of the patients. Since dual therapy usually is used in treating a sexually dysfunctional couple, the female usually will model appropriate role behavior for the female patient and a similar task is assigned to the male therapist with the male patient. As treatment progresses, disagreements between the therapists concerning strategy may occur and the need for discussion and consultation sometimes may be necessary in the presence of the couple. The ability of the therapists to model appropriate male–female relation-ship activity is very important. Patients observe the nonverbal as well as the verbal activity of the two therapists. The two therapists may well show to the patient different attitudes to the same problem but always with respect for each other's point of view. If disharmony creeps in and persists, it may disrupt the therapeutic effectiveness of the treating couple.

The happiness of the therapy team in working together is important, recognized, protected, and guarded. Some teams are husband and wife and that might work well, but, for others, working with someone other than a spouse might be more helpful and realistic. No scientifically devised studies have been published so far on the advantages and difficulties faced by the husband-and-wife team.

Advantages of dual therapy include: a separate opinion on the management of each case, a representation of the point of view of someone of the same sex as to the sexual difficulties and their consequences within a relationship, and a backup therapist if one of the therapists is personally having a difficult day.

The disadvantages are cost, inconvenience, and the energies needed to preserve a total harmony with one's cotherapist for the purpose of preserving an effective team relationship.

The Rapid Treatment Method for Treating Impotence

In 1970, Masters and Johnson reported several concepts contrary to previously prevailing psychiatric therapies. These were that, first, there is no such entity as an individual patient with sexual distress or dysfunction in a two-partner relationship; second, therapy "needed" by one partner must be undertaken by both partners; and third, the marital unit is best treated by a dual therapy team.

For the treatment of the impotent male and his partner, a two-week period of treatment away from day-to-day distraction is an important element of the treatment. The couple are together away from children and jobs and spend a majority of their time with each other. At the outset of treatment, all explicit sexual behaviors are forbidden. The couple are seen for therapy every day by a dual team, one of whom is a physician. Extensive histories are taken, the sexual value systems are determined, and a full physical examination, including pelvic and rectal examinations, is carried out. The SMA 12 blood chemistry is evaluated in each patient. On the second day, the two therapists and the couple have a four-way meeting at which the therapists reiterate the strengths and weaknesses of the couple's relationships and how the impotence reflects a breakdown in biologic and sociologic functioning.

Efforts then are made, on a daily basis, to reestablish more effective communication between the marital partners, who are also taught the functional male and female anatomy and physiology.

As authorities in the field of treatment, the therapists take away any performance demand for erection by the male by impressing on him that he cannot will an erection and that in the presence of muscle and emotional relaxation, erections will occur spontaneously and frequently and that the therapists have no interest in or expectation of the patient performing intercourse at this time. This relieves the patient of the burden of his partner's performance demand.

With the clear understanding that no attempt is to be made to enter the vagina or effect ejaculation, the couple are urged to provide sensuous pleasure for each other through varied touching and stroking of each other's bodies, at first with breast and genitals off limits so that each can enjoy the emotion of sexual arousal without demand.

On subsequent days, the stroking will include tantalizing touches of the penis itself. This technique allows the couple to witness the rise and fall of the erect penis over a period of time so that they learn that if an erection is lost it can be regained and that not every erection must end in intercourse. If the male finds this protracted stimulation discomforting, he may masturbate himself to ejaculation, for penetration must be avoided to allow the male fully to enjoy the teasing. It is usual for the partners to experience wonderment, happiness, and confident anticipation of success as the erections recur.

Usually between the fifth and eighth days, penetration is effected with the female in the astride position sliding back on the penis and arranging the insertion herself. The male can manipulate his penis to help effect penetration. Even if the erection partially subsides, an aroused female can go on to a satisfying sexual experience. The male is aroused, and pleasure at the penile containment may serve as a powerful stimulant to the male's erection and climax. The female is asked to sit quietly and allow the husband to thrust slowly as she enjoys the sensation of containment, while the two partners interact sexually with mutuality of interest and the absence of anxiety or demand from either party.

This method achieves a reversed rate of 59% for primary impotence and 73.8% for secondary impotence.

Although this technique developed by Masters and Johnson focuses largely on the communication in the relationship, the unlearning of feared sexual behavior and its replacement by successful sexual arousal, erections, and vaginal–penile containment often lead to ejaculation and climax occurring in a very nonthreatening, supportive, and trusting environment during the two-week treatment period.

Transference as such is not encouraged, nor are the therapists treating any psychopathology within either partner. It is the relationship that is important and efforts are consistently made to remove whatever factors impair that relationship so that communication and trust are established and affirmed.

Failures do occur and couples who reveal extensive and unyielding psychopathology in the relationship that was not evident in the referral process are sent home prior to completion of the two-week period.

Treatment Alternatives in a Community Practice

Not every impotent male can provide a partner nor can he go away for treatment. The senior author has developed several treatment strategies for such occurrences.

Thorough personal screening is the first prerequisite. All new referrals are seen for extensive history and physical examination. If the impotence is a sign of characterologic and neurotic distress, where the chances for continued reversal of the erective difficulty are unlikely to continue after the supportive and persuasive effect of the two-week treatment method, the patient is referred to other programs within the practice. This same recommendation is made for an impotent male without a partner. If the impotence is a reflection of a difficult marital relationship or of severe psychopathology in either partner, the couple is screened out of the two-week program.

Our criteria for the two-week program are (1) a basically compatible though disordered partner relationship, (2) impotence secondary to misinformation and ignorance, or (3) a recent onset of impotence. (After several years, the female may well have responded negatively so that the male partner's attitudes need more than two weeks to be reversed.)

The profession needs to know that although the techniques developed by Masters and Johnson work in the context of a well-trained dual team, they will not work as well for therapists who merely read the book and apply the principles. In a two-week period there is a little margin for error in judgment. A case may fail secondary to misunderstanding of the importance of daily communication or the firm requirement that the couple remain within the behavioral retraining program enjoined by the therapists. of the 5,000 clinics offering sex therapy, it is Masters and Johnson's opinion that as few as 50 may be qualified by skill to ensure success. The senior author, who has been trained and who has practiced over a three-year period under the tutelage of Dr. Masters and Mrs. Johnson, can attest to the subtle skills needed to reverse sexual dysfunctioning in a rapid-treatment program, as well as the need for supervision in the learning process of becoming a therapist in the rapid-treatment method.

The impotent male not meeting our criteria for the two-week program may be treated by several modifications of the original method.

1. The male with a partner who has characterologic or neurotic problems who needs more than two weeks to undergo the program as outlined above will be seen for one week on a daily basis and then brought back every ten days to consolidate the gains for a total of thirteen visits over a sixty-day period. This would seem to ensure a greater continuing success rate.

2. If the impotence exists in the fabric of a severely disordered marital union, the couple will be accepted in a two-week format of a daily crisis-oriented program that utilizes the communicational tools and nonverbal sexual focus techniques to further marital and sexual harmony. The couple will be informed that the sessions with the therapists may last several hours each day. There, the frequent format is both psychotherapeutic and behavioral and can be a most useful adjunctive tool in a therapist's armamentarium.

3. If the impotence is situational in that the male can function sexually with other partners but not with his spouse, he may be seen in individual therapy or jointly with his wife, if she is aware of the situation, in order to resolve his thoughts and feelings over his marital lot.

4. If the impotent male has a clinical depression, vigorous antidepressant prescription with the tricyclic antidepressants along with brief counseling of the partners may be all that is required to reverse the symptom with perhaps six visits over a three-month period.

5. If the male does not have a partner, we have used group therapy on a weekly two-hour basis to establish an adult reeducative experience involving exposure to heterosexual relationships, the group being composed of men and women suffering from some form of sexual dysfunction. Patients learn from one another in a social and occasional spontaneous extragroup fashion what is required to function effectively sexually. Weekend marathon experiences of forty-eight hours of leader-led and leaderless group exposure intensify the experience (Reckless and Fauntleroy, 1974).

Surrogate Partners

Where the impotent male is unmarried, he may be accompanied by the partner of his choice. If there exists a trust relationship, any of the appropriate treatment programs may be used. If his replacement partner is a paid replacement, treatment may be unsuccessful except where novelty and "tricks" exert a positive effect on erection.

Some practitioners have utilized paramedical females to act as professional replacement partners and this is considered by some to be effective. However, the practitioner utilizing such partners faces societal negatives that may be severe or restricting.

Surrogates are useful for the male where impotence is secondary to faulty education, negative learning, and sexual ineptness.

Masters and Johnson (1970) report that in their use of surrogate partners, female surrogates with sexually inadequate males achieved approximately equal success in the reversal of the sexual dysfunction as was true in those cases in which the sexually dysfunctional males were treated in conjunction with their wives. There clearly is a need for a female partner who can share the patient's concern for success, cooperate in the physical application of suggestions presented in therapy, and exemplify different levels of female response. Such a woman should be completely responsive sexually, secure in her female role and as much like a supportive, interested and cooperative wife as possible (Masters and Johnson, 1970). These women receive intensive indoctrination in the psychology and physiology of male sexual dysfunction, and the identity of both patient and surrogate is guarded carefully.

Hypnotherapy

A few practitioners use hypnotherapy, but such treatment should be used only by skilled individuals who can combine a knowledge of hypnotic theory with conventional psychotherapeutic skills.

Conclusion

This discussion has concentrated on disorders of impotence rather than on premature ejaculation or ejaculatory incompetence, although the latter can cause avoidance of intercourse and cause secondary impotence. Techniques for dealing with premature ejaculation, especially those developed by Semans (1956), have made this condition almost invariably reversible, and the same can be said for ejaculatory incompetence.

A review of treatment methods indicates that, with the exception of psychotherapy and psychoanalysis, almost all derive from the inspired work of William H. Masters and Virginia Johnson. The work of those who follow in the field of treatment of sexual dysfunction has benefited inestimably from their efforts.

Although long-term follow-up is hard to define in respect to the treatment of impotence, it now can be said that impotence that is secondary and/or of acute onset in the young male now is reversible, and primary impotence can be reversed more readily than before with strictly followed behavioral techniques.

However, since sexual behavior and performance are a physiologic birthright exercised in accordance with psychologic factors, the impact of life events and the quality of relationship with a particular partner will be a determinant of reversal or regression in impotence. For some men, impotence will be a recurring lifetime problem in which these relationships must be taken into account.

One should not conclude a discussion of a severe human problem without considering the importance of prophylaxis. It is clearly necessary to provide good, honest, realistic education—for the lay public as well as for physicians and medical students—about human sexuality if the fears and anxiety associated with the experience or anticipation of impotence are to be relieved. Regardless of the cause, impotence is terrifying to the man who lacks understanding of sexuality and sexual behavior.

References

Arvidson, D. *Treatment of sexual dysfunction: Preparation and training of therapists.* Master's thesis, University of Calgary, Canada, 1973.

Bulpitt, C. J., and Dollery, C. T. Side effects of hypotensive agents elicited by a self-administered questionnaire. *British Medical Journal,* 1973, *3,* 485.

Cooper, A. J. Neurosis and disorders of sexual potency in the male. *Journal of Psychosomatic Research,* 1968, *12,* 141. (a)

Cooper, A. J. Hostility and male potency disorders. *Comprehensive Psychiatry,* 1968, *9,* 621. (b)

Cooper, A. J. A factual study of male potency disorders. *British Journal of Psychiatry,* 1968, *114,* 719. (c)

Cooper, A. J. A clinical study of "coital anxiety" in male potency disorders. *Journal of Psychosomatic Research,* 1969, *13,* 143.

Cooper, A. J. The causes and management of impotence. *Postgraduate Medical Journal,* 1972, *98,* 548. (a)

Cooper, A. J. Diagnosis and management of "endocrine impotence." *British Medical Journal,* 1972, *2,* 34. (b)

Cooper, A. J., Ismail, A. A. A., Harding, T., and Love, D. R. Effect of clomiphene in impotence. *British Journal of Psychiatry,* 1972, *120,* 327.

Dingman, J. F. Endocrine aspects of impotence. *Medical Aspects of Human Sexuality,* 1969, *3, 4,* 57.

Eliot, R. J., and Miles, R. What to tell the cardiac patient about sexual intercourse. *Cardiology Consultant,* September 1973, pp. 23–25.

Espir, M. L. E., Hall, T. W., Shirreffs, J. G., and Stevens, D. L. Impotence in farm workers using toxic chemicals. *British Medical Journal,* 1970, *1,* 423.

Faerman I., et al. Impotence and diabetes: Studies of androgenic function in diabetic impotent males. *Diabetes,* 1972, *21,* 23.

Fellman, S. L. In D. W. Absc, E. Nash, and L. M. R. Louden (Eds.), *Marital and sexual counseling in medical practice.* Hagerstown, Maryland: Harper & Row, 1974.

Freud, S. *Collected papers* (Vol. 110). London: Hogarth, 1950.

Friedman, D. E., and Lipsedge, M. S. Treatment of phobic anxiety and psychogenic impotence by systematic desensitization employing methohexitone. *British Journal of Psychiatry,* 1971, *118,* 89.

Gaskell, P. The importance of penile blood pressure in cases of impotence. *Canadian Medical Association Journal,* 1971, *105,* 1047.

Gold, F., and Hotchkiss, R. Sexual potency following a simple prostatectomy. *New York Journal of Medicine,* 1969, *69,* 2987.

Greenblatt, D. J., and Koch-Weser, J. Gynecomastia and impotence: Complications of ipirandoctone therapy. *Journal of the American Medical Association,* 1973, *223,* 82.

Hallbook, T., and Holmquist, B. Sexual disturbances following dissection of the aorta and the common disc arteries. *Journal of Cardiovascular Surgery,* 1970, *11,* 255.

Hastings, D. W. *Impotence and frigidity.* Boston: Little, Brown, 1963.

Johnson, J. *Disorders of sexual potency in the male.* New York: Pergamon, 1968.

Kancz, L., and Bdodims, M. C. Impotence in diabetes mellitus. *Medical Times,* 1970, *98,* 159.

Lawrence, D. M., and Swyer, G. I. M. Plasma testosterone and testosterone binding affinities in men with impotence, oligospermia, azoospermia and hypogonadism. *British Medical Journal,* 1974, *1,* 349.

Lewis, J. M. Impotence as a reflection of marital conflict. *Medical Aspects of Human Sexuality,* 1969, *3,* 73.

Lobitz, C., and LoPiccolo, J. L. New methods in the behavioral treatment of sexual dysfunction. *Journal of Behavior Therapy and Experimental Psychiatry,* 1972, *39,* 265.

LoPiccolo, J., Stewart, R., and Watkins, B. Treatment of erectile failure and ejaculatory incompetence of homosexual etiology. *Journal of Behavior Therapy and Experimental Psychiatry,* 1972, *39,* 233.

Masters, W. H., and Johnson, V. E. The sex response of the human male. *Western Journal of Surgery*, 1963, *71*, 85.

Masters, W. H., and Johnson, V. E. *Human sexual inadequacy.* Boston: Little, Brown, 1970.

Medical Letter on Drugs and Therapeutics, The (Vol. 10). New York: Drug and Therapeutic Information, 1968. P. 97.

Morales, P. A., Ducrez, J. B., Delgado, J., and Whitehead, E. D. Penile implants after erective impotence. *Urology*, 1973, *109*, 641.

Norris, H. J., and Yunis, E. Age characteristics of seminal vesicles and vasa deferentia in diabetes. *Archives of Pathology*, 1964, *77*, 126.

Obler, M. Systematic desensitization in sexual disorders. *Journal of Behavior Therapy and Experimental Psychiatry*, 1973, *4*, 93.

Pfeiffer, E., Verwoerdt, A., and Wang, H. S. Sexual behavior in senescence. *Journal of Geriatric Psychology*, 1969, *11*, 175.

Reckless, J. B., and Fauntleroy, A. D. Treatment of sexual dysfunction: Dual therapy team approach. In D. W. Abse, E. Nash, and L. M. R. Louden (Eds.), *Marital and sexual counseling in medical practice.* Hagerstown, Maryland: Harper & Row, 1974. Pp. 127–133.

Rowan, R. L., and Hanley, T. F. The electrical pain response in impotence. *Journal of Urology*, 1965, *94*, 92.

Schoffling, K., Federlin, K., Ditschuniet H., and Pfeiffer, E. F. Disorders of sexual function in male diabetics. *Diabetes*, 1963, *12*, 519.

Semans, J. Premature ejaculation: A new approach. *Southern Medical Journal*, 1956, *46*, 353.

Simpson, G. M., Blane, J. H., and Amoso, D. Effect of antidepressants on genito-urinary function. *Diseases of the Nervous System*, 1965, *26*, 787.

Stafford-Clark, D. The aetiology and treatment of impotence. *Practitioner*, 1954, *172*, 397.

Strauss, E. B. Impotence from the psychiatric standpoint. *British Medical Journal*, 1950, *1*, 697.

Wilson, J. D., and Gloyna, R. E. The intra-nuclear metabolism of testosterone in the necessary organs of reproduction. *Recent Progress in Hormone Research*, 1970, *26*, 309.

In this chapter, Cooper reviews the available literature on treatment of male sexual dysfunction. Although this article is somewhat dated (1972), it remains valuable for its review of various psychotherapeutic approaches to male dysfunction.

It is of interest to note Cooper's suggested explanation for the failure of analytic therapy in most cases of impotence: lack of involvement of the female sexual partner in therapy.

The discussion of various patient characteristics that predict success or failure in treatment is valuable for the practicing clinician. One aspect of sex therapy that needs research is the issue of which patients benefit from which type of therapy. Given that the sex therapy procedures are generally quite effective, cases that do not respond to treatment should be carefully studied and described, in an attempt to develop more effective procedures.

25

Treatments of Male Potency Disorders: The Present Status

Alan J. Cooper

Introduction

Man's preoccupation with his masculinity and sexual prowess and his deep-rooted fear of impotence has been recorded by medical and nonmedical writers of every civilization since the dawn of history. (For recent substantive reviews or "review type" contributions on various aspects of potency and potency disorders see for example Cooper, 1967, 1968; Johnson, 1964; El-Senoussi, Coleman, and Tauber, 1959; Kinsey, Pomeroy, and Martin, 1948; Masters and Johnson, 1966.) Despite, however, the enormous volume of opinion on every facet of potency disorders that ranges diversely from a(nthropologic) to z(oologic), for one reason or another, authoritative factual information is even today sadly lacking. It is perhaps ironic that nowhere is this more true than in that area that is of the greatest potential medical significance, namely, the clinical problem of treatment; the bulk of the literature is often anecdotal, confusing, and conflicting; hard data are sparse or nonexisting.

Alan J. Cooper • Department of Psychiatry, St. Mary's Hospital Medical School, University of London, London, England

The present article, which reviews a representative sample of the literature on the treatment and prognoses of male potency disorders, asks and, it is hoped, provides some answers to the following questions: (a) What treatments are currently available? (b) What are their respective indications and therapeutic merits? (c) What associated factors (social, psychological, etc.) influence the outcome?

In the past fifty years or so, numerous and diverse treatments have been introduced for potency disorders; many, fashionable at the time, were later discarded either (a) as ineffective or (b) because of their prohibitive cost in time and money.

In the case of impotence and impotentia ejaculandi (failure to ejaculate during coitus in the presence of normal erection and desire) (Johnson, 1964), a by no means exhaustive list includes: surgical ligation of the dorsal vein of the penis and urethral cautery (Lydston, 1908/ 1963), a penile splint or brace (Lowenstein, 1947), male sex hormones (Tuthill, 1955; Hamilton, 1937), hydrotherapy, tonics, and electrotherapy and sedatives, including alcohol (Schapiro, 1947), central nervous system stimulants, including yohimbine, strychnine, marihuana, amphetamines, and LSD (Cooper, 1967; Tuthill, 1955; Allen, 1962), and foodstuffs with allegedly aphrodisiac properties; among the less exotic and most available in a Western culture are oysters and truffles (MacDougald, 1967).

More recently, unless a clear "organic" or "constitutional" cause could be established, reflecting the consensus (but unproven) view that impotence is usually "psychogenically" determined, treatments have increasingly tended to be psychotherapy of some sort or other, directed at one, the other, or both sexual partners. Psychotherapies in current use include: formal psychoanalysis and psychoanalytically oriented psychotherapy (Gutheil, 1959; Rees, 1935), psychotherapy by reciprocal inhibition—"behavior therapy" (Cooper, 1963; Rachman, 1961), and superficial psychotherapy consisting essentially of sexual education, explanation, and reassurance (Stafford-Clark, 1954).

For premature ejaculation, which has been considered perhaps by many as more "somatic" than "psycho," most therapies have tended on the whole to be pharmacologically and/or behaviorally oriented; although some purely psychological procedures remain in vogue, treatments include formal psychoanalysis (Gutheil, 1959; Abraham, 1949), "behavior therapy" with or without the simultaneous use of sedative or tranquilizer drugs (Wolpe, 1958; Friedman, 1968; Cooper, 1969), application of a local anesthetic to the glans (Aycock, 1949), and various drugs including sedatives and tonics (Schapiro, 1947), the MAOI antidepressants, isocarboxazid (Marplan) (Santanelli, 1960) and iproniazid (Marsilid) (Santanelli, 1960), and the phenothiazine thioridazine (Mellaril) (Santanelli, 1960), and various "physiological" treatments (Tuthill, 1955; Semans, 1956). No evaluation of the present status of treatments for male potency disorders would be complete without mentioning the still-evolving and controversial fourteen-day continuous therapy designed by Masters and Johnson (1964). Their method, applied by male and female cotherapists, is fundamentally based on "full and frank communication" between the partners and subsequent concern with improving stimulative techniques; it is a logical extension of the research findings published in *Human Sexual Response.*

In order to provide some rational basis for comparing the respective efficacy of the many therapies to be considered, unless stated otherwise, it has been assumed that each has fulfilled its own theoretical and technical requirements and that in each case it has been administered optimally by an experienced practitioner, adequately trained in its methodology.

Depth Psychotherapies

Psychoanalysis and psychoanalytically oriented psychotherapy (and other depth psychotherapies) that are used most often in psychoneurotics and personality-disordered individuals assume that the potency disorder is symptomatic of underlying, often deeply unconscious motives or conflicts. Permanent amelioration of the symptom is held to occur only if basic changes in personality structure are effected. However, despite its vociferous advocates and apparent patient appeal, it is difficult or impossible to comment on its efficacy; most of the claims made for it are based on single or a few case studies, or merely stated as theoretical (but nonetheless categorically so) assertions without any supporting data.

The present author believes that classical analysis, which may take up to three years to complete, should not even be entertained for potency-disordered males. The reasons for this are: (a) It is prohibitive in time and money (the author contends that any psychiatric therapy to be seriously judged as effective should produce improvement within one year. This is especially important in insidious-onset, long-standing impotence occurring in middle-aged males where a progressive and rapidly waning sex drive may prohibit a therapeutic response; unless this is achieved quickly, what little motivation there might be for change rapidly dissipates). (b) In previously published studies on vaginismus (Friedman, 1962), and frigidity (Lazarus, 1963; Brady, 1966) and male potency disorders (Cooper, 1969b), the maximum therapeutic results were attained within three to six months in each case; thereafter, further improvement was negligible or absent. This perhaps is surprising since the therapies employed were widely different in orientation, being respectively "analytic" (Friedman, 1962) and "behavioristic" (Lazarus, 1963; Brady, 1966; Cooper, 1969b). This suggests perhaps that the precise composition of treatment is less important than has been hitherto thought. (c) The requirements of analysis specifically preclude the active participation in therapy of the female spouse; this, hardly surprising, has been shown to be crucial in treating impotence (Cooper, 1969b; Masters and Johnson, 1970).

Specific references to the use of psychoanalysis in impotence include those of the pioneering giants Freud (1910/1957) and Stekel (1927) and many others (e.g., Allen, 1962; Gutheil, 1959; Rees, 1935; Abraham, 1949; Jones, 1919; Ellis, 1948). For example, Freud stated: "We are usually able to make a confident promise of recovery to the psychically impotent . . . with the exception of cases involving a typically masochistic attitude, perhaps embedded since infancy." Jones (1919) believed that impotence was an exceedingly common neurosis in man and was readily curable by psychoanalysis, etc. Rees (1935), who advocated suggestion and education "for simple cases" and detailed investigation and analysis for "serious cases," was the first to devote a complete paper to the wider issue of prognosis: On the basis of his clinical experience he cited age, duration of symptoms, intelligence of the patient, degree of desire for change or cure, social situation, and, most important, the severity of the coincident psychoneurotic symptoms as factors affecting the outcome. Rees obviously considered some factors to be of greater importance than others. For example, he believed that intelligence was often more important than age. He commented, "An intelligent man of seventy years, who has suffered a sexual neurosis (impotence) for twenty years may get perfectly well. . . ." Rees clearly and very properly recognized the crucial role of the female in the treatment and ultimately the prognosis of impotence. He considered that "readjustment" was difficult or impossible if the spouse was "demanding, unsympathetic, or querulous." Rees, without giving any figures, estimated a cure rate for impotence of 76%; he considered it "a less serious affliction."

Gutheil (1959) considered that the outcome of treatment in impotence was, on the whole, good, but he gave no figures to support his views. He contended that the extent of improvement was limited by the patient's sex drive, which he believed could not be modified (increased) to any degree. Accordingly, he defined the therapist's role as removing the inhibitory forces that prevented satisfactory sexual performance. Gutheil placed great emphasis on the patient's motivation and the degree of cooperation from the sexual partner, which he considered was a prerequisite of a successful outcome. He believed that if the sexual partners had no real affection for each other, or if the situation was complicated by an extramarital affair, then the prospect of a favorable outcome was bleak.

Increasing age and an impotence that had persisted for many years were further bad prognostic signs. Interestingly, Gutheil, who advocated psychoanalysis as the treatment of choice, considered that an "exploratory interview" with the female spouse was often a useful procedure. He elaborated, however, that if therapy was also shown to be indicated for her, this should be undertaken by a different analyst. Simultaneous treatment of both as a "sexual unit" by the same therapist was apparently inadmissible.

Allen (1962), in a textbook on psychosexual disorders exceeding 400 pages, allocated less than ten lines to personal observations, related to the prognosis of impotence. He generalized: "In my opinion the psycho-sexual disorders (including impotence) are as capable of treatment as any other neurosis." Then somewhat contradictorily, he continued, "Impotence is difficult to cure if due to primary sexual hypo-aversion or aversion. Excluding the simple impotence . . . most impotence is of this type." This author considered that patients who had never experienced sexual desire in any form, or who had never masturbated, were untreatable.

Allen did not indicate what he considered was the cure rate of disorders of potency, but suggested that intensive individual psychotherapy, including psychoanalysis, achieved the best results. For "prolonged" or "congenital" impotence, he advocated deep analysis. Allen was among many authorities (e.g., Ellis, 1948; Neustatter, 1953; Fenichel, 1953; Hirschfeld, 1944) who considered that, irrespective of the type of therapy, the prognosis was significantly worsened if impotence was associated with sexual inversion. Thus, he stated that sadism, masochism, transvestism, fetishism, and especially homosexuality all adversely influenced the outcome of deranged (coital) potency. However, he maintained that perversion, being largely the product of nurture rather than nature, was potentially reversible by appropriate therapy (analytic psychotherapy). Allen, however, did not underestimate the importance of adequate motivation in influencing the outcome of the perversion, and ultimately the impotence. He stated: "The majority of homosexuals who are seriously concerned about their condition and willing to work to improve it may . . . be distinctly helped to achieve a more satisfactory heterosexual situation." Other authors (Ellis, 1948; Neustatter, 1953; Curran, 1954; Kraft-Ebbing, 1951; Hemphill, Leith, and Stuart, 1958) considered perversions in general and homosexuality in particular to have a predominantly constitutional basis; these writers were less optimistic than Allen about the restoration of potency in such cases. These few examples are generally indicative of the psychoanalytic standpoint with respect to impotence; dogmatic statements as to its efficacy abound, but hard data are lacking. Accordingly, the case for its usefulness at this time remains unproven.

Superficial Psychotherapies

Superficial psychotherapy differs fundamentally from psychoanalysis (and other "depth procedures") in its level of intervention; this is generally at the manifest (neurotic) symptom itself, rather than the underlying personality structure. It is also very likely to be briefer in its time of application ($<$ 1 year). In the present article, the term is used generically to include such apparently unrelated and often predominantly nonverbal procedures as various physiologic maneuvers, behavior therapy, and sexual education and reassurance, etc.

Tuthill (1955), who believed that most cases of impotence and impotentia ejaculandi were physiologic in origin, considered that their prognoses were good. He elaborated: "Sexual impotence is generally regarded as a psychological disorder. . . . To assume that it is caused by a failure of emotional relationships and that treatment should be directed to adjusting these relationships is, I am sure, unwise." Tuthill, who believed that most cases of impotence could be ascribed to severe inhibition, the product of culturally imbued taboos, stated with some eloquence: "These men (impotents) approach their wives in a spirit of pure love." For therapy, Tuthill recommended that such a man should "retrace the steps of courtship, which in some cases, he may have never trod at all"; specifically, he advocated the couple spending more time in bed together and for the male to concern himself with experiencing and enhancing the sensual pleasures of the act, rather than with his performance per se. Tuthill urged abandoning restraint, increased sexual experimentation, and the incorporation of his sexual fantasies into actual sexual practices. In addition, in some cases, Tuthill prescribed testosterone implants, and various stimulants including a proprietary tablet containing amphetamine sulphate, strychnine, arsenic, and yohimbine. Tuthill, who rarely saw patients more than a few times, on the basis of a postal return claimed 136 out of 257 (57%) of impotents and 6 out of 12 (50%) with impotentia ejaculandi were satisfied with their improvement (96 of the former group failed to reply or were not treated; the present author has included these in the failed category). Tuthill did not consider individual prognostic factors.

Stafford-Clark (1954), without providing any supporting data, stated that "at least 50% of cases of impotence presenting in the psychiatric clinic can be satisfactorily treated with a dozen interviews." His interviews would appear to have consisted essentially of education, support, and reassurance and information on coital techniques, etc. As far as can be gauged, no serious attempt was made to change personality structure. Stafford-Clark distinguished "simple" cases from "complicated" ones, in which impotence was the presenting symptom of a "serious deep-seated neurosis or personality disorder"; this latter type, he believed had the poorer prognosis; Stafford-Clark emphasized the importance of positive motivation in both "simple" and "complicated" cases. However, he does not elaborate further.

Johnson's contribution (Johnson, 1965) although retrospective, is valuable and informative. He rightly pointed out that since many psychiatric disorders run a fluctuating course with spontaneous remission and exacerbation, any evaluation of the efficacy of treatment to be truly valid must appreciate and allow for these vicissitudes. He followed up sixty-two patients who presented at the Maudsley Hospital between 1950 and 1959 with primary complaint of disordered potency. Johnson's aim was "to define the natural history of disorders of sexual potency as met in psychiatric practice." His findings suggested that the prognosis for the recovery of potency, with or without treatment, was poor; 66.6% of the cases were unchanged at follow-up (mean follow-up period 5.8 years), 16.7% were improved, and the remaining 16.7% were cured.

He found that patients with impotence (persistent inability to obtain or sustain an erection sufficient to allow orgasm and ejaculation to be satisfactorily concluded during heterosexual coitus) did significantly better than patients with ejaculatory disorders (premature ejaculation or a failure to ejaculate).

A "neurotic constitution" was associated with a poor outcome, as was an "early onset" type of disorder (disorder dating from the first attempt at heterosexual coitus).

The duration of the sexual impairment was very significantly related to outcome. Patients whose condition had lasted two or more years hardly ever showed improvement.

A more favorable outcome was associated with a "late onset" (previously sexually competent), particularly when this was related to engagement, marriage, or some psychophysical stress.

Johnson found a relationship between the outcome and the type of treatment employed. In his series, twenty-three patients did not attend hospital after their initial referral, either because no treatment was advised or because they were considered "poorly motivated." At follow-up, six of these patients were found to be improved. Twelve patients received testosterone therapy; only two were improved. Twenty-one underwent some form of psychotherapeutic treatment such as superficial psychotherapy, group therapy, or counseling; eleven patients were improved at follow-up.

In Johnson's view, the significantly better results from psychotherapy, as compared with other methods of treatment or no treatment, probably reflected a higher degree of motivation on the part of the patient to overcome his difficulty. (The present author considers this interpretation unjustified on the data Johnson offers.)

Cooper (1969b), like Johnson, was dismayed with the absence of factual data in the literature; he therefore embarked on a complementary (uncontrolled) study; its aims were (1) to evaluate the efficacy of short-term (minimum of twenty fortnightly sessions) outpatient therapy in a group of sixty-seven "unselected" male patients who presented in the clinic with a primary complaint of a disorder of sexual potency (i.e., cases referred from any medical source as being completely or predominantly "psychogenic," but excluding those clearly secondary to psychoses, organic pathology, drugs, endocrinopathies, etc.); (2) to examine statistically selected clinical and psychological data (including the majority of factors that recur in the literature as being of prognostic importance) to identify factors associated with the response to treatment; and thereby (3) to suggest a prognostic scale predictive of success or failure of treatment in male potency disorders. The treatment employed, essentially practical and superficial, was directed in the main at the actual symptom of disordered potency rather than at any "underlying" cause; it consisted of an optimum combination of (a) deep muscular relaxation, (b) provision, as far as possible, of optimal sexual stimulation from the female, (c) sexual education, and (d) "psychotherapy"; it was designed and applied flexibly according to the psychopathology in the individual case. Cooper believed that such treatment might be an effective alternative to some of the other more analytical therapies; one of the purposes of the investigation was to test this hypothesis. Treatment sessions were provided fortnightly and lasted approximately 45 minutes; in addition, however, the patients were strongly encouraged to practice deep muscular relaxation daily, at home, for up to thirty minutes.

Out of the original sixty-seven patients, forty-nine (73%) satisfied the "treated criterion" of attending for a minimum of twenty fortnightly interviews during one year. Nineteen of these (39%) were recovered or improved (mean number of sessions to improvement 9.4), while thirty (61%) were unchanged or worse. Factors associated significantly ($p < .05$) with a poor outcome of treatment were: premature ejaculation, insidious onset of impotence, a disorder of long duration (> 2 years), personality abnormality in the male, absence of motivation for therapy, a sex drive other than heterosexual, absence of desire in the coital situation, unwillingness or inability of the female to cooperate in treatment, personality abnormality in the female. A better outcome ($p < .05$) was associated with: acute onset of impotence, a disorder of short duration, a heterosexual sex drive, presence of desire in the coital situation, absence of personality abnormality in the male, marital happiness in the male, a male rating of loving his spouse, motivation for treatment, marital happiness in the female, willingness and ability of the female to cooperate fully in treatment, absence of personality abnormality in the female.

Friedman (1968) is one of the increasing number of psychiatrists who have used behavior therapy in impotence and who give sufficient clinical and follow-up data to allow of meaningful comment. He treated nineteen consecutive patients with a potency disorder at weekly intervals. A graduated list of items concerning imagined situations involving lovemaking was constructed for each case. This began with a comparatively innocuous stimulus—"hand holding"—and progressed through a range of situations of increasing anxiety-evoking propensities, ending in "the maintenance of intravaginal erection for at least ten minutes before ejaculation." During the presentation of each situation, muscular relaxation was facilitated by administering a 2½% solution of methohexitone sodium ("Brietal or Brevital") intravenously. Beginning at the bottom of the hierarchy, items were presented until the patient no longer became anxious while imagining them. The criterion of cure was the ability to have sexual intercourse that was satisfactory to both partners with no erective or ejaculatory problems. Cases were rated at the end of treatment, six months later and twelve months later. Eight out of ten patients with impotence were maintaining a cure one year after treatment (mean number of treatment sessions 9.3), three out of six with premature ejaculation were doing so (mean 10.5 sessions), and none out of three with impotencia ejaculandi, despite having each received over twenty-eight treatments.

Friedman concluded that his superficial therapy was eminently successful in impotence but less conclusive in ejaculatory disorders; however, impotence is not a homogenous condition. Cooper (1967) and Johnson (1965) have suggested at least two etiologic and prognostic discrete types; perhaps his conclusion is an oversimplification.

The most exciting and most discussed treatment for male potency disorders is likely to be that of Masters and Johnson (1964) (respectively, a gynecologist and a sociologist), who followed up their cases for five years. They claim lasting relief for 50% of males who had been impotent since adolescence and 80% in those who became impotent later; for premature ejaculators, they claim a 100% cure rate. It is worth speculating on possible reasons for their high success rate. Masters and Johnson's treatment, which consists of an intensive fourteen-day exposure of the patient and his spouse to male and female cotherapists, first one, then the other, then both together, is based on their research findings; even more important is that therapy is applied under as near optimum conditions as is likely to be attained in a Western culture—thus, both partners must be prepared to devote two weeks full time to rectifying or modifying inhibitory patterns of behavior and/or improving stimulative techniques based on frank discussions with each other and the therapists. Another prerequisite is that both should see the problem as mutual and have a sincere desire arising out of affection to improve their marriage. In short, patients are only taken on for therapy if they are genuinely motivated and are willing and able to work hard to improve their situation. In addition, Masters and Johnson's method of accepting patients only from bonafide professional sources coupled with their own careful pretreatment screening is designed to eliminate those with serious coexisting psychiatric problems.

Masters and Johnson's treatment results are doubly remarkable since one of their requirements for acceptance was a previous unsuccessful therapeutic venture, of at least six months (in most cases this had been psychotherapy of some sort or other). In accounting for this success their very stringent "motivational" and "cooperational" requirements from both sexual partners would seem crucial; in essence they treat a group highly selected with "tools and in surroundings" maximally conductive to a favorable outcome. Shainess (1968), commenting on their work, succinctly points this out; she reminds us that in psychiatric practice, because of the very nature of the patients (who are often personality-disordered, etc.), these "pretreatment requirements" can rarely be met, a melancholy fact of which many psychiatrists are only too aware.

Drugs

There has recently been a revival of drug therapy for impotence and impotentia ejaculandi with, it seems, gratifying results. Miller (1968), Margolis, Sangree, Prieto, Stein, and Chinn (1967), Margolis and Leslie (1966), Leslie and Bruhl (1963), Bruhl and Leslie (1963), and Sobotka (1969) using Afrodex (each tablet contains nuxvomica extract 5 mg, methyl testosterone 5 mg, and yohimbine 5 mg) report significant improvement in a series of controlled and uncontrolled studies on over 4,000 patients. Miller (1968) and Sobotka (1969), while convinced of the specificity of the drug, attest to the importance of the psychological factors in the treatment response, since patients (a) also demonstrated significant improvement on placebo and (b) maintained potency for a prolonged period of time after the drug was stopped. Although data are understandably sparse in respect of the majority of the 4,000 patients treated, in those cases reported in detail improvement was most marked in "hypogonadal" and "climacteric" impotence; psychogenic impotence was more resistant to treatment.

Clearly widespread replication of these findings would represent a major advance in treatment.

There are comparatively few (and no controlled) studies that deal specifically with the treatment and prognosis of premature ejaculation and that are presented in a form that allows critical appraisal. Thus, although psychoanalysis and analytically oriented therapy have been used for premature ejaculation, as in the case of impotence, objective information is generally unavailable; accordingly, at this time evaluation is impossible. Most of the "reviewable" investigations are pharamacologically or behaviorally oriented.

Schapiro (1947), for example, reported on 1,130 cases treated over a twenty-year period. He distinguished two discrete and etiologicaly unrelated types, which he designated Types A and B. Type A, which was premature ejaculation associated with erectional insufficiency, usually in older males, was treated with a judicious combination of prolonged sexual rest, nerve tonics, testosterone, and general roborant measures—to induce a resurgence in a flagging sex drive. Type A had an improvement rate of 65%. Type B, which was premature ejaculation with abnormally high sexual tension and good erections, occurring in younger males, he treated with sedative drugs; the cure rate in Type B was 85%. In both types he also stressed the importance of education, support, and reassurance (superficial psycho-therapy).

Cooper (1969a) treated thirty male subjects, who presented in a psychiatric outpatient department with a primary complaint of premature ejaculation. Therapy, which was practically oriented, aimed to remove psychological factors that the therapist judged might be contributing to the prematurity; it was applied for a minimum of one year (twenty sessions) and consisted in the individual case of an optimum of (a) training in relaxation, (b) sexual education, (c) provision of optimum sexual stimulation, (d) Semans's (1956) maneuver,* and (e) psychotherapy. At the time of assessment 43% of the patients were improved, while 57% remained unchanged or were worse; Type 1† premature ejaculation had the worst outcome and Type 2** the best. Type 3†† occupied an intermediary position. Tuthill (1955) and Semans (1956) employing "physiologic treatments" (merely abandoning restraint and greater frequency of coitus in Tuthill's case) claimed success rates in 100% of cases in sixty-six and eight patients, respectively. Hastings (1963), a physician with over twenty years' experience in treating sexual disorders, has never cured a single case. These major discrepancies may be "real" (reflecting genuine differences between the efficacy of the respective treatments) or "apparent" and they may be accounted for by any one of numerous factors. For example, Schapiro's results, which were based on twenty years' experience, failed to specify either the duration of treatment or the length of follow-up. It is conceivable that his high cure rate for Type B premature ejaculators might in part have related to patients treated over many years when the natural decline in sexual responsiveness might have been paralleled by a slowing down of the ejaculatory reflex; this "improvement" might have been attributed erroneously to the therapy. Tuthill's criteria for acceptance and cure, which were not explicit, may have been different; also his results derived from a postal return may be thought questionably reliable by some. Cooper's very small sample might not have been strictly comparable to the others. These interpretations of many other possibilities are presented merely to indicate the difficulties in comparing heterogenous studies; this, at best, can be only an approximation.

More recently, arising out of clinical observations that certain MAOI and phenothiazine drugs may delay or inhibit ejaculation as a side effect (Sandison, Whitelaw, and Currie, 1960; Haider, 1966; Freyhan, 1961), some workers have used these drugs specifically for this purpose in premature ejaculation. Although the results are often unpredictable and variable, among those claiming success are Santanelli (1960), thirty-eight out of forty cases [iproniazid—Marsilid (MAOI)], Bennet (1961), six out of six cases [isocarboxazid—Marplan (MAOI)], and Mellgren (1967) [thioridazine—Mellaril (phenothiazine)]. The latter study is worthy of special mention. Mellgren studied and treated forty premature ejaculators between 1964 and 1966; he divided the cases into two groups. Twenty-seven he considered as "psychasthenic personalities" with marked obsessional features; thirteen patients he classed as primarily suffering from an anxiety neurosis.

---

*Provision by the female of manual stimulation of the erect penis until the male experiences the sensation premonitory to ejaculation; at this point, stimulation is discontinued and the sensation is allowed to dissipate; when this happens stimulation is recommenced until the feeling develops again; again it is allowed to die away. According to Semans, repeating this procedure will eventually allow ejaculation to be delayed indefinitely.

†Habitual premature ejaculation with strong erection, present since adolescence.

**Acute onset premature ejaculation often associated with erectile insufficiency in young males.

††Insidious onset premature ejaculation in older males generally with erectional insufficiency and evidence of declining sexual responsiveness.

Mellgren's treatment regime included psychosexual exploration, somatic investigation, general and special sexual education, and in twenty-nine cases conversations with the female partner, with the addition of thioridazine (Mellaril) 25–50 mg 1–3 hours before coitus. Twenty-nine out of forty (72%) were improved (able to have coitus of at least two minutes or more on over 75% of occasions).

Discussion and Conclusion

If, for the sake of argument, it is assumed that the outcome in potency disorders is better with than without treatment—and despite Johnson's (1965) investigations on the natural history of these conditions in the absence of controlled studies, this is by no means certain—there are still formidable difficulties in attempting to assess the respective merits of the many treatments reviewed above. These difficulties, which include (a) problems of semantics between different investigators, (b) variable criteria for accepting patients for treatment, (c) treatments of variable durations and intensities, (d) variable criteria of cure and follow-up periods, etc., make comparative evaluation hazardous or impossible. However, notwithstanding, the author intends, provocatively perhaps, to stick his neck out and to attempt a comparison of sorts.

For impotence (and impotentia ejaculandi), on the available data "superficial psychotherapies" biased toward practicality and especially that of Masters and Johnson (1964) with older "climacteric impotents," sexual stimulants such as Afrodex, perhaps as an adjunct, rate as vastly superior to the more traditional psychiatric depth therapies (e.g., psychoanalysis and analytically oriented psychotherapy). It may perhaps be inferred from this that either "depth psychotherapies" are the wrong treatment for impotence or, alternatively, the patients who seek out analysis are in any event the toughest and most recalcitrant cases.

The author believes that both of these are valid interpretations. However, in the light of Masters and Johnson's criteria of acceptance for their therapy (at least six months prior unsuccessful psychotherapy) and in the absence of proof to the contrary, the former (and embarrassingly so) seems more relevant. As well as having a definite "edge in efficacy," what little factual information we have on prognostic factors has also been mainly derived from "superficial treatment studies"; since these have been largely empirical and pragmatic, which are practical rather than theoretical, this is hardly surprising. Clearly, much more work is required on this very important subject.

On the practical question of which should be the treatment of choice for impotence (and impotentia ejaculandi), it would appear reasonable on empirical grounds to prescribe superficial therapy in all cases for six months or so. A failure to respond by that time might be one indication for other approaches, including deep psychiatric investigation.

In premature ejaculation, the case for superficial behaviorally oriented therapy with or without adjunctive drug therapy seems overwhelming, although for the same methodological reasons as stated above, direct comparison of individual treatments is difficult.

In looking forward, the author would first like to register regret for the past and in large measure for the present and to express a hope for the future; this applies with equal force not only to the present subject but to many others of psychiatric concern; it is the application of scientific method—specifically, in the area of comparative evaluation of different (or the same) therapies applied by different practitioners. The acceptance of (a) standard terminology, (b) agreed criteria for inclusion in any study, which as far as possible should be methodologically sound and made on a homogeneous population, and (c) standard criteria for cure, etc., is mandatory if significant advances that will stand the test of time are to be achieved.

Summary

A representative sample of the literature on the treatment and prognosis of male potency disorders (e.g., impotence, impotentia ejaculandi, premature ejaculation) is presented; despite the enormous volume of opinion, the amount of reviewable hard data is desultory.

On the available information there is no factual evidence that psychoanalysis or other depth psychotherapies are either effective or ineffective in these conditions; at the moment an objective evaluation is not possible.

If, among other qualifications, it is assumed that the natural history of the various potency disorders is that of a static process (i.e., the condition would neither have worsened nor improved spontaneously), a superficial behavioral approach, especially that of Masters and Johnson, seems vastly superior.

Some suggestions are offered which are thought would improve the quality of future work in this area.

References

Abraham, K. Ejaculatio praecox. In E. Jones (Ed.), *Selected papers on psychoanalysis*. London: Hogarth, 1949.

Allen, C. *A textbook of psycho-sexual disorders*. London: Oxford University Press, 1962.

Aycock, L. The medical management of premature ejaculation. *Journal of Urology*, 1949, *62*, 361–362.

Bennett, D. Treatment of ejaculation praecox with monoamine-oxidase inhibitors. *Lancet*, 1961, *2*, 1309.

Brady, J. P. Brevital relaxation treatment of frigidity. *Behavior Research and Therapy*, 1966, *4*, 71–77.

Bruhl, D. E., and Leslie, C. H. Afrodex, double-blind test in impotence. *Medical Record and Annals*, 1963, *56*, 22.

Cooper, A. J. A case of fetishism and impotence treated by behaviour therapy. *British Journal of Psychiatry*, 1963, *109*, 649–652.

Cooper, A. J. Unpublished M.D. thesis, University of Bristol, 1967.

Cooper, A. J. A factual study of male potency disorders. *British Journal of Psychiatry*, 1968, *114*, 719–731.

Cooper, A. J. Clinical and therapeutic studies in premature ejaculation. *Comprehensive Psychiatry*, 1969, *10*, 285–295. (a)

Cooper, A. J. Disorders of sexual potency in the male: A clinical and statistical study of some factors related to short-term prognosis. *British Journal of Psychiatry*, 1969, *115*, 709–719. (b)

Curran, D.: Sexual perversions. *Practitioner*, 1954, *172*, 440–445.

Ellis, H. *Psychology of sex*. London: Heinemann, 1948.

El-Senoussi, A., Coleman, D. R., and Tauber, A. S. Factors in male impotence. *Journal of Psychology*, 1959, *48*, 3–46.

Fenichel, O. *Collected papers* (First series). New York: Norton, 1953.

Friedman, D. The treatment of impotence by Brietal relaxation therapy. *Behaviour Research and Therapy*, 1968, *6*, 257–261.

Friedman, L. J. *Virgin wives*. London: Tavistock, 1962.

Freud, S. *Complete works* (Vol. II). London: Hogarth, 1957. (Originally published 1910.)

Freyhan, F. A. Loss of ejaculation during Mellaril treatment. *American Journal of Psychiatry*, 1961, *118*, 171–172.

Gutheil, E. H. Sexual dysfunctions in men. In S. Arieti (Ed.), *American handbook of psychiatry*. New York: Basic Books, 1959.

Haider, I. Thioridazine and sexual dysfunctions. *International Journal of Neuropsychiatry*, 1966, *2*, 255–257.

Hamilton, J. B. Induction of penile erection by male hormone substances. *Endocrinology*, 1937, *21*, 744–749.

Hastings, D. W. *Impotence and frigidity*. Churchill: London, 1963.

Hemphill, R. E., Leith, A., and Stuart, J. R.: A factual study of male homosexuality. *British Medical Journal*, 1958, *2*, 1317–1323.

Hirschfeld, M. *Sexual anomalies and perversions: Physical and psychological development and treatment*. London: Francis Aldor, 1944.

Johnson, J. Unpublished M.D. Thesis, University of Manchester, 1964.

Johnson, J. Prognosis of disorders of sexual potency in the male. *Journal of Psychosomatic Research*, 1965, *9*, 195–200.

Jones, E. *Papers on psychoanalysis*. New York: Wood, 1919.

Kinsey, A. C., Pomeroy, W. B., and Martin, C. E. *Sexual behavior in the human male*. Philadelphia: Saunders, 1948.

Kraft-Ebbing, R. Von. *Aberration of sexual life*. New York: Liveright, 1951.

Lazarus, A. A. The treatment of chronic frigidity by systematic desensitization. *Journal of Nervous and Mental Disease*, 1963, *136*, 272–278.

Leslie, C. H., and Bruhl, D. E. An effective anti-impotence agent. Statistical evaluation of 1,000 reported cases. *Memphis and Mid-South Medical Journal*, 1963, *38*, 379–385.

Lowenstein, J. *Treatment of impotence*. London: Hamish Hamilton, 1947.

Lydston (1908). Cited by Hastings, D. W. In *Impotence and frigidity*. Churchill: London, 1963.

MacDougald, D., Jr. Aphrodisiacs and anaphrodisiacs. In A. Ellis and A. Arbarbanel (Eds.), *The encyclopedia of sexual behavior*. New York: Hawthorn Books, 1967.

Margolis, R., and Leslie, C. H. Review of studies on a mixture of methyltestosterone in the treatment of impotence. *Current Therapeutic Research*, 1966, *8*, 280–284.

Margolis, R., Sangree, H., Prieto, P., Stein, L., and Chinn S. Clinical studies on the use of Afrodex in the treatment of impotence. Statistical summary of 4,000 cases. *Current Therapeutic Research*, 1967, *9*, 213–219.

Masters, W. H., and Johnson, V. E. A team approach to the rapid diagnosis and treatment of sexual incompatibility. *Pacific Medicine and Surgery*, 1964, *72*, 371–375.

Masters, W. H., and Johnson, V. E. *Human sexual response*. Boston: Little, Brown, 1966.

Masters, W. H., and Johnson, V. E. *Human sexual inadequacy*. Boston: Little, Brown, 1970.

Mellgren, A. Treatment of ejaculatio praecox with thioridazine. *Psychotherapy and Psychosomatics*, 1967, *15*, 454–460.

Miller, W. W. Afrodex in the treatment of impotence. A double-blind cross over study. *Current Therapeutic Research*, 1968, *10*, 354–359.

Neustatter, W. L. Homosexuality: The medical aspect. *Practitioner*, 1953, *172*, 364–373.

Rachman, S. Sexual disorders and behavior therapy. *American Journal of Psychiatry*, 1961, *118*, 235–240.

Rees, J. R. Prognosis in the sexual neuroses. *Lancet*, 1935, *1*, 948–949.

Sandison, R. A., Whitelaw, E., and Currie, J. D. C. Clinical trials with Mellaril in the treatment of schizophrenia. *Journal of Mental Science*, 1960, *106*, 732–741.

Santanelli, R. *Le sindrome depressive*. Turin: 1960.

Schapiro, B. Premature ejaculation: Review of 1130 cases. *Journal of Urology*, 1947, *50*, 374–379.

Semans, J. H. Premature ejaculation: A new approach. *Journal of Urology*, 1956, *49*, 533–537.

Shainess, N. The therapy of frigidity. In *Current psychiatric therapies* (Vol. 8). New York: Grune & Stratton, 1968. Pp. 70–79.

Slater, E. The neurotic constitution. A statistical study of two thousand neurotic soldiers. *Journal of Neurology*, 1943, *6*, 1–16.

Sobotka, J. J. An evaluation of Afrodex in the management of male impotency. A double-blind cross over study. *Current Therapeutic Research*, 1969, *11*, 87–94.

Stafford-Clark, D. The aetiology and treatment of impotence. *Practitioner*, 1954, *172*, 397–404.

Stekel, W. *Impotence in the male*. New York: Liveright, 1927.

Tuthill, J. F. Impotence. *Lancet*, 1955, *1*, 124–128.

Wolpe, J. *Psychotherapy by reciprocal inhibition*. Stanford: Stanford University Press, 1958.

The preceding chapters in this part dealt with the etiology of erectile dysfunction as well as the more common forms of treatment for this dysfunction.

In this article, Kockott, Dittmar, and Nusselt attempt to evaluate the effectiveness of systematic desensitization in the treatment of impotence. This study is based on a sample of twenty-four men, and care was taken to "match" the subjects in the three different treatment groups. A waiting list control group, which did not receive any treatment, was used to evaluate effectiveness of therapy. These factors are important to note as clinical outcome studies such as this are often criticized on the basis of not being methodologically rigorous.

The use of three methods for evaluating treatment outcome in this study (behavioral description, subjective report, and physiological response) is important to note. Reliance on one method alone increases the chance that the final data may not be totally accurate.

This concern is especially relevant to research in the area of sexual dysfunction where a patient's subjective report of arousal, for example, may contradict his or her physiological response (see Heiman, Part II, Chapter 8).

26

Systematic Desensitization of Erectile Impotence: A Controlled Study

G. Kockott, F. Dittmar, and L. Nusselt

Introduction

Up to 1970, there were a number of single case studies in the behavior therapy literature on impotence (Garfield, McBrearty, and Dichter, 1969; Kraft and Al-Issa, 1968; Lazarus, 1965; Salzman, 1969), and a few papers gave results on small groups of patients without controls (Friedman, 1968; Wolpe and Lazarus, 1966). The authors of these papers argued that the impotence of their patients was due to anxiety about sexual intercourse and that therefore systematic desensitization was the therapy of choice. However, Cooper (1968) questioned this approach.

The purpose of our study was to determine whether or not systematic desensitization is a useful therapeutic method for erectile impotence. The hypothesis was that systematic desensitization would produce therapeutic results better than those of routine therapy or no therapy at all. The definition of *routine therapy* was therapy that is usually provided by general practitioners, dermatologists,

G. Kockett, F. Dittmar, and **L. Nusselt** • Max Planck Institut für Psychiatrie, München, West Germany

urologists, or neurologists in their private practice, i.e., medication and some general advice.

Method

The patient group consisted of twenty-four men with a mean age of thirty-one years who for at least six months had had the problem of erectile impotence before or during sexual intercourse, which made intromission impossible. The selection of subjects was based on an intake interview, a physical examination, and a number of psychological tests (depression scale, personality question-naire, etc.). Each patient also had to have a cooperative partner. Patients whose complaints were due to organic disturbance, sexual deviation, endogenous depression, or mainly conflicts in their partnership were excluded from this study. Three groups of eight patients each were formed, the behavior therapy group (BT), the routine therapy group (RT), and a group of patients who were put on a waiting list (WL). The groups were matched (Table 1) for age, primary or secondary impotence, IQ, and neuroticism score as measured by the Brengelmann (1960) personality questionnaire.

The patients in the behavior therapy group had fourteen sessions of systematic desensitization. The patients in the routine therapy group were seen by psychiatrists a total of four times at intervals of three to five weeks. The psychiatrists tried to duplicate the routine treatment used in private practice, i.e., the giving of standardized advice and medication. The manual for the standardized advice was based on the results of an inquiry made among general practitioners and psychiatrists in Munich. The patients on the waiting list had to wait sixteen weeks on the average.

The therapeutic effect was investigated on three levels: behavioral, subjective, and physiological. The subjects were tested twice before and once each during and after therapy or waiting period.

Table 1. Matched Groups

	BT	RT	WL
Number of cases	8	8	8
Mean age (x)	29	32	32
Primary impotence	6	5	5
Secondary impotence	2	3	3
IQ			
90–110	3	3	3
Above 110	5	5	5
N score			
0–13	5	4	5
14+	3	4	3

Behavioral Level

Sexual behavior usually cannot be observed directly. The therapist has to rely on the statements of the patient and of his partner. For this reason, a semi-structured interview was developed, including, among other categorties, fourteen concerning quality and quantity of sexual behavior. These categories were (1) frequency of masturbation, (2) frequency and (3) quality of erections during masturbation, (4) frequency of masturbatory ejaculation, (5) frequency of sexual fantasies, (6) frequency of sexual fantasies with erections, (7) frequency of sexual dreams, (8) frequency of spontaneous erections, (9) frequency of sexual intercourse, (10) presence of symptoms of anxiety during sexual intercourse, (11) avoidance of sexual intercourse, (12) erection behavior during sexual intercourse, (13) ejaculation behavior during sexual intercourse, and (14) degree of sexual excitement while ejaculating.

In a given category the patient could receive from 0 to a maximum of 4 points. High scores expressed undisturbed or almost undisturbed behavior. With this system, we could then rank the data. In this way, differences among the three groups in change during therapy could be better compared. The semistructured interview was taped and then scored by the interviewer and two independent psychiatrists. Differences between the statements made before and after therapy were then used as a measure of therapeutic effectiveness.

Subjective Level

A test was constructed in which the patient was to use adjectives to describe his feelings about two standardized situations he was to imagine. The first situation was sexual intercourse with his own partner, the second with a seductive woman whom he had just met.

In this second situation, the patient was given some pictures of attractive girls to help him imagine later a girl of his taste. The patient then listened to a tape prepared by the authors. On this tape was a story about a male friend who comes to visit the patient and invites him to go to a party. At the party, the patient is without a girl and feels a bit left out. After a while he starts talking with the hostess, a very attractive girl. At the end of the party, he is the last one to say goodbye to her. She invites him to stay overnight and puts her arms around him, and they go back into the living room. The story ends with a situation in which it is completely clear to the patient that the girl wants to have sexual intercourse.

The patients were given sixteen positive and sixteen negative adjectives related to the dimension "anxiety." The adjectives were printed on small cards. Using a 5-point scale, the patients were asked to rate the adjectives as to how they described their feelings connected with the standardized scenes. As an indication of therapeutic success, it was expected that the positive adjectives would describe the feelings of the patients poorly before therapy but better after therapy and that the negative adjectives would describe their feelings well before therapy but less well after therapy.

Physiological Level

A penile plethysmograph similar to the one described by Bancroft, Jones, and Pullan (1966) was used to measure sexual arousal to only slightly stimulating material, i.e., to the two standardized situations described above. Thus the same test situations were used for both the subjective and the physiological tests. The hypothesis was that therapeutic effectiveness would be evident if there were changes in the erectile reactions during stimulus presentation. The extent of erection consists of penile volume enlargement and duration of this enlargement. Both factors should be included in quantitative evaluation. For technical reasons, only the duration of erections could be measured. Therefore, statistical comparisons were not made.

Results

Behavioral Level

According to the theoretical concept of systematic desensitization, the patients in the behavior therapy group, and only in this group, were told at the beginning of treatment not to have sexual intercourse. When the semistructured interview was developed, the assumption was made, based on the literature, that this "restriction" would be lifted as improvement was seen in the course of the fourteen desensitization sessions. But such improvement occurred in only two of eight patients. Thus at the end of the study there was an additional, therapeutically necessary variable in the behavior therapy group. Therefore, a statistical comparison among the three groups at the end of the study was not possible. However, the results can be discussed descriptively. In Table 2, those categories

Table 2.   *Behavioral Level: Total Scores on Questionnaire for Each Group Before and After Therapy*

Category of sexual behavior	(1) Frequency of masturbation	(5) Frequency of sexual fantasies	(7) Frequency of sexual dreams	(8) Frequency of spontaneous erections	(12) Erection behavior	(13) Ejaculation behavior
BT						
Before	16	15	7	19	6	5
After	13	18	15	22	12	8
Difference	−3	+3	+8	+3	+6	+3
RT						
Before	14	12	9	18	11	6
After	14	14	8	21	14	10
Difference	0	+2	−1	+3	+3	+4
WL						
Before	16	11	7	16	14	7
After	21	9	3	21	12	5
Difference	+5	−2	−4	+5	−2	−2

Table 3.　Distribution of Patients by Change in Score Following Therapy
(Behavior Level)[a]

	Number of patients	Frequency of masturbation			Frequency of sexual dream			Erection behavior		
		−	0	+	−	0	+	−	0	+
BT	8	4	2	2	1	1	6	2	2	4
RT	8	2	4	2	1	6	1	2	1	5
WL	8	0	3	5	3	4	1	4	2	2

[a]Symbols: −, decrease; 0, no change; +, increase.

are shown which seemed relevant to therapy. For each category, the total number of points scored by each group before and after therapy and the difference between these two scores are given. A composite score combining all categories is not given as it is uncertain what implications the changes in the different categories have for therapy. When the three groups are compared, it can be seen that the differences were most pronounced in categories 1 (frequency of masturbation), 7 (frequency of sexual dreams), 12 (erection behavior), and 13 (ejaculation behavior). In the BT group, frequency of masturbation decreased slightly, in the WL group, it increased. Sexual dreams were reported in the BT group much more often at the end of therapy than at the beginning, whereas in the other two groups such dreams were less frequent following therapy. The scores in categories 12 and 13 were higher for the two therapy groups and lower for the WL group after therapy.

These changes could have been caused by a single patient or by a very few patients. In order to show that these differences indicate tendencies of the whole group, the changes within each patient were examined. The patients were grouped within each category according to whether they showed an increase, a decrease, or no change in their scores following therapy. In Table 3, the three categories are shown in which the most pronounced differences were seen; here again it is categories 1, 7, and 12. In each of these three categories, the direction of change is the same as that in the group scores (Table 2).

Subjective Level

The various testings of each individual patient were compared statistically using the Fisher exact probability test. There were no significant differences between the two pretherapy tests. A comparison between the second pretherapy test and the test given after therapy showed that a number of patients in each group had changed significantly ($p < .05$). Then the numbers of significant changes per group between the second pretherapy test and the test given after therapy were compared. Again the Fisher exact probability test was used. For the description of the feelings about the party story—i.e., having sexual intercourse with an attractive woman whom the patient had just met at a party—there were significant differences for the negative adjectives. After therapy, patients in the behavior therapy group rated negative adjectives as poorly describing their feelings significantly more often than patients in the other two groups ($p < .001$).

Thus, it seems that systematic desensitization produced a change in attitude: After therapy, the patients in the behavior therapy group were able to imagine having intercourse with a woman whom they had just met with less aversion and anxiety than the patients in the two control groups. No other significant changes were found.

Physiological Level

Erections were recorded in ten patients (two BT, five RT, three WL) during stimulus presentation before, during, and after therapy or waiting period. In six patients, there was no change in the duration of the erections. In four patients (one BT, two RT, one WL), an increase in duration of the erection up to 20% was measured after therapy, but there was no association between this increase and the clinical rating of being cured or improved. In fourteen patients, no erections were recorded.

Clinical Rating

As to the change in the individual patients in the BT and RT groups, two patients each were cured; in the WL group, one patient had a spontaneous remission. "Cured" was defined as erection maintained for at least one minute after intromission with intravaginal ejaculation before loss of erection.

In the BT and RT groups, one patient each improved; however, in the waiting list group none of the patients improved. *Improved* was defined as erection maintained for at least one minute after intromission with or without ejaculation, the important point being that intromission was possible. In the BT and RT groups, five patients each showed no improvement; in the WL group, seven showed no improvement.

Conclusion

When systematic desensitization is used alone as a treatment for erectile impotence, only limited therapeutic effect is seen. This is not surprising, because systematic desensitization is a technique for dealing with anxiety-related problems alone. But during the behavior analysis of the patients it became clear that there were a great number of other factors in addition to anxiety that seemed to maintain the behavioral disturbance. Some of these factors were social anxiety, anxiety about level of performance, unrealistic sexual standards, very limited range of sexual behaviors, and the attitude that "sex is dirty." It must also be stressed that the partner plays an extremely important role in the therapy. Both the patient and the partner must understand that the disturbance is not due solely to the patient and that both have to change their behavioral patterns if therapeutic success is to be expected.

Therefore, when this project was completed the therapy strategy was changed. Those patients who had shown no improvement in this study were then treated using a modification of the Masters and Johnson (1970) technique combined with sex education. Twelve patients have been treated by this method. Of these twelve patients, eight are cured or improved according to the operational definitions stated earlier. Three patients showed no change and one patient relapsed shortly after therapy was completed. Follow-up is planned to one year. The authors' impression is that the results with this method are superior to the results obtained when systematic desensitization is used alone. Since this treatment method has not been used in a controlled study, it is not known whether or not these results are due to this therapy method only.

References

Bancroft, J. H. J., Jones, H. G., and Pullan, B. R. A simple transducer for measuring penile erection, with comments on its use in the treatment of sexual disorders. *Behaviour Research and Therapy,* 1966, *4,* 239–241.

Brengelmann, J. C. Deutsche Validierung von Fragebogen der Extraversion, neurotischer Tendenz und Rigidität. *Zeitschrift für Experimentelle und Agnewandte Psychologie,* 1960, *7,* 291–331.

Cooper, A. J. A factual study of male potency disorders. *British Journal of Psychiatry,* 1968, *114,* 719–731.

Friedman, D. The treatment of impotence by Brietal relaxation therapy. *Behaviour Research and Therapy,* 1968, *6,* 257–262.

Garfield, Z., McBrearty, J., and Dichter, M. A case of impotence successfully treated with desensitization combined with *in vivo* operant training and thought substitution. In R. D. Rubin and C. M. Franks (Eds.), *Advances in behavior therapy.* New York: Academic Press, 1969. Pp. 97–103.

Kraft, T., and Al-Issa, I. The use of methohexitone sodium in the systematic desensitization of premature ejaculation. *British Journal of Psychiatry,* 1968, *114,* 351–352.

Lazarus, A. A. The treatment of a sexually inadequate man. In L. P. Ullmann and L. Krasner (Eds.), *Case studies in behavior modification.* New York: Holt, Rinehart & Winston, 1965. Pp. 243–245.

Masters, W. H., and Johnson, V. E. *Human sexual inadequacy.* London: Churchill, 1970.

Saltzman, L. F. Systematic desensitization of a patient with chronic total impotence. In R. D. Rubin and C. M. Franks (Eds.), *Advances in behavior therapy.* New York: Academic Press, 1969. Pp. 131–137.

Wolpe, J. A., and Lazarus, A. A. *Behavior therapy techniques: A guide to treatment of neuroses.* Oxford: Pergamon Press, 1966.

In this chapter LoPiccolo, McMullen, and Watkins describe the course of treatment for one couple where homosexuality was a factor in the etiology of the male's sexual dysfunction.

   Although this is a single case study, it is significant for two reasons. First, it reports on the use of an arousal reconditioning technique that increased heterosexual arousal in the male. Second, the successful results indicate that it is sometimes possible for a time-limited behavioral approach to produce effective results even though underlying psychodynamic issues are not dealt with in therapy.

27

Treatment of Erectile Failure and Ejaculatory Incompetence of Homosexual Etiology

Joseph LoPiccolo, Rita Stewart McMullen, and Bruce Watkins

In contrast to their generally high rates of success in treating problems of sexual inadequacy, Masters and Johnson (1970) report considerable difficulty in treating impotence (erectile failure) in cases where religious othodoxy or homosexual influence are etiological factors. They state, "It is in these two areas that so much more work needs to be done. Currently there is an inexcusably high level of failure rate in therapeutic return for patients handicapped by either of these two specific etiological influences" (p. 273).

   This article reports on a learning-theory-based treatment program developed for cases of impotence where homosexuality is involved, and illustrates the use of this program in one case.

Joseph LoPiccolo • Department of Psychiatry and Behavioral Science, School of Medicine, State University of New York, Stony Brook, New York   *Rita Stewart McMullen* • Desert Counseling Clinic, Inc., Ridgecrest, California   *Bruce Watkins* • Department of Psychology, University of Oregon, Eugene, Oregon. When this chapter was originally published, Joseph LoPiccolo was with the Psychology Clinic, University of Oregon, Eugene, Oregon

Masters and Johnson consider erectile failure to be a fear reaction. "Fear can prevent erections just as fear can increase the respiratory rate or lead to diarrhea or vomiting" (Masters and Johnson, 1970, p. 196). They consider this fear to be a fear of failure, or "performance anxiety," which leads the male to assume a nonparticipant, "spectator" role in sexual relations. Their program aims to reduce this fear through what is basically an in vivo desensitization procedure, similar to that described by Wolpe (1969).

In cases of erectile failure where the male has a homosexual orientation, it seems logical to assume that lack of heterosexual arousal in addition to performance anxiety is a factor in the inability to attain and maintain an erection. A treatment that focuses only on reducing performance anxiety, and not on increasing heterosexual arousal, would seem likely to be unsuccessful in such cases.

In the case reported here, an in vivo desensitization program to reduce performance anxiety was used contiguously with a program designed to recondition sexual arousal to heterosexual stimuli through the directed use of fantasy and masturbation.

Case A

The clients were two unmarried graduate students living together in a stable and permanent love relationship. Their presenting problems were the male's lack of sexual arousal to his mate, his inability to attain or maintain an erection in sexual relations with her, and his frequent inability to become aroused enough to ejaculate (ejaculatory incompetence) on those occasions when he did achieve an erection. In support of the notion that arousal reconditioning is necessary in such cases, it might be noted that the client felt genuine revulsion and disgust at the sight or touch of the female's genitals.

The male had been an overt homosexual since early adolescence and was engaging in overt homosexual activities (mutual masturbation, fellatio, anal intercourse) at the time the couple entered treatment. He had had intercourse with six or seven other women besides his mate, but each relationship terminated because of his inability to achieve erections.

The female was sexually liberal and quite experienced (more than forty previous sexual partners). She was aware of her partner's homosexuality and did not object to it per se but only to his inability to perform sexually with her.

What they wanted of treatment was to increase his heterosexual arousal and functioning. They both stated that they did *not* want the therapists to attempt to eliminate the male's homosexuality, which they viewed as nonpathological, but merely to enhance his heterosexuality. This was agreed to with the exception that the male was to refrain from overt homosexual activities for the duration of treatment.

Treatment

Both the male and the female were seen for fifteen weekly sessions by a male and a female therapist (R. S. and B. W.).

One aspect of treatment involved the reduction of the male's performance anxiety through an in vivo desensitization approach. As this approach has been well described elsewhere (Wolpe, 1958, 1969; Masters and Johnson, 1970) it will not be detailed here. Briefly, the clients were initially forbidden to engage in any sexual activity. They were then given, each week, a "homework" assignment to increase their repertoire of sexual behaviors. In the first week only hugging, kissing, and body massage were allowed. This assignment permits the male to relearn enjoyment of sensual pleasures, without any worry about whether or not he will be able to achieve an erection. In following weeks, the behaviors successively added were breast and genital touching, stimulation of the penis in a "teasing" manner (Masters and Johnson, 1970, p. 206), simultaneous masturbation and genital manipulation by each other, penile insertion with no movement, penile insertion with male pelvic thrusting, mutual genital manipulation and masturbation to orgasm, and finally, allowing mutual pelvic thrusting with ejaculation during intercourse. To eliminate performance anxiety, the timing of introduction of these behaviors was such that they were allowed only after the male client had become confident that he could accomplish them. For example, intravaginal ejaculation was not "allowed" until after the client had been unable to restrain himself from ejaculating intravaginally.

The major innovation in the treatment of this case was the arousal reconditioning procedure. A program of directed masturbation was initially used to raise the client's heterosexual arousal. At intake, the male client was masturbating several times weekly to exclusively homosexual fantasies. McGuire, Carlisle, and Young (1965) have suggested that the orgasm experienced during masturbation is the reinforcer that conditions arousal to the fantasy or other stimuli accompanying masturbation. Davison (1968) and Marquis (1970) have made use of this principle in "orgasmic reconditioning" procedures designed to eliminate sexual perversions. In a manner similar to the procedures developed by Davison and Marquis, the male client was instructed to use homosexual fantasies to attain erection and approach orgasm in masturbation. At the instant of orgasm, however, he was to switch to fantasies of sexual relations with his mate. If arousal was lost, he was briefly to switch back to homosexual fantasies and then return again to fantasies of his partner. Over successive occasions of masturbation, the time of the switch from homosexual to heterosexual fantasies was gradually moved backward from the point of orgasm, until the client was finally using exclusively heterosexual fantasies during the entire masturbatory session.

One modification of Marquis' procedure was made. As is typical of male homosexuals (Annon, 1971), the client had difficulty in visualizing or fantasizing heterosexual stimuli during masturbation. To deal with this problem, the therapists provided the couple with a Polaroid camera and had them take pictures of the female for the male to use as heterosexual masturbation stimuli. This procedure worked quite well, and in the latter stages of therapy the male did acquire the ability to fantasize effectively without the aid of the pictures.

Because this fantasy-switching program worked well in masturbation, it was also used to facilitate arousal in the in vivo desensitization sessions with the female. The male was instructed to use homosexual fantasies as necessary to facilitate arousal in these sessions but to switch back frequently to focusing on the reality of what he and his partner were doing, and in any case always to switch back to heterosexual reality just before orgasm. This program was also successful. While initially the male was fantasizing homosexual activities during much of the time he was engaging in sexual activity with his mate, he eventually came to be highly aroused while focusing *exclusively* on the heterosexual reality.

In any type of behavioral treatment where the major therapeutic procedures are to be carried out by the client at home, there is the problem of knowing whether or not the client is following them. In the present case, both clients were required to fill out daily activity record forms at home, specifying in detail their sexual activities and emotional reactions to them. These records, as well as the clients' verbal reports in therapy sessions, indicated that the clients did follow the program procedures quite faithfully.

Outcome

At the close of the treatment, the male was able to obtain and maintain erections solely through the use of heterosexual fantasies and activities. In addition, he was able to ejaculate intravaginally on virtually every occasion. These changes were found to have been maintained at a follow-up six months after termination.

Assessing outcome on the basis of global reports is, of course, unsatisfactory in a scientific sense. An attempt to deal with this problem in cases of sexual dysfunction is being made by the senior author and his students by the use of two sexual behavior inventories. As reliability and validity research on these inventories is still in progress, however, only a few scores of high "face validity" from these inventories will be reported here. These scores are shown in Table 1.

Table 1.   Outcome Statistics

Variable	Time of assessment		
	Pretreatment	Termination	Six-month follow-up
1. Intercourse frequency	once/2 weeks	3 times weekly	twice weekly
2. Intercourse duration	1–5 min.	11–15 min.	11–15 min.
3. Achieves erection—% of coital opportunities	25%	100%	100%
4. Achieves orgasm in intercourse, if erection achieved			
male	50%	100%	100%
female	50%	75%	75%
8. Self-rating—satisfaction with sexual relationship (scale of 1–6)			
male	2	5	5
female	2	5	5

As Table 1 indicates, treatment was quite successful in dealing with this couple's presenting complaints. One additional set of scores from our assessment inventory is also interesting, as it documents the effectiveness of the reconditioning procedure in making heterosexuality more arousing and pleasurable to the male. This inventory lists seventeen different heterosexual activities, ranging from kissing to intercourse, and asks the client to rate, on a scale from 1 to 6, how pleasant he finds each activity. The mean pleasure scores in a normative sample of sixty-three couples with a satisfactory sexual relationship are 5.3 (standard deviation = .54) for males and 5.1 (standard deviation = .54) for females. Before treatment, the male client's score was 3.8, the female's 4.9. After treatment these scores had increased to 5.0 and 5.1, respectively, and were 5.0 and 5.3 at follow-up. Clearly, heterosexual behavior had become much more pleasurable and arousing for both clients.

Discussion

The results in this case are encouraging, and suggest that the addition of an arousal reconditioning procedure to the basic Masters and Johnson (1970) program for impotence may be necessary to obtain better results in cases of impotence related to a homosexual orientation. This case is also instructive in illustrating two modifications of the arousal reconditioning procedures developed by Davison (1968) and Marquis (1970).

Usually, in this procedure the client's fantasies or *Playboy* pictures (e.g., Davison, 1968; Jackson, 1969) are used as heterosexual stimulus materials during masturbation. In this case, Polaroid pictures of the client's actual sexual partner were used. This seems to offer the advantages of providing clear and explicit stimulus materials (unlike fantasy images), and of conditioning the client's arousal *directly* to his actual sexual partner, rather than to a magazine. It seems improbable that arousal conditioned to *Playboy* models will generalize completely to the client's actual sexual partner. The Polaroid camera may therefore be a useful tool in the behavior therapist's armamentarium.

The second innovation was to have the client use his homosexual fantasies to reinforce sexual arousal in actual heterosexual behavior with his mate as well as with masturbation.

Again, it should be noted that the goal of treatment was to improve the quality of the male client's sexual relationship with his partner, and not to change his homosexual orientation. The client did report a decrease in homosexual behavior at termination, but at the time of follow-up indicated a return to its pretreatment level. The client wanted treatment to make him heterosexually aroused and competent, and it was not necessary to decrease homosexual functioning in order to achieve this aim. He is now capable of adequate sexual functioning with both sexes. We consider that the use he makes of this capacity is a matter of his personal morality, which should not be intruded upon by the therapist.

References

Annon, J. S. *The therapeutic use of masturbation in the treatment of sexual disorders.* Paper presented at Fifth Annual Meeting of the Association for the Advancement of Behavior Therapy, Washington, D.C., 1971.

Davison, G. S. Elimination of a sadistic fantasy by a client controlled counter-conditioning technique. *Journal of Abnormal Psychology*, 1968, *77*, 84–90.

Jackson, B. T. A case of voyeurism treated by counterconditioning. *Behaviour Research and Therapy*, 1969, *7*, 133–134.

Marquis, J. N. Orgasmic reconditioning: Changing sexual object choice through controlling masturbation fantasies. *Journal of Behavior Therapy and Experimental Psychiatry*, 1970, *1*, 263–271.

Masters, W. H., and Johnson, V. E. *Human sexual inadequacy*, Boston: Little, Brown, 1970.

McGuire, R. T., Carlisle, J. M., and Young, B. G. Sexual deviation as conditioned behavior: a hypothesis. *Behaviour Research and Therapy*, 1965, *2*, 185–190.

Wolpe, J. *Psychotherapy by reciprocal inhibition.* Stanford: Stanford University Press, 1958.

Wolpe, J. *The practice of behavior therapy*, New York: Pergamon Press, 1969.

As the average life span grows increasingly longer, the need for a closer look at sexuality during the aging process becomes more crucial. In this chapter, Sviland attempts to examine some of the factors that seem to influence sexual activity in the elderly. She also describes a therapy program designed to increase sexual satisfaction for elderly couples. Her section on "Special Considerations Critical to Sex Therapy with the Aged" is particularly valuable.

A topic that might have been mentioned in more detail concerns physiological changes in the aging female which can interfere with sexual enjoyment. The most common such change is thinning and loss of resiliency of the vaginal walls with age. This condition affects some postmenopausal women but can be successfully treated with replacement hormones (see Abarbanel, Part IV, Chapter 18).

28

Helping Elderly Couples Become Sexually Liberated: Psychosocial Issues

Mary Ann P. Sviland

This article describes a therapy program for helping elderly couples become sexually liberated and some critical age-related sexual problems of which the counselor must be aware in working with the elderly. To provide an adequate context for the objectives and methods of the treatment, it is necessary to first describe some psychosocial issues of sexuality which influence sexuality in the elderly. These issues include negative social attitudes toward elderly sexuality, knowledge of sexual behavior in the elderly, and cultural–physiological factors interacting to restrict elderly sexuality.

Negative Social Attitudes

Sexual discrimination against the elderly still exists in this era of expanding sexual understanding and corresponding liberalization of attitudes. Until recently, society has found amusing or insignificant the sexual needs of elderly persons. Jokes involving old people and sex bring inevitable laughter. The insignificance

Mary Ann P. Sviland • Clinical Psychologist in Private Practice, Canoga Park, California; and Lecturer, California State University, Northridge, California

of elderly sexuality is reflected in sexual research. Only three out of 1,700 pages in the two Kinsey reports are devoted to the older age group (Claman, 1966). The Masters and Johnson (1966) study of sexual response included only 31 male and female subjects beyond age sixty in a total population of 694 subjects. Part of this inadequate study-subject population is an artifact of difficulty in eliciting active cooperation in elderly subjects. Apparently societal strictures make the elderly defensive regarding disclosure of their sexual life. But old people are terribly confused and vitally interested in information about the norms of sexuality in the elderly population (Feigenbaum, Lowenthal, and Trier, 1967).

The general social belief that sexuality is the domain of the young has resigned many senior citizens to premature impotence, frustration, self-depreciation, or loneliness. The cultural myth that impotence is a natural phenomenon of aging is so entrenched that even informed aging physicians are capable of becoming unexplainably panicked at one or two erectile failures. More pathetic is the elderly patient seen in counseling practice who is laden with guilt and shame at his or her continuing sexuality and masturbation because of partner unavailability. Since the feelings and behaviors of the elderly are related to societal expectations, many elderly people feel guilty about healthy feelings because they are unacceptable to themselves, the physician, or other people they live with (Newman and Nichols, 1966). Counselors too may need to examine their own social biases regarding aged sexuality and increase their understanding of elderly sexual function to foster a supporting climate for the resolution of healthy sexual function in their elderly patients.

Counseling elderly patients in improved sexual function and adjustment is not an end in itself but a means of fulfilling a deeper core—the timeless need of all humans for intimacy and love. Sexuality is one avenue of facilitating trust, affection, and caring. As Dean (1966) observed:

> We know that old people do not cease to be human just because they are old; they have many of the desires of the young, and their need for companionship is even greater. Nor does the desire for romance, intrigue or even sex necessarily disappear with advancing years.

Thwarted sexuality may be a greater contribution to depression in the elderly than previously assumed. The lack of an intimate and empathetic relationship may account for much of the clinical depression currently diagnosed as involutional. Loneliness and feelings of not being attractive or wanted or needed create depression irrespective of age. The positive value of companionship to general physical health is seen in the higher illness and morbidity rates of older single persons.

Primary opposition to sexuality in the aged arises from adult children who view their aged parents' normal urges for intimacy and romance as a threat to social disgrace and/or signs of second childhood (Dean, 1966). The negative attitude of the children toward their parents holds much more strongly for the mother than for the father, which then generalizes to all elderly females. Claman (1966) describes the identification of parent ideals with old people which blocks acceptance of their sexuality thus:

> Our aversion to serious discussion about sex in older people may be based on the fact that we identify old people with our parents, and are therefore made uncomfortable when we

think of our parents in this connection. Sam Levinson, the school-teacher–homespun-philosopher of television fame, once said: "When I first found out how babies were born, I couldn't believe it! To think that my mother and father would do such a thing! . . ." Then, after reflection, he added: "My father—maybe, but my mother—never!"

Mateless parents who express loneliness are told to take up a hobby and are pressed into household service, thereby adding to their social isolation instead of being encouraged to reenter the mainstream of life through another marriage. The horror toward parental sexual acting-out is readily observed in the strict nursing home sexual prohibitions designed to appease the bill-paying adult children. Cognizant of the positive value of sexuality in the aged, Kassel (1974) advocated the free acceptance of sexuality in homes for the aged as humanistic.

Research Findings on Physical and Circumstantial Effects on Elderly Sexuality

Contrary to popular mythology, the greater sexual interest, activity, and capacity in earlier life, the greater the interest, activity, and capacity in later years (Claman, 1966), which supports the concept of continuity of life-style. Early termination of sexual activity occurs where sex is not important in life (Pfeiffer and Davis, 1972). While prior activity and interest affect later male activity, elderly female sexuality is only related to past sex enjoyment (Pfeiffer and Davis, 1972).

Male sexual function shows a steady decline after peak responsiveness attained around age eighteen, while female sexuality reaches peak responsiveness in the late thirties and early forties and maintains this level into the sixties (Kaplan, 1974). After the fifties, frequency of orgasm and length of refractory period have changed significantly in the male; while, in sharp contrast to men, elderly women remain capable of enjoying multiple orgasms (Kaplan, 1974). Between fifty and sixty years the wife may want sex more than the husband is able to give (Kinsey, Pomeroy, and Martin, 1948; Kinsey, Pomeroy, Martin, and Gebhard, 1953).

Partner availability and good health are crucial variables to sexual continuance. Any acute or chronic illness lowers male sexual responsiveness and if his wife is ill the aging male is restricted in sexual opportunity (Masters and Johnson, 1966). Seven out of ten healthy married couples over sixty years were sexually active, some into their late eighties (Swartz, 1966). In contrast, only 7% of the single, divorced, and widowed over sixty years were found sexually active (Newman and Nichols, 1966).

Surveys undertaken at the Kinsey Institute (Kinsey et al., 1948) and at Duke University (Newman and Nichols, 1960) have disclosed that 70% of married males aged seventy remained sexually active with a mean frequency of .9 per week, with some males maintaining a frequency of three times per week. By age seventy-five, 50% of married males are still sexually active (Claman, 1966).

Regarding female sexual incidence, 70% of married females and 12% of post-married females aged sixty engaged in coitus. The incidence of masturbation was higher for postmarital females, with 25% of single females aged seventy still masturbating (Christenson and Gagnon, 1965). Sexual abstinence in the elderly woman is not primarily biological but is influenced by social and psychological factors, since they do not seek partner replacements unless they are unusually attractive and secure with exceptional personal assets (Kaplan, 1974).

Worry over sexual failure can create secondary impotence. Culture-induced unconscious sex anxiety may cause premature sex abandonment; therefore, the supernormal frequencies found in some elderly males may more accurately reflect innate capacity and could become the average expectation in a more guiltless, biologically natural culture (Stokes, 1951). Abnormal sex behavior in the elderly cannot be described when normal sex behavior is still unknown due to lack of published research (Hirt, 1966). We are realizing that the decline of sexual activity in the elderly is less a factor of physiology than an artifact of social prohibitions and lack of willing partner availability.

Interaction of Restricting Cultural and Physiological Factors

If it is true that sexuality in the elderly is primarily spouse-related and that companionship increases life expectancy and self-worth, then elderly patients who miss intimacy and sexual expression should be directed in counseling to finding a mate. Counseling should also be directed to increasing their sexual satisfaction. Given that sex and companionship are important for the elderly, the interacting physical and cultural limitations to their sex adjustment must next be examined.

Although the culture imposes some restrictions on the elderly male, his sexuality is primarily limited by physical factors. In contrast, the elderly female, where physical capabilities and responsiveness have not depreciated, is primarily limited from sexual expression by cultural factors. Understanding of this distinction is necessary for a more rational approach to sexuality in the aged.

The elderly male experiences reduced sexual stamina, which adversely affects his sex life. Biological changes include decreased orgasm frequency, longer refractory periods following orgasm, loss of awareness of pending orgasm, and greater need for direct stimulation for arousal (Kaplan, 1974). Sexual adjustment and satisfaction in the elderly male may require shifts in the sexual pattern. The female may need to take a more active role in sexual situations and both partners may need to learn new behaviors to increase compatibility and minimize the functional effects of aging on male sexuality.

Since aging does not substantially affect sexual capacity of elderly females, compared to elderly males, cultural factors such as the double standard impede sexual actualization in elderly females. Women are faced with approximately eleven years of matelessness since they tend to marry males four years older and the life expectancy for males is seven years shorter. Elderly females glut the marketplace, which makes it easier for widowed males to remarry. Females outnumber males 138.5 to 100 at age sixty-five and 156.2 to 100 at age seventy-five (Pfeiffer and Davis, 1972).

To avert the problem of protracted widowhood, solutions from prolonging the vigor and life of the male to polygamy have been proposed (Pfeiffer and Davis, 1972; Kassell, 1966). Dean (1972) proposed a more parsimonious solution:

> It is an irony of fate and an anatomico-physiological paradox that a male-oriented society
> has propagated the custom of a man's marrying a woman younger than himself. Many a

woman, after reaching the menopause and being freed of the fear of pregnancy, is more desirous of sex than ever before, but it is precisely at such a propitious time that her husband, who is five or ten years older, may begin to show impotence. Many think there would be much less sexual frustration in later years—and perhaps fewer widows—if the chronological trend were reversed so that women marry younger men to begin with.

If not initial marriage, at least dating in older life should allow elderly females access to younger males without social censure based on mother–son incest taboos. There is no need to view sexual contact with an older person as physically repugnant stemming from our cult of youth as beauty. Much of the physical signs of aging, the paunch and the wrinkles, are due to poor body caretaking, not to the aging process. Many elderly people who lived prudently are remarkably attractive without the physical signs we attribute to old age. People, both male and female, should be allowed to pick their life partners on the sole basis of compatibility. This would make acceptable the relationship of the younger male with an older female. Age-discrepant relationships do not necessarily indicate psychopathology for either party. Since the younger male would benefit from the experience of the older female, the positive sexual and psychological benefits afforded each party would make this combination as rewarding as a liaison with a partner of one's same age. In dealing with the expanding geriatric population and their sexual needs, society will have to take a more liberalized view regarding alternate life-styles. People should be allowed to choose their mates on the basis of psychological compatibility, not preconceived standards of propriety or normalcy.

Sexual Therapy to Help Elderly Couples Become Sexually Liberated

Many therapists and sexual therapy programs are now directing themselves to enhancing sexuality (Kaplan, 1974). Therapy modalities that range from weekend sexual workshops directed to body awareness and nondemand mutual pleasuring to the more traditional techniques are helping elderly people obtain a more fulfilling sexual adjustment. Their needs are no less important sexually and no less desirable socially than the needs of younger people.

I have been involved in a therapy program to help elderly couples become sexually liberated (Sviland, 1974). This included couples over the age of sixty with a basically sound marital relationship and no sexual dysfunction who wanted to decrease their sexual inhibitions and expand their repertoire of sexual behaviors to conform to recently liberated mores. Raised in a more prohibitive era, they wanted to erase still-prevalent internal taboos toward such activities as oral–genital sex or sex for pleasure.

The primary therapy goal is increased sexual satisfaction. A universal subgoal is permission to accept one's sexuality without guilt or shame. The therapist then hooks the superego and becomes a stronger authority figure granting permission for sexual curiosity and exploration. The therapist must remain flexible throughout the therapy, shifting from exercises to psychotherapy with insight as needed. Assignments are always in "the here and now" of what the couple currently feels comfortable to work on. Exercises proceed slowly with patient control to prevent anxiety or negative emotional response. The basic attitude gotten across is that sex can be playful and enjoyable and another way of expressing affection. One does what one wants when one feels like it. Sex is not a ritual.

Procedure

Voluntary treatment occurred in a hospital setting with referral from medical services. The flood of applicants attests to the needs of elderly couples in the community at large for this type of counseling.

Outpatient treatment consisted of weekly one-hour sessions with homework assignments. Treatment combined educational materials, sexual exercises, assertion training, and traditional psychotherapy techniques according to the needs and goals of each couple. Since the whole issue of sexuality is highly personal with different value systems, the therapist never advocated specific behaviors but helped the couple achieve self-stated goals.

First sessions focused on exploration of (1) current sex life, (2) subjective feelings about current sex life, (3) marital dynamics, (4) degree of attitude change mutually desired, and (5) definition of goals and approximate number of sessions required.

In the conduct of therapy with the aged it is very important to recognize that the sexual values, attitudes, and especially capabilities may differ markedly among the elderly. Therefore, the rate of progress of introducing various information and techniques requires astute pacing to fit the characteristics of the clients.

Educational materials may be introduced at this point for the purpose of (1) desensitization to previously taboo behaviors, (2) technique learning, (3) increasing eroticism, and (4) increasing sexual fantasy. Couples may be sent into the field to view X-rated movies, self-selected, and to puruse sexual handbooks such as Comfort's *Joy of Sex* (1972) and Otto and Otto's *Total Sex* (1973). Couples generally experience a sense of naughty intrigue with these assignments. Their responses to these materials are then explored and used to establish sexual exercise goals. Increasing the fantasy system and general level of eroticism facilitates later homework sex assignments. The wife may especially need help with integration of increased, explicit sex fantasies and her self-ideal—in other words, to understand that a woman can enjoy and think about sex and still be a lady.

At this stage, increased physical attractiveness and flirtation techniques may be included where the relationship is dull because the couple take each other for granted and do not satisfy each other's romantic needs. Each spouse defines explicit attire and mannerisms that would increase erotic attraction. The husband is told, "If your wife was a young secretary, how would you have to look and what would you have to say to get her to take you seriously as a potential lover?" The wife is told, "If you were widowed and wanted to trap this man in a field of rough competition, how would you have to dress and act and talk to turn him into an ardent suitor?" Simultaneous homework exercises to replicate the playfulness, intrigue, and joy of dating may include candlelight dinners, unexpected love notes, flirtatious telephone conversations, etc.

Couples write in detail their ideal sexual fantasy before body contact exercises are introduced. The couple exchange their fantasies and behavior to supplement each party's fantasy. Frequently, the wife's fantasy indicates a need for more romance with behaviors to enhance nurturance and tenderness rather than specific sex act concerns.

Next sessions involve selected sexual exercises. Sensate focus exercises involving hand, foot, and head caresses may be initially employed. Opening communication is vital so partners can frankly convey without shame or anxiety what their sexual needs are, which may not agree with what the textbooks state is normative. To this end the nonthreatening pleasuring exercises developed by Masters and Johnson (1970) and Hartman and Fithian (1974) are very useful. Specific sex techniques are approached in a graduated series of steps to prevent anxiety or negative emotional response.

This treatment was remarkably successful in changing behavior and attitudes within weeks. Following goal attainment of increased sexual happiness, therapy is extended with minor variations on the exercises to ensure a stable system of consistent positive response to recently acquired behaviors with absence of ensuing marital or intrapsychic conflict.

Problems encountered in sexual therapy with the elderly which are age-specific and must be worked through to make therapy successful will next be described.

Special Considerations Critical to Sex Therapy with the Aged

Depression and Sexual Avoidance Following Goal Success. Some couples who were delighted with their newfound sexual liberation, experimentation, and enjoyment developed a marked avoidance of sexuality shortly after treatment success. Exploration disclosed that this avoidance was a psychological defense against depression elicited by sexual liberation in confrontation of sexual limitations due to the physiological changes of aging. In essence, this was like giving them the keys to a new sports car, then rationing the gasoline to Sunday driving only. For some, sexual expansiveness, then, brought a closer identification with the dying process than with the vitality of youth.

Although this phenomenon has not been previously reported, a major shortcoming of short-term sexual therapies without follow-up is that therapy concludes before later dynamic shifts occur. In sexual therapy with elderly couples it is imperative to continue treatment until both partners have integrated mutual self-acceptance of their age-bound capacities without devaluation or wistful regrets to regain the lost capacity of youth.

Shifting Stereotyped Roles and Techniques to Minimize the Differential Effects of Aging. Although the female does not experience much shift in her sexual capacity with aging, the male undergoes distinct performance changes. Both partners must understand and accept these changes and alter their sexual techniques accordingly to minimize the effects so both partners are left feeling mutually satisfied.

With aging the male experiences a decline in orgasm although frequent and enjoyable erections can still be maintained (Kaplan, 1974). The male must be helped to understand without loss of self-esteem or anxiety that not every erection can result in orgasm. Elderly couples must be taught to lightheartedly enjoy each sexual encounter for what it brings without performance demands. The female can remain multiply orgasmic throughout her life. Therefore, Masters and Johnson (1966) suggested that the elderly man enjoy love play with the wife without the ultimate goal of orgasm each time sex play is initiated. If he is not competitive with his wife and secure in his own sexuality, he can find pleasure and stimulation in helping her achieve her capacity for orgasm. Both must understand that the touchdown mentality of our culture requiring end-product orgasm impedes sexual pleasure. Neither partner should require orgasm from him or herself or from his or her mate to consider the sexual relationship successful. This relieves the necessity of faking an orgasm.

The aging male may have distinct loss of feeling of ejaculatory inevitability. Where this occurs, couples must forego simultaneous orgasm as the ultimate satisfactory act since the male is unable to voluntarily prolong copulation to await the female orgasm. In essence, elderly couples must be shifted to acceptance of tandem nondemand pleasuring.

The elderly male may also experience a paradoxical reaction wherein in prolonged sexual activity if the erection is lost he is unable to obtain another erection for twelve to twenty-four hours, which is the same as if he had an orgasm (Kaplan, 1974). If orgasm is possible, it is psychologically better for the male to allow himself to freely experience orgasm at any stage of love play, then continue pleasuring the female, rather than concentrating on maintaining the erection and losing it.

As the male becomes older he requires more intense direct stimulation of the genital region to obtain erection and ejaculation. The female may need to become a more active participant in the sex act. This can be highly threatening to couples with rigidly stereotyped, narrowly defined sex roles. I have seen couples who viewed their sex style as mutually satisfactory where the wife never touched the male genitalia. As a first step to desensitization of direct stimulation of the male genitalia, the female must understand that this need is not a reflection of her lessening physical attractiveness to stimulate her mate but part of the aging process of the male. Both must be helped to more actively give and receive pleasure without shame or fear that this is shifting their stereotype of what is acceptable or should be reasonable for the male or female role in sexuality.

Working Through Obstructive Marital Dynamics.   Before sexual therapy can begin, it is necessary to first work through any negative transactions and remove hidden resentments. Many times the bedroom is a battleground for hostilities and resentments arising elsewhere in the relationship. Improved sexual adjustment is improbable where the partners are occupied in power struggles, uncooperativeness, and withholding of behaviors that would satisfy the partner's sexual desires.

One case comes to mind where the couple was locked into a repetitive, destructive transaction with the wife, following a transactional analysis script of "Rapo" (Berne, 1964), being extremely seductive until the husband took the bait and made a sexual overture, wherein she would angrily reject him. The script was compatible to the husband's script of "Kick Me." The wife repeatedly requested sexuality in the context of romanticism while the husband was consistently blunt, sabotaging directed homework assignments. The sexual script outcomes of outrage in the wife and anger at rejection in the husband served as fuel for revenge in a more pervasive marital power struggle. Although this couple were easily able to liberate attitudinally and expand their repertoire of sexual behavior, sexual adjustment could not take place until this transactional dynamic was broken through and there was a loosening of the competitiveness and power struggle in the sexual scene.

A major shortcoming exists in sexual therapies that narrowly focus on specific acts. Sexual behavior must be examined from the wider perspective of the total marital relationship. Increased sexual gratification requires a shift in positive feelings for the partner and will not automatically occur from technique improvement alone. There are various types of marital and sexual dynamics occurring in ongoing relationships. These must be examined individually in treatment programs specifically designed to either maintain this balance or shift the balance constructively for both parties, or the program will be defeated.

Mutuality in Sexual Goals. Another problem in sexual therapy with the elderly involves mutual acceptance of liberated sexual goals. Typically, in goal-incompatibility problem cases, the husband wants his wife to become more sexually expansive while the wife wants to avoid any form of sex. The wife's disinterest in sex may be based on years of lack of enjoyment and orgastic dysfunction due to the husband's insensitivity to the wife's needs or from a chronic deteriorated relationship. Therapy directed to opening communication and marital dynamics must precede sexual expansion techniques. Sexual therapy is contraindicated over traditional psychotherapy where deeper intrapsychic conflicts result in sexual avoidance.

In general, where elderly couples have a good relationship and no sexual problems but want to become sexually liberated, they are given permission to experiment with as wide a range of sexual behaviors as desired. Later they discard or incorporate these behaviors into their sexual patterns according to their own values of meaningfulness. It is a mistake for one partner to engage in any specific act to please the other if unconscious aversion is not extinguished. In one case where the wife was highly motivated to sexually liberalize, she expressed conscious enjoyment of recently learned fellatio, yet loss of voice occurred four days following a dream of gagging to death on a penis. When this was interpreted and she was given permission to permanently discontinue fellatio, her voice rapidly returned. Since the couple now enjoy a wide range of other learned pleasuring behaviors, discarding fellatio was no significant loss to the husband.

Summary

For maximum long-lasting therapeutic benefit, sexual therapy should focus beyond specific training of sexual behaviors to treating the total interpersonal relationship. With the elderly couple, therapy must extend to working through depression at the confrontation of age-related physical limitations to integration of acceptance of current sexual capacity. Sexual therapy directed to helping elderly couples become sexually liberated not only has positive social value but has enabled elderly couples to open communication, increase intimacy and self-esteem, and enjoy without guilt sexual pleasures society accords as acceptable to its youth. Society should provide more such services to elderly couples and publicize their availability.

References

Berne, E. *Games people play*. New York: Grove Press, 1964.

Christenson, C. V., and Gagnon, J. H. Sexual behavior in a group of older women. *Journal of Gerontology*, 1965, *20*, 351–356.

Claman, A. D. Introduction to panel discussion: Sexual difficulties after 50. *Canadian Medical Association Journal*, 1966, *94*, 207.

Comfort, A. *Joy of sex*. New York: Crown, 1972.

Dean, S. R. Sin and senior citizens. *Journal of the American Geriatric Society*, 1966, *14*, 935–938.

Dean, S. R. Sexual behavior in middle life. *American Journal of Psychiatry*, 1972, *128*, 1267.

Feigenbaum, E. M., Lowenthal, M. F., and Trier, M. L. Aged are confused and hungry for sex information. *Geriatric Focus*, 1967, *5*, 2.

Hartman, W. E., and Fithian, M. A. *Treatment of sexual dysfunction*. New York: Jason Aronson, 1974.

Hirt, N. B. The psychiatrist's view. Panel discussion: Sexual difficulties after 50. *Canadian Medical Association Journal*, 1966, *94*, 213–214.

Kaplan, H. S. *The new sexual therapy*. New York: Brunner/Mazel, 1974.

Kassell, V. Polygamy after 60. *Geriatrics*, 1966, *21*, 214–218.

Kassell, V. *You never outgrow your need for sex*. Presented at 53rd Annual Meeting New England Hospital Assembly, Boston, March 27, 1974.

Kinsey, A. C., Pomeroy, W. B., and Martin, C. I. *Sexual behavior in the human male*. Philadelphia: W. B. Saunders, 1948.

Kinsey, A. C., Pomeroy, W. B., Martin, C. I., and Gebhard, P. H. *Sexual behavior in the human female*. Philadelpha, W. B. Saunders, 1953.

Masters, W. H., and Johnson, V. E. *Human sexual response*. Boston: Little, Brown, 1966.

Masters, W. H., and Johnson, V. E. *Human sexual inadequacy*. Boston: Little, Brown, 1970.

Newman, G., and Nichols, C. R. Sexual activities and attitudes in older persons. *Journal of the American Medical Association*, 1960, *173*, 33–35.

Otto, H. A., and Otto, R. *Total sex*. New York: New American Library, 1973.

Pfeiffer, E., and Davis, G. C. Determinants of sexual behavior in middle and old age. *Journal of the American Geriatrics Society*, 1972, *20*, 151–158.

Stokes, W. R. Sexual functioning in the aging male. *Geriatrics*, 1951, *6*, 304–308.

Sviland, M. A. P. *Helping elderly couples become sexually liberated*. Presented at Western Psychological Association Convention at San Francisco. April 28, 1974.

Swartz, D. The urologist's view. Panel discussion: Sexual difficulties after 50. *Canadian Medical Association Journal*, 1966, *94*, 213–214.

This chapter reports on a study of the sexuality of pregnant women. In general, the results showed a linear decrease in sexual interest, frequency of coitus, and frequency of orgasm over the course of pregnancy. These results should be viewed with caution, however, for a number of reasons. First, this is a retrospective study. Within a few days of delivery, women were asked to recall their sexual patterns over the course of their pregnancy. Such retrospective reports of events in the distant past are often distorted by selective memory and by the active memory of more recent events. Since the subjects were generally physically uncomfortable and therefore uninterested in sex during the ninth month of their pregnancy, their reports of decreased sexual activity during the first months of pregnancy may have been influenced by this recent memory. Secondly, the interviewers were all young males. It is reasonable to expect that many women, immediately after delivery, would be reluctant to describe themselves as highly interested in sex to young male strangers.

Regardless of these methodological problems, pregnancy is obviously an event that can have profound effects on a couple's sexual relationship. The clinician treating sexual dysfunction should always inquire carefully about pregnancy and the postdelivery period when taking sexual histories from patients.

29

Sexual Behavior in Pregnancy

Don A. Solberg, Julius Butler, and Nathaniel N. Wagner

Although in most mammalian species females do not seek intercourse during pregnancy, in certain primates and in human beings intercourse does occur during this period. The female primates do not seek coitus actively, but under male pressure and in confined physical conditions, they will submit (Booth, 1962; Benirschke and Richart, 1963; Berkson and Chaicumpa, 1969). For human females intercourse during pregnancy is exceedingly common.

Despite much of the recent interest in scientific and popular literature about human sexuality, the influences of the state of pregnancy on this highly variable aspect of human behavior are not well known. Masters and Johnson (1966) studied subjective changes in the sexuality of 101 pregnant women and found an increase in

This work was supported by a grant (RF68003) from the Rockefeller Foundation. The authors are indebted to Dr. Walter L. Herrmann, chairman of the Department of Obstetrics and Gynecology, University of Washington School of Medicine, for assistance in all stages of this study; to Clinton Sanford and James Haeg, who helped plan the study and served as interviewers; and to Dr. Josephine Sanders for assistance concerning the question of sexual activity and prematurity.

Don A. Solberg • Department of Psychology, University of Washington, Seattle, Washington   **Julius Butler** • Department of Obstetrics and Gynecology, University of Washington, School of Medicine, Seattle, Washington   **Nathaniel N. Wagner** • Department of Psychology, University of Washington, Seattle, Washington

sexual tension and performance in the second trimester that they associated with increased congestion of the pelvic vasculature. Semmens (1971) found nausea and vomiting in pregnancy to be more related to the life situation of the pregnant woman than to her sexual activity. Prochazka and Cernoch (1970), in Czechoslovakia, reported that women continued having intercourse during pregnancy for fear that their husbands would become unfaithful even though fully one-half had negative feelings about their continuing sexual behavior. Over one-half of the 200 women in their study abstained from coitus in the eighth lunar month.

Bartova, Kolrova, and Uzel (1969), in a study of 500 Czechoslovakian women, also documented a marked decrease in sexual interest and activity for many pregnant women, especially in the last half of pregnancy. Women who remained sexually active in late pregnancy often characterized their partners as overly demanding.

The purpose of our study was to investigate further female sexuality during pregnancy, as well as to provide some baseline information about specific sexual behaviors within an American population.

Materials and Methods

The subjects of this study were 260 women interviewed in the immediate post-partum period. Only those having access to a sexual partner for at least seven out of the nine months during the pregnancy in question were included in the sample. Of these, 98% were married, 1% were single but maintained stable relations throughout pregnancy, and 1% were widowed or divorced late in pregnancy.

Maternal age ranged from 17 to 41 years at the time of interview, with a mean age of 26.2 (SD of 4.4 years). Of those married, 86% had had no previous marriages, 13% had had one, and 1% had been married twice before. Length of the present marriage ranged from less than six months to more than 10 years at the time of interview, with a median of 4.2 years married.

Previous obstetric history showed 35% as gravida 1, 34% as gravida 2, and 25% as gravida 3 or 4, with 7% having had five or more previous pregnancies. The median number of previous pregnancies was 2.4

Distribution of the sample and their partners by level of education is represented in Figure 1. The median education level was .8 years of college for the women, and 2.7 years of college for their partners. The high level of education in this sample probably reflects the exclusion of most out-of-wedlock pregnancies as well as the generally high educational level of the Seattle area.

Prenatal care had begun for 87% by the end of the first trimester, and for 98% by the end of the second trimester. Of the sample, 77% received care from physicians in private practice; 23% received obstetric care from the staff in a university setting.

The mean gestational age of the infants was 38.4 weeks (SD of 2.04 weeks), and the median birth weight was 3,387 g.

Caucasians made up 93% of the sample, with 4% black, 2% Asian-American, and 1% other races. Religious preferences were denied by 19%, with 25% Catholic,

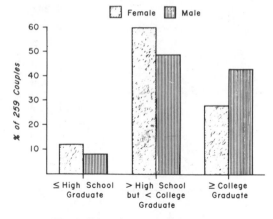

Fig. 1. Education level of the sample.

53% Protestant, 1% Jewish, and 3% other. This sample is very consistent with the ethnic and religious makeup of the Seattle area.

Each woman was interviewed by one of three trained male medical-student interviewers while in the hospital on the second or third postpartum day. Informed consent was received first from the physician in charge and then from the women themselves. All were aware of the nature and subject matter of the study: 15% of those asked refused to participate, and less than 1% discontinued the interview once it was begun.

Of those refusing to participate, the median age was 26.6 years (identical with that of the sample). The racial background and religious preference of those refusing to participate did not differ significantly from the sample except that Asian-Americans had a higher refusal rate ($p < .001$).

The interviews were conducted in private with a highly structured interview technique. For purposes of analysis, the pregnancy was divided into the following stages: first trimester (I), second trimester (II), seventh, eighth, and ninth months (7, 8, and 9), and a baseline of the year before becoming pregnant (B). Although probable date of conception was determined as closely as possible from the chart and patient information to allow accurate division of the pregnancy into stages, Stage I was considered to begin with each woman's first knowledge or strong suspicion of her pregnancy.

If a woman delivered prematurely, she was not included in the analysis of subsequent months. Data for partial months were converted to a monthly base where necessary. Data were analyzed with data-processing techniques; significance levels reflect chi-square analysis except as indicated. Minor variations in sample size within the study have occurred because some questions did not apply to all women and some women did not answer all questions.

Coitus

Data in Figures 2 and 3 were calculated from reported frequency of coitus per month. The differences between the stages of pregnancy in Figure 3 are signifi-

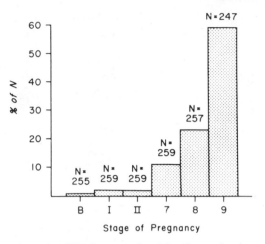

Fig. 2. Percentage of total number (*N*) of women abstaining from coitus in each stage of pregnancy.

cant at $p < .001$ except between I and II, which is significant at $p < .05$. It is note-worthy that the decrease in mean coital frequency for the women who continued to have intercourse is almost linear.

Table 1 shows a grouped frequency distribution of frequency of coitus by stage of pregnancy.

Frequency of coitus in B was significantly related to the woman's age, with older women tending to be less active ($p < .001$), and also to the length of marriage, activity tending to decrease with the duration of marriage ($p < .01$). (It is clear that age and length of marriage are interdependent measures.) Coital frequency at all stages was independent of race, religious preference, male or female education, negative feelings about being pregnant, or whether or not the pregnancy was planned. There was no significant association between coital frequency and number of previous pregnancies at any stage of pregnancy.

Despite the steady and significant decrease in sexual activity in pregnancy, few consistent relations were found between coital frequency and other data. There was some association with frequency of masturbation in the first seven months, with

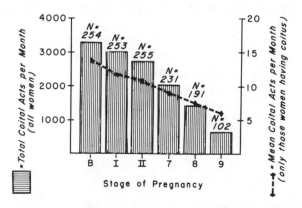

Fig. 3. Rate of coitus in each stage of pregnancy (*N* indicates the number of women still active in coitus).

Table 1. Frequency of Coitus at Different Stages of Pregnancy

Stage of pregnancy	N of women	Frequency of coitus (%)			
		None	<1/week	1–5/week	>5/week
B	255	1	7	81	12
I	259	2	11	78	9
II	259	2	16	77	5
7	259	11	23	63	2
8	257	23	29	46	2
9	247	59	19	23	1

Table 2. Rating of Sexual-Interest Level in Each Stage of Pregnancy as Compared to B

Stage of pregnancy	N of women	Sexual-interest level (%)		
		Increased	Unchanged	Decreased
I	226	23	48	28
II	226	24	32	44
7	226	16	19	65
8	224	14	14	71
9	215	13	11	75

those highly active in coitus more likely to be highly active in masturbation ($p <$ .05 to $p < .001$, depending on stage). Length of marriage became a decreasingly significant factor as pregnancy progressed, and after the seventh month, coital frequency was independent of length of marriage ($p > .05$). Women infrequently orgasmic tended to have coitus less often in Stages II and 8, although no other periods showed this relation.

The index most consistently associated with coital frequency was the woman's level of sexual interest during pregnancy as compared to the level of her interest before pregnancy. Table 2 shows the distribution of women's sexual interest level during pregnancy.

Those reporting a decrease in sexual interest tended to have lower rates of coitus than those whose interest level stayed the same or increased ($p < .05$ for Stage I, and $p < .01$ for Stages II, 7, and 8). This relation did not hold true for Stage 9, however. Interest level was not significantly associated with age, length of marriage, or parity.

Orgasmic Function

Orgasmic function during pregnancy was approached by discussion of each woman's past experience with orgasm in some detail. Only 7% of the women reported never having an orgasm. Another 9% claimed orgasmic experience, though by their description of orgasm the interviewer thought they might be

Table 3.   *Various Rates of Orgasm with Coitus at Each Stage*
of Pregnancy[a]

Stage of pregnancy	N of women	Rate of orgasm (% of women)		
		<25%	25–75%	>75%
B	233	13	36	51
I	235	20	36	45
II	237	23	41	36
7	218	40	30	30
8	186	51	25	24
9	98	57	19	23

[a]Excludes women not orgastic or abstaining from coitus.

confusing orgasm with plateau excitement. This "questionable" group of women did not differ significantly from other orgasmic women in either social or behavioral data, however, and were therefore included as orgasmic women in further analysis.

Table 3 shows the shift in percentage of coital acts leading to orgasm as pregnancy progressed. Table 4 indicates a general decrease in the strength or intensity of orgasm during as compared to orgasmic intensity before pregnancy. However, it is noteworthy that consistently a percentage of women reported an increase in orgasmic intensity at all stages of pregnancy.

Multiple orgasmic experience as described by Masters and Johnson was reported by 35% of orgastic women. Of these, the frequency of multiple orgasm during pregnancy was reported to increase by 3%, to stay the same by 35%, and to decrease by 62%. Whether or not a woman was orgastic was associated with frequency of coitus in Stages I and II $(p < .01)$, and 7 and 8 $(p < .02)$, with orgastic women more likely to have continued coitus during pregnancy. This relation did not hold true in Stage 9, however. The rate of orgasmic experience with coitus was inconsistently associated with coital frequency, as previously mentioned. There was a low-order positive relation between rate of orgasm and length of marriage $(p < .10)$ before pregnancy but no relation during pregnancy.

Table 4.   *Rating of the Strength or Intensity of Orgasm as Compared*
to Intensity in Stage B for Each Stage of Pregnancy[a]

Stage of pregnancy	N of women	Ratings of orgasm (% of women)		
		Intensity increased	Intensity unchanged	Intensity decreased
I	223	17	66	17
II	211	10	62	28
7	179	12	46	41
8	151	11	37	52
9	91	11	41	48

[a]Excludes women not orgastic or abstaining from coitus.

As with coital frequency, rate of orgasm throughout pregnancy was most significantly related to sexual-interest level. Those whose interest level decreased, as compared to the interest level in Stage B, were likely to have lower rates of coital orgasm than those whose interest level increased or stayed the same ($p < .01$ for Stage I, and $p < .001$ for Stages II, 7, 8, and 9).

Other Sexual Behavior

Masturbation as an attempt to achieve orgasm had been used in the last two years before pregnancy by 16% of 259 women. Of these, 64% had achieved orgasm with masturbation. Although some women masturbated during pregnancy only, there was a larger shift toward abstaining. Of the 44 women using masturbation in the previous two years, only 12% did not masturbate in B, whereas 50 to 60% did not masturbate during pregnancy (differences between stages were not significant). Orgasmic rate with masturbation did not change significantly during pregnancy.

Hand stimulation by the woman's partner as an attempt to reach orgasm was used in the previous two years before pregnancy by 45% of 260 women; of these 118, 57% had been successfully orgasmic at least once. Although 23% of the 118 did not use hand stimulation in Stage B, 38 to 42% did not use it during pregnancy. Orgasmic rate from hand stimulation did not seem to vary significantly during pregnancy.

Oral–genital stimulation in an attempt to reach orgasm was used by 39% of 257 women in the previous two years. Of these 99 women, fellatio was usually performed by 32%, and cunnilingus by 17%, with 50% using both with equal frequency or simultaneously. Using oral–genital stimulation, 53% of the 99 women had been successful in reaching orgasm at least once. There were no significant differences between these three methods in terms of rate of use throughout pregnancy. Of the 99 using oral–genital stimulation to attempt orgasm, 11% did not use it in Stage B, whereas 42 to 55% did not use it during pregnancy. Orgasmic rates from oral–genital stimulation did decline with pregnancy, going from 16% reporting orgasm rarely or never in Stage B to 58% in Stage 9.

Other sexual practices did not occur at a frequency sufficient for analysis.

Only five women (2%) received recommendations from their physicians or other paramedical personnel concerning sexual activities that might be substituted for coitus in pregnancy. Hand stimulation was the activity recommended to satisfy both partners.

Coital Positions

Figure 4 shows the percentage of couples who preferred using various coital positions. Notable was the decrease in the use of the male superior position and the increase in use of other positions, particularly side-by-side, as pregnancy progressed. Figure 5 shows the percentage of couples using positions other than those in Figure 4. The amount of variability in coital positions used by couples

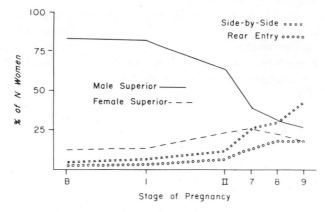

Fig. 4. Coital positions used most often.

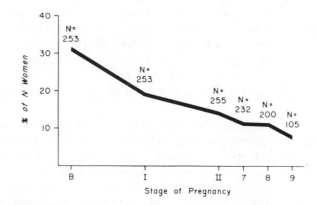

Fig. 5. Percentage of women using coital positions other than the basic four shown in Fig. 4.

tended to decrease (as coital frequency continued to decrease) throughout pregnancy.

There was no striking association between coital frequency and positions used, but there was a consistent, low-order relation, with more active women tending to use a side-by-side position in Stages 7, 8, and 9 more frequently than women of low activity. There was no association between position used and orgasmic rate.

Of the 260 women, 10% received recommendations from their physicians or other paramedical personnel about positions that might be more comfortable in pregnancy. Side-by-side or rear entry was recommended to 5%, the rest receiving other recommendations.

Reasons for Change

Women reporting a change in degree or intensity of their sexual experience during pregnancy were questioned about the reason (or reasons) in their own minds for the change. Their responses, as grouped by the interviewers, were as follows: physical discomfort, 46%; fear of injury to baby, 27%; loss of interest, 23%; awkwardness having coitus, 17%; recommendation of physician, 8%; reasons extraneous to pregnancy, 6%; loss of attractiveness in woman's own mind, 4%; recommendation of person other than physician, 1%; and other reasons, 15%. The major reason for change, if more than one reason was given, followed the same distribution.

Of 260 women, 29% received instructions from their physicians recommending coital abstention, beginning at times ranging from two to eight weeks before the estimated date of confinement. Women receiving such instructions were more likely to abstain from coitus in Stage 9 ($p < .01$). Other months showed no such relation.

Sexual Activity and Prematurity

Among the 260 women, only nineteen deliveries were premature by dates or infant birth weight, with only nine infants premature by both criteria. This sample is too small to attach any statistical significance to trends observed in the sexual behavior of mothers of premature infants.

However, out of 260 women, none had noticed the immediate onset of labor after coitus or orgasm. Also, birth weight, gestational age at delivery, and APGAR scores at one minute were all independent of either frequency of coitus or rate of orgasm in Stages 7, 8, and 9.

Discussion

Much of this study has been intended as normative information and needs no further discussion. Several points are of particular interest, however.

Masters and Johnson (1966), in the only other reported study on an American population of female sexuality in pregnancy, found several relationships not supported in this study. Most strikingly, the second-trimester increase in sexual tension and effectiveness of performance noted by 82 of 101 women in their report was evidenced by only 24% of 226 women in this study. Moreover, nearly all other measurements of sexual behavior that were monitored in this study point to an overall steady, almost linear decline in all aspects of sexuality for the majority of women as pregnancy progressed. it is possible that details of feeling and behavior were obscured into a general "impression" by the time women were interviewed in this study; however, it was our impression that most women had excellent recall of events happening during their pregnancy, and the wide differences in responses between stages for many individual women reflect this.

Also, Masters and Johnson noted a distinct association between parity and sexual-interest levels in the first trimester, with nulliparous women more likely to notice a decrease in sexual interest at this stage than parous women, whose interest level tended to remain the same. No such relation was found in our sample, however, since nulliparous and parous women did not differ significantly in interest level throughout pregnancy.

Furthermore, Masters and Johnson found a large number of women (20 of 101) reporting feelings of loss of their physical attractiveness to their partners, and cited this as a major factor in the declining sexuality noticed in the third trimester. Our results indicate that a much smaller portion (4%) listed loss of attractiveness as a reason for change. Interestingly enough, although 29% of the women in our sample received instructions to abstain toward the estimated date of confinement, only 8% of women claimed to have directly changed their behavior owing to physician recommendation. Masters and Johnson found 47% of their sample receiving direct instructions to abstain toward the estimated date of confinement, and they felt that this was a strongly influencing factor.

There is good agreement between the two studies concerning sexual-interest levels and performance in the last trimester.

The differences in results as noted above may be related to sampling error or to the procedural differences inherent in the two studies. A retrospective study such as the present one, although it may appear less precise, cannot directly effect a change in sample behavior in the process of measuring that behavior. It should also be noted that Masters and Johnson regard the portion of the work cited as primarily clinical impressions supplying groundwork for further investigation.

Whether or not there is any association between sexual activity during late pregnancy and premature birth is currently controversial. Javert (1957) contended that frequent or multiple orgasm early in pregnancy may result in spontaneous abortion. Pugh and Fernandez (1953) found no relation between coital activity and prematurity. Goodlin, Keller, and Raffin (1971) contended that orgasm after thirty-two weeks of pregnancy was significantly more frequent in patients who subsequently delivered prematurely than those who delivered at term. Masters and Johnson (1966), in their review, concluded that the whole problem of coition during the third trimester should be individualized, with the only major contraindications to coition being spotting, bleeding, or a deeply engaged presenting fetal part.

The present study cannot fully resolve this question. It is apparent that there is no linear relation between sexual activity in late pregnancy and premature birth for the large majority of women. It also appears that the approximate prematurity risk factor of 15% for women continuing to be orgasmic after thirty-two weeks as calculated by Goodlin et al. (1971) does not hold true for this sample population. For the 138 women in our study who had orgasm after the seventh month, the prematurity rate was less than 6%, which was not significantly different from that in women who did not have orgasm after the seventh month.

However, it is quite possible that there is a small subgroup of women already predisposed to prematurity for whom orgasm after thirty-two weeks is an added risk factor. This question requires a larger sample of premature births for adequate study.

Conclusions

It is obvious that the human female undergoes a complicated series of physical, hormonal, and psychologic changes during pregnancy. The response to these changes is quite variable, reflecting the highly individualistic nature of human sexuality and response to pregnancy.

Many women, however, appear to respond to these changes with a generalized loss of libido, with the number of women so affected increasing during the later stages of pregnancy. This loss of libido is usually reflected by reduced sexual performance in coital and noncoital sexual behavior. The decrease in noncoital behavior, such as mutual oral–genital stimulation, suggests that more than attitudes and comfort with sexuality are involved. Which women will be so affected is not predictable by socioeconomic or other demographic information. Pregnancy appears to be a unique event in terms of a woman's sexuality, and should be treated as such.

It is our impression that most pregnant women desire information concerning the physiologic and emotional aspects of sexual activity during pregnancy. The normative data described in this article can supply a sound basis of fact by means of which physicians and other medical personnel can counsel couples during this time when they have so many unasked and unanswered questions. It is to be hoped that this research will encourage other investigators to broaden knowledge and understanding by further studies.

References

Bartova, D., Kolrova, O., Uzel, R., et al. Sex life during pregnancy. *Ceskoslovenska Gynekologie*, 1969, *34*, 560–562.

Benirschke, K., and Richart, R. The establishment of a marmoset breeding colony and its four pregnancies. *Laboratory Animal Care*, 1963, *13*, 70–83.

Berkson, G., and Chaicumpa, V. Breeding gibbons (*Hylobates lar entelloides*) in the laboratory. *Laboratory Animal Care*, 1969, *19*, 808–811.

Booth, C. Some observations on behavior of Cercopithecus monkeys. *Annals of the New York Academy of Sciences*, 1962, *102*, 477–487.

Goodlin, R. C., Keller, D. W. F., and Raffin, M. Orgasm during late pregnancy: Possible deleterious effects. *Obstetrics and Gynecology*, 1971, *38*, 916–920.

Javert, C. T. *Spontaneous and habitual abortion*. New York: McGraw-Hill, 1957.

Masters, W. H., and Johnson, V. E. *Human sexual response*. Boston: Little, Brown, 1966. Pp. 141–168.

Prochazka, J., and Cernoch, A. Coitus in pregnancy. *Ceskoslovenska Gynekologie*, 1970, *35*, 282–287.

Pugh, W. E., and Fernandez, F. L. Coitus in late pregnancy: A follow-up study of the effects of coitus on late pregnancy, delivery, and the puerperium. *Obstetrics and Gynecology*, 1953, *2*, 636–642.

Semmens, J. P. Female sexuality and life situations: An etiologic psycho-socio-sexual profile of weight gain and nausea and vomiting in pregnancy. *Obstetrics and Gynecology*, 1971, *38*, 555–563.

In treatment of life-threatening and often fatal diseases, it is understandable that management of less urgent aspects of the patient's rehabilitation is often overlooked. In regard to sexual functioning, both the physician's and the patient's embarrassment about discussing sex adds to the probability that the patient's postcoronary sexual adjustment will not be considered. In this article, the literature on the effects of heart disease on sexual functioning is reviewed, and a number of data-based suggstions for improved patient care are offered. The type of preventive and rehabilitative program suggested would presumably prevent postcoronary patients from developing a sexual dysfunction as the result of anxiety, fear, and depression caused by a lack of knowledge about the effects of their heart condition on their sexuality.

30

Sexual Adjustment of the Postcoronary Male

Jerry M. Friedman

Cardiovascular disease remains the number one health problem in this country, with myocardial infarction, or heart attack, one of the most common forms of the disease (American Heart Association, 1974). Survivors of a myocardial infarction, and their families, are often forced to make significant social and psychological adjustments. Efforts to rehabilitate the heart attack victim usually consist of attempts to return him to an optimal physical and mental state, and an activity level compatible with the functional capacity of his heart. In view of this goal, it is surprising to find that the vast majority of rehabilitation literature has been concerned with vocational rehabilitation and, until recently, has virtually ignored the sexual rehabilitation of the cardiac patient. In a review of the recent literature on cardiovascular rehabilitation for the National Heart and Lung Institute, McGill (1975) cited only 2 studies, out of more than 100 reviewed, that dealt directly with sexual rehabilitation. In an earlier review, Hellerstein and Friedman (1969) reviewed 33 cardiology texts and found no more than 1000 words referring to sexual activity and heart disease.

In view of the limited research on postcorony sexual adjustment, several questions need to be addressed.

Jerry M. Friedman • Department of Psychology and Department of Psychiatry and Behavioral Science, State University of New York, Stony Brook, New York

What Are the Sexual Problems and Concerns of Postcoronary Patients?

The most widely accepted criteria for evaluating rehabilitation services are degree of physical improvement and the ability to return to work. The patient's own evaluation of his physical improvement, and his psychosocial adjustment in terms of sexual, familial, and interpersonal roles, are seldom included as criteria (Safilios-Rothschild, 1970). Fear of death or another heart attack seems to be a major concern of heart attack victims, and this fear is frequently associated with sexual difficulty (Bloch, Maeder, and Haissly, 1975; Dangrove, 1968; Hackett and Cossem, 1973; Renshaw, 1976; Sanne, 1973; Stein, 1975).

The primary sexual problems reported by male patients are decreased sexual desire and impotence. Bloch et al. (1975) questioned 100 postmyocardial infarction patients about their usual sexual activity prior to their heart attack and at follow-up eleven months later. They found a significant decrease in sexual activity, more marked in older patients, but present in all age groups. This reduction in sexual activity was present, in spite of the fact that almost all of the patients had resumed an otherwise normally active life. There was no correlation between work capacity and frequency of intercourse, with some physically fit patients engaging in no sexual activity, and others with poor physical fitness continuing with quite frequent intercourse. In an earlier study by Klein, Dean, Willson, and Bogdonoff (1965), 5 out of 20 postmyocardial infarction patients interviewed had resumed full sexual activity, 7 claimed abstinence, and 8 claimed diminished activity. Tuttle, Cook, and Fitch (1964) interviewed males who were being advised by a work evaluation clinic and found that two-thirds had a marked and lasting reduction in the frequency of their sexual activity, while one-third had returned to their prior level of activity. Ten percent of the sample reported permanent impotence. No pattern was found to correlate reduced sexual activity with age or severity of heart attack. The men were interviewed one to nine years after the infarct. Hellerstein and Friedman (1970) found a significant decrease in sexual activity in a group of patients who had experienced a heart attack, when compared to a matched group of coronary prone men.

These studies tend to support the contention that many cardiac patients do have sexual difficulties, ranging from reduced activity to total impotence. Furthermore, these problems are not necessarily related to age, severity of infarct, and capacity for other nonsexual activity, and they may not be evident from studies that use such criteria as return to work or degree of physical improvement as measures of successful rehabilitation. Yet sexual difficulties can be one of the most important problems a heart attack victim has to face. As one physician puts it: "I think that one of the most important problems for the post-heart-attack patient is sex life—or, rather worry and inhibitions about it. It's a major problem—a stress factor for patient and spouse . . ." (Brinner, 1972).

Reduced sexual activity can lead to marital conflict (as well as be caused by it), frustration, and irritability, thus possibly starting a cycle of behavior that may further hamper rehabilitation, and may even increase the chances of further cardiac symptomatology (Koller, Kennedy, Butler, and Wagner, 1972).

Are Postcoronary Patients Receiving Adequate Advice and Help in Dealing with Their Sexual Problems and Concerns?

Researchers and clinicians writing in the field of sexual rehabilitation are almost unanimous in their assertion that heart attack patients are not getting adequate advice and help (Douglas and Wilkes, 1975; Francis, Krosch, and Morris, 1969; Green, 1975; Hackett and Bildeau, 1971; Klein et al., 1965; Koller et al., 1972; Renshaw, 1976; Semmler and Semmler, 1974; Tuttle et al., 1964).

Tuttle and his associates found that two-thirds of their sample claimed to have received no advice on sex, and the remaining one-third claimed vague or nonspecific advice. The authors assert: "Having received little or no advice from their physicians, these patients set their own patterns which represented a considerable deviation from their previous sexual activity" (Tuttle et al., 1964).

Koller and associates state: "Standard advice to the coronary patient includes reducing or stopping smoking, reducing weight and dietary fat intake and doing regular, mild physical exercise, but not much about sexual matters. Consequently, the patient acts according to his limited knowledge, fears, opinions or superstitions. He may unnecessarily reduce his sexual activity, even to the point of abstinence" (Koller et al., 1972).

Hackett and Bildeau (1971) found that there was little information given to patients regarding sexual activity except for such generalities as "avoid overexertion" in work and recreation.

A good deal of the criticism for the inadequate advice given to cardiac patients on sexual matters is directed at the physician. Among the reasons advanced for the lack of adequate advice by physicians are cultural bias, embarrassment, lack of information, time constraints, and basic conservatism. While the data seem to indicate that some of the criticism is justified, a good deal of it may not be.

The public misconception that a person who has had a heart attack must be on an extremely limited activity schedule may militate against a physician's taking advantage of newer treatment regimes such as early exercise and return to sexual activity. If the patient died because of unrelated factors, the suspicion might remain that the activity schedule had caused the death. So, even though evidence points to the fact that there is no increase in mortality due to early yet gradual return to full activity (including sexual activity), there remains a cultural bias that doctors may be reluctant to change (Levy and McGill, 1975). Hellerstein and Ford (1957) have stated, even more directly, that if a bold approach would result in death it would reflect adversely on the doctor's professional competence, reputation, and potential earnings. Therefore, being reluctant to take this risk, a doctor may actually delay rehabilitation.

While reluctance to take risks may motivate some physicians, it should also be noted that empirical knowledge of the effects of sexual activity on the diseased heart is still fragmentary. Many doctors taking a conservative approach to treatment may be awaiting more information, and actually may be practicing more responsible medicine. As will be demonstrated below, there has been some overgeneralization of the data that do exist on the cardiac demands of sexual activity.

Koller et al. (1972) argue that two reasons for inadequate sexual advice are that the physician, like other Americans, often finds it uncomfortable to discuss sexuality, and that he usually has not been educated to deal with his patient's sexual difficulties. In a discussion of medical education, Hellerstein and Friedman (1969) state: "During their training they learn something about sexual anatomy and about conception, pregnancy and birth. Few are given any conception of the physiology of normal coitus and orgasm, or of the psychopathology of sex." This statement is most likely less true now, with the addition of courses in human sexual behavior to many medical school curricula. However, many currently practicing physicians may not be as informed as they would like to be about this central area of human functioning, and they may still hesitate to initiate discussion on the topic.

Time has also been proposed as a factor that keeps doctors from discussing problems and giving adequate information. They often cannot meet the needs of their patients for advice on sex due to time constraints, and may be reluctant to have the patient and family counseled by a nurse or other health professional (Francis et al., 1969).

The patient also is often too embarrassed to discuss the subject of sex and may be apprehensive about any sexual restrictions that may be placed on him. As noted above, Tuttle et al. (1964) found that two-thirds of those patients they interviewed received no advice on sex, with the remaining one-third receiving vague or unspecified advice. However, in another study, Hellerstein and Friedman (1969) received responses to questionnaires from over 2,000 doctors, and 94% said that they counseled on sex. The discrepancy in these data may be due to problems of communication. Even when sex *is* discussed, there may be difficulty in establishing effective communication between patient and physician, especially since the subject often is an uncomfortable one for both of them, and the time a stressful one. In a study including 307 patients and 102 physicians, patients perceived doctors as initiating discussions of sex far less frequently than the doctors said they did. Both doctors and patients agreed that patients seldom initiated discussions of sex. Of 112 patients reporting discussions of sexual matters, only 44% believed the discussions to be helpful (Pinderhughes, Grace, Reyna, and Anderson, 1972).

In summary, physicians have usually been exposed to the same cultural mores as their patients. Sex, an uncomfortable topic, is often ignored by both physician and patient alike. However, it remains the responsibility of the physician to take the initiative and begin sexual counseling when needed. This requires time, openness, empathy, sexual knowledge, and an acceptance of the importance of sex. Those physicians with limited sexual knowledge and/or limited time can make certain that their patients receive adequate counseling from other health professionals such as nurses, social workers, or psychologists.

Why Do Postcoronary Patients Experience Sexual Problems and What Are the Empirical Findings Addressing These Problems?

Clearly cardiac patients may experience sexual problems for a number of reasons, only some directly related to their cardiac condition. Bloch et al. (1975)

report that the reasons given for decreased sexual activity by patients in their study were anxiety and fear of relapse or sudden death, depression, spouse decision, fatigue, and angina pain. Other factors that may influence sexual adjustment are drugs, aging, interpersonal dynamics, and loss of self-esteem.

Fear of reinfarct or death is one of the most commonly reported problems in all areas of cardiac rehabilitation. Tuttle et al. (1964) concluded that the decreased sexual activity and impotence found among the patients they interviewed were "based on misinformation and fear." Hackett and Cossem (1973) report that one of the most common misconceptions of coronary patients is that even limited exertion can kill, and that repeat heart attacks tend to occur during orgasm. In a recent study, Sanne (1973) found that of 315 nonselected patients studied, 42% limited their physical activities because of fear rather than because of physical limitations. The questions doctors need to address to deal effectively with these fears are: Does sex produce significant strain on the heart? How does the physiological cost of sex compare with that of other activities?

Masters and Johnson (1966) have studied the physiologic effects of sexual intercourse in the laboratory with healthy subjects, and found that sexual activity is accompanied by marked cardiovascular fluctuations. These include tachycardia, increases in blood pressure, and increased respiratory rates. These changes, while dramatic, are brief, building to a peak at orgasm and returning to normal levels within a few minutes.

Hellerstein and Friedman (1970), in a most important study, provided the first significant experimental findings on the impact of sexual activity on males with a diseased heart. They questioned how much the increased heart rate found by Masters and Johnson (1966) during coitus (up to 180 beats per minute) might be due to factors such as the laboratory setting, the direct or photographic observations of the sex act, the use of people not necessarily in established marital units, and the possibly special characteristics of persons who volunteer for such a study. They wished to determine how well these data applied to middle-aged, middle-class, convalescent males, who engaged in sexual activities with wives of twenty or more years in the privacy of their bedroom. Forty-eight postmyocardial patients and forty-three normal but coronary-prone subjects were studied. Data were obtained during twenty-four- to forty-eight-hour monitoring periods with a portable electromagnetic tape recorder, which continuously recorded electrocardiogram (EKG) information on tape. Each subject kept a journal of activity during this period. Although no specific instructions were given, a subset of fourteen patients engaged in conjugal sexual activity during this monitored time period. The EKGs were analyzed for rhythm, displacement of the ST-T segment, and changes in rhythm and heart rate. Heart rate and EKG changes associated with sexual activity were compared with those occurring in other activities. These heart rates were also compared with those obtained during bicycle ergometer exercise within a few weeks of the recorded sexual activity. The object was to equate a particular heart rate with the total amount of muscular work expended. Hellerstein and Friedman found that the mean maximal heart rate during orgasm was 117.4 beats per minute (BPM) with a range from 90 BPM to 144 BPM. This dropped to 96.9 BPM one minute after and to 85.0 BPM two minutes after. The mean maximal heart rate during the performance of usual occupational or professional activity was 120.1, just slightly more than that during sexual activity.

This occurred while walking or climbing stairs, or during sedentary work. EKG changes (ST-T segment depression or ectopic beats) and symptoms during coitus and usual occupational activities were comparable in frequency and severity. Hellerstein and Friedman (1970) concluded that "physical expression of conjugal sexual activity in middle-aged men is not very impressive when compared with other common physical activities. . . . The equivalent oxygen cost is similar to that of climbing a flight of stairs, walking briskly or performing ordinary tasks in many occupations."

Further support for the safety of postmyocardial infarction sexual activity comes from Douglas and Wilkes (1975). The energy expenditure of a person at rest requires an oxygen consumption of approximately 3.5 ml per kg body weight per minute. This activity level is equal to one metabolic equivalent or 1 MET. Exercise above this level can then be described in multiples of METs. According to Douglas and Wilkes, the mean energy cost in METs of some common activities are: sleeping, .8; walking uphill at a 5% grade at three miles per hour, 4.0; sexual foreplay, 3.5; raking leaves, 4.0 to 5.0; and orgasm, 4.7 to 5.5. Heart rate has been found to correlate well with the number of METs and is also a very practical measure of oxygen consumption, and thus physical work (Green, 1975). The average man who has recovered from an uncomplicated myocardial infarction has a maximum capacity of 8–9 METs (Eliot and Miles, 1973). Thus, sexual activity is well below this upper limit.

Doctors are well aware of the possible detrimental effects of isometric exercise for coronary patients and accordingly have cautioned their patients against lifting heavy objects, shoveling snow, etc. (Douglas and Wilkes, 1975; Koller et al., 1972). For this reason, many doctors feel that the "male on top" coital position is inadvisable for most heart attack patients, to avoid the necessity of using their arms to support their body for sustained periods of time. Nemec, Mansfield, and Kennedy (1976) examined the effects of the male's position during sexual intercourse on heart rate and blood pressure. Eight normal men with an age range of twenty-four to forty years were studied in the privacy of their own bedroom while having sexual intercourse with their wives. No significant differences were found in heart rate or blood pressure as a function of coital position. The authors concluded that there is no basis for advising cardiac patients to assume the male on bottom position during sexual intercourse.

But what about the so-called coital coronary? How realistic are the fears that many patients, their spouses, and their doctors have about the danger of death or another infarct while having intercourse?

One of the most rigorous studies to date was a coroner's report from Japan (Ueno, 1963). Thirty-four out of 5,559 cases (or .6%) of sudden death occurred during some form of sexual activity, with 18 (or .3%) attributable to heart disease. Of these 18 cases, 80% occurred during or after extramarital intercourse. Another coroner reports that acute coronary insufficiency resulting from coitus is a fact, but the causal relationship of coitus to sudden death is still a matter of relative probabilities rather than absolute proof. There is indirect evidence that coital death may be more a function of stress than sexual activity alone (Massie, Rose, Rupp, and Whelton, 1969). In the same report, Massie indicated that such deaths usually follow a pattern: a male with a nonspouse in unfamiliar surroundings, engaging in sexual intercourse after food and alcohol intake. Hellerstein and Friedman (1970) have maintained that coital death is infrequent, and that those that do occur do not involve middle-aged, middle-class men of the type they studied. The facts seem to indicate that the chances of coital death, particularly within a stable sexual relationship, are quite small. In fact, the percentage of deaths directly related to any controlled exercise is very small. Out of 170,000 heart-diseased individuals taking treadmill stress tests, the deaths due to exercise occur at a rate of approximately 1 in 10,000, and heart rates during such tests commonly go much higher than those attained during sexual activity (Scheingold and Wagner, 1974). One possibility that must be considered, however, is that the coital coronary within marriage may not be reported as such by wives, and that the incidence may indeed be at a higher level than the data indicate.

The currently accepted treatment methods for most myocardial infarction patients are very different from earlier methods. During the last twenty years, doctors have learned that prolonged bed rest can severely impair cardiovascular reserve in a normal person, and that programs to rehabilitate heart attack victims can get 70% back to work within six months, while "benign neglect" returns only 20%. These facts have been reinforced by noting that people with physically demanding occupations have a lower rate of coronary artery disease than those in sedentary occupations, that physically fit people have a better chance of surviving *any* physical trauma, and that patients with coronary artery disease show dramatic improvement in cardiovascular functional capacity when they participate in a physical training program (Douglas and Wilkes, 1975). Within forty-eight hours of a heart attack, according to Douglas and Wilkes, patients who are pain-free show no signs of heart failure or other complications, and those whose resting pulses are between 50 and 90 are ready to embark on an exercise rehabilitation program. Such a program, while not guaranteeing protection from another attack, will most likely increase the chance of survival if another attack occurs. Although not all doctors agree on how much exercise is beneficial, and when to begin an exercise program, it is clear that in order to pursue sex safely, the heart must be capable of tolerating a specific work load. There is considerable evidence that the physically fit individual can perform a given level of work at a lower heart rate and systolic blood pressure than the unfit person (Douglas and Wilkes, 1975; Hellerstein, 1968; Stein, 1975).

Hellerstein and Friedman (1970) reported that 40% of their sample reported symptoms during intercourse which were mainly rapid heart action. Although normal people may experience the same sensations during coitus, the heart patient is more likely to label them as symptoms. The patient who is more physically fit due to a systematic exercise program is less likely to experience rapid heart pounding and breathlessness during sex and thus is less likely to mislabel these unusual responses to sexual activity. Therefore, exercise can have a positive psychological effect on the sexual functioning of the cardiac patient, as well as a physical one.

Other data supporting the value of systematic exercise are offered by Masters and Johnson (1966), who found that the slower the initial heart rate at resting stage (conditioning should lower the at-rest heart rate), the lower the rate during sexual stimulation. Stein (1975) found a significant decrease in peak coital heart rate in cardiac patients who were part of a systematic exercise program, and Heller-

stein and Friedman (1970) concluded that participation in an active physical conditioning program produced significant improvements in physical fitness, blood
pressure, mood, frequency, and quality of sexual activity.

With these data in mind, what kind of advice can a patient be offered regarding
sexual activity, and how can his fears be allayed? Particular advice must be tailored
to the needs of the patient. In order to be able to answer the question of when
and to what extent a patient can resume sexual activity, such factors as general
health, severity of damage, frequency of pain or arrhythmias, and age must be
considered, as well as preinfarct sexual activity. If the patient is a middle-aged
male in a long-standing marriage relationship, the physician may recall the
Hellerstein and Friedman (1970) data, which indicated that many such patients can
fulfill the physiological demands of sexual activity without undue strain. He may
also wish to recall the data on coital death, and discourage sex after large intakes
of food or alcohol, or with unfamiliar partners in unfamiliar settings (Massie et al.,
1969; Ueno, 1963). The Nemec et al. (1976) data may indicate to the doctor that it
is unnecessary to limit intercourse to certain positions. Griffith (1973) suggests
that the patient be instructed to report any of the following symptoms to the doctor:
anginal pain, palpitation continuing for more than fifteen minutes after intercourse,
sleeplessness due to sexual exertion, or unusual fatigue after intercourse.

A most important consideration, in light of the data reviewed, is an assessment of the physiological costs of sexual activity. Hellerstein and Friedman (1970)
remind us that there is wide individual variation in duration and intensity of
response to sexual stimulation. If there is any question, use of the portable electromagnetic tape EKG (or sexercise test) can be of value. If the patient is not middle-
aged and middle-class and does not match the sample in the Hellerstein and
Friedman (1970) study, the issue of assessment becomes even more important.
Hellerstein and Friedman caution: "Because the study population was highly
selected . . . generalization cannot be made about other groups. The subsample of
14 subjects engaging in sexual activity during the monitoring period may have been
a very highly selected group in terms of factors not measured in the study. As such
they may not have been representative even of the . . . sample under investigation."

Several references appear in the literature which make generalizing statements
based on this study with little or no new data. Renshaw (1976) states: "If a heart
patient is well enough to walk up a flight of stairs, he is well enough to have sexual
relations." Others make similar statements (Scheingold and Wagner, 1974; Semmler and Semmler, 1974). With more young people experiencing heart attacks, the
physician should be especially cautious about accepting the flight of stairs analogy
without making a thorough individual assessment of the physiological capabilities
of their patients, preferably with a stress test. One difficulty is that there often is a
lack of availability of exercise testing equipment and facilities, as Wenger (1973)
demonstrated in a survey of 3,600 doctors. However, Green (1975) points out that
a step test can be adequate in the absence of sophisticated equipment, along with
observation of the patient engaging in simple activities. Once such an evaluation
has been made, the physician, or his designated representative, can give the patient
specific advice on the resumption of sexual activity, offer reassurance based on his
findings, and answer any questions.

Depression, like fear or anxiety, is not an uncommon reaction to a heart attack and may lead to decreased interest in sexual activity. Depression can be one of the most important psychological complications of coronary heart disease. It can arise out of real, feared or imagined loss and may be correlated with poor outcome as measured in terms of mortality and morbidity (Bruh, Wolf, and Phillips, 1971). The health professional should be alert to such signs of depression as loss of appetite, sleeplessness, excessive fatigue, withdrawal, and a marked decrease in sexual activity. In some cases psychological intervention or the prescription of anti-depressant medication may be indicated.

Aging is another factor that may result in decreased sexual activity. Many middle-aged patients may blame this normal decline in sexual interest on their heart disease. Such an attribution is likely to increase anxiety, which may in turn exacerbate the sexual problem. Masters and Johnson (1970) have found that the sexual response slows with age in both sexes. In the male, this may take the form of longer latency to erection, lack of full erection until just prior to ejaculation, and fewer penile contractions. The health professional should make sure his patients know these facts if he suspects that these changes are being attributed to the heart disease.

Drugs are another possible source of sexual dysfunction. Many antihyperten-sive medications, as well as other drugs used for cardiac problems, may have effects on sexual functioning (Nies, 1975; Renshaw, 1976; Scheingold and Wagner, 1974). To the extent that the patient attributes any sexual problems to his heart disease, anxiety may increase. Since the drugs do not always cause sexual dysfunction, the problem a health professional faces is whether or not to mention this possibility. Telling a patient that a drug may cause impotence may indeed cause impotence, in-dependent of the drug's actual effect, for a fear of being impotent is often a major cause of impotence (Masters and Johnson, 1970; Scheingold and Wagner, 1974). If nothing is said, it is most important that the health professional continue to in-quire about efforts to resume sexual activity. If a problem occurs, then the possible link to the drug can be explained to the patient, and alternative medication pre-scribed, when possible.

One of the most important determinants of how well a cardiac patient will function sexually is how well his spouse is functioning, for fear and anxiety from either partner may have a dampening effect on sexual activity. Anxiety and depres-sion in the spouse can serve to stimulate similar reactions in the patient. The spouse, fearing another attack, may find that she can no longer enjoy sex. This may in turn produce feelings of inadequacy in the male (particularly if he is middle-aged and undergoing some physical or psychological changes) and possibly result in reduced potency.

In a study of the psychological consequences of a heart attack on sixty-five wives of male patients, Dominian and Skelton (1973) found feelings of loss, depression, and guilt to be present. The period of convalescence was very stressful to the wives, and they attributed the stress to a fear of recurrent infarct and to marital tension caused by their husband's increased irritability and dependency. Frequently after a heart attack, many areas of interpersonal functioning become disrupted. Income may change, financial troubles may begin, responsibilities may shift to the healthy spouse, time schedules and recreational patterns may change. In short, often there is a drastic change in life-style patterns, which can easily include sexual patterns. If the spouse does not have adequate information about the safety of sexual activity, she may not know how to behave. Should she be warm and responsive in bed or keep her distance? If communication about sex is difficult, as it is with many couples, the husband may label any distancing behavior as rejection, and this certainly will harm his already vulnerable self-image. Many difficulties can be avoided by counseling and providing specific guidelines for the spouse as well as the patient. If she knows the physiologic cost of sexual activity for her husband and sees him participating in an exercise program, her concerns may be greatly alleviated.

Pain, such as that caused by angina, may be a great inhibitor of sexual activity as well as other activity. Such pain may be severe enough to be truly debilitating or, even when mild, be sufficient to maintain anxiety. Hellerstein and Friedman (1970) found that although 20% of their patients had angina, drugs and physical conditioning programs in most cases helped improve sexual enjoyment. The use of prophylactic nitroglycerin may prevent angina pain during intercourse, and thus help reduce anxiety (Koller et al., 1972). If exercise and drugs do not help, the possibility of a psychological component to the anginal pain should be considered, and brief psychotherapy might be beneficial (Lane, 1973).

The most effective way to help the cardiac patient with sexual rehabilitation is to try to prevent as many problems as possible. There is encouraging information that can be given to a heart patient and his family. It might be helpful to know, for example, that after six months to one year following an uncomplicated myocardial infarction, the chances of a second infarct are no greater than for an individual of the same age and risk factor index who has *never* had a heart attack (Levy and McGill, 1975). Doctors can help reduce anxiety by being direct and specific in their instructions, so that the patient and the patient's spouse need not rely on their own opinions. Instead of telling the patient that he must abstain from sex for a particular number of weeks (which can vary from four to fourteen, depending on the physician), it might be more helpful to have the patient associate his sexual activity with his other physical activities by telling him that he can resume full sexual activity when he meets an exercise tolerance criterion. In the interim, relaxed sex play can be suggested (Douglas and Wilkes, 1975; Renshaw, 1976). The physician should tailor his remarks and his style of presentation to the individual patient and family, taking into account their anxiety level, intelligence, and mood state. Open-ended questions such as "How are you feeling about resuming your usual activities, like going back to work and having sex?" provide for more than a yes/no answer and can help him gauge how direct he can be with a particular patient. If the physician cannot take the time to do this, he should avail himself of the services of other competent professionals. A patient's expression of fear of sex should never be answered with a generality such as "don't worry," but by a full acceptance and understanding of the patient's feelings as legitimate and important.

Who Should Participate in Sexual Rehabilitation Programs?

Professional participation, as has already been pointed out, must be led by the physician since the final decision of what a given patient can and should do is a medical one. However, it is also clear that the time necessary to do an adequate job in the delicate area of sexual counseling is substantial and requires psychological skill as well as medical knowledge. Psychological assessment of the individual patient and his relationships is essential. Empathy and understanding are crucial, with efforts directed at the spouse as well as at the patient.

There are other professionals who, in cooperation with the doctor, can be of great help—nurses, social workers, psychologists, and physical therapists. There has been a movement toward a team approach to cardiac rehabilitation (Semmler and Semmler, 1974), and some good advice has been generated on how nurses can help ease the sexual fears of their cardiac patients (Lawson, 1971). Certainly, in dealing with depression, anxiety, unreasonable fear, and marital problems the psychologist can be of great value. Garrity (1973) found that a counselor could help the rehabilitee achieve a positive opinion of his present state of health, physical capabilities, possibilities for physical reconditioning, and future health status. He concluded that the importance of a person's perception of his health is what determines outcome to a great extent. Adsett (1968) found that short-term group therapy was helpful to patients and their wives. Resumption of sexual activity often evokes more concern than resumption of other physical activity. However, reassurance that sex is similar to other activities, and open discussion with a trained professional, can help alleviate anxiety.

It is clear that not all cardiac patients have sexual problems. When Hellerstein and Friedman (1970) assessed the quality of sexual activity among their patients, they found that 52.3% indicated no change following their heart attack, while 22.7% indicated improvement. Of all their patients, 41.7% indicated that there was no change in the frequency of sexual activity following their heart attack. Researchers would do well to study the characteristics of those patients who seem to be immune to the sexual problems that other patients experience.

In assessing the need for sexual counseling, the health professional should not automatically reject a patient who reports either no problems or increased frequency or pleasure. Indications of hypersexuality may identify a patient who is denying his illness and who may be pushing himself beyond his current capabilities, and who may not be complying with medical advice. The health professional should also be aware that decrease in frequency or termination of sexual activity by itself may not necessarily indicate a need for sexual counseling. For some patients and their spouses, a heart attack may provide an excuse to terminate sexual activity. If this is a decision that both partners are comfortable with, and if other reasons for termination of activity have been ruled out, it would be inappropriate for the professional to attempt rehabilitation in spite of the needs and desires of the patient and his wife.

Recently, "heart clubs" have been started in many hospitals for postmyocardial infarction patients. Through group discussion and guest speakers, an attempt is made to aid the transition back to a normal life-style. While there are few data available, such clubs most likely have a beneficial effect. However, there can be problems as well. For example, a speaker on sex may speak of activities that a more conservative physician of a particular patient may not approve of. This could lead the patient to surmise that he must be "sicker" than his fellow club members. Also, if a club member has a reinfarct, this can have a demoralizing effect on the other members and contribute greatly to continued anxiety about their own health.

This discussion has concerned itself primarily with male patients. There are few data on the sexual difficulties of females who have had a myocardial infarction. However, Masters and Johnson (1966) have demonstrated that heart function during orgasm is virtually the same in both sexes. Thus, it may be assumed that the middle-aged, long-married female has the same cardiac costs as the men in the Hellerstein and Friedman (1970) study. Sanne (1973), as well as Hellerstein and Friedman (1970), has indicated that lack of sexual desire or response in the female is a "common" result following a myocardial infarction. Sudden death during sexual activity has been reported very rarely in women (Ueno, 1963). Abramov (1976) has reported a high incidence of depression among women who have had heart attacks.

Although myocardial infarction is the only form of cardiovascular disease discussed here, it should be pointed out that patients with congestive heart failure should be advised quite differently from the advice suggested here. Any strenuous physical activity, including sexual activity, should be avoided until the heart failure is controlled (Koller et al., 1972). Hellerstein (1968) advises against a conditioning program for patients with congestive heart failure, and against resumption of intercourse until the failure is controlled (Hellerstein and Friedman, 1970).

In summary, it seems clear from the material presented that sex is often a concern of the male coronary patient. Communication between doctor and patient needs to be improved in this area. It is the responsibility of the doctor to initiate the discussion of sex in a timely and direct manner. Particularly, with the use of exercise tolerance technology, there are sufficient data available for the physician to reach safe conclusions about the capacity for sexual activity of his patient. There are sufficient data to be able to reassure the patient about his fears of sudden coital death. Exercise rehabilitation helps sexual rehabilitation as well. All sexual advice should be based on a thorough physical and psychological assessment of the patient, an assessment of his spouse's psychological state, the marital relationship, and precoronary sexual activity. Other professionals, particularly those who can offer short-term psychotherapy, can be an enormously helpful adjunct to the physician in patient management.

References

Abramov, L. A. Sexual life and sexual frigidity among women developing acute myocardial infarction. *Psychosomatic Medicine*, 1976, *38* (6), 418–425.

Adsett, C. A., and Bruhn, J. Short-term group psychotherapy for postmyocardial infarction patients and their wives. *Canadian Medical Association Journal*, 1968, *99*, 557–784.

American Heart Association. *Heart facts.* New York: American Heart Association, 1974.

Bloch, A., Maeder, J., and Haissly, J. Sexual problems after myocardial infarction. *American Heart Journal*, 1975, *90* (4), 536–537.

Brinner, D. Quoted in F. Miller and L. Galton, *Freedom from heart attacks.* New York: Simon and Schuster, 1972. P. 231.

Bruh, H., Wolf, S., and Phillips, B. Depression and death in myocardial infarction: A psychosocial study of screening male coronary patients over nine years. *Psychosomatic Research*, 1971, *15*, 305.

Dangrove, E. Sexual responses to disease processes. *Journal of Sexual Research*, 1968, *4*, 257.

Dominian, J., and Skelton, M. Psychological stress in wives of patients with myocardial infarction. *British Medical Journal*, 1973, *2*, 101.

Douglas, J. E., and Wilkes, T. D. Reconditioning cardiac patients. *American Family Physician*, 1975, *11* (1), 123–129.

Eliot, R. S., and Miles, R. What to tell the cardiac patient about sexual intercourse. *Resident-Intern Consultant*, 1973, *2*, 14.

Francis, C., Krosch, B., and Morris, M. Gaps in doctor-patient communication. *New England Journal of Medicine*, 1969, *280*, 535.

Garrity, T. Vocational adjustment after myocardial infarction. *Social Science and Medicine*, 1973, *7*, 705–717.

Green, A. W. Sexual activity and the postmyocardial infarction patient. *American Heart Journal*, 1975, *89* (2), 246–252.

Griffith, G. C. Sexuality and the cardiac patient. *Heart and Lung*, 1973, *2*, 70–73.

Hackett, R., and Bildeau, C. Issues raised in a group setting by patients recovering from myocardial infarction. *American Journal of Psychiatry*, 1971, *128*, 105.

Hackett, T. P., and Cossem, N. H. Psychological adaptation in myocardial infarction patients. In J. P. Naughton and H. K. Hellerstein (Eds.), *Exercise testing and exercise training in coronary heart disease.* New York: Academic Press, 1973.

Hellerstein, H. Exercise therapy in coronary disease. *Bulletin of the New York Academy of Medicine*, 1968, *44* (8), 1028–1047.

Hellerstein, H., and Ford, A. Rehabilitation of the cardiac patient. *Journal of the American Medical Association*, 1957, *164*, 225.

Hellerstein, H., and Friedman, E. J. Sexual activity and the postcoronary patient. *Medical Aspects of Human Sexuality*, March 1969, p. 70.

Hellerstein, H., and Friedman, E. J. Sexual activity and the postcoronary patient. *Archives of Internal Medicine*, 1970, *125*, 987.

Klein, R. F., Dean, A., Wilson, M., and Bogdonoff, M. The physician and postmyocardial invalidism. *Journal of the American Medical Association*, 1965, *194*, 123.

Koller, R., Kennedy, J. W., Butler, J. C., and Wagner, N. N. Counseling the coronary patient on sexual activity. *Postgraduate Medicine*, 1972, *51*, 133.

Lane, F. M. Mental mechanisms and the pain of angina pectoris. *American Heart Journal*, 1973, *85* (4), 563–568.

Lawson, B. Easing the sexual fears of the cardiac patient. *RN*, April 1971, pp. ICU1–ICU5.

Levy, R., and McGill, A. Target behaviors for task group on cardiac rehabilitation. *Proceedings of the NHLI Working Conference on Health Behavior, May 1975.* DHEW Publication No. (NIH) 76-868. Washington, D.C.: United States Department of Health, Education and Welfare, 1975.

Massie, E., Rose, E., Rupp, J., and Whelton, R. Sudden death during coitus—fact or fiction? *Medical Aspects of Human Sexuality*, March 1969, pp. 22–26.

Masters, W. H., and Johnson, V. E. *Human sexual response.* Boston: Little, Brown, 1966.

Masters, W. H., and Johnson, V. E. *Human sexual inadequacy.* Boston: Little, Brown, 1970.

McGill, A. M. Review of literature on cardiovascular rehabilitation. *Proceedings of the NHLI Working Conference on Health Behavior, May 1975.* DHEW Publication No. (NIH) 76-868. Washington, D.C.: United States Department of Health, Education and Welfare, 1975.

Nemec, E., Mansfield, L., and Kennedy, J. W. Heart rate and blood pressure response during sexual activity in normal males. *American Heart Journal*, 1976, *92* (3), 274–277.

Nies, A. A. Adverse reactions and interactions limiting the use of antihypertensive drugs. *American Journal of Medicine*, 1975, *58*, 493.

Pinderhughes. C. A., Grace, E. B., Reyna, L. J., and Anderson, R. T. Interrelationships between sexual functioning and medical conditions. *Medical Aspects of Human Sexuality*, October 1972, p. 52.

Renshaw, B. Emotional links to coronary disease: Impact on sexual activity. *Practical Psychology for Physicians*, March 1976, pp. 30–35.

Safilios-Rothschild, C. *The sociology and social psychology of disability and rehabilitation.* New York: Random House, 1970.

Sanne, H. Exercise tolerance and physical training of non-selected patients after myocardial infarction. *Acta Scandinavia* (Suppl.), 1973, *55*, 1.

Scheingold, L. D., and Wagner, N. N. *Sound sex and the aging heart*. New York: Human Sciences Press, 1974.

Semmler, C., and Semmler, M. Counselling the coronary patient. *American Journal of Occupational Therapy*, 1974, *28* (10), 609.

Stein, R. The effects of exercise training on peak coital heart rate in postmyocardial infarction males. *Circulation*, 1975, *51* (Abstract 456, Supplement 11).

Tuttle, W. B., Cook, W. L., and Fitch, E. Sexual behavior in postmyocardial infarction patients. *American Journal of Cardiology*, 1964, *13*, 140. (Abstract)

Ueno, M. The so-called coition death. *Japanese Journal of Legal Medicine*, 1963, *17*, 535.

Wenger, N. The early ambulation of patients after myocardial infarction. *Cardiology*, 1973, *58*, 1–6.

In this chapter, Higgins reviews the available literature on sexual function in males and females with spinal-cord injury. The number of such patients is large (approximately 100,000) and increasing as medical technology increases the life span of patients with cord injury.

Higgin's review indicates that the physiological effect of cord lesions on sexual functioning is highly variable and unpredictable. Given this variability, the role of psychological factors in the posttrauma adjustment of patients is especially important. The workshop programs for sexual rehabilitation of patients with cord injury that Higgins describes seem to be moderately effective, but as the author notes, more discussion of sexual functioning by the primary care team might be even more beneficial for most patients.

31

Aspects of Sexual Response in Adults with Spinal-Cord Injury: A Review of the Literature

Glenn E. Higgins, Jr.

Since World War II, as a result of advances in medical care, physically disabled individuals in general and in particular those with spinal-cord injury have constituted an increasingly large proportion of the population. Current estimates number the physically disabled adults in the United States at over 11,000,000 persons (President's Committee on Employment of the Handicapped, 1975). Approximately 100,000 of these are persons with spinal-cord injury as a result of various military and civilian injuries (National Institute of Neurological Diseases and Stroke, 1971).

As these people have come to live longer and more nearly normal lives, the issue of sexuality and physical disability has achieved increasing attention and importance (Eisenberg and Rustad, 1974; Gregory, 1974; Heslinga, Schellen, and Verkuyl, 1974; Mooney, Cole, and Chilgren, 1975). There has been a growing volume of research which has sought to document the social, psychological, and biological components of the sexuality of the physically disabled.

Glenn E. Higgins, Jr. • Department of Psychology, State University of New York, Stony Brook, New York

Sex is involved in so many diverse areas that the relevant literature is scattered throughout a number of different disciplines. A number of bibliographies have been prepared which catalogue this scattered literature but offer no critical evaluation (Griffith, Timms, and Tomko, 1973; *Sex and the Handicapped*, 1974; Clowers and Taylor, 1976). Some aspects of sexuality and spinal-cord injury have been reviewed (Tarabulcy, 1972; Griffith, Tomko, and Timms, 1973; Griffith and Trieschmann, 1975; Teal and Athelstan, 1975). The purpose of this chapter is to extend this earlier work by pulling together and critically evaluating the existing literature and suggesting directions for future work.

All studies involved in this review address themselves to various aspects of the sexuality or sexual behavior of adults with spinal-cord injury. That is to say that the problems of socialization into the role of sexually active individual are not addressed. These investigations assume (and it is an assumption that might well be challenged) that the subjects involved were sexually active adults prior to the sudden onset of a traumatic spinal-cord injury.

Here it might be well to briefly review the principal characteristics of spinal-cord injury:

> The diagnosis of injury to the spinal cord is made from the history of trauma and the clinical findings. The level of the injury is determined by the results of a neurological examination and the findings on roentgenographic examinations of the spine. . . .
>
> In the incomplete transverse lesions of the cord there is usually a considerable degree of return of motor and sensory function. Bladder and rectal control usually return to normal. . . .
>
> When the cord has been completely severed, the motor paralysis and sensory loss will be permanent. The further evolution of the symptoms and signs in these cases depends upon the restoration of function in the isolated segment of the cord. (Merritt, 1973, p. 346)

Damage to the spinal cord may differentially affect upper and lower motor neurons depending on the site and extent of the injury:

> The lower motor neuron . . . is the essential motor cell concerned with skeletal activity. Lesions of the lower motor neurons may be located in the cells of the ventral gray column of the spinal cord or brain stem or in their axons, which constitute the ventral roots and spinal nerves or the cranial nerves. . . .
>
> Signs of lower motor neuron lesions include flaccid paralysis of the involved muscles, muscle atrophy, and reaction of degeneration. Reflexes of the involved muscle are diminished or absent, and no pathologic reflexes are obtainable.
>
> The upper motor neuron conveys impulses from the motor area of the cerebrum and is essential to voluntary muscular activity. . . .
>
> Lesions of the upper motor neuron may be located in the cerebral cortex, the internal capsule, the cerebral peduncles, the brain stem, or the spinal cord. . . .
>
> Signs of the upper motor neuron lesions include spastic paralysis or paresis of the involved muscles, little or no muscle atrophy, and hyperactive deep reflexes, diminished or absent superficial reflexes, and pathologic reflexes and signs. (Chusid, 1970, p. 166)

It is important to keep in mind when evaluating research results that diagnosis of spinal-cord injury relies on inference from functional examination rather than definite and observable physical evidence. As Conomy (1973) puts it, "Riddoch (p. 843) stated in 1917 that 'there are no manifestations by which we can be certain that the spinal cord has been anatomically divided.' Subsequent studies have not altered this statement."

This issue is particularly important in the evaluation of those studies that attempt to differentiate between complete and incomplete transections of the spinal cord. As will be seen, a peculiarly circular logic is sometimes invoked to demonstrate the existence of complete transection.

A closely related issue is the lack of specificity in the designation of "incomplete lesion." As Comarr (1973) points out, "It is important to realize that the term 'incomplete lesion' is a very loose expression. One patient with an incomplete lesion may have minimal neurological residuals and be capable of nearly normal sexual activity; yet another patient with marked neurological involvement may for practical purposes have to be considered sexually as though he had a complete lesion" (p. 228).

Another phenomenon that must be recognized in spinal-cord injury is that of spinal shock:

> In the period immediately following the injury, the function of the isolated segment is in complete abeyance, due to the development of the state of spinal shock. During this stage there is an absence of the deep and superficial reflexes and atonic paralysis of the bladder and rectum. Recovery from the stage of spinal shock occurs in the majority of the patients within the space of a few weeks or months. Recovery is prevented or retarded by the presence of bed sores or urinary sepsis.
>
> With recovery from spinal shock there is a return of the deep reflexes, which frequently become quite brisk, although the arc of the movement and the duration of the reflex are less than those which occur with incomplete lesions of the cord. Concomitant with the return of the deep reflexes, there are signs of other reflex activity in the isolated cord. (Merritt, 1973, p. 348)

This is obviously important because any assessment of "sexual potential" made before the stabilization that occurs after recovery from spinal shock will not reflect the long-term status of the individual.

A third dimension along which many studies of sex and spinal-cord injury make a distinction is that of level of lesion. Terminology used to describe segmental level is presented in Figure 1.

Clearly this is an important variable in respect to genital physiological functioning, but as in the study of all significant variables, here, too, interpretations from data must be cautiously made. In attempting an adequate understanding of the genital physiological functioning of any single individual or group of individuals, "Sensory and motor segmental levels must be ascertained; the presence or absence of reflex activity must be ascertained; the completeness or incompleteness of the lesion must be ascertained. One can easily appreciate, therefore, why attempting to prognosticate a patient's sexual future based only on a knowledge of the injury at a given vertebral level alone is inadequate" (Comarr, 1973, p. 236).

These then are some of the issues that must be addressed in the interpretation of studies of genital sexual response in spinal-cord injury. Other issues that relate to individual studies are discussed below.

The sections that follow are organized around specific "target" behaviors. The contribution of each study to our knowledge of each specific behavior will be considered.

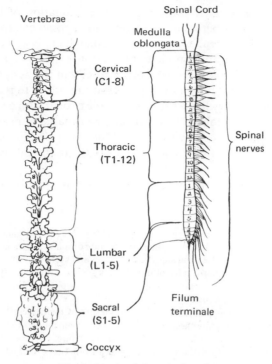

Fig. 1. Levels of the spinal cord.

Erectile Capability

The first area of sexual function to be considered will be erection. Studies distinguish between two distinct types of erection: reflexive, or reflexogenic, in which tumescence results from direct physical stimulation of the genitals; and psychic, or psychogenic, in which cognitive activity causes erection (Bors and Comarr, 1960). The individual with reflex or reflexogenic erections must have direct local stimulation and cannot produce an erection through erotic fantasy or other cognitive activity. The person with psychogenic erections, on the other hand, is able to achieve erections through the use of either arousing erotic thought or direct bodily and/or genital manipulation.

In thirteen studies reviewed (Munro, Horne, and Paull, 1948; Talbot, 1949, 1955; Kuhn, 1950; Zeitlin, Cottrell, and Lloyd, 1957; Bors and Comarr, 1960; Money, 1960; Tsuji, Nakajima, Morimoto, and Nounaka, 1961; Hohmann, 1966; Cibeira, 1970; Comarr, 1970; Jochheim and Wahle, 1970; Fitzpatrick, 1974), in spite of methodological inadequacies and differences in population, some tentative generalizations seem possible. The retention of erectile capability after spinal-cord injury varied widely in the overall samples from study to study, ranging from 48.2% (Jochheim and Wahle, 1970) to 91.7% (Fitzpatrick, 1974). In general, those studies that divided their subjects on the basis of lesion level demonstrated that erectile capability is more frequently maintained in the higher lesion level groups

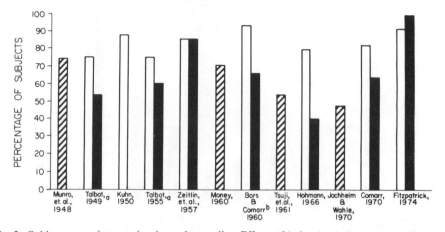

Fig. 2. Subjects reporting erection in twelve studies: Effects of lesion level. Open bars, higher level lesions (T12 and above unless otherwise indicated); solid bars, lower level lesions (below T12 unless otherwise indicated); striped bars, undifferentiated lesions. [a]Samples are divided T11 and above versus T12 and below. [b]Sample is divided T9 and above versus below T9.

(Talbot, 1949, 1955; Bors and Comarr, 1960; Tsjui et al., 1961; Hohmann, 1966; Cibeira, 1970; Comarr, 1970; Jochheim and Wahle, 1970). These results are illustrated graphically in Figures 2, 3, and 4. In examination of complete spinal-cord transections, this ranged from 100% erectile capability in cervical groups (Bors and Comarr, 1960) to no erectile capability in lesions in the T7–12 and lumbar groups (Comarr, 1970).

These findings may be at least in part attributable to the differences in the type of lesion involved at different segmental levels. Higher lesions are more likely to involve upper motor as opposed to lower motor neurons, whereas the reverse is true for the lower segmental levels. The effects of the type of lesion on erection can

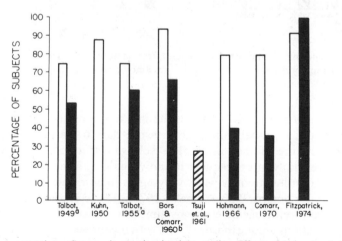

Fig. 3. Subjects reporting reflexogenic erection in eight studies: Effects of lesion level. For explanation of bars and footnotes, see Fig. 2.

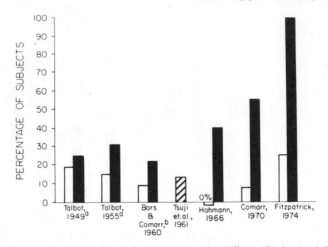

Fig. 4. Subjects reporting psychogenic erection in seven studies: Effects of lesion level. For explanation of bars and footnotes, see Fig. 2.

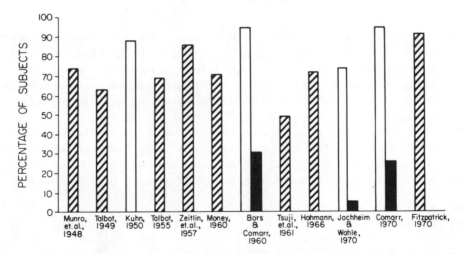

Fig. 5. Subjects reporting erection in twelve studies: Effects of upper versus lower motor neuron lesion. Open bars, upper motor neuron lesion; solid bars, lower motor neuron lesion; striped bars, undifferentiated lesions.

be seen in Figures 5, 6, and 7. The results in examining incomplete lesions are somewhat less clear, probably in large measure due to the previously discussed unsatisfactory nature of the "incomplete" classification. Suffice it to say that erections are generally more frequent in individuals with incomplete lesions, but that the range is still extremely wide, varying as in complete lesions from 0% to 100% (Bors and Comarr, 1960; Comarr, 1970). Those studies that differentiate psychogenic from reflexogenic erections similarly indicate a higher incidence of psychogenic erections among those subjects with incomplete lesions. Here the range is from 90% in an incomplete lower motor neuron group (Bors and Comarr, 1960) to 0% in some complete upper motor neuron groups, depending on segmental level

(Bors and Comarr, 1960; Comarr, 1970). These results are summarized in Figures 8, 9, and 10. Talbot (1949, 1955) takes the occurrence of psychogenic erections as sufficient evidence for the diagnosis of incomplete lesion. This would appear to be unfounded on the basis of his own data as well as on that of others (Bors and Comarr, 1960; Tsuji et al., 1961; Hohmann, 1966; Cibeira, 1970; Comarr, 1970). The reported occurrence of psychogenic erections in the presence of complete upper motor neuron lesions seems paradoxical in light of conventional neurophysiology and cannot yet be explained or fully understood on the basis of research at hand.

Another interesting phenomenon reported is the occurrence, in a small number of subjects, of psychogenic erections in the absence of reflexogenic erections.

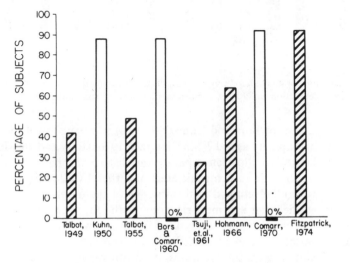

Fig. 6. Subjects reporting reflexogenic erection in eight studies: Effects of upper versus lower motor neuron lesion. For explanation of bars, see Fig. 5.

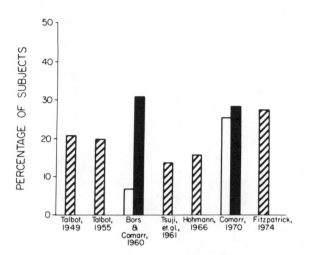

Fig. 7. Subjects reporting psychogenic erection in seven studies: Effects of upper versus lower motor neuron lesion. For explanation of bars, see Fig. 5.

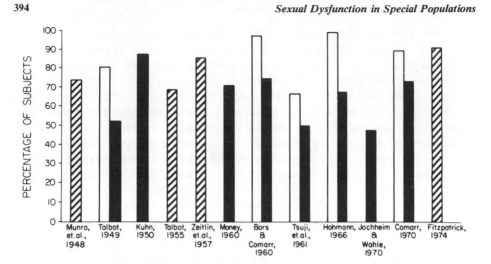

Fig. 8. Subjects reporting erection in twelve studies: Effects of complete versus incomplete lesion. Open bars, incomplete lesion; solid bars, complete lesion; striped bars, undifferentiated lesions.

Twenty-seven percent of Bors and Comarr's (1960) complete lower motor neuron group showed this capacity as did 7% in Cibeira's (1970) study and 40% in Comarr's (1970) sample. These data illustrate separate and distinct mechanisms that mediate psychogenic as opposed to reflexogenic erections, thereby allowing the possibility that one capacity can be retained in the absence of the other.

Definitive studies that meet rigorous methodological criteria are not yet in existence. Adequate statistical analysis of the data, and even collection of data, in relation to variables such as age, duration of injury, general health status, possibly significant surgical interventions, chemotherapeutic regimens, and prior sexual experience or activity, is lacking. In addition, reliance on verbal report,

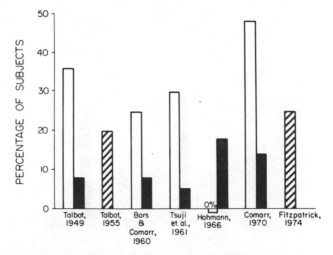

Fig. 9. Subjects reporting reflexogenic erection in eight studies: Effects of complete versus incomplete lesion. For explanation of bars, see Fig. 8.

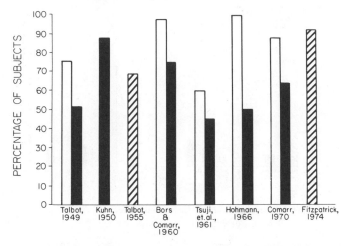

Fig. 10. Subjects reporting psychogenic erection in seven studies: Effects of complete versus incomplete lesion. For explanation of bars, see Fig. 8.

generally uncorroborated, in all investigations except one (Kuhn, 1950) compromises the validity of these studies and must detract from our confidence in their findings.

Ejaculatory Capability

Thirteen studies addressing themselves to ejaculatory capability were reviewed (Munro et al., 1948; Talbot, 1949, 1955; Kuhn, 1950; Zeitlin et al., 1957; Borrs and Comarr, 1960; Money, 1960; Tsuji et al., 1961; Hohmann, 1966; Cibeira, 1970; Comarr, 1970; Jochheim and Wahle, 1970; Fitzpatrick, 1974). Data on ejaculatory capability were collected in most studies in a manner similar to the studies on erectile capacity, that is, generally through interviews or questionnaires with only occasional corroboration by spouse or objective physiological observation.

Like the available information on erectile capability, the data on ejaculatory capability are severely flawed by numerous methodological problems. Those generalizations that can be drawn from the studies surveyed indicate that ejaculation has been reported in some cases within all the various patient subgroupings. Ejaculatory capability has been found to range in those patients with complete lesions from 0% (Money, 1960) to 7% (Jochheim and Wahle, 1970), and in those patients with incomplete lesions from 27% (Comarr, 1970) to 32% (Borrs and Comarr, 1960). Various other studies on samples in which the degree of completeness of lesion varies have reported incidences of ejaculatory capability as high as 50% (Fitzpatrick, 1974). These results are shown in Figure 11.

In regard to site and type of lesion, the data suggest a higher incidence of ejaculation in those subjects with lower motor neuron lesions as opposed to those with upper motor neuron lesions and a higher incidence in those with lower level

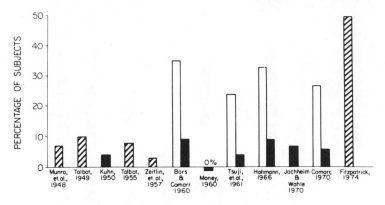

Fig. 11. Subjects reporting ejaculation in twelve studies: Effects of complete versus incomplete lesion. For explanation of bars, see Fig. 8.

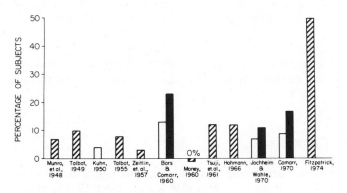

Fig. 12. Subjects reporting ejaculation in twelve studies: Effects of upper versus lower motor neuron lesion. For explanation of bars, see Fig. 5.

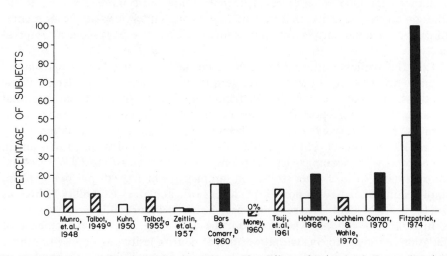

Fig. 13. Subjects reporting ejaculation in twelve studies: Effects of lesion level. For explanation of bars and footnotes, see Fig. 2.

lesions versus those with lesions higher in the cord. These differences are illustrated in Figures 12 and 13. These generalizations cannot be taken as more than suggestive, however, in light of the aforementioned methodological difficulties in general and, in particular, in view of the fact that in only one of the thirteen studies reviewed (Kuhn, 1950) was any attempt made to elicit ejaculation, or, failing that, to collect data on whether or not the subjects had attempted to achieve ejaculation, and if so, under what conditions and by what means. This is particularly important in view of evidence that ejaculation can be elicited in subjects with spinal-cord injury by a variety of unconventional means: the use of electrical stimulation (Rowan, Howley, and Nova, 1962; Bensman and Kottke, 1966), injection of prostigmin (Guttman and Walsh, 1971; Rossier, Ziegler, Duchosal, and Meylan, 1971), and the use of a vibrator (Tarabulcy, 1972).

Orgasmic Capability

In general, the question of orgasmic capability is handled with less than the desired degree of sophistication in the spinal-cord-injury literature. Rather than acknowledging the physiological, psychological, and sociological aspects of the phenomenon of orgasm as suggested by Masters and Johnson (1966), orgasm is treated in an exclusively neurophysiological context and in what Griffith et al. (1973) have referred to as an "all or none fashion reminiscent of neuronal physiology" (p. 539). In many studies (Munro et al., 1948; Tsuji et al., 1961; Fitzpatrick, 1974) orgasm and ejaculation are treated as if they are identical events. Furthermore, in those studies in which orgasm was treated independently the criteria for orgasm were not stated in the texts nor was there any explanation of the way in which questions were put to experimental subjects. Further, as with the studies on ejaculation, there were no data reported on what subjects under what conditions and by what methods attempted to reach orgasm.

Allowing for all these deficiencies, only the most tentative generalizations concerning orgams or orgasmlike phenomena in the individual with spinal-cord injury can be made. Orgasm ranges from 2% (Jochheim and Wahle, 1970) to 16% (Hohmann, 1966), although, as noted, the criteria for defining orgasm are not given.

Some generalizations emerge by taking reports from the texts of various studies and using the broader classification of orgasmlike phenomena to address the question: What is the outcome of prolonged genital stimulation in spinal-cord-injured patients? It becomes evident that in some percentage of spinal-cord-injured cases (whether labeled as orgasmic or not) a variety of extragenital responses occur, including warm sensation (Money, 1960), severe muscular spasticity (Kuhn, 1950; Zeitlin et al., 1957; Comarr, 1970), physical pleasure (Zeitlin et al., 1957), sexual excitation (Hohmann, 1966), and headaches (Comarr, 1970). These may be labeled as pleasant or unpleasant and seen as related to or completely separate from orgasm by both subjects and investigators.

Hohmann reported in his 1966 paper a phenomenon first pointed out by Bors and Comarr (1960): "Others in this group reported feelings of sexual excitement due to stimulation of erogenous zones, especially the nipples, and two reported what they considered to be peculiar erogenous zones which had appeared since injury, in the center of the back, just above the existing effective sensory level. They

said that stimulation of these areas caused some feelings of sexual tension and they felt some pressure to continue the contact (p. 149).

The development of new locations capable of providing erotic sensation has been noted by other investigators and remains an interesting if little understood area for future study (Bors and Comarr, 1960; Cole, 1975).

In his 1960 paper Money proposed the view that orgasmlike phenomena in individuals with spinal-cord injury derive largely from "cognitional eroticism" that "may be entirely independent of genitopelvic sensation and action" (p. 382). Money regarded this as similar in many ways to the phantom limb phenomenon in amputees and coined the term "phantom orgasm." This notion of phantom orgasm has remained in the literature and is often referred to in contemporary articles on sexuality and spinal-cord injury. As such, it deserves more detailed discussion here. The concept is a problematic one founded on an imprecise analogy with a neurophysiological phenomenon and has served to cloud the issue of the mediation of the orgasmic response in the spinal-cord-injured individual.

The phanton limb phenomenon refers to the perception of sensation as originating in an amputated limb, apparently due to stimulation of nerve endings in the stump. "When these nerve impulses from the nerve fibers in the stump reach the cerebrum, they are interpreted as coming from receptors in the absent limb, that is, the areas normally supplied by the fibers" (Gardner, 1968, p. 185). Clearly this situation is not completely analogous to that existing in the spinal-cord-injured individual. The end organs in this situation are intact and presumably the neural pathway itself is interrupted. However, we must, in some cases at least, raise questions about the interruptions of the neural pathway when end organ, i.e., genitopelvic, stimulation results in the kinds of responses that we have called orgasm or orgasmlike. The notion of phantom orgasm has been invoked to suggest that these orgasms or orgasmlike responses in the spinal-cord-injured individual are purely cerebrocognitional and serve interpersonal or intrapsychic functions. In some sense the implication is reminiscent of naïve psychosomatics, which might suggest that these orgasms are "all in the head" and represent an unwillingness on the part of the individual with spinal-cord injury to accept the reality of his situation. In light of our incomplete understanding of the orgasmic response and its neurological mediation, the assumptions that underlie this implication seem wholly unwarranted. Such assumptions both hinder our understanding of the orgasmic response in spinal-cord-injured individuals and discourage further examination of the neural mechanisms that are involved in it.

It should be obvious that more precise and sophisticated examination is required for meaningful assessment of the varied consequences of prolonged sexual stimulation. Psychophysiological techniques now used to study the sexual response cycle could be profitably applied to a spinal-cord-injured population and the results of such investigations should increase our understanding of the sexual response of the spinal-cord-injured population.

Coitus

Investigators have tabulated the number of subjects who have attempted intercourse and the percentage of that group that has been "successful." In general,

"successful" intercourse remains undefined, although one can infer that the investigators consider maintenance of erection sufficient for intromission and for at least some period of intravaginal containment as the criterion of "success." Thus "successful intercourse" need not involve ejaculation for the male or orgasm for either partner.

Attempts at intercourse and degree of success in attempted intercourse are tabulated in nine studies. All subject populations were found to have at least some degree of sexual activity reflected by an attempt at intercourse although the percentages varied widely ranging from 8% (Tsuji et al., 1961) to 82% (Bors and Comarr, 1960).

"Successful intercourse" was achieved by subjects ranging from 5% (Tsuji et al., 1961) to 56% (Hohmann, 1966) of the total samples. No studies collected information on the circumstances that accompanied attempts at intercourse nor were any data reported on those factors that led to successful intercourse. Several authors (Zeitlin et al., 1957; Money, 1960; Comarr, 1970) speculated that the primary motivation for intercourse was the sexual satisfaction of the partner rather than sexual gratification of the subject per se; however, no data directly addressing this point were reported. There was also speculation (Zeitlin et al., 1957; Comarr, 1970) as to why some subjects had not attempted intercourse, but data directly on this point were also unreported.

There is a need for more detailed research into the patterns of sexual behavior which naturally occur in the spinal-cord-injured population. Questions of motivation should be directly addressed and data collected concerning frequency, enjoyment, and psychological and physiological functions subserved by intercourse in particular and sexual activity in general.

Interest in Continued Sexual Activity

As can be seen from the above section, participation in intercourse, whether "attempted" or "successful," has been taken as an index of interest in continued sexual activity. It is important to reiterate that the speculation in general has been that this interest derives from a desire to satisfy nonsexual psychological needs (e.g., performing well for a partner's enjoyment) rather than to satisfy more directly sexual needs or desires. In other words, the assumption has been that the individual with spinal-cord injury is interested in sexual behavior primarily to gratify others' desires and to satisfy him/herself only secondarily if at all.

Evidence has been gathered, in some studies, which attempts to delineate more clearly the nature of the interest in sexual activity after spinal-cord injury. These data provide a valuable adjunct to the data on intercourse. Problems of validity and reliability of the self-report measures used must be recognized, however, and should, in fact, be given particular weight in this highly emotional area. Social desirability might reasonably be expected to play a large part in the subjects' responses.

Engaging in sexual intercourse is dependent upon a variety of conditions beyond the subject's direct control, such as availability of a cooperative partner, perceived ability to perform adequately, access to privacy, and numerous other considerations. The report of interest in continued sexuality can exist regardless of these situational factors and may give us a more complete picture of the sexual wishes and desires of the members of the spinal-cord-injured population. As in the other studies reviewed, the methodology leaves much to be desired. Interest in continued sexual activity is generally not operationalized in any detail in these studies. Rather vague terms, such as *normal sexual activity, libidinous interest,* and *libido sexualis,* are used to indicate this interest. Specific definitions of the concepts used in each study are not given nor are the specific questions posed reported.

The issue of interest in continued sexual activity does not lend itself to simple quantification. The criteria taken to indicate continued sexual interest are specified in only a few studies (Weiss and Diamond, 1966; Jochheim and Wahle, 1970; Cole, Chilgren, and Rosenberg, 1973) and may vary widely from study to study. The distinction has been made between local somasthetic (Talbot, 1949) or genito-pelvic (Money, 1960) erotic stimulation and psychic or cerebrocognitional eroticism. Once this distinction is taken into account, there is general agreement that psychic eroticism remains intact while genitopelvic erotic stimulation is somewhat more variable dependent upon site and type of lesion (Talbot, 1971).

Several studies (Money, 1960; Hohmann, 1966; Weiss and Diamond, 1966) asked subjects to compare their current sexual experiences with those they had had prior to their spinal-cord lesions. This method deserves some special comment because of the extreme difficulty presented in attempting to interpret responses to this sort of question. Aside from being confounded by inextricably linked variables such as changes in chronological age as well as psychological and physio-logical changes related to the simple passage of time, the implicit assumption is that were it not for the physiological effects of the spinal-cord lesion, present and past experiences would be similar or identical. This assumption is extremely tenuous. It fails to consider the whole range of psychosocial adaptations that the individual has made (including those attendant to the physical disability itself), as well as countless other extraneous changes only indirectly linked to the disability. Behavioral changes reflecting altered body image and perceptions of oneself as a sexual being, as well as corresponding feedback from the social environment, must be presumed to play a role in the experience of sexual interest.

All studies surveyed found either no change (Talbot, 1949, 1955; Bors and Comarr, 1960), some slight decrease (Money, 1960; Tsuji et al., 1961; Hohmann, 1966; Weiss and Diamond, 1966), or a marked decrease (Herman, 1950; Jochheim and Wahle, 1970) in "sexual interest," variously defined. Only Weiss and Diamond's (1966) female sample showed an increased interest in sexual activity. Since Jochheim and Wahle (1970) considered only intercourse, the degree of change regarding interest in sexual activity is rendered difficult to assess. Similarly, the other study (Herman, 1950), which claimed marked diminution of sexual desire, was based on a small sample size and has been repeatedly rebutted (Talbot, 1955; Bors and Comarr, 1960; Weiss and Diamond, 1966; Cole et al., 1973).

The data indicate that, although the nature of sexual excitation is often some-what changed, sexual activity in one form or another persists and is enjoyed by a large portion of the spinal-cord-injured population.

Female Sexual Response

For a variety of reasons, probably including societal biases against seeing women as sexual beings (Griffith and Trieschmann, 1975), the usually passive sexual role assigned to women (Romano, 1973), and the proportionately small number of women in the spinal-cord-injured population (Cole et al., 1973), the sexual response of females with spinal-cord injury has been even less adequately investigated than has that of cord-injured males.

There are no reports in the literature of systematic data collected on genital responses to sexual stimulation in cord-injured females. The counterparts to erection and ejaculation in the male, including such physiological events as genital vascular engorgement, Bartholin's glands secretions, and vaginal lubrication, have not been directly investigated in spinal-cord-injured females, although some authors suggest that these functions should show sparing analogous to that exhibited by males (Comarr, 1966; Rusk, 1967; Cole, 1975).

In regard to perceived sexual excitation, Money (1960) interviewed seven females who had been injured from six months to fourteen years and ranged in age from twenty-one to sixty-five years. His data indicate that three had been non-orgasmic prior to injury and that, of the three who had attempted intercourse, the responses ranged from "terrible," "just a waste of time" to "some pleasure but no genital sensation." Two also reported pleasurable sexual feelings as the result of breast stimulation.

A second study to consider female sexuality was Weiss and Diamond's 1966 survey, cited above. Twenty-four percent of their twenty-one female subjects reported "undifferentiated sexual sensations" prior to injury, while 33% reported that they experienced such sensations after injury. In their data on perception of "localized sexual sensations," Weiss and Diamond found that 38% of their female sample said that they had experienced such sensations prior to injury while 52% reported such experience after disability. About half (48%) of Weiss and Diamond's female sample indicated that they had had "conscious sexual desire" prior to disablement and 62% of the women reported such desire at the time of the study.

Fifty-two percent of the females questioned indicated that they had engaged in "some form of sexual activity" prior to injury, and 62% reported that they were sexually active at the time of the study.

In data collected to assess sexual interest, 29% preinjury and 38% postinjury reported daydreams and sexual fantasies, and 24% preinjury and 19% postinjury reported sexual dreams.

Weiss and Diamond's data offer evidence to contradict the assumption that females with spinal-cord injury are markedly less sexual than cord-injured males. The study lacks a nondisabled control group, which would have allowed for interesting comparisons with the general population.

Fitzpatrick's (1974) study included two females in his sample: one subject experienced no arousal, had not experienced orgasm, and had made unsuccessful attempts at intercourse. The other subject experienced sexual arousal, was orgasmic, and was sexually active engaging in intercourse approximately one time per month.

Bregman (1975) interviewed thirty-one women ranging in age from eighteen to fifty-one years whose time since cord injury ranged from six months to twenty-eight years. All women reported some sexual experience postinjury. Of seven subjects who reported "a full sexual life" before injury, six reported less satisfaction with sex postinjury and one reported more sexual pleasure. In regard to orgasm, Bregman included subjective descriptions.

It is unclear from Bregman's data what percentage of her sample had orgasms or orgasmlike experiences, or how her other subjects responded to specific genital stimulation. She did report that twenty-seven subjects indicated vaginal lubrication and that in general the subjects felt that spinal-cord injuries do not affect the functioning of sexual arousal and lubrication.

Bregman's study is the most comprehensive to date on female sexuality and spinal-cord injury. Like many other studies reviewed in this chapter, it suffers from methodological inadequacies but represents an important starting point in understanding the effects of cord injury on women's sexual response.

There has been considerable interest on the part of researchers in the reproductive capacity of cord-injured women. This work is considered outside the scope of this discussion and will not be reviewed here. It is summarized succinctly by Griffith and Trieschmann (1975) with the statement that "disabled women in the childbearing years are susceptible to pregnancy and certain associated medical risks. Whether or not fertility is significantly reduced below that of able-bodied women is uncertain" (p. 19). The reader is referred to the Griffith and Trieschmann (1975) paper for further information on the effects of cord injury on reproductive capacity.

Those authors also note that excessive spasticity, autonomic dysreflexia, and bone fractures have been reported as isolated instances of complications accompanying intercourse in cord-injured females.

The sexual response of the female with spinal-cord injury remains virtually unexplained, with only suggestive evidence thus far gathered. The area is an important one and deserves extensive further research work.

Psychosocial Aspects of Spinal-Cord-Injured Sexuality

The preceding sections have dealt primarily with the physiological aspects of sexual response in individuals with spinal-cord injury. There exists another set of investigations which attempts to examine sexuality and spinal-cord injury from a more psychosocial or psychological perspective. These studies have been reviewed recently by Teal and Athelstan (1975) and will not be individually scrutinized here. In general, these investigations, like their more physiologically oriented counterparts, suffer numerous shortcomings in a variety of methodological areas, e.g., sample size and representativeness, lack of satisfactory control groups, lack of adequately standardized data collection procedures.

It is of some interest that only one of these articles (Weiss and Diamond, 1966) records even self-report data of actual sexual behavior, and none offer partner corroboration.

The data in these investigations are gathered to shed light on hypothesized psychological states or constructs whose relationship to sexual behavior is only theoretical in nature. Investigators seek to evaluate the nature of "self-concept" in cord-injured individuals (Thom, VonSalzen, and Fromme, 1946; Nagler, 1950; Hirschenfang and Benton, 1966), to discover the integrity of the "sexual identity" (Weiss and Diamond, 1966) of these individuals, and to determine impairments in "body image" (Lindner, 1953; Wachs and Zaks, 1960; Ryan, 1961). Investigators have also approached the question of sexual adjustment indirectly by examining marriage and divorce statistics for spinal-cord-injured populations (Comarr, 1962; Guttman, 1964; Fink, Skipper, and Hallenbeck, 1968). Here, too, reference to direct sexual behavior is lacking.

As important in theory as these various concepts may be to "sexual adjustment" and therefore sexual behavior, the lack of direct data regarding sexual behavior does not allow inferences that could either substantiate or refute their importance. It seems clear that a data base concerning actual sexual behavior is a necessary precursor to the sorts of theoretical speculations that make up the majority of the literature in this area. The cart, it would seem, is somewhat before the horse.

This lack of solid behavioral data not only has implications for theory building upon a firm foundation of empirical evidence but also has very direct practical consequences. Such data are needed in order to knowledgeably counsel individuals with spinal-cord injuries regarding their sexual options and the sorts of sexual experiences and sexual deficits that they can expect to encounter.

Therapeutic Programs: Evaluations and Reports

In contrast to both the physiological studies and the psychosocial studies of sexuality and spinal-cord injury, both of which began to appear in the literature in the late 1940s, reports of therapeutic activities in reference to sexual behavior and papers that offered advice on how to proceed in sexual counseling with spinal-cord-injured individuals did not begin to show up in the literature until the 1970s. Among the first of these was an unpublished paper by Braddom (1971), which acknowledged a great debt to Masters and Johnson's (1966) work. One can speculate that until the advances by Masters and Johnson and others in the late 1960s and early 1970s, the question of sexual counseling was largely academic. Everyone was in agreement that such counseling should go on but examination of the literature would indicate that there were no publicly shared opinions as to how one should go about it.

Hohmann (1972) suggested that changes in the patient population in the early 1970s and a social climate generally more accepting of sexuality led to demands for sexual counseling, and that this, in turn, kindled professional interest. He also credits the instructional materials developed by Cole and his associates at the University of Minnesota for adding impetus to the growing interest in sexual counseling for individuals with spinal-cord injury.

Romano and Lassiter (1972) reported their clinical experience with fifty-six spinal-cord-injured patients. Their subjects, both male and female, ranged in age from sixteen to sixty-three years, had been disabled for periods ranging from two weeks to over seven years, and included injuries ranging from C4 to S2. Their format consisted of a series of small group discussions in which sexual anatomy and physiology were reviewed in both normal and spinal-cord-injured populations.

Physiological changes were explained to patients and a sharing of experiences and broadening of sexual options was encouraged. The importance of communication between partners was stressed, and methods of adapting to the limitations of disability were introduced. Specific questions were answered as directly and nonjudgmentally as possible. The counseling generally took place in two to three sixty- to ninety-minute sessions, which were spaced to allow the patients to integrate the material discussed. Romano and Lassiter do not provide any outcome data, although they make it clear that they consider the program to be successful.

Cole et al. (1973) report on their program of sex counseling. They use a format adapted from the National Sex Forum, which consists of an intensive two-day, twenty-hour workshop that includes:

> Slides, speakers, panels and films . . . sequenced in a deliberate manner to stimulate and faciltate the participant to deal . . . with progressively more explicit . . . sexual material. The presentations and films explained or graphically displayed conventional and controversial aspects of human sexuality. The formal content included summaries of some of the pertinent literature. . . . Also included were movies of selected aspects of human sexuality including fantasy, male and female masturbation, male and female homosexuality, heterosexuality, sexual therapy and sexuality of the spinal cord injured person. (p. 115)

The program also included intensive small group discussions led by experienced group leaders.

Questionnaires were administered before and after the program to assess changes in sexual attitudes. They report responses from fifty-five participants in the program, including both spinal-cord-injured individuals and a "spouse or close friend with whom he/she could discuss personal and sexual matters" (p. 115). The group included participants ranging in age from sixteen to fifty-nine years, both unmarried and married, and was composed of spinal-cord-injured individuals with injuries at various levels, their friends and/or spouses, and health professionals.

Postworkshop evaluations simply asked, "Are you glad you attended the workshop on sexual function and spinal cord injury?" "Has the workshop in sexual function and spinal cord injury been helpful/harmful to you?" and "Should a deliberate program dealing with human sexuality be offered on a voluntary basis to all spinal-cord-injured adults?" Responses indicated that 100% were glad or very glad that they had attended the workshop, 98% had found it helpful, while 2% felt it had had no effect, and 98% believed that a deliberate program should be offered to all spinal-cord-injured adults.

These overwhelmingly positive evaluations reflect, in part, of course, the very general nature of the questions and the selected nature of the participants (all had been personally invited to attend). It should not be underestimated, however, that this is the first systematic response from the spinal-cord-injured population regarding sexual counseling, and it strongly supports the kind of enthusiasm that other authors have anecdotally reported.

In 1975, Held, Cole, Held, Anderson, and Chilgren reported on a series of five workshops for both professional and spinal-cord-injured adults, similar in format to the one described above. Ninety-five spinal-cord-injured adults and their partners participated in this series. Seventy-six participants completed anonymous questionnaires and, as in Cole et al. (1973), the response was enthusiastic. Ninety-six percent reported pleasure at having attended, 82.8% felt it had been personally beneficial, and 90.8% stated that they would recommend the program to others like themselves.

As in the earlier study (Cole et al., 1973), the data indicate enthusiasm for this sort of program, but there remains the glaring lack of data on sexual behavior and sexual satisfaction. We cannot even begin to make a judgment as to whether programs such as these actually lead to changes in sexual behavior or to changes in satisfaction with behaviors already ongoing. Beyond that, of course, are the questions: If there are changes, are they long-lasting or transitory, and what stresses or benefits derive from them? Again, the need for data on actual sexual activity makes itself apparent.

Methodological Problems and Suggestions for Future Research

In regard to the entire topic of sexuality and spinal-cord injury, the problem of sampling deserves primary consideration: It is an extremely important factor which transcends target behaviors. As has been noted above, research has been almost exclusively on males, and most subject populations have been drawn from hospitals or rehabilitation centers. Lacking empirical evidence to the contrary, the possibility exists that these individuals are not representative of the total spinal-cord-injured population. For example, they might arguably be assumed to have more physical pathology than the general spinal-cord-injured population, and this might, therefore, bias the results toward an underestimation of sexual interest and sexual activity.

A second consideration in sampling lies in the often unassessed areas: Use of medication that might affect sexuality, availability of a sexually willing and interested partner, and extraneous medical procedures that might affect sexual behavior are but a few obvious examples. These issues, too, transcend specific target behaviors and should be taken into account in any investigation of sexual behavior and spinal-cord injury.

The use of psychophysiological techniques has been completely overlooked in the study of sex and spinal-cord injury, although they have been very useful in the study of normal populations (Masters and Johnson, 1966; Zuckerman, 1971). In regard to investigations of erectile capability in males with spinal-cord injury, more advanced methodology should be employed than the customary uncorroborated self-report. Direct physiological monitoring via the penile plethysmograph has been used by numerous investigators in a variety of contexts (Bancroft, Jones, and Pullan, 1966; Rosen, 1973). Data based on this sort of measurement and experimental studies employing the presentation of various erotic stimuli could yield significant data on erectile capability in general, and on the distinction between reflexogenic and psychogenic erections in particular.

Recent psychophysiological investigations (Cohen and Shapiro, 1970; Geer, Morokoff, and Greenwood, 1974; Geer, 1975; Stintchak and Geer, 1975) have contributed the methodology necessary to readily assess genital response in cord-injured females. As has been noted, there is a dearth of information on female sexuality and spinal-cord injury. This new technology could be employed to remedy this situation. The use of psychophysiology to give a more precise picture of genital response should enable investigators to disentangle some of the complex questions that exist in the area of sex and spinal-cord injury.

Similarly, psychophysiological monitoring of extragenital responses to experimental stimuli (Masters and Johnson, 1966; Zuckerman, 1971; Geer, 1975) could shed light on the relationship between genitopelvic eroticism and cerebro-cognitional eroticism. This distinction, although proposed by Money (1960), has received no experimental consideration and is an important one for experimental investigation. It has been assumed (Cole, 1975) that the extragenital responses of the individual with spinal-cord injury parallel those of the physiologically normal, but no data have been offered to support this point.

In an effort to collect ejaculate for procreative purposes, a number of investigations have been carried out into means of inducing ejaculation (Rowan et al., 1962; Guttman, 1974; Bensman and Kottke, 1966). These have met with varying degrees of success and the question of ejaculatory capability may largely turn on the question of what means one is willing to undertake to achieve ejaculation. Although these medical interventions relate much more closely to reproductive functioning than to sexual behavior, and while their relevance to everyday sexual activity seems limited, such manipulations could yield important data about the sexual response in cord-injured individuals. Perhaps even more important, at least from a behavioral point of view, are the methods by which, and the conditions under which, ejaculation and/or orgasm has been attempted. This area of investigation has been virtually totally neglected. Underlying this neglect, one can speculate, there is in operation a "biological fallacy." That is, the existence of erectile failure or ejaculatory incompetence is assumed in every case to be a direct physiological result of injury to the spinal cord. This assumption overlooks all of the psychological and sociological variables that are attendant to catastrophically disabling conditions and that might very well account for at least some percentage of the resultant diminution in sexual function and sexual activity.

This biological fallacy also leads to neglect of consideration of the effects of the sexual myths and misconceptions that have led to the societal view of the spinal-cord-injured individual as asexual, and the "self-fulfilling prophecy" aspects of this view. As we know from Masters and Johnson (1970) and others, even occasional erectile difficulties with various physical or psychological causes can lead, over time, to complete erectile failure and dysfunctional avoidance of sexual contact. To tacitly suggest, as the present investigations do, that only biological factors are involved in sexual disturbances in the spinal-cord-injured population leads to confusion about the role of physiology in spinal-cord-injury sexual dysfunction and to neglect of psychosocial influences. These psychosocial influences may not only play an important role in causing dysfunction but may also prove to be a fruitful point of intervention in alleviating such dysfunctions.

Work has been done which attempts to differentiate between biogenic and psychogenic erectile failure (Karacan, 1970; Beutler, Karacan, Anch, Salis, Scott, and Williams, 1975). Although a definitive methodology is not yet available, this technology could profitably be applied to spinal-cord-injured populations.

The research to date leaves us with only the scantiest picture of the relationship between spinal-cord injury and sexual activity. The situation with other disabling conditions in regard to research efforts is even less satisfactory. Clearly, if more is to be learned about this most sensitive psychosocial area, and if the distress of all those individuals afflicted with disabling conditions is to be significantly alleviated, a great deal of work remains to be done. Such work will not only illuminate the mechanisms underlying sexual response in the disabled populations but could potentially shed a great deal of light on the sexual functioning of the physiologically normal population as well.

As a final note, let us remain aware that those research findings that do exist, setting aside for a moment all of the serious methodological and interpretive problems presented below, can and do represent only the current status of the individual with spinal-cord injury. The physiological data are by no means clear enough to allow us to understand all of sexual behavior on a physical basis. Sexual behavior and sexuality are influenced, probably more than any other sphere of human behavior, by attitudes, beliefs, myths, and misconceptions (Bidgood, 1974). It is only recently that some open discussion and examination of sex as it relates to the spinal-cord-injured has begun (Diamond, 1974; Singh and Manger, 1975). Professionals as well as cord-injured people are still to a large extent guided by the prejudices and biases of the past. The nature of sexual behavior is such that continuing change can be expected. Future surveys of well-informed spinal-cord-injured individuals will undoubtedly reveal different patterns of sexual behavior from those that are found in the sometimes naïve and often misinformed cord-injured of the present.

Summary

Current research on sexual response in spinal-cord-injured adults has been reviewed. Data on erection, ejaculation, orgasm, coitus, interest in continued sexual activity, and evaluation of therapeutic programs have been reported.

Thirteen studies examined erectile capability and found that approximately 50–90% of subjects were capable of erections. Subjects with higher level lesions and subjects with incomplete lesions were more likely to retain erectile capability.

Thirteen studies examined ejaculatory capability, which ranged from 0 to 50%. A higher incidence of ejaculation was found in those subjects with lower segmental lesions and those subjects with incomplete lesions.

Eleven studies examined male orgasm and found that it occurred in 2–16% of subjects. Quality of orgasm showed considerable variability and was markedly changed from the preinjury experience of orgasm.

Four studies examined sexual arousal in female subjects. Specific statistics on orgasm were not presented, although it is indicated that some women with spinal-cord injury experience orgasm.

Nine studies examined attempts at intercourse. Of various sample groups, 8–82% had attempted intercourse. "Successful" intercourse was achieved by 5–56% of subjects.

Eleven studies examined interest in continued sexual activity. Eight studies found no change or a slight decrease in sexual interest variously defined. Two studies found a marked decrease and one study found an increase in interest in sexual activity.

Three reports of therapeutic programs have been reviewed, indicasting positive response to anonymous questionnaires. No specific behavioral measures are reported and concrete conclusions concerning program effectiveness cannot be made.

Further research in all areas is strongly urged. Current methodology is criticized and suggestions for future research are made.

References

Bancroft, J. H., Jones, H. G., and Pullan, B. P. A simple transducer for measuring penile erection with comments on its use in the treatment of sexual disorders. *Behavior Research and Therapy*, 1966, *4*, 239–241.

Bensman, A., and Kottke, F. J. Induced emission of sperm utilizing electrical stimulation of the seminal vesicles and vas deferens. *Archives of Physical Medicine and Rehabilitation*, 1966, *47*, 436–443.

Beutler, L. E., Karacan, I., Anch, A. M., Salis, P. J., Scott, F. B., and Williams, R. L. MMPI and MIT discriminators of biogenic and psychogenic impotence. *Journal of Consulting and Clinical Psychology*, 1975, *43*, 899–903.

Bidgood, F. E. Sexuality and the handicapped. *SIECUS Report.* 1974, *2*(3), 1–2 ff.

Bors, E., and Comarr, A. E. Neurological disturbances of sexual function with special reference to 529 patients with spinal cord injury. *Urological Survey*, 1960, *10*, 191–222.

Braddom, R. L. *Sexual adjustment in spinal cord injury.* Unpublished manuscript, Ohio State University School of Medicine, 1971.

Bregman, S. *Sexuality and the spinal cord injured woman.* Minneapolis: Sister Kenney Institute, 1975.

Chusid, J. G. *Correlative neuroanatomy and functional neurology* (14th ed.). Los Altos, California: Lange Medical Publications, 1970.

Cibeira, J. B. Some conclusions on a study of 365 patients with spinal cord lesions. *Paraplegia*, 1970, *7*, 249–254.

Clowers, M. R., and Taylor, C. St. C. Sexuality and the spinal cord injured: An annotated bibliography. *Paraplegia News*, 1976, *29*(328), 42–44.

Cohen, H. D., and Shapiro, A. A method for measuring sexual arousal in the female. *Psychophysiology*, 1970, *8*, 251 (Abstract).

Cole, T. M. Sexuality and the spinal cord injured. In R. Green (Ed.), *Human sexuality: A health practitioner's text.* Balitmore: William and Wilkins, 1975.

Cole, T. M., Chilgren, R., and Rosenberg, P. A new programme of sex education and counseling for spinal-cord-injured adults and health care professionals. *Paraplegia*, 1973, *11*, 111–124.

Comarr, A. E. Marriage and divorce among patients with spinal cord injury. *Proceedings of the 11th Annual Spinal Cord Injury Conference.* New York: Bronx Veterans Administration Hospital, 1962, 163–215.

Comarr, A. E. Observations on menstruation and pregnancy among female spinal cord injury patients. *Paraplegia*, 1966, *3*, 263–272.

Comarr, A. E. Sexual function among patients with spinal cord injury. *Urologia Internationalis*, 1970, *25*, 134–168.

Comarr, A. E. Sex among patients with spinal cord and/or cauda equina injuries. *Medical Aspects of Human Sexuality*, 1973, *7*, 222–238.

Conomy, J. P. Disorders of body image after spinal cord injury. *Neurology*, 1973, *23*, 842–850.

Diamond, M. Sexuality and the handicapped. *Rehabilitation Literature*, 1974, *35*, 34–40.

Eisenberg, M. G., and Rustad, L. C. *Sex and the spinal cord injured: Some questions and answers* (2nd ed.). Pub. No. 5100-00076. Washington, D.C.: Superintendent of Documents, U.S. Government Printing Office, 1974.

Fink, S. L. Skipper, J. K., Jr., and Hallenbeck, P. N. Physical disability and problems in marriage. *Journal of Marriage and the Family*, 1968, *30*, 64–74.

Fitzpatrick, W. F. Sexual functioning in the paraplegic patient. *Archives of Physical Medicine and Rehabilitation*, 1974, *55*, 221–227.

Gardner, E. *Fundamentals of neurology*. Philadelphia: W. B. Saunders, 1968.

Geer, J. H. Direct measurement of genital responding. *American Psychologist*, 1975, *30*, 415–418.

Geer, J. H., Morokoff, P., and Greenwood, P. Sexual arousal in women: The development of a measurement device for vaginal blood volume. *Archives of Sexual Behavior*, 1974, *3*, 559–564.

Gregory, M. F. *Sexual adjustment: A guide for the spinal cord injured*. Bloomington, Illinois: Accent on Living, 1974.

Griffith, E. R., Timms, R. J., and Tomko, M. A. (Eds.). *Sexual problems of patients with spinal injuries: An annotated bibliography*. Cincinnati: University of Cincinnati, 1973.

Griffith, E., Tomko, M., and Timms, R. Sexual function in spinal cord injured patients: A review. *Archives of Physical Medicine and Rehabilitation*, 1973, *54*, 539–543.

Griffith, E. R., and Trieschmann, R. B. Sexual functioning in women with spinal cord injury. *Archives of Physical Medicine and Rehabilitation*, 1975, *56*, 18–21.

Guttman, L. The married life of paraplegics and tetraplegics. *Paraplegia*, 1964, *2*, 182–188.

Guttman, L., and Walsh, J. J. Prostigmin assessment test of fertility in spinal man. *Paraplegia*, 1971, *9*, 39–51.

Held, J., Cole, T., Held, C., Anderson, C., and Chilgren, R. Sexual attitude reassessment workshops: Effect on spinal cord injured adults, their partners and rehabilitation professionals. *Archives of Physical Medicine and Rehabilitation*, 1975, *56*, 14–18.

Herman, M. Role of somesthetic stimuli in the development of sexual excitation in man. *Archives of Neurology and Psychiatry*, 1950, *64*, 42–56.

Heslinga, K., Schellen, A. M. C. M., and Verkuyl, A. *Not made of stone: The sexual problems of handicapped people*. Springfield, Illinois: Charles C Thomas, 1974.

Hirschenfang, S., and Benton, J. Rorschach responses of paraplegic and quadriplegic patients. *Paraplegia*, 1966, *4*, 40–42.

Hohmann, G. W. Some effects of spinal cord lesions on experienced emotional feelings. *Psychophysiology*, 1966, *3*, 143–156.

Hohmann, G. W. Considerations in management of psychosexual readjustment in the cord injured male. *Rehabilitation Psychology*, 1972, *19*, 50–58.

Jochheim, K. A., and Wahle, H. A study on sexual function in 56 male patients with complete irreversible lesions of the spinal cord and cauda equina. *Paraplegia*, 1970, *8*, 166–172.

Karacan, I. Clinical value of nocturnal erection in the prognosis and diagnosis of impotence. *Medical Aspects of Human Sexuality*, 1970, *4*, 27–34.

Kuhn, R. A. Functional capacity of the isolated human spinal cord. *Brain*, 1950, *73*, 1–51.

Lindner, H. Perceptual sensitization to sexual phenomena in the chronic physically handicapped. *Journal of Clinical Psychology*, 1953, *9*, 67–68.

Masters, W. H., and Johnson, V. E. *Human sexual response*. Boston: Little, Brown, 1966.

Masters, W. H., and Johnson, V. E. *Human sexual inadequacy*. Boston: Little, Brown, 1970.

Merritt, H. H. *A textbook of neurology* (5th ed.). Philadelphia: Lea and Febiger, 1973.

Money, J. Phantom orgasm in the dreams of paraplegic men and women. *AMA Archives of General Psychiatry*, 1960, *3*, 373–382.

Mooney, T. O., Cole, T. M. and Chilgren, R. A. *Sexual options for paraplegics and quadriplegics*. Boston: Little, Brown, 1975.

Munro, D., Horne, H. H., and Paull, D. P. The effect of injury to the spinal cord and cauda equina on the sexual potency of men. *New England Journal of Medicine*, 1948, *239*, 903–911.

Nagler, B. Psychiatric aspects of cord injury. *American Journal of Psychiatry*, 1950, *107*, 49–56.

National Institute of Neurological Diseases and Stroke. *Spinal cord injury: Hope through research.*

Pub. No. (NIH) 72-160. Washington, D.C.: Superintendent of Documents, U.S. Government Printing Office, 1971.

President's Committee on Employment of the Handicapped. *One in eleven: Handicapped adults in America.* Washington, D.C., 1975.

Riddoch, G. The reflex functions of the completely divided spinal cord in man, compared with those associated with less severe lesions. *Brain*, 1917, *40*, 326. Cited by J. P. Conomy, Disorders of body image after spinal cord injury. *Neurology*, 1973, *23*, 842–850.

Romano, M. What we've always wanted to know. In Sex: Rehabilitation's stepchild. *Proceedings of the Workshop on Continuing Education in the Treatment of Spinal Cord Injuries.* Chicago: National Paraplegia Foundation, 1973. Pp. 27–33.

Romano, M., and Lassiter, R. Sexual counseling with the spinal cord injured. *Archives of Physical Medicine and Rehabilitation*, 1972, *53*, 568–572.

Rosen, R. C. Suppression of penile tumescence by instrumental conditioning. *Psychosomatic Medicine*, 1973, *35*, 509–513.

Rossier, A. B., Ziegler, W. H., Duchosal, P. W., and Meylan, J. Sexual function and dysreflexia. *Paraplegia*, 1971, *9*, 51–58.

Rowan, R. L., Howley, T. F., and Nova, H. R. Electro-ejaculation. *Journal of Urology*, 1962, *98*, 726–729.

Rusk, H. A. (Mod.). Roundtable: Sex problems in paraplegia. Symposium presented at the New York University School of Medicine, New York City. Published in *Medical Aspects of Human Sexuality*, December 1967, pp. 46–50.

Ryan, J. H. Dreams of paraplegics. Archives of General Psychiatry, 1961, *5*, 94.

Sex and the handicapped: A selected bibliography (1927–1973). Cleveland: Veterans Administration Hospital, 1974.

Singh, S. P., and Manger, T. Sex and self: The spinal cord injured. *Rehabilitation Literature*, 1975, *36*, 2–10.

Sintchak, G. H., and Geer, J. H. A vaginal plethysmograph system. *Psychophysiology*, 1975, *12*, 113–115.

Talbot, H. S. A report on sexual function in paraplegics. *Journal of Urology*, 1949, *61*, 265–270.

Talbot, H. S. Sexual function in paraplegia. *Journal of Urology*, 1955, *73*, 91–100.

Talbot, H. S. Psycho-social aspects of sexuality in spinal cord injury patients. *Paraplegia*, 1971, *9*, 37–39.

Tarabulcy, E. Sexual function in the normal and in paraplegia. *Paraplegia*, 1972, *10*, 201–208.

Teal, J. C., and Athelstan, G. T. Sexuality and spinal cord injury: Some psychosocial considerations. *Archives of Physical Medicine and Rehabilitation*, 1975, *56*, 264–268.

Thom, D. A., VonSalzen, C. F., and Fromme, A. Psychological aspects of the paraplegic patient. *The Medical Clinics of North America.* Philadelphia: W. B. Saunders, 1946, *30*, 473–480.

Tsuji, I., Nakajima, F., Morimoto, J., and Nounaka, Y. The sexual function in patients with spinal cord injury. *Urologia Internationalis*, 1961, *12*, 270–280.

Wachs, H., and Zaks, M. Studies of body images in men with spinal cord injury. *Journal of Nervous and Mental Disease*, 1960, *131*, 121–127.

Weiss, A., and Diamond, D. Sexual adjustment, identification and attitudes of patients with myelopathy. *Archives of Physical Medicine and Rehabilitation*, 1966, *47*, 245–250.

Zeitlin, A. B., Cottrell, T. L., and Lloyd, F. A. Sexology of the paraplegic male. *Fertility and Sterility*, 1957, *8*, 337–344.

Zuckerman, M. Physiological measures of sexual arousal in the human. *Psychological Bulletin*, 1971, *75*, 297–329.

Until recently, failure of kidney function was a fatal illness. The development of renal dialysis and kidney transplants has changed this picture, and patients now survive for many years with one or both of these procedures.

In this study, the sexual functioning of 80% of dialysis or transplant patients was found to be impaired. The relative contributions of physiological and psychological factors in producing sexual dysfunction in patients with renal failure can not be identified at present. It is clear that the clinician who works with kidney patients should anticipate and be prepared to deal with problems his patients may experience in their sexual adjustment.

32

Sexual Functioning in Patients with Chronic Renal Failure

Harry S. Abram,† Larry R. Hester, William F. Sheridan, and Gerald M. Epstein

Until the early 1960s chronic renal failure represented a terminal illness for which there was no definitive treatment. The agonizing and lingering death caused by uremia is embedded in the memories of many physicians caring for these patients through the first half of this century. With the advent of intermittent hemodialysis and subsequently the availability of renal transplantation, the clinical picture and therapeutic avenues have vastly changed. Patients' lives are prolonged, and indeed many remain productive and active members of families and society, especially with a combined program offering dialysis and transplantation (Abram, 1972). Nevertheless, these treatment modalities are associated with physical, as well as psychosocial, hazards which take their toll (Abram, 1970). Complications are manifold, ranging from bone demineralization to suicide (Abram, Moore, and Westervelt, 1971) with chronic dialysis and steroid intoxication to organ rejection with transplantation. Disturbances in sexual activity, namely a decrease in

Harry S. Abram,† Larry R. Hester, and *William F. Sheridan* • Department of Psychiatry, Vanderbilt University Medical Center, Nashville, Tennessee. Dr. Abram died on September 3, 1977.   *Gerald M. Epstein* • Department of Psychology, George Peabody College for Teachers, Nashville, Tennessee

sexual potency, are mentioned, but there is little documentation or discussion of this subject in the medical literature (Goodwin, Valenti, Hall, et al., 1968; Levy, 1973; Schreiner and Maher, 1965). In this presentation we shall briefly review the psychosocial concomitants involved in the treatment of chronic renal failure, document the effect of renal disease and its treatment on sexual activity in male patients, describe sexual attitudes, and discuss the implications of the findings.

Psychosocial Concomitants

The patient with chronic renal failure does not begin hemodialysis or receive a transplant until the terminal phases of his illness. In a literal and symbolic sense he is brought from death's door and experiences a form of rebirth. Some have even spoken of a "Lazarus reaction" following a renal homograft. Dialysis and transplantation are not mutually exclusive and are frequently complementary. The former is necessary while the patient awaits a homograft, either from a related living or cadaver donor. If his body rejects the transplant then dialysis again is a necessity until he receives another. Some patients elect to remain on dialysis rather than accept the uncertainty of a transplant. The mortality with the former is approximately 10% per year, while with transplantation the one-year survival rate for a cadaver homograft or a kidney from a living related donor is 65% (excluding a homozygous twin homograft with a survival rate of 95%). Thus, prolonged life through dialysis or with a transplant has its precarious aspects and psychosocial sequelae.

With chronic dialysis the patient finds himself in the bind of imposed dependence on the "artificial kidney" (the dialyzer), the medical regimen, the medical personnel and his family, and at the same time an expected independence necessary to maintain his responsibilities in a healthy world. For the rest of his life or until he receives a transplant, he undergoes dialysis thirty hours weekly (usually divided into two or three "runs"). During this time he passively lies in bed "hooked" (connected) to a machine (the "kidney") which dialyzes or cleanses by osmosis his blood of impurities. In addition to postdialysis lethargy, he finds his life constricted by dietary and fluid restrictions, the economic burden of a catastrophic illness, the regressive pulls of a chronic disease, and physical deterrents such as anemia and intercurrent infection which hinder his sense of well-being. Yet he must support a family and be a "productive'" citizen when not on dialysis. This conflict between dependency and independency, passivity and activity, sickness and health underlies the patient's adaptation to dialysis and affects his sexual adjustment.

With a renal transplant the patient's survival is no longer dependent upon a machine. There are other crises in his life, such as awaiting the homograft and episodes of threatened organ rejection; and the side effects of his steroid and immunosuppressive medication are potentially bothersome. Yet he is freer to act in an independent fashion, and his feelings of well-being are enhanced by the physiological functioning of a natural organ not reproducible by a mechanical one. If organ rejection occurs and chronic dialysis then becomes again necessary, the psychological reverberations can be severe (Abram et al., 1971). There are other psychological issues—for example, fantasies and conflicts related to accepting the transplanted organ—which may influence behavior and sexual functioning.

Sexual Activity

With physical, psychosocial, and behavioral alterations in dialysis and transplant patients, one could hypothesize changes in the sexual sphere. A diminished sense of physical well-being, conflicts related to passivity and dependency imposed by the treatment regimen, and the regressive aspects of chronic illness, for example, could lead to a decrease in sexual functioning in the chronic dialysand; whereas improved physiological functioning and greater independency in the transplant patient could lead to improved sexual activity. It is not uncommon for male dialysis patients to complain of sexual impotence and for transplant patients to remark on their improved sexual performance. Other aspects of sexual behavior, such as masturbation while being dialyzed, male patients exhibiting themselves to dialysis nurses, sexual liaisons between nurses and patients, and wives of dialysands having extramarital affairs (Shambaugh, Hampers, Bailey, et al., 1967), are informally discussed by dialysis personnel. We suspect that sexual taboos and denial (Short and Wilson, 1969) by personnel (i.e., that such behavioral changes occur or are significant in their patients) account for the paucity of documented information in this area.

Our method of studying sexual behavior consisted of personal interviews at random with thirty-two dialysis and transplant patients (Abram, Hester, Epstein, et al., 1974). With eleven we held separate interviews with their wives. For the purposes of the initial report and in order to decrease the number of variables, we limited our sample to male veterans who had married prior to the onset of kidney disease and who had been on dialysis for a minimum of three months. Nineteen of these patients had functioning renal homografts at the time of the study, thus allowing some comparison of sexual activity prior to the onset of kidney disease, while on dialysis, and after transplantation. The major indicator of sexual activity was frequency of intercourse, although other parameters (such as the degree and type of impotency if present, the spouse's attitude, the relationship of sexual activity to physical complications, psychological complications, and the amount of time on dialysis) were also included in the overall evaluation of each patient, as well as a detailed history of renal disease. A structured Dialysis-Transplant Sexual Questionnaire completed by the interviewer in the presence of the patient or spouse was used to record the data obtained. With each interview, strict anonymity and confidentiality were assured and a noncoercive straightforward approach taken.

As noted, for purposes of the study sexual activity was measured by the frequency of intercourse before the onset of chronic kidney disease, after the onset, while on dialysis, and after transplantation if applicable. We defined "reduced potency" as a decrease in frequency of sexual intercourse of 50% or more when compared to sexual activity prior to onset of kidney disease. Table 1 summarizes the patient sampling, renal disease history, and sexual intercourse frequencies.

Table 1. Marital, Renal, and Sexual History

Patient	Patient's age	Wife's age	Years married	Age chronic renal disease diagnosed	Age dialysis begun	Months on dialysis	Age transplant performed	Present urine output (ml/24 hr)	Frequency of intercourse per month prior to renal disease	Frequency of intercourse per month after onset of renal disease	Frequency of intercourse per month on dialysis	Frequency of intercourse per month after transplant
1.	28	24	10	27	27	4	28	5000	30	5	5	(1 month postop)
2.	45	38	18	39	42		45	1500	15	15	0	(3 weeks postop)
3.	48	38	15	34	45	5	48	5000	8	6	0	5
4.	44	46	15	40	41		42	750	13	7	2	4
5.	45	38	22	33	38	3	38	2750	6	2	2	3
6.	39	36	19	20	32		34	2000	9	9	¼	3
7.	42	32	11	33	38	37	41 (3rd reject)	0	12	5	2	
8.	36	30	14	29	32	14	34 (2nd)	2500	6	6	2	6
9.	29	27	7	22	27	4	28	"very good"	10	10	1	14
10.	41	38	19	22	39		40	2000	15	3	3	3
11.	39	37	17	22	32	24	34	2000	15	15	15	15
12.	36	31	3	34	34	4	35	2000	20	0	10	20
13.	39	35	15	26	36	3	36	3500	17	4	0	12
14.	51	48	27	45	47	20	49	1300	12	6	1	4
15.	34	31	9	27	32	20	33	3000	4	4	4	4
16.	51	41	20	25	44		47	4000	5	5	5	5
17.	46	26	3	34	45	4		1500	2	2	2	
18.	29	25	6	20	27	26		2000	11	1	3	
19.	50	51	30	41	45	58		20	5	1	1	
20.	32	28	11	29	30	22	30	0	8	5	3	
21.	56	56	28	49	55	5		35	15	2	0	
22.	45	43	23	42	44	7		750	11	3	1	
23.	48	41	21	35	47	6		30	10	4	5	(1 month postop)
24.	43	39	14	25	40	15		3600	3	3	1	
25.	50	46	24	36	48	16		0	8	1	0	
26.	47	40	16	45	46			1000	2	2	1	
27.	39	36	18	22	37	20			10	10	10	
28.	41	39	20	33	37		41	0	12	12	8	(1 month postop)
29.	39	29	10	21	38	10	38	3200	4	4	1	(1 month postop)
30.	46	46	25	42	43	35	46	2900	8	0	0	(1 month postop)
31.	33	27	12	25	32	7		1500	10	6	6	
32.	38	35	18	24	36	17		0	16	11	6	

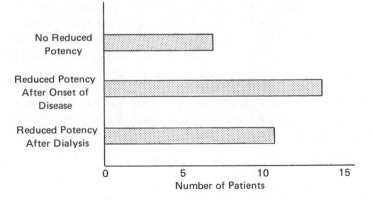

Fig. 1. Potency after onset of renal disease and dialysis.

The average age of the patients was 41.5 years and of the spouses 36.8 with 16.2 the average number of years married. Average age for the initial diagnosis of chronic renal disease was 31.3 with maintenance hemodialysis becoming necessary at 38.6 years. The average length of time on dialysis was 15.4 months. Transplantation in the 19 patients with functioning homografts took place at the average age of 38.4 years. The frequency of sexual intercourse per month for all patients before the onset of renal disease was 10.4, 5.7 after the onset, 4.0 while on dialysis, and 7.5 after transplant (where applicable).

Figure 1 depicts the effect of chronic renal disease and dialysis on sexual activity in the entire group of thirty-two patients. Seven patients had no significant decrease in sexual relations after the onset of disease or after the institution of dialysis. Fourteen patients reported reduced potency (a decrease in sexual activity of 50% or more compared to premorbid sexual functioning) after the onset of renal disease, and the remaining eleven patients with no significant decrease in sexual activity after disease onset had reduced potency after beginning dialysis. Figure 2 represents the effect of renal transplantation on sexual performance. Of those

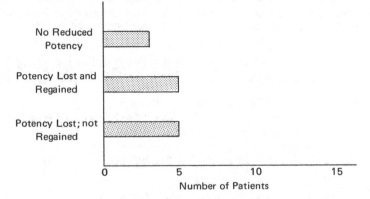

Fig. 2. Effect of transplant on potency.

patients with functioning homografts, six were not included as they were still in the convalescent postoperative stage. In the remaining thirteen patients, three maintained their sexual activity as it had been before the onset of disease and the institution of dialysis, five regained activity approximately equal to the premorbid state, and five did not.

In the twenty-five patients with reduced potency after the onset of renal disease and dialysis, decreased libido and problems having an erection appeared to be associated with reduced potency as opposed to problems ejaculating. Nocturnal emissions and morning or evening erections were rare. Table 2 summarizes these data.

Sexual Attitudes

Most patients were generally cooperative and responded to the interview session in an open fashion with little apparent attempt to please the interviewer. Only in one instance did a patient express overt hostility by refusing to participate in the study. The majority of patients with reduced sexual potency at some point during their illness believed that physical complications most likely accounted for their decreased activity. Such statements as "When you're sick sex is the furthest thing from your mind," "If you're tired, you don't have the energy," and "When you feel bad you just can't do it" were common. One patient stated the situation well, remarking, "When I was sick (during the time he required dialysis before receiving a transplant) the last problem I had was with sex. It never entered my mind to have relations with my wife. It took all of my energy to stay alive!" Indeed, with the intercurrent physical complications (the anemia, lethargy, etc.) of the dialysis patient, it is not difficult to postulate that the patient's cathexis is withdrawn from sexual objects to bodily preservation. However, some noted that when they were feeling better physically they were unable to perform sexually, making such observations as "When I am feeling good I have the desire but I can't do anything about it," and "Even when he feels good he's still the same—no sexual interest at all" (the latter comment by a spouse). One patient expressed fear of harming his transplanted kidney by having sexual intercourse; similarly, a dialysis patient was fearful of damaging his exterior arteriovenous shunt or in some fashion injuring himself.

Sexual activity appeared related to dialysis time in that patients considered themselves less likely to have intercourse immediately following a "run" (usually an eight- to twelve-hour period of being dialyzed). Likewise, they observed that

Table 2.   Reduced Potency

	Never	Almost never	Sometimes	Almost always	Always
Decreased libido	4	3	5	11	2
Problem having erection	5	3	5	7	5
Problem ejaculating	10	4	4	3	4
Nocturnal emissions	13	5	7		
Morning or night erections	8	6	10	1	

the longer they remained on dialysis at one setting the less sexually active they were afterward. For example, a patient commented, "When you come off the machine and your blood pressure is low, you don't even think about sex." With shifts in the blood–brain barrier, hypotensive episodes, fluid loss, and electrolyte changes, patients often feel "washed out" (realistically and symbolically) for twelve to twenty-four hours after dialysis. Their observations of decreased sexual activity in the postdialysis phase may thus be associated with these physiological alterations.

Our interviewing technique with the use of a structured questionnaire did not allow for an in-depth look at unconscious psychological conflicts related to decreased sexual activity. This defect, compounded by the defensive maneuver of denial which is so prevalent among dialysands (Short and Wilson, 1969), made proper assessment of psychological complications difficult. Thus with few exceptions the study patients denied that their psychological state affected their sexual performance, but some remarked that depression and anxiety decreased their sexual activity. For example, some patients who noted, "If you're depressed you're less likely to do it," "When you're upset you just don't think about sex," and "When you're worried or depressed your sexual desire decreases" at least pointed to the role of overt emotions if not to unconscious conflicts.

In separate interviews with eleven spouses, we found rather consistent attitudes and some data divergent from our interviews with their husbands. Concerning the latter, in eight there was discrepant information with regard to frequency of sexual intercourse before renal disease, after its onset, and after dialysis. Six of the spouses reported lower frequencies of sexual relations, while the other two wives gave higher frequencies. The wives tended to be more defensive than and protective of their husbands. They made such statements as "I'm really more interested in my husband's health than I am in his sex life," "I really don't see the value of this study," and "Are all these questions really necessary? I think you're getting too personal."

Generally the patients looked upon their wives as supportive and sexually nonaggressive. Several commented that the spouse was indifferent or appeared relieved not to have sexual relations. Patients with reduced potency made remarks such as "I don't believe it bothers her that we don't have relations. I feel like she is well content," "She understands me. The fact that I'm not (sexually) active anymore doesn't seem to bother her one way or the other," and "She's a very cold-natured woman, so it doesn't bother her. In fact, she almost seems happier." Some admitted that their wives were "frustrated" sexually or that the "marriage had suffered a little bit." One commented, "My wife is a passionate woman, but what could I do? No doubt it's hard on a woman unless you're married to a cold-blooded one." Two patients noted that their wives had "nervous breakdowns," requiring psychiatric treatment, at some point during the course of their illness.

Comment

Three categories of patients emerged from our initial findings: those with no decrease in sexual activity at any point during the course of their illness and treatment (approximately 20% of the patient sample), those with a decrease in sexual activity after the onset of chronic renal disease (45%), and those with reduced potency after the institution of dialysis (35%). Thus chronic dialysis cannot be implicated as of primary etiological importance in all patients with reduced sexual activity, as a significant proportion of male patients are impotent prior to its institution. In a smaller subgroup of patients with functioning homografts, 20% maintained sexual activity as before the onset of illness and while on dialysis, 40% who had reduced sexual potency after disease onset or on dialysis regained their potency, and another 40% did not regain potency. Thus renal transplantation improves sexual functioning in a significant group of patients but not all. (As one remarked, "It's like being on a honeymoon again.") From a statistical viewpoint, we found that patients less than thirty years of age were less likely to develop reduced sexual potency after onset of disease or the institution of dialysis ($p = .01$) and that patients over thirty were more likely to have decreased sexual activity after disease onset and before dialysis (i.e., earlier in the disease process). Thus the younger the patient the better the sexual prognosis. There was no significant statistical relationship between premorbid frequency of sexual intercourse and the occurrence of reduced potency.

Our sample is admittedly small and limited to married veterans with a history of renal disease prior to marriage. Future studies in this area should include not only male patients but a broader range, such as women, unmarried men, etc. More in-depth, longitudinal studies are also needed to explore further unconscious sexual fantasies and conflicts related to chronic renal failure and its treatment, as well as to determine if various phases (e.g., early, middle, or late) of dialysis or transplantation affect sexual activity differently. At this point the etiology of reduced sexual potency in this group of patients remains unclear but appears multidetermined. Decreased sexual performance does not universally accompany renal failure, chronic dialysis, or renal transplantation, and reduced potency occurs in 45% of patients prior to the onset of dialysis. These findings, along with 40% showing no improvement with transplantation, demonstrate that many variables, both physiological and psychosocial, are involved. Hopefully, more elaborate and sophisticated studies will elucidate these factors and lead to therapeutic measures beneficial to the growing patient population who now survive the ravages of chronic kidney disease.

References

Abram, H. S. Survival by machine: The psychological stress of chronic hemodialysis. *Psychiatry in Medicine*, 1970, *1*, 37–50.

Abram, H. S. The psychiatrist, the treatment of chronic renal failure, and the prolongation of life: III. *American Journal of Psychiatry*, 1972, *128*, 84–89.

Abram, H. S., Moore, G. L., and Westervelt, F. B. Suicidal behavior in chronic dialysis patients. *American Journal of Psychiatry*, 1971, *127*, 1199–1204.

Abram, H. S., Hester, L. R., Epstein, G. M., et al. Sexual activity and renal failure. In *Fifth International Congress of Nephrology*, Vol. III. Basel: Karger, 1974. Pp. 207–210.

Goodwin, N. J., Valenti, C., Hall, J. E., et al. Effects of uremia and chronic hemodialysis on the reproductive cycle. *American Journal of Obstetrics and Gynecology*, 1968, *1*, 528–535.

Levy, N. B. Sexual adjustment to maintenance hemodialysis and renal transplantation: National survey by questionnaire: Preliminary report. *Transactions of the American Society of Artificial Internal Organs*, 1973, *19*, 138–143.

Schreiner, G. E., and Maher, J. F. Hemodialysis for chronic renal failure. III. Medical, moral and ethical, and socio-economic problems. *Annals of Internal Medicine*, 1965, *62*, 551–557.

Shambaugh, P. W., Hampers, C. L., Bailey, G. L., et al. Hemodialysis in the home—emotional impact on the spouse. *Transactions of the American Society of Artificial Internal Organs*, 1967, *13*, 41–45.

Short, M. J., and Wilson, W. P. Roles of denial in chronic hemodialysis. *Archives of General Psychiatry*, 1969, *20*, 433–437.

In this chapter, Ellenberg describes a study undertaken to investigate the influence of endocrine, neurologic, and urologic factors in the etiology of impotence in diabetic males. Accurate diagnosis of the basis for diabetic impotence is crucial, as diagnosis determines which treatment strategies are indicated and what the prognosis for reversal will be.

Ellenberg mentions the use of techniques for monitoring nocturnal erections as a useful aid in the diagnosis of diabetic impotence. While he stated at the time of publication that there is "no direct method of objectively measuring impotence" new refinements in nocturnal penile tumescence research (NPT) are beginning to provide this methodology (see Karacan, Part II, Chapter 9).

33

Impotence in Diabetes: The Neurologic Factor

Max Ellenberg

The increased frequency of impotence in the male diabetic has long been recognized; furthermore, diabetes as a systemic disease is virtually unique in this regard. These facts clearly suggest that the impotence is related, in some manner, to the diabetes per se. This study was undertaken to elucidate the underlying factor(s).

A survey of the literature yields uniform corroboration of the increased prevalence of impotence in diabetes. Von Noorden, in 1903, commented on the common occurrence of loss of sexual power in diabetic men. Naunyn (1906) added the observation that impaired potency is not only more frequent but may be an early symptom of diabetes. More recent studies report an impressive prevalence of impotence in diabetic men, with an average involvement approximating 50% (Rubin and Babbott, 1953; Montenero and Donatone, 1962; Schoffling, Federlin, Ditschunheit, et al., 1963). These figures are considerably greater than that for the general population as reported by Kinsey, Pomeroy, and Martins (1948).

The author is indebted to Drs. J. L. Gabrilove and C. Nicolis, in whose laboratory many of the plasma testosterone levels were determined, and to Drs. H. Weber and S. Gandelsman, who performed the cystometric studies.

Max Ellenberg • Department of Medicine, Mt. Sinai Hospital, New York, New York

In approaching the problem it is essential to differentiate libido, potency, and fertility. These may be individually affected, and considerable confusion has arisen because of an assumed relationship and indiscriminate interchange in use of these terms. Potency may be defined as the ability to initiate, sustain, and successfully conclude the act of coitus. Thus, a satisfactory firm penile erection sufficiently maintained to secure vaginal intromission with subsequent orgasm constitutes adequate potency (Roen, 1965).

Penile erection takes place as a reflex. Stimulation of the second, third, and fourth sacral components of the parasympathetic nerves (that is, the nervi erigentes), which may be psychic or reflex, results in dilatation of the penile arteries, increase in blood flow, and tumescence of the corpora cavernosa and the corpus spongiosum. Erection is thus induced by active hyperemia of the arteries, which are partially occluded by longitudinal ridges in the resting state. With retention of blood the cavernous spaces expand and compress the veins, which have funnel-like valves, and so sustain erection. Detumescence results from vasoconstriction of the penile arteries with subsequent decrease of arterial blood flow, diminution of pressure, and release of the compressed veins (Learmouth, 1931; Bors and Comarr, 1960).

An underlying neuropathic factor in diabetes was suggested by the facts that potency depends on the integrity of the autonomic nervous system and that the latter is frequently involved in diabetic neuropathy. This hypothesis was further encouraged by a previous study that indicated a uniform association between impotence and dysfunction of the incipient, asymptomatic neurogenic bladder (Ellenberg and Weber, 1967).

The Study and the Patients

The direction of the investigation was based on the recognition that the autonomic pathways involved in micturition and erection are identical (Learmouth, 1931) (Figure 1). When these nerves are intact, bladder function is normal. Since there is no direct method of objectively measuring impotence, neurogenic bladder studies were performed, the assumption being that involvement of these nerves would be reflected simultaneously by abnormalities in both areas. The studies included cystometric readings, measurement of residual urine, bladder capacity, and cystoscopy where indicated. In addition, a complete clinical survey and detailed neurological examinations were done on the diabetic man with impotence and on a control series of diabetic men without impotence.

There were forty-five diabetic male patients in this study series, all included solely on the basis of impotence. Their age (Table 1) varied from 21 to 68 years, with 75% being less than 50 years of age. The average age was 43.2 years. The duration of diabetes (Table 1) varied from 0 to over 20 years. Three-fourths (75%) of the patients had had diabetes for less than 10 years; this early onset and lack of relationship to duration is similar to previous reports (Rubin and Babbott, 1958; Montenero and Donatone, 1962; Rubin, 1958). In six patients the initial clinical manifestation of diabetes was impotence; investigation of this symptom led to the diagnosis of diabetes.

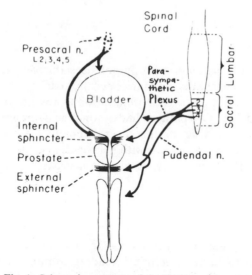

Fig. 1. Schematic anatomy of the bladder and penis.

Control was maintained with insulin in twenty-six patients, oral agents were satisfactorily used in fourteen patients, and five were controlled with diet alone. Control of the carbohydrate metabolic disorder had been satisfactory in most patients; at the time of the study it was good in all.

Table 1.   Characteristics of Study Groups

	Impotent diabetics	Control diabetics
Total diabetics (N)	45	30
Age (N)		
21–30 years	5	4
31–40 years	10	6
41–50 years	19	12
51–60 years	10	7
>60 years	1	1
Average age (years)	43.2	42.9
Duration of diabetes (N)		
0–5 years	9	6
5–10 years	18	12
10–11 years	7	5
15–20 years	6	4
20+ years	5	3
Evidence of neuropathy (N)		
Diabetic peripheral neuropathy	38	6
Neurogenic bladder without		
peripheral neuropathy	2	0
Abnormal cystometrogram	37	3
Increased bladder capacity	37	3
Psychogenic impotence (N)	4	0

Results

Neurologic Findings

Of the forty-five patients with impotence, thirty-eight had evidence of peripheral diabetic neuropathy as manifested by pain, paresthesia, absent deep reflexes—especially ankle jerks—and diminution to absence of the various sensations in the legs and feet. Two patients had autonomic neurogenic bladder involvement without accompanying peripheral neuropathy. Associated neuropathic involvement was seen in four patients with neuropathic ulcer, three with retrograde ejaculation, five with enteropathy, two with neuroarthropathy, and two with orthostatic hypotension.

Urologic Findings

Cystometrograms were performed on all forty-five patients; 500 ml was chosen as the shutoff point to ensure a definitive reading, although the average response of the normal bladder is approximately at the 250-ml level (Figure 2). Cystometric abnormalities were recorded in thirty-seven of the patients, and eight had normal findings. Residual urine was present in six patients; cystoscopy was performed in these, and no bladder-neck obstruction was observed. Cystoscopy in twenty-four other patients showed normal findings. Bladder capacity and distensibility were increased in all patients with an abnormal cystometrogram (Figure 3).

Two patients had impotence, abnormal cystometrogram readings, and a normal peripheral nervous system on examination—that is, what may be classified as a "pure" autonomic involvement. One patient with severe neuropathy had a hypertonic bladder response compatible with upper neuron involvement. Of the other five patients with neither cystometric abnormalities nor involvement of the peripheral nervous system, four were psychogenic, as indicated by the presence of morning erections and competence in an extramarital situation in two and intermittent potence in two. The fifth patient was not clearly categorized, although there appeared to be a strong psychogenic overlay.

Other complications in addition to neuropathy included twenty-six cases of retinopathy of various degrees, ten patients with hypertension, and sixteen with trace to moderate amounts of albuminuria; all occurred in the patients with bladder abnormalities. Cholesterol and urea nitrogen levels were essentially normal.

Because of the frequent implication of a possible endocrine basis for impotence in diabetes, plasma testosterone, the most accurate index of Leydig cell function, was measured (Paulson, 1968). This test is crucial in evaluating testicular involvement because testosterone is the hormonal determinant of potency. The method used was that of electron-capture gas-liquid chromatography (Kirschner and Coffman, 1968). In our patients the range varied from 350 to 1,720 μg/100 ml, and the average value was 762 μg/100 ml, all within normal limits. A comparable finding was reported by Kent in 1969 (Kent, 1969). Further corroboration has recently been obtained (Rivarola, Faerman, Jadzinsky, et al., 1970; Eliasson, Wide, Wiklund, et al., 1970).

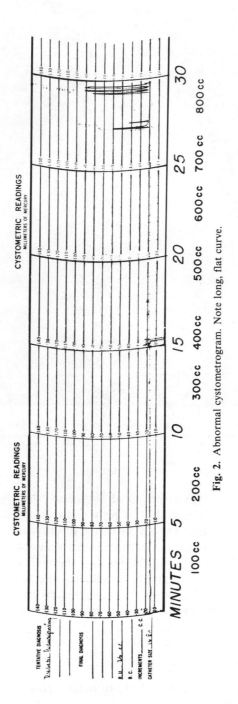

Fig. 2. Abnormal cystometrogram. Note long, flat curve.

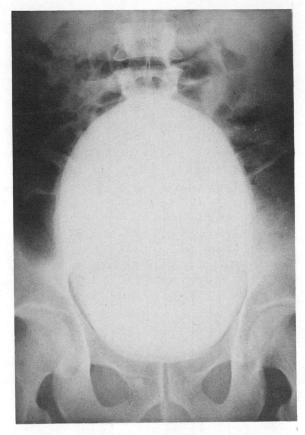

Fig. 3. Cystogram showing enlarged, dilated bladder.

Therapeutic Trials

Testosterone was administered to all impotent patients. Twenty-one of the forty-five patients received testosterone propionate, 50 mg intramuscularly, three times weekly for a minimum of two months and most for three months or more. In addition, twelve of the twenty-one patients received added therapy in the form of methyltestosterone (buccal), 10 mg, on the days they did not receive the injections. Fifteen patients received methyltestosterone, buccal, 10 to 20 mg daily, for a period of three months; the other nine patients received 400 mg testosterone cypionate injections every three weeks for four months. In no instance was there any beneficial effect on the impotence.

Control Series

The control group consisted of thirty male diabetic patients who were not impotent. They were selected to parallel the age distribution and duration of diabetes in the group with impotence. Specifically, the age range was from 22 to 72 years; the average age was 42.9 years. The duration of diabetes was from 1 to 25 years (Table 1). The man who was 72 years of age was still very potent; he had been diabetic for 25 years and required insulin for control. Of the thirty patients, three had abnormal cystometrograms, and none had residual urine. Six patients had clinical evidence of peripheral neuropathy, but none had autonomic or visceral involvement.

Clinical Aspects

A striking clinical feature was the persistence of libido despite the absence of potency. Impotence itself was gradual in appearance, and often the onset of the problem dated back to two years before impotence became complete. Although libido was virtually always present when impotence became manifest, in some it tended to become sublimated secondary to the frustrations of inadequacy. This was not always so, since in two patients with impotence for more than ten years libido had not perceptibly diminished. Inasmuch as most patients do not readily volunteer information about sex, it becomes necessary to tactfully query them; the frequency of impotence greatly increased as a result of direct questioning. Such questions generally provoked two kinds of response; many responded with such statements as "I am so happy you asked; I was embarrassed to discuss it." Those who did not mention impotence on the supposition that there was no relationship to the diabetes were surprised and interested to learn of the association. All benefited from the knowledge that impotence was organic and hence not a reflection on their "manhood," a source of great insecurity and often the basis of intense marital friction and distrust, leading to separation and even divorce. Discussion with both partners will often allay anxiety and lead to a satisfactory emotional adjustment.

Discussion

It is important to reemphasize that any and all causes of impotence in the nondiabetic may also result in impotence in the diabetic. The causes of impotence may be classified under the following headings.

Psychogenic
Organic
   Congenital abnormality
   Trauma
   Systemic disease
   Vascular disease
   Endocrine deficiency
   Neurological disease
      Central
      Spinal
      Peripheral neuropathy
Drug induced

Psychological impotence is by far the commonest type in the nondiabetic population. More than 90% of impotence in the general population is estimated to be psychogenic in origin (Simpson, 1950). There is no indication, however, that it is more prevalent in diabetics than in the nondiabetic population. In fact, in many diabetic patients impotence is the first clinical manifestation of the disease (Rubin and Babbott, 1958). Psychologic impotence is typified by its selectivity and periodicity. Additional differentiating factors include the presence of morning erection, the ability to masturbate sucessfully, or the occurrence of nocturnal emission (Johnson, 1968; Strauss, 1949, 1950). There is usually little difficulty in recognition. In those cases where the picture is not clear, however, the use of a mercury strain gauge for measuring the circumference of the penis and monitoring nocturnal erections has made possible a differential diagnosis. Reports indicate that it is a valuable clinical aid (Karacan, 1969, 1970).

Trauma and systemic disease are readily eliminated. Since erection requires an increase in blood flow, an adequate circulatory status is necessary. When impotence is caused by impaired circulation, diffuse advanced arteriosclerosis, usually with thrombosis of the aortic bifurcation or vessels immediately below it, or both, must be present. A classic example is Leriche's syndrome, where impotence has been euphemistically described as "intermittent claudication du troisième membre." The finding of diminished femoral arterial pulsation or the history of gluteal claudication suggests the diagnosis.

Drugs that have caused impotence include the estrogens, which are used, for example, in the treatment of carcinoma of the prostate. Other important drug groups are alcohol, phenothiazines, antidepressants, and some of the hypotensive drugs.

The only other causative factors are neurological and endocrine.

Endocrine Aspects

An endocrine basis for impotence has long been espoused. One of the first areas of investigation was measurement of 17-ketosteroid excretion in the urine. It should be pointed out that only 30% of the excretion is derived from the testes, whereas 70% is derived from the adrenal cortex; in addition, contradictory evidence of a relationship to potency has been presented (Schoffling et al., 1963; Miller and Mason, 1945; Horstmann, 1950; Bergquist, 1954; Ayad, 1965). Gonadotrophic secretion values were found to be normal in the patients with well-controlled diabetes (Bergquist, 1954).

Abnormalities of spermatogenesis, sperm count, motility, and seminal fluid volume have been offered in support of an endocrine basis for impotency in the diabetic. Not only are these not measures of sexual potency, there is also conflicting evidence of a relationship to potency (Schoffling, 1970; Klebanow and MacLeod, 1960). Instances of complete absence of sperm are most readily explained by retrograde ejaculation (Ellenberg and Weber, 1966). In our patients, in the absence of retrograde ejaculation, the sperm count, motility, and volume were generally within the normal range. Normal motility of sperm has previously been observed (Oakley, 1950).

Klinefelter's syndrome has been implicated as a possible significant factor because of the suggested associated higher prevalence of diabetes or family history of diabetes. This is untenable since the syndrome is fairly readily recognized, is relatively infrequent, and, like other endocrine causes of impotence, is associated with a decreased or absent libido as distinguished from the typical picture of diabetic impotence (Simpson, 1966).

Biopsy specimens were reported by Schoffling (1970) to show thickening of the basement membrane of the tubules and abnormal spermatogenesis. On the other hand, Warren, LeCompte, and Legg (1966) state that "the interstitial cells are unaffected; in the adequately treated diabetic patient, there is no apparent altera-tion of the usual picture." Oakley (1950) also found normal testicular tissue on biopsy material.

Testosterone is the hormonal determinant of potency. As noted above, the direct measure of plasma testosterone was done in our patients and found to be normal; others have confirmed this. It has been reported that, anatomically, there is a diminution in the number of Leydig cells, which produce testosterone (Schoff-ling et al., 1963). This finding has been refuted by Rivarola and colleagues (1970), who not only found no diminution but also observed no change on both light and electron microscopy.

It seems, therefore, that there is no consistent or acceptable support for an endocrine basis of impotence. The most damaging argument is the demonstration of normal amounts of plasma testosterone.

Neurologic Aspects

There is considerable clinical evidence corroborating and consistent with a neuropathic basis for diabetic impotence. Since erection takes place on a reflex basis, only local involvement of the parasympathetic plexus will predictably prevent it. Involvement of the plexus will produce impotence but will have no effect on libido. In diabetes it is striking that the impotence precedes any loss of libido.

In a routine survey of 200 diabetic male patients, I found 118 (59%) who were impotent and 82 (41%) who were not. Significantly, of the 118 impotent diabetics 104 (88%) had clinical evidence of neuropathy, whereas only 12% of the 82 potent diabetics had neuropathy (Table 2). A similar correlation was observed by Martin (1953).

Other supporting factors include the simultaneous occurrence of impotence and diabetic visceral neuropathy. Rundles (1945) noted the almost invariable association of complete impotence with diabetic atonic bladder paralysis. The presence of impotence in all cases of diabetic enteropathy has been reported by Whalen, Soergel, and Geenen (1969) and by Malins and Mayne (1969). In my own

Table 2.   Survey of 200 Male Diabetics

	Diabetics with neuropathy	Diabetics without neuropathy	Total
Impotent	104 (88%)	14 (12%)	118 (59%)
Potent	10 (12%)	72 (88%)	82 (41%)

experience all cases of diabetic neurogenic vesical paralysis, neuropathic ulcer, Charcot neuroarthropathy, enteropathy, and orthostatic hypotension have been accompanied by impotence. Other diseases affecting the spinal cord such as tabes, syringomyelia, pernicious anemia, myelitis, multiple sclerosis, and spinal cord tumor have been associated with impotence (Levens, 1964). Also pertinent, the antihypertensive and antidepressant drugs that lead to impotence are agents that act by means of the autonomic nervous system. And finally, the pathologic entities of the peripheral nervous system and spinal cord that produce impotence are all associated with retention of libido, as in the diabetic impotent male (McDowell, 1968).

Therapy and Prognosis

When impotence results from poorly controlled diabetes, it is a reflection of the associated malnutrition and weakness. In such cases proper management of the metabolic aspect of the disease, which restores normal health and vigor, will restore normal potency (Klebanow and MacLeod, 1960; Simpson, 1949). If the impotence is psychogenic in origin, the approach must be based on psychological evaluation and psychotherapy. If drugs are involved, their elimination is usually followed by return of potency. Finally, if there is an endocrine basis, the appropriate hormonal therapy should be instituted.

In most instances the cause is neurogenic. Unfortunately, there is as yet no specific prophylactic or therapeutic modality for neurogenic impotence; hence, the prognosis in these cases is poor.

Mechanical devices have been suggested and have been found to prove beneficial. In some patients with partial impotence a rubber band may be used at the base of the penis to help maintain erection; it serves as a tourniquet to prevent the return flow of blood and detumescence. For patients with total impotence a silicone prosthesis may be implanted surgically; it functions chiefly to prevent buckling of the shaft of the penis during intercourse, is not awkward in carrying on everyday activities, and does not produce discernible bulging (Pearman, 1967; Lash, 1968).

It is hoped that with the understanding of the pathogenetic mechanism involved, further investigations will yield basic, beneficial therapeutic applications.

Clinical Implications

The findings indicate lack of correlation between the occurrence of impotence and the control, duration, or severity of the diabetes. This has been repeatedly confirmed by other authors (Rubin and Babbott, 1958; Montenero and Donatone, 1962; Schoffling et al., 1963; Ellenberg and Weber, 1967). Indeed, impotence is not infrequently the initial clinical manifestation of diabetes, as has been reported by other investigators (Rubin and Babbott, 1958; Ellenberg and Weber, 1967). The implication is obvious: When a man complains of premature impotence, diabetes mellitus must be considered as a possible cause (Ellenberg, 1970).

The finding of normal plasma testosterone values and the completely negative response to the use of testosterone in full measure are strong arguments against the significance of endocrine factors in the pathogenesis of diabetic impotence. Testosterone, of course, is of real value only in organic impotence caused by a deficiency of the hormone and has no therapeutic efficacy in any other condition (Klebanow and MacLeod, 1960; Simpson, 1949; Sprague, 1963).

The results imply that neuropathy is a significant factor in the pathogenesis of impotence and minimize the importance of endocrine influences.

References

Ayad, H. Discussion of K. Schoffling, Hypogonadism in male diabetic patients. In B. S. Leibel and G. A. Wrenshall (Eds.), *On the nature and treatment of diabetes.* Amsterdam: Excerpta Medica Foundation, 1965.

Bergquist, N. The gonadal function in male diabetes. *Acta Endocrinologica*, 1954, *18* (Suppl.), 3–29.

Bors E., and Comarr, A. E. Neurological disturbances of sexual function with special reference to 529 patients with spinal cord injury. *Urological Survey*, 1960, *10*, 191–222.

Eliasson, R., Wide, L., Wiklund, B., et al. Sexual function in male diabetic patients. In *Abstracts of Excerpta Medica, VIIth Congress of International Federation of Diabetes*, Buenos Aires, Argentina, August 1970. P. 147.

Ellenberg, M. Diabetic neuropathy. In M. Ellenberg and H. Rifkin (Eds.), *Diabetes mellitus: Theory and practice.* New York: McGraw-Hill, 1970. Pp. 822–847.

Ellenberg, M., and Weber, H. Retrograde ejaculation in diabetic neuropathy. *Annals of Internal Medicine*, 1966, *65*, 1237–1246.

Ellenberg, M., and Weber, H. The incipient, asymptomatic diabetic bladder. *Diabetes*, 1967, *16*, 331–339.

Horstmann, P. The excretion of androgens in human diabetes mellitus. *Acta Endocrinologica (Copenhagen)*, 1950, *5*, 261–269.

Johnson, J. *Disorders of sexual potency in the male.* New York: Pergamon Press, 1968.

Karacan, I. A simple and inexpensive transducer for quantitative measurements of penile erection during sleep. *Behavior Research Methods and Instrumentation*, 1969, *1*, 251–252.

Karacan, I. Clinical value of nocturnal erection in the prognosis and diagnosis of impotence. *Medical Aspects of Human Sexuality*, 1970, *4*, 27–34.

Kent, J. R. Gonadal function in impotent diabetic males. In *Abstracts of the 26th Annual Meeting of the American Diabetes Association*, San Francisco, 1969, P. 537.

Kinsey, A. C., Pomeroy, W. B., and Martins, C. E. *Sexual behavior in the human male.* Philadelphia: W. B. Saunders, 1948.

Kirschner, M. A., and Coffman, G. D. Measurement of plasma testosterone and "delta-4"-androstenedione using electron capture gas-liquid chromatography. *Journal of Clinical Endocrinology*, 1968, *28*, 1347–1355.

Klebanow, D., and MacLeod, J. Semen quality and certain disturbances of reproduction in diabetic men. *Fertility and Sterility*, 1960, *11*, 255–261.

Lash, H. Silicone implant for impotence. *Journal of Urology*, 1968, *100*, 709–714.

Learmouth, J. R. A contribution to the neurophysiology of the urinary bladder in man. *Brain*, 1931, *54*, 147–176.

Levens, A. J. Impotence as a manifestation of neurologic disease. *Medical Annals of the District of Columbia*, 1964, *33*, 209–213.

Malins, J. M., and Mayne, N. Diabetic diarrhea. *Diabetes*, 1969, *18*, 858–866.

Martin, M. M. Diabetic neuropathy. *Lancet*, 1953, *1*, 560–574.

McDowell, F. H. Sexual manifestations of neurologic disease. *Medical Aspects of Human Sexuality*, 1968, *2*, 13–21.

Miller, S., and Mason, H. L. The excretion of 17-ketosteroids by diabetics. *Journal of Clinical Endocrinology*, 1945, *5*, 220–229.

Montenero, P., and Donatone, E. Diabète et activite sexuelle chez l'homme. *Le Diabète*, 1962, *8*, 327–332.

Naunyn, B. *Der Diabetes Mellitus.* Vienna: Alfred Holder, 1906.

Oakley, W. G. Discussion of E. B. Strauss, Impotence from the psychiatric standpoint. *British Medical Journal*, 1950, *1*, 697–703.

Paulson, C. A. The testes. In R. H. Williams (Ed.), *Endocrinology.* Philadelphia: W. B. Saunders, 1968. Pp. 405–458.

Pearman, R. O. Treatment of organic impotence by implantation of a penile prosthesis. *Journal of Urology*, 1967, *97*, 716–720.

Rivarola, M. A., Faerman, I., Jadzinsky, M., et al. Plasma testosterone levels in diabetic men with and without normal sexual potency. In *Abstracts of Excerpta Medica. VIIth Congress of International Federation of Diabetes*, Buenos Aires, Argentina, August 1970. P. 38.

Roen, P. R. Impotence. *New York Journal of Medicine*, 1965, *65*, 2576–2583.

Rubin, A. The influence of diabetes mellitus in men upon reproduction. *American Journal of Obstetrics and Gynecology*, 1958, *76*, 25–29.

Rubin, A., and Babbott, D. Impotence and diabetes mellitus. *Journal of the American Medical Association*, 1958, *168*, 498–500.

Rundler, R. W. Diabetic neuropathy. *Medicine (Baltimore)*, 1945, *24*, 111–160.

Schoffling, K. *Diabetes mellitus and male gonadal function.* Presented at VIIth Congress of International Federation of Diabetes, Buenos Aires, Argentina, August 1970.

Schoffling, K., Federlin, K., Ditschunheit, H., et al. Disorders of sexual function in male diabetics. *Diabetes*, 1963, *12*, 519–527.

Simpson, S. L. Impotence. *Medical Society Transactions*, 1949, *64*, 279–291.

Simpson, S. L. Impotence. *British Medical Journal*, 1950, *1*, 692–697.

Simpson, S. L. Impotence. *Fertility and Sterility*, 1966, *17*, 429–438.

Sprague, R. Impotence in male diabetics (editorial). *Diabetes*, 1963, *12*, 559.

Strauss, E. B. Impotence. *Medical Society Transactions*, 1949, *64*, 291–299.

Strauss, E. B. Impotence from the psychiatric standpoint. *British Medical Journal*, 1950, *1*, 697–703.

Von Noorden, C. *Die Zuckerkrankheit und ihre Behandlung.* Berlin: August Hirschwald, 1903.

Warren, S., LeCompte, P. M., and Legg, M. A. *The pathology of diabetes mellitus.* (4th ed.). Philadelphia: Lea & Febiger, 1966.

Whalen, G. E., Soergel, K. H., and Geenen, J. E. Diabetic diarrhea. *Gastroenterology*, 1969, *56*, 1021–1027.

As documented in the preceding article by Ellenberg, the incidence of erectile failure in diabetic men is over 50%. While recognizing that diabetes can produce both neurological and vascular damage leading to loss of erectile capability, Renshaw emphasizes that at least some diabetic impotence is functional, not organic. In this chapter, Renshaw discusses the use of sex therapy in cases of diabetic erectile failure.

In the last half of the chapter, the author discusses the use and misuse of implanted penile protheses for diabetic men. This material was written especially for this volume and updates the author's earlier work on diabetic impotence.

34

Impotence in Diabetics

Domeena C. Renshaw

Today literate men and women who have diabetes mellitus are usually well informed regarding the chronic nature of their disorder. Most are also aware of the many potential complications, including the fact that for men who have had diabetes for over six years, 48% may have impotence (Cooper, 1972; Ellenberg and Weber, 1966; Ellenberg, 1972; Faerman, Glocer, Fox, Jadinsky, and Rapport, 1973; Gee, 1977; Kolodny, 1974). Few diabetics share the euphoria noted in multiple sclerosis. Some may effectively defend by denial—"not me"—but other diabetics may become upset, anxious, and depressed at the endlessness of their difficulties.

No clinician today should neglect to check diabetic patients for the cardinal vegetative signs of a clinical depression: insomnia, anorexia, and weight loss. There is an important difference between demoralization—an appropriate dejection and frustration at facing inevitable, incurable illness—and a clinical depression, which has a high mortality rate due to suicide. In the latter, together with depression of mood and reduced appetite for sleep and food, the appetite for sex is also lowered in both males and females who are depressed (Renshaw, 1974).

Domeena C. Renshaw • Department of Psychiatry, Loyola University, Stritch School of Medicine, Maywood, Illinois

The male may volunteer an inability to have erections, yet on questioning he will say he does wake with a morning erection. The female is less likely to be aware that vaginal lubrication is her analogue of erotic male erections, but may admit to loss of sexual desire. The sexual dysfunctions of depression are as responsive to antidepressants as are the anorexia and insomnia, and usually with no specific sex counseling. There is, on further inquiry in most cases, a temporal relationship of the loss of libido to the onset of the depression. A single bedtime dose of between 100 mg and 300 mg Sinequan, Elavil, Tofranil, etc., is favored since this promotes sleep, obviates the need for hypnotics, and reduces daytime side effects. Effectiveness for the insomnia is almost immediate. The appetite for food improves within a week. Sexual arousal returns in about three to four weeks.

If, however, the impotence of depression is interpreted fatalistically by patient or physician as a complication of the diabetes, a sense of hopelessness could promote psychogenic impotence. Unfortunately, neither will realize that he has given up on a reversible and eminently treatable symptom.

The foregoing statement also applies to the uninformed male over fifty years who regards with despair the first partial erections that are known to occur with aging. What he does not know is that with further sex play or penile stimulation, he will respond with a full and excellent erection. However, if either his partner or physician responds with "What do you expect? You're diabetic and getting too old," the way is paved for psychogenic impotence, which will require vigorous sex counseling to undo.

Besides depression, there are three important *A*'s—Alcohol, Anxiety, and Anger—in the etiology of impotence (broadly used here to include male and female sexual arousal).

1. *Alcohol* in excess is perhaps the most common worldwide cause of secondary impotence and delayed ejaculation in males. Excess alcohol in females reduces sexual arousal and prevents orgasmic release. Alcohol is a central nervous system depressant. Moderate intake usually reduces sexual inhibitions, but excess causes sexual dysfunction for both sexes. It should be remembered that alcoholics have a higher-than-average incidence of diabetes; therefore, careful follow-up of diabetics should always include inquiry regarding current daily alcohol intake.

2. *Anxiety* may or may not be apparent to the individual. Frequently sexual performance anxiety—"will I make it?"—may be realized by the patient for the first time upon explicit questioning. Patients should be asked if they have a sense of watching themselves performing in bed. Other anxieties inhibiting sexual functioning may range from fear of discovery (children coming into the bedroom) to fear of venereal disease or divine punishment. Anxiety responses are mediated through the sympathetic nervous system, whereas arousal and sustained erections depend on parasympathetic dominance (relaxation). Excess anxiety suppresses enjoyable effective sexual expression.

3. *Anger* between the partners in the form of nonresponsive behavior, cutting remarks, old remembered conflicts, or current ones may all successfully block sexual responses. The sympathetic nervous system also mediates aggressive reactions, blocking relaxed sexual enjoyment.

From this preamble, it should be clear that sexual arousal is vulnerable to many factors additional to the organic ones of the endocrine, neurologic, and vascular systems. Our knowledge of the anatomy and mechanisms and human dynamics of the male and female sexual responses is now markedly improved, thanks to the pioneering work of Masters and Johnson. However, what we know about the neurophysiology, endocrinology, and hemodynamics of sex is still rudimentary (Johnson, 1965; Weiss, 1972).

In diabetes mellitus, the endocrine factors seem unrelated to the sexual dysfunction (Faerman et al., 1973; Kolodny, 1971, 1974). In severe diabetic neuropathy of the periphery, it is perhaps conceivable that the genital nerve endings may also be affected. The saddle area should be carefully tested for sensation of touch and pain to confirm or negate involvement of pudenal nerve branches. Inquiry should be made regarding erections on awakening, or through masturbation.

To separate vascular and neurological factors is always difficult, if not impossible. This applies particularly in the genital area, where interplay between the neurophysiological and hemodynamic responses results in the local manifestations of sexual arousal: erection in the penis or clitoris; vascularity of the corpora cavernosa (which is balanced by the polster valves); vascularity of the scrotum, the labia, and the vagina. This phase of peripheral vasodilatation is predominantly mediated by parasympathetic nerve endings on the vessels. The vasoconstriction necessary to complete resolution after climax, in both sexes, requires dominance of sympathetic neurohormones (Johnson, 1965; Weiss, 1972).

Recent electron microscope studies indicate that diabetic angiopathies are irreversible. If there are ischemic changes in limbs, it is possible that genital area capillaries may also be affected, which could be an organic cause for impotence. However, sexual desire persists unabated. Such a documented finding should be carefully interpreted to patient and spouse, encouraging them to exercise other-than-coital exchange—namely, sensual contact and caressing—to provide the essential human comfort of intimacy, which they require more than ever at this very difficult stage of the illness. They should also be informed about surgical prostheses being inserted if indicated (Gee, McRoberts, Raney, and Ansell, 1974) (see below).

No clinician should overlook major vascular obstruction that may be preventing genital responses in spite of intact peripheral nerves and capillaries. An arteriogram visualizing the pelvic aorta and the internal iliacs is essential to a complete investigation. Bypass surgery may assist genital functioning.

In spite of all the testing we are at this stage equipped to do, including radio-isotope penograms in Japan (Kolodny, 1971), there are numerous cases of so-called organic sexual dysfunction that are still only presumptive diagnoses by exclusion and induction. For emphasis, I repeat that when this medical indictment is categorically and authoritatively given to a vulnerable patient, iatrogenic psychogenic impotence is tragically fixed. Much costly undoing will be needed by a skilled physician sex therapist, who will be the only possible counteractive authority.

Most eloquent evident would be brief presentations of a few cases that have come to my attention almost accidentally, rather than by physician referral.

Case 1. A forty-nine-year-old executive came for assistance with marital conflict. He complained of secondary impotence of eight months' duration. He was on large divided doses of tricyclic antidepressants for a depression that had occurred two years previously. He was drinking heavily again after having stopped with the help of A. A. one year ago. He was diagnosed as diabetic eight years ago and had been on insulin throughout. Since he was not depressed when seen, the antidepressants were discontinued. The wife was seen with him and agreed to have him return home if he stopped drinking. He agreed to use Antabuse and return to A. A. The couple discussed their concern about the diabetes as a possible factor in the impotence.

They were told that both alcohol and the tricyclics could also have contributed, as well as the open angry conflict between them. Sex play was suggested, with emphasis on sensory stimulation, and avoidance of coitus for two weeks to remove any pressure to perform. He was told he could not will an erection but could relaxedly experience one. He had partial erections in the second week and full erections in the third week of this very simple, but explicit, approach.

Case 2. A fifty-seven-year-old insurance broker presented a year ago with a severe depression and was hospitalized. He was agitated and suicidal, so required twelve E.S.T.'s. He had been on 80 units of lente insulin for twenty years, the diabetic diagnosis being preceded by twenty years of heavy drinking and two episodes of "pre-D.T.'s." He had been in intensive care for a coronary six months prior to the depression and was on digoxin. On the first day of admission, in his wife's presence, he accused her of refusing sex in their younger years, when they practiced rhythm method birth control. Now, since her hysterectomy four years ago, he was impotent. He said that this made him angry at her, at himself, and at God. "I've read the books, why did this damn diabetes have to happen to me?"

Questioning the couple revealed that the first sexual problem was the occurrence of partial erections, which he tried to "force" to full erections. The performance anxiety so generated, plus his rage, of course, and the anxious association of diabetes–impotence, ensured psychogenic impotence. The expectable changes in sexual function for males over fifty years were explained to both, then and upon discharge four weeks later. Full sexual function was restored. He now uses a single bedtime dose of Sinequan 100 mg and is seen every two months for follow-up.

Case 3. A fifty-two-year-old lumber yard manager presented at the Loyola Sexual Dysfunction Clinic with secondary impotence of two years' duration, nonresponsive to twelve monthly testosterone injections. His previous coital frequency was daily. "I read about the sex clinic. My internist (endocrinologist) said you'd never take us, but please let us have a try! You've got nothing to lose!"

He was an appealing, jovial 350-pounder who blocked me in the corridor and poured out his textbook of pathology, right there. He admitted heartily to thirty-two years of ongoing heavy drinking (with diagnosed cirrhosis by liver function tests, hematemesis, hemorrhoids, gynocomastia). He had at least five medical admissions to hospitals. For twelve years he had been on 40–60 units of lente insulin for diabetes. He was on Aldomet 250 mg daily for hypertension. He had known for some twenty years that he was oligospermic. He had been married for seventeen years to a divorcee who also drank heavily, as did his domineering little eighty-year-old widowed mother. If this had been a paper or telephone intake, it is doubtful if the couple would ever have been accepted for the sex clinic.

On a compassionate rather than a scientific basis, we took on the challenge. We were amazed that they obtained symptom removal in the first week!! Both insisted that it was a wholesome marriage relationship and the impotence was their main problem. A detailed and explicit sex history was taken on the first visit by the dual-sex team of sex therapists: a resident in urology and a psychiatric social worker. They were asked to avoid coitus and focus on general sensual stimulation instead. The couple returned sheepishly for the second visit saying: "You're going to be mad at us, but we just couldn't help it—we had intercourse last night!"

They said their success was due to the sex team's:

1. Injunction that they not have coitus (this relieved the performance pressure).
2. Suggestion that they place a lock on their bedroom door to keep the children out.
3. Suggestion that they throw their mattress on the floor to prevent the bed squeaking, which could be heard by the children, and which was of concern to the husband.
4. Suggestion to use mutual body massage.
5. Explanation that alcohol, anxiety, or anger inhibited erections—and that partial erections were expectable after age fifty.

Of all of these, which really did the trick for him? Was it perhaps the stimulating image he took home of the pretty cotherapist social worker who had for four hours shared his verbal intimacies?

In summary, this brief discussion overviews what little has been done in the specific study of diabetic impotence and reveals many uncertainties regarding the actual mechanisms responsible for the symptom. Three clinical cases are presented, where psychogenic factors were dealt with, relieving long-standing impotence in the diabetic males discussed. For the physician, a diagnosis of organic impotence in a diabetic may be not only extraordinarily difficult but also professionally premature.

Use of Penile Prostheses in Organic Impotence

Remarkable progress has been made in the past two decades in the field of implants for impotent men. Earlier types were "constant erection" or "semirigid," with the use of bone, then the Small-Carrion more flexible silicone implants (Schuster, 1976). These are not complex to insert but require wearing a truss to conceal the embarrassing permanent erection (Merrill and Swanson, 1976). Physical complications of prostheses include nonhealing, infection, hematoma, fracture of the implant with vigorous thrusting, and erosion at either end. Then, in 1973, the inventive Scott's flexible "inflatable hydraulic system" penile prosthesis emerged in Texas amid headlines (Furlow, 1976; For Organic Impotence, 1974). Candidates clamored for insertion, even at the overall cost (including hospital stay) of around $7,000 (equipment alone, about $1,200).

The increasing surgeon enthusiasm for these new mechanical cures to erectile failure is of concern to many thoughtful physicians since impotent men are highly vulnerable. Also, at present there is questionable screening for and follow-up of these not innocuous inserts.

There are now two distinct "penile prosthesis philosophies" with frequent Small–Scott debates in urology circles (Controversy of Penile Implants for Impotence, 1977). While manufacturers claim that over 1,000 of their $1,200 "inflatable Scotts" have been sold and over 4,000 of the $150 "Small-Carrions," should there be pause to evaluate the men and their partners at the other end? Particularly since the alleged indications for insertion are ". . . age, diseases (?) . . . side effects of drugs. In some cases it is also being used for psychogenic erectile impotence. . ." (Controversy of Penile Implants for Impotence, 1977). Since 95% of the presenting cases of impotence are known to be psychogenic rather than organic, again the question of adequate screening is important.

Other surgical therapy for impotence includes attempts to revascularize the penis. Harry LaVeen, a surgeon at Brooklyn VA Hospital, describes deflecting the inferior epigastric artery to the penis with good results from the bypass (Controversy of Penile Implants for Impotence, 1977). Little is mentioned of case selection, numbers of cases, or follow-up in this newest surgical treatment method.

Initial enthusiasm may temper caution in the selection criteria for any new "cure" that includes the healing knife of the surgeon. Questionable and dramatic early results of the Scott prosthesis included postoperative discovery of an unrecognized exhibitionist. He was in his twenties and merely wanted a guaranteed erection on demand. Another failure was in an "impotent" middle-aged man, forced to the "penis doctor" by his angry wife. Postoperatively, he has had impotence of his dominant index finger and is "unable" to inflate the device. A surgical success, certainly. To a passive man with a hostile, demanding wife, his "impotence" (often selective) may be either relief or retaliation. Prediction is difficult in any medical specialty. However, clinical experience and some failures indicate a need for more careful screening of "impotent" males before referral for penile prostheses (Gee, 1977). To illustrate the importance of screening evaluation before recommending a penile prosthesis for organically impotent men, consider the following case example.

Case Report. Joe, thirty-seven, and Kathy, thirty-one, married ten years, presented to the Loyola Sex Clinic with a chief complaint of secondary impotence of six years' duration. On taking the history, it was found that Kathy was primary nonorgasmic, and that indeed Joe had at no time been concerned with her sexual satisfaction. He was clinically depressed as well as being a very sick man. He had lack of all skin sensation from T12 to S4, a true neuropathy. No morning erections had been seen for the past five years. During the course of the seven-week sex therapy, he was placed on tricyclic antidepressants and responded positively by the fifth week by mood elevation, restored sleep and appetite, and stability of his blood sugar and insulin dose. However, no erections resulted from their sensate pleasuring. On the other hand, Kathy had been encouraged, in Joe's presence in therapy, to masturbate. She became orgasmic in the fourth week of therapy. She was afraid to tell him at home and waited until the clinic session. "I was afraid he would be jealous," which indeed he was. He wept in self-pity and was unable to share her elation in experiencing sexual release for the first time at age thirty-one!

In the following weeks we discussed Joe's fantasies regarding having a penile prosthesis fitted. To him it was a "rebirth" phenomenon, denial of death, and an entirely narcissistic search for magic—a new life. It did not include Kathy at all. He expected a "big climax." We directed our efforts toward his sharing Kathy's sexual pleasure by masturbating her to climax. It was not more than a token attempt and seemed to upset him that "she can and I can't." Would any urologist implant this patient?

Screening Outline for Penile Prosthesis

An assessment of how well a penile prosthesis will meet the needs of a patient should consider physical functioning, the patient's personal sexual pattern and attitude, and the nature of the sexual relationship with the spouse. What follows are suggested questions in each of these areas.

A. *Physical Factors*
   1. Do you have partial erections now?
   2. Do you have orgasms now?
   3. Do you ejaculate now? (frequency?)
   4. Do you masturbate now? (frequency?)
   5. Do you ejaculate when you masturbate? (frequency?)
   6. Do you have morning erections?

As part of the physical evaluation, nocturnal penile plethysmography can be done to measure sleep erections to differentiate organicity (gives a flat tracing, i.e., no nocturnal erections). Vascular studies of pelvic and penile vessels are not free of risk and are, therefore, not standard tests (Shiraim, Nakamura, and Matsuda, 1973). However, nocturnal penile plethysmography is innocuous. Penile monitors are now readily available for about $1,400 with strip chart records (American Medical Systems).

B. *Personal Sexual Pattern and Attitudes*
   1. What does the penile implant mean to you?
   2. What do you expect to feel after you have it?
   3. Do you expect a climax/ejaculation?

4. Do you expect to masturbate after you have it?
5. How accepting (relieved?) or upset (preoccupied) are you about being impotent?

C. *Sexual Relationship with the Spouse* (or sexual partner)

The prosthesis is predominantly for giving of sexual pleasure to his partner; it does not of itself provide new arousal, ejaculation, or orgasm for the patient. Therefore, the following questions should be routine:

1. What does your partner's sexual enjoyment mean to you?
2. Would you feel satisfied to share her climax?
3. Prior to becoming impotent, were you concerned with your partner's having orgasm?
4. Since becoming impotent, what alternative sexual techniques (masturbation/oral/vibrator) have you employed to provide sexual stimulation for your partner?
5. What was your coital frequency preimpotence?
6. What has been your sex play frequency since the impotence?
7. How frequently per week do you feel sexual desire?
8. How frequently per week does your partner feel sexual desire?
9. Is your partner pressuring you to have an implant?
10. What do you think her coital demands will be postimplant?
11. Have you discussed divorce in the past year?
12. Have you thought of or tried sex therapy?
13. Have you thought of or tried marital therapy?
14. What were the gains and the problems of therapy?

After such questioning of *both* sexual partners, it is important that adequate information be given to the patient by the physician that:

1. The implant is predominantly for the male to be able *to give* pleasure to his partner.
2. The implant does not provide a sensation of arousal or sensation of erection for the male.
3. The implant does not provide ejaculation or orgasm for the male.

Thus, the crucial issue becomes whether the male patient is able to enjoy and obtain satisfaction from his partner's sexual arousal. To such a man, it can be exhilarating once more to share closely in his partner's orgasm.

Use of Penile Prosthesis in Diabetic Males

In the past, diabetic males were presumed to have organic impotence. Therefore, in large numbers they have been presumed to be "prime candidates" for referral for prostheses. However, they merit the same thorough evaluation as outlined above, since observations from sexual dysfunction clinics are now beginning to challenge these assumptions (Renshaw, 1976). The question is raised: Diabetic impotence—inevitable or imposed?

The case discussed above (Joe) is our first sex therapy failure in eleven cases of diabetic impotence so far treated. Ten responded remarkably well; they ranged in age from thirty-three to sixty. In the general enthusiasm with any "easy" treatments, both evaluations and follow-ups tend to be less than adequate, yet both are essential if we are to provide quality medical care.

Internists usually serve as the referring physicians of diabetic impotent men who should, before being sent for surgery, be considered for "immediate screening," namely, referral to a reputable sex dysfunction clinic. In this way, today, sexual medicine becomes part of a holistic approach to patient management (Levin, 1976). Many cases will respond to the new sex therapy; some will not.

For those cases where sex therapy has failed to assist a diabetic impotent male, the therapy itself will have provided evaluation of the relationship, his desire to perform sexually not only for self but also for partner. The primary motive for penile prosthesis must be partner satisfaction, if clinical success is to be a goal. The couple together should be informed of all of the current options for surgical help, what can and cannot be expected postoperatively. They will, in sex therapy, have learned many sexual alternatives to coitus. If together they decide on penile prosthesis, then sex therapy would appropriately have served as the final screening.

References

American Medical Systems, 3312 Gorham Avenue, Minneapolis, Minnesota 55426.

Controversy of penile implants for impotence. *Medical World News*, 1977, *16*(1), 25–27.

Cooper, A. J. The causes and management of diabetes. *Postgraduate Medical Journal*, 1972, *48*, 548–554.

Ellenberg, M. Impotence in diabetics: The neural factor. *American Internal Medicine*, 1972, *75*, 213–219.

Ellenberg, M., and Weber, H. Retrograde ejaculation in diabetic neuropathy. *American Internal Medicine*, 1966, *65*, 1237–1246.

Faerman, I., Glocer, L., Fox, D., Jadzinsky, M., and Rapaport, M. Impotence and diabetes. *Excerpta Medica. 8th Congress of International Diabetes Federation*, Brussels, Belgium, July 15–20, 1973.

For organic impotence: Implants. *Medical World News*, June 21, 1974, p. 17.

Furlow, W. L. Surgical man of impotence using the inflatable penile prosthesis (experience with 36 patients). *Mayo Clinic Proceedings*, 1976, *51*(6), 325–328.

Gee, W. F. Ejaculatory difficulties with penile prosthesis. *Medical Aspects of Human Sexuality*, 1977, *11*(2), 97.

Gee, W. F., McRoberts, J. W., Raney, J. O., and Ansell, J. S. The impotent patient: Surgical treatment with penile prosthesis and psychiatric evaluation. *Journal of Urology*, 1974, *111*, 41–43.

Johnson, J. Sexual impotence and the limbic system. *British Journal of Psychiatry*, 1965, *111*, 300.

Karacan, I. Clinical value of nocturnal erection in the prognosis and diagnosis of impotence. *Medical Aspects of Human Sexuality*, 1970, *4*, 27–34.

Kolodny, R. D. Sexual dysfunction in diabetic females. *Diabetes*, 1971, *20*, 557–559.

Kolodny, R. D. Sexual dysfunction in diabetic men. *Diabetes*, 1974, *23*, 306–309.

Levin, S. B. Marital sexual dysfunction: Erectile dysfunction. *Annals of Internal Medicine*, 1976, *85*, 342–350.

Merrill, D. C., and Swanson, D. A. Experience with the Small-Carrion penile prosthesis. *Journal of Urology*, 1976, *115*(3), 277–279.

Renshaw, D. C. Psychosomatic manifestations of depression. Sexual dysfunctions in depression. *Excerpta Medica*, 1974, 86–105.

Renshaw, D. C. Impotence in diabetes mellitus. *Comprehensive Therapy*, 1976, *2*(11), 47–50.

Schuster, K. Small-Carrion penile prosthesis. *Mayo Clinic Proceedings*, 1976, *51*(6), 336–338.

Shiraim, M., Nakamura, M., and Matsuda, S. Differential diagnosis between functional and organic impotence by radio-isotope penogram following visual sexual stimulation. *Tohoku Journal of Experimental Medicine*, 1973, *111*, 187–195.

Weiss, H. D. The physiology of human penile erections. *Annals of Internal Medicine*, 1972, *76*, 793–799.

The question of whether or not sex therapy is an effective and viable treatment option for minority groups has never been addressed directly. Although there has been some research done, most of it has centered on the disparity in life-style between the patient and therapist and has not dealt with sex therapy per se.

In this chapter the authors examine some of the issues that need to be dealt with when attempting to do sex therapy with Afro-American couples. They use the case report of one couple to illustrate their points and give an outline of the structure of therapy.

Many of the issues the authors raise are likely to be relevant for sex therapy with any minority or ethnic group. Such issues include the effects of racial myths and stereotypes about sexual performance on a patient's self-image, and the patient's mistrust of the therapist.

35

Issues in the Treatment of Sexually Dysfunctioning Couples of Afro-American Descent

Gail E. Wyatt, Richard G. Strayer, and W. Charles Lobitz

Following the model of Masters and Johnson (1970), directive treatment programs have been developed for a variety of sexual dysfunctions, ranging from primary and secondary orgasmic dysfunction in women to premature ejaculation and erectile failure in men (Kaplan, 1974; Lobitz and LoPiccolo, 1972; LoPiccolo and Lobitz, 1973). Although many of the treatment procedures are amplifications of the general anxiety-reduction approach common to behavior therapy (Wolpe, 1969), other aspects of the treatment derive from cognitive, personality and humanistic psychology (cf. Lobitz, LoPiccolo, Lobitz, and Brockway, 1974). Direct retraining approaches to treating sexual dysfunctions have been effective with a Caucasian population (Kaplan, 1974; Lobitz and LoPiccolo, 1972; Masters and Johnson,

Gail E. Wyatt • Neuropsychiatric Institute, University of California at Los Angeles, School of Medicine, Los Angeles, California   *Richard G. Strayer* • The Wheeler Clinic, Plainville, Connecticut   *W. Charles Lobitz* • Division of Clinical Psychology, Department of Psychiatry, University of Colorado School of Medicine, Denver, Colorado. The first two authors served as cotherapists in the Sexual Dysfunction Clinic, UCLA Neuropsychiatric Institute, under the direction of the third author.

1970; Obler, 1973), even where one partner has a psychotic diagnosis (Tanner, 1973). However, the treatment of Afro-American couples is a relatively new and un-researched area. Because of widely held stereotypes about black sexuality, a number of factors must be considered in applying the above treatment programs to an Afro-American population. This chapter reviews the literature describing the myths of black sexuality and delineates the issues involved in the treatment of sexually dysfunctioning Afro-American couples by an interracial therapy team. A case history elucidating these factors is presented.

Myths of Black Sexuality

Myths about the sexual practices of black Americans originated with the country's history. As early as 1550, African religion, skin color, and behavior were perceived as inferior to that of the Anglo-Americans (Vontress, 1971). Missionaries who first traveled to Africa to convert "heathens" to Christianity were shocked by the "polygamy and diversity of sexual relationships" that they observed (Goldstein, 1948). African and Christian religions differed in their view of sexuality. Early American Christians believed that many sexual behaviors were offenses against God, whereas the African nationals followed a religious standard that did not include sexual morality. The violation of laws was perceived by the latter as an offense against a person and not against God (Staples, 1967).

The sexual prowess of blacks has been isolated throughout history as a dimension of special interest. Written accounts of Anglos' obsession with black genitalia and sexual abilities date back to the sixteenth century (Thomas, 1972; Vontress, 1971). These myths have always been sustained in a negative context. Reported hypersexuality of blacks was often equated with their potential to be savage and bestial with their partners (Thomas, 1972). Credibility was added to these accounts by physicians who, fearing attacks on Anglo women, warned of black males' dangerous sexual potential (Thomas, 1972). To quote one early American physician, "A few emasculated Negroes scattered around and through the thickly settled Negro communities would really prove the conservation of energy, as far as the repression of sexual crimes is concerned" (Haller, 1970).

Although black males occasionally have been reported to be undersexed and unconcerned about their partner's sexual gratification (Kardiner and Ovesey, 1951), the myth of black hypersexuality is still the most widespread today. The recent abundance of "black sexploitation" films perpetuates this image of the black male's sexual prowess. Accounts of black female sexuality are more contradictory. A limited study of black women suggested that they suffer "quite frequently" from "frigidity" (Kardiner and Ovesey, 1951). In the popular press black females have been described as being sexually aggressive and having fewer sexual hang-ups about sexual role-playing than white women (Young, 1974), while another comparison saw them as more sexually restrained and traditional in their sexual expression than white women today (Staples, 1974). The variety of myths that circulate in the lay press only confuse blacks about their sexual abilities and the overall importance of sexual expression in the total relationship. Many black men and women internalize the expectation that they have extraordinary genitalia and sexual prowess. This situation can create both identity and sexual dysfunction problems when an individual does not live up to these stereotyped images. These problems can be compounded by the highly competitive and exploitative attitudes that blacks have been found to have toward sexual relations (Rainwater, 1966).

There is little behavioral data to support any of the black hyper- or hypo-sexuality myths. For example, information gathered by the Kinsey Institute on penis length of black and white males revealed no significant differences in the length of the erect penis (Bell, 1968). Similarly, black teen-age women are reported to have a higher incidence of premarital sex than white teen-agers (Zelnik and Kanfner, 1972), but these differences disappear at older ages (Hunt, 1974). In another study of adolescents, blacks and males were found to be more sexually permissive than whites and females (Reiss, 1967). The paucity of research on actual behavior only perpetuates confusion about the sexual behavior of black men and women. In addition, the absence of normative data handicaps professionals who attempt to help dysfunctioning black couples through reeducation.

The Influence of Race in the Therapy Process

There has been relatively little research on the issues involved when the therapist and patient are of different races. Furthermore, the majority of studies have described interracial practice in the more traditional psychotherapies. The largest proportion of the studies has examined the social and economic disparity between white therapists and black clients (Oberndorf, 1954; Kardiner and Ovesey, 1951; Bernard, 1972; Sager, Brayboy, and Waxenberg, 1972), and the resulting problems that appear to influence treatment (Hollingshead and Redlich, 1958). Much of this research has involved documenting the value and life-style differences between the middle-class therapist and the lower-class client. However, life-style differences and similarities between white therapists and middle- to upper-class Afro-Americans have yet to be examined.

A second major focus has been the emerging black consciousness and the attendant antagonism toward whites (Bernard, 1972). This has been explored in terms of both the client's distrust and anger toward his white therapist (Kennedy, 1952; Schachter and Butts, 1968) and the therapist's reactive fear and lessened sense of competence as he receives, or expects to receive, hostility and rebuffs from his black clients (Bernard, 1972; Reiss, 1971; Bernard, 1953; Schachter and Butts, 1968).

The third issue, raised by only a few studies, is that of the therapist's own racial attitudes and stereotypes (Bernard, 1953, 1972). Schachter and Butts (1968) suggest that this not only is a problem when encountered in the form of prejudicial discrimination but is equally destructive when the therapist is *too* racially conscious. This leads to the therapist overemphasizing the existence of racial conflict, thereby depriving the patient of working through the nonracial aspects of his difficulties.

Although there has been little research on interracial practice in the more traditional psychotherapies, even fewer such studies have developed from a behavioral perspective. This is particularly true regarding behavioral approaches to sexual dysfunctions. It would appear that cross-racial treatment considerations in a behavioral modality emphasize the individual's conscious control of his own behavior and minimize the role of the unconscious. As a result, transference and countertransference reactions are not the primary focus of therapy. The most salient dynamics in this form of treatment exist within the client couples, rather than between the therapists and clients. Thus, the therapist's role is based more on the expert-technician/educator model than on the analytic modes (LoPiccolo and Lobitz, 1973). Sexual dysfunction therapy, by its very nature, focuses explicity on sexual behavior, thoughts, and feelings. Because of the myths surrounding black sexuality and their partial acceptance by both the black and white populations, such an emphasis may increase the already emotionally charged nature of the relationship between client and therapist.

In view of these special factors involved in a behavioral approach to sexually dysfunctioning black couples, as well as the literature regarding interracial therapy in general, the following three issues should be considered: First, the distrust and anger that Bernard (1972) suggests black clients often feel toward their white therapists may well be exacerbated by the specific focus on sexual difficulties, particularly because this has stereotypically been the black individual's area of strength. In addition, the behavioral approach places the therapist in the role of sexual expert, thus accentuating both the disparity between the client and the therapist and the attendant antagonism. Secondly, as previously noted, for centuries black sexuality has generated strong emotions in the white population. It is reasonable to assume that such responses may continue to occur even within the therapeutic relationship. The therapist's attempt to compensate for such stereotypic reactions may also cause treatment difficulties of another nature. In this instance the therapist, in attempting to present a liberal bias, may tend to dilute the power of his presence, thereby reducing the effect of therapy. A third major issue that is often overlooked is the effect of cultural variables on treatment. What white therapists may assume is sexually deviant may in fact be accepted as normal within the client's culture. In addition, the therapist's unfamiliarity with differences in cultural values may lead to unrealistic expectations regarding the client's attitude toward therapy in general and sex dysfunction therapy in particular. Such a lack of awareness may also cause the therapists to attempt to mold marital relationships in accordance with their own expectations rather than allowing the clients to choose on the basis of their own needs and desires.

Case History

Sarah and Nick (pseudonyms) are middle-class Afro-Americans in their early thirties who sought treatment at the Sexual Dysfunction Clinic, NPI, UCLA. Nick was experiencing premature ejaculations, which restricted his ability to bring Sarah to orgasm through intercourse, resulting in frustration for both of them. The couple was having intercourse slightly less than once a week with both partners describing their sexual relationship as "extremely unsatisfactory." Approximately 75% of the time Nick had difficulty maintaining an erection prior to intercourse. His latency to ejaculation was reported to be less than one minute with only minimal foreplay.

Sexual Histories. Sarah had been raised in a predominantly black community in another state. At an early age, she became aware of the sexual mores, expectations, and stereotypes of her culture, especially the myths regarding black male and female roles. She had been previously married and had a child, age eight. Prior to meeting Nick she experienced no sexual problems in the marriage or in any other relationship in which she was involved. Based upon her past experiences and background, she maintained high expectations of spontaneous sexual relationships where both partners could perform genital intercourse with mutual orgasm without prolonged foreplay.

Nick's father was a career army enlistee; consequently, Nick was raised and educated in predominantly white areas surrounding army bases where his early social contacts and dating experiences were minimal. His first sexual encounters took place while in the armed forces in Germany. Nick was reluctant to admit a prior history of premature ejaculations because he was quite conscious of the stereotyped image of the hypersexual abilities of black males. He finally revealed that he felt inadequate, that he "couldn't do his job" of performing up to the stereotyped expectations for his culture. This performance anxiety served only to heighten Nick's sexual dysfunction.

The couple was highly achievement-oriented: Sarah was a college student, and Nick was in a competitive executive training program. Both individuals had well-defined conceptions of each other's sexual role in the relationship. Yet, there was little discussion of the growing discrepancy between Nick's expectations for himself and his current performance level. In addition, Sarah failed to directly express her disappointment with the sexual aspects of the relationship.

Nick and Sarah were seen one hour a week by a female–male, black–white cotherapy team (G. E. W. and R. G. S.) for a total of thirteen therapy sessions. Therapy followed the general format prescribed by Masters and Johnson (1970) as modified by Lobitz and LoPiccolo (1972), in which the couple was given "homework" assignments of sexual activities to be carried out in the privacy of their own home. Concurrent with the general directive approach of therapy, several treatment issues emerged which were pronounced for black couples.

Issues Related to Black Sexual Stereotypes

Myth. "Black males are 'naturally' sensual lovers."

Example. Nick felt inadequate and inferior because his body build and sexual performance did not "naturally" match the hypersexual black image. His resulting anxiety inhibited him from experiencing physical pleasure during sexual relations.

Management. Nick was assigned self-pleasuring sessions in which he explored his own body through the tactile, visual, and olfactory modalities. These sessions were designed to increase his acceptance of his body and awareness of those parts from which he could experience pleasurable sensations. Second, he was instructed to explore areas of his body, which increased his sexual arousal in order to make him aware of body areas, in addition to genitalia, that could be aroused. Third, during the couple's mutual sessions, he was encouraged to communicate the methods of pleasure and arousal that he had discovered. This was designed to increase Sarah's appreciation of Nick as a sensual person and to help her to realize her role in awakening that sensuality in him that previously had been dormant. She was also instructed as to how she could lessen her partner's performance anxiety by supportive verbal statements and by attempting some of the methods that Nick described as arousing in their mutual sessions.

Myth. "Black women can only be satisfied through intercourse."

Example. Sarah perceived herself as a highly sensual individual who had an increasing need for sexual satisfaction through intercourse. This placed a great deal of performance pressure on Nick. In spite of her self-image, she was not aware of her body's response to physical stimulation other than genital intercourse.

Management. Sarah was assigned individual pleasuring sessions in which she explored her body visually and tactually. This was expanded to include masturbation. Her self-image as a highly sensual individual was enhanced by her developing a means of sexual satisfaction in addition to genital intercourse with her partner.

Myth. "Black men and women do not require sexual foreplay before intercourse."

Example. Sarah perceived spontaneous, immediate genital intercourse as the "ideal" form of sexual expression. Her early learning history included sexual mores that proscribed sexual contact other than intercourse.

Management. The couple was given assignments that broadened their range of foreplay skills. They were also instructed in means of genital stimulation, in addition to intercourse, which they incorporated into their repertoire. During the course of therapy, Sarah discovered that genital stimulation prior to intercourse greatly enhanced her arousal.

Myth. "Black men have unusually long latencies to ejaculation."

Example. Prior to treatment, Nick denied that he had prematurely ejaculated, attempted to demonstrate longer retention abilities than he had, and refused to admit that there was a history of the dysfunction.

Management. While Nick was given support in understanding his frustrations, he was also made aware of the frequency of this problem among men and how his denying the problem only served to exacerbate it and further alienate him from Sarah. He was told to expect premature ejaculations to occur from time to time during the stepwise desensitization procedure of the program. Both partners were instructed to reinitiate sexual contact if a premature ejaculation occurred. The therapists stressed the importance of verbally supporting each other at this point. In a stepwise fashion Nick mastered the "squeeze technique" (Masters and Johnson, 1970) in individual sessions, which increased his awareness of the phase prior to ejaculation and heightened his self-confidence over his control. He then taught Sarah to apply the "squeeze" during intromission. Her perception of his ability to overcome the premature ejaculation problem increased as Nick exhibited more self-control.

Myth. "All black males are sexually aggressive and highly physical partners."

Example. Nick failed to be as sexually demonstrative and aggressive as Sarah desired.

Management. This problem was handled with a two-pronged approach: Sarah was encouraged to note the aspects of Nick's personality and approach toward her that she *liked*, as well as to communicate those things she wanted him to change. Second, Nick was encouraged to respond to Sarah's requests if he felt he could comfortably change his behavior. He also worked on understanding the sexual, nonverbal cues from his partner. Sarah learned to provide more verbal and nonverbal cues to increase the likelihood that her partner would understand when and how her sexual needs could be met. As a means of illustrating to the couple how increased communication should take place, the therapists role-played simulated conversations in which both partners expressed their desires and yet attempted to compromise with each other.

Issues Related to Cross-Racial Treatment

Issue. "Black couples may feel distrust and anger toward the white therapist."

Example. The therapists were concerned about Sarah and Nick's reaction to the directive nature of sex dysfunction therapy, since the structure and authority were emanating from a black–white therapy team.

Management. The primary means of dealing with this possibility was to emphasize collaboration with the clients as colleagues rather than maintaining a client/therapist dichotomy. Throughout the therapy process the treatment team attempted to maximize the couples' involvement in both developing future homework assignments and in understanding and resolving their own problems when they arose. The educational model used in this mode of therapy enabled the clients and therapists to work together through sharing information and discussing alternative means of alleviating the dysfunction, thus minimizing the directive/authoritative aspects of sexual dysfunction therapy.

Issue. "A white therapist working with a black client may often be so invested in maintaining a nonprejudicial stance that his normal style of interacting with a client is inhibited."

Example. The male therapist in this treatment team experienced initial difficulty in limit setting and assertive confrontation, particularly with the male client.

Management. This problem was resolved mainly through postsession consultation with the black cotherapist. She pointed out the male therapist's inhibited approach and reassured him that he could maintain his characteristically assertive style without jeopardizing his liberal attitudes. Subsequently, the male therapist was able to relate more openly with Nick.

Issue. "Cultural relevance is often overlooked in developing treatment goals."

Example. The cotherapists were aware of the pitfall of suggesting to their clients treatment goals that lacked continuity with their cultural experiences.

Management. Since Sarah and Nick had internalized certain sexual stereotypes, it was the function of therapy not to destroy these "ideal" images but to broaden the couple's level of self-awareness and sexual skills. A great deal of the reeducation process included discussions of how myths of black sexuality have been a means of focusing upon an aspect of the behavior of Afro-Americans which has led to exploitation but minimal understanding within and between races. The purpose was not only to dispel myths but to make the clients aware of how these myths affect the behavior of Afro-Americans.

Outcome

At the end of therapy, Sarah and Nick were having intercourse about three times a week. Nick's ability to sustain an erection increased from 25% to 90% of the time prior to intercourse. His latency during intromission ranged from ten to fifteen minutes before ejaculation occurred, allowing Sarah to achieve orgasm, frequently more than once per session. They reported feeling more comfortable with masturbation as a valuable asset to their sexual repertoires. Both partners verbalized their satisfaction with their improved sexual relationship and their ability to communicate their needs to one another during sexual and nonsexual contact.

Implications for Future Treatment and Research

Treatment programs for sexual dysfunctions have largely been staffed by white therapists and have treated white, middle-class populations. Recently, in Los Angeles and in other urban areas, black couples have sought therapy for a variety of sexual dysfunctions. The above case is presented to highlight the management of issues that may arise in cross-racial sex therapy. Several implications for future treatment and research emerge.

First, the therapist's receptivity to working with individuals whose sexual behavior is influenced by their cultural background is believed essential to treatment success. It is difficult, if not impossible, to maintain an objective approach in the treatment of black couples without the therapists' commitment to accept aspects of the clients' experience which might be expressed in forms of sexual behavior different than their own.

Second, it is the therapist's responsibility to obtain information regarding the sexual myths that permeate the greater community and influence the self-concept of the Afro-American subculture. Prior to therapy, it is also important to examine how the myths of sexuality, culture, and ethnicity tend to influence the therapist's attitude toward the clients. This kind of self-examination might lessen the likelihood of these variables interfering with the development of the therapeutic relationship.

Black clients may enter treatment with feelings of discomfort and even distrust and resentment toward white therapists, especially where sexual behavior is the focus. As Bernard (1972) has cautioned, these feelings may produce counterfeelings in the therapist which could seriously jeopardize treatment outcome. The therapist needs to facilitate an open exploration of this possibility. The use of self-disclosure by the therapist can often allay the clients' apprehensions about revealing their feelings in the therapy session (Jourard, 1964). Therapist self-disclosure legitimizes the clients' expressions of discomfort when it becomes apparent that they are shared by more than one individual in the client–therapist relationship. In addition, interracial tension can be minimized by assuring that the clients set their own goals. Thus, the clients are enlisted as "therapeutic colleagues" in the treatment process.

Not only does the present discussion elucidate several issues involved in treating sexual dysfunctions in black couples, but it also exposes a critical need for descriptive research on black sexuality. Of particular importance are normative data, beyond that collected by the Kinsey Institute (Bell, 1968), which compare sexual behavior in black and white populations. Studies need to examine whether there are differences between racial groups in the quantity of sexual contact, forms of sexual expression, and incidence and prevalence of sexual dysfunction. Research of this type would be a valuable asset to therapists and laypersons alike in validating or dispelling the myths regarding black sexual behavior. Hunt (1974), for example, has collected the necessary data but has reported little of them separately for each race.

In addition to descriptive research, there is a need for therapy outcome studies on sexual dysfunctions in black populations. In the present case, the black co-therapist facilitated resolution of several issues involving the interracial nature of therapy. The question remains as to how the race of the therapists affects the success of the treatment program. Systematic outcome research comparing white, black, and interracial therapy teams is required to provide a definitive answer.

References

Bell, A. *Black sexuality, fact and fancy*. Bloomington, Indiana: Black America Series, Indiana University, 1968.

Bernard, V. W. Psychoanalysis and members of minority groups. *American Journal of Psychiatry*, 1953, *1*, 256–267.

Bernard, V. W. Interracial practice in the midst of change. *American Journal of Psychiatry*, 1972, *128*, 92–98.

Calneck, M. Racial factors in the countertransference: The black therapist and the black client. *American Journal of Orthopsychiatry*, 1970, *40*, 39–46.

Curry, A. Myth, transference and the black psychotherapist. *Psychoanalytic Review*, 1964, *51*, 7–14.

Fisher, N. An interracial analysis: Transference and counter transference significance. *Journal of the American Psychoanalytic Association*, 1971, *19*, 736–745.

Goldstein, N. *The roots of prejudice against the Negro in the United States*. Boston: Boston University Press, 1948.

Haller, J. The physician versus the Negro: Medical and anthropological concepts of race in the late nineteenth century. *Bulletin of the History of Medicine*, 1970, *44*, 154–167.

Hollingshead, A. B., and Redlich, F. C. *Social class and mental illness: A community study*. New York: Wiley, 1958.

Hunt, M. *Sexual behavior in the 1970's*. Chicago: Playboy Press, 1974.

Jourard, S. M. *The transparent self*. Princeton, New Jersey: Van Nostrand, 1964.

Kaplan, H. S. *The new sex therapy*. New York: Brunner/Mazel, 1974.

Kardiner, A., and Ovesey, L. *The mark of oppression*. Cleveland: World Publishing, 1951.

Kennedy, J. A. Problems posed in the analysis of Negro patients. *Psychiatry*, 1952, *15*, 313–327.

Lobitz, W. C., and LoPiccolo, J. New methods in the behavioral treatment of sexual dysfunction. *Journal of Behavior Therapy and Experimental Psychiatry*, 1972, *3*, 265–271.

Lobitz, W. C., LoPiccolo, J., Lobitz, G. K., and Brockway, J. A closer look at "simplistic" behavior therapy for sexual dysfunction. In H. J. Eysenck (Ed.), *Case studies in behavior therapy*. London: Routledge and Kegan Paul, 1974.

LoPiccolo, J., and Lobitz, W. C. Behavior therapy of sexual dysfunction. In L. A. Hamerlynck, L. C. Handy, and E. J. Mash (Eds.), *Behavior change: Methodology, concepts, and practice*. Champaign, Illinois: Research Press, 1973.

Masters, W. H., and Johnson, V. E. *Human sexual inadequacy*. Boston: Little, Brown, 1970.

Oberndorf, C. P. Selectivity and option for psychotherapy. *American Journal of Psychiatry*, 1954, *110*, 754–758.

Obler, M. Systematic desensitization in sexual disorders. *Journal of Behavior Therapy and Experimental Psychiatry*, 1973, *4*, 93–101.

Rainwater, L. Some aspects of lower-class sexual behavior. *Journal of Social Issues*, 1966, *22*, 96–108.

Reiss, B. Observations of the therapist factor in interethnic psychotherapy. *Psychotherapy: Theory, Research and Practice*, 1971, *8*, 71–72.

Reiss, I. *The social context of pre-marital sexual permissiveness*. New York: Holt, Rinehart & Winston, 1967.

Sager, C., Brayboy, T., and Waxenberg, B. Black patient–white therapist. *American Journal of Orthopsychiatry*, 1972, *42*, 415–423.

Schachter, J. S., and Butts, H. Transference and countertransference in interracial analysis. *Journal of American Psychoanalysis*, 1968, *16*, 792–808.

Staples, R. Sex behavior of lower income Negroes. *Sexology*, October 1967, pp. 52–55.

Staples, R. Is the sexual revolution by-passing blacks? *Ebony*, March 1974, pp. 111–114.

Tanner, B. A. Two case reports on the modification of the ejaculatory response with the squeeze technique. *Psychotherapy: Theory, Research, and Practice*, 1973, *10*, 297–300.

Thomas, A., and Sillen, S. *Racism and psychiatry*. New York: Brunner/Mazel, 1972.

Vontress, C. The black male personality. *Black Scholar*, June 1971, pp. 10–16.

Waite, R. R. The Negro patient and clinical theory. *Journal of Consulting and Clinical Psychology*, 1968, *32*, 427–433.

Wolpe, J. *The practice of behavior therapy*. New York: Pergamon, 1969.

Young, L. C. Are black women taking care of business? *Essence*, May 1974, p. 58.

Zelnik, M., and Kanfner, J. Sexuality, contraception, and pregnancy among young unwed females in the United States. In U.S. Commission on Population Growth, *Demographic and social aspects of population growth*, 1972.

Research in the area of sexual dysfunction has occasionally resulted in development of sex therapy techniques that are applicable and beneficial for nondysfunctional couples as well. The Semans pause technique for extending ejaculatory control or the squeeze technique of Masters and Johnson, for example, have often been recommended as a means of increasing pleasure for nondysfunctional couples who just want their sexual experiences to last longer.

Many of the elements of the program described in this chapter were developed by LoPiccolo and Miller on the basis of their experience in treating sexual problems. Unlike many other group therapies, this program has a relatively structured format and attempts to integrate behavioral and group systems techniques.

36

A Program for Enhancing the Sexual Relationship of Normal Couples

Joseph LoPiccolo and Vinnie H. Miller

Two of the most publicized recent developments in psychotherapy have been the success of behavioral techniques in the treatment of sexual dysfunction and the use of group methods to promote personal growth in normal people. This chapter reports on a combination of these two developments; a behavioral training program designed to help normal, nondysfunctional people realize their full potential for sexual expression and satisfaction.

Within the past few years, considerable evidence has accumulated to support the effectiveness of direct behavioral methods in the treatment of sexual dysfunctions such as erectile failure or premature ejaculation in men, and orgasmic dysfunction in women (Masters and Johnson, 1970; Wolpe and Lazarus, 1966; LoPiccolo and Lobitz, 1972; Kaplan, 1974). While the details of treatment vary somewhat from program to program, this behavioral approach generally focuses on skill training in effective sexual behavior, reducing anxiety about performance, and increasing communication between partners.

Joseph LoPiccolo • Department of Psychiatry and Behavioral Science, School of Medicine, State University of New York, Stony Brook, New York   *Vinnie H. Miller* • Counseling Center, University of Oregon, Eugene, Oregon

Oddly enough, with the documented success of such behavioral techniques in treating specific symptomatic dysfunctions, there do not seem to have been any attempts to apply behavior technology to enhancing and enriching the sexual relationship of normal, nondysfunctional couples. Indeed, as Walker (1974) has pointed out, mental health professionals have by and large focused "most of our efforts in working with the pathological, the disturbed and the emotionally crippled," to the exclusion of "helping normal people realize their full potential." Only within the encounter group–humanistic movement has there been any focus on promoting growth in the normal person (Walker, 1974), and it is therefore not surprising that previous efforts to promote sexual growth have been "encounter group" oriented.

For example, Bindrum (1968, 1969) has described nude encounter-group marathons which he reports improve the sexual relationships of the participants. Hartman and Fithian (1970, 1971) have reported on enhancing sexual satisfaction through group nudity and sensitivity groups. Gunther (1971) has also advocated group sensory awareness training as a means of increasing sexual satisfaction. Lacking in these reports has been any formal evaluation of the group's effectiveness.

It is puzzling that behavioral clinicians have not attempted to enhance the sexual relationship of normal couples, as it is generally agreed that many normal couples are lacking in information and skill in both sexual technique and interpersonal communication (Ford and Beach, 1951; Mace, 1971). A behavioral, social learning approach, directly teaching people about sexual technique and communication, would seem to have at least as much to offer as a less focused "encounter group."

In the course of a long-term clinical research project on behavioral treatment of sexual dysfunction (LoPiccolo and Lobitz, 1972, 1973; Lobitz and LoPiccolo, 1972; LoPiccolo, Stewart, and Watkins, 1972), a group training procedure for teaching basic sexual skills to normal, nondysfunctional couples has been developed. This program is aimed at the dissatisfied couple who find their sexual life unrewarding, despite the absence of any specific sexual dysfunction. Estimates of the prevalence of such dissatisfaction ranges from 30% of young, liberal couples (Athanasiou, Shaver, and Tavris, 1970) to 54% of lower-class couples (Rainwater, 1966), indicating a clear need for a procedure of basic skill training.

In designing the program reported on here, an attempt was made to capitalize on the features of the encounter-group movement most relevant to a good sexual relationship. Particularly important were the emphasis on open and honest communication, direct interpersonal feedback, and a focus on the here and now. Several general procedural aspects of the group movement were also adopted, such as the format of a small group meeting together extensively over a weekend, and the role of the leaders as participant-models and facilitators. On the other hand, many of the specific techniques used were adopted from behavioral treatment programs for sexual dysfunction. These techniques emphasize education, attitude change, and specific skill training. It was hoped that the group procedure would thus be a happy marriage of behaviorism and humanism, avoiding the reductionism of behavior therapy on the one hand (Koch, 1971) and the group movements' "catch phrases, vagueness and unspecified relationship of goals to the techniques employed to achieve them" (Lakin, 1972) on the other.

The Group Procedure

The group procedure varies somewhat in response to the needs of the particular participants. All groups share the common features of having three client-couples and a male–female coleadership couple, meeting for three three-hour sessions over a weekend, completing a "homework" assignment for sexual activities to be carried out in private Saturday night, and meeting again for a follow-up session two weeks later.

The group follows a moderately structured format, which is shown in Table 1 and described briefly below.

Session 1

1. Ground rules and name game: The leaders begin by briefly stating the ground rules of the group experience—no alcohol or drugs, first names only, focus on the here and now, and so forth. The "name game" of having participants sequentially recite the name of each group member is then used to familiarize the participants with each other.

2. Verbal disinhibition: To facilitate open discussion on the sensitive topic of sex, the leaders then supply the participants with a verbal list of common sexual terms such as *penis, vagina, intercourse*, etc. The participants respond to each term by saying out loud all the common synonyms they know for each term. The leaders then initiate a discussion of how inability to use sexual words can prevent effective communication during lovemaking. This exercise usually produces a good deal of embarrassment and anxiety, often expressed as laughter, and seems to facilitate the rest of the group discussion.

3. Fears and hopes: The participants next write out anonymously a list of things they hope will happen in the group and as a result of the group, and a similar

Table 1. Timetable for Sexual Enrichment Groups

Saturday 9:00 AM to 12:30 PM
1. Ground rules and name game, 15 minutes.
2. Verbal disinhibition, 15 minutes.
3. Fears and hopes, 15 minutes.
4. Initiation and refusal, 1 hour and 30 minutes.
5. Masters and Johnson positions, 15 minutes.

Saturday 2:30 to 5:30 PM
1. Share turn-ons and turn-offs, 1 hour.
2. Instantaneous feedback, 30 minutes.
3. Sensate focus, 30 minutes.
4. Movie and homework assignment, 15 minutes.

Sunday 11:00 AM to 2:00 PM
1. Debrief the Saturday night homework assignment, 20 minutes.
2. *Berkeley Barb* ad, 20 minutes.
3. Unfinished business, 1 hour.
4. Planning two weeks assignment, 30 minutes.

list of outcomes they fear. These lists are shuffled, distributed, and read aloud. This exercise, designed to build group supportiveness and a sense of commonality, typically leads to a discussion of interpersonal competitiveness, anxieties about sexual competence, and fears that the spouse will disclose something embarrassing. The leaders respond by pointing out that "pleasure, not prowess" is the hallmark of a good sex life, and model self-disclosure and openness about their own sexual life.

4. Initiation and refusal: This exercise is designed to teach the couples how to initiate sexual activity clearly and how to decline such an initiation by the spouse in a nonhurtful way. Most couples report that initiation takes place in a very tentative, indirect way. This patter serves to minimize risks; if the spouse is not in the mood for sex, both partners can easily pretend that nothing at all ever happened. The attendant danger, of course, is that such indirect communication is open to a good deal of misunderstanding. The leaders bring the couples into touch with their maladaptive patterns by having each person reverse-role-play his or her spouse, making an initiation that they do not like. Next, they role-play what would be a good initiation for them and discuss the differences. This role-play-reversal procedure is then repeated around the issue of declining intercourse when the spouse initiates it. Participants are initially rather upset and emotional during this exercise (a reverse role-play can be a rather hostile mockery of the spouse's behavior) but generally reach resolution of those feelings as they learn specifically what it is that they have been doing wrong and what to do differently in the future.

At this point, to resolve great differences in desired frequency of intercourse, the leaders focus a discussion on masturbation and nonmutual sexual activity (i.e., manipulating your partner's genitals to orgasm when you do not want to have intercourse).

5. Masters and Johnson positions: To end the first session on a pleasant note, the participants next learn the genital-caressing positions recommended by Masters and Johnson (1970). This exercise includes a discussion of the value of "selfishness," that is, learning to just relax and receive sexual pleasure with no pressure to simultaneously please your partner.

Session II

1. Turn-ons and turn-offs: This exercise has two purposes. First, many couples complain of a routine, dull sex life with little variety and a narrow repertoire of sexual activities. Secondly, many people have fantasies of new sexual activities they would like to try but are ashamed to share these fantasies with their spouse. Accordingly, each person in the group describes various things that make sex more pleasurable for him or her and specific sexual activities he or she enjoys. This discussion usually begins with a listing of "atmosphere" elements (candlelight, bearskin rugs, etc.), and the leaders press for more specific (and embarrassing) material by modeling open self-disclosure of their own preferences. This sharing is repeated for "turn-offs" and again in terms of perception of the partner ("I think it turns my wife off if . . ."). Throughout this exercise, the leaders stress

that there is no such thing as an objective or absolute standard for sexual preferences. What turns one couple *on* turns another *off*; the leaders accent both as normal variation in "taste" or preferences. Couples typically enjoy this exercise. Comments of "Wow, we never thought of that, I want to try it" and "You mean you think about trying that sort of thing too?" are very common.

2. Instantaneous feedback: A factor in many couples' dissatisfaction is inhibition about giving feedback to their partner during sexual activity. Without such feedback, partners may persist for years in ineffective techniques of kissing, caressing, and intercourse. Accordingly, in this exercise, couples are trained to give effective feedback. The emphasis is a shift from "Stop, I don't like it" to "Just a little bit lighter and slower is better for me"; that is, good feedback should tell the spouse exactly what to do differently. Following discussion, couples practice this style of feedback, during clothed massage, as an analogue for sexual behavior, which we see as inappropriate in a group setting.

3. Sensate focus: The leaders discuss the distractions of daily life and how worries about jobs, finances, and so forth can interfere with becoming sexually aroused. To counteract these distractions, a session of sensory awareness and sensate focusing is included in the group. This procedure is modeled very directly after that described by Gunther (1971).

4. Movie and homework assignment: A movie showing a wide variety of foreplay and intercourse techniques is then presented. Then couples, with the leader's help, plan for their sexual activity for Saturday night. Typically, couples are directed to use their new initiation skills, to try some new techniques they've learned, and to use feedback during sexual activity. They are instructed not to try to have a fantastic sexual experience but rather to just enjoy some experimentation, free of pressure for "results."

Session III

1. Debrief: The third session begins with each couple reporting on their "homework" session Saturday evening. If couples report difficulties, the leaders respond with suggestions and a reminder that the first try at something new is often difficult, but future attempts will probably go more smoothly.

2. *Berkeley Barb* advertisement: To reintroduce a light, positive note, participants next write and read aloud an advertisement for an underground newspaper, offering their mate for sale or rent as a sexual partner. The importance of reinforcing and rewarding each other for changes in sexual behavior is stressed at this point.

3. Unfinished business: The remainder of the group is relatively unstructured. Participants write out "unfinished business" (unresolved problems, questions, etc.) on cards and the leaders and other group members respond. In some groups, divisions into male-only and female-only groups are useful while discussing unresolved issues. In these subgroups, the women tend to talk about masturbation and techniques for reaching orgasm; the males tend to discuss issues of frequency of sex, duration of intercourse, and changes in sexual response with aging. The leaders need a good general knowledge of sexuality in order to correct misinformation and offer advice in these less structured discussions.

4. Two-week assignment: At the end of the weekend, each couple writes out a plan for their sexual activity over the next two weeks. Issues such as making sex a higher-priority activity rather than the last thing done before falling asleep, further technique experimentation, the use of feedback, and changing usual initiation patterns are often stressed in these plans. The plans are read aloud and the leaders and other group members respond with suggestions.

Follow-Up

Two weeks later, the group reconvenes for a follow-up session. The two weeks are reviewed, a plan for future growth is written out by each couple, and assessment data are gathered (see below).

Results

After a good deal of preliminary work, this group procedure has been used on four groups, led by a total of seven different leaders. Additionally, an untreated control group was administered the assessment battery at the same intervals as the group participants, as a check for instrument reactivity and spontaneous change. As this chapter has focused on the techniques themselves, only a brief summary of the assessment data is presented. Assessment took place before the group met, at the two-week postsession and three months later as a follow-up check on long-term results. Assessment was done with the Sexual Interaction Inventory (SII) (LoPiccolo and Steger, 1974) to check for sex-specific effects and the Fundamental Interpersonal Relationship-Orientation-Behavior scale (FIRO-B) (Schutz, 1966). The most relevant measure of the group's effect is the Sexual Interaction Inventory. The SII, developed as a diagnostic and outcome measure for sexual dysfunction, assesses a couple's sexual relationship in terms of pleasure derived from a list of seventeen heterosexual behaviors (kissing to intercourse). From these ratings, scales for satisfaction with range and frequency of sexual activity, acceptance of one's own and one's partner's sexual responsiveness, and accuracy of perception of partner's sexual preferences are derived. The SII profiles for the twelve couples who have experienced the group thus far are shown in Figure 1.

Briefly, statistical analysis indicates that the gains shown for the clients are significant both in comparison to the control group and in relationship to their own pregroup score. These differences maintain at follow-up three months later, a finding that is generally not found for less focused encounter-type groups (Campbell and Dunnette, 1968). Changes in the FIRO-B were not significant for the clients, nor did their scores differ from the control group. This finding suggests that the effects of the group are, as intended, specific to changes in sexual behavior. Furthermore, the lack of change in the FIRO-B scores suggests that the changes in the SII scores do not reflect some sort of placebo, social desirability, or expectancy effect as a function of group participation. Furthermore, the four groups were run by seven different leaders, suggesting that the procedures themselves, rather than the personality of a charismatic leader, produce the results obtained.

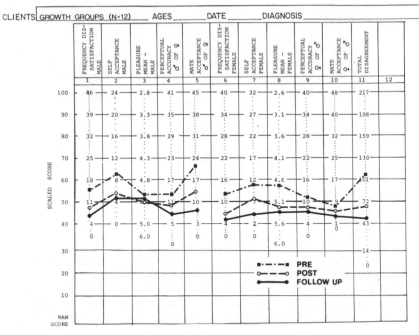

Fig. 1. Sexual interaction of clients.

Further research will investigate the effectiveness of this procedure in comparison to other types of group experiences focused on sex. In the interim, it is hoped that the rather lengthy description presented above will encourage others to experiment with this procedure. It would be especially gratifying if college counseling centers began to define such training in basic sexual skills as part of their responsibility to students. Being exposed to such training at this time in their life cycle would seem likely to reduce the probability of sexual dissatisfaction or sexual dysfunction occurring later in marriage. While deans and the community are likely to look askance at "sex classes," such training could probably be included in "marriage preparation" programs without causing public relations problems.

References

Athanasiou, R., Shaver, P., and Tavris, C. Sex. *Psychology Today*, 1970, *4*(2), 37–52.

Bindrim, P. A report on a nude marathon: The effect of physical nudity on the practice of interaction in marathon groups. *Psychotherapy*, *Theory*, *Research and Practice*, September 1968, *5*, 180–188.

Bindrim, P. Nudity as a quick grab for intimacy in group therapy. *Psychology Today*, June, 1969, pp. 24–28.

Campbell, J. P., and Dunnette, M. D. Effectiveness of T-group experiences in managerial training and development. *Psychological Bulletin*, 1968, *70*, 73–104.

Ford, C. S., and Beach, F. A. *Patterns of sexual behavior*, New York: Signet, 1951.

Gunther, B. Sensory awakening and sensuality. In H. Otto (Ed.), *The new sexuality*. Palo Alto, Caliia: Science & Behavior Books, 1971.

Hartman, W. E., and Fithian, M. A. Enhancing sexuality through nudism. In H. Otto (Ed.), *The new sexuality*. Palo Alto, California: Science & Behavior Books, 1971.

Hartman, W. E., and Fithian, M. A. Desert retreat. In J. and J. Robbins (Eds.), *An analysis of human sexual inadequacy*. New York: New American Library, 1970.

Kaplan, H. S. *The new sex therapy*. New York: Brunner/Mazel, 1974.

Koch, S. The image of man implicit in encounter group theory. *Journal of Humanistic Psychology*, 1971, *11*(27), 109–128.

Lakin, M. *Experimental groups: The uses of interpersonal encounter, psycho-therapy groups and sensitivity training*. Morristown, New Jersey: General Learning Press, 1972.

Lobitz, W. C., and LoPiccolo, J. New methods in the behavioral treatment of sexual dysfunction. *Journal of Behavior Therapy and Experimental Psychiatry*, 1972, *3*(4), 265–271.

LoPiccolo, J., and Lobitz, W. C. The role of masturbation in the treatment of organic dysfunction. *Archives of Sexual Behavior*, 1972, *2*, 153–164.

LoPiccolo, J., and Lobitz, W. C. Behavior therapy of sexual dysfunction. In L. A. Hammerlynck, L. C. Handy, and E. J. Mash (Eds.), *Behavior change: Methodology, concepts, and practice*. Champaign, Illinois: Research Press, 1973, Chap. 13.

LoPiccolo, J., and Steger, J. The Sexual Interaction Inventory: A new instrument for assessment of sexual dysfunction. *Archives of Sexual Behavior*, 1974, *3*, 585–595.

LoPiccolo, J., Stewart, R., and Watkins, B. Case study: Treatment of erectile failure and ejaculatory incompetence in a case with homosexual etiology. *Journal of Behavior Therapy and Experimental Psychiatry*, 1972, *3*, 233–236.

Mace, D. R. Counseling a sexually inhibited couple. *Sexual Behavior*, 1971, *1*(9), 32–37.

Masters, W. H., and Johnson, V. E. *Human sexual inadequacy*. Boston: Little, Brown, 1970.

Rainwater, L. Some aspects of lower class sexual behavior. *Journal of Social Issues*, 1966, *22*(2), 96–109.

Schutz, W. *The interpersonal underworld*. Palo Alto, California: Science and Behavior Books, 1966.

Walker, C. E. Training in clinical psychology: The future. *The Clinical Psychologist*, 1974, *27*(2), 12–13.

Wolpe, J., and Lazarus, A. A. *Behavior therapy techniques*. New York: Pergamon Press, 1966.

The use of a group format for the treatment of sexual dysfunction in couples is a relatively new phenomenon. In 1974 Kaplan et al. reported on a group treatment program for premature ejaculators that involved couples (see Part V, Chapter 21).

In this chapter, McGovern, Kirkpatrick, and LoPiccolo describe a group treatment program for couples which focused on two dysfunctions: premature ejaculation in three out of the four males and primary orgasmic dysfunction in the females.

One important aspect of this article is the authors' evaluation of the advantages and disadvantages of using a group format for the treatment of sexual dysfunctions. For this group, increased efficiency in terms of therapist time per couple did not turn out to be the case. However, the group seemed to have a positive effect on the couples' ability to make changes in attitudes and behaviors.

The issue of the relationship between the reinforcing value of the group and its influence on maintenance of treatment gains is an important one raised by the authors.

37

A Behavioral Group Treatment Program for Sexually Dysfunctional Couples

Kevin B. McGovern, Carole C. Kirkpatrick, and Joseph LoPiccolo

Recent publications have established that couples with sexual dysfunctions can be successfully treated through behaviorally oriented therapy programs (Masters and Johnson, 1970; LoPiccolo and Lobitz, 1972; Kaplan, 1974; Kohlenberg, 1974). Treatment is typically carried out by a male and female cotherapy team, meeting with the dysfunctional couple for fifteen to twenty sessions. Through these programs, clients with erectile failure, premature ejaculation, and orgasmic difficulties receive communication and skills training aimed at teaching more adaptive patterns of sexual behavior.

A version of this chapter was presented at APA, Chicago, 1975, by Dr. Kirkpatrick. Dates of research: January–June 1973. The first two authors served as cotherapists for the project. First and second authorship was decided by the flip of a coin.

Kevin B. McGovern • Columbia Psychiatric Clinic, Portland, Oregon   **Carole C. Kirkpatrick** • Independent Practice, Psychology, Eugene, Oregon   **Joseph LoPiccolo** • Department of Psychiatry and Behavioral Science, School of Medicine, State University of New York, Stony Brook, New York. When this chapter was originally published, Carole Kirkpatrick was Visiting Assistant Professor, Psychology Department, University of Oregon, Eugene, Oregon.

The overall efficacy of these treatment programs for sexually dysfunctional couples has been demonstrated, and the treatment procedures have been described elsewhere (LoPiccolo and Lobitz, 1972; McGovern, Stewart, and LoPiccolo, 1975; Snyder, LoPiccolo, and LoPiccolo, 1975). The most frequently noted drawback to these programs, however, is that the modification of sexual behavior can be an expensive and time-consuming process. One solution would be to treat dysfunctional clients in a group setting, thereby treating more people in a less costly format. At this point, though, there is very little evidence available to indicate that the techniques employed in sexual treatment programs can be applied to a group setting. With the exception of a few groups designed for single clients (Romano, 1973), or groups for one partner only (Mann, 1975), no behaviorally based group treatment programs for couples have yet been reported in the literature.

Method

The purpose of this chapter is to describe a group treatment program for dysfunctional couples. The overall success of this program demonstrates that a behaviorally oriented group approach to sexual dysfunctions shows promise as an equally effective and efficient alternative to individual treatment.

Client Selection

Since treatment procedures for women with primary inorgasmic dysfunctions and men with premature ejaculation have already been well established (Masters and Johnson, 1970; LoPiccolo and Lobitz, 1972), four couples with these presenting problems were selected from our treatment program's waiting list. Of the eight individuals, the four females were primary inorgasmic and three of the males were considered premature ejaculators. A primary inorgasmic woman is one who has not experienced an orgasm through any mode of physical stimulation (i.e., masturbation, oral stimulation, or intercourse). Prematurely ejaculating men often reach orgasm several seconds before or after vaginal penetration.

Each couple came in for a standard screening interview conducted by the authors. The purpose of this interview was to assess the couple's current sexual functioning and to explain the group program. In this explanation, the therapists emphasized the need to learn new behavioral skills and communication patterns. The first four couples interviewed were considered acceptable for treatment and agreed to the group method. Although homogeneous with respect to their sexual problems, the couples were heterogeneous regarding demographic characteristics of age, education, number of children, and life-styles. For example, the oldest couple was in their forties, had been married seventeen years, had two children, and were religiously active; while the youngest couple was in their twenties, married three years, had no children, and professed no religious beliefs.

Assessment

Prior to the start of group treatment, each couple completed the standard assessment package consisting of (a) a general background information form assessing current sexual attitudes and behaviors; (b) the Sexual Interaction Inventory, an assessment device that gives couples specific ratings of current sexual satisfaction across a variety of dimensions (LoPiccolo and Steger, 1974); (c) the Locke–Wallace Marital Adjustment Test, used in order to provide an index of marital satisfaction as a whole.

Each couple was asked to complete the assessment package two weeks prior to treatment, at termination, and at a follow-up point six months after termination. Thus, data at three points in time are available for all couples except one who did not respond to our follow-up request.

Treatment

The treatment program consisted of fifteen three-hour evening group sessions. The first thirteen sessions were held on a weekly basis; the last two sessions were spread over a six-week period to maximize the fading of treatment into self-directed maintenance.

The therapists provided the couples with an informal atmosphere. The clients were encouraged to dress informally and sit on cushions placed on the floor. After the first ninety minutes of each session, there was a fifteen- to twenty-minute coffee break. The therapists used this time to consult with the observers. With this information, the therapists decided if it was necessary to make program changes for the second part of the training session.

At the end of each group session, the therapists gave the four couples their weekly homework assignments. The couples kept detailed records of their assignments on prepared data sheets. These records were collected six hours prior to the next treatment session to aid the therapists in planning treatment strategies for the next session.

A number of treatment techniques were adapted or designed specifically for the group treatment program. Those treatment components unique to the group treatment mode, as opposed to individual therapy, are briefly described below.

1. Warm-Up Exercises: Several activities were constructed to get participants acquainted and feel at ease with each other. Such activities were done at the beginning of the session and included: (a) Group milling: Members walked around ("milled") and either verbally or nonverbally greeted each other. After a period of this greeting activity, participants then exchanged one written piece of information about themselves to another group member (e.g., "I like drag races," "I was born in New York," and so on). Verbal conversation between pairs ensued. (b) Blind trust walk: People paired off and one person led the other person who was blindfolded through various experiences. The therapists usually arranged the pairing off so spouses would be partners. (c) Hopes and fears exercise: The participants wrote each of his or her hopes and fears pertaining to the

group experience on index cards. The cards were collected, shuffled, and then read out loud with discussion.

2. Relaxation Training: Group members were taught deep muscle relaxation in the group and were given a relaxation tape to take home for further use.

3. Roundtable Procedure: At each group meeting, the four couples would take turns giving a five-minute overview of their weekly activities. This provided an opportunity to share common cognitive, emotional, and behavioral reactions of the previous session or homework assignments.

4. Behavioral Rehearsal: Many problems shared by all couples, or specific to one couple, were worked on by direct behavioral rehearsal. For example, if the same couples had difficulty initiating or refusing sexual behavior, then all persons in turn would be directed to turn to their partner, give several initiation and refusal responses, and receive their partner's feedback. Also, if a couple had experienced a specific problematic situation during the week, the therapists would reconstruct a similar scene for the group and let each couple role-play their "solution." These role-play procedures are described in detail elsewhere (LoPiccolo and Miller, 1975).

5. Subgroups: In order to deal with issues not shared by the whole group, the group was occasionally subdivided into male and female halves, or two couples with each therapist. The smallness and homogeneity of such subgroups fostered much personal sharing.

Treatment Results

The primary focus of the group treatment was to change the orgasmic responses of the men and women. Accordingly, the women were taught methods of increasing the probability of an orgasmic response, while the men were taught how to control the ejaculatory latency. The data displayed in Table 1 demonstrate that the group therapy program was effective in changing the sexual behavior of

Table 1.   *Pre, Post, and Follow-Up Mean Scores on Sexual Response Items*
($N = 4$ females, 4 males)

Sexual response	Pre	Post	Follow-up	
1. Male's ejaculatory latency	3	8	8	Male 1
(minutes of continuous intromission)	3	8	7	Male 2
	3	11	5	Male 3
	30	30	30	Male 4
2. Female orgasmic response				
(percentage of time orgasmic)				
a. in masturbation	0%	100%	92%	
b. through manual stimulation	0%	81%	60%	
c. in intercourse	0%	75%	33%	
3. Duration of foreplay (minutes)	7	18	10	
4. Frequency of intercourse				
(times per month)	5	10	5	

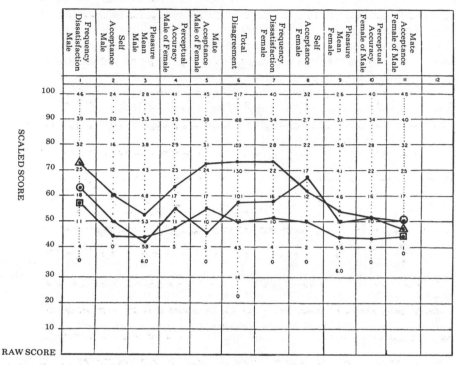

Fig. 1. Sexual Interaction Inventory: pre (△), post (□) and follow-up (○) mean scores. $N = 4$ couples (follow-up, 3 couples).

the three premature ejaculators. The fourth male reported a thirty-minute latency during the program.

As can also be seen in Table 1, dramatic increases in female orgasmic performance took place during treatment. Mean responses are given because all four women performed similarly. By the end of treatment all four females were orgasmic 100% of the time in masturbation. In addition, each woman reported experiencing an orgasm with the penile insertion and concomitant manual stimulation on at least two consecutive occasions. The percentage of orgasmic response is lower for genital caressing and intercourse than masturbation. It was

Table 2. Pre, Post, Follow-Up Scores
on Locke–Wallace Marital
Adjustment Inventory
($N = 8$)

	Pre	Post	Follow-up
Mean	96.12	116.25[a]	109.42[b]
SD	11.75	15.97	9.79

[a] Pre–post t test = 2.77 (p .05, one-tailed).
[b] Pre–follow-up t test = 2.45 (p .05, one-tailed).

expected that greater stimulus generalization would occur over time with continued practice. However, the follow-up data do not demonstrate that the high-frequency orgasmic response learned through masturbation had sufficiently generalized to intercourse. Increases during treatment in the length of foreplay and frequency of intercourse are also evident in Table 1.

The couples' responses to the Sexual Interaction Inventory (Figure 1) and the Locke–Wallace Inventory (Table 2) demonstrated, in addition, that the group treatment was effective in changing not only the couples' general level of sexual satisfaction but also their marital happiness.

Follow-Up

Although the major goals of the group treatment program were met by each of the four couples, several of the follow-up data suggest some behavioral regression following termination. Already noted was the low female orgasmic generalization. Likewise, the amount of time spent in foreplay activities and the frequency of intercourse decreased after the program had terminated (Table 1). Similar trends were observed on other treatment measures, including the Sexual Interaction Inventory (Figure 1). However, in terms of self-reported satisfaction with the quality of sex at follow-up, all couples remained at termination levels of satisfaction—either 5 or 6 on a 6-point scale of sexual satisfaction.

Discussion

The results of this preliminary report suggest that the group treatment program for sexually dysfunctional couples is an effective mode of treatment. Furthermore, group treatment may have some additional advantages over individual treatment. First of all, the presence of other couples seemed to act as a disinhibitor, rather than as a stimulus for anxiety. Our couples reported feeling more comfortable knowing that others had similar problems. Couples may also feel less pressure in a group setting since the therapists do not focus solely on them. In addition, the more informal structure afforded by the group may be more comparable to clients' other experiences with organizational groups, class discussions, and so forth. For many of our clients, individual therapy would be a novel experience, creating anxiety regarding social norms.

The presence of other couples also seemed to have a powerful modeling effect in our group. As therapists, we were impressed with the ease of teaching alternative behaviors via role-playing and behavioral rehearsal. In fact, each couple developed proficient behavioral rehearsal skills. During some sessions the couples would model alternative methods of interacting for the other couples. On other occasions, a couple would mirror or replicate the behaviors of another couple. Through these procedures, the couples learned alternative viable behavior that could be incorporated.

The presence of other couples also seemed to produce more rapid attitude change. This change was seen most dramatically in the group division by sex.

For the women especially, having the opportunity to share thoughts and feelings with three other women produced rapid attitude change toward their own sexuality. Within three weeks women who had never experienced orgasm or sexual arousal were sharing fantasies, noticing genital sensations, enjoying masturbation, and eagerly looking at nude males displayed in magazines.

In summary, the group treatment program presented above seemed to have afforded some distinct advantages over individual treatment. The direct comparison, modeling, and disclosure with peers made possible a therapeutic climate that was safe, supportive, and conducive to rapid attitude and behavior change.

Although our group was surprisingly free of competitiveness, romantic entanglements between different spouses, reluctance to self-disclosure in front of strangers, or strong personal dislikes, these are important issues to consider, especially for couples with sensitive sexual problems. These burdensome problems that often hamper group therapy were avoided through careful preplanning sessions. Prior to each therapy meeting, the therapists and observers carefully read each couple's daily record forms. After reviewing these forms, the therapists developed a treatment plan for the next therapeutic session, carefully structuring activities to maximize positive feelings and constructive problem solving.

In addition, the authors recognized that each couple would demonstrate different rates of therapeutic progress. In order to discourage competitiveness or fear of failing, the therapists met individually with one of the couples each week for half an hour before the general group session. During these brief sessions, the therapists dealt with any issues that were impeding the couple's progress. In no case, however, did the therapist give different homework assignments to any of the couples. Each couple was expected to continue with the regular weekly assignments. However, some of the couples were encouraged to repeat a number of their past assignments.

One of the more intriguing issues raised by this study is whether group therapy can be too powerful. Is it possible that the couples' changes in attitude and behavior may have been affected more by the group process, rather than a product of a new husband and wife relationship? Is it possible that after the group disbanded, the primary source of reinforcement was withdrawn? This hypothesis is consonant with the regression effect observed at follow-up. Although maintenance lists had been thoroughly constructed, the therapists gradually became less direct, and treatment eventually faded over a number of weeks; these data revealed that the couples were not spending as much time in sexual activities.

Once the program was terminated, each couple lost an important source of continuous reinforcement. As one couple reported when the group did not meet one week, "This has been the highlight of our week. We didn't know what to do without the group." This loss of support and encouragement may account largely for the regression effect. The fact that attendance and camaraderie were extremely high also supports this hypothesis. If the same effect is observed in other programs utilizing a group treatment approach, alterations of the treatment procedures are suggested, and perhaps a more comprehensive maintenance program should be established.

On the other hand, some behavioral regression is to be expected as well as the fact that measures of frequency and foreplay often do not correspond to the subjective experience of sexual satisfaction.

In addition, the question of efficiency as opposed to efficacy is somewhat unresolved. Mean therapist time per session was six hours per therapist, as compared with an average of three hours per session when seeing a couple individually. In part, additional time spent in the group therapy design was caused by a lack of previously established treatment procedures. A major portion of the therapists' time was spent carefully designing, discussing, and debriefing each treatment session. Additionally, it is not known what effects reducing group sessions to two hours would have had. Research is currently under way to reduce the amount of therapist time spent in group treatment. It is hoped that these studies will shed new light on a promising treatment approach.

References

Kaplan, H. *The new sex therapy*. New York: Brunner/Mazel, 1974.

Kohlenberg, R. Directed masturbation and the treatment of primary orgasmic dysfunction. *Archives of Sexual Behavior*, 1974, *3*, 349–356.

Lobitz, W. C., and LoPiccolo, J. New methods in the behavioral treatment of sexual dysfunction. *Journal of Behavioral Therapy and Experimental Psychiatry*, 1973, *3*, 265–271.

LoPiccolo, J., and Lobitz, W. C. The role of masturbation in the treatment of orgasmic dysfunction, *Archives of Sexual Behavior*, 1972, *2*, 163–171.

LoPiccolo, J., and Miller, V. A program for enhancing the sexual relationship for normal couples. *Counseling Psychologist*, 1975, *5*, 41–46.

LoPiccolo, J., and Steger, J. The Sexual Interaction Inventory: A new instrument for assessment of sexual dysfunction. *Archives of Sexual Behavior*, 1974, *3*, 585–595.

Mann, Jay. Is sex counseling here to stay? *Counseling Psychologist*, 1975, *5*, 60–64.

Masters, W., and Johnson, V. E. *Human sexual inadequacy*. Boston: Little, Brown, 1970.

McGovern, K., Stewart, R., and LoPiccolo, J. Secondary orgasmic dysfunction. I: Analyses and strategies for treatment. *Archives of Sexual Behavior*, 1975, *22*, 505–512.

Romano, M. Sexual counseling in groups, *Journal of Sex Research*, 1973, *9*, 69–78.

Snyder, A., LoPiccolo, L., and LoPiccolo, J. Secondary orgasmic dysfunction. II: Case study. *Archives of Sexual Behavior*, 1975.

In the history of the development of psychotherapeutic procedures, a common sequence has been for a particular technique to be developed in individual therapy, then applied to group treatment. Group treatment offers certain advantages in terms of lower cost and wider availability of therapy to more patients, as well as the supportive atmosphere created in a group of people with similar problems.

In this article, the authors describe the application of individual therapy procedures for nonorgasmic women (see Part III) to a group setting. While the results were generally quite good, it should be noted that only one of the twenty women treated gained the capacity for orgasm during coitus. This result compares poorly with the coital orgasm rates generally reported for individual couple therapy. Unfortunately, the cause of this difference cannot be clearly identified. The group therapy format used differed from individual therapy in one additional and probably crucial way: Male sexual partners were not included in this group therapy program, as they are in most individual therapy. Whether the poorer results were caused by the group format or by failure to include the male partners is an issue awaiting further research.

38

Group Therapy for Nonorgasmic Women: Two Age Levels

Barbara Schneidman and Linda McGuire

Introduction

Current research involves experimentation with new modes of treatment for sexual dysfunction. Whereas, formerly, treatment of those individuals who defined themselves as sexually inadequate was primarily psychoanalytic, since 1970 a behavior modification approach to the treatment of sexual dysfunction, developed by Masters and Johnson, has been widely adopted by clinicians.

We report here the results of a group method of therapy for the treatment of female orgasmic dysfunction. In the development of the group paradigm, there was concern for the isolation of the female partner from the male. The consequences of creating a situation in which the female partner might feel responsible for the sexual inadequacy as a result of being singled out for treatment were considered. The treatment was an adaptation of the Masters and Johnson behavior modifica-

Barbara Schneidman • Department of Obstetrics and Gynecology, United States Public Health Service Hospital, Seattle, Washington   *Linda McGuire* • Department of Obstetrics and Gynecology and Department of Psychiatry, School of Medicine, University of Washington, Seattle, Washington

tion style of therapy plus a masturbation desensitization program developed by LoPiccolo and Lobitz (1972). The former program involves successive instructional steps that lead to a modification of sexual behavior by skill training and anxiety reduction. The latter technique involves a sequence of specific masturbation-related activities that the woman practices at home.

Subject Selection

Subjects met the following criteria: They had a stable relationship with their partner and had never experienced orgasm under any circumstances (except dreams). Thirty-five women were ultimately diagnosed as primary nonorgasmic, and were subdivided into those above age thirty-five (group B) and those below thirty-five (group A). Names were then chosen by random selection until two groups of ten women were selected.

Subject Preparation for Study

An appointment was made for an interview with the subject and her partner. The one-hour interviews were to determine the stability of the relationship and the degree of marital discord. Subjects with a recent history of extensive marital counseling or threat of divorce were excluded from therapy.

It was emphasized that although only the woman would be a group member the problem was not solely hers but rather a problem in the sexual relationship of the couple. It was determined whether male sexual dysfunction existed. If the couple expressed a concern over ejaculatory control, they were told that they would be instructed in the use of the squeeze technique. There was no evidence for other types of male dysfunction in the subjects selected.

The treatment program was outlined with emphasis on the duration of therapy and its associated required period of abstinence from intercourse. It was suggested that the man masturbate to orgasm with the same frequency that he had been having intercourse prior to therapy. This suggestion was made in order to decrease sexual tensions, relieve the female partner of sexual pressure, and allow the woman to be comfortable learning masturbatory techniques with the knowledge that her male partner was engaging in the same activity.

Measures

Three tests were administered. The short form of the Minnesota Multiphasic Personality Inventory (MMPI) was used to detect serious psychopathology that would exclude the couple from therapy. The Locke–Wallace Marital Adjustment Test (MAT) was used to provide information as to the subjective degree of happiness and areas of disagreement expressed by the couple in their relationship. A score of 100 or more on the MAT indicates a stable marriage with little evidence for disagreement (Locke and Wallace, 1959). The Sexual Responsiveness

Table 1.   Baseline Subject Data

	N	Female mean age	Male mean age	Age range Female	Age range Male	Number of years married	Number of children	Intercourse prior to marriage (%) Female	Intercourse prior to marriage (%) Male
Group A	10	29.4	34.4	23–34	24–37	6.6	1.6	30	40
Group B	10	40	43	35–48	36–53	17	2.9	60	70

Survey (SRS) was given to evaluate individual attitudes toward masturbation, premarital and extramarital sex, menstruation, genital size, simultaneous orgasm, nudity, and homosexuality (Pion, Anderson, and Wagner, 1970).

Subject Baseline Data

Group A consisted of ten white, middle-class, college-educated couples (Table 1). MAT scores averaged 114 for the women and 117 for the men. MMPIs were all within normal range. Seventy percent of the females and 60% of the males were virgins prior to marriage.

Group B consisted of ten white, middle-class, college-educated couples. MAT scores averaged 109 for the women and 108 for the men. MMPIs were all within normal range. Forty percent of the females and 30% of the males were virgins prior to marriage.

Treatment Methodology

The treatment program consisted of four components: educational and audiovisual instruction, group discussion, couple-oriented therapy, and self-stimulation therapy.

Educational and Audiovisual Component

Didactic presentations on areas of male and female reproductive anatomy, physiology of human sexual response with emphasis on the female response pattern, historical overview of social attitudes including cultural sources of inhibition of female sexuality, cross-cultural perspectives on human sexuality, use of sexual fantasy in promoting sexual arousal, and the use of communication techniques were given. Multimedia sexual education films were also used as well as the Glide Foundation *Yes* book on masturbation. Appropriate articles dealing with female sexuality were distributed to group members.

Group Discussion Component

Each session began with a brief report of each woman's reactions to the previous week's homework exercises. Further clarification and description of the instruction were often necessary at this time, as was reassurance when the outcome of the past week's exercise had been negative. In this latter instance, the other women in the group invariably became positive and supportive.

Each woman was given the opportunity to give a sexual history to the group and all of the women participated by giving a twenty- to thirty-minute history. Major background information was requested such as parental attitudes toward sex, religious attitudes, first dating experiences, first sexual experiences, and feelings about the relationship with the present partner.

"Masters and Johnson" Component

The "Masters and Johnson" component is similar to that described in *Human Sexual Inadequacy* (1970) for couples with female orgasmic dysfunction. Explicit instructions were given weekly to each woman to practice with her partner at home. They were told to abstain from intercourse, and a gradual program of sensual stimulation was introduced in order to build up natural tension increments and to increase sexual communication.

If the couple were concerned that premature ejaculation (by their own definition) was a problem, verbal as well as written instructions were distributed on the use of the squeeze technique, as described in *Human Sexual Inadequacy*. However, the method was modified in that the woman employed the squeeze on the man at her discretion rather than at his instruction, thus eliminating the need for the man to be "spectatoring" on himself and creating additional anxiety relating to his performance.

Self-Stimulation Component

Self-stimulation or training in masturbation is a logical adjunct to a learning theory approach to orgasmic dysfunction. Kinsey, Pomeroy, Martin, and Gebhard, (1953) reported that approximately 95% of women are successful in their masturbatory attempts whereas only 70% of the married women in their sample achieved orgasm during intercourse after at least one year of marriage. Therefore, it is more likely that a first orgasm can be achieved by oneself than with one's partner. Furthermore, Masters and Johnson (1966) reported that, based on various indices of physiological arousal, the highest responsivity was recorded during orgasms obtained through masturbation when compared to those obtained during intercourse or manual stimulation by a partner. In adopting a learning theory format, one would select the most intense and readily obtainable response to ensure its occurrence.

From a social and learning framework, it was decided that instruction in self-stimulation would desensitize the fears that many of these women voiced regarding their bodies in general and their genitals in particular. The self-stimulation program is a progressive nine-week technique that begins with visual exploration of the body and genitals, becoming more focused and intense each week. Vibrators were introduced if self-stimulation did not result in orgasmic response by the sixth week of therapy (LoPiccolo and Lobitz, 1972).

Data Evaluation

The success of the therapeutic program was determined by the ability of the woman to achieve an orgasm and by her attitude change. The latter was measured by the Marital Adjustment Test (MAT) and the Sexual Responsiveness Survey (SRS).

The first follow-up was made three months after treatment, when each woman was interviewed privately by the cotherapy team. The second contact was a mailed follow-up questionnaire, which dealt with the ability of the female partner to achieve orgasm and documented new sexual behaviors practiced by the couple. Change was evaluated for statistical significance across groups.

Results

Seventy percent of group A women reported that they were orgasmic with vibrator stimulation, masturbation, or partner stimulation by the end of the ten-week treatment. None was orgasmic with intercourse. The three-month follow-up showed no change. With 100% follow-up participation, the six-month follow-up reported 80% of the women orgasmic with vibrators, masturbation, or a vibrator used with intercourse. Group B women reported that 40% were orgasmic at the termination of therapy. None was orgasmic with intercourse. The three-month follow-up showed no change. With all ten members participating, the six-month follow-up reported 60% of the women orgasmic with vibrators, self-stimulation, or partner-related activities. One woman was orgasmic with intercourse 50% of the time (see Tables 2A and 2B).

In group A, the frequency of intercourse had increased from one or two times a week to two or three times a week. The single individual whose frequency decreased became pregnant shortly after treatment started and volunteered that this was the contributing cause. One subject, who remained nonorgasmic at therapy termination, was in her second trimester of pregnancy during the treatment, was uncomfortable with her body, and was not motivated to do the self-stimulation exercises. In group B, three of the ten women had totally ceased self-stimulation: one because of lack of interest, another because of her failure to attain orgasm, and the third because of a "frightening" experience associated with vibrator stimulation (the episode was not described further). The frequency of intercourse had increased for one and remained the same for nine. Seven subjects reported that sexual communication had improved.

Table 2A.   Incidence of Noncoital Orgasmic Frequency

	N	Termination of therapy	N	3-month follow-up	N	6-month follow-up
Group A	10	70%	10	70%	10	80%
Group B	10	40%	10	40%	10	60%

*Table 2B.   Methods by Which Orgasm Was
Attained at 6-Month Follow-Up*

Group A
  Vibrator only   2 (self or with partner)
  Self-stimulation
    or vibrator   3
  Vibrator used with
    intercourse or alone   3

Group B
  Self-stimulation only   2
  Self-stimulation,
    partner stimulation,
    vibrator alone, or
    intercourse alone   1
  Vibrator only   1 (self or with partner)
  Self-stimulation or
    partner stimulation   1

In group A, the SRS revealed seven couples with no change in areas of agreement or disagreement and three couples who stated that there was more agreement after treatment. In group B, the SRS revealed ten couples with no change in areas of disagreement or agreement.

MAT scores were tabulated for the two groups (see Table 3), showing a significant positive change for the group A female partners.

Discussion

Group treatment appears to be a highly effective method of changing patterns of sexual response in women as shown by the high percentages of women who were able to achieve an orgasmic response during or after treatment. Group A women (under age thirty-five) experienced orgasm at an earlier time in therapy, and a greater percentage of them were orgasmic at the termination of therapy. Masters

Table 3.   MAT Scores

		Pretreatment			Posttreatment			
	N	Mean	Median	Range	Mean	Median	Range	p value[a]
Group A								
Female	10	114	123	89–138	124	128	106–139	$.05 < p < .10$
Male	10	117	118	99–138	124	125	114–144	.01
Group B								
Female	10	109	118	62–135	113	120	61–138	.20
Male	10	108	107	63–142	111	112	82–148	.20

[a]Using Wilcoxon signed-rank test.

and Johnson report a success rate of 83% at follow-up (which they do not define as coital vs. noncoital orgasm) for all primary nonorgasmic women. The group method appears to be less successful for older women, who may have better results in a couple-oriented therapy. Masters and Johnson report a success rate of 60% at follow-up for all women over fifty. However, this figure includes all varieties of sexual dysfunction.

During the treatment program, some of the women in both groups stated that this therapy appeared to be a potential threat to their partners in that as they became more assertive the men became increasingly anxious while observing their partners' new behaviors. Before their partners' therapy, the men had generally been the initiators of the coital experience and the women had usually been passive recipients who felt obligated to participate. Once the women were instructed to initiate sexual activity as homework exercises, the men reacted either by being very supportive of their mates' activities or, in four couples, by becoming increasingly resistant and refusing to cooperate fully with the exercises. It was necessary to call a meeting of all the male partners of group A, between the fifth and sixth sessions, to discuss their anxieties and treatment goals. This was not necessary with group B men, perhaps because the sexual behavior change was slower in this group.

Although weekly meetings were satisfactory at the beginning, two meetings per week after the fifth session might have been more effective because new sexual feelings were developing rapidly and needed clarification. For example, there were several women who urinated with their initial orgasms, thereupon ceasing self-stimulation.

Lack of attainment of coital orgasm did not appear to be an issue with these couples. In the educational sessions dealing with the anatomy and physiology of human sexual response, information about orgasmic response being dependent on direct or indirect clitoral stimulation made it apparent that achievement of an orgasm during coitus may be difficult unless a coital position is maintained where there is effective clitoral stimulation. Also, there was such an obvious enhancement of sexual relations and communication techniques that coital orgasm was not a therapy goal. Most couples found that the sexual relationship continued to improve after therapy, which is consistent with Barbach's findings (1974) in her preorgasmic women's groups that the transfer of orgasmic capacity to partner-related activities usually occurred within eight months of termination.

In utilizing group therapy, the issue of why not treat five couples instead of ten women arises. The group members were candid about and supportive of other members' experiences and might have felt inhibited with men present. This method could certainly be used with women whose partners were not available on a weekly or regular basis and could also be adapted for use with single women without partners.

Two men manifested secondary impotence when the demand was placed on them to "perform" and provide an erect penis. The problem was easily solved by having the woman share with her partner the fact that this was also happening with the other men occasionally and was not atypical under these stressful circumstances. In reality, a small number appear to have this complaint, and it was not felt to be a major problem. Perhaps because the male partners are not seen weekly some of these issues or problems are hidden.

Table 4.   *Orgasmic Success at 6-Month Follow-Up*
versus History of Premarital Coitus

		Orgasmic	Nonorgasmic
Females ($N = 20$)			
Virgins	11	9	2
Nonvirgins	9	5	4
Males ($N = 20$)			
Virgins	9	8	1
Nonvirgins	11	6	5

The ten-week format implied that the subjects would have ten weeks in which to achieve an orgasm. This produced considerable goal-oriented anxiety. It was emphasized, however, that orgasm is a small part of one's sexuality and that pleasure seeking between partners would be a more appropriate goal. The exercises have a tendency to program sexual activity for the ten weeks, and several women reported that their "libido" increased after therapy.

Nine of the twenty men in both groups had never had sexual intercourse at the time of their marriage. Kinsey's data suggest that we dealt with an atypical population in regard to incidence of premarital intercourse. Otherwise, the groups were fairly representative of white middle-class Americans. Table 4 compares orgasmic success at the six-month follow-up to the history of both mates' sexual activity prior to marriage. From these data, it is unclear whether any conclusions can be drawn as to predicting the success of the therapy based on the knowledge of a couple's previous sexual activity. Perhaps the naïveté experienced by the virginal couples and lack of negative sexual experiences led to greater success in these couples.

In conclusion, the overall success rate for the women under age thirty-five was consistent with the experience of Masters and Johnson. It was easier to change behavior and attitudes in this group than in the older group B women. The group B women were more resistant, having a lower rate of orgasmic success at the end of therapy.

References

Barbach, L. G. Group treatment of preorgasmic women. *Journal of Sex and Marital Therapy*, 1974, *1*, 139–145.

Hastings, D. W. *A doctor speaks on sexual expression in marriage.* Boston: Little, Brown, 1966.

Kinsey, A. C., Pomeroy, W. B., Martin, C. E., and Gebhard, P. H. *Sexual behavior in the human female.* Philadelphia: Saunders, 1953.

Locke, H. J., and Wallace, K. M. Short marital adjustment and prediction tests: Their reliability and prediction. *Marriage and Family Living*, 1959, *21*, 251–258.

LoPiccolo, J., and Lobitz, W. C. The role of masturbation in the treatment of orgasmic dysfunction. *Archives of Sexual Behavior*, 1972, *2*, 163–171.

Masters, W. H., and Johnson, V. E. *Human sexual response.* Boston: Little, Brown, 1966.

Masters, W. H., and Johnson, V. E. *Human sexual inadequacy.* Boston: Little, Brown, 1970.

Pion, R. N., Anderson, S. N., and Wagner, N. N. *Sexual responsiveness survey.* Seattle: Northwest Counseling Associates, 1970.

Stone, A., and Levine, L. Group therapy in sexual maladjustment. *American Journal of Psychiatry,* 1952, *197*, 195–202.

Perhaps no aspect of sex therapy has received so much notoriety as the use of surrogate partners in the treatment of patients who do not have a sexual partner. Although advocating the incorporation of actual sexual experiences (body work exercises) between male patient and female cotherapist, Williams clearly distinguishes the surrogate experience from what he calls "individual sex therapy."

The premise on which individual sex therapy is based is an intriguing one: that an important part of therapy is eliciting genuine reactions in the patient by placing him in stressful "real-life" sexual situations. In this way, the patient is forced to confront and express those thoughts, feelings, and fears that have served to inhibit sexual arousal in the past. With the help of the female cotherapist, the patient learns to deal with these feelings in a nonhostile environment.

A serious criticism of this approach is the lack of any validating data on patient characteristics or treatment outcome, including follow-up to see if treatment effects generalize to sexual partners other than the female cotherapist. Before such a radical therapy approach can receive serious professional consideration, methodologically sound controlled studies need to be done to answer the question "When, and for what types of patients, with what dysfunctions, is this treatment effective?" Williams's statement that "our approach does not require us to screen out severely disturbed patients" seems to imply that this form of sex therapy is appropriate for all patients. It would seem, however, that a careful evaluation of a patient's ability to cope with the stress inherent in the program should be made. This is often done in the more traditional forms of sex therapy, which also involve a degree of stress for the couple or individual (see Lobitz, Part II, Chapter 5).

One limitation of this approach as presented here is its focus on dealing with the stresses of new relationships. The usefulness of using such an approach with a patient who is experiencing sexual dysfunction in the context of a monogamous committed relationship has not been shown.

39

Individual Sex Therapy

Martin H. Williams

Individual sex therapy is a direct, behavioral approach, which is intended to supercede the surrogate technique described by Masters and Johnson (1970). This new approach has been contrasted with the old elsewhere (e.g., Apfelbaum, 1977; Greene, 1977), and the present effort will focus only on describing the new one. I will talk about individual sex therapy in two parts: First, I will go through its procedures, and then I will present a brief overview and statement of its rationale.

Procedures

Patients seeking individual sex therapy have been almost exclusively men. More than 500 have consulted with us during the past five years. About half are

This paper was originally presented at the Second Annual Meeting of the Eastern Association for Sex Therapy, Philadelphia, Pennsylvania, March 1976.

Martin H. Williams • Berkeley Sex Therapy Group, Berkeley, California

self-referred, having heard of us through the media, and the rest are referred by mental health professionals or physicians. Currently, most of our new patients come from outside the San Francisco Bay area, either from elsewhere in California, from out of state, or from abroad.

New patients begin with one or more individual consultation sessions. This brief psychotherapy or sex counseling is sufficient to resolve the presenting problems of many who consult with us, and they do not go on to individual sex therapy. For those who do continue, the initial consultation sessions require at least two hours, with part of that time serving as an orientation helping the patient relate his specific problem to the procedures of our program. Our approach does not require us to screen out severely disturbed patients.

Following the initial consultation, the patient begins the four-hour daily sequence that constitutes individual sex therapy. There are two separate sessions in this sequence: body work followed by review. These may be repeated any number of times depending on the severity of the symptom. Ten days, scheduled consecutively, has been the typical treatment duration for the 246 cases we have seen over the past five years.

The Body-Work Session

The body-work session takes place at the office of a female cotherapist, whom we call the body-work therapist, and lasts 2½ hours. This session is the part of our therapy that has received the most publicity. Its central element is the *prospect* of structured sexual body work. Although the patient's emotional state will force us to avoid or curtail the body work on certain days, its prospect is always psychologically significant. It is this prospect that provokes the patient's idiosyncratic emotional reactions to situations that seem potentially sexual. Because such reactions can be analyzed and changed when they occur in the therapeutic context, the body work serves as the catalyst that enables us to work rapidly even when dealing with severe or long-standing problems.

For example, the body-work therapist and patient might begin a session by talking about the patient's reactions to what took place on the previous day. This might be enough to start the patient worrying about whether *he* should be instigating the assignments: "Is she waiting until I make the first move?" "Is this a test to see how shy I am?" Or he might start wondering if *she* is stalling: "She wants to keep me talking so she won't have to do the body work." Reactions with this degree of specificity might be unavailable for years in conventional verbal psychotherapy.

The body work itself consists of structured behavioral assignments like those developed by Masters and Johnson for couples. Although we have added or altered specific assignments, their metamessage is unchanged: Sexual arousal can occur in a noncompulsive, unhurried way, and it can be interrupted and resumed. For individual sex therapy, most of the exercises put the patient in the passive role with his, rather than his partner's, arousal being the focus.

Although similar in structure, the assignments are not used for the same purpose in individual sex therapy as they are in standard couple sex therapy. The patient is not encouraged to focus on sensation or even to stick with the assignment. Instead, he is taught to notice and talk about the emotional reactions to his partner and to himself that the assignments arouse in him.

For example, while stroking the body-work therapist the patient might find himself thinking: "She is bored, she's just doing this out of pity for me; I can't stroke her well like other men can" or "Why don't I have an erection yet?"

These thoughts are, obviously, worrisome for the patient. He fears that as long as he continues to think like this, he won't get turned on. Our position, however, is the opposite of his. We find that as long as he tries to suppress such thoughts, as long as he desperately tries to "think sexy" he will feel pressured and turned-off. So we interrupt his self-defeating cycle and encourage him to allow *all* his thoughts. He is taught for the first time in his life to become conscious and analytical of his stress reactions to the sexual situation.

The body-work therapist plays an active role in these sessions. On one hand, she is a therapist; she "alter-egos" the patient's emotional reactions in order to help him become more aware of them. She might say something like this, for example, during a body-work session: "At that point when you saw me look out the window, you seemed hurt. You looked like you felt rejected, like I really didn't care about you and I was daydreaming, and you wouldn't want to say anything to me about that because you'd be afraid that would alienate me." She helps bring out his inner voice—the voice he is convinced his sex partners can't stand knowing about.

At the same time, she is a candid *partner*. She notices the reactions that he evokes in her, and she discusses them with him. An example might be something as simple as: "At that point when you told me you felt scared, I felt relieved and closer to you." Her disclosure of such emotional reactions is a central element of the therapy. These reactions of hers, and of women in general, rather than any particular physical event, are what the patient needs the most help coping with. He is afraid that he will cause her to feel rejected and that any such feelings which he evokes in her will be irreversible, ending any possibility of their becoming turned on. By being exposed to her reactions, he has an opportunity to learn how to handle them.

The dual role of therapist and partner is very difficult for this sex therapist to perform. It is based on the premise that a relationship can exist primarily for the benefit of one of the partners—the same idea on which talk therapy is predicated. For this premise to be actualized, the body-work therapist must make decisions in the relationship based solely on considerations of the patient's dynamics and our theory of sexual arousal. In other words, what she does in the relationship should be based on real decisions, instead of on her unconscious defenses and impulses that might be disguised as decisions. This is a tall order, and the danger exists that she will fall into the kind of unconscious acting-out that would victimize the patient or jeopardize the therapy. She would have difficulty maintaining her objectivity when, for example, the patient says: "You are only doing this kind of work because you're afraid of men. You have to be so analytical and talk about feelings in order to keep me at a distance. You really enjoy watching me suffer, and you don't want me to improve." (I took these quotations from a borderline patient we recently saw.) Were it not for her cotherapist serving in a detached role and helping her maintain perspective on the relationship, this therapy would be impossible.

The Review Session

Her cotherapist enters the picture as the review therapist in the daily, hour-long review session, which is held following the body work. In this second half of our daily sequence the patient and cotherapists compare their three viewpoints on what took place in the body work. The review therapist helps them analyze the dynamics of the relationship from the point of view of someone who has heard both descriptions of what went on. Unlike a therapist listening to a standard couple, however, he has the advantage of conferring daily with one member of this special couple and sharing her theoretical stance.

On a typical day, the review therapist might include an observation like this one in his remarks: "So you thought that Bill just wanted to talk to get some ideas straight about his feeling of desperation. But now it seems that, really, Bill was afraid to be stroked again and he was stalling. He was afraid to let you touch him because he'd then have to get turned on, and he was afraid that he wouldn't. He couldn't tell you this because he imagined that you'd force him to do the assignment." The patient is often surprised to find in these sessions that sense can be made of what he had thought to be meaningless or immutable behaviors. He discovers what causes his idiosyncratic ways of coping with the structured assignments and with his therapist-partner.

For the body-work therapist these sessions are invaluable. She often feels rescued, either from a sense of helplessness that the patient has induced or from unconsciously participating in the patient's self-defeating system. The omission of such sessions from the Masters and Johnson surrogate approach may have been the chief cause of what they called "psychosocial strain," which they felt limited the number of patients the surrogate could see to no more than one per year.

Because we have found these review sessions so helpful, we began making duplicate audio cassettes of them about two years ago. The second copy is given to the patient, and he studies it before the next day's body work.

During this same interval, between review and body-work sessions, the co-therapists confer without the patient. They discuss his progress, suggest plans for the next day, and share any perspectives on him which could not be discussed in his presence due to considerations of timing.

Overview

I would like to give an overview of how we think about the individual sex therapy situation, especially what we see the patient getting from it.

I would say that the main thing we are doing is showing the patient how he can turn on by *including himself* in sexual relationships. We are teaching him how to confront his partner with his complaints, insecurities, and doubts—with all of the feelings that are very real to him but that he has always excluded from sexual relationships. He had considered these feelings countersexual.

The individual male patient, regardless of his performance symptom, is consistent in his wish to bypass his frightened, hopeless, depressed, or, in general, *turned-off* side. He fears that thinking or talking about these feelings in a relationship will lead to a more lasting turn-off rather than resolution. Yet his attempts to bypass these feelings fail. He unsuccessfully tries to be: up for the party, just out for a good time, turned on, and lighthearted. He tries to fantasize, or focus just on sensation, but he is too insecure in new relationships for such bypassing strategies to work. They fail, and the failures intensify the crisis.

The idea of seeing a surrogate, by the way, fits right into this wish to become better at bypassing. "If only the women could be made a little less real," he hopes, "perhaps I'd be able to practice performing without encountering my insecurities." Unfortunately, he discovers that even this partner remains too real for him to feel secure. What he really needs to learn is how to stop trying to bypass.

In a way, you could say that the individual male patient believes too strongly in the "joy of sex" (Comfort, 1972). So much so that he is left with no way to deal with the stress of sex, the numbness of sex, or the depression of sex—feelings that he does experience. He keeps trying to concentrate on the joy, and in the midst of so doing his performance symptom occurs. What he needs to notice, first of all, is that he is experiencing *something other than joy*.

Now there is nothing new about this part of what we do. Other forms of intensive psychotherapy also take unconscious sexual and relationship insecurities and make the patient conscious of them. What *is* unusual is our access to a situation that intensifies a person's sexual insecurities to such an extent that they take on a vivid reality. It is one thing for an individual patient to announce that he fears rejection from women. It's quite another for him to be visibly shaken because he fears that he has caused this woman sitting across from him to wish never to see him again.

Almost every patient finds individual sex therapy a crisis. He feels that he must turn on to a stranger, a woman who seems sexually secure, and who, by virtue of her professional relationship to him, gives him no basis to believe that she feels caring, or even concerned, let alone loving. Our program allows him to project onto this sex therapist the same insecurities he feels with any partner. Thus, the reactions he has to our time-limited sessions parallel those to his time-limited dates. His idea that the body-work therapist can't possibly get any gratification from him is the same idea he always has about women.

Once the patient becomes more aware of his insecurities, we teach him how to feel more secure. We teach the patient to achieve a state we call a *contact turn-on*. If the usual way of turning on is a matter of friction plus fantasy, the contact turn-on is based on friction plus intimacy. *The patient turns on by virtue of being able to express his turned-off emotions to his partner.* He learns to talk about feeling afraid, rejected, hostile, hopeless about the therapy, and helpless to change himself. He talks about, rather than defending against, his depression or anxiety.

This can have dramatic effects. It is not uncommon for the patient to finally admit during the genital stroking assignment: "I am turned off. I find you mechanical, this whole therapy feels mechanical, and I'm getting nothing out of what you're doing now." Nor is it uncommon for such an admission to be immediately followed by a strong surge of sensation, and a full erection.

Surrogates Not Viable

Because of its relationship focus, our approach is viable where the surrogate one is not. Apart from the body work, the surrogate approach bears little resemblance to ours. It does not focus on the relationship but only on certain sexual events. Its model is Masters and Johnson's (1970) couple therapy, a therapy that is specifically designed for existing couples *who do not have significant psychodynamic problems.* Yet the surrogate approach would be applied by some, Masters and Johnson's warnings notwithstanding, to a brand new relationship in which one of the partners is sexually insecure. We tried this ourselves when we first started treating individuals.

The surrogate approach requires, like the couple approach after which it is modeled, that the partners: are not afraid of each other, trust each other, and *are able to keep their neuroses out of the bedroom.* Yet that approach includes no techniques to create such conditions; one can only hope that they occur spontaneously. The exclusive therapeutic maneuver of the surrogate approach is the behavioral assignment, and the only strategy available to keep the patient focused on these assignments is the standard behavioral one of authoritative exhortation.

Because of these technical limitations, this approach seems suited only for the rare male patient who *is* comfortable with women and *is* able to feel secure in new relationships but who has a highly specific sexual dysfunction that is not psychodynamically determined. We have treated such patients, but they account for no more than 5% of our population. Treatment in such cases has been a simple matter of specific desensitization and sex education.

The majority of individual patients need the more complex relationship focus offered by individual sex therapy. Their symptoms occur due to the stress of new relationships, and a new relationship is what they need if their symptoms are going to be addressed. A new relationship highlights the patient's insecurities because it provides no opportunity for him to develop the protective and avoidant habits that one finds in established couples. Yet the original surrogate approach, which we have obviously revised radically, is based on ignoring the stressful aspects of the relationship that are due precisely to its newness; the relationship is treated as if it were an established marriage.

These patients who need to be confronted with their real reactions to a new relationship should not get a surrogate instead.

References

Apfelbaum, B. The myth of the surrogate. *Journal of Sex Research*, 1977, *13*(4) (in press).
Comfort, A. *The joy of sex*. New York: Simon and Schuster, 1972.

Greene, S. Resisting the pressure to become a surrogate: A case study. *Journal of Sex and Marital Therapy*, 1977, *3*(1), 40–49.

Masters, W. H., and Johnson, V. E. *Human sexual inadequacy*. Boston: Little, Brown, 1970.

This chapter discusses the traditional psychodynamic objections to symptom-focused sex therapy and offers the sex therapist's reply. Although the article was written some years ago, this debate still goes on.

An emerging trend, however, is for therapists no longer to hold to an exclusively psychodynamic or behavioral position on the etiology and treatment of sexual dysfunctions, but instead to attempt to integrate these different viewpoints. Most clinicians agree that there are personality and life-history factors in the etiology of sexual dysfunctions; a dysfunction is not just a "bad habit." Yet it is not necessary to spend large amounts of time on these factors in some cases to get good results; a direct symptomatic focus can work. There is nothing logically inconsistent in this position, as the original cause of a dysfunction can be entirely separate from the factors that currently maintain it.

40

The Psychiatrists versus Masters and Johnson

Vivian Cadden

Once upon a time—and it seems like a long time ago—there was no doubt in anyone's mind that sex problems were the result of a childhood gone astray. Mother and Father were the villains, of course, and it was certain that the impotent man and what used to be called the "frigid" woman got that way around the age of three or four, reinforced by some further horrendous experiences during adolescence.

It followed, therefore, like the night upon the day, that the only way to unravel a current sexual dilemma was indeed to unravel it—to take the long, long trail from the unsatisfactory marriage bed back to childhood and Mother and there find the source of the trouble. This meant some kind of therapy, whether psychoanalysis or less ambitious forms, which dealt not only, or even specifically, with the sex problem at issue, but which ranged over a whole gamut of recollections, experiences, and problems.

Today, while many experts would give at least a nodding agreement to the first proposition—that sexual inadequacy probably has some origins in the whole web of an adult's childhood experiences, there are nevertheless an increasing number who

Vivian Cadden • New York, New York. Ms. Cadden is an editor of *McCall's* Magazine. She was formerly on the board of the Sex Information and Educational Council of the United States (SIECUS).

find the second proposition a non sequitur. Even if Mother is the culprit, they don't believe that it is necessary or even wise to dredge up the details of her villainy. They believe that most sex problems can be treated in the here and now.

Dr. William Masters and Mrs. Virginia Johnson are the apotheosis of the here-and-now treatment of sex problems. Their two-week clinic sessions in St. Louis with couples seeking help spend a minimum of time excavating the past. True, Masters and Johnson take a very detailed sexual history and their account of the treatment process contained in their new book, *Human Sexual Inadequacy*, has passing references to such familiar and baleful factors and figures as The Dominant Mother, The Dominant Father, Religious Orthodoxy, and GUILT. Nevertheless Masters and Johnson are committed to the treatment of sexual dysfunction regardless of its origin. And it is this short shrift that they give to the sources of the problem and their belief that in a sense sexual problems can be isolated from other problems that first earned them the enmity of those specialists in origins and interrelatedness, the psychoanalysts and psychoanalytically oriented therapists.

The rift between Masters and Johnson and certain wings of psychiatry got off to an early start even before the publication of their first book, *Human Sexual Response*. In a brilliant and often uproariously funny article, entitled, "I'm Sorry, Dear," Dr. Leslie H. Farber, a Washington, D.C., psychoanalyst, mercilessly spoofed the cult of simultaneous, self-conscious, split-second satisfaction, used Masters and Johnson as the prime examples of his thesis that "sex for the most part has lost its viability as a human experience," and delivered a withering blast against what he considered the tasteless and atypical aspects of sex as studied in the laboratory.

Farber was followed, upon publication of the book, by a goodly number of others. "Mechanical," "mechanistic," "dehumanizing," "depersonalizing" were among the favorite words of the critics.

Now, with the publication of *Human Sexual Inadequacy* the battle lines have been drawn again but with one very important difference. In the four years between the appearance of these two books there has been a significant shift within psychiatry from the long-term delving into the origins of problems and the global aim of changing "the whole person" to the here-and-now treatment of current difficulties. This applies not only to sex problems but to many, varied, specific complaints and distresses that patients may bring to a therapist.

"Mechanical," "mechanistic," "dehumanizing," and "depersonalizing" are still the favorite adjectives of the critics of the new Masters and Johnson study. But there are fewer voices and even those that are heard are, for the most part, somewhat muted.

One pillar of psychoanalytic orthodoxy still remains to state the pure, classical position. Dr. Natalie Shainess, a New York psychoanalyst, was one of the most vocal critics of the earlier study. Not surprisingly, reporters sought her out upon publication of the new book and Dr. Shainess was quoted as calling the study "oversimplistic and naïve." It was, she said, merely a way of "papering over" symptoms, which, because they arose from deep-seated and fundamental problems, would be certain to reappear.

Dr. Shainess feels something of a sense of mission in her attack on the whole range of Masters and Johnson's work. She is particularly blistering about their therapy for the problem of premature ejaculation, since it involves a specific technique that can be easily taught, is reportedly almost 100% foolproof, and has all the hallmarks of a sexual "gimmick."

"Is that sex?" Dr. Shainess asks with withering scorn. "That's manipulation! What happens to a person's ego in that kind of sex? A man must feel like a puppet. What kind of ongoing process can it be when a woman must do this or do that? That's just a parody of sexual intercourse! Press here. Touch there. That's joyless sex!"

Behind sexual inadequacy, Dr. Shainess believes, there is always anxiety, fear, hatred or rage—or a combination of these. The genesis of sexual disturbances lies somewhere deep in the past and there are no shortcuts to their alleviation. While Dr. Shainess does not claim that psychiatry is always successful in freeing people so that they may know joyful sex, she dismisses the Masters and Johnson approach as a kind of "coaching that reduces one partner to a push-button operator."

But, as Dr. Shainess is the first to admit, hers is fast becoming an extreme minority position within her profession. "I'm on lonely ground," she says. "I don't know why the psychiatrists are jumping on the Masters and Johnson bandwagon. I wish I knew. They seem glad to have a sexual bible."

If not all psychiatrists have "jumped on the bandwagon" it is true that most of them are viewing the Masters and Johnson work with greater respect than they did four years ago. The change has paralleled their greater respect for the treatment of symptoms, behavioral problems, and inadequate functioning of all kinds, apart from and regardless of their source. It is not that they have altogether given up their search for reasons and origins and sources but rather their growing conviction that help need not wait upon complete understanding.

John H. Gagnon, associate professor of sociology at State University of New York and formerly a senior research fellow at the Kinsey Institute, points out that what Masters and Johnson are doing is akin to "behavior therapy."

"Behavior therapy," Gagnon says, "treats the presenting problem. If you have a phobia about rats, it tries to desensitize you to rats. If you have a fear of high places, it tries to tackle that fear of high places. No need to drag Mother into it."

Gagnon believes that the trouble with traditional psychoanalysis is that it assumed too much continuity between childhood and adulthood. The man who is afraid of flying may never have fallen out of the apple tree as a child and even if he did, and now understands that he did and remembers how unpleasant that was, it may have very little bearing on his ability to muster the strength to board a plane. A kind of psychiatric Dramamine (plus Dramamine) might be of greater help.

Until relatively recently, Gagnon says, psychiatry has proceeded on the premise that if you understand something, you can do something about it. If you know how someone made a lock you can then make keys to open it. If you understand the etiology of a symptom or a disease—if you know how it came about—you can cure it. "But," Gagnon says, "it's not necessarily so—as psychiatrists are more and more admitting.

"What Masters and Johnson (and behavior therapy) recognize is that the symptom takes on a life of its own, a functional autonomy, that in turn creates other problems. Regardless of where it came from—and obviously sexual inadequacy can come from a myriad of sources—it's there, operating as a here-and-now factor in a marriage. And if the symptom can be treated who are we to say that this is not a *profound* change in the life of a human being."

Gagnon believes that some psychiatrists, "particularly run-of-the-mill ones," have had a tendency to be "uptight" about Masters and Johnson because prior to their advent it was the psychiatrist and the psychiatrist alone who was "Dr. Sex."

"It was threatening enough to the profession when Masters and Johnson set about with their original research into the nature of sexual response. But now that they have gone into therapy many traditional therapists will be as jittery as the plumbers union is when faced with a possible incursion of blacks into their ranks."

Gerald Caplan, professor of clinical psychiatry at the Harvard Medical School and director of the Laboratory of Community Psychiatry, feels that the point of view exemplified by Dr. Shainess is probably related to the very skewed sample of the population that analysts are likely to see.

"These are often extremely disturbed people whose sex problems are only one part of some very deep pathology," Dr. Caplan says. "I can understand how in such cases dealing with the sex problem can be thought of as merely 'papering over' symptoms—although in some cases that in itself can be helpful. In other cases, if the sex problem is the only outlet for the pathology, removing it might make matters even worse.

"There are fat people whose obesity is one expression of deep disturbances. Solving the obesity problem would 'paper over' other problems yet it might be a positive step forward. There are other fat people whose fatness is the *sole* expression of deep disturbances. If you take away their obesity, they might become depressed and psychotic."

But such considerations, Dr. Caplan believes, whether about sex or obesity, apply only to a very tiny minority—perhaps 5%—of the people who need help.

"For most people," Dr. Caplan says, "sex problems may very well have emerged from relatively mild conflicts. The symptoms have then perpetuated themselves and thus brought on secondary symptoms. Removing such symptoms is not only possible, it produces an ego strength that is good. It makes people feel better."

Dr. Caplan estimates that at least 60% of sexual problems arise out of problems that are no longer active—ignorance at some past time, failing on a wedding night and having failed once, failing twice and feeling then psychologically inept.

"Masters and Johnson's approach is a reeducation approach," Dr. Caplan says, "a kind of retraining approach. To call it 'mechanistic' plainly misses the pole. It is certainly true that sexual intercourse has its basis in instinctual life. It is a form of human interaction. But people often have to learn modes of interaction; they don't necessarily spring forth in full bloom. One might say that dancing and singing together are forms of human interaction—very ancient and important forms indeed—yet they can be learned.

"And sexual intercourse, like almost everything else, is a learned experience. Nor is there any inherent conflict between training and spontaneity. At the moment of being trained one must be highly conscious. But that training having been accomplished, one can be entirely spontaneous. One might even say that the training of a ballet dancer or a pianist or an actor is precisely what frees him to be spontaneous. Having mastery, he can throw away the book."

Dr. Caplan thinks that Masters and Johnson are up to something besides behavior therapy or symptom relief. In many cases of sexual inadequacy, the failing is not necessarily a "symptom." It's what Dr. Caplan calls "ineffective behavior." Masters and Johnson, he believes, are modifying ineffective behavior.

Traditional psychiatry and Masters and Johnson are at odds not only on the importance of the origins of sexual inadequacy and the efficacy of treating it ad hoc but also on the question of whether to treat one or both partners.

It is a cornerstone of the Masters and Johnson method that both partners in a marriage or a sexual relationship be treated together even though it may seem that only one has the problem. Not only do Masters and Johnson consider this approach crucial to their work; they suggest that the failure of traditional therapy in problems of sexual inadequacy can be laid at the door of the single-partner-treatment concept.

If only one partner is in treatment, Masters and Johnson say, the other partner may "destroy or negate" the treatment simply because he or she is not privy to what is going on and has no clues on how to act.

"For example," Masters and Johnson say, "if little or no information of sexual import, or for that matter of total treatment progress, reaches the wife of an impotent husband, she is in a quandary as to the most effective means of dealing with the ongoing marital relationship while her husband is in therapy. She does not know when, or if, or how, or under what circumstances to make sexual advances, or whether she should make advances at all. Would it be better to be simply a 'good wife' available to her husband's expression of sexual intent, or on occasion should she take the sexual initiative? During actual sexual functioning should she maintain a completely passive, a somewhat active, or a mutually participating role? None of these questions, all of which inevitably arise in the mind of any intelligent woman contending with the multiple anxieties and performance fears of an impotent husband, finds answers in the inevitable communications void that develops between husband and wife when one is isolated as a participant in therapy."

Dr. Caplan agrees completely with Masters and Johnson on the importance of treating both partners. But he feels that so many of his colleagues share this point of view that Masters and Johnson are "beating a dead horse" on this point. "I wouldn't conceive of treating a married couple or a pair of lovers with sexual problems without seeing each individually and/or both together," he says.

Harold Lief, professor of psychiatry and director of the Division of Family Study at the University of Pennsylvania School of Medicine, and one of the earliest and most enthusiastic supporters of the Masters and Johnson research, also concurs heartily that sexual problems can best be treated within the context of the marriage relationship. Dr. Lief, who is a past president of the Sex Information and Education Council of the United States (SIECUS), feels that the chances for success are much greater when both partners are involved.

"There are occasional exceptions as when one partner has deep-seated fears and phobias and inhibitions," Dr. Lief says. "Here psychiatry for that person seems to be indicated. But there's no guarantee that psychiatry will be able to do any better with such cases. For the vast bulk of cases of sexual inadequacy it makes eminently good sense to treat the couple."

Dr. Lief tells of a woman patient whom he had had in therapy for a long while, with no success. He referred her and her husband to Masters and Johnson and they went out to St. Louis for two weeks.

"She was paranoid, in a constant state of rage against her husband and what she described as his cruelty to her," Dr. Lief says. "He was an obsessive–compulsive and if not cruel, at least wholly insensitive to her needs."

After the couple had been in St. Louis for eleven days, Mrs. Johnson called Dr. Lief to report that the couple was having successful sexual relations for the first time in many years.

But five months later the wife was in a lawyer's office, raging again, and instituting divorce proceedings against her husband. Mrs. Johnson had taught them some tricks, she said. But that was the extent of it.

"Well," Dr. Lief remarks, "here was a case where we all failed."

No one knows better than Masters and Johnson that there will be failures. And indeed, it is probably the disarming modesty of their claims that will eventually serve to erase any conflict of interest between them and the psychiatrists.

The *New York Times* headlined its front-page story on the publication of *Human Sexual Inadequacy*, "80% Success Claimed for Sex Therapy." But that was the *Times* interpretation of Masters and Johnson's report of a 20% failure rate in their work. Masters and Johnson know that "success" is not the opposite of failure. By talking about failure, Masters and Johnson carefully put a limit on their goals. With calculated understatement, Masters and Johnson in effect define their objective as seeing to it that a sexually dysfunctional couple with a presenting complaint of, say, secondary impotence does not have that complaint upon leaving St. Louis after two weeks of therapy and continues not to have that complaint five years later.

The Masters and Johnson "successes," as some people call them, or non-failures, as Masters and Johnson would call them, may indeed find that "success" is not all that it is advertised to be. The nonorgasmic woman, orgasmic after therapy, may find that this experience is not the be-all and end-all of marriage. She may find that it's not sufficient to have a fundamentally poor relationship. The happy-go-lucky premature ejaculator may turn into a responsible, anxious, joyless provider of satisfaction to a wife who doesn't know which version of him is preferable. Possible. But Masters and Johnson have never pretended to solve all the ills of mankind, or even to save marriages.

In this article Linda Wolfe provides some appropriately caustic commentary on the use and misuse of surrogates in sex therapy. At present there is a great deal of variability of practice, with some surrogates working independently and others working closely with a therapist who is responsible for supervision and structure of therapy.

A large criticism of the work with surrogates that has been done so far is the absence of data on treatment effectiveness. The major question is whether or not any gains made in therapy will generalize to other relationships.

Recently, the American Psychological Association stated that sexual contact between patient and therapist is unethical. In light of this, the use of surrogates will probably be the subject of more intense scrutiny in the future.

41

The Question of Surrogates in Sex Therapy

Linda Wolfe

The woman I am talking with is getting dressed for her evening's work and is very much annoyed at the amount of preparation it is taking. "I hate getting dressed up only to get undressed," she says. "This guy tonight wants to have me look like I stepped out of a bandbox. I know that it's a cop-out when a guy says he'll never be able to make it with me because I'm too heavy for him, or he doesn't like the way I dress. But still, I may not be able to help him at all if I don't go along with it. I mean, I've got preferences, too. I won't take on a fat man, myself. So I'll spend forty-five minutes tonight getting dolled up."

I'll have to give her a fictitious name, and Pandora comes to mind, Pandora because she is, as far as I know, the first New York sexual surrogate to talk to the press, the first to open up that box of potential ugliness and ephemeral hope the lid of which has been kept tightly closed by most sex therapists. Pandora is in her early thirties, divorced, a mother—which is, she explains, her main reason for not wanting her name revealed—and a college graduate with a major in psychology. She has only recently become a sexual surrogate, a woman who treats men who are premature ejaculators or have potency problems by engaging in step-by-step sexual activity with them.

Pandora takes her referrals from various physicians and psychiatrists around town. She started out charging $500 for a set of twelve sessions, spread over a

Linda Wolfe • *New York* Magazine, New York, New York

fourteen-day period, three to four hours the session. She has just raised her fee to $750 and has found no decrease in the demand for her services. She has had, she reports, 100% success, but won't reveal the number of her cases. "If it's too few, people will say I'm inexperienced—which I'm not—and if it's too many, they'll say I'm a hooker—which I'm not."

The case Pandora is on tonight started four evenings ago with the "social session." She had instructed the patient to choose a place where they could get to know each other over dinner, but where they would be able to draw a bit closer after the meal by dancing to quiet music. He had picked a restaurant on Long Island. "A very good steak house." Pandora said admiringly. "A really good choice." She likes the social session. "And I do pet on the way home," she adds. "I know it's ridiculous, but I like to know what I've got coming to me."

The man, who was referred to her by a physician, had reported that he suffered from both premature ejaculation and occasional impotence. But later tonight after the fourth session, Pandora, breathless, reports to me that "it was incredible. I think I've discovered something entirely new. This guy didn't have premature ejaculation at all. He could keep going for a long time as long as I was doing the thrusting. And he wasn't impotent either. He went limp only when he had to do the thrusting. I haven't seen anything in the literature that quite describes it. It's so exciting. I think I'm going to write a paper on it."

Pandora is one of a small number of sexual surrogates now practicing in the New York area, and one of an ever-increasing and rather larger number of sex therapists here. Only a year and a half ago* I reported that New York had the then surprising number of five sex therapy clinics—surprising in that sex therapy itself had ballooned only in 1970 with the publication of Masters and Johnson's second volume, *Human Sexual Inadequacy*. Since that time, at least seven more hospital-related clinics have opened in the New York area. In addition, a handful of private sex clinics has sprouted.

The small town that was sex therapy is rapidly expanding, grabbing up territory, crossing the tracks, even sending up skyscrapers. Just a few weeks ago I met with Norman C. King, a media consultant who has now decided to become emperor of sex in New York by building a chain of clinics called "Male Potency Centers of America." He has polled 1,500 Wall Street executives earning over $40,000 and 1,500 men earning around $12,000 to see how many of them were (a) sometimes impotent and (b) interested in doing something about it. "In the mail-order business," King explains to me, "even a 5% return is considered fantastic. Imagine my astonishment when close to one-fourth of the men I wrote to actually phoned back to me and said they were sometimes impotent and wanted to know what to do about it. That's how Male Potency Centers of America got born."

Actually, King's chain of clinics is still fetal. It exists in a detailed financial prospectus in King's office in the Seagram Building. But like a host of other new and privately run sex clinics, it will be born next year. Sex therapy, what a friend of mine in the field calls "America's greatest cultural contribution after jazz," is about to become big business.

The use of sexual surrogates is one of the more controversial techniques available to sex therapists, although it is one of the best researched. Masters and

*This article was first published in 1973.

Johnson used it first, providing what they originally called "partner surrogates"—women they themselves selected—to engage in sexual activity with men who not only had sexual problems but also had personality problems that prevented them from finding partners of their own. When surrogate and man were carefully matched and guided, Masters and Johnson found that their therapy worked about as well as it did for men who entered treatment with their own loving wives and girl friends. Yet the use of surrogates is still considered questionable, largely because of the doubtful legal status of the surrogate (Is she a therapist? Or is she a prostitute, since she exchanges sexual services for money?).

Although there is no doubt that sexual surrogates are being used in New York, finding one to talk to is as difficult as finding an abortionist used to be. None of the prominent hospital-related sex clinics use surrogates, although, as Dr. Helen Kaplan, head of the sex education program at New York Hospital's Payne Whitney Clinic, points out, "Not a week goes by that we don't get a request for a surrogate. The prevalence of the request and the fact that we have real difficulty in helping the single person who has a sexual dysfunction makes the question very important." At a private clinic I was told, "Even if we were using them, we wouldn't admit to it."

I have spoken to several private practitioners here who admit to using surrogates—usually call girls who charge $100 a night—but they will not let me interview their call girl/surrogates. Nor do they want their own names mentioned. Surrogates are about the last clandestine thing in town. Only one psychologist was willing to discuss the practice with me, and then only because he has given it up. This was Dr. Herbert Fensterheim, the behavior therapist, who found his first surrogate when an impotent patient himself brought a call girl into therapy. Fensterheim gave her instructions. "I assigned her chapter and verse of Masters and Johnson." And she proved a very adept student. The patient was cured; the call girl later expressed interest in taking on other cases. She tried a few and so did a friend she recommended. But Fensterheim, who was not secretive about his work, was soon besieged by colleagues who either criticized him or else wanted the women's phone numbers for use with their own impotent patients. "I began to feel like a procurer," Fensterheim says, "so I gave it up."

I finally found Pandora through the New York City Health Commissioner's office, which this fall was considering the nagging question of how to license various psychotherapy practitioners. Assistant Commissioner Robert Doud, in response to a question of mine concerning the licensing of surrogates, said his department had not yet given this matter heavy thought, but that he knew of one surrogate I might speak with. He gave me a number, which turned out to be Pandora's, and she, curiously, turned out to be a woman I already knew, in quite a different capacity.

I had met her and interviewed her a year ago when, as a student on a nearby campus, she was running a sex information club for students—not your ordinary garden-variety campus sex club with leaflets explaining birth control and listing low-cost abortion centers, but one that was, at Pandora's insistence, delving deeply into the heavier philosophical issues of sex. "We had rap sessions on everything," she told me then. "Like incest. Who better than a parent can introduce a child to sexuality? And on bestiality? Why not bestiality? Why is there any harm if some man or woman has only a pet and needs some sexual gratification and has no one but the pet to turn to?" She wasn't kidding. Indeed, she planned, she had told me then, to make sex her life work and had asserted, "I hope that ten years from now they'll speak of Pandora the way they speak of Masters and Johnson." I had known at that moment that all that ambition would have to lead somewhere.

So I got back in touch with Pandora. How had she fared since she left school? Quite well, it appeared. There were new clothes, a new hairdo, and, most surprising, a new confidence in her cultivated voice.

She began by telling me that "nothing could be less romantic, even less sexual, than a surrogate. You should make that clear. It's very manipulative; it's as if you were giving instruction in tennis." She went on to explain that basically what she does is program sexual activity for men complaining of premature ejaculation or secondary impotence—the kind that occurs often, or sometimes, or rarely, or only under certain circumstances and only with certain women. She spends one social session with her patients, and then holds at least one session of "sensate focus," during which both partners stroke and caress each other nongenitally. When the patient feels comfortable with these sensual stimuli, Pandora proceeds to the sexual. Now she and the man caress each other genitally until he is able to achieve and maintain erections for long periods of time. Ultimately she arrives at intercourse. During intercourse Pandora will strive first to make the man feel easy at just being inside her vagina; later she will progress to thrusting in the female-superior position. She rarely attempts the man-on-top position with her patients because, she tells me, it brings back memories for them of all the times they've tried it and failed; it is, she warns, the least promising position for a man with potency problems.

Pandora sees herself as a crusader for sexual freedom. Her interest in sex as a career dates back, she explains, to the time when she split up with her husband. She had become fond of sex during the marriage and then had the common female experience of finding it difficult to replace her husband with another appealing sexual partner. "I found this so hard. There are so few people around who are healthy sexually. And I got into a crusade."

Pandora went back to school and organized her sex club. Her new crusade gives her a daily conviction of usefulness that matters more than money; she points out that her fees are lower than those charged by call girls for comparable time, and lower than those charged by many sex therapists.

Still, she wants me to know it isn't all easy. There is, for one thing, her weight problem. She is five-foot-seven and weighs a hefty number above 165. "I always tell guys during the initial consultation that perhaps my weight will turn them off, and sometimes it does." She cannot handle more than two cases a month and has had to train a second surrogate to work with her to enable her to pursue her other interests, like lecturing at the Anthos Center on East 22nd Street on the joys of loving for singles. And she gets a lot of flak from friends and relatives. "My sister once wrote me an accusing letter," she told me. "She wrote, 'There are hundreds of thousands of people in the United States with gonorrhea and it's all due to people like you.'" Slurs like this deeply wound Pandora, among whose long-range goals are training a male surrogate to treat single women with orgasmic difficulties.

Although she receives referrals from physicians and therapists, Pandora does not work in conjunction with any other professional but is at once both therapist and sexual partner. Any other system would be costly and unproductive, she tells me, and since she has a background in psychology she feels competent to do the work she has chosen.

Because it was difficult to find a surrogate to talk to does not mean that Pandora is unique. In California this summer a mixed bag of sexual surrogates (some for men, some for women) banded together to form the first national surrogates' association. There were enough of them to set the goal of lobbying the state legislature to license them.

Many of the California surrogates consider themselves, as Pandora does, therapists first and foremost, and one of them, male "surrogate-therapist" Emerson Symonds, has even coined a name for the previously unchristened occupation: Direct Action Therapy. It is a far cry, and almost a primal scream, from the kind of therapy Masters and Johnson espoused. While they were the first therapists to design a program utilizing surrogates, they also were the first to point out that many doctors were sleeping with patients and that such treatment could be deleterious.

I have talked with several of the California surrogates—two of whom act as both therapists and surrogates at the Berkeley Group for Sexual Development, run by psychoanalyst Dr. Bernard Apfelbaum—and have found some surprising similarities among the women. Like the turn-of-the-century social workers, they view themselves as dedicated, as bent on service to mankind—in the old-fashioned sense of the expression. While Sharie Marler, a Berkeley surrogate, criticized her colleague, Sandi Enders, for describing to me her frequent orgasms with her male patients ("She [Enders] *gives* them to the male like gifts"), she too expressed all her qualifications as a surrogate in terms of giving. "What you need to be a surrogate is being able to go at somebody else's pace and being patient and being able to hear what somebody is saying other than just through their words." One of the California surrogates has treated a paraplegic; Pandora tells me she is starting surrogate therapy with a victim of cerebral palsy next week.

Who are the clients? Middle-class men exclusively. Apfelbaum's program costs $1,800 and often involves air fare to Berkeley and a hotel stay; Pandora says her clients are "mostly professionals or, if not, then educated men in any event; the kind of men to whose apartments I am not afraid to go, which is necessary since I cannot practice at home." They tend, in Apfelbaum's words, to be "super-responsible, driven individuals"; in Pandora's, "fussy and afraid of contact." Masters and Johnson had found the men who needed sexual surrogates to be "extremely vulnerable."

There are apparently many such men. Ralph Slovenko, prominent lawyer-philosopher of sex, feels that the current "sexual revolution" is more than just a reaction to Victorian-inherited repression. It is also, he says, "related to the prevalent society-wide sense of loneliness and self-estrangement." Slovenko finds isolation on every level of our lives: "Instead of walking or strolling or sitting outside, the American roams in a car, his box, and he encounters other boxes, not people. He lives isolated, lonely. . . . Man's work, be it on the assembly line or in the office, is fragmented to the point that it is replete with stereotyped, repetitive motions. . . . It is now necessary to readjust erections for daylight-saving time."

It is the kind of gloomy assessment of our world as alienating that underlies the hesitant acceptance that even some conventional therapists have given to the concept of the sexual surrogate. People are lonely, isolated; any contact is better than none. But the acceptance is merely theoretical. Few practitioners are ready to introduce surrogates into practice because they do not quite see how to translate the concept into reality. "It's more than just having a call girl or a woman who's paid," says Dr. Wardell Pomeroy, the city's most eminent sexologist and Kinsey's biographer. "The surrogate really has to be a paraprofessional, a psychological aide. She'd have to be supervised and brought into the treatment program, given homework and exact instructions for dealing with each case.

This isn't considered easy, although recommendations abound. In her forthcoming book, *Psycho-Sexual Transactions*, Martha Stein, a young social worker, advocates call girls as surrogates. Tucked away in closets and hidden behind one-way mirrors, she has observed over 1,200 transactions between johns and prostitutes and has found that many of the women she watched seemed downright supportive and therapeutic when confronted with timid or impotent males. The heads of two separate hospital sex therapy clinics here decided to act on Stein's recommendations and attempted to make contact with a few of her more therapeutic-sounding call girls. But the search for the proverbial golden-hearted hooker proved as difficult as Jason's search for the golden sheepskin. None of the women was willing to take on patient referrals; none contacted the clinic heads. Stein may have been less than forceful in urging the women to accept the proferred assignment since, as she says, "It did make me feel like I was being asked to be a madam," but the two clinicians are convinced that the call girls themselves did not want the supervision and exchange that working for a clinic would have entailed.

Masters and Johnson had made it clear that they didn't want to draw their surrogates from the call girl population. "To have used prostitutes," they wrote, "would have been at best clinically unsuccessful and at worst psychologically disastrous." So they used volunteer surrogates, 75% of whom held full-time employment in offices, academia, or medicine. A large number of the surrogates had experienced "sexually oriented trauma" within their immediate families—rape, homosexuality, impotence—and had humanistic yearnings to create a healthier sexual world. Yet even these surrogates sometimes disappointed Masters and Johnson. Musing, they once said to me, "You could call it coincidence if you like, but we never had a surrogate become emotionally involved with a man who didn't have money."

Masters and Johnson are no longer using surrogates, apparently because a lawsuit against them was undertaken by the husband of a woman suspected of being a surrogate. Yet they have never fully abandoned their support of the surrogate as a therapy approach that, when carefully utilized, is dramatically effective. "And who knows?" Masters said this summer. "Someday we might go back to the idea again." But they are emphatically opposed to the idea of the therapist as surrogate. They view all such arrangements as exploiting "the vulnerability of men and women lost in the maze of human sexual inadequancy," and simply want the practice stopped.

Lawyer Harriet Pilpel, who was honored last month by SIECUS, the Sex Information and Education Council of the United States, for her lifelong championship of legal sexual reforms, takes a similar stand; "If a practice is responding to some felt need in the community, then we'd better pay attention to that need. But if it has so many disadvantages that it oughtn't to be done—which is a possibility—then we ought to be figuring out what can be done that would make sense for people with the need."

What do I make of it? I became enamored of sex therapy and determined to be its biographer when it was a humble gadfly nipping at mighty psychoanalysis, and later, when it became a dragon breathing the fiery notion "Hurry up" at lengthy psychotherapy. The tone of that old sex therapy was scientific. Masters and Johnson studied 733 people over an eleven-year period and did not charge fees during the first five years of their investigations. But the tone of the new sex therapy is self-aggrandizing and vague. Hartman and Fithian, a West Coast team who like to call themselves the Masters and Johnson of the Far West, have written a book on their techniques in which they refuse to give statistics about their successes, since these might create "a numbers game where centers such as ours will enter into a kind of spurious competition based on numbers," as if competition for the best results were *bad* for patients. New techniques are being blazoned all across the country, from testosterone for all varieties of male impotence to surgical procedures on the clitorises of women with orgasmic difficulties, all done for fees, and without being tried on enough people to know for whom they will work and for whom they will fail.

The training of some sex therapists is at present almost casual. Masters and Johnson are no longer training. Hartman and Fithian offer diplomas in sex therapy, complete with golden seal and parchment paper, to people who take an eight-hour, $85 seminar with them. Those who "graduate" often set up training seminars of their own. Compared with that, surrogates don't bother me much. In a way I have a grudging sympathy for surrogates. Like small shopkeepers, they hardly stand a chance against the big sex-therapy supermarkets—with middlemen and entrepreneurs and lecture-circuit mafiosi—that the next few years are likely to bring. Of course, I wish surrogates didn't have to be clandestine, so that accurate records of when they succeed and how they work could be kept. But surrogate therapists *are* a problem. Therapists who practice alone always seem to exaggerate the virtues of their private methods. I wish all psychotherapists had to work in supervised teams and be answerable to someone besides the patient. But short of that, there seems little point in bemoaning sexual surrogates, other than to sigh with Orwell, "I wasn't born for an age like this. Was Smith? Was Jones? Were you?"

In this chapter, the authors describe the training program for sex therapists developed by the Reproductive Biology Research Foundation in 1971. A number of the difficulties that were encountered as the program progressed are described. The relationship between the cotherapist trainees and the relationship between the trainees and their staff supervisors were both crucial elements in the training process.

This article raises some interesting questions. First, is it necessary to have a male–female cotherapy team in order to do effective sex therapy? Since a great many of the difficulties in the training process involved the relationship between the cotherapists, it would seem that single-therapist therapy might offer some real advantages. There have been some studies that indicate that a poor relationship between cotherapists is detrimental to patient progress.

Second, is it possible to take people who are not psychotherapists by training and train them to be successful sex therapists in a limited amount of time? The answer to this question depends a great deal on how sex therapy as a whole is viewed: as a set of independent techniques or as an area of specialization within the field of psychotherapy. The very limited success of the training program the authors describe and the complexity of the issues often encountered in cases of sexual dysfunction would argue for the latter definition of sex therapy and would suggest that sex therapy training be limited to mental health professionals.

42

Training Dual Sex Teams for Rapid Treatment of Sexual Dysfunction: A Pilot Program

Raymond W. Waggoner, Emily H. Mudd, and Marshall L. Shearer

A continuing education program was developed at the Reproductive Biology Research Foundation in 1971 to train male/female cotherapy teams to treat human sexual inadequacies and marital conflict by the rapid treatment method reported in Masters and Johnson's *Human Sexual Inadequacy.* The results reported in the above-mentioned publication by this method are better than results claimed for many other treatment methods. It was recognized that there were many complexities, complications, and possible limitations inherent in such training, because the rapid treatment method was an additional complicating factor. Follow-up contacts and evaluation of the therapeutic results of former trainees were built into the program.

Raymond W. Waggoner • Department of Psychiatry, University of Michigan Medical School, Ann Arbor, Michigan   ***Emily H. Mudd*** • Department of Psychiatry, University of Pennsylvania, School of Medicine, Philadelphia, Pennsylvania   ***Marshall L. Shearer*** • Department of Psychiatry, University of Michigan Medical School, Ann Arbor, Michigan

At the foundation it is not considered that sexual dysfunction is necessarily a manifestation of basic emotional disorder. Constantly emphasized is the fact that there cannot be an uninvolved partner in a sexually dysfunctional marriage, even though the presenting complaint is primarily from one spouse. Treatment procedures take into consideration the many situational factors that may lead to sexual distress. Childhood experiences, biological difficulties, the attitudes of society, and poor communication between the spouses are some of the factors that may be responsible.

Treatment Procedures at the Foundation

In order to understand the complexities of training, it is essential first to understand the usual procedure for staff and patients at the foundation. All patients at the foundation, other than physicians, must be referred by a professional source: a physician, psychologist, social worker, minister, etc., before coming to St. Louis. Before coming to the foundation, each member of the marital unit completes a questionnaire individually and submits a statement describing the dysfunction.

In order to resolve the difficulty presented by the marital unit, it is important to obtain a complete history. The first day at the clinic the female therapist takes a history from the female member of the marital unit and the male therapist from the male member. The next day the order is reversed; the female therapist takes a history with the male patient and the male therapist with the female patient. Intervening time between histories gives the cotherapists an opportunity to review significant or sensitive areas that should be explored further. On the third day a complete medical history is obtained and a careful physical examination of both members of the marital unit is performed by the physician member of the staff team, who also orders thorough laboratory tests. The histories previously obtained are discussed with the marital unit by the two staff therapists in what is described as a round-table discussion. Points at variance are discussed and clarified, but specific material that either spouse does not want brought into the discussion is held in confidence.

The fourth day or so the patients are given specific instructions to explore the pleasure to be obtained from tactile contacts but are specifically instructed to avoid any direct sexual activity. This is described as sensate focus. This kind of sensual response is usually a new experience for the patients. Subsequently, fondling and caressing the breasts and genitals may be incorporated in this tactile experience but again with the advice not to attempt intercourse or attempt to produce orgasmic reaction in either partner. The process produces considerable sexual stimulation without fear of inadequate performance. This is particularly important, because the significant factor in sexual dysfunction is the anxiety produced by fear of a potential inability to perform satisfactorily.

Errors in the interrelationship between husband and wife and further suggestions for improving this aspect of communication are discussed in succeeding interviews, with recommendations for specific changes as deemed appropriate.

Various kinds of dysfunction such as impotence, premature ejaculation, or non-orgasmic response require differing kinds of instructional intervention.

The Masters and Johnson method of treatment combines education, understanding, communication, suggestion, conditioning, and confrontation by the dual sex therapy team within definite time limits. It recognizes the interrelationship in each patient of environmental, emotional, and physical components. Desired results usually can be achieved more quickly than is possible with many other methods of treatment. This is believed to be due to the intensity of the two-week time-limited therapy. The actual hours of therapy may differ little from the hours spent in other forms of marriage and sexual therapy requiring weekly appointments. However, this approach tends to increase significantly the difficulty and complexity of training.

Philosophy and Goals for Training

The philosophy and goals of this pilot training program were based on the following premise: If it could be demonstrated after training at the Reproductive Biology Research Foundation that results obtained by trained teams were within the same range of success as those obtained by Masters and Johnson, the possibility for such treatment of sexual inadequacy and marital conflict would become more readily available. The training of additional dual sex teams then would be definitely indicated if financial resources became available.

Criteria for Acceptance of Trainees

Acceptance for training required the following professional qualifications based on the initial team approach of Dr. Masters and Mrs. Johnson. One member of the team was required to be a physician willing to undertake the complete physical examination of the patient unit. The other member of the team should have a degree in one of the behavioral sciences, such as psychology, social work, or nursing.

Candidates for participation in the continuing education program were screened from requests for training from individuals in academic and private practice positions. Some attention was given to selection of candidates from diverse geographic areas and to those with an academic appointment.

Screening involved the following sequential steps:

1. Only training teams combining male and female therapists meeting the qualifications listed above were selected.
2. An information form was completed by each member of the applicant trainee team and submitted together with his or her curriculum vitae to the foundation's review committee, consisting of the codirectors of training, the directors of the foundation, and selected staff members.
3. If the applicant team's credentials were found to be satisfactory, they were

invited to visit the foundation to become familiar with its format. This visit enabled staff specifically responsible for training to interview the team as individuals and as a working unit. The interviewers' impressions of each applicant's attitude, values, goals, and personality, as well as their inter-action as a team, were made a part of the record.

4. Originally, a continuous four-week period of training at the foundation was planned. It became clear that four weeks was not sufficient time, and the final team had a total of six weeks.

Organization and Content of Training

From the experiences of Dr. Masters and Mrs. Johnson, it is clear that a female point of view is needed to evaluate and express the observed female responses, and by the same token it is necessary for a male member of the team to understand and explain the male reactions. It was hoped that through training, individuals properly selected might understand and utilize these concepts. Since the codirectors could be present only part time, it was necessary to have permanent staff constantly responsible for the trainees. Mrs. Virginia Johnson and Dr. Marshall Shearer, a staff psychiatrist, accepted this responsibility, and other members of the permanent staff gave significant assistance.

The trainees were expected to have a thorough knowledge of *Human Sexual Response* and *Human Sexual Inadequacy* prior to their arrival at the foundation. Invariably it was found that the trainee's knowledge of sexual psychology was limited in both the interview and the treatment situation. Consequently, additional attention had to be given to teaching sexual physiology.

The foundation does receive information on the patients prior to their arrival, and case assignments are made on the basis of information available. However, the case that appears one of the simplest on paper often gives this impression because the patient has intentionally omitted, for various reasons, pertinent information. It must be understood that at the foundation no individual is treated as an individual; rather, the interrelationship between husband and wife is treated.

With the patient's written permission, all interviews are tape-recorded. The trainees were oriented to the treatment method by listening for a day or two to recorded staff interviews at various stages of the treatment process. Then each trainee was assigned to work with a permanent staff member of the opposite sex in the treatment of regularly accepted patients, the male trainee with a female staff member, the female trainee with a male staff member. After experience in work-ing with a permanent staff member with two or more patient units, the two trainees, working together as a team, were assigned a patient unit for therapy. Every inter-view of the trainees was recorded and, in addition, was monitored from another room by staff supervisors. This provided protection for the patients through possible interruption of the interview by office phone and later supervision discussion. The importance of the various aspects of treatment, beginning with the individual histories taken during the first two days, the round table the third day, and subsequent therapeutic sessions, was brought to the attention of the trainees by their active participation, by seminars, by the availability of their taped interviews, and by continuing supervision of their cases.

As already described, complete physical examinations were conducted for husband and wife patients by the physician member of the trainee team, who also ordered thorough laboratory studies.

Qualifications and Response of Trainees

Of those interviewed, six teams were selected. Males in the six teams included four board-certified psychiatrists and two board-certified obstetrician–gynecologists. Female team members included three nurses, one anthropologist, one social worker, and one psychiatrist.

Four of the trainee teams were husband and wife and two were not. Experience indicated that there were both advantages and disadvantages if the trainee team were husband and wife. The number of teams was obviously too small to come to any definite conclusion concerning the value of the married training teams versus the teams not married to each other. Training of the dual sex team, especially husband and wife, is incredibly more difficult than training a single individual, because of the inevitable complexity of interacting factors. With the positive interrelationship of the husband and wife, there was a tendency for one or the other, usually the wife, to retreat from the true peer relationship and assume a secondary role that is out of consonance with the concept of the dual sex team in which each member has equal status and responsibility. On the other hand, there appeared to be certain positive advantages to the husband–wife team whose previously established forms of communication were helpful in the therapeutic situation. Obviously, this did not exist in the non-husband–wife team.

Each trainee, regardless of background, had some difficulty with the two initial history interviews. Those with a background in nursing and the behavioral sciences seemed to have greater difficulty than those whose training and experience had included therapeutic interventions with the concept of a structured but open-ended interview, during which essential basic material is elicited without checking a list of questions. Trainees with a background in obstetrics–gynecology, social work, or psychiatry had no difficulty with the concept of an open-ended, structured interview. Histories by the gynecologists had a great deal of factual material but were often sparse or devoid of information in regard to how the patient reacted emotionally to life experiences. This was true in both the sexual and nonsexual areas. On the other hand, the psychiatrists would tend to ask questions about the meaning of historical events in many areas in a patient's life, but they did not do this in sexual areas. For example, if a man reported that he was unable to have an erection the first time he attempted intercourse, it was surprising if the patient were asked how he felt, or what explanation he gave himself, or how he perceived the reaction of his female partner.

All trainees had a great deal of difficulty following the development and progression of the sexual distress. This was unexpected in view of the fact that in most instances their professional background embodied the concept that, to be understood, the course of an illness must be traced from its onset to the present. They seemed content to establish the fact that sex in the beginning of marriage may or may not have been adequate and that now a sexual dysfunction existed, without establishing when the difficulty began, what explanation the patient himself gave, or what he and his wife had done to attempt to correct the situation. There is a usual, or expected, history of the development of sexual disorders just as there is for any other disorder. If behooves the therapists to know where the patient is in the natural progression of the particular dysfunction.

The treatment process is specific to each type of sexual distress and is tailored to the individual needs of the patients. The trainees tended to over-generalize their learning experiences from one disorder to another or from one patient to another. The concept of pacing a patient through the course of treatment was one that seemed entirely new to the trainees, and no one grasped more than an appreciation of this concept during the training period. For example, if a couple presented the problem of male impotence there was no need for them to undertake the mounting process in coitus until midway into the second week of therapy, whereas if a couple presented the problem of nonorgasmic return they needed to be mounting no later than the end of the first week. Also, the concept of pacing the patient's physiological sexual appetite was new to the trainees.

Almost all couples seen in treatment at the foundation have a communication problem of varying degrees. Certain couples would not have had sexual difficulty if their communication had been adequate. Consequently, it was important to teach the trainees how to encourage patients to communicate at all levels, both verbal and nonverbal.

All trainees had difficulty with the concept of the role of the therapist vis-à-vis the role of cotherapist. The psychiatrist understandably had more trouble in sorting out these roles than any of the other trainees. Most of the psychiatrists had experience in treating couples as the sole therapist. It was difficult for the trainees to understand that the basic concept of the male therapist representing and being responsible to the male patient and the female therapist being responsible to the female patient must be adhered to. To the extent these roles become blurred, the door opens to misunderstanding by both patient and therapist and to major transference difficulties as well as to lack of open communication. As these roles are adhered to, transference difficulties can be handled or, in large part, avoided.

The overriding trainee response was anxiety. It is understandable and to be expected that these professionally equipped men and women, many of whom had been engaged in active clinical practice for several years, would find their role of learner both new and difficult. The experience of exposure from having each interview monitored was inevitably anxiety-provoking. Feelings of resistance and irritation produced ambivalence toward the program.

Training candidates had been screened to determine that they were able to deal comfortably with sexual problems. However, as already mentioned when discussing the patient interview, they seemed inhibited from taking a logical history of the progression of the sexual dysfunction. They did not pursue material in the sexual area with the kind of professional curiosity that physicians use daily in regard to other disabilities. The trainees naturally are a product of our society and as such evidenced some of its sexual conditioning. This was a contributing factor to their anxiety early in training. Anxiety about the topic of sex seemed to be relatively non-existent by the third week.

The psychiatrists had some anxiety with the recognition that they would need to unlearn some psychiatric patterns, particularly in regard to the role with their cotherapist, and to be more direct and more educative to the patients in regard to the nature of sexual functioning. Other trainees experienced some anxiety from the realization that they were dealing with feelings and emotions and using psycho-therapeutic principles with which they felt unqualified. This was especially true for the female trainee, whose anxiety might be focused on her relationship to her co-therapist, and in turn her anxiety was also felt by her cotherapist. Some female trainees tried to deal with the inequality between team members by assuming equality, others by denying their skills and withdrawing, others by taking on an air of superiority. Such struggles sometimes resulted in depression, but the most common reaction was one of anxiety. Such anxiety was undoubtedly augmented by the phenomenon of information overload. Four weeks of training was grossly too short. It has been extended to six weeks, and it is realized that this period of time is also inadequate because of the trainee's need to carry more cases under supervision. However, few of the best qualified candidates felt they could afford to be away from their professional activities for more than six weeks.

It is a recognized tenet in both medicine and the behavioral sciences that a trainee will take longer to treat a patient or accomplish a given procedure than an experienced expert in the field. However, patients coming to the foundation have agreed upon a two-week time period for treatment, and frequently needed extra time was not available. This created additional anxiety in both the trainees and the supervisors. All trainees were introduced to the patients as staff of the foundation.

When, during the last two weeks of their training, the trainees began to work with each other as cotherapists, the anxiety associated with problems of working with a cotherapist resurfaced with renewed intensity. In addition, the dynamics of the relationship between the cotherapist trainees and between trainees and staff supervisors were thrown into bold relief. The interactional dynamics between the cotherapists reflected the dynamics of their overall relationship, including the relationship of their marriage in those instances where the trainees were husband and wife. Anxiety was generated by the trainees facing the new awareness of their relationship or by an attempt at avoidance. There were specific areas in these interactional dynamics that were detrimental to the progress of therapy with the patients.

Staff Response to Trainees

The Reproductive Biology Research Foundation functions currently with a small staff of four male/female teams. The addition of a training team is therefore felt closely by all staff members. The basic response of the staff to the trainees was in regard to the trainees' anxiety. In the first few days, when the trainees' anxiety was due to the newness of the situation, the staff's response was concern and empathy. As the trainees' anxiety increased, staff concern and empathy reached the point where the staff members, other than the supervisors, withdrew, which undoubtedly added to the trainees' anxiety. Anxiety is infectious and was transmitted to the staff and then transmitted back again to the trainees. The infectious component was recognized in relatively short order and, in the main, the cycle was broken.

In the last two weeks of training when the trainees worked together as cotherapists, in contrast to the first two weeks when the trainees worked with an experienced staff therapist, small errors of treatment could not be immediately corrected. This, in addition to the fact of the trainees working together as cotherapists for the first time at the foundation as well as the limitation of treatment time to two weeks, created concern for the outcome of patient therapy and, hence, more anxiety. The small treatment errors were cumulative and frequently had an effect in the latter part of therapy out of proportion to the original error. The responsibility of the supervisors for the patients versus their responsibility to the trainees was often in conflict. This conflict of interests by the supervisors was picked up by the trainees and added to their anxiety. At times, if treatment was not going well, a staff supervisor moved in to replace the trainees in treatment of the case. At other times the trainees succeeded; and at still other times the patients returned after several months for additional treatment by the permanent staff at no further fee.

There was one very unusual and particularly exhausting frustration that the supervisors experienced. This was the frustration of having seen a particular dynamic emerging in the treatment process, of talking to the trainees about it with their apparent understanding, only to realize in monitoring the next session that the concept had been poorly understood or misunderstood.

At the end of the year (1971) the statistical results of overall treatment failure were higher than those in previous years. Investigation suggested a significant difference in the treatment results of the professional staff not involved in training when the trainees were at the foundation as opposed to when they were not. Obviously, other variables in staff also were involved. However, it would appear that the presence of the trainees resulted in an additional affective load, which may have accounted in part for this result. Another contributing factor came from the fact that conferences and seminars, geared to the individual trainee's needs, usurped the formal and informal time the experienced staff therapists had used to consult one another about problem cases.

Evaluative Procedures

One important aspect of a pilot program is to ferret out guidelines for the future based on an assessment of results together with their implications for future training after suggested modifications. In this connection various procedures were planned and undertaken in setting up this training program:

Before Acceptance

A systematic graded estimate was made of each applicant for training by at least four staff members following in-person interviews at the foundation. No applicant was accepted for training whose rating averaged less than B on a scale of A to D.

After Training Concluded

Staff discussion of training indicated the importance of determining what had been gained during training in the following areas:

- Facility and content of history taking
- Physical examination ability
- Ability to relate to patients
- Understanding patient dynamics; ability to use these dynamics in promoting positive change in patient
- Ability to use self as a therapeutic instrument: Natural
  Acquired
- Basic concept of psychophysiology of sexual functioning
- Therapy, unit interaction
- Ability to accept and make use of criticism
- Ability to absorb material
- Overall therapeutic effectiveness
- Degree to which concept was mastered
- Patient referral restrictions, if any
- Points to observe for follow-up

Subjective assessments were made of each trainee's ability after training from an overall viewpoint, taking into account the various aspects of therapy as listed above. These estimates were based on conferences with the permanent staff and program directors.

It became apparent at completion of one month that the time period allowed was too brief. Trainees, supervisors, and staff, individually and as a group, were emotionally and physically exhausted. The highest motivation on everyone's part to succeed, together with continuous overtime work, did not appear to make possible the achievement of goals completely acceptable to trainees or staff. However, four additional teams had been scheduled for the four-week training period and were unable to extend the training time. It was thought that as staff and supervisors became acclimated to the demands of a training program, the strain would decrease and comfort and progress in all aspects would increase. This hoped-for result did not occur. The sixth team was able to accept six weeks for training. As has been emphasized repeatedly, even this period was felt to be too brief.

Follow-Up Seminar

As planned in advance, on May 8 and 9, 1972, the posttraining seminar was held. It had been built into the program plan and, therefore, was organized by the foundation staff. Prior to arrival the trainees submitted material that included the number of cases they had treated since completing training, the diagnosis, the outcome, and a protocol of one of their difficult cases. All six trainee teams and all professional staff attended. The mood included a sense of unity, eagerness to learn, working through of posttraumatic training experiences, and evidence of current anxiety.

The seminar consisted of formal case presentations, open discussions, informal gatherings in a social atmosphere, as well as one session where the men and women from the staff and former trainee teams separated for a discussion period aimed primarily at any problems in regard to working with their respective cotherapist. No significant problems emerged in the male group at this time in regard to current work with their cotherapist, either from the men who were married to their co-therapist or from those who were not. The women, on the other hand, expressed concern about their professional adequacy and their role as cotherapists rather than as assistants. The married women working with their spouses related episodes of feeling competitive with their cotherapist and indicated meaningful change had subsequently occurred in their marital situation.

The major problem presented by the trainees seemed to be how to adapt the treatment methods to local clientele. In contrast, 95% of the cases seen at the foundation are from such a distance that commuting is impractical. This means that the patients at the foundation are away from home and job responsibilities. The trainees with a psychiatric background seemed to be attempting to treat some patients whose prognosis was extremely poor and who would not have been accepted for treatment at the foundation. However, they seemed to feel that these patients had a better prognosis with this mode of therapy than with other modes of therapy they had been using.

The trainees indicated that in their local communities they had continued their former professional work as their main activity. They maintained a low profile as sex therapists and had not let it be widely known that they were doing this kind of treatment. Partly this was because they carried prior full-time professional activities. Also, part of it seemed to be that they were not secure with their own new skills, nor were they sure that the foundation had confidence in their ability in their new work, in spite of referrals of patients through the foundation. Thirdly, and most importantly, they seemed to be anticipating a negative community reaction. It was clear that the trainees were quite reluctant to enhance their own identities in their community as those of sex therapists. However, there was no single incident mentioned in which the community had in any way rejected or indicated a negative reception to any of the six trainee teams. Once again, these reactions point up that the reluctance of the helping professions to deal actively with sexual problems is their own reluctance rather than the reaction of the general population to their so doing.

The follow-up seminar served to promote definite feelings of camaraderie and mutual supportiveness. In this way it removed much of the still free-floating anxiety concerning the handling of cases, fees, referrals, reports, etc. In addition, it promoted feelings of greater confidence between the former trainees and the foundation staff. One concrete illustration of these feelings was the decision on the part of the former trainees at this May meeting to organize on their own another get-together seminar and to invite the foundation directors of training and staff. Dates were set to meet in Bethesda, the home base of two former trainee teams, the last weekend of July 1972.

Independently Organized Seminar of Former Trainees

The meeting, as agreed upon at the Foundation Follow-up Seminar in May 1972, was held July 28-30. All six trainee teams were represented, although in two instances one member of the team was unavoidably absent. Drs. Waggoner and Mudd attended voluntarily and Dr. Spitz was sent from the foundation staff. All except Dr. Spitz covered their own expenses.

Discussions were held Saturday afternoon and Sunday morning, with friendly informal contacts and buffet at the home of trainee hosts Saturday evening. There was much less evidence of anxiety in the handling of details of criteria for acceptance of patients, fee setting, variation in time limits, reports on case outcome, and most importantly, the actual treatment dynamics. Again, each member of the group seemed to gain, and in turn give, mutual support to the others. Desire was expressed to keep in touch with foundation plans. Unanimous agreement was arrived at to meet voluntarily about twice yearly. The next seminar was invited by one of the team members to meet in January 1973 in Durham, North Carolina. At this meeting it was hoped that sufficient time would have elapsed following training to scrutinize results of treatment by the former trainees and to compare these results to those obtained in St. Louis.

Summary and Conclusion

Because of the many complexities inherent in this type of training, it is not surprising that the foundation is left with certain unresolved dilemmas regarding future training. How much time can qualified professional persons afford to take off for training? Could more than one team be trained at one time? How large a staff would be necessary to supervise longer training and how would costs be covered?

The program as reported has obvious limitations as well as intriguing potentials. Its very uniqueness among ventures in training raises stimulating questions concerning learning theory. It is clear that adequate evaluation of their acquired ability was not possible within the short time allotted each training team. Other vital questions fall in the categories of admission requirements, supervisory relationships of a man/woman treatment team, and time span necessary for the goals expected or desired. As of June 1971, the foundation had no definitive plans to reestablish a training program unless adequate funds became available. If and when such a program might be reestablished, staff involved in training would have to explore intensively modifications in the program based on the pilot experience.

Finally, however, because of the intensity of contact with each trainee individually and as a cotherapist in this pilot training program, the authors feel assured that the skills of each trainee in the areas listed above were improved during their training. These professional persons will be able to be more helpful to patients with problems of sexual dysfunction.

Attitudes towards sexuality have been gradually changing in America over the last thirty-five years. Increasing emphasis on the positive role of sexuality throughout the life cycle has focused professional and public attention on the practice of sex therapy.

In this final chapter, Lo Piccolo addresses some of the most crucial questions concerning sex therapy as a profession: What exactly is sex therapy, who is qualified to be a sex therapist, and how can the profession ensure high standards and protect the consumer?

In his discussion, the author pulls together many of the ideas presented in preceding chapters of this book. Beginning with a brief overview of the development of sex therapy, the author goes on to evaluate the current uncontrolled state of the "profession" of sex therapist.

Given that sex therapy has been shown to be effective, it seems destined to become a permanent part of the psychotherapy scene. The issues of training and licensure that the author raises, along with his proposals for regulation, deserve serious consideration.

43

The Professionalization of Sex Therapy: Issues and Problems

Joseph LoPiccolo

Much has been made, in the last two decades, of the "sexual revolution" in America. Frequently cited components of this revolution include greater openness about sex in media and conversation, greater public acceptance of "taboo" activities such as pre- and extramarital intercourse, the legalization of abortion, and, in several states, the decriminalization of all sexual acts between consenting adults in private settings. These changes are primarily attitudinal; whether or not there has been a significant change in actual sexual behavior is less clear. Allowing for differences in sampling procedures and for a greater willingness of people to answer truthfully, recent surveys (e.g., Hunt, 1974) show remarkably few behavioral changes from the original Kinsey surveys (1948, 1953), the publication of which might be viewed as one catalyst for the sexual revolution.

Preparation of this article was supported in part by a grant from the National Institute of Mental Health. The author would like to express his appreciation to the following persons for their helpful comments on an earlier draft of this article: Albert Ellis, Julia Heiman, Lewis Klebanoff, Nechama Liss-Levinson, W. Charles Lobitz, Leslie LoPiccolo, William Masters, Susan Price, and David A. Rodgers.

Joseph LoPiccolo • Department of Psychiatry and Behavioral Science, School of Medicine, State University of New York, Stony Brook, New York

The publication of Kinsey's books, with their emphasis on "total outlet" (number of orgasms), produced a new theme in American attitudes toward sexuality. Sex, once a devalued activity, gradually came to be viewed as a required ability (LoPiccolo and Heiman, 1977). The public acceptance of Freudian theory also contributed much to this new emphasis on sexual adequacy and ability. Freudian theory (especially its popularized versions) stressed sexual maturation and functioning as the cornerstone of healthy personality. Kinsey's data added substance to this Freudian theoretical skeleton, in that anyone could now evaluate his/her own sexual functioning: Were you having as many orgasms as the average person of your sex and age? Did your "coital contacts" last as long as the national average?

This emphasis on sexual functioning had a number of long-range effects. "Marriage manuals"—a euphemism for sex technique training books—became best sellers in the 1950s and, with the passage of time, became very direct in both title and approach [contrast, for example, Eichenlaub's *The Marriage Art* (1961) with Comfort's *The Joy of Sex* (1972)]. While many people who were uninformed about sexual techniques undoubtedly were greatly helped by these books, many others turned to psychotherapy for aid with more serious sexual dysfunctions such as lack of orgasm ("frigidity") in women, and erectile failure ("impotence") or premature ejaculation in men.

In the 1940s and 1950s, the psychotherapy establishment had relatively little to offer the person suffering from sexual dysfunction. American psychology and psychiatry were primarily Freudian psychoanalytic in orientation. In a seeming paradox, although one of Freud's greatest contributions was his emphasis on sexuality as a central element of personality, psychoanalysis proved to be a rather ineffective technique for treating sexual dysfunctions. Psychoanalytic treatment, focusing on uncovering repressed childhood experiences, resolving unconscious conflicts, resolution of the Oedipal complex, and development of a "transference" relationship with the analyst, is necessarily of great duration. For "frigidity," it was stated that "an appointment several times a week for a minimum of eight months" was required and that, therefore, "as a mass problem, the question of frigidity is not to be solved" (Bergler, 1947, 1951).

Even when a woman could afford treatment of this length, the results were generally poor. Following several years of analysis, many, if not most, women remained inorgasmic (Sherfey, 1972). Results were not any better for men suffering from erectile problems or premature ejaculation (Moore, 1961).

In retrospect, it seems remarkably naïve to have expected analytic treatment to have major effects on sexual functioning. For one thing, the psychoanalytic theory of sexual functioning was developed in the absence of any empirical knowledge of the physiology of human sexual response. The Freudian belief in a transfer from clitoral to vaginal orgasm in the mature woman has not been substantiated by research on the physiology of female sexual arousal (Masters and Johnson, 1970; Sherfey, 1972).

As another problem, psychoanalytic theory did not take into account the role of the sexual partner in contributing to sexual dysfunction. Consider, for example, an inorgasmic woman who is having sex with a man who is extremely abrupt and unskilled as a lover. Further assume that the man and woman are both ignorant of the physiology of female sexual arousal, as is commonly the case. How could one possibly expect analytic therapy, with its focus on the past and on the woman's intrapsychic mechanisms, to have any effect in such a case?

In the late 1950s, a quiet revolution began in American psychotherapy. In the place of historically oriented, long-term analytic treatment, a variety of new short-term approaches, based on learning theory and stressing direct behavioral retraining procedures in the "here and now," emerged. Therapists such as Joseph Wolpe (1958), Donald Hastings (1963), and Albert Ellis (1966), in dealing with sexual problems, focused on various procedures such as reducing anxiety about sexual performance, changing negative attitudes toward sexuality, increasing communication between the couple, and education and training in sexual physiology and sexual techniques.

While this approach was remarkably successful (cure rates of 60–80% were reported), it was ignored by the mainstream of American psychology and psychiatry, as well as by the media. It was only with the landmark publication of Masters and Johnson's *Human Sexual Inadequacy* (1970) that the general public became aware of the existence of a new and effective "sex therapy."

In the years since 1970, there has been a virtual explosion of interest in sex therapy. The publicity sex therapy has received has been generally positive, stressing the effectiveness and rapidity of the treatment. This positive press has had the beneficial effect of encouraging people to go for therapy. However, the resultant high demand for sex therapy, coupled with a shortage of sex-therapy-trained psychotherapists, has created a set of unique problems that might be termed "the professionalization of sex therapy."

Sex Therapy: Procedures or Profession?

It is assumed that most people are now at least generally aware of the basic elements of sex therapy programs, as perhaps best described by Masters and Johnson. As noted above, sex therapy is a brief (often ten to fifteen sessions) therapy, with the emphasis on directly changing the client's sexual attitudes and sexual behaviors.

In an analysis of the theoretical basis for sex therapy procedures, it has been pointed out (LoPiccolo, 1977) that there seem to be seven major underlying elements in the total therapy package for sexually dysfunctional couples.

1. Mutual responsibility: Sex therapy considers any sexual dysfunction to be a mutual problem between the couple. Much therapy time is spent discussing the husband–wife interaction.

2. Information, education, and permission: Couples are instructed in sexual physiology and sexual techniques and are given "permission" by a respected authority (the therapist) to try out the new sexual techniques they learn.

3. Attitude change: Much therapy time is spent in attempts to change negative attitudes toward sexuality. These attitudes are usually the result of societal or parental injunctions against sexuality, which are internalized during childhood and

adolescence. Although the patient often has intellectually rejected these prohibitions, their emotional components are not so easily changed. Many of the attitude change techniques are adaptations of Ellis's rational-emotive psychotherapy (1962).

4. Anxiety reduction: Anxiety about sexual performance leads to goal orientation and the taking of a destructive, self-evaluative "spectator role" during sex. Various anxiety-reduction procedures, including behavioral psychotherapy techniques such as systematic desensitization, are used to reduce performance anxiety.

5. Communication and feedback: To increase the patients' ability to communicate and give each other feedback during sexual activity, a number of communication training procedures adapted from marital therapy programs are often included in sex therapy.

6. Intervention in destructive sex roles, life-styles, and family interaction: Since sex exists in the context of an emotionally complex couple relationship, a variety of marriage therapy and family systems therapy procedures are used to restructure negative elements of the relationship which are interfering with sexual functioning.

7. Prescribing changes in sexual behavior: Typically, in sex therapy the couple is initially forbidden to engage in actual intercourse. Instead, the couple is instructed in a series of "nondemanding" or "sensate focus" activities, consisting of body massage, hugging, and kissing. Gradually, more sexual activities such as breast and genital caressing are included, eventually leading to intercourse. (As will be discussed later, with a few well-publicized exceptions, the patients perform their sexual activities at home in private, without the therapists present or participating.) Throughout this behavioral retraining, the six elements listed above are concurrently being used to produce therapeutic change. Unfortunately, media coverage of sex therapy has emphasized only the element of changing the couple's actual sexual behavior and has led to the view that sex therapy consists *only* of the therapist prescribing body massages, genital caressing, and other sexual activities.

What Is Sex Therapy?

Given this brief summary of the elements of sex therapy, the question arises as to what "sex therapy" *is*. Is it, as proposed above, a complex, multifaceted psychotherapy procedure to be used only by those with formal training (and a license) to practice psychotherapy? Is it, as many sex therapists argue, a form of educational activity not requiring psychotherapeutic skills on the part of the sex therapist? Is sex therapy merely a form of physical skill training, like golf or tennis lessons?

This is not just an academic question, for the issue of what sex therapy is interacts with the most pressing issue facing the would-be consumer of sex therapy: What sort of training and skills does a "sex therapist" need to have to be effective?

There are at least two schools of thought on this issue of the qualifications needed to do sex therapy. On the one hand, the established mental health professionals tend to argue that sex therapy is a set of specialized procedures for use only by trained psychotherapists. On the other hand, a number of the new sex therapists argue that sex therapy is a separate new profession.

The point of view held by many if not most psychologists and psychiatrists is that sex therapy is a subspecialty of psychotherapy. It logically follows, then, that only those persons who are qualified by training and experience to do psychotherapy should be doing sex therapy. This viewpoint stresses that sexual dysfunction does not exist in a vacuum, but that it often is related to problems in the couple's emotional relationship, such as poor communication, hostility and competitiveness, or sex-role problems. Furthermore, even in those cases in which the sexual dysfunction is not related to relationship problems, the couple's emotional relationship is often damaged by the sexual problem and the feelings of guilt, inadequacy, and frustration that usually accompany sexual dysfunction. Therefore, it is stressed that training in psychotherapy (especially marital or family systems therapy) is required to deal with these problems. Finally, this viewpoint notes that sex therapy itself is a stressful procedure, and that psychotherapeutic expertise is required to deal with the patient's emotional reactions to the sex therapy process.

While the logic of this argument is certainly compelling, the new sex therapists point out that it is not based on any empirical research data. No one has conducted a study of effectiveness of sex therapy procedures when used by trained psychotherapists as opposed to laypersons trained only in sex therapy procedures. Outside the sex area, comparisons of effectiveness of therapy for emotional problems have generally *not* provided strong evidence that professional psychotherapists do better than nonprofessional psychotherapists (e.g., ministers, family doctors, etc.) (Bergin, 1971).

Certainly those "sex therapists" who are not psychotherapists claim results every bit as good as those obtained by psychologists and psychiatrists (Hartman and Fithian, 1972). Indeed, even a written educational program without *any* contact with a sex therapist has been shown to be remarkably effective for premature ejaculation (Mikulas and Lowe, 1975). In this vein, a number of "self-help" books for sexual dysfunction (Heiman, LoPiccolo, and LoPiccolo, 1976; McCarthy, Ryan, and Johnson, 1975) have recently appeared on the market. While formal research on their effectiveness is lacking, the authors all have numerous clinical examples to support the likely effectiveness of this "therapy without a therapist."

Even while acknowledging the truth of these counterarguments, it might be pointed out that those people who seek out a sex therapist may be more severely dysfunctional (or in a more troubled relationship) than those people who attend an educational program or choose only to read a self-help book. It may well be that the professional psychotherapists are correct in their assertion that their patients need their psychotherapy skills. It may also be true, however, that not all couples suffering from a sexual dysfunction need the services of a psychotherapist. For couples who have a loving and strong emotional relationship, but who are simply unskilled and naïve sexually, education rather than therapy may be the treatment of choice.

The question may ultimately be reduced, then, to one of the nature of the patients seeking sex therapy. Most clinics that specialize in sexual dysfunction report that there has been a change in the characteristics of their patient applicants over the last few years. Some years ago, most couples seeking therapy were basically very naïve about sex; an education and training approach was usually quite successful. Recently, fewer and fewer such cases appear. The current greater cultural acceptance of sexuality and the widespread availability of good information about sexual physiology and technique have apparently resulted in a lower incidence of sexual dysfunction caused by naïveté and ignorance. Current cases more commonly involve deep-seated negative attitudes about sexuality, relationship problems, or other factors not responsive to a sex therapy program that only includes education and behavioral retraining exercises.

If the "easy" cases are becoming less common, it becomes a matter of some concern that individuals with no psychotherapy training, such as most health educators, experimental psychologists, sociologists, and clergy, can represent themselves as "sex therapists."

This total lack of control over who can be a sex therapist is indeed the current state of affairs. There are absolutely no legal restraints to prevent anyone from hanging up a shingle proclaiming his status as a sex therapist. Anyone familiar with the national scene in sex therapy can cite any number of "sex therapists" who, before they became sex therapists, were not involved in any sort of therapy or human health services activity. While state licensing laws and professional societies prevent quacks from representing themselves as physicians, psychologists, psychiatrists, and, in some states, marriage counselors, the field legally is wide open for anyone who wants to open the "Jones County Center for Sex Therapy."

While some of the new sex therapists are obviously unqualified and seem to be attracted to the field because there is money to be made and no controls to keep them out, a perhaps more serious problem concerns those well-intentioned people who believe themselves to be competent, but who may not be. This may be a more serious problem because such people usually have some sort of credentials to establish their credibility to the reasonably suspicious and sophisticated consumer, who will not patronize the outright quacks.

Many of these marginally competent sex therapists are qualified mental health professionals, but have very little or no training in the specialized techniques of sex therapy. Again, if sex therapy is considered a subspecialty of psychotherapy, seeing your local psychiatrist or psychologist for sexual dysfunction may be analogous to seeing a general practitioner for a medical condition that really requires specialized treatment.

It seems that the ideal situation would be for all mental health professionals to acquire, as part of their training, at least some passing familiarity with sex therapy techniques. Again, ideally, intensive training would be available for those who wish to specialize in the area, as would continuing education for practicing professionals.

Unfortunately, the actual situation in professional training schools is about as far from this ideal as it is possible to be. While most medical schools now have a general, broad content course in human sexuality as an elective part of the curriculum, opportunities for training and supervised experience in sex therapy are almost nonexistent. Similarly, most clinical psychology and psychiatry residency programs simply do not provide such training. Those institutions that do have such opportunities for their students generally do so out of fortuitous circumstances rather than by design—someone on the faculty happens to have a research interest in sex therapy.

Even if training programs in psychiatry and psychology come to include sex therapy training in the future, the question remains as to how the current practitioners of psychotherapy can learn the specialized skills of sex therapy. When new treatment procedures are developed, the issue of continuing education for the already licensed professionals becomes a major issue.

It is again the case that such continuing education is simply not widely available. What is available are lectures and "workshops," usually consisting of a few evening or weekend lectures. It is certainly debatable that therapeutic skills can be learned by passively reading and listening to lectures. Like all complex and inexact arts, therapy skills are best learned by supervised practical experience under a master practitioner.

What is especially disturbing about the continuing education scene is that, once again, the high demand for sex therapy means there is money to be made here. Consequently, a number of people and institutions now offer high-priced brief "training" in sex therapy. The graduates of such courses can then represent themselves as "trained sex therapists" and can charge their clients high fees for their "expertise." As one concrete example, one sex therapy group offers a one-day workshop in a number of cities each year. The admission requirements for this workshop are minimal. After sitting in a large room with perhaps a hundred others for a total of eight hours, the graduate receives an impressive diploma (complete with blue ribbon and gold seal) certifying status as a trained sex therapist. There is no examination to see if the trainee was awake and learning anything (or even physically present) during the course; if you pay your $85 fee in advance you can merely show up Sunday afternoon to pick up your diploma (Wolfe, 1973).

There are some legitimate continuing education programs. Masters and Johnson periodically run training programs, as does the Human Sexuality Program of the University of California medical school. To take the California program as an example, their trainees are required to have a formal training background in marital or family therapy, to complete seventy-five hours of relevant course work, and to be personally interviewed before entering the training program. The program itself consists of training for two days per week for six months, including case work under intensive supervision. At the end of the course, the trainee receives a letter stating he or she has satisfactorily completed the course. No diploma or certification as a sex therapist is given.

Apparently, there is at least some legislative awareness of this lack of training in human sexuality in most professional schools and continuing education programs. Two laws recently passed in California (Assembly Bill 4178 and 4179, signed into law by the governor in September of 1976) require, as of January 1, 1978, evidence of training in human sexuality as a condition for licensure (or renewal of licensure) as a physician, psychologist, social worker, or marriage, family, and child counselor. If other states follow this model, professional schools and professional associations will be forced by law to do what they should have been doing in any case, as part of their professional responsibility to the public.

Problems in the Professionalization of Sex Therapy

As this chapter has discussed, the major problem in the professionalization of sex therapy is that the high demand for sex therapy has drawn many minimally qualified and untrained persons into the field. Reflecting both this high demand and the freedom of these new sex therapists from the ethical and legal controls of the established psychotherapy professions, at least two major problems have also arisen. These problems revolve around fees and the issue of sex between patient and therapist.

Fees and Insurance Payment for Treatment

It is remarkable to consider that in the United States, the average cost range for fifteen hours of outpatient psychotherapy with a private practice psychologist or psychiatrist is between $300 and $750. Yet the average cost range for fifteen hours (the usual duration) of sex therapy from one of the many new sex therapy centers is between $2,500 and $4,000. While there is an obvious reason for higher fees when two therapists see a given couple—a male–female cotherapy team is common sex therapy practice—the five to ten times higher fee level cannot be justified on any rational grounds. Sex therapists, as discussed above, often have *less* formal training and experience than do psychotherapists. The sex therapy consumer is *not* paying for longer training or expensive equipment, which are the usual reasons for higher fees of specialty practitioners. Regarding the necessity for higher fees to pay two therapists, there is at least some clinical evidence that a single therapist can be as effective as cotherapy teams (Kaplan, 1974). If further research supports this conclusion, the preference of sex therapists to work in dual sex teams may be just a luxury, the cost of which is unreasonable to expect the patients to underwrite.

As we move slowly toward a system of national health insurance in the United States, the issue of licensing of mental health care practitioners becomes more crucial. The question of who will be eligible for reimbursement under a national health insurance system is currently the subject of vigorous lobbying efforts in Washington. Each of the health professions (not just the various psychotherapeutic professions) argues that they must be included, for the national welfare, of course, and not out of any self-interest. Before national health insurance for mental health problems (such as sexual dysfunction) can become a reality, someone is going to have to make some hard decisions about who can actually *do* psychotherapy.

Even if the issue of which practitioners should be eligible for national health insurance payment can be resolved, it is still very doubtful that sex therapy would be covered. Currently, most private health insurance does pay for psychotherapy by psychologists and psychiatrists. However, payment for psychotherapy (even by these practitioners) for marital or sexual problems usually is specifically excluded. Some psychologists and psychiatrists routinely give their sexually dysfunctional patients fraudulent diagnoses on insurance forms so that the patient's insurance will pay for the cost of therapy. The ethics of this practice may be questionable, but it is unreasonable that treatment of anxiety and depression caused by job problems is covered by insurance, while treatment of anxiety and depression caused by marital or sexual problems is not. Perhaps this represents a last vestige of our society's Victorian heritage, or alternatively, the insurance companies may simply fear that with the divorce rate approaching 40% nationally, such coverage would break the bank. However, given the social cost of broken marriages (welfare aid to dependent children, tying up the court system with divorce cases, etc.), inclusion of sexual and marital psychotherapy under national health insurance might be a bargain at almost any price.

Sex Between Therapist and Patient: Trick or Treatment?

The procedures of sex therapy as described by Masters and Johnson have a firm theoretical basis in learning theory and behavioral psychotherapy, and they are also empirically based in that they have been shown to work when properly used. In contrast to this mainstream approach, there is now a growing trend for sex therapy to include some fort of quasi-sexual or directly sexual contact between therapist and patient, or between patient and "sexual surrogate"—a para-professional who serves as a sexual partner for those individuals who do not enter therapy in the context of an established sexual relationship. Such procedures are as yet rare outside of California, which most psychotherapists consider to be the "weirdness" capital of the profession. Yet, if it is true that California is the cultural bellwether for the rest of the country, such procedures may become more wide-spread and common.

One variety of quasi-sexual therapist–patient contact is the "sexological exam" (Hartman and Fithian, 1972). In this procedure each of the nude patients is sexually stimulated by the opposite-sex therapist. This stimulation usually includes breast and genital manipulation. The purpose of the exam is described as being to check for sexual response and demonstrate it to the patient. Of course, anyone with any reasonable degree of sophistication might note that whether or not sexual response is elicited by a stranger in an examining room doesn't necessarily tell anything about how the patient responds to his or her spouse in a private setting. In any case, the possibilities for abuse of this sexological exam by therapists are obvious.

Another variety of quasi-sexual contact between patient and therapist involves nudity and massage (Hartman and Fithian, 1970, 1971; Bindrum, 1968; Lawrence, 1969). The assumption here is that nudity per se is somehow therapeutic. This nude therapy is usually done in groups and sometimes includes procedures such as having the patients float across a warm swimming pool thinking, "I give myself com-pletely," or having the patients buy fruits and nuts because they are "symbol-ically speaking . . . reminiscent of early sexual symbols" (Hartman and Fithian, 1970, p. 156). While it would seem requisite for therapists who use such procedures to provide some data on their effectiveness, this has not been done. What one sees instead are global unsubstantiated statements that the procedures are beneficial.

The most direct form of sexual contact between therapist and patient is, of course, for the therapist—or a "surrogate partner" provided by the therapist—to actually go through the therapy program with the patient. Masters and Johnson started this approach, using carefully screened and trained surrogates under close supervision in cases where a man lacked a sexual partner. They discontinued this approach partly because of legal problems and partly because they noticed a selective tendency for their surrogates to become emotionally involved with wealthy patients (Wolfe, 1973).

Today, there is an International Professional Surrogates Association (based in California, of course), which makes surrogates available to therapists who would like to use them. While the use of surrogates has been described as "thinly veiled prostitution" (Holden, 1974), the use of a surrogate is at least a seemingly logical approach (although not the only approach, as the surrogate advocates claim) for the dysfunctional patient who does not have a sexual partner. Again, there is an obvious problem: While the advocates of surrogate therapy claim high success, data on whether or not the patient's newfound ability to function generalizes from the surrogate to a "real-life" sexual partner are almost totally nonexistent. In the absence of such data, the practice of providing surrogates to married men with wives who are unwilling to enter therapy with their husbands is at best question-able, even ignoring the other problematic issues involved in such cases (Apfelbaum, 1976). Perhaps more disturbing, there is a current trend for these surrogates to move toward becoming independent therapists, and to operate without any professional consultation or supervision.

In all procedures involving nudity, touching, and sexual activity between patient and therapist, even the most charitable observer must question the therapist's motives for using such procedures. Is there a theoretical rationale or are there actual data to support the utility of such risky procedures? Is the enjoyment and gratification of the therapist, rather than patient welfare, a major factor in the decision to use such procedures?

While less relevant in cases where the therapist provides a surrogate for the patient, in cases of direct patient–therapist sexual contact, the issue of exploita-tion of the patient is an enormous one, yet one that is simply denied by the advocates of this approach. Because of the obvious risks of exploitation of patients, sex between patient and therapist is considered to be unethical by all of the professional psychotherapy disciplines.

Given that there are few trained professional sex therapists around, that many nonprofessionals are calling themselves sex therapists, that many questionable activities are practiced under the guise of sex therapy, and that many professionals are doing sex therapy with little or no specific sex therapy training, what is to be done? This question really has two components: (1) What can be done legally or professionally to protect the consumer (a long-term social policy question) and (2) what can a couple seeking sex therapy do to make sure that they find a competent practitioner (an immediate personal question)?

Consumer Protection: The Failure of Legal and Professional Quality Controls

The sorry state of affairs in regard to sex therapy is only slightly worse than that found in the mental health field in general. Licensing and certification laws for psychiatrists, psychologists, and social workers (the three major psychothera-peutic professions) have been under recent attack by consumer groups (Adams and Orgel, 1975). Basically, the current licensure laws can be faulted on at least two major counts:

1. The laws are more effective in protecting the status of the professions than in ensuring competence for the consumer seeking therapy. Most states' licensure laws restrict *only the use of the title* of psychiatrist, psychologist, or social worker to those who have met certain qualifications. The actual *practice* of psychotherapy is unregulated. As is true of the title "sex therapist," anyone can advertise and practice as a "psychotherapist" or "counselor."

2. Even within the three legally regulated professions, the requirements do not begin to ensure competence. It is neither unethical nor illegal for *any* licensed physician to practice as a psychiatrist; no special training or competence is re-quired. The vast majority of psychiatrists do complete a psychiatric residency training program, but the quality control the American Medical Association exercises over such programs has been severely criticized (Torrey, 1974a,b). Similarly, certification as a psychologist in most states is not limited to those trained as *clinical* psychologists—experimental psychologists whose entire training has been limited to laboratory work are eligible. Social work licensure is also not restricted to clinically trained social workers. However, even completion of a *clinical* training program is no guarantee of competence. Both the American Psychological Association and the National Association of Social Workers have recently been criticized for failure to adequately evaluate and control quality of clinical training programs (Adams and Orgel, 1975). This failure is critical, as bad psychotherapy is not merely ineffective. Some psychotherapists have been shown to consistently make their patients *worse*. Bad psychotherapy produces a "deterio-ration effect"; it is worse than no therapy at all (Bergin, 1971).

All three major mental health professions do have additional, more rigorous *voluntary* examination and certification (by the American Board of Psychiatry and Neurology, the American Board of Professional Psychology, and the Academy of Certified Social Workers). However, this certification is completely voluntary, and since the average consumer-patient is unlikely to be aware of the existence of such boards, lack of certification really has little or no negative effect on private prac-titioners. Nationally, for example, only 33% of psychiatrists are board-certified (Adams and Orgel, 1975).

It would seem, then, the issue of ensuring competence of sex therapists cannot be separated from the larger issues of ensuring competence of all mental health professionals. While a discussion of the complexities involved in such a general reform of training and licensure is beyond the scope of this chapter, some specific recommendations can be made in regard to sex therapy.

Both to control the sex therapy explosion and for general consumer pro-tection, uniform laws need to be passed regulating who can engage in the *practice* of psychotherapy or provision of mental health services. Licensure that simply restricts the use of the three major professional titles is not enough. The proliferation of nonprofessional "sex therapists" who are legally exempt from current laws is a good example of this inadequacy. The issues involved in such a "license-to-practice" law are extremely complex. Such laws have to define what "psychotherapy" and "mental health services" are. Does a clergyman doing pastoral counseling need to be licensed? What about marriage counseling, vocational rehabilitation, encounter groups, sensitivity training, EST, and a whole host of other procedures that might or might not be considered "mental health services"?

A feasible solution might be a law that restricted to licensees the practice of "psychotherapy, personal counseling, marriage counseling, hypnosis, sexual therapy, or related procedures aimed primarily at the amelioration of psychological distress through direct personal intervention by a practitioner." Rather than trying to write a law that covered all possibilities, individual borderline cases could be handled by a licensure board, which would include a variety of professional disciplines, legal experts, and consumer representatives. Consumer representatives would be necessary both to ensure that the professional societies upgrade their quality controls on training programs and to ensure that qualified persons were not arbitrarily excluded from licensure simply because they lacked a "union card" in one of the major mental health fields. Licensure would be based on evaluation of actual psychotherapeutic competence, not just on professional degree status (although formal clinical training would be a necessary prerequisite for evaluation). Furthermore, such competence-based licensure would be reevaluated at periodic (three- to five-year) intervals, to ensure that effective continuing education to keep the practitioner abreast of new developments in the field was indeed taking place. Such mandatory evaluation of competence and enforcement of such laws would obviously be very expensive but worthwhile, given the current almost total lack of protection for the consumer seeking psychotherapy. Under some such competence-based "license-to-practice psychotherapy" system, the issue of incompetent sex therapists being able to practice would not arise.

An alternative approach to ensuring competence of sex therapists is to similarly certify (or license) sex therapists directly, not as a subfield of psychotherapy practice. Indeed, there is at least one nationwide voluntary certification program, started by AASECT—the American Association of Sex Educators, Counselors, and Therapists—in 1974. AASECT was just AASEC for many years; it was primarily an organization of educators involved in teaching sex education. The *T* for *Therapist* was added only last year.

AASECT's standards for certification are probably too low to guarantee uniform competence, although many expert therapists are AASECT-certified. A person can be certified by AASECT in one of two ways. As a "grandperson" (already established sex therapist) one must have an M.A. degree or its equivalency (not defined) plus 1,000 hours of paid clinical experience as a sex therapist, or an M.A. degree plus an internship (not defined) with a Certified Sex Therapist in a recognized agency. If the applicant can not meet the "grandperson" requirements, certification is available by having a master's degree or its equivalent (not defined) in a clinical field. However, for nonclinicians, workshop programs can satisfy the equivalency requirement. In addition to the degree (or equivalency), certification requirements include 1,000 paid hours of experience as a sex therapist, a written examination, a personal interview, and attendance in a two-day AASECT workshop on sexual attitudes and values. Obviously, the AASECT focus is on sex therapy rather than on psychotherapy training. If one certifies, as sex therapists, persons who have a nonclinical master's degree plus "workshops," one is assuming that general psychotherapy training and experience are not necessary to be an effective sex therapist.

When AASECT established this program in 1974, there was a good deal of resistance from the professional community. Were the standards too low to ensure competence? Was it appropriate for any one membership organization to coopt the field and arbitrarily announce, "*We* will be *the* certification body for sex therapy"? (This issue, some years ago, led the Association for Advancement of Behavior Therapy to decide not to begin a certification program for behavior therapists.) In any case, was AASECT, basically an organization of health educators specializing in sex education, and an organization without any formal ties to mental health services or psychotherapy, the appropriate one to certify therapists? Was voluntary certification by an educational association with little public visibility worthwhile? Given that AASECT certification is not backed up by any legal constraints on who can use the title "sex therapist" or who can practice sex therapy, is it at all meaningful?

On the other hand, were the professional psychotherapists opposing AASECT certification as part of an elitist attempt to keep sex therapy as part of their exclusive (and suddenly profitable) domain? Were the professional organizations themselves doing anything about the unqualified "sex therapists" who were suddenly getting lots of publicity, and with it, lots of unsuspecting patients?

The situation today has clarified only somewhat. A good deal of squabbling still goes on between psychiatry, gynecology, urology, clinical psychology, AASECT, and various marriage and family therapy organizations as to who properly "owns" sex therapy. The AASECT program has slowly gained acceptance. Several of the nationally prominent therapists who initially declined "grand-person" certification when it was offered by AASECT recently accepted it, including Masters and Johnson.

AASECT has recently started, in conjunction with a local college, a training program for sex therapists. While this is a laudable idea, there are obvious potential conflict of interest problems in the certification organization offering training (will a candidate who has paid AASECT the substantial tuition for this program ever be found unworthy of certification?). Because of these obvious problems, in all other health-related disciplines, the license or certification is granted by an independent state-regulated board, not by the professional school or the professional association.

In recent telephone conversations with several AASECT board members, there seemed to be a general feeling that certification is only a marginally useful first step. Statutory regulation of practice was mentioned as the most desirable option, with two current board members feeling that the current voluntary certification was essentially meaningless. Others voiced concern about the low level of professional psychotherapy training required, but as one initially opposed but now certified therapist put it, "It's the only game in town." Whether or not the AASECT certification program has social utility in protecting the consumer, or at least in guiding the consumer to a competent sex therapist, remains to be seen.

As a first step in providing some consumer protection, AASECT has recently proposed a code of ethics for sex therapists which would forbid nudity (except in same sex groups), sexological exams, and all sexual contact between patient and therapist. Dr. Albert Ellis, the chairman of the ethical standards committee, indicated in a recent conversation that there is some resistance to this proposed code, primarily from California-based sex therapists. It will be interesting to see if AASECT adopts this code, and if so, whether or not it will be enforced by withdrawing certification from those therapists who use such procedures. Again pointing out the limited value of voluntary certification by a membership organization such as AASECT, some California therapists who disagree with the proposed AASECT code are talking about starting a national certification program of their own.

This review of the current state of affairs in the enterprise of sex therapy makes it clear that quality controls are sadly lacking. The existing laws, the professional psychotherapy disciplines, and AASECT have not been effective in guaranteeing the competence of the practitioners of sex therapy. In the absence of such effective controls, the patient couple seeking sex therapy must be vary wary in entering treatment.

Let the Buyer Beware: A Brief Guide to Choosing a Sex Therapist

To turn to the personal issue of just how a couple seeking sex therapy can find a qualified practitioner, several brief guidelines can be mentioned. If you are considering sex therapy and seeking a practitioner, you should keep the following principles in mind:

1. Don't respond to paid advertising, in any medium. Such advertising is against the ethical codes of virtually all professional organizations. AASECT is on record as recommending that sex therapists "use traditional professional forums for announcing their practices."

2. On the other hand, media *news* coverage (not advertising) of university, medical school, or social agency-sponsored sex therapy clinics is often an excellent way to locate qualified sex therapy centers. In general, institutional clinics, with their higher standards of in-service staff training and supervision, are more likely than private practice settings to exercise quality control on patient care. Additionally, fees are usually lower in such institutional settings than the going rates in private practice. In psychotherapy, the best is not always the most expensive. Psychoanalysis, usually the most expensive form of psychotherapy, seems to be among the least effective for sexual dysfunction, as previously mentioned.

3. Be sure that your prospective therapist is licensed as a psychiatrist, psychologist, or social worker in your state. There are obviously other types of qualified therapists (and not all psychiatrists, psychologists, or social workers are even minimally competent), but this provides you with certain legal protections that are worth having. (Employees of state agencies are often exempt from licensure, so this is less relevant if you are going to a university- or agency-based therapy program.)

4. Check on the qualifications of your therapist. Beyond state licensure, is the therapist board-certified by his or her profession, as discussed above? Does

the therapist have training and experience in marriage or relationship therapy, as well as in the specialized sex therapy techniques? A board-certified therapist who simply has read Masters and Johnson (1970) and has now decided to see sexual dysfunction cases is not the optimal choice.

5. A call to your local medical society or state psychological association for a referral is not likely to be helpful. Usually, these organizations are required to simply give you the names of three of their members, sequentially taken from the membership roster without prejudice. Even in those cases where referral to particular practitioners is allowed, this referral is based on the member's *self-described* (not evaluated) area of competence and interest. A phone call to the nearest university department of psychiatry, clinical psychology program, or school of social work may, however, help you locate a specialist in sex therapy. Within the reservations noted previously about the level of standards, the AASECT list of certified therapists may be helpful. If someone is both licensed and boarded as a psychologist, psychiatrist, or social worker *and* is AASECT-certified, you can be reassured about his or her competence.

6. Take referrals from your family doctor, pastor, or other professionals with a grain of salt. Often such referrals are to a friend, classmate, or golfing partner, rather than being based on actual evaluation of the therapist's skills. Such referrals are a useful starting point, but still check out the therapist's qualifications in accordance with points 3, 4, and 5 above.

In Conclusion

This chapter has focused on how changing cultural attitudes about sex and the development of new psychotherapeutic techniques have combined to create high public demand for "sex therapy." As a combined result of this demand, a lack of action by the professional psychotherapy disciplines, and the inadequate laws regulating psychotherapeutic practice, a major problem has arisen regarding the competence of those people who call themselves sex therapists. Currently, there is virtually no legal or professional protection of the consumer seeking such therapy. Again reflecting high demand, the fees charged for sex therapy are irrationally high when compared to other forms of outpatient psychotherapy. Finally, there is a small but growing trend for sex therapy to include a variety of both quasi-sexual and frankly sexual interactions between therapist and patient. These sexual interactions lack a theoretical basis, are of unproven utility, and may be exploitive of or harmful to the patients. Therapists who engage in such interactions may be gratifying their own needs at the client's expense, and the ethicality and legality of such procedures are dubious.

Taking these three issues in the professionalization of sex therapy together, it is apparent that long-term consumer protection reforms in the training and licensure of therapists are indicated. On a short-term basis, consumer education is indicated to enable prospective sex therapy patients to protect themselves. In seeking out sex therapy, the current situation suggests that the appropriate strategy is indeed *caveat emptor.*

References

Adams, S., and Orgel, M. *Through the mental health maze: A consumer's guide to finding a psycho-therapist.* Washington D.C.: Public Citizens Health Research Group, 1975.

Apfelbaum, B. *Theoretical and clinical issues in individual body-work sex therapy.* Paper presented at University of California, Los Angeles, conference on Professional and Legal Issues in the Use of Surrogate Partners in Sex Therapy, May 1976.

Bergin, A. E. The evaluation of therapeutic outcomes. In A. E. Bergin and S. Garfield (Eds.), *Handbook of psychotherapy and behavior change.* New York: Wiley, 1971.

Bergler, E. Frigidity in the female: Misconceptions and facts. *Marriage Hygiene,* 1947, *1,* 16–21.

Bergler, E. *Neurotic-counterfeit sex.* New York: Grune and Stratton, 1951.

Bindrum, P. A report on a nude marathon. *Psychotherapy: Theory, Research and Practice,* 1968, *5,* 180–188.

Comfort, A. *The joy of sex.* New York: Crown, 1972.

Eichenlaub, J. E. *The marriage art.* New York: Dell, 1961.

Ellis, A. *Reason and emotion in psychotherapy.* New York: Lyle Stuart, 1962.

Ellis, A. *Sex without guilt.* New York: Lancer Books, 1966.

Hartman, W. A., and Fithian, M. A. Desert retreat. In J. Robbins, *An analysis of human sexual inadequency.* New York: Signet, 1970.

Hartman, W. A., and Fithian, M. A. Enhancing sexuality through nudism. In H. Otto, *The new sexuality.* Palo Alto, California: Science and Behavior Books, 1971.

Hartman, W. A., and Fithian, M. A. *Treatment of sexual dysfunction.* Long Beach, California: Center for Marital and Sexual Studies, 1972.

Hastings, D. W. *Impotence and frigidity.* Boston: Little, Brown, 1963.

Heiman, J., LoPiccolo, L., and LoPiccolo, J. *Becoming orgasmic: A sexual growth program for women.* Englewood Cliffs, New Jersey: Prentice-Hall, 1976.

Holden, C. Sex therapy: Making it as a science and an industry. *Science,* 1974, *186,* 330–334.

Hunt, M. *Sexual behavior in the 70's.* Chicago: Playboy Press, 1974.

Kaplan, H. S. *The new sex therapy.* New York: Brunner/Mazel, 1974.

Kinsey, A., Pomeroy, W. B., and Martin, C. E. *Sexual behavior in the human male.* Philadelphia: W. B. Saunders, 1948.

Kinsey, A., Pomeroy, W. B., Martin, C. E., and Gebhard, P. H. *Sexual behavior in the human female.* Philadelphia: W. B. Saunders, 1953.

Lawrence, S. B. Videotape and other therapeutic procedures with nude marathon groups. *American Psychologist,* 1969, *24,* 476–479.

LoPiccolo, J. Direct treatment of sexual dysfunction. In H. Musaph and J. Money (Eds.), *Textbook of sexology.* New York: Elsevier-North Holland Press, 1977.

LoPiccolo, J., and Heiman, J. Cultural values and the therapeutic definition of sexual function and dysfunction. *Journal of Social Issues,* 1977, *33*(2), 50–65.

Masters, W. H., and Johnson, V. E. *Human sexual inadequacy.* Boston: Little, Brown, 1970.

McCarthy, B. W., Ryan, M., and Johnson, F. A. *Sexual awareness.* San Francisco: Boyd and Fraser, 1975.

Mikulas, W. L., and Lowe, T. C. Self-control of premature ejaculation. *Psychological Reports,* 1975, *37,* 295–298.

Moore, B. Frigidity in women. *Journal of the American Psychoanalytic Association,* 1961, *9,* 571–584.

Sherfey, M. J. *The nature and evolution of female sexuality.* New York: Vintage Books, 1972.

Torrey, E. F. Plumbers and psychiatrists: A consumer's view of mandatory evaluation. Paper presented at annual meeting, American Psychiatric Association, Detroit, 1974. (a)

Torrey, E. F. *The death of psychiatry.* Radnor, Pennsylvania: Chilton, 1974. (b)

Wolfe, L. The question of surrogates in sex therapy. *New York* magazine, 1973.

Wolpe, J. *Psychotherapy by reciprocal inhibition.* Stanford: Stanford University Press, 1958.

Index